Comparative Government

STORIES OF THE WORLD

FOR THE AP® COURSE

Karen Waples

Holy Family High School, Colorado

Adapted from
Introducing Comparative Politics
Fifth Edition
Stephen Orvis
Carol Ann Drogus

bedford, freeman & worth publishers

Boston | New York

Vice President, Social Sciences and High School: Shani Fisher
Executive Program Director, High School: Ann Heath
Senior Development Editor: Donald Gecewicz
Media Editor: Gina Forsythe
Editorial Assistant: Sophie Dora Tulchin
Director of Marketing, High School: Janie Pierce-Bratcher
Marketing Assistant: Nicollette Brady
Director, Content Management Enhancement: Tracey Kuehn
Senior Managing Editor: Michael Granger
Executive Content Project Manager: Gregory Erb
Senior Workflow Project Manager: Lisa McDowell
Production Supervisor: Robin Besofsky
Director of Design, Content Management: Diana Blume
Interior Designer: Tamara Newnam
Senior Cover Designer: William Boardman
Art Manager: Matthew McAdams
Illustrations: Troutt Visual Services
Executive Permissions Editor: Cecilia Varas
Photo Researcher: Krystyna Borgen/Lumina Datamatics, Inc.
Text Permissions Researcher: Michael McCarty
Senior Director of Digital Production: Keri deManigold
Lead Media Project Manager: Jodi Isman
Composition: Lumina Datamatics, Inc.
Printing and Binding: Transcontinental Printing

Library of Congress Control Number: 2022932868
ISBN-13: 978-1-319-44323-8
ISBN-10: 1-319-44323-0

Printed in Canada.
2   3   4   5   6   27   26   25   24   23

Acknowledgments
Unit icons: Abror kumpeh Daaruttauhid/Shutterstock (gears); Zarifamm/ Shutterstock (bank building); Arcady/Shutterstock (raised hands); Tri Setya/ Shutterstock (election vote); Oleksandr Yuhlichek/Shutterstock (graph with arrow).

Text and art acknowledgments and copyrights appear on the same page as the text and art selections they cover.

For information, write: BFW Publishers, 120 Broadway, New York, NY 10271
hsmarketing@bfwpub.com

Brief Contents

Contents

Unit 1
Introduction to Comparative Government: Political Systems, Regimes, and Governments

Abedin Taherkenareh/EPA/Shutterstock

Chapter 1
Introduction to Comparative Politics   4

Chapter 2
Political Systems

26

Chapter 3
Case Study: Mexico 53

Unit 2
Political Institutions

Jonathan Brady—PA Images/Getty Images

Chapter 4
Political Institutions 100

Chapter 5
Case Study: United Kingdom

122

Unit 3
Political Culture
and Participation

Extreme-Photographer/iStock/Getty Images

Chapter 6
Political Culture and Participation   170

Chapter 7
Case Study: Russia   198

Unit 4
Party and Electoral Systems and Citizen Organizations

Chapter 8
Party and Electoral Systems and Citizen Organizations 242

Chapter 9
Case Study: Nigeria   264

Isabelle Eshraghi/Agence VU/Redux

Unit 5
Political and Economic Changes and Development

Fatemeh Bahrami/Anadolu Agency/Getty Images

Chapter 10
Globalization   310

Chapter 11
Case Study: China

332

Chapter 12
Political and Economic Change and Development

371

Chapter 13
Case Study: Iran   393

About the Authors

Courtesy Cherry Creek High School

Karen Waples
Holy Family High School, Colorado

Formerly a trial attorney, Karen Waples has taught since 1989 and currently teaches AP® Comparative Government and Politics and AP® U.S. Government and Politics at Holy Family High School in Broomfield, Colorado. Karen has served as a reader, table leader, question leader, and exam leader for the AP® Comparative Government and Politics Exam and as a reader for the AP® U.S. Government and Politics and AP® U.S. History Exams. She is an endorsed consultant for the College Board® and leads workshops and institutes throughout the country for both the AP® Comparative Government and Politics course and the AP® U.S. Government and Politics course. Karen was the chair of the College Board® Social Science Academic Advisory Committee and was a member of the Curriculum Re-design Committee for AP® U.S. Government and Politics. She received the Colorado Governor's Award for Excellence in Education in 1997 and was recognized as a Cherry Creek High School Teacher of the Year in 2002.

Stephen Orvis
Hamilton College, New York

Stephen Orvis is Professor of Government at Hamilton College. He is a specialist on sub-Saharan Africa (Kenya in particular), identity politics, democratic transitions, and the political economy of development. He has been teaching introduction to comparative politics for more than twenty-five years, as well as courses on African politics, nationalism and the politics of identity, political economy of development, and weak states. He has written a book and articles on agricultural development in Kenya, as well as several articles on civil society in Africa and Kenya, and is currently doing research on political institutions in Africa.

Carol Ann Drogus
Carol Ann Drogus is a retired Professor of Government at Hamilton College. She is a specialist on Brazil, religion, and women's political participation. She taught introduction to comparative politics for more than twenty years, as well as courses on Latin American politics, gender and politics, and women in Latin America. She has written two books and numerous articles on the political participation of women in religious movements in Brazil.

Acknowledgments

I love teaching the AP® Comparative Government and Politics course, and when given the opportunity to write a book specifically for the needs of high school students and teachers, I jumped at the chance. I was fortunate to be able to draw on the exceptional text, *Introducing Comparative Politics*, Fifth Edition, written by Stephen Orvis and Carol Ann Drogus as the foundation for this work. I am indebted to them for providing outstanding core content from which I could build.

Stan Lugar, professor and chair of the Political Science Department at the University of Northern Colorado, wrote the stories that begin each chapter and bring this book to life. He is an excellent researcher, storyteller, and writer, and I am grateful for his collaboration and friendship, which spans twenty years.

I want to express my gratitude to the following wonderful teachers who reviewed the manuscript and contributed their expertise in teaching the AP® Course content. Their keen eyes and insightful input made this book better. I am grateful for their help.

- Sarah Fisher, Central Kitsap High School (WA)
- Jennifer Horan, University of North Carolina at Wilmington (NC)
- Jason Knoll, Verona Area High School (WI)
- Bonnie Sussman, Bishop O'Dowd High School (CA)

We asked reviewers who are experts on each of the six course countries to offer advice about how to present the history, politics, and society of each country so that the case studies can conform to the needs of high-school students. Special thanks to the following experts for reviewing the country chapter indicated:

- Nick Clark, Susquehanna University (PA)–United Kingdom
- Carrie Currier, Texas Christian University–China
- Jennifer Horan, University of North Carolina at Wilmington (NC)–Mexico
- Heather Tafel, Grand Valley State University (MI)–Russia
- Greg Williams, University of Northern Colorado–Nigeria and Iran

Thanks to the following teachers for helping to create the Teacher's Resources. They provided materials that make the AP® Comparative Government and Politics course accessible for teachers and students, and I am grateful for their help.

- Suzanne Bailey, Virgil I. Grissom High School (AL)
- Sarah Fisher, Central Kitsap High School (WA)
- Daniel Lazar, John F. Kennedy High School (Berlin, Germany)
- Terry Newman, Hempfield School District (PA)
- Scott Rivinius, Broward College (FL)
- Lisa Silverman, Milton High School (GA)
- Rebecca Small, Fairfax County Schools (VA)
- Benwari Singh, Cherry Creek High School (CO)

This book is a testament to the hard work and professionalism of the team at BFW. Special thanks to Don Gecewicz, Development Editor. His thoughtfulness and sense of humor made writing this book a pleasure. This book is immeasurably better because of his eagle eyes. Greg Erb, Executive Content Project Manager, has a terrific eye for detail, and I appreciate his thoroughness. Ann Heath, Executive Program Director, guided me throughout the process of writing this book. Her insight, experience, and patience made me a better author.

Reviewers of the College Book

We wish also to thank the many reviewers who read chapters of the college book by Orvis and Drogus at various stages and for various editions. They have collectively made it a much better book that the authors hope will serve students well.

William Avilés, University of Nebraska–Kearney

Jody Baumgartner, East Carolina University

Laura N. Bell, West Texas A&M University

Dilchoda Berdieva, Miami University

Michael Bernhard, University of Florida

Gitika Commuri, California State University–Bakersfield

Jeffrey Conroy-Krutz, Michigan State University

Carolyn Craig, University of Oregon

William Crowther, University of North Carolina–Greensboro

Andrea Duwel, Santa Clara University

Clement M. Henry, University of Texas–Austin

Eric H. Hines, University of Montana

Jennifer Horan, University of North Carolina–Wilmington

John Hulsey, James Madison University

Christian B. Jensen, University of Iowa

Neal G. Jesse, Bowling Green State University

Alana Jeydel, American River College

Eli C. Kaul, Kent State University

Jeffrey Key, Sweet Briar College

Eric Langenbacher, Georgetown University

Ricardo René Larémont, Binghamton University, SUNY

Carol S. Leff, University of Illinois at Urbana–Champaign

Paul Lenze, Northern Arizona University

M. Casey Kane Love, Tulane University

Mona Lyne, University of Missouri–Kansas City

Rahsaan Maxwell, University of Massachusetts

Mary McCarthy, Drake University

Scott Morgenstern, University of Pittsburgh

Stephen Mumme, Colorado State University

Immanuel Ness, City University of New York, Brooklyn College

Sandra K. Rana, Tulsa Community College

Nils Ringe, University of Wisconsin–Madison

David Sacko, U.S. Air Force Academy

Edward Schwerin, Florida Atlantic University

Brian Shoup, Mississippi State University

Erika Cornelius Smith, Nichols College

Tony Spanakos, Montclair State University

Boyka Stefanova, University of Texas–San Antonio

Sarah Tenney, The Citadel

Erica Townsend-Bell, University of Iowa

Kellee Tsai, Johns Hopkins University

Dwayne Woods, Purdue University

Eleanor E. Zeff, Drake University

Darren Zook, University of California, Berkeley

Welcome to a New Way of Exploring the World

Dear AP® student:

I've taught AP® Comparative Government and Politics for a long time. It's one of my favorite classes to teach. My goal in writing *Comparative Government: Stories of the World for the AP® Course* is to meet the requirements of the College Board® curriculum in understandable language and organize the book in a way that makes it easier for you to grasp the key concepts in the course, practice core skills, and apply them to the six required countries.

The subtitle of this book, "Stories of the World," refers to the narratives that begin each chapter. Each story describes a person or group whose activities illustrate the concept or country studied. These stories start each chapter vividly and will grab your attention, helping you to put the information that follows in context.

In the first chapter or chapters that begin each unit, you will learn about the important ideas in comparative politics. These thematic chapters address the five units in the College Board curriculum—Political Systems, Political Institutions, Political Culture and Participation, Party and Electoral Systems and Citizen Organizations, Globalization, and Political and Economic Change and Development. They provide you with a broad-based framework of the key concepts in the course. The country chapter or chapters in each unit present case studies of government and politics, highlighting one of the six countries that are required in the AP® course—Mexico, the United Kingdom, Russia, Nigeria, China, and Iran (in the order in which you will meet them). Focusing on each country in a specific chapter allows you to examine the details of other cultures and systems of government.

Because this is a *comparative* government course, you need to learn how to build on your understanding of government and politics so that you can explain the similarities and differences between countries and systems. Interweaving the thematic chapters with the country cases gives you a chance to start applying core concepts to real-life situations beginning with the first Unit.

At the end of the course, you will take the AP® Exam. The AP® Exam focuses on disciplinary practices that will lead you to think like a political scientist. The Exam provides a chance to demonstrate your ability to understand and interpret data, graphs, speeches, and debates about laws and policies. AP® Tips throughout the book help you navigate the Exam. Watch for them.

AP® Political Science Practices features provide you with opportunities to build skills (handy things like making comparisons, doing an analysis, and organizing your writing) that will give you confidence and help to do well on the AP® Exam. Read them carefully. The features in Chapter 13 focus on how to be more successful on the Exam.

Besides introducing you to valuable ideas, and helping you to do well on the AP® Exam, I have an even bigger goal: I want to increase the number of students taking this class, because this is a phenomenal course that will help you better understand the world.

Karen Waples

Tips for Taking the AP® Exam

The AP® Exam consists of 55 multiple-choice questions and 4 free-response questions. The Exam is 2 hours and 30 minutes long. Here is what to expect:

Multiple-Choice Questions

You will have an hour (60 minutes) to complete the multiple-choice part of the Exam. Budget your time wisely. If you get stuck on a question, mark it in the Exam booklet, bubble in a random answer, move on, and come back to the question later, if you have time.

The multiple-choice exam has three categories of questions:

1. Individual questions:

Up to 44 of the questions are of this type, meaning that they are written questions without a display of data or a reading (excerpt).

2. Two kinds of question sets:

- Quantitative analysis: three sets of questions asking you to analyze a quantitative stimulus like a line graph, bar chart, table of data, map, or infographic.

- Qualitative analysis: two sets of questions asking you to analyze text-based secondary sources like speeches, interviews, articles, laws, or paragraphs of a constitution.

Country focus:

The six countries addressed in AP® Comparative Government and Politics are China, Iran, Mexico, Nigeria, Russia, and the United Kingdom.

What the MC questions look like:

Each multiple-choice question has four answer choices. You will earn one point for each correct answer, and there is no penalty for guessing, so answer every question. The multiple-choice portion makes up half of your score on the AP® Exam.

Free-Response Questions

You will answer four written questions in an hour and 30 minutes (90 minutes).

Question 1: Conceptual analysis (suggested time: 10 minutes; Exam weight = 11%). Define or describe a political concept and explain and/or compare political systems, principles, institutions, processes, policies, or behaviors.

Question 2: Quantitative analysis (suggested time: 20 minutes; Exam weight = 12.5%). Analyze quantitative data, identify a trend or pattern, or draw a conclusion from a display of data and explain how it relates to political systems, principles, institutions, processes, policies, or behaviors.

Question 3: Comparative analysis (suggested time: 20 minutes; Exam weight = 12.5%). Compare political concepts, systems, institutions, or policies among different course countries.

Question 4: Argument essay (suggested time: 40 minutes; Exam weight = 14%). Write an essay with an analytical thesis that develops an argument about a topic. You will also use evidence from course countries and reasoning to explain how the evidence is related to the course concepts in the question prompt. You will also have to provide an alternative perspective and respond to that alternative perspective using refutation, rebuttal, or concession.

The free-response section makes up half of your score on the exam. The free-response questions have slightly different weights. The argument essay will take you longer to write and is worth a bit more in exam weighting. Again, budget your time carefully.

Helpful organization

Combining concept chapters with engaging country case studies gives you a framework for *comparison*, which is at the heart of the comparative government and politics course.

Integrating the AP® Course Framework's content themes with the required countries helps make the information concrete so that you can start drawing comparisons in the first unit. The spiraling increases in complexity as the book progresses so you are fully prepared for the AP® Exam by Unit 6.

Five Thematic Units mirror the AP® Course Framework

In the first chapter(s) that begin each unit, you learn about the comparative concepts that are central to the course. Because the comparative concepts are more broad-based and abstract, we introduce them patiently. Colorful icons identify the theme in each unit

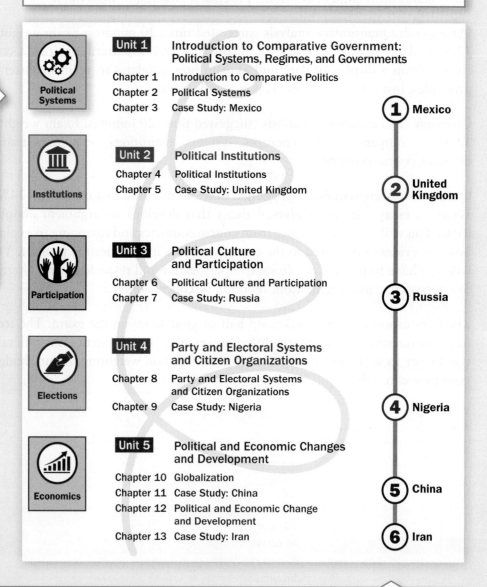

Political Systems

Unit 1 Introduction to Comparative Government:
Political Systems, Regimes, and Governments

Chapter 1   Introduction to Comparative Politics
Chapter 2   Political Systems
Chapter 3   Case Study: Mexico

1 Mexico

Institutions

Unit 2 Political Institutions

Chapter 4   Political Institutions
Chapter 5   Case Study: United Kingdom

2 United Kingdom

Participation

Unit 3 Political Culture and Participation

Chapter 6   Political Culture and Participation
Chapter 7   Case Study: Russia

3 Russia

Elections

Unit 4 Party and Electoral Systems and Citizen Organizations

Chapter 8   Party and Electoral Systems and Citizen Organizations
Chapter 9   Case Study: Nigeria

4 Nigeria

Economics

Unit 5 Political and Economic Changes and Development

Chapter 10   Globalization
Chapter 11   Case Study: China
Chapter 12   Political and Economic Change and Development
Chapter 13   Case Study: Iran

5 China

6 Iran

Six Integrated Country Case Studies

The country chapter in each unit follows as a case study of government and politics, highlighting one of the six course countries. It's fun and interesting to learn about other cultures and systems of government. The more specific and detailed information in these chapters empowers you to explain the similarities and differences between countries and systems.

Engaging Stories

Each chapter begins with a story about a person or group whose activities illustrate the concept or country being studied. These stories bring the content to life.

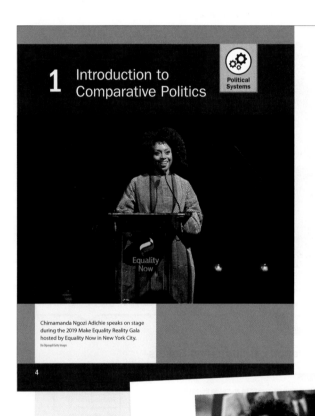

1 Introduction to Comparative Politics

Political Systems

Chimamanda Ngozi Adichie speaks on stage during the 2019 Make Equality Reality Gala hosted by Equality Now in New York City.

4

The Power of a Single Story

In one of the most watched TED Talks ever, having been viewed more than 18 million times, the writer Chimamanda Ngozi Adichie warns us of the danger of the single story. Born in Nigeria in 1977, Adichie has received dozens of awards for her novels, many honorary degrees, and the prestigious MacArthur Foundation "genius grant" in 2008. (Adichie Web site.)

By 2015, her 2009 TED Talk, "The Danger of a Single Story," had become one of the top-ten most-viewed TED Talks. (Adichie TED Talk, 2009.) She was listed among *The New Yorker's* 20 Under 40 in 2010. In 2015, *Time* magazine named Adichie one of the most influential people in the world. (100 Most Influential, 2015.) She has become a sought-after college commencement speaker. (Eastern Connecticut, 2015.)

Her novel *Half of a Yellow Sun* won the world's top prize for female authors. (Women's Prize, 2021.) It is set in Nigeria during the Biafran War, which took place between 1967 and 1970, causing the deaths of as many as 2 million people. The novel has been described as "about the end of colonialism, ethnic allegiances, class, race and female empowerment—and how love can complicate all of these things."

Adichie came to the United States
lege. She graduated from Eastern Con
degree in creative writing from John
tion, her parents worked at the Unive
statistics in Nigeria after receiving h
Her mother was the first female regis

An early reader and writer, she
Adichie recalled that the first stories
was written by American and British

All my characters were white and blu
they talked a lot about the weather, l
despite the fact that I lived in Nigeria.
We ate mangoes.

Adichie concludes from this me
stories we read and absorb. Although
tion, her discovery of African authors
are" and, in a larger sense, how to u

Once she came to the United Sta
of Africa—one of catastrophe, hunge
together all the nations of Africa (o
understood that English was the off
music was well known in Nigeria.

Until she came to the United St
as Nigerian, or as Igbo, her family's
Nigeria's 200 million people. Only w
as a Black person or thought of herr
story that characterized her.

For Adichie, the stories told by ot
shape the perception of those withou
of colonialism.

I've always felt that it is impossible
engaging with all of the stories of tha

The Man behind Brexit

In June 2016, the electorate in the United Kingdom shocked the country and the rest of Europe by voting to leave the European Union (EU).

Comprised of twenty-seven European nations, the EU is a type of international organization known as a supranational organization, with a total population of roughly 450 million. Countries that join the EU give up some sovereignty in exchange for the benefits of membership. This gives the EU the power to act in a given policy area on behalf of all members—trade being the number-one example. It provides for the free movement of people, goods, and services, and it sets the rules of commerce between member states. Citizens of one country can freely move to another to work or live.

In 1951, when six nations formed the European Coal and Steel Community, the original goal was to integrate their economies and lessen the extreme nationalism that had led to World War I and World War II. At first, free trade among member nations was its mission. Over time, other nations joined, and tighter economic and political integration among nations was implemented.

The British remained outside these agreements until 1973, when the United Kingdom joined what was then called the European Economic Community. In 1993, further integration resulted in the EEC becoming the EU, as more nations joined. Yet the British remained ambivalent about the EU and opted out of the common currency, the euro, that was fully implemented in 2002, retaining the pound sterling (£).

EU member countries agree to give up some of their sovereignty over domestic and international affairs to centralized EU institutions—a parliament, a court of justice, a central bank, and more. Yet, each nation retains some sovereignty over domestic budgetary affairs and welfare state spending. Sovereignty is the ability of a state to act without internal or external interference. While the state is seen as the central ingredient of the modern world, no state is fully independent of the impact of trade, the global environment, and international conflicts.

Dominic Cummings, special adviser to U.K. Prime Minister Boris Johnson, walks from the meeting hall in Manchester of the 2019 Conservative Party conference.

The Man behind Brexit 27

Climate-change activist Noga Levy-Rapoport participates in a May Day rally in London in 2019.

Learn about leaders and activists who are changing the political landscape in their respective countries, including:

- Claudia Sheinbaum Pardo, mayor of Mexico City (Chapter 3)
- Ebrahim Raisi, president of Iran (Chapter 4)
- Noga Levy-Rapoport, climate-change activist (Chapter 5)
- Vladimir Putin, president of Russia (Chapter 7)
- Andrés Manuel López Obrador, president of Mexico (Chapter 8)
- Mo Abudu, Nigerian multimedia mogul (Chapter 9)
- Jack Ma, founder of Alibaba (Chapter 10)
- Rebiya Kadeer: Uyghur human-rights activist (Chapter 11)

Well-paced content to keep you on track

This course can be challenging because there are so many concepts and skills to learn. Each chapter is made up of three to five sections, and each section is designed to be covered as a single lesson to deliver content, skills, assignments, and assessments in a brief and easy-to-use "chunk."

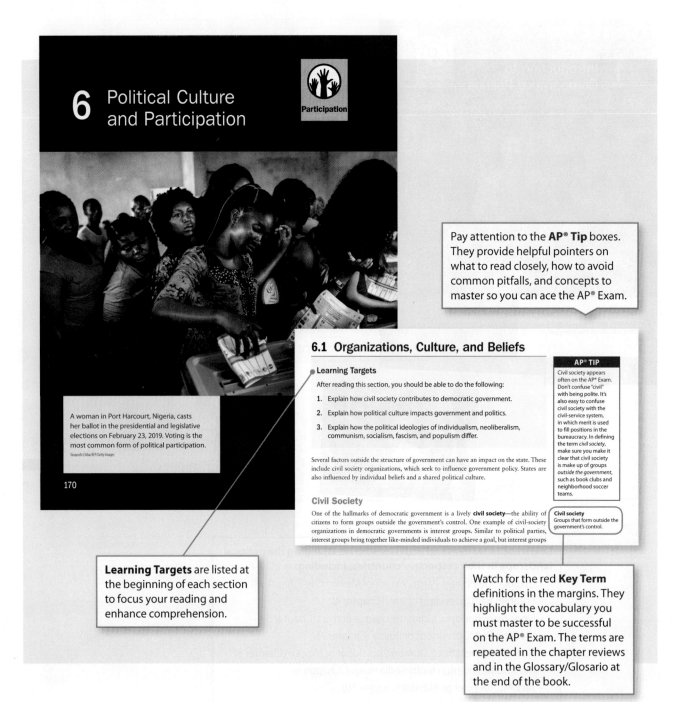

6 Political Culture and Participation

Participation

A woman in Port Harcourt, Nigeria, casts her ballot in the presidential and legislative elections on February 23, 2019. Voting is the most common form of political participation.

Yoayoshi Chiba/AFP/Getty Images

170

Pay attention to the **AP® Tip** boxes. They provide helpful pointers on what to read closely, how to avoid common pitfalls, and concepts to master so you can ace the AP® Exam.

6.1 Organizations, Culture, and Beliefs

Learning Targets

After reading this section, you should be able to do the following:

1. Explain how civil society contributes to democratic government.

2. Explain how political culture impacts government and politics.

3. Explain how the political ideologies of individualism, neoliberalism, communism, socialism, fascism, and populism differ.

Several factors outside the structure of government can have an impact on the state. These include civil society organizations, which seek to influence government policy. States are also influenced by individual beliefs and a shared political culture.

Civil Society

One of the hallmarks of democratic government is a lively **civil society**—the ability of citizens to form groups outside the government's control. One example of civil-society organizations in democratic governments is interest groups. Similar to political parties, interest groups bring together like-minded individuals to achieve a goal, but interest groups

AP® TIP

Civil society appears often on the AP® Exam. Don't confuse "civil" with being polite. It's also easy to confuse civil society with the civil-service system, in which merit is used to fill positions in the bureaucracy. In defining the term *civil society*, make sure you make it clear that civil society is make up of groups *outside the government*, such as book clubs and neighborhood soccer teams.

Civil society
Groups that form outside the government's control.

Learning Targets are listed at the beginning of each section to focus your reading and enhance comprehension.

Watch for the red **Key Term** definitions in the margins. They highlight the vocabulary you must master to be successful on the AP® Exam. The terms are repeated in the chapter reviews and in the Glossary/Glosario at the end of the book.

Consistent presentation and visual tools empower country comparisons

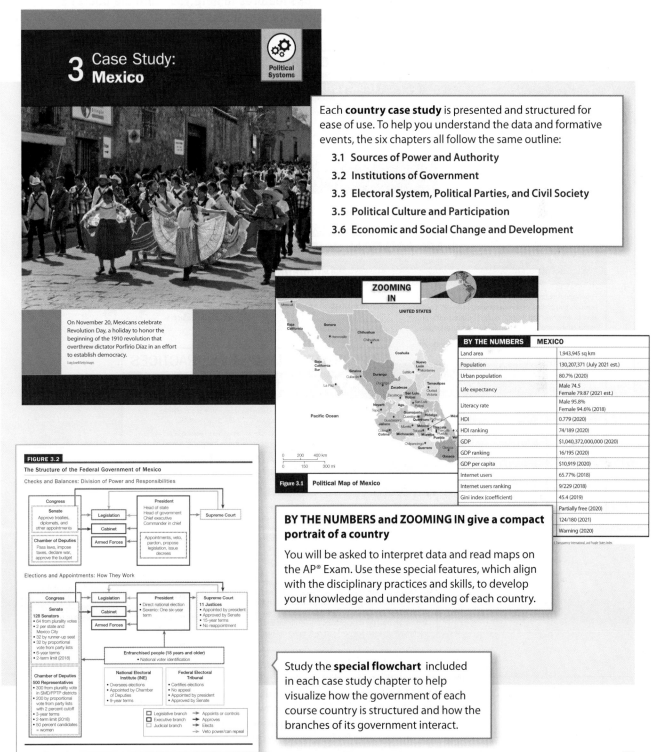

Each **country case study** is presented and structured for ease of use. To help you understand the data and formative events, the six chapters all follow the same outline:

3.1 Sources of Power and Authority

3.2 Institutions of Government

3.3 Electoral System, Political Parties, and Civil Society

3.5 Political Culture and Participation

3.6 Economic and Social Change and Development

BY THE NUMBERS and ZOOMING IN give a compact portrait of a country

You will be asked to interpret data and read maps on the AP® Exam. Use these special features, which align with the disciplinary practices and skills, to develop your knowledge and understanding of each country.

Study the **special flowchart** included in each case study chapter to help visualize how the government of each course country is structured and how the branches of its government interact.

Get comfortable with the AP® Political Science Skills

Each chapter includes two AP® Political Science Practices features to help you learn the course's disciplinary practices and the skills related to the disciplinary practices.

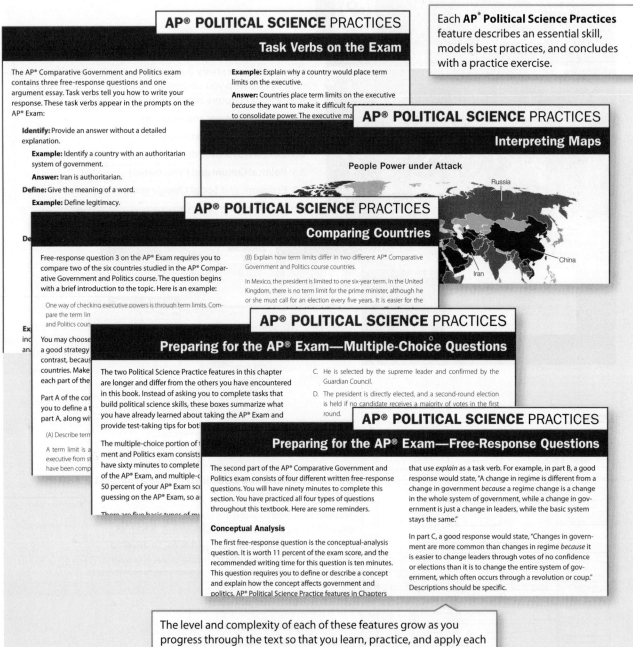

AP® POLITICAL SCIENCE PRACTICES

Task Verbs on the Exam

The AP® Comparative Government and Politics exam contains three free-response questions and one argument essay. Task verbs tell you how to write your response. These task verbs appear in the prompts on the AP® Exam:

Identify: Provide an answer without a detailed explanation.

    Example: Identify a country with an authoritarian system of government.

    Answer: Iran is authoritarian.

Define: Give the meaning of a word.

    Example: Define legitimacy.

Example: Explain why a country would place term limits on the executive.

Answer: Countries place term limits on the executive *because* they want to make it difficult for to consolidate power. The executive ma

Each **AP® Political Science Practices** feature describes an essential skill, models best practices, and concludes with a practice exercise.

AP® POLITICAL SCIENCE PRACTICES

Interpreting Maps

People Power under Attack

Russia

China

Iran

AP® POLITICAL SCIENCE PRACTICES

Comparing Countries

Free-response question 3 on the AP® Exam requires you to compare two of the six countries studied in the AP® Comparative Government and Politics course. The question begins with a brief introduction to the topic. Here is an example:

    One way of checking executive powers is through term limits. Compare the term lim and Politics cour

(B) Explain how term limits differ in two different AP® Comparative Government and Politics course countries.

In Mexico, the president is limited to one six-year term. In the United Kingdom, there is no term limit for the prime minister, although he or she must call for an election every five years. It is easier for the

AP® POLITICAL SCIENCE PRACTICES

Preparing for the AP® Exam—Multiple-Choice Questions

The two Political Science Practice features in this chapter are longer and differ from the others you have encountered in this book. Instead of asking you to complete tasks that build political science skills, these boxes summarize what you have already learned about taking the AP® Exam and provide test-taking tips for bot

The multiple-choice portion of ment and Politics exam consists have sixty minutes to complete of the AP® Exam, and multiple-c 50 percent of your AP® Exam sc guessing on the AP® Exam, so a

C. He is selected by the supreme leader and confirmed by the Guardian Council.

D. The president is directly elected, and a second-round election is held if no candidate receives a majority of votes in the first round.

AP® POLITICAL SCIENCE PRACTICES

Preparing for the AP® Exam—Free-Response Questions

The second part of the AP® Comparative Government and Politics exam consists of four different written free-response questions. You will have ninety minutes to complete this section. You have practiced all four types of questions throughout this textbook. Here are some reminders.

Conceptual Analysis

The first free-response question is the conceptual-analysis question. It is worth 11 percent of the exam score, and the recommended writing time for this question is ten minutes. This question requires you to define or describe a concept and explain how the concept affects government and politics. AP® Political Science Practice features in Chapters

that use *explain* as a task verb. For example, in part B, a good response would state, "A change in regime is different from a change in government *because* a regime change is a change in the whole system of government, while a change in government is just a change in leaders, while the basic system stays the same."

In part C, a good response would state, "Changes in government are more common than changes in regime *because* it is easier to change leaders through votes of no confidence or elections than it is to change the entire system of government, which often occurs through a revolution or coup." Descriptions should be specific.

The level and complexity of each of these features grow as you progress through the text so that you learn, practice, and apply each skill. Chapter 13 contains two special **AP® Political Science Practices Features** to make sure you are prepared for the AP® exam: one helps you prepare to answer multiple-choice questions and another offers advice on preparing for free-response questions.

Practice for the AP® Exam

Free-response questions at the end of each section that test your mastery of concepts and skills, and help you practice the art of drawing sound comparisons between countries, are integrated throughout the text to give you daily practice.

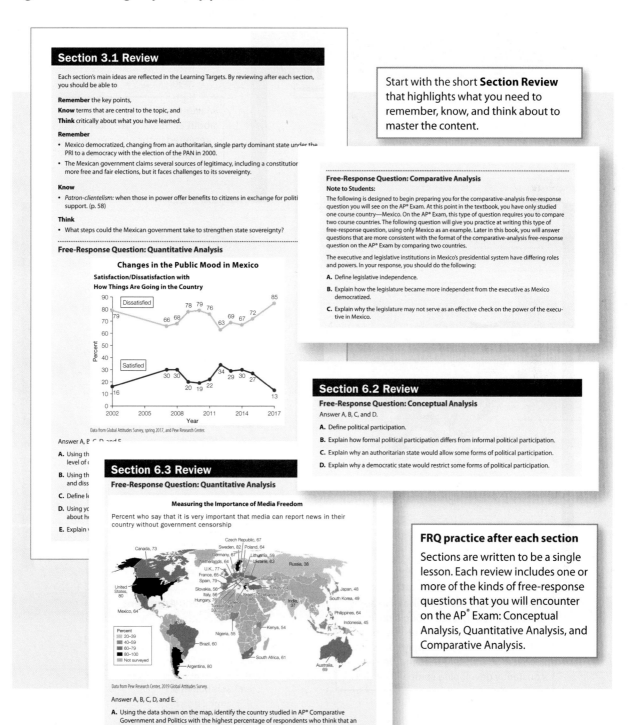

Section 3.1 Review

Each section's main ideas are reflected in the Learning Targets. By reviewing after each section, you should be able to

Remember the key points,

Know terms that are central to the topic, and

Think critically about what you have learned.

Remember

- Mexico democratized, changing from an authoritarian, single party dominant state under the PRI to a democracy with the election of the PAN in 2000.
- The Mexican government claims several sources of legitimacy, including a constitution more free and fair elections, but it faces challenges to its sovereignty.

Know

- *Patron-clientelism*: when those in power offer benefits to citizens in exchange for politi support. (p. 58)

Think

- What steps could the Mexican government take to strengthen state sovereignty?

Free-Response Question: Quantitative Analysis

Changes in the Public Mood in Mexico

Satisfaction/Dissatisfaction with How Things Are Going in the Country

Dissatisfied: 79, 66, 68, 78, 79, 76, 63, 69, 67, 72, 85
Satisfied: 16, 30, 30, 20, 19, 22, 34, 29, 30, 27, 13

Years: 2002, 2005, 2008, 2011, 2014, 2017

Data from Global Attitudes Survey, spring 2017, and Pew Research Center.

Answer A, B, C, D and E

A. Using th
level of

B. Using th
and diss

C. Define le

D. Using yo
about ho

E. Explain

> **Start with the short Section Review** that highlights what you need to remember, know, and think about to master the content.

Free-Response Question: Comparative Analysis

Note to Students:

The following is designed to begin preparing you for the comparative-analysis free-response question you will see on the AP® Exam. At this point in the textbook, you have only studied one course country—Mexico. On the AP® Exam, this type of question requires you to compare two course countries. The following question will give you practice at writing this type of free-response question, using only Mexico as an example. Later in this book, you will answer questions that are more consistent with the format of the comparative-analysis free-response question on the AP® Exam by comparing two countries.

The executive and legislative institutions in Mexico's presidential system have differing roles and powers. In your response, you should do the following:

A. Define legislative independence.

B. Explain how the legislature became more independent from the executive as Mexico democratized.

C. Explain why the legislature may not serve as an effective check on the power of the executive in Mexico.

Section 6.2 Review

Free-Response Question: Conceptual Analysis

Answer A, B, C, and D.

A. Define political participation.

B. Explain how formal political participation differs from informal political participation.

C. Explain why an authoritarian state would allow some forms of political participation.

D. Explain why a democratic state would restrict some forms of political participation.

Section 6.3 Review

Free-Response Question: Quantitative Analysis

Measuring the Importance of Media Freedom

Percent who say that it is very important that media can report news in their country without government censorship

Canada, 73; Czech Republic, 67; Sweden, 82; Poland, 64; Germany, 67; Lithuania, 59; Netherlands, 64; Ukraine, 63; Russia, 38; U.K., 77; France, 65; Spain, 79; Slovakia, 56; Italy, 56; Hungary, 7?; Japan, 48; South Korea, 49; India, 37; United States, 80; Mexico, 64; Philippines, 64; Indonesia, 45; Kenya, 54; Nigeria, 55; Brazil, 60; South Africa, 61; Argentina, 80; Australia, 69

Percent
- 20–39
- 40–59
- 60–79
- 80–100
- Not surveyed

Data from Pew Research Center, 2019 Global Attitudes Survey.

Answer A, B, C, D, and E.

A. Using the data shown on the map, identify the country studied in AP® Comparative Government and Politics with the highest percentage of respondents who think that an independent press is important.

> **FRQ practice after each section**
>
> Sections are written to be a single lesson. Each review includes one or more of the kinds of free-response questions that you will encounter on the AP® Exam: Conceptual Analysis, Quantitative Analysis, and Comparative Analysis.

Practice for the AP® Exam

At the end of each chapter, use your developing knowledge to answer Multiple-Choice Questions and to practice writing a compelling Argument Essay.

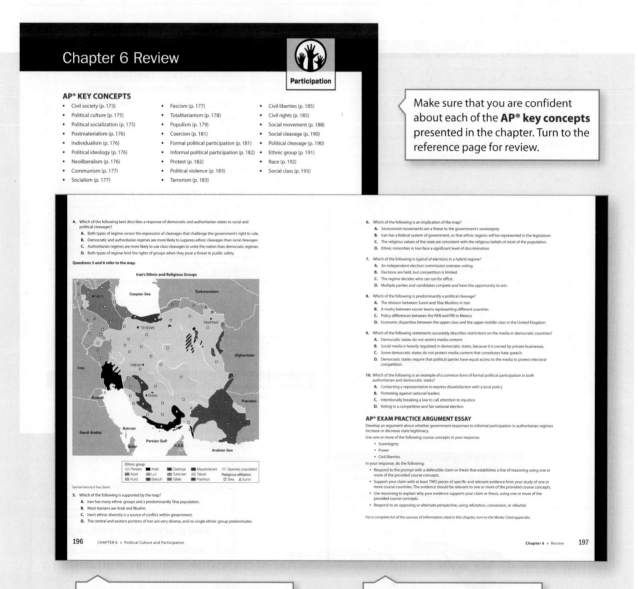

> Make sure that you are confident about each of the **AP® key concepts** presented in the chapter. Turn to the reference page for review.

> Questions push you to think and to apply concepts broadly. Even though Iran is not featured until Chapter 13, this question in Chapter 6 asks you to apply your skills to reading a map of Iran so that you are constantly developing comparative skills.

> Writing a strong **Argument Essay** takes practice! These end-of-chapter questions prompt you with a thought-provoking question and clear instructions.

Put it all together in the Unit Reviews and Practice AP® Exam

After the end of each unit, you will find AP®-style practice questions that mirror the AP® Exam. Practice includes multiple-choice questions, free-response questions, and an argument essay. Finally, test your readiness by taking the AP® Comparative Government and Politics Practice Exam at the end of the book.

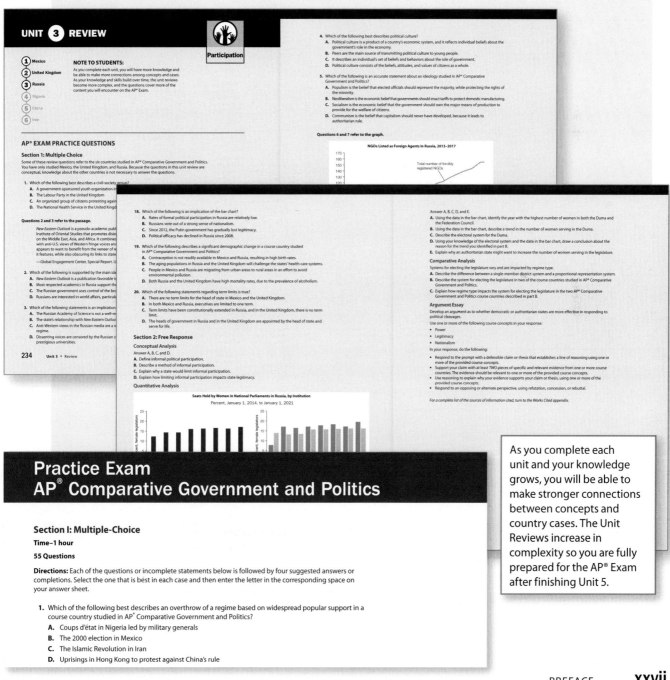

As you complete each unit and your knowledge grows, you will be able to make stronger connections between concepts and country cases. The Unit Reviews increase in complexity so you are fully prepared for the AP® Exam after finishing Unit 5.

Comparative Government

STORIES OF THE WORLD

FOR THE AP® COURSE

UNIT 1

Introduction to Comparative Government: Political Systems, Regimes, and Governments

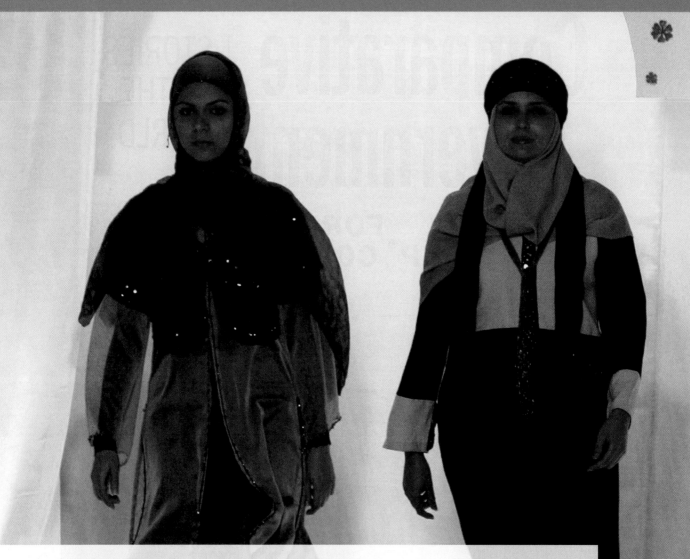

In this unit, you will start to learn how to observe political and social behavior to understand how people act toward their governments and how governments maintain authority and legitimacy. Iran is a theocracy, but it has a young population that has, at times, been restless. One way of maintaining a government's legitimacy is by allowing some civil liberties, giving citizens some latitude in public and in private. The Iranian government requires women to wear headscarves in public. Here, we see how Iranian fashions adapt to government restrictions.

Chapter 1	**Chapter 2**	**Chapter 3**
Introduction to Comparative Politics	Political Systems	Case Study: **Mexico**

C omparative political scientists seek to understand similarities and differences between states, evaluate how different government systems operate, and explain why political changes occur. Unit 1 sets the foundation for you to start thinking like a comparative political scientist by reading and analyzing qualitative and quantitative data related to the six required course countries—China, Iran, Mexico, Nigeria, Russia, and the United Kingdom. You will begin to learn about the key concepts that help political scientists compare countries, and you will encounter your first country, Mexico. Using these concepts, you will begin building the skills necessary for success on the AP® Exam.

After completing Unit 1, you will be able to:

- Describe what political scientists do
- Define political organizations
- Compare democracy and authoritarianism
- Explain how democratization occurs
- Describe sources of power and authority
- Explain why power and authority change over time
- Compare federal and unitary systems
- Define political legitimacy
- Explain how legitimacy is sustained
- Define political stability
- Examine government and politics in Mexico

Mexico is a highly diverse nation. More than 60 indigenous languages are spoken in Mexico. In the states of Oaxaca and Chiapas, much of the population speaks Native American languages. Many do not speak Spanish. This young man, a poet and speaker of Mixtec, is participating in a poetry "slam" in Oaxaca.

Thomas F. Aleto

1 Introduction to Comparative Politics

Political Systems

Chimamanda Ngozi Adichie speaks on stage during the 2019 Make Equality Reality Gala hosted by Equality Now in New York City.

Dia Dipasupil/Getty Images

The Power of a Single Story

In one of the most watched TED Talks ever, having been viewed more than 18 million times, the writer Chimamanda Ngozi Adichie warns us of the danger of the single story. Born in Nigeria in 1977, Adichie has received dozens of awards for her novels, many honorary degrees, and the prestigious MacArthur Foundation "genius grant" in 2008. (Adichie Web site.)

By 2015, her 2009 TED Talk, "The Danger of a Single Story," had become one of the top-ten most-viewed TED Talks. (Adichie TED Talk, 2009.) She was listed among *The New Yorker*'s 20 Under 40 in 2010. In 2015, *Time* magazine named Adichie one of the most influential people in the world. (100 Most Influential, 2015.) She has become a sought-after college commencement speaker. (Eastern Connecticut, 2015.)

Her novel *Half of a Yellow Sun* won the world's top prize for female authors. (Women's Prize, 2021.) It is set in Nigeria during the Biafran War, which took place between 1967 and 1970, causing the deaths of as many as 2 million people. The novel has been described as "about the end of colonialism, ethnic allegiances, class, race and female empowerment—and how love can complicate all of these things."

Adichie came to the United States, where she now lives most of the time, to attend college. She graduated from Eastern Connecticut State University and then received a master's degree in creative writing from Johns Hopkins University. No strangers to higher education, her parents worked at the University of Nigeria. Her father was the first professor of statistics in Nigeria after receiving his Ph.D. from the University of California, Berkeley. Her mother was the first female registrar at the university.

An early reader and writer, she began writing and illustrating stories at age seven. Adichie recalled that the first stories she wrote reflected the literature that she read that was written by American and British authors in English. As she recalled:

> All my characters were white and blue-eyed. They played in the snow. They ate apples. And they talked a lot about the weather, how lovely it was that the sun had come out. Now, this despite the fact that I lived in Nigeria. I had never been outside Nigeria. We didn't have snow. We ate mangoes.

Adichie concludes from this memory how impressionable we are in response to the stories we read and absorb. Although she loved these books, and they opened her imagination, her discovery of African authors saved her from "having a single story of what books are" and, in a larger sense, how to understand her own identity.

Once she came to the United States to attend college, she encountered the single story of Africa—one of catastrophe, hunger, and violence. Many of her fellow students lumped together all the nations of Africa (currently fifty-four) as if Africa was a country. Few understood that English was the official language of Nigeria or that American popular music was well known in Nigeria.

Until she came to the United States, she had not thought of herself as African, but as Nigerian, or as Igbo, her family's ethnic group that accounts for about 18 percent of Nigeria's 200 million people. Only when she came to the United States was she perceived as a Black person or thought of herself as such. In the United States, that was the single story that characterized her.

For Adichie, the stories told by others about a people, or a nation, reflect the power to shape the perception of those without power. For Africans, it has often reflected the power of colonialism.

> I've always felt that it is impossible to engage properly with a place or a person without engaging with all of the stories of that place and that person. The consequence of the single

story is this: It robs people of dignity. It makes our recognition of our equal humanity difficult. It emphasizes how we are different rather than how we are similar.

Another of her TED Talks, "We Should All Be Feminists," viewed more than 6 million times since it was first delivered in 2012, was turned into a book that has been handed out to every sixteen-year-old in Sweden, and whose title was used by the French fashion house Dior on one of its T-shirts. Her words were borrowed by Beyoncé in her song, "Flawless." (Adichie TED Talk, 2012.)

The danger of the single story is not always easy to escape, even for Adichie. It is often something that we bring along with us unwittingly. In her 2009 TED Talk, she recalled visiting Mexico a few years earlier amid heated debates in the United States over immigration characterized by repeated negative portrayals of Mexicans. On her first day in Guadalajara, a city of almost 1.5 million people, she watched people going about their everyday lives in the market, going to work, and more:

> . . . they had become one thing in my mind, the abject immigrant. I had bought into the single story of Mexicans and I could not have been more ashamed of myself. So that is how to create a single story, show a people as one thing, as only one thing, over and over again, and that is what they become.

Her hope in warning about the dangers of the single story is that "when we reject the single story, when we realize that there is never a single story about any place . . ."

As you begin your journey in AP® Comparative Government and Politics, keep in mind that countries, and the people who live in them, are complex. The stories that open each chapter will give you perspective, and they provide context for the countries and concepts you will study. But no single story can describe the complicated world of government and politics. Do not set aside your own moral compass, but try to keep an open mind. Enjoy the stories, knowing that they represent just a small fraction of experiences in a much larger world.

1.1 Why Study AP® Comparative Government and Politics?

Learning Targets

After reading this section, you should be able to do the following:

1. Recognize the important questions studied in comparative politics.

2. Describe the field of comparative politics.

AP® Comparative Government and Politics is a fascinating course that examines the most interesting questions facing political scientists today. How can a government convince people that it has the right to rule? Why do some governments last longer than others? Why do some forms of government serve their people's interests better than others? How do democracies form, and how do they fall apart? Can democracy work anywhere, or only in particular countries and at particular times? Why are some political institutions more democratic than others? What policies can governments enact to reduce poverty and improve economic well-being? This book introduces you to the conflicting answers to these questions by examining them comparatively.

The AP® Comparative Government and Politics course focuses on six countries—China, Iran, Mexico, Nigeria, Russia, and the United Kingdom. Comparing these six countries will help you decide which answers are the most convincing and why.

Political Scientists Study Politics and Power

Comparative politics is the study of similarities and differences between states, how different government systems operate, and why political changes occur. As the name of this course implies, comparativists also *compare* by systematically examining political phenomena in more than one place and during more than one period and drawing conclusions from those observations. Comparative politics focuses mainly on power and decision making within countries. The study of how countries deal with one another is the focus of a different political science course called international relations.

Remember to compare what you have learned as you go through the course. This course is not a march through unrelated countries or concepts. Each chapter builds on the others, and soon, you will see a bigger picture emerge.

Comparative politics
The study of similarities and differences between states, how different government systems operate, and why political changes occur.

How the AP® Comparative Government and Politics Course Is Organized

The AP® Comparative Government and Politics course is organized into five units and focuses on six countries. Instead of focusing mostly on units or mostly on countries, this book uses a hybrid approach. You will learn about a unit and its concepts and then have the opportunity to apply what you have just learned through the case study of a country.

Unit 1 covers political systems, regimes, and governments (Chapters 1 and 2 of this book). Unit 2 is about political institutions (Chapter 4). Unit 3 examines political culture and participation (Chapter 6). Unit 4 covers party and electoral systems as well as citizen organizations (Chapter 8). The book ends with Unit 5, which looks into political and economic changes and development (Chapters 10 and 12).

In addition to units and countries, the AP® Comparative Government and Politics course includes five themes, which the College Board calls Big Ideas. The first Big Idea is power and authority. Governments use different methods to maintain control. Consider how effective these methods are in maintaining control as you study each country.

The second Big Idea is legitimacy and stability. There is a connection between citizens' belief that the government has the right to rule and whether a state is strong or weak. Look for these connections as we study each country.

The third Big Idea is democratization. Some states successfully make the transition from being an authoritarian state to democracy, while others never fully complete the transition or backslide into authoritarianism. We will examine how Mexico and Nigeria democratized and why Russia backslid into authoritarianism.

The fourth Big Idea is the impact of internal and external forces. Governments face challenges from people within the country and from outside forces. As you study each country, consider the impact of these internal and external forces and how the government responds.

The last Big Idea is methods of political analysis. Political scientists collect data to describe patterns and trends that explain political behavior. Some of these data come from other disciplines, like history, geography, and economics. The key indicators used by political scientists to compare countries are discussed later in this chapter.

The AP® Comparative Government and Politics exam contains three free-response questions and one argument essay. Task verbs tell you how to write your response. These task verbs appear in the prompts on the AP® Exam:

Identify: Provide an answer without a detailed explanation.

> **Example:** Identify a country with an authoritarian system of government.
>
> **Answer:** Iran is authoritarian.

Define: Give the meaning of a word.

> **Example:** Define legitimacy.
>
> **Answer:** Legitimacy is the people's belief that the government has a right to rule.

Describe: State the characteristics of a topic.

> **Example:** Describe a referendum in the United Kingdom.
>
> **Answer:** An example of a referendum in the United Kingdom is Brexit, which was a question sent by parliament to citizens on the issue of whether or not citizens wanted the United Kingdom to leave the European Union or remain a member.

Explain: To give a cause or reason. Explanations usually include the word *because*. "Explain how" means to analyze a process. "Explain why" means to analyze the reasons why something occurs.

> **Example:** Explain how the legislature can check the executive in a presidential system.
>
> **Answer:** In a presidential system, the legislature can check the executive, *because* it has the power to ratify treaties and confirm cabinet appointments. This prevents the executive from acting unilaterally, *because* he or she must rely on the legislature to finalize treaties and fill cabinet positions.

> **Example:** Explain why a country would place term limits on the executive.
>
> **Answer:** Countries place term limits on the executive *because* they want to make it difficult for one person to consolidate power. The executive may stay in office for only a limited span of time, and this reduces the chance of the executive becoming a dictator.

Compare: Describe or explain similarities or differences, using a comparison term, such as *similarly*, or *in contrast*.

> **Example:** Compare the term limits of the executives in Mexico and Nigeria.
>
> **Answer:** The Mexican president serves for one six-year term. *In contrast*, the president in Nigeria may serve two terms of four years each. The president of Mexico never faces reelection, *unlike* the president in Nigeria, who faces reelection after his or her first four-year term.

Develop an argument: Take a position and support it with facts. Arguments usually contain the word *because*.

> **Example:** Develop an argument about whether democratic or authoritarian systems are better at maintaining security.
>
> **Answer:** Authoritarian systems are better at maintaining security, *because* they do not respect civil rights and liberties, making it easier to crack down on potential threats.

Draw a conclusion: Make an accurate statement based on evidence or information provided.

> **Example:** Based on the data shown in the table (of Human Development Index values), draw a conclusion about the level of development in the United Kingdom.
>
> **Answer:** The United Kingdom has a Human Development Index value of 9.32, which means it has a high level of development.

Section 1.1 Review

Each section's main ideas are reflected in the Learning Targets. By reviewing after each section, you should be able to

Remember the key points,

Know terms that are central to the topic, and

Think critically about what you have learned.

Remember

- Political scientists who study comparative government and politics *compare* by systematically examining political phenomena in more than one place and during more than one period and drawing conclusions from those observations.

Know

- *Comparative politics:* the study of similarities and differences between states, how different government systems operate, and why political changes occur. (p. 7)

Think

- How does studying political phenomena over different times and in different places help political scientists draw conclusions about government and politics?
- Why is it important to study different systems of government and compare their responses to similar events?

....

Free-Response Question: Conceptual Analysis

Answer A, B, C, and D.

A. Describe comparative politics.

B. Explain how political scientists compare countries.

C. Explain how political scientists reach conclusions by comparing countries.

D. Explain why it is difficult for political scientists to make predictions about future political events.

1.2 Thinking Like a Political Scientist

Learning Targets

After reading this section, you should be able to do the following:

1. Describe the difference between causation and correlation.

2. Describe the difference between empirical and normative statements.

3. Describe the role of quantitative information and source analysis in political science.

> **AP® TIP**
>
> **Vocabulary matters!**
>
> The AP® Comparative Government and Politics Exam assesses the knowledge and application of important concepts. Pay attention to the bold terms in the textbook. Understanding key concepts means much more than just memorizing words. It's crucial to understand why each concept is important and to be able to apply it to new scenarios and use the concept to compare countries.

Political scientists do not have perfect scientific conditions in which to do research. They do not work in a laboratory where they can control the variables of an experiment. Political scientists cannot control the real world of politics. Physicists can use a laboratory to monitor all elements of an experiment, and they can repeat that same experiment to achieve similar results because molecules do not notice what the scientists are doing, think about the situation, and change their behavior.

In political science, however, political actors think about the changes going on around them and modify their behavior accordingly. Governments are not lab rats. Nevertheless, there are standard methods that political scientists use to study the behavior of people and their governments. Although political scientists cannot introduce experiment-like controls, they still engage in systematic research to reach conclusions. For example, political scientists are highly successful at predicting things like voter behavior and turnout.

An Iranian woman shows ink on her index finger—it is proof of having voted in the election for parliament. Although Iran is an authoritarian state, elections are a source of participation and political engagement for Iranian citizens.

Atta Kenare/AFP/Getty Images

Comparative method
Examining the same phenomenon in several cases and reaching conclusions.

Scholars use the **comparative method** to examine the same phenomenon in several cases and reach conclusions from the individual cases. In studying political events and making comparisons, it's also important to differentiate between causation and correlation.

Looking for Causes and Connections

Causation
When a change in one variable precipitates a change in another variable.

Causation occurs when a change in one variable precipitates a change in another variable. In science classes, causation may be easy to prove. For example, a temperature below 32 degrees Fahrenheit causes water to freeze. Causation can be difficult to prove in political science, because political events are usually the result of several factors. Government officials, politicians, and citizens do not act according to a predictable set of scientific rules.

Correlation
An apparent connection between variables.

Unlike causation, which is a provable connection between variables, **correlation** is an apparent connection between variables. A positive correlation occurs when two variables move in the same direction. For example, when people have a strong sense of political efficacy—the belief that their vote may make a different in the political process—they are more likely to vote. This is a positive correlation because as political efficacy increases, so does voter turnout. An inverse correlation occurs when one variable increases and a second variable decreases. For example, when a state increases arrests and detentions of protestors, the number of protests usually decreases.

Sometimes two variables are correlated with a third variable, but there is no causal connection between the first two variables. Every summer, both ice cream sales and the number of forest fires increase. (Silver.) These factors are correlated, because both factors increase at the same time and for the same reason—hot, dry weather. However, there is no causal connection between them. Forest fires do not make people want to eat more ice cream.

Assessing Facts and Judgments

Empirical statement
An assertion of fact that can be proven.

Political scientists distinguish between empirical and normative statements. An **empirical statement** is an assertion of fact that can be proven. For example, "Mexico has a presidential system of government." This can be proven by examining the structure of government in Mexico and comparing it to the structure of a presidential system. Empirical statements are often based on data. An example of a data-based empirical statement is, "According to the *CIA World Factbook*, Mexico's GDP per capita in 2020 was $19,900."

A **normative statement** is a value judgment. For example, "The United Kingdom should eliminate the monarchy because it is expensive and unnecessary," is a normative statement. An empirical statement describes what *actually occurs*, and a normative statement describes what *should occur*.

Normative statement
A value judgment, usually in the form of a *should* or *ought* statement.

Examining Statistics and Written Sources

Political scientists rely on quantitative and qualitative data to reach conclusions about political outcomes. **Quantitative data** are observations made using statistical techniques. Quantitative data are often conveyed in charts, graphs, tables, and maps. On the AP® Comparative Government and Politics Exam, you will be asked to analyze quantitative data in these formats. **Qualitative data** are text-based descriptions, including explanations of how government and political institutions function. Both quantitative and qualitative data can be conveyed in infographics. You will encounter qualitative data on the AP® Exam in the form of source-analysis questions that ask you to analyze a passage and understand an author's point of view.

Quantitative data
Observations made using statistical techniques, which are often conveyed in charts, graphs, tables, and maps.

Qualitative data
Text-based descriptions, including explanations of how government and political institutions function.

AP® POLITICAL SCIENCE PRACTICES

Source Analysis

On the AP® Exam, you will be asked to analyze passages, such as excerpts from journal articles and official government documents. For example, you might be asked to interpret a law or a constitutional passage from one of the six countries studied. Journal articles may be controversial and often make an argument or present a point of view. Laws and constitutional provisions may or may not reflect the way a country's government really operates.

Your first task is to determine the source of the passage or provision. This information is provided in the citation. The name of the author might not be useful in analyzing the passage unless the author is a prominent leader, such as a president. Look at the article title, which often contains clues about the author's viewpoint or the purpose of the law or constitutional provision. Read carefully, and underline language that explains the motive of the author or the purpose of the provision. Pay special attention to language meant to elicit an emotional response from the reader. For example, an author might choose language to demonize an opponent. In a famous speech by Ayatollah Khomeini, who led the Islamic Revolution in Iran, he called the United States "the Great Satan," accusing it of imperialism and corruption. (Khomeini.)

Read and analyze the following passage:

As for protecting its content, well, every event has a content and a meaning. What was the content of that event? We should gain a correct understanding about its content and then protect and guard it. Why should we guard it? Because treacherous narrators and analysts with ulterior motives try to distort the content of great events to their own benefit and to the benefit of usurping powers in the world. This practice has existed since long ago: narrators with ulterior motives narrate an event in a way that the opposite meaning is portrayed in the minds of the audience.

Today, with the development of means of mass communication and numerous other technologies, corrupt powers and treacherous hands are capable of changing events and their content. They analyze them in the wrong way and misguide public opinion—in particular, future generations and those who were not present when the event took place, who did not see it up close, and who did not hear about it in times close to the event itself.

—Ayatollah Ali Khamenei, Supreme Leader of Iran, televised speech delivered January 8, 2021

A. Identify the author of the speech.

B. Describe the author's point of view.

C. Explain how the author chose his or her words to persuade the audience.

The multiple-choice portion of the exam will require you to understand and interpret quantitative and qualitative data. The quantitative free-response question will require you to understand and interpret data in the form of a chart, graph, table, or map.

Another important skill in political science is **source analysis**, which is the ability to read and analyze texts. You will encounter source analysis on the multiple-choice portion of the AP® Exam. Passages might be drawn from journal articles or official government documents, such as constitutions. Source analysis gives insight into how governments function and how leaders react to events.

Political science can never be a pure science because of imperfect laboratory conditions: In the real world, we have very little control over social and political phenomena. Nevertheless, we can use the tools of political science to understand political behavior and how governments evolve.

Section 1.2 Review

Remember

- Scholars use the comparative method to examine the same phenomenon in several cases and reach conclusions.
- Political scientists rely on quantitative and qualitative data in reaching conclusions.

Know

- *Comparative method:* examining the same phenomenon in several cases and reaching conclusions. (p. 10)
- *Causation:* when a change in one variable precipitates a change in another variable. (p. 10)
- *Correlation:* an apparent connection between variables. (p. 10)
- *Empirical statement:* an assertion of fact that can be proven. (p. 10)
- *Normative statement:* a value judgment, usually in the form of a *should* or *ought* statement. (p. 11)
- *Quantitative data:* observations made using statistical techniques, which are often conveyed in charts, graphs, tables, and maps. (p. 11)
- *Qualitative data:* text-based descriptions, including explanations of how government and political institutions function. (p. 11)
- *Source analysis:* reading and analyzing text. (p. 12)

Think

- Why is it easier to find correlation in comparative government than it is to find causation?
- Why do political scientists make both empirical and normative statements in reaching conclusions?

Free-Response Question: Conceptual Analysis

Answer A, B, C, and D.

A. Describe the difference between an empirical statement and a normative statement.

B. Explain how political scientists use empirical evidence to support conclusions.

C. Describe a criticism of making normative statements when comparing countries.

D. Explain why political scientists make normative statements a part of the research process.

1.3 Comparing Economic Development

Learning Targets

After reading this section, you should be able to do the following:

1. Describe the economic indicators political scientists use to compare countries.

2. Describe the advantages and disadvantages of the indicators used by political scientists in comparing countries.

Countries can be compared using different indicators. This section will cover some of the most common measures used to compare countries' economies. Each indicator measures a specific factor or factors, and it's important not to draw unsupported conclusions about factors that are not measured. All measures have strengths and weaknesses. For example, comparing production and growth rates may be useful in measuring overall economic growth, but it doesn't convey much information about what it is like for the average citizen to live in a country.

The Human Development Index

The word *development* conjures up images of impoverished children and gleaming new skyscrapers. Since World War II, an entire industry and several major international organizations—the International Monetary Fund (IMF) and the World Bank in particular—have arisen to try to help poor countries "develop." Both of these organizations provide advice and financial assistance to member countries in an effort to improve the global economy, and you will learn more about them in Chapter 10. Governments of the Organisation for Economic Co-operation and Development (OECD), the wealthiest countries of the world, spent $147 billion on foreign aid toward this effort in 2017.

In the past, social scientists and policymakers viewed "development" as being about the poor countries of the world—what they called the "Third World" or "underdeveloped countries"—looking more like wealthy, Western countries. Politically, this meant becoming independent, democratic states. Economically, it meant becoming wealthier, which meant industrializing and urbanizing. Some countries have been spectacularly successful. China's economic growth has helped make it a global superpower, and the World Bank lists China as an "upper-middle-income" country.

Some political scientists question whether poor countries in the current era of globalization can realistically follow the same path as the West and question whether wealth generation and economic growth should be the main goals of development. Economic growth does not always reduce poverty, critics argued, and should not be seen as development. Instead, development should focus on the "poorest of the poor."

Economist and philosopher Amartya Sen profoundly influenced thinking on the concept of development in the new millennium with his focus on human capabilities. He argued that neither growth nor poverty reduction alone were adequate goals. The real goal of development anywhere in the world (including in wealthy countries) should be enhancing the capabilities of individuals to lead fulfilling lives as people define them. Economic growth that provides higher incomes and reduces poverty would certainly be part of that, but helping people achieve greater capabilities also means they need to be healthy, educated, and free. (Sen, 1999.)

Sen argued that freedom is essential. He argued that people need to be free politically and live in democracies—only then could they define for themselves what a fulfilling life would be—and they needed to be free from social restrictions, such as traditional gender norms that limit their capabilities.

Sen's theory has become the leading conceptualization of development. It is the basis for a widely used index of development, the Human Development Index (HDI) developed by the United Nations. The **Human Development Index (HDI)** is an aggregate measure, which means it takes into account several factors that impact people's standard of living, including life expectancy, education, and per capita income. Countries are sorted into four categories of development: very high, high, medium, and low. They are also ranked from 1 to 189. Countries are given an HDI value that ranges from zero to 1.0, with 1.0 representing the highest level of development. In 2020, Norway was ranked first in human development, with an HDI value of 0.957.

The HDI scores for the six countries studied in AP® Comparative Government and Politics are shown in Table 1.1.

Critics of using HDI to measure development point out that it weights factors, such as education and per capita income, equally. (Chowdhury, 1991.) As a result, a country with a low level of education and a high level of income would receive a score similar to a country with lower income and a higher level of education. The standard of living in two countries with nearly identical HDI values may differ greatly. Furthermore, a high level of national wealth does not mean wealth is distributed evenly or that the government provides social welfare benefits to citizens, because HDI doesn't take income inequality into account. (Investopedia, 2020.) Also, as discussed above, the term *development* can have several differing meanings. Notions of development that focus mainly on economic growth differ from other ideas about development that focus on quality of life.

Human Development Index (HDI)
An aggregate measure of life expectancy, education, and per capita income.

TABLE 1.1 Countries by Human Development Index Value

Country	HDI Value
United Kingdom	0.932
Russia	0.824
Iran	0.783
Mexico	0.779
China	0.761
Nigeria	0.539

Data from 2020 Human Development Index.

Gross Domestic Product, GDP per Capita, and GDP Growth Rate

Gross domestic product (GDP)
The total value of goods and services produced in a country in a year.

Economic indicators are another way to compare countries. **Gross domestic product (GDP)** represents the total value of goods and services produced in a country in a year. GDP is a comprehensive measure of all economic activity within a country, and it is a prominent indicator of the health of a country's economy. The 2020 GDP for each of the six countries studied is shown in Table 1.2.

The six countries studied in this course are all ranked in the top 12 percent of countries in terms of GDP. However, GDP is not a sound basis for comparison, because it does not take into account how many people are living in a country. Another criticism of GDP as an economic measure is that many countries have significant underground black markets,

TABLE 1.2 Countries Ranked by Gross Domestic Product

Country	2020 GDP (in millions/USD)	Rank (out of 195)
China	14,860,775	2
United Kingdom	2,638,296	5
Russia	1,464,078	11
Mexico	1,040,372	16
Iran	610,662	22
Nigeria	442,976	27

Data from International Monetary Fund, 2020 estimates.

Beijing's main business district sparkles. The many new skyscrapers indicate a high gross domestic product, yet gross domestic product is not an indicator of how people lead their daily lives or how much they earn.

Wang Yukun/Moment/Getty Images

where economic activity is not reported or taxed, and GDP does not take this activity into account. Furthermore, GDP relies on official government data, which may not be accurate.

GDP forms the basis for other comparative indicators, such as **GDP per capita**, which is a nation's GDP divided by its population. GDP per capita measures economic production per person. This is a very rough estimate of the standard of living within a country. Don't confuse GDP per capita with average per capita income—the amount the average person makes. The GDP per capita for our six countries is shown in Table 1.3.

GDP per capita
Gross domestic product divided by population.

As shown in Table 1.3, GDP per capita is a better comparative measure than GDP. For example, while China's GDP was the second largest in the world in 2020, it ranked fifty-ninth in GDP per capita. This is because China has the largest population in the world, more than 1.4 billion people. (Statista, 2021.) Nigeria offers another striking example. It was ranked twenty-first in GDP, but its rank in GDP per capita was 135th, in the bottom half of countries. Like China, this is because of Nigeria's large population, estimated at 206 million in 2020. (Statista, 2021.)

TABLE 1.3 Countries Ranked by Gross Domestic Product per Capita

Country	GDP per capita (in USD)	Rank (out of 187)
United Kingdom	39,229	21
China	10,839	59
Russia	9,972	62
Mexico	8,069	71
Iran	7,257	78
Nigeria	2,149	135

Data from International Monetary Fund, 2020 estimates.

One weakness of GDP per capita is that it is an average, and it does not tell us much about how income is distributed. If most of the income is concentrated among the wealthiest citizens, then GDP per capita is not an accurate picture of the economic status of most citizens.

Another way GDP forms the basis for economic comparison is the **GDP growth rate**. This measures how much GDP has grown over a period of time. GDP growth rate shows how fast the economy of a country is improving over time. Keep in mind that GDP can continue to grow even when the GDP growth rate slows. The GDP growth rates for the six countries are shown in Figure 1.1.

GDP growth rate
The percentage of GDP growth over a period of time.

GDP statistics provide indicators of a country's economic performance, but they do not tell us much about how wealth is distributed.

FIGURE 1.1

Twenty Years of GDP Growth Rates (Percent)

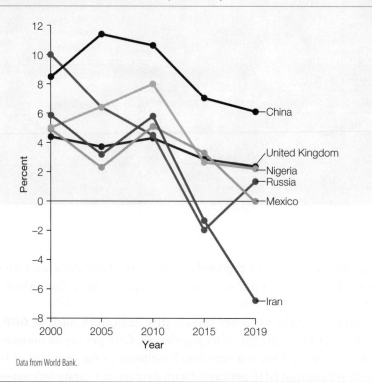

Data from World Bank.

Gini Index

A high rate of income inequality is associated with greater poverty and has a negative effect on the notion of equality in a democracy. Countries with higher inequality have lower intergenerational mobility—the rich stay rich and the poor stay poor. A team of economists at the International Monetary Fund demonstrated that greater inequality also results in slower economic growth. (Ostry et al., 2019.)

Since the 1980s, when the current era of globalization began, the Gini index, the most common measure of inequality, increased across all thirty-seven of the member countries in the Organisation for Economic Cooperation and Development. The Gini index increased from 0.29 in 1980 to 0.33 by 2016, an increase of about 10 percent. (OECD, 2020.) In 1980, the poorest half of the population in OECD countries had a slightly larger share of after-tax national income than the richest 10 percent. By 2017, the richer group had 5 percent more than the bottom half. (World Inequality Database, 2019.)

The **Gini index**, also called the Gini coefficient, measures income inequality. A score of zero indicates complete equality, and a score of 1 indicates complete inequality. The higher the score, the bigger the gap between the rich and the poor. A high level of equality might not be beneficial, especially if everyone is poor. However, high levels of inequality or a widening wealth gap may lead to civil unrest. As is true of all comparative indicators, the Gini index must be considered in the context of the country being studied. The Gini index scores for the six countries are shown in Table 1.4.

Gini index (coefficient)
A measure of income inequality within a country.

TABLE 1.4 Gini Index, 2019

Country	Gini index (coefficient)
United Kingdom	33.12
Nigeria	35.1
Russia	35.32
Iran	41.14
Mexico	42.79
China	46.5

Data from Statista.

Migrant workers Wang Qin (at left) and her sister Wang Jun eat lunch during a break from collecting scrap materials from the debris of demolished buildings at the outskirts of Beijing. As China moved to a market economy, the income gap widened. The Gini index is a measure of income inequality in a country.

Thomas Peter/Reuters/Alamy

Note that there is less income inequality in the United Kingdom, which has a regulated free-market economy, than there is in China, which moved from a command economy in the Mao Zedong era to a market-socialist economy in the 1980s. Although China's rapid economic growth lifted millions of people out of poverty, the wealth gap increased.

There is a popular saying that "a rising tide lifts all boats." In other words, economic growth improves the lives of all citizens. The rising tide of China's economy lifted all boats, but some boats were lifted a lot higher than others.

Economic development is just one way to compare countries. It's also important to look at political factors, such as human rights.

Section 1.3 Review

Remember

- Development refers to the political and economic improvements in people's lives.
- Some commonly used indicators of economic development include the Human Development Index (HDI), Gross Domestic Product (GDP), GDP per capita, GDP growth rate, and the Gini index (coefficient).

Know

- *Human Development Index (HDI):* an aggregate measure of life expectancy, education, and per capita income. (p. 14)
- *Gross domestic product (GDP):* the total value of goods and services produced in a country in a year. (p. 14)
- *GDP per capita:* gross domestic product divided by population. (p. 15)
- *GDP growth rate:* the percentage of GDP growth over a period of time. (p. 15)
- *Gini index (coefficient):* a measure of income inequality within a country. (p. 16)

Think

- What are the drawbacks of the economic indicators discussed in this section in drawing conclusions about the level of development within a state?

Free-Response Question: Quantitative Analysis

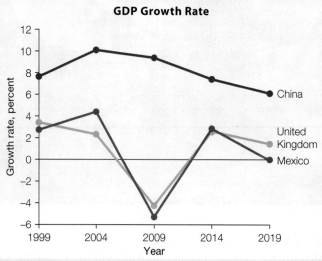

GDP Growth Rate

Data from World Bank.

Answer A, B, C, D, and E.

A. Using the data in the line graph, identify the state with the highest GDP growth rate in 2019.

B. Using the data in the line graph, describe a trend in the GDP growth rate for the country you identified in part A.

C. Define GDP growth rate.

D. Using your knowledge of development and the data in the line graph, draw a conclusion about economic development in China.

E. Explain a limitation of the data shown in the line graph in measuring economic development.

1.4 Comparing Political Development

Learning Targets

After reading this section, you should be able to do the following:

1. Describe the political indicators that political scientists use to compare countries.

2. Describe the advantages and disadvantages of the political indicators used by political scientists in comparing countries.

This section will cover some of the most common measures used to compare political development. Each indicator measures a specific factor or factors, and it's important not to draw unsupported conclusions about factors that are not measured. For example, comparing levels of personal freedom will tell you whether a country is democratic or authoritarian, but it doesn't convey much information about citizens' standard of living.

Freedom House

Freedom House is a nongovernmental organization, founded in the United States, that advocates for democracy and human rights and measures freedom around the world. Freedom House studies countries, makes policy recommendations, and provides articles about government accountability, transparency, and human rights.

Countries are given Freedom House scores based on political rights and civil liberties and are classified as free, partially free, and not free. Political rights scores are based on free and fair elections, pluralism, and participation. Civil liberties scores are based on freedom of expression and belief, the right of association, rule of law, and individual rights and autonomy. Scores for political rights range up to 40, and scores for civil liberties range up to 60. It is possible to receive a negative score. You may encounter earlier Freedom House scores on the AP® Exam. Until 2021, Freedom House scores for political rights and civil liberties ranged from 1 to 7, with lower scores indicating higher levels of freedom.

Freedom House scores for the six countries are shown in Table 1.5.

Freedom House
A nongovernmental organization that advocates for democracy and human rights and measures freedom around the world.

TABLE 1.5 Freedom House Ratings, 2020

Country	Status	Personal rights	Civil liberties
China	NF	−2	11
Iran	NF	6	10
Mexico	PF	27	34
Nigeria	PF	21	24
Russia	NF	5	15
United Kingdom	F	39	54

Note: Personal-rights scores range from 1 to 40. Civil-liberties scores range from 1 to 60. Higher scores indicate higher levels of freedom. F indicates that a country is classified as free, PF indicates that a country is classified as partially free, and NF indicates that a country is classified as not free.
Data from Freedom House.

Note the differences in the scores between China, which offers its citizens few personal rights and the United Kingdom, which has a nearly perfect score. This is one of the reasons why the United Kingdom is considered to be a consolidated democratic state. **Democratic consolidation** is the process by which a regime has developed stable democratic institutions and significant protections of civil liberties and is unlikely to revert to authoritarianism. Democratic consolidation means that democracy has become widely accepted by both government officials and the people as the permanent system of government in a country.

Democratic consolidation
The process by which a regime has developed stable democratic institutions and significant protections of civil liberties and is unlikely to revert to authoritarianism.

Critics of Freedom House's methodology argue that assigning a mathematical score to the concept of freedom is overly simplified. Critics also contend that the report is biased toward Western conceptions of freedom. (Lozovsky, 2016.) Nevertheless, Freedom House is a valuable tool in comparing political rights.

Transparency International and the Corruption Perceptions Index

Transparency International is a nongovernmental organization devoted to reducing corruption by encouraging transparency and accountability. **Corruption** is the abuse of official power for personal gain.

Corruption
The abuse of official power for personal gain.

There are two types of corruption. Grand corruption occurs at the highest levels of society. It causes significant harm, and because the perpetrators are among the political elite, it often goes unpunished. For example, a high-ranking official might divert government revenues into a personal bank account, enriching the official and reducing the amount of money available to support government programs. Petty corruption is the everyday abuse of power by government workers in their interactions with citizens. For example, if a clerk at a department of motor vehicles asks for a bribe to process an application for a driver's license, he or she is engaging in petty corruption. Corruption hinders democracy, because it harms citizens' faith in the government and undermines the rule of law.

Transparency International created the **Corruption Perceptions Index** to measure how corrupt a system is believed to be according to experts and business leaders. It's difficult to measure the actual amount of corruption within a system because officials do not admit to corruption. Instead, the Corruption Perceptions Index measures people's experiences in encountering corruption. Countries are scored on a scale of 0 to 100, with 0 representing absolute corruption and 100 representing completely clean government.

Corruption Perceptions Index
A measure of how corrupt a system is believed to be.

TABLE 1.6 Corruption Perceptions Score and Rank 2019

Country	Score	Rank (out of 180)
United Kingdom	77	12
China	41	80
Mexico	29	130
Russia	28	137
Nigeria	26	146
Iran	26	146

Data from Transparency International.

The 2019 Corruptions Perceptions Index scores and ranking for the six countries are shown in Table 1.6.

The United Kingdom, the most democratic country studied, has the lowest level of corruption. However, there is not a clear pattern between levels of corruption in emerging democracies and authoritarian states. For example, China, an authoritarian state, has a lower level of perceived corruption than the emerging democracies in Mexico and Nigeria.

Another way to compare countries is by how stable they are and the likelihood of collapse.

The Fragile States Index

Strong state
A state that is capable of providing necessary government services to its citizens.

A **strong state** is generally capable of providing necessary government services to its citizens. State strength, however, exists on a continuum, with no state being perfectly strong in all categories. Stronger states tend to be wealthier and have healthier national economies. They also are less corrupt, indicating the presence of stronger bureaucracies, and tend to be more legitimate.

Weak states, on the other hand, are often characterized by what Thomas Risse termed "limited statehood"—the government widely distributes some goods and services, but others exist only in certain areas of the country. (Risse, 2015.) Other actors—local strongmen, religious institutions, nongovernmental organizations (NGOs), or even drug cartels—may substitute for a weak state in some regions, providing goods and services that the state cannot or will not deliver.

Failed state
A state that has lost control over all or part of its territory.

A state that is so weak that it loses control over all or part of its territory is a **failed state**. Failed states make headlines when their governments collapse. The elements of state strength are interconnected. If a state lacks the resources to provide basic infrastructure and security, its support among citizens most likely will decline. Lack of resources also may mean civil servants are paid very little, which may lead to corruption and an even further decline in the quality of state services. Corruption in some bureaucracies, such as the military and border patrol, can cause a loss of security and territorial integrity. If the state cannot provide basic services, such as education, citizens will likely find alternative routes to success that might involve illegal activity, like smuggling and selling goods on the black market, undermining sovereignty even more. Citizens go outside of the legal system to settle disputes (mafias are a prime example of this phenomenon), threatening law and order.

Continuing patterns of lawless behavior create and reinforce the public perception that the state is weak, so weak states can become caught in a vicious cycle that is difficult to break.

Measuring State Strength

In response to growing international concern about state failure, the Fund for Peace developed a **Fragile States Index** to highlight countries of imminent concern. In 2019, the fifteenth annual index ranked 178 countries on twelve factors in four categories considered essential to state strength:

Fragile States Index
A measure of state strength, highlighting concerns about fragile and failed states.

Social indicators
- Demographic pressures
- Refugees or internally displaced persons
- Intervention by external political actors

Economic indicators
- Uneven economic development
- Poverty/severe economic decline
- Sustained human flight and educated people leaving the country (the brain drain)

Political indicators
- The people's belief in the government's right to rule (legitimacy)
- Deterioration of public services
- Rule of law/human-rights abuses

Cohesion indicators
- The military and police forces (security apparatus)
- Factionalized leadership
- Groups seeking vengeance

The index measures those twelve indicators and then adds them up, weighting them all equally, to arrive at an overall score for each country. Table 1.7 shows the Fragile States Index score and classification for the six countries. Countries are classified as very sustainable, sustainable, very stable, more stable, warning, elevated warning, high warning, alert, high alert, and very high alert. The Fragile States index gives countries a score, with 120 points maximum. Higher scores indicate greater instability.

TABLE 1.7 Strength of States from the Fragile States Index

Country	Rating	Classification
United Kingdom	38.3	Very Sustainable
China	69.9	Warning
Mexico	67.2	Warning
Russia	76	High Warning
Iran	83.4	High Warning
Nigeria	93.7	Alert

Data from Fragile States Index, 2020.

Countries can take several steps to strengthen the state, including diversifying the economy and improving infrastructure. Improving education and protecting the environment also enhance stability. Policies to make a country more democratic, such as free and fair elections, protecting civil rights and liberties, and media independence, may also make a state more stable. States can encourage stability by enacting policies to prevent overpopulation. States with large refugee populations can prevent unrest by providing them with resources and support to help them become a part of the community.

Critics of the Fragile States Index assert that it creates a false distinction between strong and weak states. They also claim the term "fragile" is vague. Finally, critics argue that the index is not useful in predicting which states are likely to collapse. (Beehner and Young, 2014.)

There is no perfect indicator to compare countries. However, by examining the measures discussed in this chapter, we can get a clearer comparison of the six countries studied in AP® Comparative Government and Politics.

Section 1.4 Review

Remember

- Some commonly used indicators of political development include Freedom House ratings, the Corruption Perceptions Index, and the Fragile States Index.
- There is no perfect measure of political development, but by looking at several measures, political scientists can draw conclusions about the level of political development within a country.

Know

- *Freedom House:* a nongovernmental organization that advocates for democracy and human rights and measures freedom around the world. (p. 19)
- *Democratic consolidation:* the process by which a regime has developed stable democratic institutions and significant protections of civil liberties and is unlikely to revert to authoritarianism. (p. 19)
- *Corruption:* the abuse of official power for personal gain. (p. 19)
- *Corruption Perceptions Index:* a measure of how corrupt a system is believed to be. (p. 20)
- *Strong state:* a state that is capable of providing necessary government services to its citizens. (p. 20)
- *Failed state:* a state that has lost control over all or part of its territory. (p. 20)
- *Fragile States Index:* a measure of state strength, highlighting concerns about fragile and failed states. (p. 21)

Think

- Are political factors, such as freedom, or economic factors, such as GDP per capita, more important in measuring the level of development within a state?

Free-Response Question: Quantitative Analysis

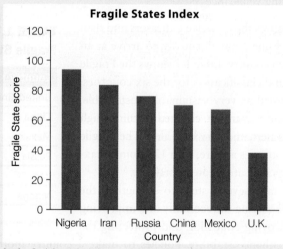

Data from Fragile States Index, 2020.

Answer A, B, C, D, and E. Keep the following in mind: Maximum score is 120. Higher numbers mean less stability.

A. Using the data in the bar chart, identify the state with the highest level of fragility.

B. Using the data in the chart, explain why the country you identified in part A has a high level of fragility.

C. Draw a conclusion about democratic government and the level of fragility in a country.

D. Using your knowledge of fragility, describe a policy a state could enact to increase stability.

E. Explain a limitation of the Fragile States Index in measuring the strength of states.

Political Systems

AP® KEY CONCEPTS

- Comparative politics (p. 7)
- Comparative method (p. 10)
- Causation (p. 10)
- Correlation (p. 10)
- Empirical statement (p. 10)
- Normative statement (p. 11)
- Quantitative data (p. 11)
- Qualitative data (p. 11)

- Source analysis (p. 12)
- Human Development Index (HDI) (p. 14)
- Gross domestic product (GDP) (p. 14)
- GDP per capita (p. 15)
- GDP growth rate (p. 15)
- Gini index (coefficient) (p. 16)
- Freedom House (p. 19)

- Democratic consolidation (p. 19)
- Corruption (p. 19)
- Corruption Perceptions Index (p. 20)
- Strong state (p. 20)
- Failed state (p. 20)
- Fragile States Index (p. 21)

AP® EXAM MULTIPLE-CHOICE PRACTICE QUESTIONS

1. Which of the following statements represents a correlation?
   A. Authoritarian states restrict civil rights and liberties to control potential threats to the regime.
   B. Consolidated democracies tend to have more accountability and transparency than authoritarian states.
   C. An increase in gross domestic product (GDP) causes a country's GDP growth rate to increase.
   D. Mexico should reduce corruption in an effort to increase citizens' trust in government.

2. Which of the following is a normative statement?
   A. Foreign direct investment often causes a decline in environmental conditions.
   B. The Human Development Index is a relatively accurate measure of a country's standard of living.
   C. Iran should ease social restrictions in an effort to encourage young people to remain in the country.
   D. Development is difficult to measure because every country has a different political culture and economy.

3. Which of the following is an empirical statement?
   A. In 2020, China received a Fragile States Index rating of 69.9, which places the country at the "warning" level.
   B. To improve its relationship with the United States, Mexico should pay for a portion of the border wall.
   C. The monarchy in the United Kingdom is a costly and unnecessary tradition.
   D. Russia's president has consolidated power, and he is likely to become a dictator.

4. Which of the following measures takes income, education, and life expectancy into account?
   A. GDP per capita
   B. The Gini index (coefficient)
   C. Freedom House Ratings
   D. The Human Development Index (HDI)

Questions 5 and 6 refer to the table.

Country	GDP (in billions USD)	GDP per capita (in USD)	GDP growth rate
China	$14,327,359	$8,041	6.14
United Kingdom	$2,827,918	$43,111	1.26
Mexico	$2,156,946	$10,275	−0.3
Russia	$1,702,361	$12,842	1.34
Nigeria	$475,062	$5,900	0.8 (2017)
Iran	$581,252	$20,100 (2017)	3.7 (2017)

Data from International Monetary Fund, 2019, except for data from 2017 as indicated.

5. Which of the following is accurate according to the table?
   A. Mexico has a higher GDP per capita than Russia.
   B. China has the highest standard of living of the countries shown.
   C. Mexico is the only country shown with a negative GDP growth rate.
   D. Iran has the lowest GDP of the countries shown.

6. Which of the following is an implication of the table?
   A. China's GDP per capita is relatively low, but it is likely to improve due to China's GDP growth rate.
   B. There is a correlation between having a democratic government and having a strong GDP growth rate.
   C. Nigeria is unlikely to improve its standard of living due to a low GDP growth rate and a high rate of population growth.
   D. Mexico is more likely than Russia to raise its status from a middle-income country to a high-income country.

7. Which of the following is a criticism of the Gini index (coefficient) in comparing countries?
   A. It does not take into account that a high level of income inequality is a positive development, because it encourages people to work harder.
   B. Countries with similar Gini index scores may have different living standards.
   C. It is difficult to measure income inequality because countries with a high level of inequality are hesitant to share data.
   D. GDP is a better comparative measure than the Gini index because it accounts for population size.

Questions 8 and 9 refer to the map.

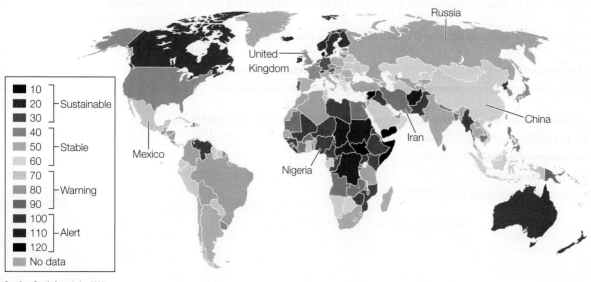

Data from Fragile States Index, 2020.

8. Which of the following is an accurate statement according to the map?
   A. China is more fragile than Russia.
   B. Iran is the most fragile state in the Middle East.
   C. Mexico is considered to be a very fragile state.
   D. Nigeria is at the alert level and is considered unstable.

9. Which of the following is an implication of the map?
   A. Western Europe is the most stable region in the world.
   B. Most of the states rated as very unstable are in Africa.
   C. Authoritarian states are more stable than democratic states.
   D. Stability is difficult to measure because it differs from region to region.

10. Which of the following is a criticism of the Corruption Perceptions Index?
    A. Corruption is difficult to measure because government officials rarely admit to engaging in corrupt behavior.
    B. Corruption is difficult to define and there are no universally accepted criteria for measuring it.
    C. Citizens rarely experience grand corruption firsthand, and as a result, grand corruption is underreported.
    D. Citizens rarely report their experiences with corruption.

AP® EXAM PRACTICE ARGUMENT ESSAY

Note to Students:

The following is designed to begin preparing you for the argument essay prompt that you will see on the AP® Exam. You will build on this skill throughout the book.

The argument question on the AP® Comparative Government and Politics Exam will require you to use knowledge from at least two of the six countries studied. But at this point in the textbook, you have not had an opportunity to study any of the countries. (You will get to the first country—Mexico—in Chapter 3.) For that reason, this preliminary question will give you practice at developing an argument in the form of an essay.

Later in this book, you will answer questions that are more consistent with the format of the argument essay on the AP® Exam.

Here is a simplified argument question:

Develop an argument as to whether indicators used by political scientists are accurate measures of the level of development within countries.

- Use one or more of the following course concepts in your response:
  - GDP per capita
  - Gini index (coefficient)
  - Freedom House ratings

In your response, do the following:

- Respond to the prompt with a defensible claim or thesis that establishes a line of reasoning using one or more of the provided course concepts.
- Use reasoning to explain why your evidence supports your claim or thesis, using one or more of the provided course concepts.
- Respond to an opposing or alternate perspective, using refutation, concession, or rebuttal.

For a complete list of the sources of information cited in this chapter, turn to the Works Cited appendix.

2 Political Systems

Crowds in Parliament Square in London celebrate Brexit. Supporters of Brexit believed that the United Kingdom gave up too much sovereignty as a member of the European Union.

Guy Corbishley/Alamy

The Man behind Brexit

In June 2016, the electorate in the United Kingdom shocked the country and the rest of Europe by voting to leave the European Union (EU).

Comprised of twenty-seven European nations, the EU is a type of international organization known as a supranational organization, with a total population of roughly 450 million. Countries that join the EU give up some sovereignty in exchange for the benefits of membership. This gives the EU the power to act in a given policy area on behalf of all members—trade being the number-one example. It provides for the free movement of people, goods, and services, and it sets the rules of commerce between member states. Citizens of one country can freely move to another to work or live.

In 1951, when six nations formed the European Coal and Steel Community, the original goal was to integrate their economies and lessen the extreme nationalism that had led to World War I and World War II. At first, free trade among member nations was its mission. Over time, other nations joined, and tighter economic and political integration among nations was implemented.

The British remained outside these agreements until 1973, when the United Kingdom joined what was then called the European Economic Community. In 1993, further integration resulted in the EEC becoming the EU, as more nations joined. Yet the British remained ambivalent about the EU and opted out of the common currency, the euro, that was fully implemented in 2002, retaining the pound sterling (£).

EU member countries agree to give up some of their sovereignty over domestic and international affairs to centralized EU institutions—a parliament, a court of justice, a central bank, and more. Yet, each nation retains some sovereignty over domestic budgetary affairs and welfare state spending. Sovereignty is the ability of a state to act without internal or external interference. While the state is seen as the central ingredient of the modern world, no state is fully independent of the impact of trade, the global environment, and international conflicts.

Dominic Cummings, special adviser to U.K. Prime Minister Boris Johnson, walks from the meeting hall in Manchester of the 2019 Conservative Party conference.

Chris Ratcliffe/Bloomberg/Getty Images

Geographically and historically, the British have seen themselves as both a part of Europe and, at the same time, separate. The United Kingdom is made of distinct regions, including England, Scotland, Wales, and Northern Ireland. Regional identity is so strong that the British do not field one team to represent them in the World Cup (soccer) championship. There are four—England, Scotland, Wales, and Northern Ireland, each with its own flag.

The vote to leave the EU was fueled by a reaction to the effects of globalization, immigration from poorer countries, and the aftermath of the worldwide 2008–09 financial crisis. The goal was to retake power over domestic economic affairs and immigration policy and, more broadly, to protect the nation's cultural identity. The slogan coined for the 2016 referendum for those who favored withdrawal from EU membership was "Take Back Control." The architect of the Leave campaign and author of this slogan was Dominic Cummings.

Born in 1971, Cummings went to a private secondary boarding school and then to the University of Oxford, a training ground for Britain's elite. One of his professors at Oxford recalled decades after he graduated, "He was fizzing with ideas, unconvinced by any received set of views about anything." (Lambert.) He was "something like a Robespierre— someone determined to bring down things that don't work." (Lambert.) After he graduated, Cummings moved to Russia to establish an airline that later failed.

Cummings moved back to Britain in 1997 and began his rise in politics. Soon he was a key advisor to the campaign to keep the United Kingdom from joining the monetary union that became a centerpiece of the EU, with the new currency, the euro. Known for his blunt style, Cummings became the director of strategy for the Conservative Party and then a key aide to Michael Gove, a member of parliament who then served as minister of education. While serving in the government, he was known for hurling insults to all who stood in his way, whether of his own party or the opposition. Fellow Conservative David Cameron, while prime minister, called him a "career psychopath." Cummings described himself as an iconoclast and uber-revolutionary. (Collini.)

The movement to leave the EU accelerated in the aftermath of the 2010 British parliamentary elections, when the British government began its austerity program and started cutting back social services to spur economic recovery from the recession that began in 2008. Some voters felt that being entangled with the EU only made economic matters worse, and with rising economic frustration, anti-immigrant feeling grew. Prime Minister Cameron's worries about the rising anti-EU sentiment in the country grew when, in 2014, in elections for the European Parliament, the UK Independence Party (UKIP), dedicated to leaving the EU, won more votes than either the Conservative or the Labour Party.

Dominic Cummings seized the moment and in 2015 co-founded Vote Leave, which was the official campaign organization leading the effort to exit the EU. The Leave campaign cut across party lines, with David Cameron, the Conservative Party leader and prime minister, against it, but other Conservatives supporting it. The same pattern was evident in the Labour Party. (Cummings.)

For many voters, the abstraction of issues such as "sovereignty" was crystallized in the concern over immigration, which some blamed for the nation's economic woes. Those who supported remaining in the EU were worried about the economic dislocation that would result from severing ties with the EU.

As the campaign unfolded, Cummings claimed that the cost of EU membership was draining the National Health Service, and the money saved could be redirected to the nation's universal health-care system. Large ads were placed covering the entire side of buses with the claim, which was proved to be demonstrably false, but it resonated with many voters. (Cummings.) In 2019, he refused to appear before a committee of parliament investigating "fake news" central to the Leave campaign.

In fact, in 2017 Cummings did not hide the rhetorical power of his efforts: "Would we have won without immigration? No. Would we have won without £350 million for NHS? All our research and the close result strongly suggest no. Would we have won by spending our time talking about trade and the single market? No way." For Cummings, "Immigration was a baseball bat that just needed picking up at the right time and in the right way." (Cummings.) He argued that continued membership in the EU posed a threat to member nations due to the influx of immigrants that led to a rise in political extremism.

The vote split both main political parties. The Leave vote was higher in areas of economic decline and in areas with higher numbers of deaths of despair (deaths by suicide, or drug and alcohol abuse). Leave voters indicated that they were very concerned about immigration. They were older, less educated, and less well off. Geographically, Leave voters were from small towns and rural areas, while Remain voters were clustered in cities, were more educated, younger, and better off.

On a broader scale, voters in England and Wales supported Leave, while voters in Scotland and Northern Ireland supported Remain. Studies of voters' motivations showed that there was a strong anti-immigrant and anti-globalization divide between the winners and losers of globalization. Fears of the cultural and economic threats of globalization were a key element dividing voters. (Hobalt.)

In 2019, Dominic Cummings became a key senior advisor to Boris Johnson, who was able to capture the leadership of the Conservative Party and become prime minister. Although Johnson defended Cummings as an essential member of his government, Cummings, always a controversial figure, was forced to resign in spring 2020 when it was reported that he had broken the COVID-19 lockdown rules, which he himself had helped to formulate. Cummings had already exposed himself to criticism for his role in discussions among science advisors concerning how to respond to the global pandemic even though he had no formal scientific training. As public opinion turned on him for the hypocrisy of breaking the rules he made for others to follow, he had no choice but to resign.

Although Cummings no longer serves an official role in government, the Leave campaign he spearheaded and the United Kingdom's exit from the European Union changed politics in the United Kingdom. The Brexit vote demonstrates that citizens worry about the sovereignty and strength of their states in an increasingly globalized world.

2.1 States, Governments, Regimes, and Nations

Learning Targets

After reading this section, you should be able to do the following:

1. Describe the difference between a state and a nation.

2. Describe the difference between a change in government and regime change.

State
Political institutions with international recognition that govern a population in a territory.

The state is the starting point for studying comparative politics. In everyday language, *state* is often used interchangeably with both *country* and *nation*, but political scientists use the term *state* in a specific way. A **state** consists of political institutions with international recognition that govern a population in a defined territory. Courts of law, police headquarters, and social service agencies are all part of the state. States collect taxes and provide public goods such as roads and schools, enforce laws, and raise revenue through taxes. If you are also taking AP® U.S. Government and Politics, you may think of states as subunits of government, such as the state of Colorado. Around the world, subunits of government are referred to variously as states, provinces, and districts. In AP® Comparative Government and Politics, the term *state* is much broader.

What Is a State?

States have four characteristics:

—The first characteristic of the modern state is that it must have institutions of **government** that make legally binding decisions for the state, such as an executive, a legislature, and a judiciary. States also have bureaucracies to implement the law. A **bureaucracy** is a set of appointed officials and government workers who carry out policies. The bureaucracy carries out tasks like paving roads, building schools, and providing retirement pensions. Governments have the lawful right to use power to enforce their decisions without outside interference. **Sovereignty** is a state's ability to act without internal or external interference.

—The second characteristic of a state is that it must have a permanent population that is subject to the government's rule.

—The third characteristic of a state is that it must have territory, an area with clearly defined borders. Borders are one of the places where the state is "seen" most clearly through the signs that welcome visitors and the customs and immigration officers who enforce border regulations. The size of modern states varies enormously. Russia is geographically the largest at 6,601,242 square miles of land. (Worldometer, Largest Countries in the World by Area.)

—Finally, the fourth characteristic of a state is that it must have **international recognition**. One of the tools of diplomacy is to grant a state official recognition and begin treating it as a member of the international community.

Regimes, Governments, and How They Change

The *long-standing* nature of the state sets it apart from both a regime and a government. **Regimes** are types of political systems, such as liberal democracy or authoritarian. **Regime change** happens when there is a change in the fundamental rules and system of government. This might occur through a coup d'état (coup) or a revolution. A **coup d'état** is an overthrow of government by a small number of people, often military leaders. A **revolution** is an overthrow of a regime based on widespread popular support. For example, regime change occurs when a democratic government is overthrown in a military coup that establishes an authoritarian regime.

Regime changes can also occur without upheaval. For example, Mexico experienced a regime change in 2000. After many years of one-party rule, a different party won control of government through a mostly free and fair election. The year 2000 marked Mexico's regime change from an authoritarian state to one that was partially democratic.

A **change in government** is a change in leaders without systematic changes in the system of government. For example, when prime minister Theresa May was replaced by Boris Johnson, the United Kingdom experienced a change in government. Changes

---

Government
Institutions and individuals, such as the executive, legislature, judiciary, and bureaucracy, that make legally binding decisions for the state and that have the lawful right to use power to enforce those decisions.

Bureaucracy
A set of appointed officials and government workers who carry out policies.

Sovereignty
A state's ability to act without internal or external interference.

International recognition
A formal step taken by a state to grant official status to another state and begin treating it as a member of the global community.

Regime
A type of government, such as liberal democracy or authoritarian.

Regime change
A change in the fundamental rules and system of government.

Coup d'état (coup)
An overthrow of government by a small number of people, often military leaders.

Revolution
An overthrow of a regime based on widespread popular support.

Change in government
A change in leaders, without fundamental changes in the system of government.

in government occur from one election to the next, even when one party is voted out of office and another party takes its place. Changes in government happen more often than regime changes, and they are typically peaceful. However, government can also be changed through violence, such as the military coups that occurred in Nigeria in the mid-to-late twentieth century, when one military dictator was replaced with another.

The Meanings of Nation and State

In everyday conversations, the terms *state* and *nation* are used interchangeably, but in comparative government they have different, and very specific meanings. The term **nation** refers to a group of people who share a sense of belonging and who often have a common language, culture, religion, race, ethnicity, political identity, or set of traditions or aspirations. Defining the word *nation* is no easy task. A nation is a group that is connected by a shared sense of history and identity and common goals. People are members of a nation when they feel a sense of pride, connection, and duty to a group that shares a common identity. For example, the Scottish have a common identity separate from their identity as citizens of the United Kingdom.

Nationalism occurs when a group has a strong sense of identity and the desire to create its own destiny. Nationalism is sometimes the basis for a claim that the group should form its own state. An example is the Scottish nationalist movement that wants Scotland to be independent from the United Kingdom. Separatist nationalism undercuts the stability of the state.

Nationalism can become a valuable tool for politicians who want to unify and strengthen their states. However, nationalism can be used to force unwilling people to assimilate to the dominant culture, infringe upon civil rights and liberties, and even invade other states.

Nation
A group of people who share a sense of belonging and who often have a common language, culture, religion, race, ethnicity, political identity, or set of traditions or aspirations.

Nationalism
When a group has a strong sense of identity and believes it has its own destiny.

Demonstrators take part in a pro-independence rally in autumn 2012 in Edinburgh, Scotland. A referendum on whether Scotland should be an independent state was sent to voters two years later, and independence was defeated. The Brexit vote brought the topic of independence for Scotland back to the forefront.

David Moir/Reuters/Alamy

Section 2.1 Review

Each section's main ideas are reflected in the Learning Targets. By reviewing after each section, you should be able to

Remember the key points,

Know terms that are central to the topic, and

Think critically about what you have learned.

Remember

- States, governments, regimes, and nations are building blocks in comparative government, and each term has a specific meaning unique to political science.

Know

- *State:* political institutions with international recognition that govern a population in a territory. (p. 29)
- *Government:* institutions and individuals, such as the executive, legislature, judiciary, and bureaucracy, that make legally binding decisions for the state and that have the lawful right to use power to enforce those decisions. (p. 30)
- *Bureaucracy:* a set of appointed officials and government workers who carry out policies. (p. 30)
- *Sovereignty:* a state's ability to act without internal or external interference. (p. 30)
- *International recognition:* a formal step taken by a state to grant official status to another state and begin treating it as a member of the global community. (p. 30)
- *Regime:* a type of government, such as liberal democracy or authoritarian. (p. 30)
- *Regime change:* a change in the fundamental rules and system of government. (p. 30)
- *Coup d'état (coup):* an overthrow of government by a small number of people, often military leaders. (p. 30)
- *Revolution:* an overthrow of a regime based on widespread popular support. (p. 30)
- *Change in government:* a change in leaders, without fundamental changes in the system of government. (p. 30)
- *Nation:* a group of people who share a sense of belonging and who often have a common language, culture, religion, race, ethnicity, political identity, or set of traditions or aspirations. (p. 31)
- *Nationalism:* when a group has a strong sense of identity and believes it has its own destiny. (p. 31)

Think

- How can an understanding of regime change help political scientists understand how political systems evolve?

Free-Response Question: Conceptual Analysis

Answer A, B, C, and D.

A. Define regime change.

B. Explain how a regime change differs from a change in government.

C. Explain why changes in government are more common than changes in regime.

D. Describe a policy a government might enact to strengthen the state.

2.2 Democracy and Authoritarianism

Learning Targets

After reading this section, you should be able to do the following:

1. Describe the difference between democratic and authoritarian states.

2. Explain why some states democratize and others backslide into authoritarian practices.

In democratic systems, leaders answer to citizens. In authoritarian systems, citizens answer to leaders. States fall along a spectrum, with liberal democracies at one end and authoritarian states at the other, and no state is completely democratic.

A **liberal democracy** is a system with free and fair elections that provides its citizens with a wide array of civil rights and liberties. Of the six countries studied, the United Kingdom is the only one rated by Freedom House as "free." Although both Nigeria and Mexico are democracies, Freedom House rates them as "partially free." **Authoritarian states** often hold elections, but they are not free and fair, and civil rights and liberties are restricted. Freedom House lists Russia, China, and Iran as "not free," classifying them as authoritarian states. A **totalitarian state** is a type of authoritarian state in which the government has total control of nearly all aspects of citizens' lives. None of the six countries studied is considered to be totalitarian.

Illiberal, flawed, or hybrid democracies fall somewhere in the middle. They have some, but not all, of the attributes of democratic states. For example, elections may be somewhat competitive but marred by fraud, or the state might provide some civil liberties, like the right to worship, but not others, such as freedom of the press.

Political scientists ask several questions in deciding how to classify regimes. Do citizens have the ability to directly or indirectly control political leaders and institutions? How much power should be given to the majority? Liberal democracies are based on majority rule, but majority rule is balanced with the protection of civil rights and liberties of minority groups. What is the trade-off between popular participation in the government and representation of many viewpoints, on the one hand, and effective governance, on the other?

> **Liberal democracy**
> A system with free and fair elections in which a wide array of civil rights and liberties is protected.
>
> **Authoritarian state**
> A system without free and fair elections in which civil rights and liberties are restricted.
>
> **Totalitarian state**
> A type of authoritarian government where the state controls nearly all aspects of citizens' lives.
>
> **Illiberal, flawed, or hybrid democracy**
> A system in which elections may be marred by fraud and the state protects some civil rights and liberties but restricts others.

Rule of Law, Rule by Law

Rule of law is a cornerstone of democratic government. It means that no one, not even the leaders, is above the law. Rule of law is based on a clear set of rules that does not change arbitrarily. For example, if you drive through a school zone at 20 miles an hour above the speed limit, and you get caught, you will get a ticket for an amount specified by law. The rules are clear, and so are the penalties. It shouldn't make a difference whether you are a student who is late for school or the governor of your state—the law should apply to everyone uniformly.

Rule by law means government officials are not subject to the same rules as everyday citizens. The government may apply the law arbitrarily and as a tool for maintaining power. Laws may be written in vague language and enforced selectively to punish perceived opponents of the regime. Nearly all regimes, including authoritarian ones, claim to

> **Rule of law**
> A clear set of rules where government officials are subject to the same laws and penalties as citizens.
>
> **Rule by law**
> Where the law is applied arbitrarily, and government officials are not subject to the same rules and penalties as citizens.

uphold the rule of law, at least in theory. To understand politics, we must ask not just what a country's institutions look like on paper, but to what degree a government's promises are honored in practice.

Democratic and Authoritarian Regimes

In democratic systems, citizens have the ability, directly or indirectly, to control political leaders and institutions. Free and fair elections provide citizens an opportunity to choose between candidates with different ideas about how to govern. A free election is one in which almost all citizens have the right and ability to vote. A fair election is one in which parties are free to form and the media are independent. (Bishop and Hoeffler, 2016.)

Members of underrepresented groups have the ability to run for office, and multiple political parties have the right to form. In some democratic systems, like Mexico, there are quotas that require political parties to run a certain percentage of women on the ballot. In other democratic systems, there are election rules that allow parties who receive even a small percentage of the vote to earn seats in the legislature. One method of ensuring fair elections is the creation of an independent election commission to oversee registration, voting, and ballot counting. Independent election commissions in Mexico and Nigeria furthered democratization in those countries.

In democratic systems, leaders are accountable to voters, who may vote them out of office. Democratic governments also provide checks within the government to thwart potential nondemocratic abuse of power by other institutions or leaders. Examples include the legislature's ability to ask the executive to justify his or her actions and the judiciary's ability to overrule legislative or executive actions as unconstitutional. In other words, democracies balance power among governing institutions.

Along with accountability, democratic systems provide **transparency**, which is the ability of citizens to know what the government is doing. Citizens have access to information about government revenues and spending. Many democratic governments have freedom of information laws, which allow citizens to request information about what the government is doing and obtain government records about citizens. **Table 2.1** shows the major differences between democratic and authoritarian states.

Transparency
The ability of citizens to know what the government is doing.

In Mexico, the Instituto Nacional Electoral (INE), an independent commission, organizes elections. Since 2014, the INE has had responsibility for federal, state, and local elections. Here, people vote at a polling station in Mexico City during general elections in 2018. The signs, produced by INE, translate as "Your vote is free and secret."

Benedicte Desrus/Alamy

TABLE 2.1 Differences between Democratic and Authoritarian States

Democratic states	Authoritarian states
Elections	
Competitive, fair, and transparent elections. Election commission to oversee fairness and prevent fraud.	Electoral competition is limited. One party is given an advantage on the ballot or in the media. Election results are not honored.
Participation	
Citizen participation in policy making.	Government-sponsored groups limit advocacy by citizens.
Franchise	
Universal suffrage for adults.	Minority or opposition groups are disenfranchised.
Transparency and secrecy	
Transparency allows citizens to see what the government is doing and how funds are being spent.	The government operates in secret, and citizens cannot access information about government actions.
Civil rights and civil liberties	
Civil rights and liberties are protected.	Civil rights are not guaranteed, and the government infringes on liberties.
Equality	
Equal treatment of all citizens.	Some groups are favored by the government and others face discrimination.
Application of laws	
Rule of law.	Rule by law.

> **AP® TIP**
>
> The difference between democratic and authoritarian states is a key concept in AP® Comparative Government and Politics, and it appears often on the exam. Make sure you know the attributes of both types of regimes.

Authoritarian regimes take several forms—one-party, military, personalist, theocratic, and electoral authoritarian. In a one-party state, as the name implies, a single political party controls the government, and other parties are not allowed to win elections. In one-party regimes, such as China, a single party is allowed to run candidates for office and controls all aspects of government. Although one-party regimes may allow other state-approved parties to form, those parties never have an opportunity to control government. In personalist regimes, decisions can be made and implemented at the whim of the executive, who rules based on his or her personal power. In military regimes, like those in Nigeria in the mid-to-late twentieth century, leadership is controlled by a high-ranking military official, usually following a coup. Theocratic regimes, like Iran's, are based on religious rule.

A distinct regime type of authoritarianism is an electoral authoritarian regime. These regimes "allow little real competition for power . . . [but] leave enough political space for political parties and organizations of civil society to form, for an independent press to function to some extent, and for some political debate to take place." (Ottaway, 2003, 3.) In electoral authoritarian regimes, such as Russia under President Vladimir Putin, opposition parties are allowed to exist and win some elected offices, but the ruling party manipulates electoral rules enough to ensure that it maintains virtually all effective power. Such regimes typically allow some limited freedom of expression as well, but they ensure that it does not threaten the ruling party's grip on power.

Authoritarian regimes around the world all rule through some combination of repression, cooptation, and efforts at maintaining legitimacy. *Repression* is the popular image that pops into people's minds when they think of dictators, but it is an expensive way to rule.

Even the most ruthless dictator has to find other ways to ensure citizens' loyalties. Authoritarian states restrict the civil rights of groups that might pose a threat to the regime, such as the Chechens in Russia, who engaged in two civil wars against the Russian Federation in an effort to create an independent state. Civil rights, such as the free press and freedom of association, are also restricted. State-sponsored media control the viewpoints citizens are allowed to access and present the government in a favorable light.

Authoritarian regimes use *cooptation*—offering citizens benefits and official positions—which often goes hand in hand with corruption, as a way of securing political support. Most authoritarian regimes attempt to improve their economies to maintain citizen support. If citizens believe the government is acting in their best interests, they are less likely to rebel.

Security is important for all states, and this is especially true for authoritarian regimes, because they often have limited legitimacy. The loyalty of the military is crucial. Mao Zedong, who ruled China as a dictatorship, summed this up with his famous quote, "Political power grows out of the barrel of a gun." Personalist leaders often place close supporters, even family members, in key security positions. Authoritarian regimes also create vast networks of spies who gather intelligence on opponents. In the age of electronic surveillance technology and artificial intelligence (AI), surveillance threatens to become even more extreme. AI can allow a regime to follow masses of people very quickly and correlate vast amounts of data to identify patterns that might threaten the regime. China is the leading example of this trend.

Authoritarian regimes curtail the rule of law and judicial independence, although some allow the courts slightly more leeway, typically only in nonpolitical cases. In some authoritarian regimes, like China, citizens can go to court to hold local officials accountable for wrongdoing, which reveals local problems to national leaders. There are different kinds of authoritarian states, and some of them are more responsive to citizens than others.

Democratic Transitions

Democratization
The process of transitioning from an authoritarian to a democratic regime.

Democratization is the process of transitioning from an authoritarian to a democratic regime. In 1972, Freedom House classified forty-four countries as "free," meaning that they were fully functioning liberal democracies. In 1990, the number of "free" countries rose to sixty-one.

In the new millennium, though, democratic progression has slowed and even reversed. Freedom House reported that 2019 was the thirteenth straight year in which the number of countries that became less free was greater than the number that became freer.

In 2021, Freedom House described democracy as "under siege." Although democracy has advanced in some countries, many others are backsliding. Comparativists have tried to understand the expansion of democracy and its more recent decline by asking why and how countries become democratic, what obstacles they face, how democratic they are, how likely they are to continue to democratize, and whether democratic government will become consolidated.

Democratization is often triggered by an event, such as a natural disaster, economic crisis, major change in the international community, widespread civilian protests, or death of a personalist dictator. An authoritarian regime's inadequate response to a natural disaster may lead to massive protests in the streets. An economic crisis may starve an authoritarian regime of the resources it needs to maintain power. Events may trigger a broad-based and well-organized social movement for democracy. For example, after years of citizen protest against fraudulent elections in Mexico, the ruling party promised cleaner elections.

Protests and unrest among citizens may press authorities to change, although democratization is not an automatic response. During a demonstration in Tehran in January 2020, Iranians chant and hold a placard reading in Farsi, "Your mistake was unintentional. Your lie was intentional." The demonstrations broke out after the government admitted to having shot down a passenger jet, killing all 176 people on board.

STR/AFP/Getty Images

The 2000 election was freer and fairer than past elections, and an opposition party gained control of the Mexican government for the first time, marking a transition to democracy.

Creating a democracy is one thing. Sustaining it over the long term is another. Political history is littered with democracies that reverted to authoritarian rule. **Democratic consolidation** is the process by which a regime has developed stable democratic institutions and significant protections of civil liberties and is unlikely to revert to authoritarianism. Democracy has become "the only game in town"—citizens and political elites accept democratic rules and are confident that everyone else does as well. Democracy requires faith that, in the future, any significant party or group might gain power through an election.

How can we know whether the people in a country have accepted democracy unquestionably? Huntington (1991) argued that a country must pass the "two-turnover test" before it can be considered a consolidated democracy: One party must win the initial election, and then a different party must win a later election and replace the first party. For example, in Nigeria's 2015 election, the political party that had controlled the government for many years was voted out of office, and the candidate from another party won the presidency. This was a positive sign for democracy in Nigeria. Others rely on surveys to demonstrate that the elite and citizens express support for democratic values and democracy in their country in particular. (Winke and Shumacher, 2020.) Whatever measure is used, many new democracies have not fully consolidated, and doing so can take decades.

Democratic backsliding is a decline in the quality of democracy, including a decrease in citizen participation, the rule of law, transparency, and accountability. This can ultimately result in democratic breakdown and the rise of a new authoritarian regime. Democracies can protect themselves from backsliding through fair election rules, checks on government, and the protection of civil rights and liberties.

Illiberal, flawed, or hybrid democracies are more likely to backslide than liberal democracies. Illiberal, flawed, or hybrid democracies hold reasonably free and fair elections but do not fully respect civil rights and liberties or the rule of law. They are at risk of becoming electoral authoritarian regimes in which a ruling party rigs elections and manipulates institutions to stay in power, like Putin's regime in Russia. Democratization is not a one-way street, and while some countries become liberal democracies, others backslide into authoritarianism.

Democratic consolidation
The process by which a regime has developed stable democratic institutions and significant protections of civil liberties and is unlikely to revert to authoritarianism.

Democratic backsliding
Decline in the quality of democracy, including a decrease in citizen participation, rule of law, transparency, and accountability.

The free-response portion of the AP® Comparative Government and Politics Exam follows a standard format. Questions appear in the following order: (1) conceptual analysis, (2) quantitative analysis, (3) comparative analysis, and (4) argument essay. The conceptual analysis question will assess your understanding of the major ideas in the course. It is broken into parts A through D, and each part is worth one point. Here is an example:

A. Define democratization.

Response: *Democratization is the process of moving from an authoritarian state to a liberal democracy.*

B. Describe a policy a state could enact to become more democratic.

Response: *States can enact policies to become more democratic by creating independent commissions to ensure elections are freer and fairer, and they can pass laws or amend their constitutions to provide more rights to citizens, such as the rights of free speech and assembly.*

C. Explain why a leader would choose to democratize a state.

Response: *Leaders would choose to democratize a state because the leader wants to maintain his or her power, especially if a large group of citizens is pressuring the state for more rights and freedoms.*

D. Explain why democratic backsliding occurs.

Response: *A powerful executive can cause democratic backsliding because he or she can enact policies, such as rigging elections and jailing opponents, to prevent citizens from exercising democratic rights.*

Note that the conceptual-analysis question does not require you to discuss any of the countries studied, although you can use examples from the countries as evidence to support your analysis.

1. How does the level of difficulty within the question change as you progress through each part?

2. Look at the sample response to part A. What skills are important in answering part A of the conceptual analysis question?

3. Look at the sample responses to parts B and C. How is the language in the prompt incorporated into the response?

4. Look at the response to part D. What evidence is provided to support the response?

Section 2.2 Review

Remember
- Rule of law is a cornerstone of democracy.
- Democratic states provide free and fair elections and protect civil rights and liberties, while elections in authoritarian states are not free and fair, and civil rights and liberties are not protected.
- Democratization is a process, and while some states become consolidated democracies, others backslide into authoritarianism.

Know
- *Liberal democracy:* a system with free and fair elections in which a wide array of civil rights and liberties is protected. (p. 33)
- *Authoritarian state:* a system without free and fair elections in which civil rights and liberties are restricted. (p. 33)
- *Totalitarian state:* a type of authoritarian government where the state controls nearly all aspects of citizens' lives. (p. 33)
- *Illiberal, flawed, or hybrid democracy:* a system in which elections may be marred by fraud and the state protects some civil rights and liberties but restricts others. (p. 33)
- *Rule of law:* a clear set of rules where government officials are subject to the same laws and penalties as citizens. (p. 33)

- *Rule by law:* where the law is applied arbitrarily, and government officials are not subject to the same rules and penalties as citizens. (p. 33)
- *Transparency:* the ability of citizens to know what the government is doing. (p. 34)
- *Democratization:* the process of transitioning from an authoritarian to a democratic regime. (p. 36)
- *Democratic consolidation:* the process by which a regime has developed stable democratic institutions and significant protections of civil liberties and is unlikely to revert to authoritarianism. (p. 37)
- *Democratic backsliding:* decline in the quality of democracy, including a decrease in citizen participation, rule of law, transparency, and accountability. (p. 37)

Think
- Why do some states become consolidated liberal democracies while others backslide into authoritarianism?

....

Free-Response Question: Conceptual Analysis

Answer A, B, C, and D.

A. Define rule of law.

B. Describe the difference between rule of law and rule by law.

C. Explain how transparency strengthens rule of law.

D. Explain how a state can improve transparency.

2.3 Sovereignty, Authority, and Power

Learning Targets

After reading this section, you should be able to do the following:

1. Describe the sources of state power.

2. Explain how states use power and authority to maintain sovereignty.

States have power and authority over their citizens. **Power** is the ability to make someone do something they would not otherwise do, such as paying taxes. **Authority** is the legitimate power a state has over the people within its territory.

Sources of Power

Some sources of power and authority include constitutions, elections, religion, popular support, and the military. Governments rely on more than one source of authority. The unwritten constitution in the United Kingdom, and the written constitutions in Mexico, Russia, Nigeria, China, and Iran, are sources of authority.

In China, one source of authority is the Chinese Communist Party, which maintains its power partly through its control of the military, which has been used against citizens. For example, in the Tiananmen Square massacre of 1989, troops fired on thousands of students and workers who had gathered over the course of the preceding two weeks to protest in favor of government reform. (Westcott, 1999.)

Power
The ability to make someone do something they would not otherwise do.

Authority
The legitimate power a state has over people within its territory.

Theocracy
A system based on religious rule.

Iran is a **theocracy**—a system based on religious rule—and religion is an important source of the government's authority. In Russia, one source of authority comes from the popularity of a strong president who is affiliated with a political party that has created rules to ensure its dominance. States use their power and authority to maintain sovereignty—the ability to rule free from internal or external interference.

Challenges to Sovereignty

External sovereignty means a state is able to defend its territory without relying too much on other states or international organizations. If most of a state's important decisions are controlled by an outside authority, then it lacks sovereignty. Internal sovereignty means that a state has the sole authority to make and enforce laws and policies within a territory. The state must be able to defend its internal sovereignty against domestic groups that challenge it.

Internal challenges typically take the form of a declaration of independence from some part of the state's territory and perhaps even civil war. For example, when secessionists in the Russian region of Chechnya led an armed insurrection, the Russian government bombed the capital of Chechnya and deployed troops to preserve its sovereignty over its recognized territories. (Human Rights Watch, 1995.)

States try to enforce their sovereignty by claiming, in the words of German sociologist Max Weber, a "monopoly on the legitimate use of physical force." (Weber, 1970.) Put simply, the state claims to be the only entity within its territory that has the right to hold a gun to your head and tell you what to do. Some governments claim a virtually unlimited right to use force when and how they choose. At least in theory, liberal democracies follow strict guidelines about when force is allowed. For example, the government can punish a citizen who runs a red light or fails to pay taxes, but not when she criticizes government policy. Both democratic and authoritarian states claim the right to use force to ensure their internal and external sovereignty. The use of force, or the threat of force, to get someone to do something they would not otherwise do, is called **coercion**.

Coercion
The use of force, or the threat of force, to get someone to do something they would not otherwise do.

Sovereignty does not mean that a state is all-powerful. Wealthier states can defend their territories from attack better than poorer ones, and they can also more effectively ensure that their citizens comply with the law. Like many of the concepts studied in comparative government and politics, sovereignty exists on a spectrum, and no country is completely free from challenges to its ability to rule.

Section 2.3 Review

Remember

- Sources of power and authority include constitutions, elections, religion, popular support, and the military. Governments rely on more than one source of authority.
- External sovereignty means a state is able to defend its territory without overly relying on other states or international organizations.
- Internal sovereignty means that a state has the sole authority to make and enforce laws and policies within a territory.

Know

- *Power*: the ability to make someone do something they would not otherwise do. (p. 39)
- *Authority*: the legitimate power a state has over people within its territory. (p. 39)
- *Theocracy*: a system based on religious rule. (p. 40)

- *Coercion:* the use of force, or the threat of force, to get someone to do something they would not otherwise do. (p. 40)

Think

- What are the drawbacks for a state in using force against citizens in an effort to maintain sovereignty?
- How do sources of authority differ between democratic and authoritarian regimes?

··

Free-Response Question: Quantitative Analysis

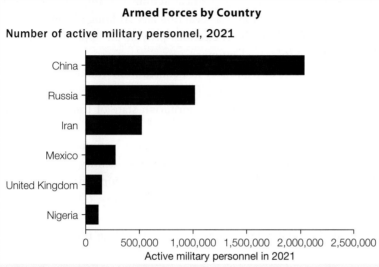

Armed Forces by Country

Number of active military personnel, 2021

Data from World Population Review.

Answer A, B, C, D, and E.

A. Using the data in the bar chart, identify the country with the largest number of members in the active-duty military in 2020.

B. Using the data in the bar chart, describe the difference between the number of active-duty military members in Russia and in China.

C. Define authority.

D. Using the data in the bar chart and your knowledge of authority, explain how the number of active-duty members in the military impacts authority in authoritarian states.

E. Describe a difference between the ways in which authoritarian and democratic states maintain authority.

2.4 Legitimacy and Stability

Learning Targets

After reading this section, you should be able to do the following:

1. Describe sources of legitimacy.

2. Explain how states maintain legitimacy.

Legitimacy is the citizens' belief that the government has the right to rule. Virtually all states claim that they are legitimate. The issue is whether or not their populations accept the government's claim. Legitimacy strengthens the state's authority and power.

Sources of Legitimacy

Some sources of legitimacy are the same for both democratic and authoritarian states. Both democratic and authoritarian states hold elections to maintain legitimacy. Elections for members of the House of Commons in the United Kingdom give citizens a sense of **political efficacy**—the belief that their political actions can impact government. China, an authoritarian state, holds elections for local officials. Although Chinese citizens cannot elect leaders at the national level, local elections provide an opportunity for meaningful political participation and increase legitimacy.

Political efficacy
A citizen's belief that his or her actions can impact the government.

Another common source of legitimacy is a constitution. Mexico's long-standing constitution, adopted in 1917, forms the basis for a democratic system of government and is a source of the state's legitimacy. In the authoritarian state of Iran, the constitution is a source of legitimacy for clerical rule.

Most states claim more than one source of legitimacy. Nationalism can unify the state and increase legitimacy. Conversely, the lack of a national identity can weaken legitimacy. In Nigeria, for example, there are more than 250 ethnic groups, making it difficult for the government to unify citizens under a shared national identity. (U.S. Embassy in Nigeria, Nigeria Fact Sheet.)

Tradition is another source of legitimacy. The monarch in the United Kingdom does not hold political power, but Queen Elizabeth II serves as a symbol of tradition, increasing legitimacy.

Governmental effectiveness and economic growth are also sources of legitimacy. People are more likely to support the state's right to rule when it improves their lives. Market reforms in China lifted 850 million people out of poverty between 1981 and 2015. (World Bank.)

A shared ideology can also provide legitimacy. When Mao Zedong was chairman of the Chinese Communist Party, students were required to study the "Little Red Book" of Mao's sayings in an effort to indoctrinate the population into communist thought. A dominant political party is a source of legitimacy when that party endorses candidates. China is a one-party state, and the Chinese Communist Party dominates political life and selects the country's leaders. In Russia, Vladimir Putin's legitimacy is strengthened by his association with United Russia, the dominant party.

States also claim legitimacy through religion, such as Iran's theocratic state, which governs its largely Shia Muslim population. The Russian state has formed a relationship with the Russian Orthodox Church, increasing legitimacy. Sources of state legitimacy are numerous, and most states claim several reasons for their right to rule.

Traditional legitimacy
The right to rule based on a society's long-standing patterns and practices.

Charismatic legitimacy
The right to rule based on personal virtue, heroism, or other extraordinary characteristics.

Maintaining Legitimacy

Sociologist Max Weber described three types of legitimacy: traditional, charismatic, and rational-legal. **Traditional legitimacy** is the right to rule based on a society's long-standing patterns and practices. Although the monarch in the United Kingdom has no political power, he or she provides traditional legitimacy to the state. **Charismatic legitimacy** is the right to rule based on personal virtue, heroism, or other extraordinary characteristics.

Wildly popular leaders, such as Ayatollah Ruhollah Khomeini, who led the Islamic Revolution in Iran, and Vladimir Putin in Russia, have charismatic legitimacy. People recognize their authority to rule because they trust them and believe they are exceptional.

Rational-legal legitimacy is the right to rule based on an accepted set of laws. Free and fair elections and leaders who rule according to a set of laws, such as a constitution, are examples of rational-legal legitimacy. Rational-legal legitimacy is an important feature of legitimacy in democratic systems.

States often claim legitimacy through a combination of the three types. For example, the United Kingdom claims rational-legal legitimacy based on free and fair elections and the rule of law, but it also has traditional legitimacy because of its long-standing traditions. In addition, a charismatic prime minister may enhance legitimacy.

Rational-legal legitimacy
The right to rule based on an accepted set of laws.

Stability

Legitimacy enhances a state's sovereignty and stability. If most citizens obey the government because they believe it has a right to rule, then little force will be necessary to maintain order. Stable countries are able to attract investment from foreign companies and private capital, because investors have confidence that their assets will be protected.

Free and fair elections, political efficacy, the peaceful transfer of power, and a strong economy enhance stability. In Mexico, the National Electoral Institute (INE) is an independent commission that oversees elections in an effort to prevent fraud and increase stability. Citizens are less likely to rebel when they believe their participation matters and they trust the state to follow established rules, even when their party loses an election. States that resolve conflicts peacefully and reduce corruption are more stable. For example, China is making efforts to reduce corruption, especially at local levels, in an effort to maintain legitimacy and stability.

Economic development also enhances stability. Mexico has grown into a prosperous nation, with a growing middle class. (Smith.) Although Mexico faces instability due to corruption and the influence of drug cartels, strong economic growth is a positive sign for the country going forward.

As part of its anticorruption campaign, the Chinese government removed Meng Hongwei, then head of Interpol, an international law-enforcement agency, on charges of taking bribes. Meng was sentenced in 2020 to 13.5 years in jail for accepting more than $2 million in bribes and for abusing his position.

Remember

- Sources of legitimacy include elections, a constitution, nationalism, tradition, religion, economic performance, and support from a dominant party.
- There are three types of legitimacy—traditional, charismatic, and rational-legal—and states may claim more than one type of legitimacy.
- Free and fair elections, political efficacy, the peaceful transfer of power, and a strong economy strengthen stability.

Know

- *Legitimacy:* the citizens' belief that the government has the right to rule. (p. 42)
- *Political efficacy:* a citizen's belief that his or her actions can impact the government. (p. 42)
- *Traditional legitimacy:* the right to rule based on a society's long-standing patterns and practices. (p. 42)
- *Charismatic legitimacy:* the right to rule based on personal virtue, heroism, or other extraordinary characteristics. (p. 42)
- *Rational-legal legitimacy:* the right to rule based on an accepted set of laws. (p. 43)

Think

- Why are some states better than others at maintaining sovereignty and legitimacy?

Free-Response Question: Conceptual Analysis

Answer A, B, C, and D.

A. Define legitimacy.

B. Describe sources of legitimacy.

C. Explain how legitimacy impacts state sovereignty.

D. Explain why an authoritarian state may face more challenges to sovereignty than a democratic state.

2.5 Federal and Unitary Systems

Learning Targets

After reading this section, you should be able to do the following:

1. Describe the difference between federal and unitary states.

2. Explain why unitary states devolve power.

Unitary system
A political system in which the central government has sole constitutional sovereignty and power.

Federal system
A political system in which a state's power is legally and constitutionally divided among more than one level of government.

In every country, there are governments in towns, cities, and states or provinces below the national level. These lower-level governments are called subnational governments or subgovernments. Subgovernments have differing amounts of power and autonomy. In **unitary systems**, the central government has sole constitutional power. In **federal systems**, the national government shares constitutional power with subunits, such as states, provinces, or regions. Local governments exist in unitary systems, but they derive their powers from the central government, which can take their power away. In federal systems, subnational governments have constitutionally derived powers that the national government cannot take away.

Federalism

While federal systems are a minority of the world's governments, they include most of its geographically largest countries, including Mexico, Russia, and Nigeria. Larger countries adopt federal systems to provide a level of government closer to the people than the national government. Regional and local governments are familiar with the political culture in their areas and with the challenges citizens face. They can tailor policies to meet the needs of local communities.

A second purpose of federalism is to limit the power of the majority by decentralizing and dividing governmental power. Federal systems usually have bicameral legislatures. The upper house of the legislature in a federal system usually represents state or provincial governments, while the lower house represents individual voters. Russia, Mexico, and Nigeria are examples of federal states with bicameral legislatures. Bicameral legislatures give subnational governments power to check national legislation, because the upper house often has the power to reject a bill from the other chamber.

Federalism is also designed to protect the interests of religious or ethnic minorities, especially when they are concentrated in a region. When regional minority communities feel threatened by other groups' control of the national government, a federal system can ease tensions. States or provinces with clear ethnic or religious majorities can make their own local policies, reducing the potential for conflict.

Subnational governments in federal systems may have significant power in making and carrying out policies, or their power may be very limited. The constitutions of all federal systems lay out the powers of both the central government and the states or provinces. The federal structure in Nigeria, for example, has allowed twelve states in the north to implement sharia law as part of their judicial systems. States or provinces typically have power over education, transportation, and some social services. The national government always has power over the military, foreign, and monetary policies. States can raise money through property and income taxes, but most rely on the national government for money. Underfunded states are at the mercy of the national government, and they have little autonomy in policymaking.

In federal systems, the national government may treat states equally or may favor some states over others. Mexico is an example of a symmetrical federal system—all states have the same relationship with and rights in relation to the national government.

In an asymmetrical federal state, some states or provinces have special rights or powers that others do not. In Russia, regions controlled by Bashkirs, Chechens, Yakuts, and Tatars have less autonomy than regions controlled by ethnic Russians, which are more likely to support the regime. In 2000, the Russian government created seven federal districts to consolidate national authority and decrease the powers of regional and local governments. (Srebrnik, 2019.) In Russia, as democracy at the national level withered, the Putin administration enacted policies, such as ending the direct election of governors, that weakened federalism and re-centralized control in the national government.

Unitary Systems

In unitary states, such as the United Kingdom, China, and Iran, power is centralized in the national government. Like federal states, unitary states are divided into provinces and

FIGURE 2.1

Unitary and Federal Systems of Government

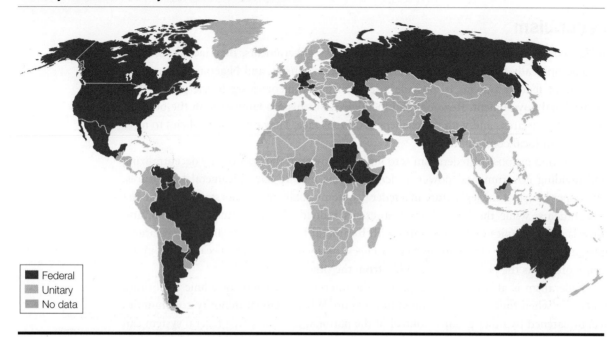

Federal
Unitary
No data

states with some self-government. However, subnational governments in unitary states ultimately are under control of the national government, which can enlarge or restrict their authority. Some unitary states have unicameral legislatures, because there is no need to create a separate house for states and provinces that have little power. Other unitary states have a bicameral legislature, but the upper house does not represent subnational governments. In the United Kingdom, for example, the House of Lords represents the traditional elite and has little policymaking authority.

In some unitary systems, such as in the United Kingdom, decentralization has taken place. **Devolution** occurs when the national government gives regional governments more power and authority. As in federal systems, giving subgovernments more power helps them tailor policies to local needs and takes some policymaking pressure off the central government.

A unitary state with a significant amount of devolved power is still not a federal state, because the devolution of power is reversible. For example, in the late 1990s, regional assemblies were created in Northern Ireland, Scotland, and Wales. These assemblies have significant authority to make policies affecting their regions. As another example, NHS Scotland is accountable to the Scottish Cabinet Secretary for Health and Sport instead of the United Kingdom's Secretary for Health. As a result of devolution, health-care policy and funding are responsibilities of the Scottish government. Northern Ireland, Scotland, and Wales each have their own set of devolved responsibilities (Leeke, Sear, and Gay, 2003), which parliament can modify or eliminate.

Devolution hasn't fully satisfied the members of the Scottish National Party (SNP), which used its newly devolved powers to demand a referendum on independence. The 2014 referendum failed to pass. However, after Britain's vote to leave the EU in 2016, the party promised to hold another referendum on independence, which most observers believe would pass, separating Scotland from the United Kingdom. In the 2021 elections for the Scottish Parliament, the SNP won a plurality but fell one vote short of a majority, which may stall the push for a new referendum on independence. While members of the

Devolution
Granting of powers by the central government to regional governments.

SNP claim the right to hold a referendum without the approval of the House of Commons, Prime Minister Boris Johnson has asserted that the House of Commons must consent to the referendum and that he would deny permission for a referendum to proceed. (Sim, 2021.) The Scottish independence movement demonstrates that devolution of power may result in pressure from subgovernment for even more autonomy.

All governments struggle with how much power to give subnational units of government and how much to keep for themselves.

AP® POLITICAL SCIENCE PRACTICES

Refutation, Concession, and Rebuttal

The AP® Comparative Government and Politics Exam contains an argument question that requires you to use the skills of refutation, concession, and rebuttal.

Refutation is using evidence to prove that an opponent's contention is false.

Rebuttal means discrediting an argument by offering a different point of view.

Concession means acknowledging a point and demonstrating an understanding of a differing viewpoint.

Read the following statements about whether unitary or federal systems are more efficient in policymaking and decide if each statement represents refutation, rebuttal, or concession.

Statement A: A proponent of unitary systems would argue that the national government in a unitary system has significant resources to efficiently carry out policies. Although national governments usually have significant resources, efficiency is not the most important aspect of policymaking. It is more important that policies be effective at meeting citizens' needs. Federal systems produce more effective policies, because government officials are closer to the people.

Statement B: Some would argue that unitary systems are more efficient in policymaking, because they are

centralized and can make decisions for the entire nation. However, this argument is flawed. Because local officials understand the needs of their region, they can act more quickly than the national government because they have a better understanding of what needs to be done. Therefore, policymaking is more efficient in a federal system.

Statement C: Some would argue that unitary systems are more efficient in making policy because decision making is centralized. However, unitary systems are not more efficient at policymaking than federal systems. Centralized policymaking requires consensus among different factions, which is time consuming. Policymaking by local officials in federal systems is faster because representatives share similar views as their constituents and can act quickly.

1. Explain whether Statement A represents refutation, concession, or rebuttal. Why?

2. Explain whether Statement B represents refutation, concession, or rebuttal. Why?

3. Explain whether Statement C represents refutation, concession, or rebuttal. Why?

4. Why might it be easier to use refutation and rebuttal than concession in your argument essay?

Section 2.5 Review

Remember

- In unitary systems, power is centralized in the national government, and although subnational governments may be given power, the national government can always take it away.

- In federal systems, subnational governments have some protected powers that the national government cannot take away.

- Unitary systems devolve policymaking authority to subnational governments to make policymaking more efficient and to enable local officials to tailor policies to local needs.

Know

- *Unitary system:* a political system in which the central government has sole constitutional sovereignty and power. (p. 44)
- *Federal system:* a political system in which a state's power is legally and constitutionally divided among more than one level of government. (p. 44)
- *Devolution:* granting of powers by the central government to regional governments. (p. 46)

Think

- What are the advantages and disadvantages of federal and unitary systems in the policymaking process?

....

Free-Response Question: Conceptual Analysis

Answer A, B, C, and D.

A. Define federalism.

B. Compare the power of subnational governments in unitary and federal systems.

C. Explain why a multi-ethnic state would adopt a federal system.

D. Explain why it might be more difficult to make policies in a federal system than in a unitary system.

Chapter 2 Review

AP® KEY CONCEPTS

- State (p. 29)
- Government (p. 30)
- Bureaucracy (p. 30)
- Sovereignty (p. 30)
- International recognition (p. 30)
- Regime (p. 30)
- Regime change (p. 30)
- Coup d'état (p. 30)
- Revolution (p. 30)
- Change in government (p. 30)
- Nation (p. 31)
- Nationalism (p. 31)

- Liberal democracy (p. 33)
- Authoritarian state (p. 33)
- Totalitarian state (p. 33)
- Illiberal, flawed, or hybrid democracy (p. 33)
- Rule of law (p. 33)
- Rule by law (p. 33)
- Transparency (p. 34)
- Democratization (p. 36)
- Democratic consolidation (p. 37)
- Democratic backsliding (p. 37)
- Power (p. 39)

- Authority (p. 39)
- Theocracy (p. 40)
- Coercion (p. 40)
- Legitimacy (p. 42)
- Political efficacy (p. 42)
- Traditional legitimacy (p. 42)
- Charismatic legitimacy (p. 42)
- Rational-legal legitimacy (p. 43)
- Unitary system (p. 44)
- Federal system (p. 44)
- Devolution (p. 46)

AP® EXAM MULTIPLE-CHOICE PRACTICE QUESTIONS

Note: Some of these review questions refer to the six countries studied in AP® Comparative Government and Politics. You will study these countries in later chapters. Because the questions in this chapter review are conceptual, knowledge about the countries is not necessary to answer the questions.

Questions 1 and 2 refer to the map.

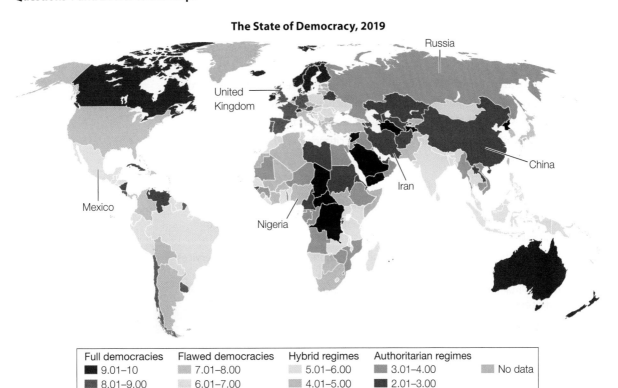

The State of Democracy, 2019

Full democracies	Flawed democracies	Hybrid regimes	Authoritarian regimes	
■ 9.01–10	■ 7.01–8.00	■ 5.01–6.00	■ 3.01–4.00	■ No data
■ 8.01–9.00	■ 6.01–7.00	■ 4.01–5.00	■ 2.01–3.00	
			■ 0–2.00	

Data from the Democracy Index from the Economist Intelligence Unit.

1. The map supports which of the following statements?
    A. Russia is more authoritarian than China.
    B. Mexico is more democratic than Nigeria.
    C. China is more authoritarian than Iran.
    D. The United Kingdom is the most democratic state in Western Europe.

2. Which of the following is an implication of the information shown on the map?
    A. The countries most likely to democratize are in Southeast Asia.
    B. The most recent wave of democratization did not reach countries in eastern Europe.
    C. The global South has not democratized as fully as the northern hemisphere.
    D. China is likely to continue a trend away from authoritarianism and toward a hybrid model of democracy.

3. Which of the following is the best example of a nation?
    A. People in Scotland who support the independence movement.
    B. Drug lords in Mexico whose presence challenges state sovereignty.
    C. The Nigerian people because they share a common religion and language.
    D. High-ranking members of the Chinese Communist Party.

Questions 4 and 5 refer to the quote.

> Where power is seen as legitimate, the cost of citizen compliance with government is reduced. In the absence of legitimacy, three outcomes are possible. In repression, the state incurs the high costs necessary to enforce its decisions on citizens. In conflict, the state attempts this process but is not strong enough to prevent violent opposition. In theater, the state abandons the attempt to impose its will merely mimicking the actions of a functional government.
>
> —Paul Collier, "Culture Politics, and Economic Development,"
> *Annual Review of Political Science*, 2017

4. Which of the following is supported by the main idea of the passage?
    A. Legitimacy is the citizens' belief that the government has the power and authority to rule.
    B. Governments can maintain legitimacy by copying the actions of other states.
    C. Authoritarian states are more likely to use repression in an effort to maintain their power.
    D. It is in a state's best interest to maintain the support of citizens, because loss of legitimacy is costly and causes violence.

5. Which of the following is an implication of the argument presented in the passage?
    A. Democratic states have higher levels of legitimacy than authoritarian states.
    B. Authoritarian states have an incentive to respond to citizens' concerns in an effort to maintain legitimacy.
    C. States can increase their level of legitimacy by spending more money on security services to identify and punish dissenters.
    D. Maintaining legitimacy is expensive, because states must spend money to enforce their decisions on citizens.

6. Which of the following is an example of rule of law?

   A. The Supreme Court in Iran overturns a law passed by the parliament on grounds that it violates the principles of Islam.

   B. A citizen in Nigeria avoids getting a traffic ticket by giving money to the officer who stopped her vehicle.

   C. The Supreme Court in the United Kingdom rules that the prime minister unconstitutionally suspended parliament.

   D. The Russian president orders parliament to investigate the business transactions of a political rival.

7. Which of the following is the best example of democratization?

   A. Following decades of military rule, Nigeria adopts a new constitution that creates three branches of government, with checks and balances.

   B. A revolution in Iran, with broad popular support, resulted in the overthrow of the Shah and the establishment of an Islamic state.

   C. China holds competitive elections for townships and villages.

   D. President Putin's approval ratings remain high, and he is reelected with a large percentage of the vote.

8. Which of the following is an accurate description of two key concepts studied in AP® Comparative Government and Politics?

   A. A nation is a country with a population and defined borders, and a state is a subnational government.

   B. Sovereignty is the state's ability to govern without interference, and legitimacy is the citizens' belief that the government has the right to rule.

   C. Rule of law is a set of common law decisions written by judges that serve as precedent, and rule by law is the code law enacted by legislatures.

   D. Democratization is a process that begins when a state adopts a constitution, and an illiberal, flawed, or hybrid democracy is a state that lacks free and fair elections and restricts civil rights and liberties.

9. Which of the following is a change in government?

   A. Following an election in the House of Commons, a Conservative prime minister is replaced by the leader of the Labour Party.

   B. The military government in Nigeria voluntarily cedes power and a new democratic constitution is ratified.

   C. China switches from a command economy to a market economy and encourages foreign direct investment.

   D. In 2000, a member of the opposition party in Mexico is elected, following decades of single-party rule.

10. Which of the following is a reason why a state would adopt a federal system?

   A. Small states adopt federal systems because it is easier to decentralize power over districts with manageable populations.

   B. States with an official religion adopt federal systems because there is less potential for revolt and little need for strong centralized power.

   C. Federalism is adopted in states with ethnic diversity granting groups some autonomy and preventing revolts.

   D. Federalism is adopted in an effort to make more consistent policies throughout the state.

AP® EXAM PRACTICE ARGUMENT ESSAY

Note to Students:

The following is designed to begin preparing you for the argument essay prompt that you will see on the AP® Exam. At this point in the textbook, you have not had an opportunity to study any of the countries. This question will give you practice at developing an argument in the form of an essay. Later in this book, you will answer questions that are more consistent with the format of the argument essay on the AP® Exam.

Develop an argument as to whether democratic or authoritarian states are better at maintaining legitimacy.

Use one or more of the following course concepts in your response:

- Rule of law
- Power
- Transparency

In your response, do the following:

- Respond to the prompt with a defensible claim or thesis that establishes a line of reasoning using one or more of the provided course concepts.
- Use reasoning to explain why your evidence supports your claim or thesis, using one or more of the provided course concepts.
- Respond to an opposing or alternate perspective, using refutation, concession, or rebuttal.

For a complete list of the sources of information cited in this chapter, turn to the Works Cited appendix.

3 Case Study: Mexico

Political Systems

On November 20, Mexicans celebrate Revolution Day, a holiday to honor the beginning of the 1910 revolution that overthrew dictator Porfirio Díaz in an effort to establish democracy.

Craig Lovell/Getty Images

A Story of Many Firsts:
Mayor Claudia Sheinbaum

In 2018, Claudia Sheinbaum Pardo was the first woman to be elected as mayor of Mexico City. Her victory was not only a personal triumph but part of a broader, long-term movement to bring more women into elected office in Mexico. She is also the first Jewish person to be mayor of the city.

In 1996, Mexico's legislature passed the country's first gender-quota laws that mandated that at least 30 percent of the candidates for the federal legislature be women. Responding to pressure from women's groups, the quota was raised to 50 percent by 2014. The 2018 election brought women into the national and state legislatures in unprecedented numbers. At the national level, 49 percent of those elected to the lower house were women, while in the senate 51 percent were women. Within most state legislatures, women make up 50 percent of the representatives. As of 2018, Mexico ranked fourth in the world in the percentage of women serving in legislatures. This is notable because women in Mexico did not gain the right to vote until 1953.

Electing more women to office corrects historic underrepresentation by providing greater access to power and is essential for descriptive representation—the idea that elected officials should mirror the characteristics of the people they represent. Gender quotas requiring parties to run a certain percentage of female candidates are grounded in the view that traditional notions of patriarchy caused harm to women and unfairly advantaged men. (Piscopo, *Boston Review*.) By 2020, eighty countries had gender-quota laws.

Once women are in office, women's issues are no longer ignored. Women legislators are more likely to support policies directed at women's rights and policies related to social welfare issues such as health and education. Female legislators from both the left and the right are more likely to support access to contraception and abortion, stronger protections against violence toward women, and enhanced family-oriented policies, including day-care policies and parental leave. (Piscopo, "Beyond Hearth and Home.")

Claudia Sheinbaum's rise to power was grounded in these evolving ideas and new quota requirements: "What happened in Mexico City is the result of a movement during the last twenty years, led by feminists and women in politics," noted the head of one Mexican nongovernmental organization focused on women's rights. (Pskowski.)

Sheinbaum comes from a family of scientists. Her father was a chemical engineer, her mother an internationally renowned biologist, and her brother a physicist. Both of her parents were professors at the National Autonomous University of Mexico (UNAM), as well as political activists.

Mexico's Jewish population is small, only about 67,000 out of the country's 130 million, with most living in Mexico City. Sheinbaum's grandparents were Jewish immigrants from Europe. Her father's parents came to Mexico in the 1920s from Lithuania, while her mother's parents fled Bulgaria in the 1940s to avoid the Holocaust. Seldom identifying herself as Jewish, and raised as an atheist, she prefers to focus on her scientific achievements and her role as a woman in public office. Speaking before a Mexican Jewish women's group, though, she recounted celebrating Jewish holidays at her grandparents' homes.

Born in 1962, Sheinbaum followed her parents' careers. Sheinbaum studied physics at Mexico's National Autonomous University (UNAM) as an undergraduate and received a doctorate in energy engineering in 1995. As part of her doctoral research, she studied at the U.S. Department of Energy's prestigious Lawrence Livermore National Laboratory in California. Upon completion of her degree, she became a professor at UNAM and in 1999

After taking the oath of office, Mayor Claudia Sheinbaum Pardo introduces her cabinet and her governmental programs in a ceremony at the Theater of the City.

Lucía Godinez/Newscom

received the university's prize for the best young scholar in engineering and technological innovation. She has published more than 100 scholarly articles and two books.

Sheinbaum's research concentrated on energy science and engineering with a focus on vehicle emissions and climate-change mitigation. In 2007, she was a contributing author to the U.N. Intergovernmental Panel on Climate Change (IPCC) report that won the Nobel Peace Prize for its "efforts to build up and disseminate greater knowledge about man-made climate change, and to lay the foundations for the measures that are needed to counteract such change." (Nobel Peace Prize 2007.)

She credited her scientific background with giving her the skills to tackle public policy. "Training in physics," she said, "makes you always look for the root causes. Why is something happening? And then engineering is much more focused on the 'how.' How can I solve it?" In 2018, the British Broadcasting Company selected her as one of the top 100 "inspiring and influential women from around the world."

As a student activist in the 1980s, she contributed to the formation of the social-democratic political party, Partido de la Revolución Democrática (PRD). The party was formed in 1988 by leftists upset with the ruling political party (PRI) in the aftermath of that year's election that was generally considered to be fraudulent. It was through the PRD that she met Andrés Manuel López Obrador (known as AMLO), Mexico's current president.

AMLO was elected mayor of Mexico City in 2000 and appointed Sheinbaum the city's secretary of the environment. In 2015, she was elected mayor of Tlalpan, a borough in Mexico City with a population of almost 700,000. Sheinbaum's political career has been closely tied to AMLO. When he left the PRD in 2014 to form a new political party known by its Spanish acronym MORENA, which is also Spanish for brown-skinned, she joined him. She is seen by many as a potential successor to AMLO when his term as president ends in 2024.

Some in the Mexican media labeled 2018 "*el año de la mujer*," or "year of the woman," because 3,000 women ran for public office across the country. In her race, four of the six candidates were women. Sheinbaum won just over 50 percent of the vote. Although the position of the head of the government of Mexico City is translated into English as mayor, the position is closer to a U.S. governor and has a seat at Mexico's national governors' conference alongside 31 state governors. With an overall population of 22 million, Mexico City is the fifth-largest metropolitan area in the world.

As mayor, Sheinbaum has tried to tackle the city's environmental challenges. In 2019, for example, she announced a plan to invest 145 billion pesos ($7.4 billion) over the next six years to reach a variety of environmental goals: reducing air pollution by 30 percent and planting 15 million trees around the city, reducing solid waste by banning single-use plastics and encouraging recycling, improving public transit, and expanding solar energy.

Claudia Sheinbaum's political career has spanned almost one-third of the time that women have been able to vote. A measure of the progress during this time is evident in how she recounted meeting AMLO for the first time decades ago. He had come to meet with her then-husband, a political activist involved in the formation of the PRD. As Sheinbaum recounted: "I prepared the coffee and the cookies."

Mexico is a democracy. It holds lively elections, where multiple parties compete, and power is transferred peacefully. As Claudia Sheinbaum's story illustrates, Mexican politics is becoming more inclusive of groups, such as women, who had little power in the past. However, the state faces significant challenges that have prevented it from fully realizing its democratic potential. Corruption and human-rights abuses prevent Mexico from being a liberal democracy. Mexico is an upper-middle-income country with a growing middle class. Despite the challenges facing the state, Mexicans have reasons to be optimistic about the future of their powerful country.

BY THE NUMBERS	MEXICO
Land area	1,943,945 sq km
Population	130,207,371 (July 2021 est.)
Urban population	80.7% (2020)
Life expectancy	Male 74.5 Female 79.87 (2021 est.)
Literacy rate	Male 95.8% Female 94.6% (2018)
HDI	0.779 (2020)
HDI ranking	74/189 (2020)
GDP	$1,040,372,000,000 (2020)
GDP ranking	16/195 (2020)
GDP per capita	$10,919 (2020)
Internet users	65.77% (2018)
Internet users ranking	9/229 (2018)
Gini index (coefficient)	45.4 (2019)
Freedom House rating	Partially free (2020)
Corruption Perceptions ranking	124/180 (2021)
Fragile States Index classification	Warning (2020)

Data from *CIA World Factbook*, World Bank, Freedom House, International Monetary Fund, Transparency International, and Fragile States Index.

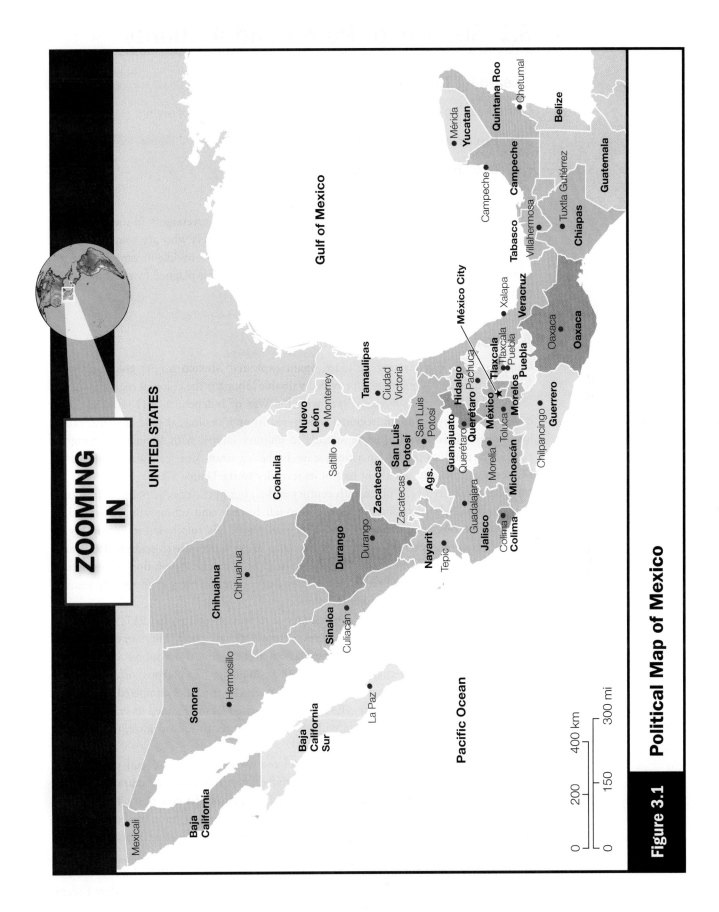

ZOOMING IN

UNITED STATES

Gulf of Mexico

Pacific Ocean

Baja California

Mexicali

Sonora

Hermosillo

Baja California Sur

La Paz

Chihuahua

Chihuahua

Sinaloa

Culiacán

Durango

Durango

Coahuila

Saltillo

Nuevo León

Monterrey

Zacatecas

Zacatecas

Tamaulipas

Ciudad Victoria

San Luis Potosí

San Luis Potosí

Nayarit

Tepic

Ags.

Guanajuato

Querétaro

Querétaro

Hidalgo

Pachuca

México City

México

Toluca

Tlaxcala

Tlaxcala

Puebla

Puebla

Morelos

Veracruz

Xalapa

Jalisco

Guadalajara

Colima

Colima

Michoacán

Morelia

Guerrero

Chilpancingo

Oaxaca

Oaxaca

Tabasco

Villahermosa

Chiapas

Tuxtla Gutiérrez

Campeche

Campeche

Yucatan

Mérida

Quintana Roo

Chetumal

Belize

Guatemala

200   400 km

0   150   300 mi

0

Figure 3.1   Political Map of Mexico

3.1 Sources of Power and Authority

Learning Targets

After reading this section, you should be able to do the following:

1. Explain how Mexico democratized.

2. Describe challenges facing the Mexican state.

Mexico is a democracy but faces challenges to its internal sovereignty in the south from indigenous groups and, more threateningly, from drug cartels who are sometimes more powerful than the state's security forces. This important upper-middle-income country has seen significant economic success in the last few decades but is plagued by growing threats to its sovereignty.

A Brief History of Mexico

Under colonial rule starting in 1519, Spain exploited Mexico for its gold and silver. Mexico's indigenous population provided valuable labor for the colonial regime.

Mexico became a sovereign state with the War of Independence (1810–1821), but it was bitterly divided along regional (north–south) and ideological (liberal–conservative) lines. These divisions resulted in successive military coups, with strongmen vying for power. The conflicts resulted in a weak state. In the Mexican-American War (1846–1848), Mexico was forced to sell about half of its territory to the United States.

The instability of the nineteenth century ended, but at the cost of political freedoms. Porfirio Díaz, who consolidated power through bribery and intimidation, founded an authoritarian regime and ruled from 1876 until 1910. His rule based its legitimacy on political order and economic growth. When Díaz broke a promise to retire in 1910, anti-Díaz forces, supported by the rural poor, started the Mexican Revolution. The Mexican Revolution created the modern Mexican state but resulted in more than seventy years of rule by one party, the Institutional Revolutionary Party (PRI).

Although the PRI embraced a democratic constitution written in 1917, it formed an authoritarian regime that governed Mexico from 1929 to 2000. The party maintained power through corruption, bribery, intimidation, and effective voter mobilization tactics. It also engaged in **patron-clientelism**, where those in power (the patrons) offer benefits to citizens (the clients) in exchange for political support. Other parties competed in elections, such as the National Action Party (PAN). However, the PRI maintained its grip on power. The PRI used oil wealth and trade with the United States to industrialize, transforming Mexico into a middle-income country.

Starting in the early 1980s, the PRI moved away from traditional policies that protected the rural poor, adopting policies more favorable to a free market economy with less government intervention. This led to the creation of a new party, the National Democratic Front (FDN). The 1988 election was a three-way race between the PRI, PAN, and FDN, which won 30 percent of the vote, amid widespread claims of electoral fraud.

Given the tense political climate following the controversial 1988 election, the PRI was forced to enact policies to make elections freer and fairer. IFE, the independent Federal

Patron-clientelism
When those in power offer benefits to citizens in exchange for political support.

Electoral Institute (now called the National Electoral Institute or INE), was formed in 1990 as an autonomous agency to oversee elections.

The next election took place in 1994, and the PRI's presidential candidate, Ernesto Zedillo, won. Although the PRI kept the presidency, the days of one-party rule were numbered. A new, democratic, three-party system emerged. In 2000, the election of the National Action Party's Vicente Fox broke the PRI's seventy-one-year monopoly on the presidency, ushering in a new era in Mexican politics.

Democratization

Mexico completed a transition to democracy in 2000. Citizens and major political actors (except for the drug cartels) accept the electoral process as "the only game in town." Citizens gained trust in elections, because the IFE, and the later INE, oversees elections independent from executive influence.

Since 2000, political power on the national level has changed hands between political parties three times. In 2018, voters elected President Andrés Manuel López Obrador (who is nicknamed AMLO). He ran an anticorruption campaign at the head of a new, left-leaning party, MORENA (an acronym from the Spanish form of its name, National Regeneration Movement). MORENA's ability to emerge as a new party and elect not only the president but also majorities in both houses of congress might be considered another democratic success.

Yet serious challenges remain. By early 2019, many observers wondered if López Obrador's presidency would reduce corruption and enhance social welfare as promised or put Mexico on a path back to authoritarianism. Mexico's young democracy is still plagued by the problems of a weak state, including corruption, clientelism, and drug-related violence.

Federalism

Mexico has a federal system. The country is divided into thirty-one states and Mexico City, the capital. Each state is governed by a governor and a unicameral legislature, which has power over taxation, police, education, and other policy areas. Under the PRI, federalism was weak. The party and the president used power over revenue to punish states that did not follow central directives and reward those that did. Governors were expected to preserve law and order and follow central party directives.

Following democratization in 2000, federalism strengthened, and states gained power. Governors and state legislatures became much more autonomous. Governors from all parties created a national association. They resisted the central government's attempts to make the states carry out programs without sufficient revenue from the national government. They also succeeded in getting the congress to reform the fiscal system: By 2004, some 31 percent of the federal budget went to the states, and by 2010, the states were providing 21 percent of their own revenue, up from 5 percent a decade earlier. (Camp, 2014.) Because of these reforms, states have more funding to provide services to their citizens.

Continued corruption and clientelism plague some states, however. Several state governors and other local leaders have been implicated for supporting various drug cartels. The state government and police of Guerrero were involved in the disappearance of a group of forty-three students at a rural teachers' college in Iguala in 2014, who allegedly were turned over by local police to drug cartels and executed. (Garcia-Navarro, 2018.) Human-rights groups claimed several state governments violated basic rights at the local level, one of the biggest problems for Mexico's young democracy. While Mexican federalism remains relatively centralized, democracy has allowed for some decentralization, creating both benefits and costs to the country's new democratic system.

Legitimacy and Challenges to the State

There are several sources of the Mexican state's legitimacy. Mexico's longstanding constitution, written in 1917, provides for a democratic system of government with three independent branches. Although the constitution did not create a democracy when it was written, because of single-party dominance under PRI, it now provides a well-established framework for Mexico's democratic government and is a source of legitimacy. Although there are still instances of fraud, the independent National Electoral Institute has made elections freer and fairer. Political parties may form freely, run candidates, and have a chance of winning. President López Obrador is a fiery speaker who gives daily speeches, and his charisma is also a source of legitimacy.

Economic development also enhances legitimacy. Mexico is an upper-middle-income country, with a growing middle class. (Smith, 2019.) Strong economic growth is an encouraging sign for Mexico's legitimacy in the future.

Other aspects of Mexico's democracy remain fragile. Threats to democracy include clientelism and corruption, which allow the wealthy to continue to enjoy disproportionate political power. Drug cartels pose the biggest threat to Mexico's stability. Drug gangs are so powerful in some states that entire police departments are corrupt. Drug lords finance their own candidates for governor, mayor, and other offices. Some even provide social services, such as distributing aid during the 2020 coronavirus outbreak. (de Córdoba, 2020.) By offering benefits to citizens that the government is unable to provide, drug cartels weaken state sovereignty. Both PAN and PRI governments tried to battle the drug lords with increased military action, which produced tens of thousands of deaths and 6,000 detentions but failed to reduce drug-related violence.

The 2014 Iguala massacre is a famous example of the connection between government officials and drug cartels. Forty-three students from a teachers' college in the state of Guerrero, who were on their way to a political protest, disappeared. An investigation into the killings implicated corrupt local politicians, police, and the Mexican military, which worked in connection with drug gangs to kill the students. Changing explanations and inconclusive investigations led to a political crisis. (Garcia-Navarro, 2018.)

The case remained unsolved, and in 2019, President López Obrador created a truth commission to investigate the massacre as one of his first acts as president. As of June 2021, the remains of three students have been identified, and all of the students are presumed dead. Insecurity became so great that in one state, residents formed illegal self-defense groups who use vigilante justice to protect themselves. (Magaloni and Razu, 2016.)

Although Mexico successfully transitioned from a single-party-dominant authoritarian state to a democracy, it faces significant challenges that may hinder further democratization.

<aside>
AP® TIP

The free-response portion of the AP® Exam may ask for examples of policies countries can enact to further democratization. Both Mexico and Nigeria created independent commissions to make elections freer and fairer. These commissions are a specific example of democratization that you can use as evidence on the AP® Exam.
</aside>

Section 3.1 Review

Each section's main ideas are reflected in the Learning Targets. By reviewing after each section, you should be able to

Remember the key points,

Know terms that are central to the topic, and

Think critically about what you have learned.

Remember

- Mexico democratized, changing from an authoritarian, single party dominant state under the PRI to a democracy with the election of the PAN in 2000.
- The Mexican government claims several sources of legitimacy, including a constitution and more free and fair elections, but it faces challenges to its sovereignty.

Know

- *Patron-clientelism:* when those in power offer benefits to citizens in exchange for political support. (p. 58)

Think

- What steps could the Mexican government take to strengthen state sovereignty?

Free-Response Question: Quantitative Analysis

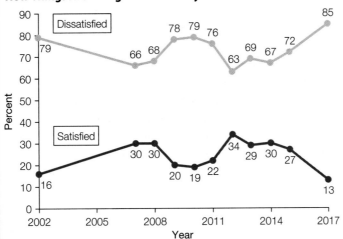

Changes in the Public Mood in Mexico

Satisfaction/Dissatisfaction with How Things Are Going in the Country

Data from Global Attitudes Survey, spring 2017, and Pew Research Center.

Answer A, B, C, D, and E.

A. Using the data in the line graph, identify the year in which people in Mexico had the highest level of dissatisfaction.

B. Using the data in the line graph, describe a trend in the gap between levels of satisfaction and dissatisfaction in Mexico from 2012 to 2017.

C. Define legitimacy.

D. Using your knowledge of political legitimacy and the data in the graph, draw a conclusion about how the level of citizen satisfaction impacts state sovereignty.

E. Explain what the data illustrate about the strength of democracy in Mexico.

3.2 Institutions of Government

Learning Targets

After reading this section, you should be able to do the following:

1. Describe the roles and powers of Mexico's executive, legislative, and judicial institutions.

2. Explain how President López Obrador has expanded executive power.

3. Describe the limits on judicial independence in Mexico.

Mexico has a presidential system of government. Presidential systems have separate executive, legislative, and judicial institutions, which have the power to check each other. While the Mexican president has a significant amount of power, democratization increased checks on executive power. Presidential systems of government will be covered in more detail in Chapter 4.

The Executive

Head of state
The symbolic representative of a country.

Head of government
The key executive in the policymaking process.

Mexico's president serves as both head of state and head of government. A **head of state** is the symbolic representative of the country. A **head of government** is the key executive in the policymaking process. In presidential systems, these roles are fused in a single executive.

When Mexico was an authoritarian state under the single-party dominance of the PRI, there were few checks on presidential power, because the legislative and judicial branches were under the PRI's control. Since the end of one-party dominance, the president has often faced divided government, when one or both houses of the legislature are controlled by a political party different from the political party of the president. This makes it more difficult for presidents to get their proposed policies passed. Furthermore, the judiciary is gaining independence. As a result, Mexican presidents recently faced more checks on their power. Despite this trend, the Mexican president is still very powerful.

Cabinet head
An official appointed to run a government department with a specific policy area.

The Mexican president has the power to appoint **cabinet heads**, who run departments in specific policy areas, like the treasury and defense. The president is the commander-in-chief of the military, a role that gives him the power to deploy troops. The president proposes a program of legislation, and once a bill is passed in the lower house, he has the power to sign or veto it. One of the president's strongest powers is the ability to issue a decree that has the force of law, bypassing the legislature. In foreign affairs, the Mexican president is the chief diplomat and has the power to negotiate treaties with other countries.

Sexenio
The single six-year term for the Mexican president.

Mexico's president is limited to a single six-year term, called the **sexenio**. This prevents the executive from consolidating power over a long time span and becoming a dictator. As a result of the one-term limit, policies may change fairly often if a new president is elected from a different political party and he reverses course from his predecessor.

With congressional majorities and little organized opposition, President López Obrador was able to issue decrees and pass reforms quickly early in his term. López Obrador's programs have strengthened the power of the executive relative to the legislature and the states. López Obrador has used populist appeals, focusing on the interests of everyday citizens and criticizing the elites, while consolidating power in the presidency.

His anticorruption campaign cut the federal budget and public funds for **nongovernmental organizations (NGOs)**, which are nonprofit groups outside of the government's control. López Obrador questioned the need for government transparency and human-rights commissions. He declared he will govern "without intermediaries" and appointed friends and allies to handle local delivery of promised social programs, bypassing local government institutions and stating that new social programs "would link recipients to him personally." (Dresser, 2019.)

No one was prosecuted for corruption during his first few months in office, and as many as 70 percent of government contracts were awarded without a bidding process. He appointed close associates to key positions.

He has criticized the media in his frequent press conferences, creating tension in a country where journalists are often assassinated. (Ahmed and Semple, 2019.) López Obrador opposed the social media bans on President Trump following the insurgency at the U.S. Capitol, and he has suggested the creation of a social network run by the Mexican government. (Taylor, 2021.)

Two years into his term, President López Obrador expanded executive power even further by giving the military a broader role in battling drug cartels. Record numbers of troops have been deployed in an effort to prevent Mexico's security situation from deteriorating. Troops are raiding suspected drug labs, patrolling city streets, and protecting strategic locations. Using the military against citizens poses risks. Civilian oversight of government activities has diminished, and soldiers have been accused of human-rights violations. (Sheridan, 2020.)

Nongovernmental organization (NGO) A nonprofit group outside the government's control.

Andrés Manuel López Obrador, of the MORENA party, at a campaign rally before the 2018 election. A popular leftist, López Obrador won the presidency with more than 50 percent of the vote. His six-year term began in December 2018.

Jessica Espinosa Sánchez/Notimex/Newscom

The López Obrador government has also faced criticism for its handling of the COVID-19 pandemic. At the beginning of the outbreak, the president downplayed the seriousness of the virus and undermined the messages of public health officials. In a television appearance in March 2020, he held a prayer card and claimed that his faith in Jesus and good deeds would protect him from the virus. The response to COVID-19 was left up to the governors, and those who acted decisively to impose public health orders were criticized by the president for being too heavy-handed. Later in the year, López Obrador switched course and advocated social-distancing policies that he had rejected earlier. (Enriquez et al., 2020.)

López Obrador's critics worry that his actions rely too much on personal appeals and are undoing checks and balances. They fear that he may concentrate power in the presidency and in MORENA, essentially creating a new single-party-dominant authoritarian regime.

The legislature may remove the executive in a presidential system, such as Mexico. Article 108 of the Mexican constitution provides that the president may be charged with "treason and serious crimes of the common order." However, it is very difficult to impeach the executive in a presidential system, who can usually get enough support from the members of his or her party in the legislature to remain in power.

The Legislature

Bicameral
A legislature with two chambers.

Chamber of Deputies
The elected lower house of the Mexican Congress, which has the power to pass legislation, levy taxes, approve the budget, and certify elections.

Lower house
The legislative body in a bicameral system that typically has more members, shorter terms, and less prestige than the upper house, but it may be the more powerful body in the legislature.

Senate
The elected upper house of the Mexican Congress, which has the power to confirm appointments, ratify treaties, and approve federal intervention in the states.

Upper house
The legislative body in a bicameral system that typically has fewer members and may have more prestige but less power than the lower house.

Mexico's Congress of the Union is **bicameral**, which means it has two chambers. The **Chamber of Deputies** is the **lower house**, which is the legislative body that typically has more members and may have less prestige. The lower house in a legislature is unusually considered to be closer to the people (because there are fewer representatives per person) and has shorter terms than the upper house.

Ironically, in many systems, the lower house has more power over legislation than the upper house. The Chamber of Deputies has the power to debate and pass legislation, levy taxes, approve the budget, and certify elections.

The **Senate** is the **upper house**, which is the legislative body that typically has fewer members and may have more prestige. It has the power to confirm presidential appointments to the cabinet and Supreme Court, ratify treaties, and approve intervention by the federal government into events occurring in states. Because Mexico has a federal system of government, the Senate represents the states.

The ability of the congress to limit the president's power and the existence of three, ideologically distinct parties became the defining elements of Mexico's young democracy. Members of congress successfully initiated legislation, regularly amended the president's legislative initiatives, and were able to form coalitions of at least two parties to pass legislation. (Casar, 2016.) Independent congressional candidates with no party affiliation were allowed to stand for election starting in 2012. By 2016, though, the stability of Mexico's multiparty system seemed shakier.

During the first three years of his presidency, MORENA, President López Obrador's political party, held the majority of seats in both the Chamber of Deputies and the Senate. As a result, he was able to pass policies easily. MORENA lost seats in the 2021 election, although it held on to a majority. However, it lost the supermajority necessary to pass constitutional amendments.

Should government in Mexico become divided, with opposing parties controlling one or both houses, the legislature could serve as more of a check on the executive branch, which might curtail the expansion of presidential power.

FIGURE 3.2

The Structure of the Federal Government of Mexico

Checks and Balances: Division of Power and Responsibilities

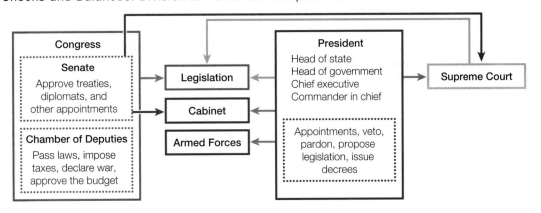

Elections and Appointments: How They Work

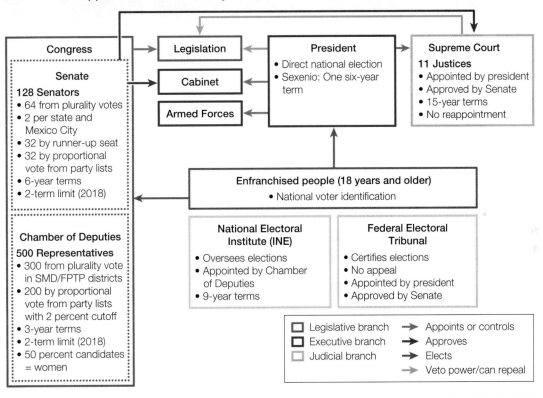

Figure 3.2 is a summary of the federal government of Mexico. The upper part shows relationships of the branches of the Mexican federal government and the powers of the branches. The lower part shows how each institution is elected or appointed.

The Judiciary

The judiciary in Mexico is an independent branch of government with the power of judicial review. Supreme Court magistrates are appointed by the president and approved by the Senate for fifteen-year terms. During rule by the PRI, the judiciary was controlled by the party and lacked independence. The Mexican government enacted reforms to increase the judiciary's professionalism and autonomy, and in the late twentieth and early twenty-first centuries, the Supreme Court has been more active in striking down executive actions.

The judicial branch, especially at the local level, is plagued by corruption, however, and rule of law remains weak. Gladys McCormick and Matthew Clearly argued in 2018 that "the single most pressing issue for the future of Mexico's fragile democracy is the renovation of the judiciary. The combination of rampant impunity, the lack of accountability and the failure of law enforcement, including the judicial branches, to counter the security crisis affecting large swaths of the country rends this the most difficult issue to tackle." (McCormick, 2018.)

If Mexico is able to reduce corruption and further professionalize the court system, the judiciary may eventually become a coequal branch of government, furthering democratization.

Section 3.2 Review

Remember

- Mexico has a presidential system of government, with separate executive, legislative, and judicial institutions.
- Mexico's president is both head of state and head of government and serves a single six-year term.
- The Congress of the Union is bicameral, with the lower house representing the people and the upper house representing the states.
- Mexico's judiciary is becoming more independent, but corruption, especially at the local level, hinders rule of law.

Know

- *Head of state:* the symbolic representative of a country. (p. 62)
- *Head of government:* the key executive in the policymaking process. (p. 62)
- *Cabinet head:* an official appointed to run a government department with a specific policy area. (p. 62)
- *Sexenio:* the single six-year term for the Mexican president. (p. 62)
- *Nongovernmental organization (NGO):* a nonprofit group outside the government's control. (p. 63)
- *Bicameral:* a legislature with two chambers. (p. 64)
- *Chamber of Deputies:* the elected lower house of the Mexican Congress, which has the power to pass legislation, levy taxes, approve the budget, and certify elections. (p. 64)
- *Lower house:* the legislative body in a bicameral system that typically has more members, shorter terms, and less prestige than the upper house, but it may be the more powerful body in the legislature. (p. 64)
- *Senate:* the elected upper house of the Mexican Congress, which has the power to confirm appointments, ratify treaties, and approve federal intervention in the states. (p. 64)
- *Upper house:* the legislative body in a bicameral system that typically has fewer members and may have more prestige but less power than the lower house. (p. 64)

Think

- How did democratization decrease the power of the Mexican president?
- What steps could Mexico take to increase judicial autonomy?

Free-Response Question: Comparative Analysis

Note to Students:

The following is designed to begin preparing you for the comparative-analysis free-response question you will see on the AP® Exam. At this point in the textbook, you have only studied one course country—Mexico. On the AP® Exam, this type of question requires you to compare two course countries. The following question will give you practice at writing this type of free-response question, using only Mexico as an example. Later in this book, you will answer questions that are more consistent with the format of the comparative-analysis free-response question on the AP® Exam by comparing two countries.

The executive and legislative institutions in Mexico's presidential system have differing roles and powers. In your response, you should do the following:

A. Define legislative independence.

B. Explain how the legislature became more independent from the executive as Mexico democratized.

C. Explain why the legislature may not serve as an effective check on the power of the executive in Mexico.

3.3 Electoral System, Political Parties, and Civil Society

Learning Targets

After reading this section, you should be able to do the following:

1. Describe the system used to elect the Mexican president and the mixed system used to elect the legislature.

2. Explain how the ideology of Mexico's political parties differs.

3. Describe the difference between corporatism and pluralism.

4. Explain how the Zapatista rebellion impacted policies in Mexico.

Free and fair elections, the ability of political parties to form and run candidates for office, and **civil society**—groups that form outside the government's control—are hallmarks of democracy. Despite its authoritarian past, Mexico has taken steps to encourage free and fair elections, party competition, and political participation by citizens. Nevertheless, groups not officially associated with the government, such as drug cartels, have assassinated politicians, reporters, and human-rights activists, repressing civil society.

Civil society
Groups that form outside the government's control.

Elections

The Mexican president is directly elected by a plurality of the vote. This means that the candidate who gets the most votes wins, even if he or she does not earn more than

50 percent of the vote. This can pose a problem for presidents entering office. Presidents who do not win with a majority may find it difficult to claim a **mandate**—the broad support of the people to carry out their proposed policies.

Presidential elections in Mexico have become freer and fairer. During PRI rule, the sitting president chose his successor through a process known as *el dedazo*. Although the president was limited to one term, he chose the next president. This gave the president the power to reward a strong supporter with the promise of future power. *El dedazo* strengthened authoritarian rule, because citizens had no say over who the next PRI candidate for the presidency would be. The PRI eliminated *el dedazo* in 1988, paving the way for party primaries, in which party members choose the nominee.

The creation of the National Electoral Institute reduced voter fraud, making elections more competitive. In addition, Mexico privatized state-owned corporations, which reduced opportunities for patron-clientelism. With fewer high-level government jobs to offer influential supporters, politicians had less leverage over elections.

Like the president, Mexico's legislature is directly elected. Mexico's Congress of the Union has two houses—the Chamber of Deputies and the Senate. The Chamber of Deputies is the lower house and has 500 members. Representatives are elected through a **mixed electoral system**, which includes both single-member districts and seats awarded through proportional representation.

Three hundred members of the Chamber of Deputies are elected through a **single-member plurality system (SMD)**. In an SMD system, the country is divided into districts that have roughly equal populations. Each district elects one representative, and the candidate with the most votes wins. If you took AP® U.S. Government and Politics, you are familiar with an SMD system, because it is used to elect members of the U.S. House of Representatives.

Two hundred seats in the Chamber of Deputies are elected through a **proportional representation (PR) system**, in which parties receive seats according to the percentage of the vote the party earns. Each political party submits a list of candidates who will be placed in office depending on how many PR seats the party wins. There is a 2 percent threshold for a party to win seats in the legislature. This means that parties earning less than 2 percent of the vote are not awarded seats, and the seats they would have earned are distributed among the parties that met the threshold.

The Senate, which represents the states in Mexico's federal system, has 128 members. Each of Mexico's thirty-one states as well as the federal district of Mexico City elects two senators, through an SMD system, for a total of sixty-four. One seat is awarded to the party that came in second in each state and in the federal district of Mexico City, for a total of thirty-two. Thirty-two additional senators are chosen through proportional representation. We will study election systems in more depth in Chapter 8.

Political parties in Mexico are allowed to form alliances or coalitions to run in a specific election. These alliances must be registered with INE, and the coalition must identify itself with a specific name and logo. PR seats are assigned to the alliance based on the total number of votes earned by the alliance in the election, and then the coalition reassigns the seats to a political party that is a member of the alliance. Interestingly, once a coalition has assigned a seat to a member of a political party, that representative does not have to work with the coalition. Major parties use this system to prevent small parties from running members for SMD seats, which might dilute the control of the major parties, in exchange for offering smaller parties some PR seats. (Alverez-Rivera.)

In an effort to increase female representation in the legislature, Mexico requires that women make up at least 50 percent of the candidates run by political parties for SMD seats and on party lists for proportional representation. Following the 2018 election, women made up 51 percent of the Senate and 49 percent of the Chamber of Deputies. (Ramirez, 2018.)

Political Parties

Mexico has a multiparty system, which includes the Partido de la Revolución Institucional (PRI), the Partido de la Revolución Democrática (PRD), the Partido Acción Nacional (PAN), and the Movimiento de Regeneración Nacional (MORENA). Smaller parties represent specific interests, such a environmentalists and workers.

The PRI was founded in 1929, and it controlled government until 2000. Ideologically, the PRI claimed legitimacy partly on the basis of the legacy of the Mexican Revolution of 1910–1920. While the revolution included many different leaders and groups, the bulk of its support came from its promises to end the extreme inequality of nineteenth- and early-twentieth-century Mexico. The PRI claimed it represented peasants, workers, and the downtrodden, and for a long time it maintained their loyalty and support. It mobilized that support through patron-clientelism.

While it allowed official opposition, the PRI made sure that it won virtually every election. The party's dominance was unquestioned for sixty years. Opposition parties won a handful of seats but never enough to threaten the regime. This system provided the illusion of democracy, and the PRI pursued policies that kept many workers and peasants loyal to it for decades. The PRI based its legitimacy partly on the claim it was modernizing the country, and it achieved significant economic development.

In the 1980s, the PRI's grip on power loosened. The PRI began to lose support in congressional and local elections. Allegations of widespread fraud in the 1988 presidential election led to the creation in 1990 of the predecessor of the INE, the Federal Electoral Institute, which, unfortunately for the PRI, reduced fraud at the polls. Although the PRI won the presidency in 1994, its single-party dominance ended in 2000 with the election of Vicente Fox, from the PAN party.

The PRI made a temporary comeback in 2012, with the election of Enrique Peña Nieto as president, who tried to characterize the party as modernized and reformed. Nevertheless, it's hard to define PRI's ideology, which has shifted over the decades between socialist policies and, more recently, free market reforms. Despite attempts to change the party's image, the PRI still relies on patron-clientelism to garner support at the local level, and the party is still plagued by allegations of electoral fraud. (Rodriguez, 2018.)

PAN is the party on the right, representing conservative interests. It was founded in 1939, and it won the presidency with the election of Vicente Fox in 2000 and Felipe Calderón, in a contested election, in 2006. The party is socially conservative, and it supports the Catholic Church. PAN's economic policies support pro-business, free market reforms. Much of its support is concentrated in the north. Both PAN presidents had difficulty passing their programs of legislation due to opposition in the Congress.

In addition, both presidents faced internal challenges from drug cartels. As will be discussed in the next section. President Calderón declared war on the drug cartels, taking a hard-line approach. Almost 200,000 people were killed and 28,000 disappeared in drug-related violence during his term in office. (*Guardian*.)

In 2012, PAN nominated the first female candidate for the presidency in Mexico—Josefina Vásquez Mota, who came in third. In 2018, PAN's candidate came in second but earned only 22 percent of the vote.

In the 1980s, the PRD emerged as the party on the left. The PRD opposed free market reforms and advocated social policies to help workers and the poor. In 2006, Andrés Manuel López Obrador was the PRD's candidate for the presidency. He lost to Felipe Calderón, the PAN candidate, by a razor-thin margin. López Obrador refused to acknowledge Calderón's victory, setting off weeks of protests, which harmed PRD's image. López Obrador won the PRD's nomination again in 2012, losing to the PRI candidate Enrique Peña Nieto. Following his defeat in the 2012 election, López Obrador left the PRD.

In 2016, the leftist PRD split into two parties when López Obrador created MORENA. López Obrador was a popular figure, and MORENA was a vehicle for him to win the presidency using his charismatic personality. MORENA capitalized on the policy failures and corruption of the administrations of Vicente Fox, Felipe Calderón, and Peña Nieto. López Obrador promised a more honest government that was closer to the people. However, the administration has been criticized for making vague promises and shifting policy proposals that send mixed signals to the public. According to political scientist Hugo Concha, "MORENA is everything, and nothing at the same time . . . One day you hear crazy proposals, and the next day they change their opinion." (Versa, 2020.)

MORENA's electoral dominance in 2018, along with the weak showing of the PAN (22 percent) and spectacular fall of the PRI (16 percent) in the presidential race and similar losses in congress (where the PRI lost 158 seats in the Chamber of Deputies), make the future of Mexico's multiparty system uncertain. On a positive note, the party in control of Mexico's presidency has changed hands twice since the 2000 election (in 2012 and 2016). The split of the PRD and weakening of the PAN and PRI, coupled with the rise of MORENA, may mean that Mexico is headed in the direction of becoming another state with a single dominant party. However, although MORENA maintained its majority in the legislature in the June 2021 midterm elections, it lost seats, and it no longer held a supermajority, which would be needed to change the constitution.

Interest Groups and Social Movements

The Transition from Corporatism to Pluralism

Corporatism
A system in which the state controls interest groups and chooses the ones it wishes to recognize.

Peak association
An organization authorized by the government to represent a group, such as labor, business, or agriculture.

When Mexico was a single-party dominant state under PRI rule, the government used state **corporatism** to control interest groups. Corporatism is the idea that each important interest in society, such as labor unions, business groups, and agricultural associations, should be represented by one organization authorized by the government, known as a **peak association**. In a corporatist system, the state controls interest groups and chooses the ones it wishes to recognize.

Mexico's authoritarian regime under the PRI was a classic example. The PRI recognized and included within the party a single labor organization, a single peasant association, and a single association for "popular groups"—small businesses, women's interests, and various others. These organizations were meant to represent their constituents within the party. PRI's policies tended to favor big businesses over smaller, family-owned operations. The workers' organization, in particular, was very powerful within the party, and real wages rose for most of the PRI's long rule, even though the unions rarely contradicted official party policies.

Over time, the corporatist system became increasingly corrupt and was controlled by the elite at the top of the party, who used the system to reward interests favorable to the regime. As the PRI began losing elections, it also lost the ability to deliver on promises made to its allies in the corporatist system.

As Mexico democratizes, **pluralism** is replacing corporatism. In a pluralist system, groups are allowed to form and advocate for their interests outside of government control. New groups have the ability to form and compete in the policymaking process. Pluralism is more democratic than corporatism, because small groups are not left out of the policymaking process, and the government does not favor a few groups over others. Interest groups in Mexico include those advocating for environmental protection, and representing the interests of women, teachers, students, journalists, and peasants.

As Mexico's corporatist system weakened, a social movement arose to challenge state power and sovereignty.

Pluralism
A system in which groups are allowed to form and advocate for their interests outside of government control.

The Zapatista Rebellion

Chiapas is Mexico's southernmost and poorest state. In the 1980s, a national leftist organization sent a handful of activists to start building a secret armed group for an unspecified future rebellion. It focused on an area of the state that had been unoccupied jungle terrain until several different indigenous groups migrated to the jungle and carved out farms. The Zapatista Army of National Liberation, or EZLN (Ejército Zapatista de Liberación Nacional), was formed from among these indigenous migrants, with several nonindigenous leaders from elsewhere in the country. The EZLN is named after Emiliano Zapata, an agrarian reformer and hero of the Mexican Revolution, who was assassinated by the military in 1919.

In 1993 the government discovered the group and engaged in a small battle with it. Afterward, the group decided the rebellion had to start soon or the government would wipe out its efforts.

The North American Free Trade Agreement (NAFTA) was an important catalyst for the Zapatista Rebellion. To implement NAFTA, the Mexican government had to remove Article 17 from the Mexican constitution. Article 17 protected *ejido* rights—communal land ownership supported by the state. Privatization of *ejido* land meant that instead of the government holding the land for the use of indigenous persons, the land could now be bought and sold to wealthy individuals, giving them an advantage over subsistence farmers.

Ejido rights were very important to the continued existence of subsistence farming. The rebels in Chiapas objected to the removal of communal land rights, and this was the main reason for the rebellion. The EZLN broadcast their intention to rebel and to take up arms against the Mexican government. On January 1, 1994, the day NAFTA officially took effect, 2,000, mostly indigenous, armed rebels wearing ski masks took control of several cities in Chiapas.

This poster celebrates years of action by the Zapatistas. The Zapatistas have grown from an armed rebellion into an internationally recognized social movement for indigenous rights, including the right to engage in communal subsistence farming. Note the EZLN slogan at the top, which translates as *Here the people command and the government obeys.*

Rommy Torrico

A nonindigenous spokesman who called himself Subcomandante Marcos announced that the EZLN had taken over the state. The EZLN's message called for social justice and democracy and advocated a national uprising to remove the long-ruling, authoritarian PRI government. The government sent in 10,000 troops to quell the uprising. Within two weeks, the rebels returned to their jungle hideouts. The military situation would remain in a standoff for years.

The Zapatista uprising was unusual in that it began with political violence and then shifted to nonviolent tactics. Although only about 2,000 armed rebels took part in the uprising, they had the support of tens of thousands of others in Chiapas. The government's heavy military response led the rebels to change their focus. Instead of advocating the overthrow of the government, they focused on indigenous rights and class-based inequality.

The military repression of indigenous rights caught the attention of activists and NGOs around the world on the internet, which was relatively new. NGOs formed highly networked, loosely coordinated, cross-border coalitions to wage an information-age social network campaign that would constrain the Mexican government and assist the EZLN's cause. (Fuller et al., 1999, 3.)

The international attention may have kept the government from pursuing the rebels militarily into the jungle. Instead, a military standoff and multiyear negotiation took place. An agreement was initially reached in 1996, but the government failed to pass the legislation to put it into effect, and the standoff continues to this day. Only after democratization in Mexico in 2000 did the national government finally approve some of the Zapatistas' demands, as Vicente Fox promised during his presidential campaign.

The Zapatistas hosted two significant conferences in the 1990s in the territory they controlled, inviting national and international activists to attend. While nothing concrete came of these efforts, they kept global attention on the movement. The Zapatistas continue to clash with non-Zapatista militias and government forces, although the overall level of violence has been reduced significantly, with the last serious clash occurring in 2014.

The Zapatista Rebellion is an example of a successful social movement in Mexico that garnered the attention of the government and the world, raising awareness of the plight of indigenous people. You will study social movements in more depth in Chapter 8.

The Chiapas region is known for its stunning landscape, but it is home to some of Mexico's poorest citizens, many of whom are indigenous Mayan people. In the town of San Juan Chamula, men taking part in a religious holiday are wearing traditional woolen tunics. A Catholic bishop in Chiapas said in 2014 that "[t]he EZLN remains alive, not as a military option, but as a social and political organization that fights for a dignified life." (*USA Today*, 2014.)

Agustin Paullier/AFP/Getty Images

Section 3.3 Review

Remember

- Mexico uses a plurality system for electing the president and a mixed system for electing the legislature.
- Mexico has a multiparty system, with three strong parties—MORENA, PRI, and PAN.
- Mexico is transitioning away from corporatism toward a pluralist system of interest group activity.
- The Zapatista Movement was a successful social movement that called attention to the plight of indigenous people.

Know

- *Civil society:* groups that form outside the government's control. (p. 67)
- *Mandate:* the broad support of the people to carry out proposed policies. (p. 68)
- *Mixed electoral system:* a system for electing members of the legislature that includes both single-member districts and seats awarded through proportional representation. (p. 68)
- *Single-member plurality system (SMD):* a system in which the candidate who earns the most votes in a district wins a seat in the legislature. (p. 68)
- *Proportional representation (PR) system:* a system in which seats in the legislature are awarded according to the percentage of votes a party receives. (p. 68)
- *Corporatism:* a system in which the state controls interest groups and chooses the ones it wishes to recognize. (p. 70)
- *Peak association:* an organization authorized by the government to represent a group, such as labor, business, or agriculture. (p. 70)
- *Pluralism:* a system in which groups are allowed to form and advocate for their interests outside of government control. (p. 71)

Think

- Will Mexico's multiparty system continue to be competitive, or will MORENA become a dominant party in Mexican politics?

Free-Response Question: Quantitative Analysis

Chamber of Deputies Election 2018

	District / Direct		Proportional		Total seats, by party	Change in number of seats, +/−
	Percent of vote	Seats	Percent of vote	Seats		
Results by party						
National Regeneration Movement	1.27	8	37.25	84	189	+154
National Action Party	1.25	5	17.93	41	83	−25
Institutional Revolutionary Party	7.78	1	16.54	38	45	−158
Party of the Democratic Revolution	0.22	0	5.27	12	21	−35
Ecologist Green Party	2.55	0	4.79	11	16	−31
Citizens' Movement	0.48	0	4.41	10	27	+1
Labor Party	0.12	0	3.93	4	61	+55
New Alliance Party	1.26	0	2.47	0	2	−8

(Continued)

	District / Direct		Proportional		Total seats, by party	Change in number of seats, +/−
	Percent of vote	Seats	Percent of vote	Seats		
Social Encounter Party	0.10	0	2.40	0	56	+48
Results by party coalitions						
MORENA, Labor, Social Encounter	42.01	210	–	–	–	–
PAN, Democratic Revolution, Citizens' Movement	25.70	63	–	–	–	–
PRI, New Alliance, Greens	12.26	13	–	–	–	–
Independents	0.96	0	0.96	0	0	−1
Write-ins	0.06	–	0.06	–	–	–
Invalid/blank votes	3.98	–	3.98	–	–	–
Total	**100**	**300**	**100**	**200**	**500**	**0**
Registered voters/ turnout	62.20	–	63.21	–	–	–

Note: The total number of seats earned by each party reflects seats earned independently plus the seats earned as part of party coalitions.
Data from Instituto Nacional Electoral.

Answer A, B, C, D, and E.

A. Using the data in the table, identify the political party that lost the greatest number of seats in the Chamber of Deputies in the 2018 election.

B. Using the data in the table, describe how the balance of power shifted in the Chamber of Deputies following the 2018 election.

C. Define a multiparty state.

D. Using the data in the table and your knowledge of AP® Comparative Government and Politics, draw a conclusion about the strength of Mexico's multiparty state.

E. Using the data in the table, explain how party competition in Mexico might impact Mexico's efforts to further democratize.

3.4 Political Culture and Participation

Learning Targets

After reading this section, you should be able to do the following:

1. Describe human-rights abuses in Mexico.

2. Describe the social cleavage between the north and south in Mexico.

3. Explain why indigenous Mexicans are poorer than mestizos and experience discrimination.

Mexico's democratic constitution guarantees basic rights to its citizens and fosters a political culture where many citizens are active in politics. **Political culture** is a set of collectively held attitudes, values, and beliefs about government and politics, and the norms of behavior in the political system. According to an online survey conducted in 2020 by the Latin American Public Opinion project, 64 percent of Mexicans agreed that democracy is the best form of government. However, only 40 percent were satisfied with how democracy functions in the country. (Topline Report, 2020.)

Mexico is a democracy, and even though elections are becoming freer and fairer and rights are guaranteed on paper, citizens report significant human-rights abuses. As a result, lack of trust and confidence in government is one feature of the political culture in Mexico. Political culture and participation will be discussed in greater detail in Chapter 6.

Political culture
A set of collectively held attitudes, values, and beliefs about government and politics, and the norms of behavior in the political system.

Civil Rights and Civil Liberties

The Mexican constitution protects **civil liberties**, the fundamental rights and freedoms protected from infringement by the government, including freedom of expression, freedom of the press, and the right to peaceably assemble. For example, the Mexican government does not restrict access to the internet, and it does not censor online content. Although most Mexicans are Roman Catholic, the law provides for the separation of church and state, and Mexicans have the right to freely exercise their religious beliefs. (State Department.) The government also guarantees **civil rights**—protections granted by the government to prevent people from being discriminated against when engaged in fundamental political actions, such as voting. Civil rights include the protection of individuals from discrimination as members of a particular group, such as ethnic and religious minorities.

Civil liberties
Fundamental rights and freedoms protected from infringement by the government.

Civil rights
Protections granted by the government to prevent people from being discriminated against when engaged in fundamental political actions, such as voting.

Although civil rights and liberties are protected on paper, rule of law is weak. Criminal organizations use violence to achieve their goals. Government officials and non-state actors engage in human-rights abuses. Those who perpetrate the abuse often escape justice. (Amnesty.)

One of the most serious challenges facing Mexico is the danger facing journalists. Reporters who investigate police wrongdoing, drug cartels, and government corruption are at high risk of being hurt or killed. The National Human Rights Commission reported that 148 journalists were killed between 2000 and 2018, not counting 21 reporters who disappeared. (Human Rights Watch.) Reporters Without Borders reported that at least nine journalists were killed in 2018 and deemed Mexico to be the most dangerous country for journalists, after Afghanistan and Syria. (Reporters Without Borders). The Mexican government created the Federal Protection Mechanism for Human Rights Defenders and Journalists in an effort to provide more security for reporters. The program provides panic buttons, safe houses, and bodyguards to those who enroll. (Freedom House.)

The Committee to Protect Journalists reported that five journalists were assassinated in 2019, although Amnesty International reports that the actual number is at least double. A Special Prosecutor's Office investigates crimes against journalists. It brought 186 criminal charges from 2010 to 2018. However, it won only ten convictions. Intimidation and the fear of violence prevent reporters from covering stories involving organized crime and government corruption. Although the law makes it a federal crime to harass journalists, the government has been slow to respond to complaints and prosecute offenders. (Freedom House.)

Like journalists, human-rights advocates report intimidation and threats of physical harm. From January to July 2019, at least thirteen people defending human rights have been killed. Crimes against human-rights defenders often go unpunished. (Human Rights Watch.)

Mexican citizens face violence from a number of sources, including drug cartels, police officers, and the military. In 2019, the death rate was high, especially in states where drug cartels have a large presence, including Baja California, Chihuahua, Colima, Guanajuato, Michoacán, and Morelos. Mass killings included the murder of fourteen people attending a family gathering in the city of Minatitlán and the deaths of twenty-six patrons at a bar that was set on fire in Coatzacoalcos, both in the state of Veracruz. (Freedom House.)

In October 2019, the National Guard captured drug lord Ovidio Guzmán López, the son of Joaquín "El Chapo" Guzmán, in Sinaloa. Following the capture, heavily armed cartel members surrounded the patrol and forced them to release Guzmán. At least thirteen people were killed, and twenty-nine prisoners escaped during the firefight. In November 2019, nine members of the LeBarón Family, which holds dual citizenship in the United States and lived in a Mormon community in Sonora state, were executed on orders of a drug lord. Federal prosecutors detained seven suspects, including a local police chief. (Freedom House.)

In addition to well-publicized killings, disappearances are a serious problem. One example already mentioned is the forty-three students in rural Iguala in 2014 who were kidnapped and are presumed dead. In 2019, President López Obrador created a commission to investigate the case. One hundred forty-two people were detained, but at least seventy-seven of them were released following allegations of torture. (Freedom House.) Findings from the U.N. Committee against Torture expressed concern about the high incidence of torture, including sexual violence and other ill treatment of civilians, by the military, security forces, and the police. (Amnesty.)

Women in Mexico face an especially high threat of violence and discrimination. The Mexican constitution and the law prohibit gender discrimination and provide for the equal treatment of women. However, according to a 2017 survey by the National Institute for Statistics and Geography, 12 percent of women were illegally asked to take a pregnancy test as a condition for employment. Women faced discrimination in working hours and benefits and earned significantly less than men for the same work. (State Department.) In 2018, official data indicated that 3,752 women were victims of homicide. As of 2016, an estimated two-thirds of women and girls over the age of 15 had experienced gender-based violence. (Amnesty.) Demonstrations against sexual violence against females have been held in Mexico City and other cities.

A General Law on Women's Access to a Life Free from Violence set up alert mechanisms to coordinate efforts to confront violence against women and girls, but as of 2018, there was no evidence that the law was effective in reducing violence. Although the government pledged to investigate and prosecute cases of violence against women, perpetrators are rarely brought to justice. (Amnesty.)

Despite protections under the Mexican constitution and laws, human-rights abuses persist. While many of these abuses come at the hands of private citizens, the government's failure to effectively prosecute these crimes is a failure to protect the guaranteed rights of citizens.

Divisions in Mexico

Mexican citizens share a strong sense of national identity. Nevertheless, Mexican citizens are divided along the lines of ethnicity, class, religion, and language. These are known as **social cleavages**. **Political cleavages** divide citizens according to their political beliefs.

The North–South Divide

Southern Mexico is beautiful, with majestic mountains and lush green fields. A few lovely hotels cater to tourists who want to hike and visit waterfalls. Behind the landscape lies poverty and inequality. Southern states are the poorest in Mexico, lagging behind Mexico City and the north on almost all economic measures, including the Human Development Index. In 2008, 95 percent of the places ranked in the bottom tenth of Mexico were in the south. In the south, 47 percent of people were poor, compared to 12 percent in the north. (The Economist.) The population in the south is spread out, which makes it hard to attract foreign companies. Incompetent, corrupt and violent local officials are common. Infrastructure and education are less developed than in the north.

Agricultural subsidies benefit the north more than the south, and agreements like the North American Free Trade Agreement and United States–Mexico–Canada Agreement make it difficult for rural farmers in the south to compete with sophisticated agribusinesses, widening the income gap.

The Zapatista rebellion in the state of Chiapas highlighted regional inequality and rural poverty. As of 2018, Chiapas was the poorest state in Mexico, with 74.6 percent of its residents living in poverty. (Statista.) Although there have been some federal efforts to redistribute wealth to the south, they remain underfunded. (O'Neil.) The economic and social inequality between the north and the south is a persistent social cleavage in Mexico.

Social cleavage
A division in society among social factors such as ethnicity, class, religion, or language.

Political cleavage
A division among citizens according to political beliefs.

The breathtaking beauty of El Chiflon, the tallest waterfall in Chiapas, Mexico. The Chiapas region is known for stunning landscapes, but it is home to some of Mexico's poorest citizens.

aindigo/Shutterstock

Divisions between Indigenous People and Mestizos

The north–south social cleavage overlaps with the division between indigenous people and mestizos. Indigenous Mexicans are the descendants of groups that lived in the country before the arrival of the Spanish. Sixty-two different languages are spoken by different indigenous groups. Mestizos are people of mixed Spanish and indigenous descent. These ethnic classifications are left over from the Spanish caste system, a color hierarchy in which Europeans placed themselves at a higher social status. (Social Sciences, LibreTexts.)

The Mexican constitution provides indigenous people the right to education, autonomy, and self-determination. However, indigenous communities report that the government does not consult them in making decisions about development projects and exploits sources of energy, minerals, timber, and other natural resources. Indigenous groups have less access to health care and education. In a 2017 study conducted by the Latin American Public Opinion Project at Vanderbilt University, data showed that people with white skin (who are more likely to be mestizo) completed 3.5 years more schooling than people with darker skin (who are more likely to be indigenous). Similar disparities were found in wealth. Those with the lightest skin fell into the highest wealth brackets in comparison with those with the darkest skin, concentrated at the bottom. (Zizumbo-Colunga and Martinez, 2017.)

Indigenous people face violence. In February 2019, Samir Flores Soberanes, an environmental-rights activist with the Peoples in Defense of the Earth and Waterfront, was gunned down, likely as a result of his opposition to plans to build two thermoelectric plants and a natural-gas pipeline in indigenous communities. (State Department.) Indigenous women, in particular, are vulnerable to racism and discrimination and are frequent victims of violence.

Social cleavages in Mexico highlight regional and ethnic inequality and prevent Mexico from fully realizing its potential as a democratic state.

AP® POLITICAL SCIENCE PRACTICES

Putting Sources in Context

The AP® Exam requires you to analyze sources. It is important to examine these sources in the context of what you have learned about the countries studied in the course. The following is an excerpt from Mexico's constitution.

> In the United Mexican States, all individuals shall be entitled to the human rights granted by this Constitution and the international treaties signed by the Mexican State, as well as to the guarantees for the protection of these rights. Such human rights shall not be restricted or suspended, except for the cases and under the conditions established by this Constitution itself.
>
> The provisions relating to human rights shall be interpreted according to this Constitution and the international treaties on the subject, working in favor of the broader protection of people at all times.
>
> All authorities, in their areas of competence, are obliged to promote, respect, protect and guarantee Human Rights, in accordance with the principles of universality, interdependence, indivisibility and progressiveness. As a consequence, the State must prevent, investigate, penalize and rectify violations to Human Rights, according to the law.

—Constitution of 1917, with Amendments through 2015, Article 1

As you have studied, the Mexican government has been accused of violating the civil rights of indigenous groups, torturing suspected criminals, and failing to protect the security of journalists and human-rights advocates. Yet the constitution provides that the Mexican government is under a duty to protect these rights. Constitutions may be aspirational. In other words, they may describe what the country hopes to achieve, without accurately reflecting government actions. Read text sources with a healthy dose of skepticism.

1. Describe the circumstances that allow Mexican authorities to violate Article 1 of the constitution.

2. Explain why Mexico's constitution claims to fully protect civil rights and liberties, even though the government does not fully provide these rights in practice.

3. Describe the drawbacks of providing constitutional protections that are not fully realized.

Remember

- Although the Mexican constitution protects civil rights and liberties, human-rights abuses and lack of prosecution prevent Mexico from being a liberal democracy.
- There is a social cleavage in Mexico between the north and south, and the north is better educated and more prosperous.
- There is a social cleavage in Mexico between mestizos and indigenous peoples, who are poorer and face discrimination.

Know

- *Political culture:* a set of collectively held attitudes, values, and beliefs about government and politics, and the norms of behavior in the political system. (p. 75)
- *Civil liberties:* fundamental rights and freedoms protected from infringement by the government. (p. 75)
- *Civil rights:* protections granted by the government to prevent people from being discriminated against when engaged in fundamental political actions, such as voting. (p. 75)
- *Social cleavage:* a division in society among social factors such as ethnicity, class, religion, or language. (p. 77)
- *Political cleavage:* a division among citizens according to political beliefs. (p. 77)

Think

- What steps could the Mexican government take to increase protection for civil rights and liberties?
- Explain how the Mexican government could address inequalities between the north and south and between mestizos and indigenous people.

....

Free-Response Question: Comparative Analysis

Note to Students:

On the AP® Exam, this type of question requires you to compare two course countries. The following question will give you practice at writing this type of free-response question, using only Mexico as an example.

Governments adopt policies in response to social cleavages. In your response, you should do the following:

A. Define social cleavage.

B. Describe a social cleavage in Mexico.

C. Explain how the Mexican government could address the social cleavage you described in part B.

3.5 Economic and Social Change and Development

Learning Targets

After reading this section, you should be able to do the following:

1. Describe how globalization impacted the Mexican economy.

2. Explain why Mexico adopted economic-liberalization policies.

3. Describe social policies adopted in Mexico.

4. Describe demographic shifts in Mexico.

5. Describe the reasons for both optimism and pessimism about Mexico's future.

Economic liberalism
Economic policies that support the free market and reduce trade barriers.

Mexico is an upper-middle-income country with a growing middle class. In the late twentieth and early twenty-first centuries Mexico embraced **economic liberalism**—economic policies that support the free market and reduce trade barriers.

Globalization

Globalization
The increased interconnectedness of people, states, and economies.

Protectionist economic policies
Policies designed to protect domestic industry and reduce foreign influence.

Nationalized industry
A state-owned company controlled by the government.

Import substitution industrialization (ISI)
Enacting high tariffs and providing incentives to encourage the growth of domestic manufacturing.

Globalization, which you will learn about in detail in Chapter 10, is the increased interconnectedness of people, states, and economies. In the 1980s, Mexico moved away from **protectionist economic policies**, which were designed to protect domestic industries and reduce foreign influence, in favor of free market policies. Under the PRI-led regime, leaders followed protectionist policies. The oil industry was nationalized. **Nationalized industries** are state-owned companies controlled by the government. Land was redistributed from the wealthy elite to peasants. Mexico adopted **import substitution industrialization (ISI)** policies to encourage economic growth. ISI policies aim to reduce dependence on other countries. ISI policies included enacting high tariffs to make foreign products more expensive so that consumers would purchase goods made within Mexico. The government offered subsidies and incentives to encourage the growth of domestic manufacturing. ISI was an economic success from 1940 through 1982, when economic growth averaged a relatively strong 3.1 percent, bolstering the legitimacy of PRI rule.

This success was in large part funded through Petróleos Mexicanos (Pemex), the company that oversaw all of Mexico's oil production. Pemex was nationalized in 1938, when the government confiscated the property of foreign oil companies. It was the world's sixth-largest oil producer at its peak. However, Mexico's haphazard infrastructure development limited Pemex's ability to reap the full benefits of its oil fields. The state used oil revenue to fund public programs in an effort to maintain the PRI's popularity and legitimacy. In 1976, extensive new oil reserves were discovered in the Gulf of Mexico, but state spending canceled out many of the expected gains.

In the mid-1970s, oil revenue and a U.S. recession caused the Mexican peso to fall sharply in relation to the dollar, making it much more expensive for Mexico to pay back its debt. As this happened, billions of dollars of capital fled the country. Mexico had borrowed money from the United States and the IMF to fund its social programs, and the global debt crisis put the IMF and the U.S. government in a position to demand fundamental changes in Mexico's economic policy. This is an example of the impact of globalization. A recession in one country or region of the world can impact the global economy and force other countries to change their economic policies.

Mexico's move toward economic liberalization began during the 1980s. Foreign-educated experts controlled Mexico's economic policy. By the late 1980s, Mexico's commitment to liberalizing its economy was well established and strongly supported by the

IMF and the U.S. government. The country joined the General Agreement on Tariffs and Trade (GATT, the predecessor of the World Trade Organization (WTO)) in 1986 and signed the North American Free Trade Agreement in 1992.

NAFTA eliminated most trade barriers between the United States, Mexico, and Canada. NAFTA not only gave Mexican manufacturers access to the vast U.S. market but invited companies from all over the world to set up manufacturing plants, or *maquiladoras*, just south of the U.S.–Mexico border to take advantage of inexpensive labor and then export their goods to the United States tariff free. Chinese and Korean firms opened plants in northern Mexico. After the 1990s boom in *maquila* manufacturing, the sector slowed down in the new millennium in the face of competition from even cheaper labor in China.

While NAFTA increased productivity, it has had only marginal impact on employment, and Mexico remains one of the most unequal societies in the world. Inequality increased as the wealthy benefited from the new business opportunities provided by economic liberalization, while the average wage dropped by 40 percent over the 1980s and 1990s and the minimum wage dropped by 70 percent.

The 2008–09 global recession hit Mexico very hard. Its GDP dropped by 6.5 percent in 2009, although as the United States began to recover, so did Mexico. Growth returned to 5.6 percent in 2010, but it slowed again to about 4 percent through 2012. After 2013, growth dropped further, to 1.5–2.5 percent, largely due to declining world oil prices. The recession also meant higher levels of poverty and reduced migration to the United States, as the U.S. job market for immigrants dried up.

In late 2013, the Mexican government proposed a constitutional amendment partially privatizing Pemex. **Privatization** occurs when a government transfers ownership and control of a nationalized industry to the private sector. The reforms left Pemex with control over significant oil fields, but in 2014, international investment was allowed for the first time. By 2017, Mexico had positive but moderate growth of about 2 percent. Over the long term, however, the effects of economic liberalization in Mexico remain unclear.

Privatization
When a government transfers ownership and control of a nationalized industry to the private sector.

The Recent Mexican Economy

After U.S. President Trump threatened to pull out of NAFTA, Mexico's President Peña Nieto participated in renegotiating the agreement and signed the new U.S.–Mexico–Canada Agreement (USMCA) just days before President López Obrador's inauguration in 2018. As the ratification process dragged on in all three countries in 2019, the Mexican government passed labor legislation to bring Mexico into compliance with the labor section of the new agreement. López Obrador had campaigned on reforming and democratizing Mexico's unions, so this was not unexpected. With few significant changes from the original NAFTA agreement, the USMCA's effect on Mexico's economic prospects remains to be seen.

In mid-2019, President Trump threatened to impose tariffs on Mexican goods to try to pressure Mexico into changing its immigration policies, a potentially serious threat to Mexico's economic well-being. During the Trump administration, the symbiotic relationship between the United States and Mexico was contentious. As the former dictator, Porfirio Díaz said, "Poor Mexico, so far from God and so close to the United States."

In his 2018 campaign, López Obrador promised to move away from Mexico's economic-liberalization model and toward more state-led development focused on the poor. He promised to renationalize key industries and build infrastructure in the poorest areas, double the minimum wage at the U.S. border, and raise the salaries of teachers, police, and doctors. He also wanted to revive Pemex, including building a major new oil refinery. He promised to increase economic growth to 4 percent per year and balance the budget. López Obrador appeared to be moving quickly on new policies in 2019, but it remains unclear how much he could change in one six-year term and during the COVID-19 pandemic that started a year later. MORENA lost seats in the 2021 legislative elections, and its majority is slim, which may make it more difficult for López Obrador to enact the policies he proposes.

Social Policies

Mexico has adopted social policies in an effort to address issues facing women, children, the elderly, and the poor. One example is its controversial policy on abortions. Mexico is a predominantly Catholic country, and the Church opposes abortion. However, church and state are separated in Mexico, and Mexico has a federal system. As a result, abortion policy varies by state. In 2007, Mexico City legalized abortion up to 12 weeks into pregnancy, a policy the Mexican Supreme Court later upheld. In September 2019, Oaxaca decriminalized abortions during the first trimester. (Freedom House.)

Abortion remains illegal under federal law, punishable with one to three years in prison. Most states criminalize abortion, both for the woman seeking an abortion and for those who perform the procedure. All states waive the penalty for abortion in the case of rape, and some states include other exceptions. (Human Rights Watch.) In 2020, President López Obrador proposed an amnesty bill for women jailed for violating abortion laws. (Freedom House.)

In addition to its policies regarding women, Mexico has adopted social programs to improve the lives of poor people. One example is Mexico's Prospera program (formerly called Oportunidades), a conditional cash-transfer program administered by the federal government. Eligible poor and vulnerable households are given cash in exchange for an agreement to send their children to school. Mothers and children have access to regular preventive health care at local clinics. Eligible households receive grants to improve the quantity and quality of the food they eat. Program staff worked closely with the families they were serving, developing trust. The program improved food consumption, decreased malnutrition, and increased school enrollment.

Prospera demonstrates the link between social and economic policies, because people who are healthy and educated can contribute more to the economic success of their families and country. (World Bank.) The model was so successful that it was adopted by 50 other countries.

In 2021, the Mexican government ended the Prospera program. López Obrador opposed the program, claiming its facilitators used cash benefits to control aid recipients. Some people alleged that program facilitators were agents of political parties and that some of them accepted bribes in exchange for medical care. Providing cash payments to poor people was unpopular with the general public. The Mexican government has proposed new social policies, including payments to finish secondary school and a universal old-age pension. (Kidd, 2019.)

Scatterplot graphs are a way of conveying multiple data points and identifying trends in the data. In this graph, each dot represents a country. The data points demonstrate a trend, which is shown by the line.

To analyze a scatterplot, first look at the title. In this case, the title indicates that people are less satisfied with democracy when economic conditions are poor.

Examine the *y*-axis, which goes from zero to 100 percent. The *y*-axis measures the percentage of respondents who are dissatisfied with the way democracy is working in their country. For example, more than 80 percent of Mexicans are dissatisfied. The *x*-axis measures the percentage of respondents who report that their current economic situation is good. For example, more than 80 percent of respondents from the Netherlands report being in a good economic situation. As you can see, the trend is that better economic conditions lead to more support for democracy within a country.

Is the Economy Linked to Democratic Discontent?

Note: Correlation = −0.81.
Data from Global Attitudes Survey, spring 2018, and Pew Research Center.

1. Describe two questions respondents asked to generate the data shown on the graph.

2. Describe the advantages of using a scatterplot graph to convey information in political science.

3. Describe the limitations of using a scatterplot graph to convey information.

Shifting Demographics

As the Mexican economy became more dependent on trade, regional disparities widened. Northern states have better access to U.S. markets. The less-developed southern states have lagged behind. In the free-trade economy, cheap, state-subsidized corn from the United States displaced traditional and less-developed agriculture meant for local consumption. This resulted in billions of dollars in losses to local growers, negatively affecting already impoverished rural communities and driving many residents to seek better opportunities by migrating to other parts of Mexico or to the United States.

People are moving from the south to the north. Northern Mexico has historically been more prosperous, and it is now even more wealthy due to trade agreements with the United States. People are also moving from rural areas, which have been hit hard by cheaper foreign agriculture, to urban areas like Mexico City.

FIGURE 3.3

Unauthorized Immigrants in the United States: Recent Estimates of Numbers from Mexico and Other Countries

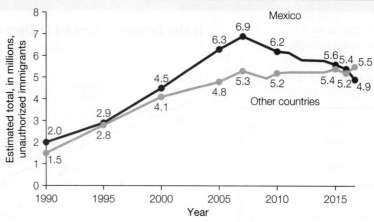

Data are estimates from Pew Research Center based on augmented data from the U.S. Census Bureau.

Mexicans are also migrating—legally and illegally—to the United States. Immigration to the United States is still a substantial source of remittances—money sent home from workers abroad. However, Mexican immigration to the United States is slowing. As shown in Figure 3.3, the Pew Research Center reports that since 2009, Mexican immigration to the United States has declined, likely due to the 2008 recession and President Trump's stance against illegal immigration from Mexico. (Gonzales-Barrera and Krogstad, 2019.)

Mexico and the Future

Mexico has been a democratic state since 2000, and since that time, power has transferred between political parties peacefully. There is hope that democratic institutions will continue to evolve and consolidate. As an upper-middle-income country, Mexico has a growing middle class. The worldwide economic downturn caused by the COVID-19 pandemic slowed Mexico's economic growth, but in the long run, Mexico's strong economic growth may continue. Lively civil society groups participate in policymaking, and pluralism is replacing corporatism. Increasingly, Mexican citizens have a voice in government. There is reason to be optimistic about Mexico.

Nevertheless, Mexico faces continued challenges. The quality of democracy in Mexico, especially at the local level, is far from ideal. Unabated drug violence and corruption threaten the state's sovereignty and legitimacy. Human-rights abuses tarnish the government's reputation and decrease citizens' trust and confidence in government. While programs like Prospera have had some success in reducing widespread poverty, much more needs to be done. Income inequality between the north and south and between mestizos and indigenous people has worsened under economic-liberalization policies.

President López Obrador won a majority of the vote because he promised to crack down on corruption and improve the lives of everyday Mexican citizens. Time will tell whether he can make good on his promises, or whether the MORENA party will consolidate power at the expense of Mexico's democracy.

Remember

- In the past, Mexico adopted protectionist economic policies, including import substitution industrialization (ISI).
- In the 1980s, Mexico adopted economic reforms, including NAFTA and the USMCA.
- Social policies in Mexico include the decriminalization of abortion in Mexico City and Oaxaca and programs to provide poor people with cash, education, and health care.
- Migration occurs within Mexico from the south to the north and from rural areas to cities and from Mexico to the United States.
- There are reasons to be both optimistic and pessimistic about Mexico's future.

Know

- *Economic liberalism:* economic policies that support the free market and reduce trade barriers. (p. 80)
- *Globalization:* the increased interconnectedness of people, states, and economies. (p. 80)
- *Protectionist economic policies:* policies designed to protect domestic industry and reduce foreign influence. (p. 80)
- *Nationalized industry:* a state-owned company controlled by the government. (p. 80)
- *Import substitution industrialization (ISI):* enacting high tariffs and providing incentives to encourage the growth of domestic manufacturing. (p. 80)
- *Privatization:* when a government transfers ownership and control of a nationalized industry to the private sector. (p. 81)

Think

- What are the benefits and drawbacks of Mexico's economic-liberalization policies?
- What types of social policies could Mexico enact in an effort to reduce income inequality?

Free-Response Question: Quantitative Analysis

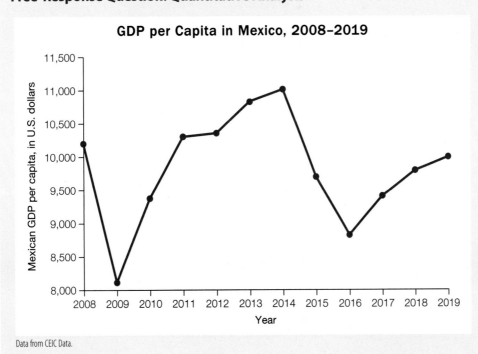

Data from CEIC Data.

Answer A, B, C, D, and E.

A. Using the data in the graph, identify the year in which Mexico had the lowest GDP per capita.

B. Using the data in the graph, describe a trend in GDP per capita from 2009 to 2014.

C. Describe economic liberalization.

D. Using your knowledge of economic liberalization and the data in the graph, draw a conclusion about the trend you described in part B.

E. Explain a limitation of the data in the graph in measuring the standard of living in Mexico.

Political Systems

AP® KEY CONCEPTS

- Patron-clientelism (p. 58)
- Head of state (p. 62)
- Head of government (p. 62)
- Cabinet head (p. 62)
- Sexenio (p. 62)
- Nongovernmental organization (NGO) (p. 63)
- Bicameral (p. 64)
- Chamber of Deputies (p. 64)
- Lower house (p. 64)
- Senate (p. 64)
- Upper house (p. 64)

- Civil society (p. 67)
- Mandate (p. 68)
- Mixed electoral system (p. 68)
- Single-member plurality system (SMD) (p. 68)
- Proportional representation (PR) system (p. 68)
- Corporatism (p. 70)
- Peak association (p. 70)
- Pluralism (p. 71)
- Political culture (p. 75)
- Civil liberties (p. 75)

- Civil rights (p. 75)
- Social cleavage (p. 77)
- Political cleavage (p. 77)
- Economic liberalism (p. 80)
- Globalization (p. 80)
- Protectionist economic policies (p. 80)
- Nationalized industry (p. 80)
- Import substitution industrialization (ISI) (p. 80)
- Privatization (p. 81)

AP® EXAM MULTIPLE-CHOICE PRACTICE QUESTIONS

1. Which of the following is an accurate description of Mexico?
   A. The state gained sovereignty over economic policy by signing NAFTA and the USMCA.
   B. Since the late twentieth century, the government gained legitimacy through freer and fairer elections.
   C. Mexico is a liberal democracy, because civil rights and liberties are protected in the constitution.
   D. Mexico is a state but not a nation, because the country lacks a shared sense of cultural identity.

2. Which of the following best describes civil rights and liberties in Mexico?
   A. Mexican citizens have the right to freedom of speech and assembly, and they may freely exercise their religious beliefs.
   B. Mestizos have fewer rights than indigenous groups, because indigenous groups are the basis for Mexican history and culture.
   C. Women are guaranteed 50 percent of seats in the legislature, and women in the legislature have passed reforms to end gender discrimination in the workplace.
   D. People living in rural areas have more civil liberties than people living in cities, who often face violence perpetrated by drug cartels and other criminals.

Questions 3 and 4 refer to the passage.

> Women's longstanding frustration with government passivity and neglect—which precedes López Obrador—has been exacerbated by a president who seems impervious and even disdainful of their demands, including calls to legalize abortion at the national level . . . his government has closed publicly subsidized day care centers, eliminated shelters for victims of domestic violence, [and] defunded the National Women's Institute . . .
>
> —Denise Dresser, *Foreign Affairs*, October 6, 2020

3. Which of the following is supported by the main idea of the passage?

   A. President López Obrador is a progressive who promised to promote gender equality and then broke that promise after he was elected.

   B. In the past, the Mexican government did not take the demands of the women's movement seriously, and budget cuts have prevented President López Obrador from promoting gender equality.

   C. Like his predecessors, President López Obrador has neglected women's issues, and his administration has enacted policies that harm women and children.

   D. President López Obrador believes that women should be wives and mothers, and his programs provide few opportunities for women to work outside of the home.

4. Which of the following statements is an implication of the argument presented in the passage?

   A. As a result of López Obrador's programs, fewer women will be elected to serve in the legislature.

   B. Increasing the budget for social services, such as women's shelters, provides a long-run benefit to the economy as a whole.

   C. More women are likely to vote for the PAN and PRI parties in 2024 than they did in 2018.

   D. The recession that occurred as a result of the COVID-19 pandemic had a disproportionate impact on women, who were forced to stay home to care for children.

5. Which of the following is an accurate statement about the results of economic-liberalization policies in Mexico?

   A. The wealth gap narrowed, because more citizens and small businesses were better able to compete in the global economy.

   B. Mexico became an upper-middle-income country, with a growing middle class.

   C. The south benefited more than the north, because agricultural products could be exported tariff-free.

   D. It resulted in a migration from urban areas to rural areas, because citizens wanted to move away from the increased pollution caused by factories.

Questions 6 and 7 refer to the map.

Affiliation with Political Parties Varies across the Globe

Percent of Citizens Who Are Not Affiliated with a Party

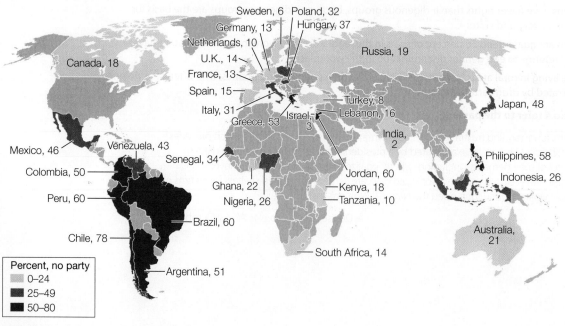

Sweden, 6 | Poland, 32
Germany, 13 | Hungary, 37
Netherlands, 10
U.K., 14
France, 13
Russia, 19
Canada, 18
Spain, 15
Turkey, 8
Italy, 31
Lebanon, 16
Greece, 53
Israel, 3
Japan, 48
India, 2
Mexico, 46
Venezuela, 43
Senegal, 34
Philippines, 58
Colombia, 50
Jordan, 60
Indonesia, 26
Ghana, 22
Kenya, 18
Peru, 60
Nigeria, 26
Tanzania, 10
Brazil, 60
Australia, 21
Chile, 78
South Africa, 14
Argentina, 51

Percent, no party
- 0–24
- 25–49
- 50–80

Data from Global Attitudes Survey, spring 2017, and Pew Research Center.

6. Which of the following is accurate according to the map?
   A. Mexican citizens are more attached to a political party than citizens in South American countries.
   B. A majority of Mexicans has no attachment to a political party.
   C. People in the United Kingdom have less loyalty to a political party than people in Mexico.
   D. Mexico has the highest level of political party affiliation among countries in North America.

7. Which of the following is an implication of the map?
   A. Illiberal or hybrid democracies have higher levels of party attachment than liberal democracies.
   B. Although Mexico has a multi-party system, it has a lower level of political attachment than the United Kingdom, which has a two-party system.
   C. The establishment of the MORENA party decreased party attachment to the PRI and PAN in Mexico.
   D. Patron-clientelism in Mexico increases citizens' attachment to a political party.

8. Which of the following best describes a regime change in Mexico?
   A. In the 2018 election, power in the executive branch changed from PRI control to MORENA control.
   B. In the 1994 election, an independent electoral commission reduced fraud at the polls and increased voter trust and confidence.
   C. In the 2000 election, a candidate from the PAN party won the presidency, ending decades of rule by the PRI.
   D. In the mid-1980s, Mexico began the transition toward economic-liberalization policies and a free market economy.

9. Which of the following best describes an economic policy in Mexico during the twenty-first century?
   A. Mexico nationalized the telecommunications industry, providing broadband internet access to urban residents.
   B. Import substitution industrialization policies were adopted to protect domestic manufacturing from foreign competition.
   C. A policy was passed requiring that 40 percent of government contracts be awarded to female and indigenous-owned businesses.
   D. The nationally owned oil company was partially privatized and opened to some foreign investment.

10. Which of the following accurately describes an institution of government in Mexico?
   A. The president has strong power, including rule by decree, and he cannot be removed by the legislature before the end of his term.
   B. The lower house of the legislature has the power to enact legislation, and the upper house reflects Mexico's federal structure.
   C. The Mexican Supreme Court does not have the power of judicial review.
   D. Because positions in the bureaucracy are filled though patron-clientelism, it is not effective in carrying out policy.

AP® EXAM PRACTICE ARGUMENT ESSAY

Note to Students:

The following is designed to begin preparing you for the argument essay prompt that you will see on the AP® Exam. On the AP® Exam, you will have the opportunity to compare countries. At this point in the textbook, you have studied only Mexico. This question will give you practice at developing an argument in the form of the essay. Later in this book, you will answer questions that are more consistent with the format of the argument essay on the AP® Exam.

Develop an argument as to whether states that allow interest groups and social movements to operate freely are better at maintaining stability.

- Use one or more of the following course concepts in your response:
  - Civil liberties
  - Power
  - Legitimacy
- In your response, do the following:
  - Respond to the prompt with a defensible claim or thesis that establishes a line of reasoning using one or more of the provided course concepts.
  - Support your claim with at least TWO pieces of specific and relevant evidence from your study of Mexico. The evidence should be relevant to one or more of the provided course concepts.
  - Use reasoning to explain why your evidence supports your claim or thesis, using one or more of the provided course concepts.

  Respond to an opposing or alternate perspective, using refutation, concession, or rebuttal.

For a complete list of the sources of information cited in this chapter, turn to the Works Cited appendix.

Political Systems

(1) **Mexico**

(2) United Kingdom

(3) Russia

(4) Nigeria

(5) China

(6) Iran

NOTE TO STUDENTS:

This unit review covers what you learned in Chapters 1 through 3. As you continue through the book, unit reviews become more cumulative. For example, the Unit 2 review will focus mostly on what you will learn in Chapters 4 and 5, but it will also test your knowledge from Unit 1.

As you complete each unit, you will have more knowledge and be able to make more connections between concepts and cases. As your knowledge and skills build over time, the unit reviews become more complex, and the questions cover more of the content you will encounter on the AP® Exam.

AP® EXAM PRACTICE QUESTIONS

Section 1: Multiple Choice

Some of these review questions refer to the six countries studied in AP® Comparative Government and Politics. You have studied only Mexico so far. Because the questions in this unit review are conceptual, knowledge about the other countries is not necessary to answer the questions.

1. Which of the following is an empirical statement?
    A. The Mexican president would have more legitimacy if he were elected in a two-round system, which would enable him to earn a majority of the vote in the second round.
    B. The Mexican Congress is not an effective check on the executive, because it lacks power to override presidential decrees.
    C. The Supreme Court in Mexico has the power of judicial review, and justices serve for fifteen-year terms.
    D. The consolidation of power by President López Obrador puts Mexico on a path toward single-party authoritarian rule.

Questions 2 and 3 refer to the passage.

> Although the constitution and law provide for an independent judiciary, court decisions were susceptible to improper influence by both private and public entities, particularly at the state and local level, as well as by transnational criminal organizations. Authorities sometimes failed to respect court orders, and arrest warrants were sometimes ignored. Across the criminal justice system, many actors lacked the necessary training and resources to carry out their duties fairly and consistently in line with the principle of equal justice.
>
> —*2019 Country Reports on Human Rights Practices: Mexico.* U.S. Department of State

2. Which of the following is supported by the main idea of the passage?
    A. The judiciary in Mexico is independent, and those suspected of crimes have several constitutionally protected due-process rights.
    B. Mexico has professionalized the judiciary, especially at the federal level.
    C. Although the constitution provides for due-process rights, lack of judicial autonomy and professionalism hinders protection of defendants' rights.
    D. Mexico values the rule of law, and the judiciary acts in accordance with the principle of equal justice.

3. Which of the following statements is an implication of the passage?
   A. An independent and professionalized judiciary would further democratization in Mexico.
   B. Mexican citizens do not have faith in the court system, and they often seek justice through vigilantism.
   C. The Supreme Court in Mexico has the power of judicial review, but it rarely uses its authority to check executive actions.
   D. Criminal organizations control the judicial branch in Mexico, and they recommend candidates for appointment to the bench.

4. Which of the following is the most accurate measure of citizens' standard of living?
   A. The Gini index, because it measures income inequality, which impacts citizens' attitudes about their economic circumstances.
   B. GDP per capita, because it serves as a rough measure of average income, taking purchasing power into account.
   C. The Corruption Perceptions Index, because it measures the amount of wealth being diverted from government programs that could improve quality of life.
   D. The Human Development Index, because it is an aggregate measure that takes several factors into account.

5. Which of the following is a criticism of the Freedom House Index?
   A. The organization is not transparent about the methods it uses to assign each country a score.
   B. The index does not consider economic performance in scoring countries.
   C. It is difficult to assign a mathematical score to a subjective concept like freedom.
   D. Ranking countries by their levels of freedom is not a useful basis for cross-country comparison.

Questions 6 and 7 refer to the bar chart.

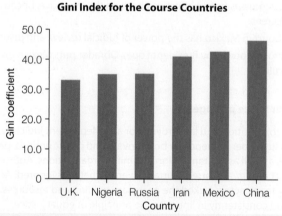

Gini Index for the Course Countries

Note: A score of zero indicates complete equality. The higher the score, the higher the level of inequality.
Data from Statista.

6. Which of the following is accurate according to the bar chart?
   A. China has the lowest level of inequality of the countries shown.
   B. Nigeria and Russia have very similar levels of income inequality.
   C. Income inequality is greater in countries with developed economies than in countries with developing economies.
   D. Democratic states have lower levels of income inequality than authoritarian states.

7. Which of the following is an implication of the bar chart?
   A. Former communist countries, such as Russia and China, have greater income equality than countries with a history of market economies, such as the United Kingdom.
   B. Russia and Nigeria have the highest levels of poverty of the countries shown in the table.
   C. Economic-liberalization policies in Mexico did not significantly reduce its comparatively high level of income inequality.
   D. As China completes the transition to a market economy, income inequality is likely to decrease.

8. Which of the following is an accurate statement about a concept studied in AP® Comparative Government and Politics?
   A. A nation is a sense of belonging, based on shared territory and common views about the role of government.
   B. Sovereignty exists when the government has the power to carry out its policies without significant interference.
   C. A constitution confers legitimacy and authority on the state, whether or not the state has widespread support among citizens.
   D. Authority is the ability to make citizens do something they otherwise would not do, such as joining the military.

9. Which of the following is an accurate statement about a concept studied in AP® Comparative Government and Politics?
   A. A change in government is a change in the fundamental system, such as the transition from democracy to authoritarianism.
   B. A regime is a fundamental system of government that endures over time, even though the leaders may change.
   C. A coup is an overthrow of government with widespread popular support.
   D. A revolution is a fundamental change in the system of government, based on a new constitution.

10. Which of the following best explains why Freedom House rated Mexico as partially free?
    A. Mexico's elections are marred by widespread fraud, because the election commission is controlled by the ruling party.
    B. President López Obrador has consolidated power in the executive, reducing checks and balances within government.
    C. Mexico's federal system is designed to underrepresent ethnic minorities in the Senate.
    D. Despite constitutional protections, government officials at the national, state, and local levels engage in human-rights abuses.

Questions 11 and 12 refer to the passage.

> Democratic backsliding (meaning the state-led debilitation or elimination of the political institutions sustaining an existing democracy) has changed dramatically since the Cold War. Open-ended coups d'état, executive coups, and blatant election-day vote fraud are declining while promissory coups, executive aggrandizement, and strategic electoral manipulation and harassment are increasing. Contemporary forms of backsliding are especially vexing because they are legitimated by the very institutions democracy promoters prioritize, but overall, backsliding today reflects democracy's advance and not its retreat. The current mix of backsliding is more easily reversible than the past mix, and successor dictatorships are shorter-lived and less authoritarian.
>
> —Nancy Bermeo, "On Democratic Backsliding," *Journal of Democracy*, January 2016

11. Which of the following is supported by the main idea of the passage?

   A. Democratic backsliding is occurring for different reasons than in the past.

   B. The outlook for democratization is poor, because there is a trend in states retreating from democratic institutions.

   C. There is an increase in obvious instances of fraud on election day.

   D. Corruption hinders democratic development, because citizens lose trust and confidence in the government.

12. Which of the following is an implication of the argument presented in the passage?

   A. Authoritarian states are more likely to use brute force to maintain power than they did in the past.

   B. The chance of long-term dictatorships increases when elected leaders become authoritarian rulers.

   C. Voter suppression and the manipulation of voting systems have become tools for consolidating power.

   D. In the twenty-first century, authoritarian leaders have maintained power by dismantling existing institutions of government.

13. Which of the following is an accurate statement regarding a course concept studied in AP® Comparative Government and Politics?

   A. An independent judiciary enhances rule of law, because it has the authority to hold government officials, as well as citizens, accountable for their actions.

   B. Patron-clientelism enhances democracy, because it provides a way for citizens to participate in politics.

   C. Democratic consolidation occurs when single-party rule ends and an executive from an opposing party is elected.

   D. Political efficacy is a group's shared values about the role of government and politics.

14. Which of the following is an accurate statement about legitimacy?

   A. To have legitimacy, a state must also have sovereignty over all of its territory.

   B. The Constitution of 1917 is one source of legitimacy for the Mexican government.

   C. Economic performance is not a source of legitimacy in authoritarian states.

   D. Rule by law is a source of legitimacy in democratic states.

15. Which of the following is an example of devolution of power?

   A. The government in Mexico seeks to professionalize the judiciary, especially at the state and local levels.

   B. In China, the National People's Congress is selected by delegates from smaller, provincial congresses.

   C. In the United Kingdom, parliament created regional assemblies in Northern Ireland, Scotland, and Wales.

   D. In Russia, states have different degrees of autonomy, depending on their support for the party in power.

16. Which of the following best describes the system for electing the Mexican Congress?

   A. A high threshold for receiving PR seats prevents most small parties from winning seats in the legislature.

   B. Because the Senate represents the states, an SMD system is used for electing senators.

   C. Mexico uses a mixed electoral system, in which individual candidates run for office and some seats are filled through party lists.

   D. To win an SMD seat in the legislature, a candidate must earn more than 50 percent of the vote.

Questions 17 and 18 refer to the line graph.

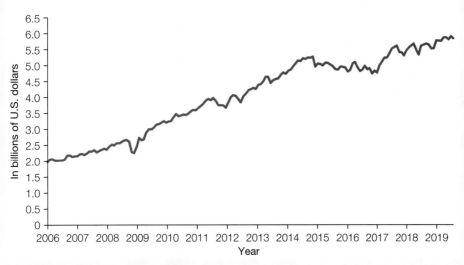

Mexican Government Debt, 2006–2020

Monthly data from CEICDATA.com.

17. Which of the following is true according to the graph?
    A. Mexico's debt declined every year from 2014 to 2017.
    B. From 2006 to 2019, Mexico's debt tripled.
    C. Mexico's highest level of debt occurred in 2019.
    D. Economic-liberalization policies increased Mexico's foreign debt.

18. Which of the following is an implication of the graph?
    A. Mexico's economic growth slowed in the decade between 2009 and 2019.
    B. The NAFTA agreement benefited the United States and Canada more than Mexico.
    C. From 2014 to 2017, the Mexican government was able to keep debt at a relatively stable level.
    D. If its debt continues to rise, Mexico will have to raise taxes and cut social programs.

19. Why was the Zapatista Rebellion significant?
    A. It called international attention to the plight of indigenous people in Mexico.
    B. It was crushed by the Mexican government and became an underground terrorist movement.
    C. Several Zapatista leaders were appointed to cabinet positions, where they were able to propose policies beneficial to the south.
    D. It posed a significant threat to sovereignty, because the Chiapas region nearly seceded from Mexico.

20. Which of the following statements regarding executive term limits in Mexico is true?
    A. Presidents can circumvent term limits through rule by decree.
    B. Limiting the executive to a single term may result in frequent policy shifts within government.
    C. Term limits in the 1917 constitution were unsuccessful in preventing dictatorships.
    D. Term limits in Mexico are undemocratic, because they encourage consolidation of power in the executive.

Section 2: Free Response

Conceptual Analysis

Answer A, B, C, and D.

A. Define sovereignty.

B. Describe a threat to sovereignty.

C. Explain how a state could strengthen sovereignty.

D. Explain how joining a supranational or an international organization impacts state sovereignty.

Quantitative Analysis

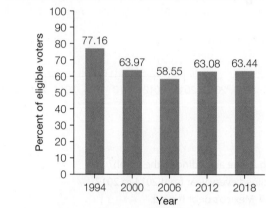

Voter Turnout in Mexican Presidential Elections, 1994–2018

Data from the Wilson Center and the Instituto Nacional Electoral (INE).

Answer A, B, C, D, and E.

A. Using the data in the bar chart, identify the year with the highest level of voter turnout in Mexican presidential elections.

B. Using the data in the bar chart, describe a trend in voter turnout in Mexican presidential elections from 1994 to 2018.

C. Define political efficacy.

D. Using your knowledge of political efficacy and the data in the bar chart, draw a conclusion about the pattern of voter turnout in Mexico's presidential elections from 1994 to 2018.

E. Explain how the Mexican government could encourage higher voter turnout in presidential elections.

Comparative Analysis

The election system impacts representation in Mexico's legislature. In your response, you should do the following:

A. Describe the system for electing the Chamber of Deputies.

B. Explain why the legislature has members from multiple political parties.

C. Explain how having multiple parties in the legislature impacts policymaking.

Argument Essay

Develop an argument as to whether using force to prevent internal threats harms legitimacy.

Use one or more of the following course concepts in your response:

- Sovereignty
- Power
- Rule of law

In your response, do the following:

- Respond to the prompt with a defensible claim or thesis that establishes a line of reasoning using one or more of the provided course concepts.
- Support your claim with at least TWO pieces of specific and relevant evidence from your study of Mexico. The evidence should be relevant to one or more of the provided course concepts.
- Use reasoning to explain why your evidence supports your claim or thesis, using one or more of the provided course concepts.
- Respond to an opposing or alternate perspective, using refutation, concession, or rebuttal.

For a complete list of the sources of information cited, turn to the Works Cited appendix.

UNIT 2

Political Institutions

In this unit, you will learn about the institutions of government—the executive, the legislature, and the judiciary. The power of institutions to check each other's actions varies and depends on whether a state is democratic or authoritarian. Here, the U.K. chief justice (in red) and the chancellor (in black and gold) follow the mace bearer after leaving the service that marks the start of the new legal year. The mace is a traditional symbol of the authority of an official.

Chapter 4
Political
Institutions

Chapter 5
Case Study:
United Kingdom

Institutions

I n Unit 2, you will learn about the institutions of government as well as how each institution uses the structure of government to wield and maintain power. Once you understand the responsibilities of the executive, legislative, and judicial systems, you will examine the government of the United Kingdom. Comparing countries with similar and different political structures will help you identify problems, analyze policymaking, and explain implications of policy decisions. This unit will help you understand the advantages and disadvantages of different institutional arrangements. You will also be able to explain how different systems impact the government's stability, legitimacy, and policymaking. Using these concepts, you will continue to refine the skills necessary for success on the AP® Exam.

After completing Unit 2, you will be able to:

- Describe parliamentary, presidential, and semi-presidential systems
- Compare parliamentary, presidential, and semi-presidential systems
- Describe the roles of heads of state and heads of government
- Describe the duties of the executive
- Describe the difference between term limits and term of office
- Describe different ways that executives can be removed
- Describe the difference between unicameral and bicameral legislatures
- Describe the responsibilities of the legislature
- Describe the role of the judicial system
- Explain how judiciaries maintain their independence
- Examine government and politics in the United Kingdom

The U.K. House of Commons maintains a tradition called Baby of the House. When Mhairi Black won her race in Scotland in 2015, at the age of 20 years, 8 months, she became the youngest person elected to Parliament—possibly since the 1830s. Black is a member of the Scottish National Party. A bigger achievement was that her first speech in Parliament was a major success—with more than 10 million views online.

Courtesy Mhairi Black

Political Institutions

Institutions

A meeting of the National People's Congress in China. With almost 3,000 members, it is the largest parliamentary body in the world. According to the Chinese constitution, the National People's Congress is the most powerful institution in the state. In reality, the body has little power and approves policies submitted to it by the Chinese Communist Party.

Ebrahim Raisi: The Rise to Power in an Authoritarian Theocracy

One mid-twentieth-century political commentator noted "that there is no greater necessity for men who live in communities than that they be governed, self-governed if possible, well-governed if they are fortunate, but in any event, governed." (Lippmann.)

How states organize their governing institutions becomes key to understanding how political conflict is organized, and how rules and procedures shape political forces that compete for power. Governments are structured through institutions—the executive, legislature, and judiciary. There are differences in how institutions in democracies are governed, and the same is true for authoritarian states. Some authoritarian states are ruled by a hereditary monarch, others by dictators, some by a single political party, and still others are theocracies ruled by religious leaders.

Iran, formally known as the Islamic Republic of Iran, is a theocracy. Its current constitutional order was established in 1979 after the Iranian Revolution toppled the secular authoritarian monarchy ruled by Shah (king) Mohammad Reza Pahlavi. New political institutions were created to enshrine the role of clerics in the nation's governance.

Although the revolution was fueled by both religious and secular opposition to the shah's repressive regime, a charismatic religious leader, Ayatollah Ruhollah Khomeini, consolidated power and became Iran's first supreme leader, which, as the title implies, is the most powerful government official. Good governance was understood to follow the word of God. The shah was seen as corrupt, brutal, and too closely aligned with the United States. The United States had backed a coup in 1953 that overthrew a democratically elected prime minister, Mohammad Mosaddegh, and returned the shah to power. Religious leaders also opposed the shah's efforts at modernization, seen as Westernization.

Religious authority can be seen in many institutions in which clerical power is exercised. At the top is the supreme leader, who exercises ultimate authority. Since 1989, Grand Ayatollah Ali Khamenei, now in his eighties, has been in power with no formal successor. A leading cleric seen as a successor to Khamenei is the conservative Ebrahim Raisi. In 2019, he was appointed by the supreme leader to be Iran's chief justice. Raisi, a former student of Khamenei, is a *seyyed*, a direct descendent of the Prophet Mohammed, just like Khamenei and Khomeini. Most countries in the Middle East follow Sunni Islam, but Iran is predominantly Shia Islam. The split in Islam occurred after the death of the Prophet Mohammed and concerned who was qualified to succeed him. Followers of Shia Islam believe that only direct descendants of Mohammed are eligible to lead.

Born in 1960, Raisi has been steadily moving up the ranks of government since a relatively early age. He was prosecutor for the city of Karaj (1982–1985); prosecutor for the city of Hamadan (1982–1985); deputy prosecutor-general of Tehran (1985–1988); prosecutor-general of Tehran (1989–1994); head of the State General Inspectorate Organization (1994–2004); first deputy to the chief justice (2004–2014); prosecutor-general of the Special Court for Clergy (2012–present); and prosecutor-general (2014–2016).

Raisi has also had prominent positions outside the legal system. He has been a member of Iran's leading conservative clerical association, and since 2007, he has been a member of the Assembly of Experts, a clerical body with eighty-eight members, all male, elected by Iranian citizens for eight-year terms. The Assembly of Experts is charged with supervising the supreme leader and choosing his successor. In 2016, Khamenei appointed Raisi to be the guardian of Iran's holiest shrine in Mashhad, further strengthening his religious prominence.

Raisi's appointment as chief justice was controversial because of his role in the 1988 massacre of political prisoners. Following the end of the Iran–Iraq War (1981–1988), a militant opposition group based in Iraq invaded Iran. In response, the regime sought to crush its opponents and rounded up political dissidents, leftists, and others sympathetic to the armed invasion. They were then subjected to "death commissions" and tested for their religious devotion. Thousands were executed. Those who were executed simply disappeared. Their families were never told of their fate or allowed to bury their loved ones. Their bodies allegedly were dumped in unmarked graves. (Lumsden.)

In 2017, Amnesty International called for the Iranian government to give a full accounting of what happened and estimated that at least 5,000 political prisoners were subjected to extrajudicial execution. (Amnesty International, 2018.) The U.N. Human Rights Council, along with several human-rights NGOs, estimated that as many as 30,000 were executed. In 2013, decades after these events, Canada became the first nation to call these executions crimes against humanity.

Ebrahim Raisi was Tehran's deputy prosecutor at the time and a member of its provincial tribunal responsible for administering the execution policy. Raisi was long silent on his role in these events, but in 2018, he claimed that the executions were not improper. Amnesty International responded that his claim was unsubstantiated and part of a long-running disinformation campaign to cover up the massacre.

As the chief justice in Iran, Raisi had responsibility for the entire Iranian judiciary and could appoint and dismiss all judges, including justices of the Supreme Court. The chief justice selects a list of candidates for the position of minister of justice from which the president makes the final selection. The chief justice appoints individuals to the state agencies that censor the media and internet. He also can investigate corruption among government officials. (Lumsden.)

Acting as both judge and prosecutor, Raisi could also propose bills to the unicameral parliament, known as the Majles, and could appoint half of the twelve members of the Guardian Council. The Guardian Council vets candidates for the three elected institutions in Iran: the Assembly of Experts, the presidency, and the parliament. It also can block any legislation passed by the parliament. This formal authority gave Raisi, as chief justice, a large amount of institutional power in Iran.

As a candidate for president in the Iranian election held in June 2021, Ebrahim Raisi, casts his ballot at a polling station in Tehran. He won the election.

Meghdad Madad/ATPImages/Getty Images

In 2017, Raisi ran for president but garnered only 38 percent of the vote, losing to incumbent president Hassan Rouhani, who earned 57 percent of the vote—a substantial margin of victory. The final vote totals indicate that Iranian citizens preferred the relatively moderate Rouhani to Raisi, who is considered to be a hard-line conservative. Despite his loss in 2017, Raisi was once again a candidate in the 2021 election. The Guardian Council allowed four candidates—all hard-liners—to run for president. Raisi won. Voter turnout was the lowest in the history of the Islamic Republic, at 48.8 percent. (Hafezi.)

Raisi's ascension to the presidency is the next step in his rise to power in Iran. In announcing his candidacy for the presidency in 2021, Raisi wrote: "God, you are witness that I have never been after position or power, and even at this stage I have entered the field despite personal will and interests, and only to serve my duty to answer the people and elites and create hope."

4.1 Systems of Government

Learning Targets

After reading this section, you should be able to do the following:

1. Describe the features of a parliamentary system of government.

2. Describe the features of a presidential system of government.

3. Explain how a semi-presidential system incorporates features of both parliamentary and presidential systems.

4. Explain why it is more difficult to make policy in a presidential system than it is in a parliamentary system.

Schools in almost every country teach students about the formal institutions of their government and how they are supposed to work. These **institutions** are made up of the executive branch and bureaucracy, the legislature, and the judiciary. Understanding politics requires knowing what powers are given to different institutions, yet it also means understanding how institutions function in practice. The story of Ebrahim Raisi demonstrates how government operates on both the formal and informal level. Although Raisi was elected as president under the formal rules of the constitution, his connections with the supreme leader helped him rise to power.

Presidents in different countries may have the same powers on paper, but some may be able to exercise much more power than others. Similarly, presidents in the same country at different times may have more or less actual power. To really understand politics, you have to consider what a country's institutions look like on paper and whether the constitution and laws are honored in practice.

The **executive** is the chief political power in a state, typically the single most powerful office in government. The position is usually referred to as a president or prime minister. The executive branch includes a **bureaucracy**, which is a large set of unelected officials who implement the laws, as directed by the chief executive. The **legislature**, which is typically a group of lawmakers representing citizens, passes laws. The **judiciary** is the system of courts that interprets the law and applies it to individual cases. In most countries, the supreme court is the highest level of the judiciary. The power and autonomy of

Institutions
The executive and bureaucracy, the legislature, and the judiciary.

Executive
The chief political power in a state, usually a president or prime minister.

Bureaucracy
A large set of unelected officials who implement the laws.

Legislature
A group of lawmakers that passes laws and represents citizens.

Judiciary
The system of courts that interprets the law and applies it to individual cases.

each institution varies significantly and depends on whether the state is democratic or authoritarian.

There are three systems for allocating executive power and structuring the relations between the executive and the legislature: parliamentary, presidential, and semi-presidential.

Parliamentary Systems

If you ask Americans to define democracy, many will start with "separation of powers," which you may have learned about in an AP® U.S. Government and Politics course. The oldest model of modern democracy, however, does not separate the executive and legislature. Commonly known as the Westminster, or parliamentary, model, it originated in Britain.

Parliamentary systems often have two executives—a head of state who performs ceremonial duties, and a head of government who is in charge of policymaking. Power is concentrated in one place, parliament, and there are few checks within government institutions.

The fusion of the executive and legislative branches provides for a powerful head of government. The **prime minister** is not only the executive but also a member of the legislature. He or she is the leader of the majority party in the legislature. If no party wins a majority of seats in the legislature, two or more parties will form a **coalition government** and select the prime minister.

Citizens cast one vote for an individual to represent their district in parliament. The majority party or majority coalition in parliament then selects the prime minister. In a parliamentary system, citizens do not vote for the executive directly. In practice, when citizens vote for parliament, they know who the prime-minister candidate is for each party, so their vote for their preferred **member of parliament (MP)** or party is indirectly a vote for that party's leader to serve as prime minister.

The prime minister serves at the pleasure of parliament. Should a parliamentary majority lose confidence in the prime minister, members can cast a **vote of no confidence** that forces the prime minister to resign. The leading party in parliament can choose a new leader as prime minister, or the resigning prime minister can ask the head of state to call new parliamentary elections. Parliamentary systems often do not have fixed terms of office, which means prime ministers can serve for long terms, as long as they maintain the support of their party and their party maintains its power in parliament.

Presidential Systems

American students are familiar with a **presidential system** because the best-known and most enduring example is the United States. In a presidential system, the roles of head of state and head of government are filled by the president. The defining aspect of a presidential system is the **separation of powers**. The executive and legislative branches are elected in separate (though possibly concurrent) elections, and the president is independently and directly (or nearly directly) elected. How easily a president can get his preferred policies approved by the legislature depends on whether the legislature is controlled by his or her own party, as well as the ability to bargain with legislators.

The president and legislature are elected independently, which can create **divided government**, which is when one or both houses of the legislature are controlled by a political party other than the party of the president. Presidents serve a fixed term, and it is very difficult for a legislature to remove the president from office before the end of his

Parliamentary system
A system in which the executive and legislature are fused.

Prime minister (PM)
The head of government in a parliamentary or semi-presidential system. In a parliamentary system, the PM is a member of the legislature and is selected by the majority party.

Coalition government
When two or more parties agree to work together to form a majority and select a prime minister.

Member of parliament (MP)
A representative in the legislature elected by citizens.

Vote of no confidence
In parliamentary systems, a vote by parliament to remove a government (the prime minister and cabinet) from power.

Presidential system
A system in which the executive and legislature are elected independently and have separate and independent powers.

Separation of powers
A division of power among the major branches of government.

Divided government
When one or both houses of the legislature are controlled by a political party other than the party of the president.

or her term, although most countries provide for some kind of impeachment and removal from office. Mexico and Nigeria have presidential systems of government.

Semi-Presidential Systems

Semi-presidential systems split executive power between an elected president and a prime minister. The president is elected directly by the citizens, serves as the head of state, and has significant powers in running the government. The prime minister is the head of government. In some semi-presidential systems, like Russia, the president appoints the prime minister with the consent of the lower house of parliament, the Duma. The parliament can also force the prime minister and cabinet to resign through a vote of no confidence.

For semi-presidentialism to be successful, the powers and duties of the president and prime minister as dual executives must be spelled out clearly in the constitution. For example, the president may be given power over military decisions or foreign policy, while the prime minister typically concentrates on domestic policies. The specific division of powers varies greatly, however, and is not always clearly delineated. In semi-presidential systems in which powers are blurred, the president may be far more powerful than the prime minister, and the president may be able to dismiss the prime minister at will. Russia has a semi-presidential system, with strong presidential power.

> **Semi-presidential system**
> A system that divides executive power between a directly elected president and a prime minister.

> **AP® TIP**
>
> The relationship between the executive and the legislature is a key feature of government in the six countries studied. Pay special attention to executive-legislative relations in each of the countries studied, because the topic is likely to appear on the AP® Exam.

Comparing Systems of Government

In a review of the political science literature, David Samuels (2007) concluded that, overall, presidential systems are less likely to pass legislation to change policies, and when they do, change will take longer and be more expensive than in parliamentary systems. In presidential systems, divided government renders lawmaking more complex and time-consuming, and it is hard to create new policies. In semi-presidential systems, much depends on whether the president, prime minister, and parliamentary majority are from the same party. If so, policy can pass easily and without the need to compromise. Parliamentary systems can change policy quickly and with little compromise, because the prime minister is from the majority party (or majority coalition).

The biggest debate about executive-legislative systems in recent years has been which system is more stable. Political scientist Juan Linz (1990) initiated the debate. Looking mainly at new democracies, Linz argued that presidential systems have many potential disadvantages. Since the legislature and the executive are independently and directly elected, each has legitimacy. He also argued that the direct election of the president could lead to chief executives with a "winner-take-all" mentality who would overemphasize their level of public support and be less willing to compromise. Finally, Linz claimed that presidential systems are too inflexible. It is hard to remove an executive in a presidential system.

Presidential systems are not likely to cause instability in established democracies. In stable democracies, the fixed term in a presidential system provides continuity and predictability. In parliamentary systems, the legislature may be fragmented among many parties. The best system of government depends on the history, political culture, and circumstances within a country. Each system has advantages and disadvantages in making policies that will benefit citizens.

Political scientists debate whether parliamentary or presidential systems are more likely to lead to democratic consolidation. They also disagree about which type of system produces the best economic results. The following passage argues in favor of a parliamentary system:

It has long been argued that parliamentary systems are more conducive to stable democracy. . . .

Our recent work shows that parliamentary systems also produce superior economic outcomes. . . . On average, annual output growth is up to 1.2 percentage points higher, inflation is less volatile and 6 percentage points lower, and income inequality is up to 20 percent lower in countries governed by parliamentary systems.

—Gulcin Ozkan and Richard McManus, "Parliamentary Systems Do Better Economically Than Presidential Ones," *The Conversation*, February 11, 2019

The authors of the passage state their claims and use data to support their assertions. In evaluating the persuasiveness of their argument, respond to the following:

1. Explain why the authors believe parliamentary systems are more effective in achieving stability.

2. Describe the authors' use of data in supporting their conclusions.

3. Describe political factors that the authors did not take into account in reaching their conclusions.

Section 4.1 Review

Each section's main ideas are reflected in the Learning Targets. By reviewing after each section, you should be able to

Remember the key points,

Know terms that are central to the topic, and

Think critically about what you have learned.

Remember

- In a parliamentary system, executive and legislative power are fused, and the prime minister is a member of parliament chosen as leader by the majority party or coalition.

- Presidential systems feature the separation of powers between the executive and legislature, with separate elections for members of each institution.

- Semi-presidential systems have a president, who serves as head of state, and a prime minister, who serves as the head of government.

- Policymaking can be difficult in a presidential system, especially when the executive and legislative institutions are controlled by different parties.

Know

- *Institutions:* the executive and bureaucracy, the legislature, and the judiciary. (p. 103)

- *Executive:* the chief political power in a state, usually a president or prime minister. (p. 103)

- *Bureaucracy:* a large set of unelected officials who implement the laws. (p. 103)

- *Legislature:* a group of lawmakers that passes laws and represents citizens. (p. 103)

- *Judiciary:* the system of courts that interprets the law and applies it to individual cases. (p. 103)

- *Parliamentary system:* a system in which the executive and legislature are fused. (p. 104)

- *Prime minister (PM):* the head of government in a parliamentary or semi-presidential system. In a parliamentary system, the PM is a member of the legislature and is selected by the majority party. (p. 104)

- *Coalition government:* when two or more parties agree to work together to form a majority and select a prime minister. (p. 104)
- *Member of parliament (MP):* a representative in the legislature elected by citizens. (p. 104)
- *Vote of no confidence:* in parliamentary systems, a vote by parliament to remove a government (the prime minister and cabinet) from power. (p. 104)
- *Presidential system:* a system in which the executive and legislature are elected independently and have separate and independent powers. (p. 104)
- *Separation of powers:* a division of power among the major branches of government. (p. 104)
- *Divided government:* When one or both houses of the legislature are controlled by a political party other than the party of the president. (p. 104)
- *Semi-presidential system:* a system that divides executive power between a directly elected president and a prime minister. (p. 105)

Think

- What are the advantages and disadvantages of parliamentary, presidential, and semi-presidential systems in making policy?
- Why do different countries which use the same type of system have executives with differing levels of power?

Free-Response Question: Conceptual Analysis

Answer A, B, C, and D.

A. Describe a parliamentary system of government.

B. Explain why it is easier for a prime minister to make policy in a parliamentary system of government than it is for a president to make policy in a presidential system.

C. Explain why a state would adopt a presidential system of government.

D. Explain how an executive may be removed in a parliamentary system.

4.2 Executives

Learning Targets

After reading this section, you should be able to do the following:

1. Describe the typical powers of a head of state and a head of government.

2. Describe the advantages and disadvantages of term limits.

3. Explain why it is more difficult to remove a president than a prime minister from office.

4. Describe the role of the bureaucracy within the executive branch.

The executive is indispensable to any state and fills two major roles. First, as head of state, the executive is the official, symbolic representative of a country, authorized to speak on its behalf and represent it, particularly in world affairs. Historically, heads of state were monarchs, who still exist as symbolic heads of state in a number of countries, including the United Kingdom. Second, as head of government, the executive's task is to implement

This political cartoon illustrates the power of China's president, Xi Jinping. Note that the scale of his image in comparison to the images of members of the party's Central Committee. The image of the boxing glove represents strong executive power.

Dave Simonds

the nation's laws and policies. The two parts of the executive function may be filled by one individual or two, but both are essential in governing the state.

The head of state usually serves as commander-in-chief of the military, which gives that person the authority to deploy troops abroad and, under certain circumstances, at home. In democratic systems, troops are not usually used against civilians, but they can be deployed to assist in times of crisis, such as a natural disaster. Authoritarian states are more likely to use troops against their own citizens to prevent unrest and protect the regime from internal threats to sovereignty. The head of state serves as the public face of the country and typically negotiates treaties and conveys diplomatic recognition on other countries.

Executives typically have the power to submit a program of policies to the legislature, including the national budget. In presidential systems, the executive is more likely to have to compromise with the legislature in getting his or her proposed policies passed, because the legislature may be controlled by an opposing party. It is easier for the prime minister to get his or her policy passed in a parliamentary system, because he or she is from the majority party in the legislature.

The executive is usually the most powerful institution within a state. This is especially true in authoritarian regimes. In democratic states, the legislature and judiciary serve as important checks on executive power.

Term Limits

Term limit
A restriction on the number of terms the executive may serve.

Executives may face a **term limit** on the number of times they are allowed to serve. States may limit an executive to a total number of terms or to consecutive terms, leaving the door open for the executive to return later. In parliamentary systems, such as the United Kingdom, the prime minister is able to retain office as long as he or she maintains the support of the party and is not removed through a vote of no confidence, so there are no term limits in these systems.

Term of office
A specified number of years that an executive can serve.

In a presidential system, the executive's term is a specified number of years. This is called a **term of office**. In presidential systems, fixed terms provide a predictable schedule of elections. In parliamentary systems, terms are not as rigid as they are in presidential systems. In the United Kingdom's parliamentary system, the prime minister must call for an election within a five-year period, although he or she has the power to call an election earlier, which is called a snap election.

States impose executive term limits to prevent an executive from consolidating too much power, personalizing rule, and becoming a dictator. Executives who are in their final term can focus on governing instead of campaigning. Term limits ensure that voters have an opportunity to elect a different executive with new policy goals. Term limits may prevent unrest, because voters who are unhappy with the executive can look forward to automatic removal from office at the end of that politician's final term.

Term limits have disadvantages. They prevent popular executives from being reelected, even when they have enacted successful policies and have broad popular support. Term limits also reduce policy continuity, because a new executive can shift policies before a previous policy has been tested. An executive who is term-limited may rush to pass policies at the end of the term, which can result in programs that are not well designed. Democratic systems have differing terms of office, usually four or six years. The terms of office balance the advantages and disadvantages of term limits by allowing the executive enough time to develop policies without staying in power for too long.

Removing an Executive

It is easier to remove an executive in a parliamentary system than in a presidential system. Prime ministers in parliamentary systems can be removed in three ways. Technically, a prime minister can lose an election for his or her individual seat in parliament, although this seldom happens because party leaders are slotted in a safe district where their party has a strong majority of voters, ensuring that their party almost always wins elections. Second, prime ministers can be removed by the majority party when they have lost favor. The party simply replaces the current prime minister with a new one. Third, a prime minister can be removed by a vote of no confidence in the legislature. When the prime minister proposes a major piece of legislation that fails, this means the prime minister has lost the votes of some of the members of his or her own party. A vote of no confidence follows, which can remove the prime minister from office, and new elections for parliament are called. Successful votes of no confidence are rare, because prime ministers usually bargain with party members before a vote on a crucial issue to ensure they have the support of their members.

Presidents are harder to remove before the end of their terms. In presidential systems, the legislature has the power to remove the president through **impeachment**. The term *impeachment* refers to the process in which the legislature determines whether or not the president meets the constitutional standard for removal. The standard for removal is usually very high and requires proof that the president has committed a serious crime. Removal from office usually requires a supermajority vote of more than half of the legislature, and in some presidential systems, both houses of the legislature must agree on impeachment and removal. If members of the president's party hold enough seats in the legislature, it is nearly impossible to remove a president before the end of his or her term.

The difficulty of removing the executive in a presidential system, as compared to a parliamentary system, is a function of the separation of power between the legislature and the executive branch. In a parliamentary system, where power is fused, it is easier to remove a prime minister, because the prime minister is a member of the legislature.

Impeachment
The process of removing a president from office before the end of his or her term.

Bureaucracies

The ideal modern bureaucracy consists of officials appointed on the basis of merit and expertise who implement policies lawfully, treat all citizens equally, and are held accountable by the elected head of the executive branch. In liberal democracies, bureaucratic officials are insulated from the personal and political desires of top leaders. Before modern reforms, bureaucratic positions in most states were based on political patronage–leaders appointed officials to suit the leaders' interests. Although the bureaucracy is part of the executive institution, knowledge, expertise, and the large size and scope of the bureaucracy give bureaucrats the ability to act independently of the executive.

The government bureaucracy is a part of the executive institution, which means that the executives selects a cabinet that formulates, implements, and enforces policies through ministries or agencies. A **cabinet** is composed of the heads of major departments, or ministries, within government that organize the bureaucracy. These departments oversee policy in major areas, such as the treasury, defense, and education. In a parliamentary system, cabinet members hold seats in the legislature and are usually chosen from the leadership of the majority party or majority coalition. In a presidential system, the executive can appoint his or her own cabinet ministers or secretaries, subject to confirmation by the legislature. Once appointed and confirmed by the legislature, the cabinet heads serve at the president's pleasure, and the legislature can interfere only minimally with their daily activities.

In democracies, legislators may write laws that are as specific as possible to limit bureaucratic discretion in implementing them. On the other hand, the legislature may intentionally write vague laws to give the bureaucracy wide discretion over tricky policy areas that require expertise. In both presidential and parliamentary systems, the legislature may have the power to investigate cabinet heads and other members of the bureaucracy. **Legislative oversight** is when members of the legislature, usually in committees, oversee the bureaucracy by interviewing key leaders, examining expenditures, and assessing how successfully a particular department has carried out its tasks.

Reforming the bureaucracy is a key step in democratization. When bureaucratic rules and norms are extremely weak, corruption and widespread inefficiency are likely. (O'Dwyer, 2006.) Political elites may be able to use a weak bureaucracy to pursue their own personal or financial interests, citizens may be able to use bribery to gain favors from the state, and bureaucrats may steal from the state. In weak states, citizens often have to bribe officials to get them to carry out their functions. Leaders may not be interested in stopping this behavior because they benefit from their ability to purchase favors from bureaucrats. Sometimes, they may simply have lost the ability to control members of the bureaucracy, often because of very low salaries that tempt bureaucrats to take bribes. In democracies with stronger parties and greater political competition, corruption is lower, because voters can hold corrupt officials accountable in elections.

Cabinet
The heads of major departments, or ministries, in the bureaucracy.

Legislative oversight
The power of the legislature to hold cabinet officials and members of bureaucracy accountable for their actions and policies.

Section 4.2 Review

Remember

- The head of state is the symbolic representative of a state, and the head of government implements laws and policies.
- Term limits are designed to prevent an executive from consolidating power, but term limits have disadvantages.
- It is harder to remove an executive in a presidential system than in a parliamentary system.

- The cabinet consists of the heads of key departments within the bureaucracy, which implements and enforces policy.

Know

- *Term limit:* a restriction on the number of terms the executive may serve. (p. 108)
- *Term of office:* a specified number of years that an executive can serve. (p. 108)
- *Impeachment:* the process of removing a president from office before the end of his or her term. (p. 109)
- *Cabinet:* the heads of major departments, or ministries, in the bureaucracy. (p. 110)
- *Legislative oversight:* the power of the legislature to hold cabinet officials and members of bureaucracy accountable for their actions and policies. (p. 110)

Think

- Are term limits a prerequisite for democratic government?
- What actions could a state take in an effort to limit corruption within the bureaucracy?

....

Free-Response Question: Quantitative Analysis

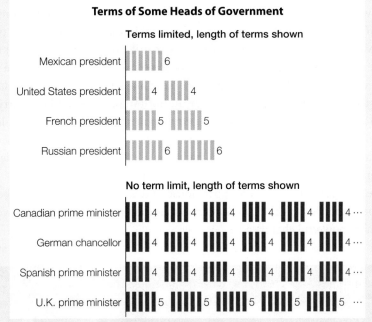

Terms of Some Heads of Government

Data from Statista.
Notes: The presidents of France and Russia share executive power with their prime ministers.
Some countries allow reelection after a certain period of time.

Answer A, B, C, D, and E.

A. Using the data in the infographic, identify the two countries studied in AP® Comparative Government and Politics with the longest terms of office.

B. Using the data in the infographic, identify the country studied in AP® Comparative Government and Politics with no term limits.

C. Describe the role of a head of government.

D. Using the data in the infographic and your knowledge of AP® Comparative Government and Politics, draw a conclusion about the impact of term limits on policy continuity.

E. Explain what the data illustrate about term limits in democratic regimes.

4.3 Legislatures

Learning Targets

After reading this section, you should be able to do the following:

1. Describe the differences between unicameral and bicameral legislatures.

2. Explain why legislatures in democratic states have more independence than legislatures in authoritarian states.

The legislature represents citizens, providing a link between constituents and policymaking. In democratic systems, the legislature has independent powers and may check executive actions. In authoritarian systems, the legislature has less autonomy.

Legislative Structures

Unicameral legislature
A legislature with one chamber.

There are two main ways to structure a legislature. A **unicameral legislature** consists of one house. As you saw in the study of Mexico, a bicameral legislature is made up of two houses.

An advantage of a unicameral legislature is that it can pass policies quickly, because bills do not have to go through two houses to become law, and less compromise is required to make new policies. Authoritarian states are more likely to have unicameral legislatures. There is usually less political competition in authoritarian states, and the party in power generally does not have to compromise in getting policies passed. Unicameral legislatures are more efficient and lack intra-branch checks that slow down the process of making policy. Because laws do not have to pass both houses, however, there is less deliberation, and laws may pass quickly without careful consideration.

Bicameral legislatures have an upper house and a lower house. Remember that the terms "upper" and "lower" refer to prestige rather than power. In fact, the lower house is often the more powerful chamber.

A female legislator during a session of the Iranian parliament. Several of her colleagues are conferring and reviewing documents. The legislature represents citizens, and its function is to debate and pass policies. The Islamic Consultative Assembly, which is also called the Majles, is Iran's unicameral legislature.

Atta Kenare/AFP/Getty Images

One reason for having a bicameral legislature is to give each house different powers. In Mexico, for example, the lower house, the Chamber of Deputies, is the more powerful lawmaking body, while the upper house, the Senate, confirms treaties and cabinet appointments. Another reason to have a bicameral legislature is so that each chamber can represent different constituencies. Federal systems typically have bicameral legislatures, with the lower house representing the people and the upper house representing the states. This is true of the federal systems of Mexico, Nigeria, and Russia. As you may have studied in AP® U.S. Government and Politics, the United States has a federal system of government, and the House of Representatives represents the people, while the Senate represents the states.

Unitary systems may also have bicameral legislatures. Instead of representing the states, which do not have protected powers in a unitary system, the upper house may represent other interests, such as the elite class. In the United Kingdom, for example, the House of Lords is an appointed body that has little power in the lawmaking process. The House of Lords has the power to delay legislation, but the House of Commons can pass legislation even when the House of Lords does not support it.

When both houses are required to enact legislation, the policymaking process is more deliberative, which may result in more effective policy being passed. However, when legislative chambers are controlled by different parties or interests, gridlock may delay policymaking, even in times of crisis.

Figure 4.1 depicts the percentages of women in legislatures worldwide. Of the six countries studied in the AP® Comparative Government and Politics course, Mexico has the highest percentage of women serving in its legislature. Mexican law requires political parties to run 50 percent female candidates.

FIGURE 4.1

Women in National Legislatures
Percentage of women, by country

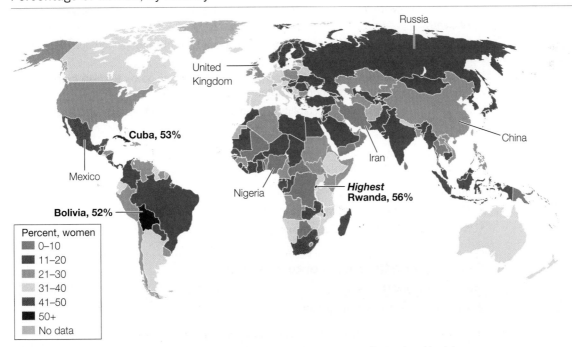

Women, who make up 51 percent of the population, are underrepresented in national legislatures. Only three countries, Rwanda, Cuba, and Bolivia, have female majorities.

Note: As of January 1, 2019.

Data from the Inter-Parliamentary Union and Pew Research Center.

Legislative Independence

Legislatures are crucial to democratic regimes because they represent citizens and are the main source of policymaking—they debate and pass laws. Independent legislatures have the power of bureaucratic oversight. They can investigate cabinet members and bureaucratic agencies for wrongdoing and oversee how policies are being implemented. Legislatures in democratic systems have the power to approve the budget for executive departments. In democratic states, the legislature can extend civil liberties to individuals and pass legislation to protect the civil rights of groups facing discrimination.

Independent legislatures also have the power to remove the executive from office before the end of his or her term. Legislatures in presidential systems usually have the power to remove the president through impeachment, although the process is usually difficult. In a parliamentary system, the legislature may remove the prime minister through a vote of no confidence.

In authoritarian regimes, the legislative branch may have little power over policymaking. Furthermore, elections for seats in the legislature may not be competitive, and one party may control policymaking. In authoritarian states, the legislature does not serve as an effective check on executive actions. Nevertheless, the legislature can provide stability in an authoritarian state. Members of the legislature can convey information about local problems, and they connect citizens with government. By allowing nondominant parties to compete in elections, and win seats in the legislature, authoritarian states can increase political efficacy and legitimacy.

In both democratic and authoritarian states, legislatures have the potential to reinforce legitimacy and stability by responding to public demand, debating policy, and facilitating compromise between factions.

Section 4.3 Review

Remember

- Unicameral legislatures consist of one chamber, which enables them to pass policies efficiently.
- Bicameral legislatures consist of two chambers that may have different powers and represent different constituencies.
- Democratic legislatures have more independence and have more power to check executive actions than legislatures in authoritarian states.
- Legislatures serve as a source of stability and legitimacy in both authoritarian and democratic states.

Know

- *Unicameral legislature:* a legislature with one chamber. (p. 112)

Think

- Why are authoritarian states more likely to have unicameral legislatures?
- What are the advantages and disadvantages of bicameralism?

Free-Response Question: Conceptual Analysis

Answer A, B, C, and D.

A. Describe a unicameral legislature.

B. Explain why an authoritarian state would have a unicameral legislature.

C. Explain how the legislature in a democratic system serves as a check on executive power.

D. Explain why an authoritarian system would provide the legislature with some power over policymaking.

4.4 Judiciaries

Learning Targets

After reading this section, you should be able to do the following:

1. Describe the role of the judiciary as an institution of government.

2. Explain why an independent judiciary enhances democracy.

The job of the judiciary is to decide cases based on the law. The judiciary's more important political role, however, is to interpret the law, especially the constitution.

Judicial Systems

The judicial system is usually made up of trial courts that hear evidence, courts that hear appeals, and a supreme court that is the final court of appeals. In federal systems, there are separate courts at the national and state levels. The highest court in most democracies has the power of judicial review, the authority to overturn a law or an executive action that violates the constitution. Judicial review supports judicial independence. However, courts do not need the power of judicial review to maintain their independence in democratic countries. For example, the Supreme Court in the United Kingdom exercises judicial independence, but it does not have the power of judicial review.

Members of the highest court may serve for long terms, such as the fifteen-year term for supreme court justices in Mexico, or they may serve for life or until a mandatory retirement age. For example, judges in Nigeria must retire at the age of seventy.

In democratic systems, the legislature may remove justices, but only for serious wrongdoing. Lengthy terms, the difficulty of removal, and the power of judicial review make the supreme court a powerful player in the political system, with the power to check the actions of other institutions of government.

There are two types of legal systems—common law and code law. **Common law** was developed in the United Kingdom. In a common-law system, judges make decisions by applying precedent, a previous written decision that establishes a rule to be applied in similar cases in the future. In common-law systems, parties to a case may file an appeal if they believe a lower court made an error in applying the law. Common-law systems can enhance the rule of law, because the facts, issues, decisions, and rulings are written down and applied as precedent in future cases. This predictability means no one should be above the law.

Code law is most closely associated with the French emperor Napoleon Bonaparte. In a code-law system, judges follow the law as written by the legislature instead of following precedent set by previous court decisions. Code-law countries usually have a special court that handles constitutional questions. Most also have abstract judicial review, meaning that certain public officials or major political groups can call on the courts to make a constitutional ruling before a law is fully in effect.

Judicial Independence

Judicial independence is the ability of judges to decide cases according to the law, free of interference from politically powerful officials or other institutions. Judicial systems

Common law
A legal system in which previous written opinions serve as precedent for future cases.

Code law
A legal system in which judges follow the law written by the legislature, and previous court decisions do not serve as precedent.

Judicial independence
The ability of judges to decide cases according to the law, free of interference from politically powerful officials or other institutions.

that lack independence are weak institutions where corruption is common. Judges may accept bribes to decide cases in a particular way or refuse to rule against powerful individuals. This can affect everyday criminal and civil cases as well as constitutional questions.

An independent judiciary protects minority rights that might be trampled by a legislature or executive acting on majority opinion. Judges who are appointed do not have to worry about reelection. They can uphold the law and the constitution, even when doing so is unpopular with the public or other institutions of government. An independent court system depends not only on formal rules but also on the strength of the judiciary as an institution. For example, judicial review is one way for the courts to exercise independence by checking the actions of the executive and legislature. However, without a strong, autonomous court system, judicial review can be meaningless in practice, even if it is clearly established in a constitution.

New democracies often have to build new judicial institutions. As you saw in the case study of Mexico, the effort to build a stronger judiciary included requiring that judges have formal legal training and increasing their pay, in an attempt to reduce corruption. The courts have played a crucial role in helping young democracies resist efforts to undermine democratic principles. Because the judiciary lacks both military and financial resources, legitimacy is crucial to its institutional strength. Without broadly recognized legitimacy, the judiciary has little power. Judiciaries typically gain legitimacy over time as people begin to trust their fairness and are satisfied with key court decisions.

AP® POLITICAL SCIENCE PRACTICES

Analyzing Sources for Point of View

On the multiple-choice portion of the AP® Exam, you will encounter passages that you most likely have never seen before. One of the keys to analyzing text sources is to analyze information about who wrote the passage, its title, where it was published, and the date of publication. It is important to consider the point of view of the author, which may impact his or her perception of political events. In addition, you should put the passage in the context of what you already know about the topic. Take a look at the passage below:

China has executed [Lai Xiaomin] the former head of one of its biggest asset management companies who was convicted of corruption.... One person who personally knew Lai attributed the severity of the punishment to his close ties to others in China's elite. The person suggested that officials "wanted to set him as an example to scare other corrupt officials."

—Edward White and Sun Yu, "China Executes Former Asset Management Chief for Corruption," *Financial Times,* January 29, 2021

You probably don't know anything about Edward White and Sun Yu, the authors of the article, and you most likely will not know much about the subject of the passage, unless they are famous leaders. The title of this article tells you that an asset manager in China was executed for corruption. You know that China is an authoritarian state, and you may know that it imposes the death penalty for a wide range of offenses. The article is published in *Financial Times.* You may not know that *Financial Times* is a daily international newspaper or that it is based in London, but it is reasonable to conclude that it is published in the West, and it may have a Western perspective.

With that information in mind, answer the following questions.

1. What is the authors' focus in writing the article?

2. How does the focus of the article reflect Western values?

3. How would the focus of the article be different if the story had appeared in a Chinese journal?

Political institutions impact who has the most power in a society and how they can exercise it. In democratic systems, leaders are held accountable by the voters, and between elections, they are held accountable by other institutions of government. In authoritarian systems, the legislature and judiciary have few checks, centralizing power in the executive. As you continue the country case studies, pay close attention to how governments are structured on paper, and compare their formal structure to how they function in practice.

Section 4.4 Review

Remember

- The highest court in most democracies has the power of judicial review.
- Judicial independence gives courts the power to check other institutions of government and protect civil rights and liberties.

Know

- *Common law:* a legal system in which previous written opinions serve as precedent for future cases. (p. 115)
- *Code law:* a legal system in which judges follow the law written by the legislature, and previous court decisions do not serve as precedent. (p. 115)
- *Judicial independence:* the ability of judges to decide cases according to the law, free of interference from politically powerful officials or other institutions. (p. 115)

Think

- What steps can democracies take in an effort to increase the professionalism and independence of the judiciary?

(Continued)

Free-Response Question: Quantitative Analysis

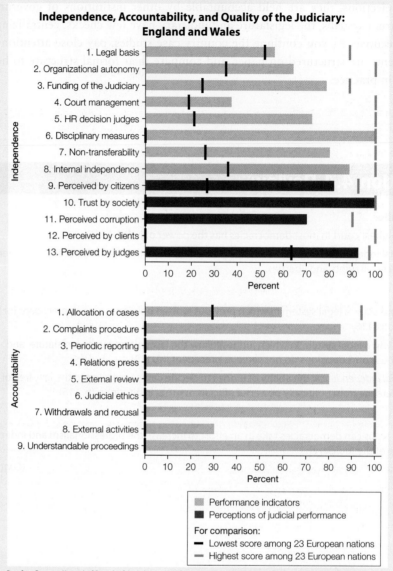

Independence, Accountability, and Quality of the Judiciary: England and Wales

Data from European Network of Councils of the Judiciary, *2017 Report on Independence, Accountability and Quality of the Judiciary.*

Answer A, B, C, D, and E.

A. Using the data in the bar chart, identify the percentage who believe members of the judiciary in England and Wales act ethically.

B. Using the data in the bar chart, describe the level of citizen understanding of judicial proceedings in England and Wales.

C. Describe judicial independence.

D. Using the data in the bar chart and your knowledge of AP® Comparative Government and Politics, draw a conclusion about how the United Kingdom could increase judicial independence.

E. Explain why the data support the classification of the United Kingdom as a liberal democracy.

AP® KEY CONCEPTS

- Institutions (p. 103)
- Executive (p. 103)
- Bureaucracy (p. 103)
- Legislature (p. 103)
- Judiciary (p. 103)
- Parliamentary system (p. 104)
- Prime minister (p. 104)
- Coalition government (p. 104)

- Member of parliament (MP) (p. 104)
- Vote of no confidence (p. 104)
- Presidential system (p. 104)
- Separation of powers (p. 104)
- Divided government (p. 104)
- Semi-presidential system (p. 105)
- Term limit (p. 108)
- Term of office (p. 108)

- Impeachment (p. 109)
- Cabinet (p. 110)
- Legislative oversight (p. 110)
- Unicameral legislature (p. 112)
- Common law (p. 115)
- Code law (p. 115)
- Judicial independence (p. 115)

AP® EXAM MULTIPLE-CHOICE PRACTICE QUESTIONS

1. Which of the following accurately describes executive-legislative relations in a system of government studied in AP® Comparative Government and Politics?

   A. In a parliamentary system, the supreme court has the power to remove the prime minister before the end of his or her term.

   B. In a presidential system, the legislature has the power to impeach the executive, but it is difficult to get the required number of votes for conviction and removal.

   C. In a parliamentary system, the lower house of the legislature has more independent checks on the executive than the lower house in a presidential system.

   D. Legislatures in presidential systems have the authority to enact policy without executive approval because they are the institution closest to the people.

2. What is the function of a bureaucracy?

   A. It carries out the executive's wishes without legislative input.

   B. The bureaucracy implements and enforces policy.

   C. It serves as a check on legislative actions.

   D. The bureaucracy represents the will of the people.

Questions 3 and 4 refer to the passage.

> Policymaking is a profession in and of itself . . . Crafting legislative proposals is a learned skill; as in other professions, experience matters. In fact, as expert analysis has shown . . . policy crafted by even the most experienced of lawmakers is likely to have ambiguous provisions and loopholes that undermine the intended effects of the legislation. The public is not best served if inexperienced members are making policy choices with widespread, lasting effects.
>
> —Casey Burgat, Brookings Institution, January 18, 2018

3. Which of the following is supported by the main idea of the passage?

   A. Policymaking is more effective when new representatives are elected to introduce novel ideas.

   B. It is important that members of the legislature have experience, because it is hard to write effective legislation.

   C. Inexperienced members of the legislature may find it difficult to handle all of their responsibilities, making it hard for them to represent the public.

   D. Experienced lawmakers purposely write legislation that has loopholes and vague language.

4. Which of the following is an implication of the argument made in the passage?
   A. Term limits for the legislature result in poorly drafted legislation.
   B. Short terms of office for the legislature improve representation and policymaking efficiency.
   C. Legislative terms should be relatively long so that representatives gain experience, but legislators should face term limits to keep them from becoming too powerful.
   D. Term limits are undemocratic, because they prevent voters from returning effective representatives to the legislature.

5. Which of the following is an argument against allowing the supreme court in a democratic country to have the power of judicial review?
   A. The power of judicial review gives too much authority to the courts and prevents the executive from gaining more power.
   B. Judicial review prevents the development of civil rights and liberties, because justices often strike down the claims of groups that have faced discrimination.
   C. Democracies are based on the principle of majority rule, and judicial review enables supreme court justices to make unpopular decisions to uphold the constitution.
   D. Supreme court justices are appointed and not elected, and it is difficult for citizens to hold them accountable for their actions in using judicial review.

Questions 6 and 7 refer to the infographic.

Share of Votes received by Vladimir Putin in Russian Presidential Elections

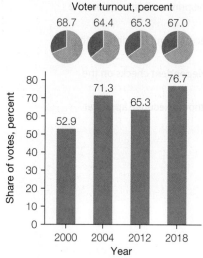

Data from Central Election Commission of the Russian Federation.

6. Which of the following is accurate according to the infographic?
   A. President Putin received the highest percentage of votes in 2004.
   B. In every election from 2000 to 2018, Putin earned a higher percentage of the vote than he did in the previous election.
   C. Voter turnout was higher in 2000 than in any other year shown in the graphic.
   D. Voter turnout in Russia is inversely correlated with the percentage of the vote earned by Putin.

7. Which of the following statements is an implication of the infographic?
   A. President Putin will likely extend his hold on power and continue to win elections.
   B. Russians have a low sense of political efficacy, and relatively few citizens participate in politics.
   C. Putin's personal charisma is one of the reasons for the legitimacy of the Russian state.
   D. The Putin administration does not allow political parties to compete in elections, concentrating power in the executive.

8. Which of the following statements best describes the role of the judiciary in democratic states?
    A. It promotes rule by law.
    B. The judiciary increases stability by deferring to executive actions.
    C. The judiciary clarifies laws enacted by the legislature.
    D. It prevents other institutions from violating constitutional principles.

9. Which of the following is a check on the executive in a parliamentary system?
    A. The head of government may be impeached for serious wrongdoing.
    B. During a parliamentary election, the prime minister's party may run the prime minister in a district controlled by the opposing political party.
    C. The head of government may be removed through a vote of no confidence.
    D. Members of the public may sign a petition for a special recall election to remove the head of government.

10. Which of the following is a disadvantage of policymaking in a presidential system?
    A. Divided government may result in gridlock, even in times of crisis.
    B. Policies favored by the executive are easily enacted, even when the public opposes them.
    C. Legislative oversight is weak, and the bureaucracy has the power to carry out policies with few restrictions.
    D. The executive is unable to act quickly to protect the country in times of international crisis.

AP® EXAM PRACTICE ARGUMENT ESSAY

Note to Students:

The following is designed to begin preparing you for the argument essay prompt that you will see on the AP® Exam. On the AP® Exam, you will be asked to compare two countries. At this point in the textbook, you have studied Mexico, and you have learned some basic information about the parliamentary system in the United Kingdom. This question will give you practice at developing an argument in the form of the essay. Later in this book, you will answer questions that are more consistent with the format of the argument question on the AP® Exam.

- Develop an argument as to whether parliamentary or presidential systems are better at making effective policy.
- Use one or more of the following course concepts in your response:
    - Accountability
    - Transparency
    - Legitimacy

In your response, do the following:

- Respond to the prompt with a defensible claim or thesis that establishes a line of reasoning using one or more of the provided course concepts.
- Support your claim with at least TWO pieces of specific and relevant evidence from one or more course countries. The evidence should be relevant to one or more of the provided course concepts.
- Use reasoning to explain why your evidence supports your claim or thesis, using one or more of the provided course concepts.
- Respond to an opposing or alternate perspective, using refutation, concession, or rebuttal.

For a complete list of the sources of information cited in this chapter, turn to the Works Cited appendix.

5 Case Study: United Kingdom

Institutions

In June 2017, Queen Elizabeth II meets schoolchildren as she arrives at Slough Station in Berkshire (just west of London) to mark the 175th anniversary of the first train journey made by a British monarch. Although the monarchy has lost virtually all of its political power, the queen still represents history and tradition.

Andrew Matthews—PA Images/Getty Images

An Inexplicable Feeling of Urgency and Necessity

Protests and demonstrations are as essential to democracy as political parties, voting, and elections. While democratic regimes require free and fair elections open to all citizens, elections are not enough, and have never been enough, to make a country fully democratic.

Citizens groups have pushed government officials by means of protest movements that include strikes, sit-ins, marches, demonstrations, and even riots to have their voices heard. In these instances, the normal routines of politics can be disrupted, coalitions split apart and reorganize, and new issues rise to the surface. Unlike routine electoral politics, protests demonstrate the intense feelings of those who take to the streets, sometimes at the risk of life and limb.

Even if their power is based upon fear, leaders of nondemocratic nations worry that their hold on power depends on maintaining at least some support from the population. Despite the prospect of brutal repression, citizens in authoritarian states sometimes turn to the streets to demand change.

Citizens organizations and protests are part of what is known as civil society. This term refers to a combination of voluntary organized groups, online activists, and social movements that exist independently of government institutions. Also included in civil society are independent media, unions, and other social and religious groups. The existence and vitality of democratic states depends on an active civil society in which citizens can develop and express political views without fear of surveillance, infiltration, and repression from government officials. (Piven and Cloward.)

The United Kingdom has a long history of protest movements. Since the Middle Ages, protest movements have engaged in battles over taxation, religious freedom, the right to unionize, and the imposition of machinery in factories and farms. From the late nineteenth to early twentieth centuries, mass protests demanded the right to vote. All men and women over thirty who met minimal property requirements won the right to vote in 1918 in the aftermath of World War I. All women over the age of twenty-one won the right to vote in 1928. Since the nineteenth century, Hyde Park, in London, has become famous for its Speaker's Corner where open debate has flourished.

One of the largest examples of mass protest that has swept the world in recent years concerns climate change. In fact, in 2019, *Collins English Dictionary*, a publication started in Scotland 200 years ago, selected "climate strike" as the word of the year. Picked from a list of new and notable words, a climate strike is "a form of protest in which people absent themselves from education or work in order to join demonstrations demanding action to counter climate change." The expression first came to notice in 2015 during mass demonstrations in Paris during the U.N. Climate Change Conference. It later became synonymous with the Swedish teenager Greta Thunberg. Recognized worldwide, she became famous in 2018 after skipping school every Friday to protest in front of the Swedish parliament.

Climate strikes soon spread throughout the world, and in September 2019, more than 7.5 million people participated in climate protests across 4,500 locations in 150 countries.

Climate-change activist Noga Levy-Rapoport participates in a May Day rally in London in 2019.

Johnny Armstead/Shakeyjon/Alamy

In the United Kingdom, 200 events were held, with more than 300,000 participants. In London, more than 100,000 joined together. One of the leaders of that protest was 17-year-old Noga Levy-Rapoport.

Born in Israel, Levy-Rapoport and her family immigrated to the United Kingdom when she was a toddler. She has quickly become the face of the climate-change protest movement in the United Kingdom, often described as the British Greta. She led the February 2019 London climate strike and was a lead organizer of the UK Student Climate Network, a group of students under 18 that supports youth strikes to demand systemic change to halt the climate crisis. In October 2019, Levy-Rapoport was selected by the *London Evening Standard* as one of London's most influential people.

Levy-Rapoport's climate activism began almost inadvertently. She attended a relatively small demonstration of just 5,000 people in February 2019 that she had heard about from a friend's Instagram post. Upon seeing the post, she later wrote,

> I immediately knew I had to go, overwhelmed by an inexplicable feeling of urgency and necessity. Images of young people organizing and leading social movements throughout time came to my mind—was this our generation's moment to take the stage, when the world had been quiet about the climate emergency for so long?
>
> That powerful feeling—of anger at the climate crisis, of fury at lack of government action, and of being surrounded by like-minded young people who would no longer be afraid or silent—carried me through that day. Without thinking, I asked to borrow a megaphone from a fellow protestor and started shouting through it for others to join me and march.... (Levy-Rapoport, 2021. Reproduced with permission of Book of Beasties Ltd.)

Levy-Rapoport, whose first name means brightness, light, or sparkle in Hebrew, has been at the forefront of youth climate protests in the United Kingdom, which have centered on calls to reduce or eliminate carbon emissions. These protests call upon political and business leaders to focus on creating a sustainable future. As opposed to the muddled path of bureaucratic foot-dragging and empty rhetoric, she has argued that concrete actions for a just transition to a clean energy system are long overdue.

A sought-after spokesperson, Levy-Rapoport has become a media celebrity in her own right. In July 2019, she gave the keynote address at the annual Children's Media Conference. Amid a gathering of delegates and executives involved in film, publishing, and other media directed at children, she criticized how the media cover climate change. Climate-related information, she said, typically offers false equivalence between fossil fuels and renewable energy and does not provide an understanding of the existential challenges of climate change. She was named as one of CMC's Changemakers of the year.

To address the climate crisis, Levy-Rapoport has become an advocate for the Green New Deal, a potential program modeled after the U.S. New Deal, the set of policies that addressed the Great Depression of the 1930s. Its aim is to combat climate change and economic inequality. She became a spokesperson for Labour for a Green New Deal, a grassroots campaign that seeks to transform the British economy and advocate the Labour Party's agenda. In 2019, the party endorsed the Green New Deal at its annual conference.

In response to critics who have challenged her support of school strikes, she said, "To disrupt the educational system the way we are doing now is newsworthy. I prioritize my education above nearly everything, but unfortunately I can't prioritize my education above survival." For Levy-Rapoport, the point of student strikes is not merely to highlight the threats of climate change to future generations, but also to highlight the need for curriculum reform.

> For far too long, the national curriculum has restricted students, forcing them to concentrate on a limited range of subjects rather than truly developing their understanding of the world. This is encroaching on the right of students to view the educational framework as a place of opportunity, development, and understanding. Students must be encouraged to step out onto the streets, to look at the injustices of the world around them and rise up against it. They can only do so when they are taught, in full, about the climate crisis—the greatest threat we have ever faced. An education system that works for rather than against our future would be one that has compulsory climate emergency classes, with quantifiable activities to ensure that students grasp the ecological crisis in depth. (Levy-Rapoport, 2019.)

Aside from dedicating her energies to fighting climate change, she hopes one day to become an opera singer. For now, fighting climate change has become her life's mission. "Inaction," she wrote, "will not be my epitaph." In seeking to mobilize her nation's youth, she remarked, "A million snowflakes make a blizzard."

Noga Levy-Rapoport's work in fighting climate change illustrates the ability of citizens to form groups and advocate for the policies they support—a key characteristic of liberal democracies.

The United Kingdom is the only liberal democracy studied in AP® Comparative Government and Politics. Elections for members of the House of Commons are free and fair,

AP® TIP

A reminder about how to deal with the statistical details of the country cases: You will be asked to interpret data on the AP® Exam, but don't worry! You do not need to memorize demographic data. The prompts will provide all of the information you need.

BY THE NUMBERS	THE UNITED KINGDOM
Land area	150,680 sq. km
Population	66,052,076 (July 2021 est.)
Urban population	83.9% (2020)
Life expectancy	Male 79.02 Female 83.7 (2021 est.)
Literacy rate	Male 99% Female 99%
HDI	0.932 (2020)
HDI ranking	14/189 (2020)
GDP	$2,638,296,000,000 (2020)
GDP per capita	$40,285 (2020)
GDP per capita ranking	21/187 (2020)
Internet users	94.9% (2018)
Internet users ranking	13/229 (2018)
Gini index (coefficient)	35 (2019)
Freedom House rating	Free (2020)
Corruption Perceptions ranking	11/180 (2021)
Fragile States Index classification	Very sustainable (2020)

Data from *CIA World Factbook*, World Bank, Freedom House, Transparency International, Fragile States Index

and multiple parties compete, although policymaking is controlled by two major parties. The government protects a full range of civil rights and liberties, although discrimination still exists against members of marginalized groups. The United Kingdom is an upper-income country with a large middle class.

Although democratic and prosperous, the United Kingdom faces challenges related to slow economic growth and the ability to provide social and economic opportunity to the disadvantaged. Despite these challenges, the United Kingdom remains a model of democratic government.

Shetland
Islands
• Lerwick

Orkney
Islands
• Kirkwall

Western
Isles
• Stornoway

SCOTLAND

Inverness •
Grampian
Highland
• Aberdeen

Tayside
• Dundee
Central **Fife**
• Glenrothes
Edinburgh
Glasgow • **Lothian**
Strathclyde

Borders
Dumfries and
Galloway **Northumberland**
Dumfries •

Tyne and Wear
• Londonderry
NORTHERN **Cumbria** **Durham**
IRELAND • Belfast
ENGLAND
North Yorkshire

Lancashire
Preston • **West** **East Riding**
Yorkshire **of Yorkshire**
Merseyside Manchester
REPUBLIC Liverpool • **South Yorkshire**
OF IRELAND **Cheshire** **Derbyshire**
Clwyd • Lincoln
Marlock
Gwynedd Stafford
Shrewsbury • Nottingham **Norfolk**
Shropshire **West** • Norwich
WALES **Midlands**
Hereford and Warwick • Cambridge **Suffolk**
Powys **Worcester** • Bedford • Ipswich
Dyfed Gloucester **Essex**
Carmarthen • • Oxford
Gwent — **Greater**
West Glamorgan **Avon** Reading ★ London **London**
Mid Glamorgan **Wiltshire**
Cardiff **Surrey** **Kent**
South Glamorgan
Somerset **Hampshire** **West** **East**
Sussex **Sussex**
Devon **Dorset** **FRANCE**
Exeter Dorchester • Newport
Cornwall **Isle of Wight**
English Channel

Atlantic
Ocean

North
Sea

0   100   200 km
0   50   100 mi

5.1 Sources of Power and Authority

Learning Targets

After reading this section, you should be able to do the following:

1. Describe the development of the state in the United Kingdom.

2. Explain how the United Kingdom democratized gradually over time.

3. Describe the devolution of power in the United Kingdom.

4. Explain why the United Kingdom faces challenges to its sovereignty and legitimacy.

A Brief History of the United Kingdom

Many of the most important developments in the history of liberal democracy occurred in the United Kingdom, a state that consists of England, Wales, Scotland, and Northern Ireland. The earliest important milestone was the Magna Carta, signed by King John in 1215 under pressure from feudal lords. It included the first right to trial by peers, guaranteed the freedom of the Catholic Church from intervention by the monarch, created an assembly of twenty-five barons that became the first parliament, and guaranteed nobles the right to assemble to discuss any significant new taxes. All of these rights and guarantees were designed to preserve the dominance of the nobility, but they were a significant first step in limiting the monarch's power.

Four centuries later, the greatest threat to the early English monarchs' sovereignty came from religious wars between Protestants and Catholics. After King Henry VIII broke with the Catholic Church in 1534 and established the Church of England (known as the Episcopal Church in the United States), religious conflicts dominated politics for well over a century. This culminated in a civil war in the 1640s that brought to power a Protestant dictatorship under a commoner, Oliver Cromwell. The monarchy was restored after about twenty years, only to be removed again, this time peacefully, by Parliament in the Glorious Revolution of 1688. Slowly the two faiths learned to live under the same government. The Glorious Revolution began a gradual transition in the basis for legitimacy from the traditional monarchy to liberal democracy.

The Glorious Revolution began a dramatic expansion of parliamentary power over the monarch. The following year, Parliament passed a Bill of Rights that substantially expanded the rights of citizenship. From that point forward, Parliament gained increasing power over the monarchy, and the power of the prime minister (PM)—an individual appointed by the king but who worked closely with Parliament—grew significantly. While the power of the elected Parliament increased, political citizenship remained restricted primarily to men with substantial property holdings, less than 5 percent of the population.

During the nineteenth century, the right to vote was extended to the growing middle class. In 1918, the Representation of the People Act granted the right to vote to men over the age of twenty-one and to women over thirty, if they met minimum requirements for owning property. Large-scale efforts from social movements pressured the government to expand the right to vote.

Starting in the mid-eighteenth century, Britain began industrializing. By the nineteenth century, rapid economic transformation helped it become the most powerful state in the world, controlling a global empire. Industrialization expanded the domestic strength of the state and helped create a modern bureaucracy. The government began filling jobs in the bureaucracy through a **civil-service system**, a method of staffing the bureaucracy based on competitive testing results, education, and other qualifications, shifting away from government appointments based on patronage.

In the twentieth century, Britain's democracy expanded the notion of social rights. After World War II, there was a sense that all citizens had shared in the sacrifices necessary to win the war and that citizens should receive benefits from the state they had fought to defend. The British government expanded its **welfare state**, creating programs to benefit the health and well-being of citizens, which increased the size of the bureaucracy and enhanced legitimacy. The National Health Service was created, making access to health care a universal right, plus other universal benefits such as an annual "child allowance" from the government for all parents raising children. New rules instituted in 2013 reduced the number of people eligible for the child allowance, restricting it mainly to parents with incomes of less than 50,000 pounds sterling (about $75,000). The debate over what should and should not be a social right in Britain's liberal democracy continues.

Democratization

The development of the liberal democratic regime in Britain was gradual and occurred over centuries. The constitution in the United Kingdom is not a unified single document. The constitution is a collection of documents, such as the Magna Carta and laws passed by Parliament, along with unwritten rules that are a part of British tradition. The government is organized based on **parliamentary sovereignty**—the principle that parliament's power is supreme and extends over all aspects of the state. Civil rights and liberties are protected because they have existed for a long time, and there is a consensus that once rights are granted, the government should not take them away.

There have been two important recent changes to Britain's democratic regime. The first is the devolution of power from the central government to regional governments, which is discussed later in the chapter. The second major change involves the judiciary, with the creation of an independent Supreme Court in 2005 to serve as a final court of appeals.

Before creation of the Supreme Court, Law Lords in the upper house of Parliament served as the highest court of appeal. The Supreme Court lacks the power of judicial review. This is because the United Kingdom's unwritten constitution is easily amended by Parliament. Even though it lacks the power of judicial review to reverse acts of Parliament, the Supreme Court has the power to overturn executive and administrative actions that violate the rights and liberties of citizens. By creating a high court with independent powers, the United Kingdom further enhanced the protection of rule of law.

A Unitary System with Devolution

The United Kingdom has a unitary system, which means that all power is held by the national government. Because unitary systems centralize power, policymaking can be quicker and more efficient. As you saw in Chapter 2, unitary systems may devolve some powers to regional governments.

Civil-service system
A method of staffing the bureaucracy based on competitive testing results, education, and other qualifications, rather than patronage.

Welfare state
Government programs to benefit the health and well-being of citizens.

Parliamentary sovereignty
The principle that parliament's power is supreme and extends over all aspects of the state.

In Scotland, Brexit led to renewed calls for independence. Here, demonstrators in Glasgow gather in March 2019 to show that they favor a new referendum.

Jeff J Mitchell/Getty Images News/Getty Images

The difference between a unitary system with devolved powers and a federal system is that regional power is constitutionally protected in a federal system. In a unitary system, the national government has the authority, at least in theory, to take back all of its power.

In 1997, the British Parliament allowed devolution in some policy areas (such as education and social services) to newly created Scottish and Welsh parliaments. In Northern Ireland, however, the relatively poor, Catholic minority was engaged in a long struggle to join the Republic of Ireland. While most Irish secessionists used peaceful tactics, the Irish Republican Army engaged in terror attacks against British targets. The wealthier Protestant majority, supported by the British, prevented Northern Ireland from leaving the United Kingdom. In 1998, the United Kingdom and parties in Northern Ireland signed the Good Friday Agreement. In exchange for an end to hostilities, power was devolved to a newly created assembly in Northern Ireland, which has the authority to make policy over issues affecting the region.

Regions welcomed assemblies, but devolution did not reduce nationalist sentiment, especially in Scotland. The Scottish National Party (SNP) seeks to create an independent Scotland, threatening to break away from the United Kingdom. In 2014, Parliament allowed Scotland to hold a referendum on Scottish independence. English political leaders across the political spectrum campaigned to preserve the United Kingdom. The referendum failed by a vote of 55 to 45 percent.

The 2014 referendum did not end Scottish nationalism. In 2016, voters in the United Kingdom passed the Brexit referendum to leave the European Union. Brexit was very unpopular in Scotland, where 62 percent of voters supported remaining in the EU. Brexit strengthened the independence movement in Scotland, raising questions about whether Scotland will be a part of the United Kingdom in the future.

Legitimacy and Challenges to the State

Starting in the 1960s, the British state slowly gave up some sovereignty to what became the European Union (EU). Its embrace of the EU, however, has always been partial.

The United Kingdom did not adopt the common currency, the euro. In 1975, the United Kingdom held its first national referendum about continued membership in the EU, which at the time was called the European Economic Community (EEC). British voters decided to remain in the EEC by a vote of 67 percent to 33 percent, but by 2016, British sentiment about the EU had changed.

The 2016 Brexit referendum sent economic shockwaves throughout the world and forced Prime Minister David Cameron, a member of the Conservative Party who opposed the referendum, to resign. Those who voted to leave the EU were concerned about what they perceived to be a high rate of immigration. They were also worried that trade rules imposed by the European Commission weakened U.K. sovereignty. "Remainers," who opposed leaving the EU, were worried that ending EU membership would cause severe negative economic consequences.

On June 7, 2019, nearly three years after Britain voted to leave the European Union, beleaguered British Prime Minister Theresa May resigned following a Conservative Party mutiny over her repeated failure to secure a vote in Parliament for a negotiated Brexit. Brexit challenged Britain's political system, long regarded as one of the world's most stable. Parliamentary procedures and both major parties were disrupted by the process, and the final outcome raised concerns about sovereignty, the economy, and even the possible secession of Scotland. After a deal negotiated by British Prime Minister Boris Johnson, the United Kingdom left the EU on January 31, 2020, and entered a transition period that lasted for nearly a year.

Immigration policy is a divisive issue in the United Kingdom. Since World War II, the previously homogenous Britain has seen large-scale immigration from its former colonies in the Caribbean, Africa, and South Asia. More recently, many Eastern Europeans have been able to enter Britain because their home countries are part of the EU, creating a backlash that fed the Brexit vote. A growing debate over the place and role of Muslim immigrants has raised questions about national identity. The government's response to the challenges posed by immigration is likely to impact the state's legitimacy.

Section 5.1 Review

Each section's main ideas are reflected in the Learning Targets. By reviewing after each section, you should be able to

Remember the key points,

Know terms that are central to the topic, and

Think critically about what you have learned.

Remember

- The United Kingdom is a liberal democracy, and the state developed over centuries.
- Democratization in the United Kingdom evolved gradually over time, as Parliament gained more power over the monarch.
- Parliament devolved power to regional assemblies in Wales, Scotland, and Northern Ireland.
- The United Kingdom faces challenges to its sovereignty and legitimacy.

Know

- *Civil-service system:* a method of staffing the bureaucracy based on competitive testing results, education, and other qualifications, rather than patronage. (p. 129)

- *Welfare state:* government programs to benefit the health and well-being of citizens. (p. 129)
- *Parliamentary sovereignty:* the principle that parliament's power is supreme and extends over all aspects of the state. (p. 129)

Think

- Are states more likely to become consolidated liberal democracies when they democratize gradually?
- What were the benefits and drawbacks for the United Kingdom in devolving power to regional assemblies?

....

Free-Response Question: Conceptual Analysis

Answer A, B, C, and D.

A. Define devolution of power.

B. Describe a measure that a government could take to devolve power to regional governments.

C. Explain why a unitary state would devolve power to regional governments.

D. Explain how devolution of power impacts state sovereignty.

5.2 Institutions of Government

Learning Targets

After reading this section, you should be able to do the following:

1. Explain why the prime minister in the United Kingdom has more power than the executive in a presidential system.

2. Describe the function of each chamber of parliament.

3. Explain why the Supreme Court enhances judicial independence and the rule of law.

The United Kingdom has a parliamentary system of government, with fusion of power between the executive and legislature.

The Executive

Monarch
A hereditary ruler who serves for life.

The United Kingdom has a separate head of state and head of government. Although the United Kingdom still has a **monarch**, the position is ceremonial. The king or queen is a symbol of national identity. The monarch provides stability and continuity regardless of which party governs the nation, and he or she encourages patriotism and service.

Technically, the monarch names the prime minister, but he or she has no authority to reject the prime minister, who is chosen by the majority party in the House of Commons. The monarch serves for life. Under a law passed in 2011, upon the death of the monarch, his or her oldest son or daughter becomes the next king or queen.

The hereditary king or queen serves as the head of state and has the technical power to appoint the prime minister. In practice, the head of state appoints the prime minister selected by the House of Commons. Britain's prime minister, who serves as the head of government, oversees the House of Commons and is considered to be one of the most powerful democratic executives in the world.

As you learned in Chapter 4, the prime minister is first elected as an MP in the House of Commons. Parties run leaders in safe districts where the party is overwhelmingly favored to win the seat. MPs are not required to live in the district they represent, although they usually do. The candidates for prime minister are announced by their parties before elections, so a vote for a party is also an indirect vote for the prime minister. After the election, the party that wins more than 50 percent of the vote selects the prime minister. If no party earns more than 50 percent of the vote, the party that earned the most votes will form a coalition with a smaller party so that together they control a majority of the seats. In a coalition government, which occurred most recently in 2010 and 2017, two (and rarely more) parties negotiate an agreement to rule together.

Because the prime minister's party or coalition has a majority of the seats in the House of Commons, he or she never faces divided government, and it is relatively easy to get policies passed. Due to fusion of powers, members of the cabinet are also chosen from the majority party in the House of Commons. The prime minister appoints approximately twenty cabinet ministers who run the individual departments of government.

The PM is supposed to consult the cabinet before making major decisions. These cabinet members are usually called ministers (in the United States, they are called secretaries). The practice of collective responsibility means that all cabinet members must publicly support all government decisions. A cabinet member who cannot do so is expected to resign. For example, during Prime Minister Theresa May's negotiations over the terms of leaving the EU following Brexit, sixteen cabinet members resigned because they could not support her. Because cabinet members are senior leaders of the majority party and MPs, collective responsibility amounts to a mutual agreement to support policies before their formal introduction in Parliament. When all cabinet members are from the same party, once they have agreed to put forth a piece of legislation, it should pass through the legislature quite easily.

The cabinet, especially in a coalition, serves as a check on the PM. In a coalition government, the prime minister must consult with the other party in the coalition about the distribution of "portfolios" (cabinet seats). Normally, both parties in the coalition have some representation in the cabinet.

Besides selecting the cabinet, the prime minister has the power to propose a program of legislation, serve as chief executive of the bureaucracy, set the agenda in foreign policy, act in the capacity of de facto commander-in-chief (even through this is technically a role of the monarch), and call elections. In the United Kingdom until 2011, the maximum term allowed between elections was five years, but a PM could call earlier elections to take advantage of high approval ratings for the party. Boris Johnson called a snap election in December 2019, increasing the Conservative Party's majority, which gave him a mandate to complete Brexit negotiations.

The coalition government that ruled from 2010 to 2015 passed the Fixed-Term Parliaments Act of 2011. The act established fixed, five-year terms for Parliament for the first time in the country's history. The Fixed-Term Parliaments Act does not set a term of office, because elections can be called within a five-year period, but it does set forth a regular election cycle. An early election can occur only if two-thirds of Parliament vote for one, or if a vote of no confidence removes a prime minister and Parliament cannot form a new government in two weeks.

Parliament approved Prime Minister Theresa May's request for an early election in 2017, which she hoped would give her strong popular support to negotiate Brexit. The political risk badly backfired, and her party ended up with fewer seats in the House of Commons than they held before. The new election law clearly increased Parliament's power over the executive and makes coalition government more likely (because the PM cannot call an election when it is likely his or her party will win a majority). (Schleiter and Belu, 2016.)

There are three ways a prime minister can be removed from office. He or she could lose the popular vote for a seat as an MP in Parliament. This is almost impossible, because prime ministers are run in districts filled with voters who support their party. A more common means of removing unpopular PMs is for the majority party to replace them. This has happened twice since 2010. In that year, Prime Minister David Cameron resigned after losing the referendum vote he called on whether Britain would remain within the European Union. Within days, Theresa May emerged as the cabinet minister with the strongest support among Conservative MPs (the majority party) and was duly approved by the queen as the new prime minister. May became the second woman to hold the position of prime minister. Facing strong opposition to her Brexit strategy, and having survived three votes of no confidence, May stepped down as party leader and PM in June 2017. Conservative Party members chose Boris Johnson as party leader and Johnson was named prime minister.

Note that control of the executive branch changed hands (though it remained within the same party) without a national election. In both cases, this happened when the PM had become exceptionally unpopular, so the change reflected popular will at least to some extent.

A prime minister can also be removed through a vote of no confidence. The majority or opposing party may call for a vote of no confidence. A vote of no confidence also occurs after a major piece of legislation supported by the prime minister and cabinet fails. There is strong party discipline in the United Kingdom, which means that political parties have a great degree of control over how their members vote. The failure of a major piece of legislation means that some of the MPs from the majority party or coalition broke with the government and voted against the proposal. The vote of no confidence that follows such a political reversal is a vote on whether the prime minister and cabinet should remain in office.

Votes of no confidence are rare, because disagreements are usually resolved before a vote on a major policy proposal. A vote of no confidence is far more likely in a coalition government. If the smaller party in the coalition is unhappy with a PM's policies, it can leave the coalition, causing the coalition to lose its majority.

A successful vote of no confidence requires calling new elections for all members of the House of Commons. MPs who cross party lines will be punished by their party, and the party will not sponsor them in the new election. MPs are understandably hesitant to risk their own jobs by supporting a vote of no confidence.

The prime minister's formal powers are extensive, but in the United Kingdom's liberal democracy, he or she must maintain the support of the party and, ultimately, of the voters to maintain the authority to rule. Removing a prime minister in a parliamentary system is not easy, but it is much more likely than removing the executive in a presidential system through a difficult impeachment process.

The Legislature

Parliament is bicameral. The **House of Commons** has 650 members. It is the lower house and is the more powerful chamber in policymaking. It has the power to debate and pass legislation, approve the budget, hold committee hearings, and formally question the prime minister. Members of the House of Commons (MPs) run in districts established by a Boundary Commission based on population. MPs are elected in a plurality SMD system—the candidate who wins the most votes in a district wins a seat in the House of Commons.

As of September 2021, the **House of Lords** had 791 members. It is the upper house of Parliament. Most of its members are appointed by the monarch, on recommendation of the prime minister and an independent commission, the House of Lords Appointments Commission, and they serve for life. With the House of Lords Reform Act of 1999, most hereditary peers lost their seats. Ninety-two hereditary peers in the House of Lords, who had inherited their positions through their families, retained their seats—a remnant of the status of the nobility. Twenty-six members are high-ranking clergy in the Church of England, who serve to hold the government accountable and are often successful at making suggested changes to proposed legislation.

The House of Lords has the power to review and amend bills passed by the House of Commons. The House of Lords may delay budgetary bills for up to a month and other legislation for up to a year. However, the House of Commons can reject suggested amendments, and the House of Lords cannot prevent the House of Commons from eventually passing bills into law.

Compared to the executive in a presidential system, prime ministers have fewer checks on their power. The most powerful check is the ability to remove a prime minister through a vote of no confidence, which is much easier than removing the executive in a presidential system through impeachment.

Parliament has long served an important watchdog function. The PM must attend Parliament weekly for Prime Minister's Question Time, a very lively, televised debate among leading politicians and ordinary members of Parliament. During Question Time, the PM is expected to respond to queries from members of his or her own party and leaders and members of the opposing party and smaller parties. The prime minister must be prepared to defend the government's policies. In addition, MPs have the right to question cabinet

House of Commons
The directly elected lower house of Parliament, which holds most of the policymaking power.

AP® TIP

Regional parties, such as the Scottish National Party, often win some seats in the House of Commons. This is because they dominate elections in certain regions, such as Scotland, and win some SMD seats. Don't mislabel the United Kingdom as a PR system, which is a mistake students commonly make on the AP® Exam. Even though small parties win a few seats in the legislature, the SMD system in the United Kingdom leads to two main parties.

House of Lords
The unelected upper house of Parliament, which has the power to suggest amendments to bills and delay legislation.

AP® TIP

Although they are both upper houses, the House of Lords in the United Kingdom has less power than the Senate in Mexico. Make sure you understand the powers of the legislative chambers in each of the countries studied.

FIGURE 5.2

The Structure of the Government of the United Kingdom
Power in a System with Parliamentary Sovereignty

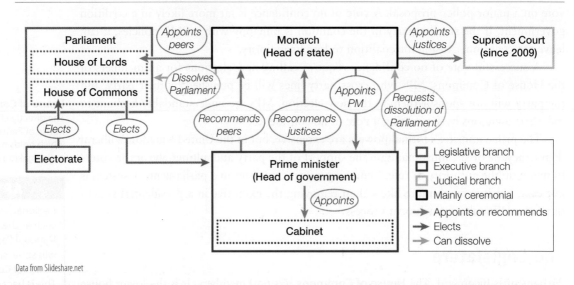

Data from Slideshare.net

ministers about the activities of their departments, who must respond personally in Parliament. This is an opportunity for the public to learn about issues of concern, both large and small. Question Time provides governmental transparency and accountability to the public.

The House of Commons recently created more committees that hold hearings on proposed legislation. The committees allow MPs to investigate the implications of proposed laws, and at times, the majority party will allow legislation to be amended if committees identify problems. Parliamentary debate also provides a means for dissident MPs to voice their opinions and communicate the concerns of their constituents. (Proksch and Slapin, 2015.)

Figure 5.2 shows the structure of the bicameral legislature of the United Kingdom. It also shows the relation between the monarch and the government, as well as who has the power of appointment.

The Judiciary

The United Kingdom has a common-law system in which written judicial opinions serve as precedent for future cases. This enhances rule of law by ensuring that the law is applied consistently and that no one is above the law. In 2009, a separate **Supreme Court** was established. Before 2009, Law Lords in the upper house served as the highest officials in the judiciary. Justices of the Supreme Court are appointed by the monarch based on a referral by the prime minister, following the recommendation of an independent judicial selection commission. Appointments are based on merit, and candidates must have previously served in a high judicial office.

The Supreme Court does not have the power of judicial review, which means it cannot overturn acts of Parliament. However, it has the authority to overturn government actions that violate civil rights and liberties. It can also rule on disputes concerning the devolution of power between the national government and regional assemblies.

Supreme Court
A high court. In the United Kingdom it cannot overturn acts of Parliament but has the authority to protect civil rights and liberties and rule on cases involving devolution.

The Supreme Court was established to create a separation of powers between the judiciary and the fused executive and legislature. The Supreme Court provides the court system with more independence and increases government transparency, enhancing rule of law.

Free-response question 3 on the AP® Exam requires you to compare two of the six countries studied in the AP® Comparative Government and Politics course. The question begins with a brief introduction to the topic. Here is an example:

> One way of checking executive powers is through term limits. Compare the term limits in two different AP® Comparative Government and Politics course countries.

You may choose which countries to compare. It is usually a good strategy to pick countries that provide a strong contrast, because the prompt asks you to compare different countries. Make sure you note the different task verbs in each part of the question.

Part A of the comparative-analysis question usually requires you to define a term or describe a process. Here is a sample part A, along with a response:

> (A) Describe term limits.

> A term limit is a law or constitutional provision that prevents an executive from staying in office after a set number of terms of office have been completed.

In answering part A, begin by using the language in the prompt, such as, "A term limit is . . ." and then use language that is not in the prompt to describe the process, such as "prevents an executive from staying in office after a set number of terms of office have been completed." The response should explain that term limits are set by law or constitutional provisions.

Part B usually requires you to compare processes or institutions in two course countries. Here is a sample part B:

> (B) Explain how term limits differ in two different AP® Comparative Government and Politics course countries.

> In Mexico, the president is limited to one six-year term. In the United Kingdom, there is no term limit for the prime minister, although he or she must call for an election every five years. It is easier for the prime minister in the United Kingdom to stay in office for a longer period than it is for the president in Mexico, who must leave office after six years and, unlike the prime minister, cannot run for reelection.

In answering part B, you have to do three things. First, describe the term limit in one country. Second, describe the term limit in a different country. Third, write a sentence making a direct comparison between the term limits in the two countries.

Part C of the comparative comparative-analysis question requires you to make another comparison between the same countries you used in part B. Here is an example:

> Explain how the term limit in the AP® Comparative Government and Politics course countries discussed in part B impacts the executive's ability to make policy.

Write a response to part C, and do the following:

1. Explain how the term limit in Mexico impacts the president's ability to make policy.

2. Explain how the absence of a term limit in the United Kingdom impacts the prime minister's ability to make policy.

3. Write a sentence making a direct comparison between the two countries.

Section 5.2 Review

Remember

- The prime minister in the United Kingdom has more power than the executive in a presidential system because he or she is from the majority party or majority-party coalition in the House of Commons.
- The elected House of Commons has more policymaking power than the unelected House of Lords, which has the power to suggest amendments to bills and delay legislation.

- Although the Supreme Court does not have the power to overturn acts of Parliament, it increases judicial independence, protects civil rights and liberties, and enhances the rule of law.

Know
- *Monarch:* a hereditary ruler who serves for life. (p. 132)
- *House of Commons:* the directly elected lower house of Parliament, which holds most of the policymaking power. (p. 135)
- *House of Lords:* the unelected upper house of Parliament, which has the power to suggest amendments to bills and delay legislation. (p. 135)
- *Supreme Court:* a high court. In the United Kingdom it cannot overturn acts of Parliament but has the authority to protect civil rights and liberties and rule on cases involving devolution. (p. 136)

Think
- To what extent do the legislature, judiciary, and voters serve as an effective check on the actions of the prime minister in the United Kingdom?

Free-Response Question: Comparative Analysis

Note to Students: This question asks specifically about Mexico and the United Kingdom, because those are the two countries you have studied so far. The comparative-analysis question on the AP® Exam will allow you to use any of the six countries studied in the AP® Comparative Government and Politics course in your response.

Compare how the legislature and judiciary can constrain executive power in Mexico and the United Kingdom. In your response, you should do the following:

A. Define institutional independence.

B. Explain how the legislature can constrain executive power in Mexico and the United Kingdom.

C. Explain how the judiciary can constrain executive power in Mexico and the United Kingdom.

5.3 Electoral System, Political Parties, and Civil Society

Learning Targets

After reading this section, you should be able to do the following:

1. Explain how the United Kingdom's SMD electoral system benefits the Labour and Conservative parties.

2. Describe the two major parties and smaller parties in the United Kingdom.

3. Explain how interest groups in the United Kingdom can impact the policymaking process.

The United Kingdom is a liberal democracy. Elections are free and fair, and political parties can form and run candidates for office. The United Kingdom also has a lively civil society, where citizens can form autonomous groups outside of government control and advocate for the policies they favor.

Elections

MPs are the only directly elected officials at the national level. As you learned earlier, representatives in the House of Commons are elected through an SMD system. Parties run candidates in legislative districts, and the candidate who wins the most votes (a plurality) wins the seat. This is also called a **first-past-the-post (FPTP) electoral system**, because it is like a horse race. The candidate that crosses the finish line with the most votes wins. It doesn't matter if the winning candidate won more than 50 percent of the vote or how many other "horses" are in the race. There is only one winner. FPTP is also called a winner-take-all system.

The SMD/FPTP system in the United Kingdom results in two dominant parties—the Labour Party and the Conservative Party. A third party, the Liberal Democrats, offers a middle ground between the two major parties, but it is disadvantaged by the SMD voting system. As an extreme example, suppose the Liberal Democrats earned 30 percent of the vote nationwide but did not earn the most votes in any district. In this scenario, the Liberal Democrats would not earn a single seat in the House of Commons. Between 1974 and 2010, the Liberal Democratic Party won between 15 and 25 percent of the vote, but always a much smaller share of seats, thanks to the FPTP electoral system.

Although the electoral system in the United Kingdom usually results in one of the two major parties winning a majority of seats in the House of Commons, the SMD system does not guarantee a majority. In 2010, neither major party was very popular. The two major parties' combined share of the vote fell to just over 65 percent, the lowest total in decades. Despite the effects of FPTP, decreasing support for the two major parties denied either party a parliamentary majority, resulting in a coalition government for the first time since World War II. The Conservative PM, David Cameron, invited the Liberal Democrats to join his government to form a parliamentary majority. Cameron, who had advocated a more pro-Europe position for Conservatives and whose coalition government was being criticized for not sufficiently limiting immigration, decided to promise an up-or-down vote on Brexit if his party won the next general election in 2015.

In the 2015 election, the incumbent Conservatives secured a majority in Parliament and the Liberal Democrats' vote share collapsed. They won only eight seats, showing that their 2010 strength clearly had been in part a "protest vote" against both major parties. Once the Liberal Democrats were part of government, their support evaporated. As the traditional third party lost votes, two others gained: the Scottish National Party and the United Kingdom Independence Party (UKIP).

The coalition government from 2010 to 2015 was the first since World War II, and the 2017 election came close to producing another. It resulted in a "hung parliament," meaning that the Conservatives won the most seats but fell just short of a majority. As a result, they made a deal, though not a formal coalition, with the Democratic Unionist Party (DUP) in Northern Ireland, which agreed to shore up the Conservative majority by supplying their ten MP votes on key issues, including the budget and Brexit, in exchange for support for their own economic policies. (Tonge, 2017, 412–416.)

The 2019 parliamentary election ended coalition government and returned the Conservative Party to dominance. The Conservative Party earned 43.6 percent of the popular vote and secured an eighty-seat majority in the House of Commons. Figure 5.3 on page 140 shows how the electoral system in the United Kingdom disadvantages smaller parties, especially when their popularity is not concentrated within a certain region. An SMD system is less likely to result in coalition government than a PR system, in which several parties must cooperate to form a majority in government.

First-past-the-post (FPTP) electoral system
Another term for an SMD plurality system, in which the candidate with the most votes wins the seat in a legislative district. This is also called a winner-take-all system.

FIGURE 5.3

The 2019 Parliamentary Election, Comparing Percentages

Votes, 2019 Election   Seats in House of Commons, 2019

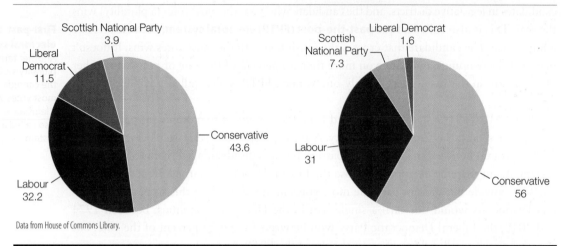

Data from House of Commons Library.

Political parties whose voters are concentrated within a certain region, such as the Scottish National Party, are not disadvantaged by the SMD system. Although the SNP won 3.9 percent of the votes in the 2019 parliamentary elections, the party received 7.3 percent of the seats in the House of Commons. This is because the party was able to capture the most votes in several districts in Scotland.

Regional parties in the United Kingdom are not popular enough nationwide to control a majority in the House of Commons, but they may be in a position to join a majority-party coalition if the Labour or Conservative Party does not earn more than 50 percent of the seats. In contrast, other smaller parties in the United Kingdom, such as the UKIP, have supporters scattered across the country but they do not typically command sufficient support to win in a given constituency. Smaller parties, like the UKIP, that do not have a regional base of support are disadvantaged by the SMD-FPTP rules. Although they may command significant vote share overall, they are not usually able to win many seats in Parliament, because the only way to win a seat in a district is to defeat the candidates from both major parties.

Political Parties

Political parties in the United Kingdom are private entities with national and local branches. One of Britain's two major parties usually wins a majority of legislative seats. Government is always controlled by either the Labour Party or the Conservatives.

The Labour Party's initial organization was unusual, because it was created by unions that wanted to give workers a voice in Parliament. Union members were automatically party members through their union membership, whatever their individual party preference. Initially, unions controlled 90 percent of the voting power in the party, so they could set the party's policy agenda. The Labour Party advocated socialism and supported the establishment of a welfare state. As labor unions declined in power in the 1980s, the Labour Party became a moderate party on the left. Party rules made it harder for labor unions to control Labour's proposed policies, and the party abandoned socialism in favor of a regulated free market.

Under PM Tony Blair, who was elected prime minister in 1997 with a Labour victory, the party enacted democratic reforms, including the devolution of power to regional assemblies. The Labour Party lost control of the government in 2010. Like the Conservatives, the Labour Party was split over the issue of Brexit. Labour leaders suggested that they would recommend a second referendum on Brexit, if they were able to win back control of government in 2017 (which they did not).

The Conservative Party, which is also called the Tory Party or the Tories, began in the late eighteenth century. It is the party on the political right, and originally it was founded to represent the elite. However, the party has always been practical. The Conservative Party expanded the welfare state following World War II and supported the Labour Party's creation of the National Health Service (NHS).

During the 1980s, under PM Margaret Thatcher, the Conservatives advocated free-market reforms, fewer regulations on businesses, and a reduction in welfare programs, which they claimed were wasteful and inefficient. With the election of David Cameron as PM in 2010, the Conservative Party became more centrist on domestic policy issues, but it faced divisions over the role of the United Kingdom in the European Union. Cameron resigned as PM in 2016, following voters' approval of the Brexit referendum, which Cameron had opposed. The Conservative Party replaced Cameron with PM Theresa May.

Until recently, parties in the United Kingdom were highly disciplined in the legislature, meaning that MPs almost always vote in support of their party's position on legislation. This is partly an effect of the parliamentary system. Ambitious MPs want to become cabinet ministers, and the head of the party controls these positions. In an effort to become future party leaders, MPs demonstrate loyalty to the current party leadership. As head of the majority party, the prime minister can usually get legislation passed with ease.

Since the 1970s, though, party discipline has slowly declined. The number of times at least one MP voted against the party has grown, reaching 39 percent of all votes under the coalition government of 2010–2015. (Russell and Cowley, 2016.) Before the 1970s, prime ministers never saw Parliament defeat a legislative proposal entirely, but since then, every prime minister has suffered a defeat at least once. Theresa May suffered multiple defeats over her Brexit plans as MPs, even in her own party, openly defied her.

May survived no-confidence votes by Conservative MPs in 2018 and the full Parliament in 2019. In the end, May had to resign over her inability to pass a plan for exiting the European Union. Conservative Party members chose Boris Johnson, a strong proponent of Brexit, to replace May. He quickly quarreled with MPs, expelling many critical Conservative MPs from the party, and attempted to prorogue (suspend) Parliament for five weeks in September and October 2019. About two weeks into the suspension, the Supreme Court ruled it invalid.

In October 2019, an agreement was reached with the EU extending the timeline for the United Kingdom's departure to January 31, 2020. At midnight on that date, the United Kingdom left the European Union. (Walker.) The aftermath of Brexit may affect the future of Britain's two-party system.

Minor parties in the United Kingdom seeking nationwide support are disadvantaged by the SMD electoral system. The traditional third party, the Liberal Democrats, is the party ideologically positioned between Labour and the Conservatives, and it is a haven for those unhappy with the two major parties. Because it appeals to voters through the country, it fails to capture many seats in Britain's electoral system.

The United Kingdom Independence Party, largely reliant on voters in England, saw its star rise and peak (at least for now) in 2015. Its longtime leader, Nigel Farage, was a leader of the successful campaign for Brexit through the 2016 referendum, as he and the

party rode a wave of populist support for anti-immigration policies. Farage stepped down after the referendum, however, and one analysis concluded that while UKIP successfully pursued the targeted referendum campaign, the party did not have the resources, experience, or capabilities to turn support into seats in Parliament. (Cutts et al., 2017.) The success of a new Brexit Party led by Farage in the 2019 EU elections suggests that many UKIP votes may have been based on his personal popularity. The Brexit Party has since renamed itself Reform UK.

Besides the minor parties that try to appeal to the whole country, the United Kingdom also has several regionally based parties. The SNP arose with Scottish nationalism. It has controlled the government in Scotland most of the time since devolution gave the region its own parliament in 1999. Although it lost the 2014 referendum on Scottish independence, the SNP's membership swelled dramatically after that loss, and it subsequently swept Scotland's seats in the U.K. Parliament in 2015. People in Scotland voted to remain in the European Union in the Brexit referendum, enhancing the movement for Scottish independence. Similar to the SNP, Plaid Cymru is the Welsh nationalist party, which advocates that Wales become an independent state.

As of 2020, the Democratic Unionist Party and Sinn Fein are the two main parties in the Northern Ireland Assembly. Sinn Fein is an Irish nationalist party, which runs candidates in both Northern Ireland and the Republic of Ireland, and it favors the reunification of Ireland. The DUP is a socially conservative party that favors union with the United Kingdom and opposes Irish nationalism.

Although he has been a highly influential politician, leading the United Kingdom out of the European Union, Nigel Farage hasn't made it into the House of Commons. From 1999 to 2020, he served as a member of the European Parliament. Although successful as a politician, he could not make UKIP successful as a parliamentary party. UKIP's supporters are scattered throughout the country, and it had difficulty winning a plurality of votes in the SMD system used in the United Kingdom. UKIP has won only a single seat in the House of Commons.

Danny Lawson/PA Images/Getty Images

In early 2019, a *New York Times* headline blared, "Is Britain's Political System Breaking?" (Castle, 2019.) From the beginning, the pressures of Brexit seemed to be crashing in on the historically stable, predictable party system in Parliament. PM David Cameron resigned the day after the national Brexit vote. A 2017 election resulted in the second hung parliament of the twenty-first century (there were only four from 1900 to 1999). In 2018 and 2019, Conservatives tried (and failed) to oust their leaders through no-confidence votes. Conservative cabinet members resigned over PM Theresa May's proposed Brexit agreements, and Parliament repeatedly refused to pass any Brexit proposal, even when given a choice of several options. In early 2019, a handful of Conservative and Labour MPs resigned from their parties. It's too soon to tell whether these challenges represent a short-term response to the Brexit vote or signal a long-term weakening of Britain's party system.

Interest Groups and Social Movements

The United Kingdom is a liberal democracy with a pluralist system, meaning that interest groups have the right to freely form and advocate for the policies they favor. Historically, the United Kingdom had a corporatist interest-group system. Remember from your study of Mexico that in a corporatist system, certain large interest groups are sanctioned by the government and included in the policymaking process. In the United Kingdom, business and labor are each represented by one major association—the Confederation of British Industry (CBI) for business and the Trades Union Congress (TUC) for labor.

In the 1960s and 1970s, the Labour Party consulted regularly and formally with both the CBI and the TUC to set wages and other economic policies. The limited ability of both groups to control their members, though, resulted in widespread strikes in the 1970s and in Labour's electoral defeat in 1979 at the hands of Margaret Thatcher, the new Conservative leader. Thatcher immediately ended the corporatist arrangements and largely shunned not only the TUC but also the CBI, preferring the advice and support of various conservative think tanks and ideological pressure groups.

Because decision making in Britain's parliamentary system is centralized in the cabinet, interest groups focus much more on lobbying the executive than the legislature. Interest groups that lobby MPs are mostly trying to gain access to cabinet members. The influence of a particular group depends on which party is in power. The prime minister decides which groups he or she is willing to work with in making policy.

Despite some limitations on the ability of interest groups to directly influence Parliament, the United Kingdom has a pluralist system. Interest groups have multiple methods of influencing policy, such as petitioning, gaining attention through traditional and social media, contributing to campaigns, and holding protests. British interest groups can have a powerful influence. (Moosbrugger, 2012.) The main farmers' union worked with relevant ministries to block several significant environmental policies that would hurt farmers, even though the vast majority of people in the United Kingdom supported the proposed changes.

The number of environmental, women's, antinuclear, and racial justice groups has exploded since the 1960s. At the same time, the TUC in particular has declined as its membership base of labor-union members has diminished. Recently, the Brexit movement has been very influential, crossing multiple parties and mobilizing people to protest and vote for fundamental changes that impact Britain's sovereignty and economic policies.

Section 5.3 Review

Remember

- The United Kingdom's SMD electoral system benefits the Labour and Conservative parties.
- The United Kingdom has a two-party system, with smaller national and regional parties.
- Interest groups in the United Kingdom use various methods to impact the policymaking process.

Know

- *First-past-the-post (FPTP) electoral system:* another term for an SMD plurality system, in which the candidate with the most votes wins the seat in a legislative district. This is also called a winner-take-all system. (p. 139)

Think

- What are the challenges facing the United Kingdom's two-party system in the future?

Free-Response Question: Quantitative Analysis

2019 Parliamentary Elections, House of Commons

Party	Percent of Seats	Percent of Votes
Conservatives	56	43.6
Labour	31	32.2
Liberal Democrats	1.6	11.5
Scottish National Party	7.3	3.9

Answer A, B, C, D, and E.

A. Using the data in the table, identify the political party with the highest percentage of seats in the House of Commons.

B. Using the data in the table, identify the political party with the biggest gap between the percentage of votes received and the percentage of seats earned in the House of Commons.

C. Describe a first-past-the-post/single-member district election system.

D. Using the data in the table, draw a conclusion about how a FPTP/SMD system impacts the number of parties that are able to control government.

E. Explain what the table illustrates about regional or minor parties.

5.4 Political Culture and Participation

Learning Targets

After reading this section, you should be able to do the following:

1. Describe the referendums sent to voters in the United Kingdom, and explain how the outcome of those referendums affected the political system.

2. Describe the civil rights and liberties protected in the United Kingdom, and describe the discrimination faced by religious and ethnic groups.

3. Explain how social and political divisions impact the political system.

In the United Kingdom's liberal democracy, citizens have many opportunities for political participation. Citizens vote for members of Parliament and regional assemblies. They also have a direct say on policy issues by voting on referendums. People enjoy a full range of constitutionally protected civil rights and liberties. However, despite a high level of freedom, social divisions and inequality remain.

Referendums

Referendum
A vote on a policy issue sent by the government to the people.

A **referendum** is a vote on a policy issue sent by the government to the people. Referendums give citizens a direct say in approving policy. Referendums enhance citizens' political efficacy and strengthen the government's legitimacy.

In the United Kingdom, the government does not have to abide by referendum results, because of parliamentary sovereignty. In theory, the prime minister and the rest of the government could decide to ignore a vote by the people. However, doing so would risk losing the next election.

The first nationwide referendum ever held in the United Kingdom occurred in 1975, when voters approved U.K. membership in the European Economic Community, two years after the United Kingdom joined the common market that would later become the EU.

Some referendums have addressed regional power. In 1997, regional referendums were sent to voters in Scotland and Wales, who approved the creation of regional assemblies as a part of the central government's devolution plan. In 1998, voters in Northern Ireland approved

FIGURE 5.4

A Timeline of Brexit

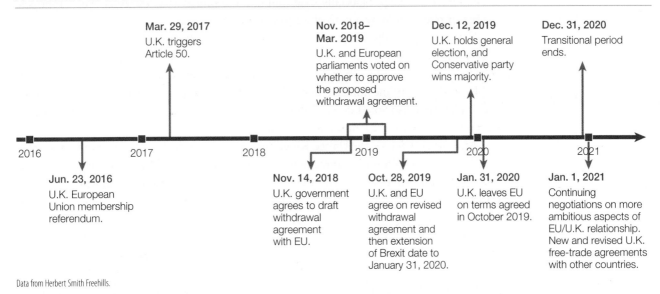

Mar. 29, 2017
U.K. triggers Article 50.

Nov. 2018–Mar. 2019
U.K. and European parliaments voted on whether to approve the proposed withdrawal agreement.

Dec. 12, 2019
U.K. holds general election, and Conservative party wins majority.

Dec. 31, 2020
Transitional period ends.

2016 2017 2018 2019 2020 2021

Jun. 23, 2016
U.K. European Union membership referendum.

Nov. 14, 2018
U.K. government agrees to draft withdrawal agreement with EU.

Oct. 28, 2019
U.K. and EU agree on revised withdrawal agreement and then extension of Brexit date to January 31, 2020.

Jan. 31, 2020
U.K. leaves EU on terms agreed in October 2019.

Jan. 1, 2021
Continuing negotiations on more ambitious aspects of EU/U.K. relationship. New and revised U.K. free-trade agreements with other countries.

Data from Herbert Smith Freehills.

the Good Friday Agreement and a simultaneous referendum creating an assembly in Northern Ireland. In 2014, a referendum was sent to voters in Scotland about whether to establish Scotland as an independent state. The proposal failed, with a vote of 55 percent to 45 percent. The failed referendum did not end Scottish nationalism or the independence movement.

In 2011, voters rejected a nationwide referendum that would have changed the method for electing members of Parliament to an alternate voting system in which voters would rank candidates in order of preference. The proposal was favored by the Liberal Democrats, because, as you have seen, the SMD system disadvantages those minor parties that try to gain support nationwide (as opposed to regional parties). Because most voters identify with one of the two major parties, it is not surprising that they rejected a proposal that would have weakened the relative power of the Labour and Conservative parties.

The Brexit referendum of 2016 and its aftermath are controversial. (See Figure 5.4.) In 1973, the United Kingdom joined the European Economic Community, which became the EU in 1992 with the signing of the Maastricht Treaty. The EU is a supranational organization. States join voluntarily and agree to the rules of the organization. In doing so, they voluntarily give up the power to make policy in specific areas. They are willing to give up sovereignty over specified policy areas because they believe the benefits of membership are worth it. Countries must apply for membership, and they must be democratic enough to be accepted. Citizens of EU member countries elect representatives to a European Parliament.

The EU sets policy in three areas: (1) the European economic community, (2) justice and home affairs, and (3) foreign relations and collective security (including immigration). EU members must abide by the decisions of the European Court of Justice.

The EU created a common market, which means that EU member countries act mostly like a single economy, with free trade and travel. Products made in EU member countries can be exported and sold with few restrictions throughout the EU. The United Kingdom never adopted the euro, the EU's common currency, which means it was never fully integrated into the EU and did not give up sovereignty over its monetary policy.

In joining the EU, the United Kingdom voluntarily gave up some sovereignty in exchange for the benefits of membership. By 2016, a majority of British voters decided that the loss of sovereignty, especially over immigration policy, was too great. They approved the Brexit referendum by a vote of 52 percent to 48 percent.

Voting to leave the EU was much easier than negotiating an exit agreement. Prime Minister Theresa May triggered Article 50 of the Treaty on European Union, which allows countries to leave the EU. Prime Minister May's exit plans were voted down three times. In May 2019, the prime minister stepped down and was replaced by Boris Johnson, whose Brexit plan was also voted down. Johnson called for new parliamentary elections, and on December 12, 2019, the Conservatives won in a landslide.

After several delays, the United Kingdom formally left the European Union on January 31, 2020, once a withdrawal agreement had finally been passed by Parliament, and began a one-year transition period. The EU-UK Trade and Cooperation Agreement took effect on January 1, 2021. It covers topics such as trade in goods and services, digital and intellectual property, infrastructure, energy, fisheries, security, defense, and intelligence sharing.

Brexit demonstrates both the benefits and drawbacks of referendums. Referendums allow citizens to have a direct say in policymaking. This increases political participation and efficacy. Referendums enhance the government's legitimacy, because they are a way for the government to respond to citizens' demands, making people less likely to rebel. Failed referendums can undercut regional movements for independence, at least temporarily. However, as Brexit demonstrates, proposals passed by citizens may be difficult to put into effect, and their long-range consequences may not be apparent for years.

Civil Rights and Civil Liberties

The unwritten constitution of the United Kingdom provides for the full protection of civil rights and civil liberties. In addition to national laws, regional assemblies have also passed legislation protecting human rights. People have civil liberties, such as freedom of expression, including speech, assembly, and the press. Newspapers regularly criticize the government without repercussions. The United Kingdom does not restrict access to the internet or social media or censor content, although hate speech is banned. Although the British Broadcasting Corporation is state-funded, it is guaranteed its independence. This sets it apart from the state-sponsored media in less democratic states. Workers are free to organize and form labor unions. Citizens are free to practice their religious beliefs. Although Protestant Christianity is the official state religion, and twenty-six members of the House of Lords are high-ranking clergy, the church is not actively involved in policymaking.

Those accused of crimes are afforded due-process rights. In certain high-crime areas, police have the authority to stop suspects without reasonable cause. Authorities are required to inform detained persons of the charges against them, although terrorism suspects may be held for fourteen days without being charged with a crime. Defendants are presumed innocent, and indigent defendants have the right to free legal counsel if they cannot afford it.

The United Kingdom also protects a wide array of civil rights. Women, ethnic and religious minorities, the disabled, and LGBTQ persons are guaranteed equal treatment under the law and protected from discrimination. The law criminalizes rape, domestic violence, and female genital mutilation (FGM), which has occurred within some refugee communities. Medical professionals are required to report cases of FGM. Sexual harassment is a criminal offense. There are also laws against child abuse, child trafficking, and forced labor. (U.S. Department of State, 2019.)

The United Kingdom fully protects human rights under the law, but members of minority religious and ethnic groups have been targeted for violence and discrimination. For example, according to a report by the NGO Community Security Trust (CST), anti-Semitism is on the rise. In 2019, 158 violent anti-Semitic assaults were reported, a 25 percent increase over 2018. There were 88 reports of desecration or damage to Jewish property, 98 anti-Semitic threats, and 1,442 incidents of abusive behavior, including graffiti and face-to-face and online hate speech. (U.S. Department of State, 2019.)

Although the law prohibits discrimination based on race or ethnicity, the Romani people and persons of Middle Eastern, African, Afro-Caribbean, and South Asian descent have reported mistreatment and discrimination. Continued tension between whites and nonwhites in the United Kingdom is a legacy of its colonial history. Racial tensions are also reflected in views on immigration, which are more negative in the United Kingdom than in most of the rest of Europe. (Migration Observatory, Public Opinion.) "Right to rent" laws require landlords in England to verify the legal immigration status of their tenants. The Supreme Court ruled that the law discriminates against noncitizens, although the law is still in place. (U.S. Department of State, 2019.)

Verbal abuse and violence against Muslims is a continuing problem. This tension is partly a result of U.K. support for the wars in Iraq and Afghanistan. It increased following bombings of buses and subways in London, which were carried out by Islamic extremists on July 7, 2005. The Home Office reported that there were 3,530 hate crimes against Muslims in England and Wales in 2018–2019. Social media and tabloid newspapers are sources of hate speech. They continue to disseminate biased, unfounded misinformation about Muslims. Scotland penalizes religious hatred through the mail, on the internet, and at soccer matches. (U.S. Department of State, 2019.)

Divisions in the United Kingdom

British political culture is often characterized by emphasizing its stability and the willingness of citizens to accept the authority of the state. Gabriel Almond and Sidney Verba's 1963 book *The Civic Culture* was based on a broad survey of citizens of five countries in North America and Europe, including the United Kingdom. The authors argued that more stable and democratic countries, such as the United Kingdom, had a civic culture. This meant that their citizens held democratic values and beliefs that supported their democracies. These attitudes led citizens to participate actively in politics but also to defer enough to the leadership to let it govern effectively. Despite the long-term stability of the state, several political and social divisions exist in the United Kingdom.

Anyone who has watched the historical drama *Downton Abbey* has some idea of class divisions in Britain in the early twentieth century. The British have long recognized class differences as a significant component of their society. As in all of Europe, the main class division before the nineteenth century was between the landed aristocracy and the peasantry. Industrialization created the early bourgeoisie—business owners who grew wealthy but had no aristocratic title—and an industrial working class.

British class distinctions went beyond economic status. The aristocracy sent their children (initially, only boys) to expensive private boarding schools (confusingly for Americans called "public" schools because, for the aristocracy, they replaced having private tutors at home). Their height of influence was in the nineteenth and twentieth centuries. These schools educated the students who would go on to the universities of Oxford and Cambridge, known informally as Oxbridge, from which almost all of the economic, social, and political elite of the country emerged.

Students at Eton College, an elite "public" school founded in 1440. In English usage, public schools are private schools attended by children of the upper class. Public school attendance is seen as a way to gain an advantage in college admissions, running for office, and working in business and industry.

Grant Rooney Premium/Alamy

Class distinctions were also clear from social symbols—accent, manners, preferred sports, and preferred entertainment. After World War II, the government created large-scale public housing for the working class to rent at subsidized rates. This created another clear class distinction, with middle- and upper-class people generally owning their own homes while most working-class people lived in neighborhoods of publicly provided rental housing.

While the traditional industrial working class shrank as the United Kingdom became an advanced service economy, people continue to see class as an important characteristic that distinguishes people by occupation, income, education, and attitudes. The BBC launched an online survey in 2011 to which millions responded. The survey showed that while the great majority thought class still mattered in many ways, only a third of respondents were willing to identify their own class position. (Savage et al., 2015.) The number of times the media and political parties mentioned class distinctions plummeted from the 1970s to 2010. (Evans and Tilley, 2017.)

Class is still important, but not as much as in the past. The Conservative Party used to be associated with the elite class, while working-class people tended to vote for the Labour Party. In recent years, working-class voters are more likely to vote on the basis of nationalism than on class-based politics.

As you learned in the discussion of political parties, regional separatist movements and groups demanding greater autonomy have emerged as a result of social and religious divisions within the United Kingdom. Wales, Scotland, and Northern Ireland each have their own language and culture distinct from other parts of the United Kingdom. Further, 45 percent of the people living in Northern Ireland are Catholic. According to a poll conducted by Lord Ashcroft Polls in 2017, 51 percent of those living in Northern Ireland support reunification with the Republic of Ireland. (McCarthy, 2019.)

Power has been devolved to local assemblies in each region, and they have been given significant policymaking authority. For example, Scotland runs its own health service. The question is whether devolution of power has done enough to satisfy secessionist movements.

The Scottish National Party favors independence from the United Kingdom and supported the failed regional referendum on Scottish independence in 2014. In the 2016 Brexit referendum, Scotland voted 62 percent to 38 percent to remain in the European Union. Voters in Northern Ireland also rejected Brexit, by a vote of 56 percent to 44 percent. The Brexit referendum strengthened nationalist movements in both regions, and Scotland may request a second referendum on independence in the future.

The United Kingdom remains a stable liberal democratic state, with multiple opportunities for political participation and legal protection of a wide range of civil rights and liberties. Nevertheless, divisions within the state may pose a challenge to its sovereignty in the future.

Section 5.4 Review

Remember

- The United Kingdom uses referendums to allow citizens to decide questions about policy issues.
- A wide range of civil rights and civil liberties is protected in the United Kingdom; nevertheless, ethnic and religious groups still face discrimination.
- Social and political divisions, including social class and separatist movements, continue to influence the political system in the United Kingdom.

Know

- *Referendum:* a vote on a policy issue sent by the government to the people. (p. 144)

Think

- How did the Brexit referendum and its aftermath impact state legitimacy in the United Kingdom?
- What further steps can the United Kingdom take to ensure that the civil rights and civil liberties protected by law are respected in practice?

....

Free-Response Question: Quantitative Analysis

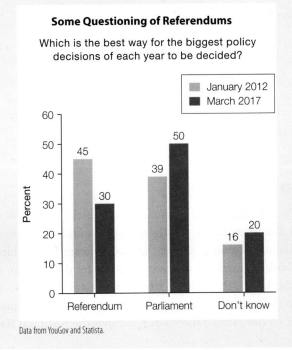

Some Questioning of Referendums

Which is the best way for the biggest policy decisions of each year to be decided?

January 2012
March 2017

Referendum: 45, 30
Parliament: 39, 50
Don't know: 16, 20

Percent

Data from YouGov and Statista.

5.5 Economic and Social Change and Development

Learning Targets

After reading this section, you should be able to do the following:

1. Describe the United Kingdom's economic policies in the period following World War II.

2. Explain how the United Kingdom liberalized its economy in the late twentieth century.

3. Describe the social welfare state in the United Kingdom, including the National Health Service.

4. Describe demographic changes in the United Kingdom.

5. Explain why the United Kingdom will face challenges in the future.

Regulated market economy
An economy in which wages, prices, and production are mostly set by supply and demand, with some regulation, and mostly private control of businesses and natural resources.

National Health Service (NHS)
The government-financed and managed health-care system in the United Kingdom.

The United Kingdom has a **regulated market economy**, in which wages, prices, and production are mostly set by supply and demand, with some government regulation, and mostly private control of businesses and natural resources.

Globalization

Following World War II, the global economy grew quickly. From World War II to the 1970s, the United Kingdom had a mostly market economy, but the government was prominent in managing economic activity with significant ownership of the means of production. The Bank of England was nationalized by the Labour government after World War II. In the 1940s, the Labour government nationalized several major industries in addition to the central bank, such as airlines, mining, automobile manufacturing, and telephone service. Simultaneously, it created the **National Health Service** and built government-owned housing for millions of working-class people. These social programs gained popular support after World War II because of a sense of shared sacrifice in the war effort. Most citizens believed the country needed a less class-based, more egalitarian society.

The strong economy in the global boom after World War II fell apart in the 1970s, a period of unparalleled economic crisis in the United Kingdom. Rising oil prices and a global recession hit the country particularly hard, reducing growth and increasing inflation. As inflation grew, unions demanded that wage increases keep up with prices, which fueled more inflation. Unions and management could not find common ground in reaching collective-bargaining agreements. This culminated in the "winter of discontent" in 1978–1979, when the Labour government lost control following massive strikes.

Margaret Thatcher led the Conservatives to victory in the 1979 election. She won by promising a new approach to economic policy, unions, and the welfare state. Unions were her first target. Parliament passed legislation making it much more difficult for unions to strike and reducing their organizational power. The coal and steel industries were privatized, and most coal plants were closed, destroying many of the country's coal-mining communities.

The Thatcher government privatized state-owned companies. She began selling off the state-owned companies to private investors, ultimately privatizing 120 corporations. Some became profitable private-sector companies, yet others simply went bankrupt. Unemployment increased as the unprofitable companies laid off workers. Unemployment rose from an average of 4.2 percent in the late 1970s to 9.5 percent in the 1980s. (Huber and Stephens, 2001, A11.) Prime Minister Thatcher also privatized a great deal of Britain's publicly owned housing for the working class, selling much of it to tenants.

The Thatcher government shifted the source of taxation, reducing individual and corporate income taxes and compensating by raising Britain's national sales tax (the value-added tax, or VAT). This increased the tax burden on lower-income groups and reduced taxes on the wealthy. Her programs did not significantly reduce the size of the government's budget or social spending.

Even though social spending did not drop, inequality increased more in the United Kingdom under Thatcher than in any other wealthy country. The share of the population living on less than half of the average national income increased from 9 to 25 percent under Thatcher and has since dropped only slightly. (Ginsburg, 2001, 186.) Regional inequality increased a great deal as well. Many of the unprofitable state-owned companies and older manufacturing firms were in the northern half of the country. Thatcher's reforms hurt that region severely, causing increased unemployment and poverty, while the southern part of the country, especially London, became one of the wealthiest regions in Europe.

Thatcher's reforms reshaped the British economy by making it more of a market economy, and subsequent governments continued economic-liberalization policies. The Labour government (1997–2010) took its most dramatic action immediately after coming into office—it gave autonomy to the Bank of England to set monetary policy. If you took AP® U.S. Government and Politics, you learned that the Federal Reserve is a similar independent body with the authority to make monetary policy.

After 2002, the government invested more heavily in education and job training in a successful effort to lower the unemployment rate, which dropped to 5.5 percent. A policy to eliminate child poverty elevated more than 1 million children out of poverty between 2005 and 2007, although overall inequality was reduced only slightly.

The United Kingdom had unprecedented economic success until the financial crisis of 2007–2009. GDP growth averaged 2.6 percent annually, well above other European countries. Inflation averaged only 1.5 percent; the deficit was kept low; and the United Kingdom attracted more direct foreign investors. (Faucher-King and Le Galès, 2010.)

The Recent Economy in the United Kingdom

The exceptional economic success up to 2007 was partly based on the financial, stock, and real estate markets. All of these markets were heavily hit by the global financial crisis that occurred between December 2007 and 2009. The British economy shrank nearly 5 percent in 2009, and unemployment hit 8 percent—up from 4.5 percent a couple of years earlier. The government responded with large infusions of cash to struggling banks and then with a stimulus program, mainly through tax cuts, that dramatically increased the deficit. These measures failed, and the Labour Party lost its majority in the May 2010 election, which brought a Conservative-led coalition government to power.

Austerity measures
Raising taxes and/or cutting spending in an effort to reduce the deficit and the national debt.

The new government quickly reversed course on economic policy and enacted **austerity measures**, raising taxes and cutting spending to reduce deficit spending and the national debt. The government argued that the country's growing debt threatened to undermine Britain's financial standing in the global economy. The government instituted spending cuts, averaging 19 percent. The government also raised the retirement age, required those on long-term unemployment benefits to actively seek work, and capped unemployment benefits at one year. Protests erupted several times after the announcement of the new policies. University students rallied against major tuition increases.

Thousands of people turned out for a 2016 protest in Central London against the government's austerity measures, which cut funding for social services.

Stefan Rousseau/PA Images/Alamy

The only sectors spared the ax were the National Health Service and primary and secondary education. In 2011, the government increased the value-added tax—the biggest tax average citizens pay—to reduce the deficit. Though the economy slipped into a second recession in 2012, by 2014 growth was up to about 3 percent and unemployment was falling.

In the aftermath of the 2016 Brexit vote, the pound plummeted to a thirty-year low and forecasts predicted falling GDP growth. The pound did not regain its pre-Brexit strength, but by 2019, it was above the low it reached in late 2016, when it traded at $1.46. (Statista.) By late 2018, years of spending cuts to policing, housing, and welfare had taken a toll. Local governments, whose funds had been slashed and were reluctant to raise taxes, were cutting services to the legal minimum and some were facing bankruptcy. Recognizing that the situation could not be sustained, Theresa May declared that "austerity is over," promising that, once a successful Brexit was achieved, the government would boost investment in public services while keeping the debt burden low.

Brexit led to fears that the vast financial sector would shrink as banks shifted their activities to EU member countries. (London is second only to New York in global banking.) There are also concerns that Britain's extensive trade with the rest of Europe would drop significantly. The full economic impact of Brexit on the U.K. economy may not be apparent for several years.

The COVID-19 pandemic, which began in late 2019, posed a daunting challenge for the United Kingdom and the rest of the world. The Johnson government was criticized for not responding quickly enough or seriously enough early in the pandemic. However, after Boris Johnson was hospitalized with COVID-19, the government took stronger measures to reduce the spread of the virus.

As 2020 unfolded, the government gave conflicting advice about social gatherings, mask wearing, and how safe it was to attend school. The government did not ban large gatherings until March 13, two and a half months after the first death occurred. On March 17, Boris Johnson predicted that the United Kingdom could "turn the tide" on the virus by summer 2020. On March 23, a lockdown was announced. On April 13, the death total hit 20,000, but the government did not encourage people to wear masks in public spaces until May. In early September, the United Kingdom recorded its highest level of infections, and on November 1, England went into a second lockdown. By the end of 2020, the economy declined sharply, and a new, more contagious, strain of the virus had appeared.

In early January 2021, Prime Minister Boris Johnson announced that children should no longer attend school. On January 7, the death toll reached 100,000. (McMullan et al., 2021.) On February 3, 2021, AstraZeneca, a pharmaceutical company based in the United Kingdom, announced that its COVID-19 vaccine was highly effective in preventing severe disease and hospitalization. The AstraZeneca vaccine joined others on the market in the fight against COVID-19.

Social Policies

The United Kingdom is a welfare state, which means the government provides benefits aimed at improving citizens' standard of living. These benefits include the Universal Credit, which provides income and housing assistance for low-income individuals. Income assistance is also available for low-income individuals over the state retirement age and people who cannot work because of disabilities. Child tax credits are available to those who qualify. A system of unemployment insurance provides benefits to people who have lost their jobs. The largest social welfare policy, in terms of budget and the number of people who benefit, is the National Health Service. (CABA.)

In a nationalized health-care system, the government owns clinical facilities and hospitals. The majority of medical professionals are paid directly by the government, which controls the cost of medical care by setting standard payments for procedures, equipment, and drugs.

The NHS traditionally functioned like one giant managed-care system. It signed contracts with general practitioners (GPs) in each region of the country to deliver primary services to patients. British patients can sign up with the GP of their choice, usually in their neighborhood, who provides basic care and functions as a gatekeeper, referring them to a specialist or hospital as needed. Most services (except for some pharmaceuticals) are free to the patient at the point of service, having been paid for by general taxes.

No one can opt out of the NHS, because it is funded by general taxation, but patients can buy private supplemental insurance that allows them to see private doctors and get hospital services without the delays in receiving care of the public system. As people in the United Kingdom have grown wealthier and have demanded more health care, a growing number have supplemented NHS coverage with private insurance. Over the decade from 2008 to 2018, about 11 percent of the population typically had private insurance. Patients can use the NHS for routine illnesses and private insurance for procedures that have long waiting lines in the NHS. Some of the recent growth in private insurance may be due to growing concerns about wait times and reflects class differences, with wealthy people more likely to purchase private insurance.

Reforms in 2012 replaced regional authorities, who used to negotiate for health-care services for their constituents, with groups of general practitioners. The government claimed the reforms would reduce administrative costs by a third and make the NHS more efficient. These groups of doctors handle most of the NHS budget and purchase services for their patients. They can use tax money to purchase services from NHS hospitals or private hospitals and specialists. Competition works only if knowledgeable people operate in the market, and it was not clear that groups of physicians were up to the task. Many feared that the reform would lead to privatization of the system and create greater inequities. However, fears of privatization appeared to be unfounded. With little real competition in the system, the vast majority of services continued to come from within the NHS. (Ham and Murray, 2015.)

The NHS allows the national government to control the costs of medical procedures and drugs. The NHS remains very popular with British citizens, but some people are unhappy with long wait times for certain procedures. The NHS is facing a funding crisis, because, as you will learn later in this chapter, the average age is increasing, people are living longer, and there is an increase in the number of older people. At the same time, the number of new workers is not growing fast enough to generate enough tax revenue to make up for the increased expenses.

Britain's 2016 vote to leave the EU may also impact the NHS. An economic downturn would harm funding for the NHS. Furthermore, a significant number of medical practitioners in the system are citizens of other EU countries whose continued status in the United Kingdom would be uncertain.

Graphs provide a way to display data, and they can help explain trends better than a table with numbers. Line graphs are often used to show trends over several years. Here is an example of a line graph that shows the Gini Index (coefficient) in the United Kingdom from 1999 to 2019. On a line graph, the horizontal *x*-axis is often divided into time intervals. In this case, the graph reports data over five-year periods. The vertical *y*-axis on a line graph usually represents a numerical range of data.

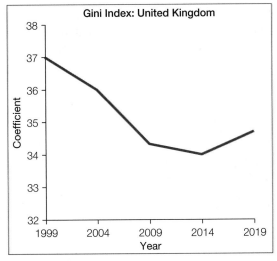

Gini Index: United Kingdom

Data from World Bank and Statista

Remember that the Gini Index measures income inequality, with zero representing perfect equality and 100 indicating absolute inequality. The first graph shows that income inequality in the United Kingdom decreased slightly from 1999 to 2014 and then rose a little in 2019.

The next graph is based on the same data, but the *y*-axis has been extended.

The second graph makes it appear that income inequality dropped sharply between 1999 and 2014, which is not

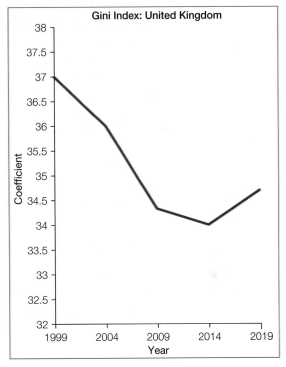

Gini Index: United Kingdom

Data from World Bank and Statista

accurate. In examining graphs, look carefully at the horizontal and vertical axes to determine whether or not the scale is appropriate. A distorted horizontal or vertical axis may be a signal that the person who made the graph wants the data to appear more or less dramatic.

1. How would the trend in the first graph appear if the *x*-axis were extended?

2. Why would someone intentionally create a distorted graph?

3. What are some steps you can take to prevent yourself from being misled by distorted graphs and charts?

Shifting Demographics

Two population shifts are having a big effect on the United Kingdom—immigration, and an aging population. Migration from other countries is the main source of population growth. (Office for National Statistics.) In 2019, 9.5 million people born in other countries lived in the United Kingdom, representing 14 percent of the population. Sixty-two percent of immigrants came from countries outside of the EU, and India was the most common birth country for immigrants. Seventy percent of migrants are working-age adults between 26 and 64. (The Migration Observatory, Overview.) Before the Brexit referendum in 2016, polls identified immigration as the biggest issue facing the United Kingdom. In 2019, 44 percent of people supported reducing the level of immigration.

Because most immigrants are of working age, citizens worry that immigrants will take jobs away from British citizens. Some people are also concerned that recent immigrants are not adopting British culture and values. Anti-Muslim sentiment also influences the debate on immigration. In addition to concerns about the loss of sovereignty, Brexit was a result of concerns about too many new immigrants coming to the United Kingdom.

Another important population shift is the rise in the average age. Over the next twenty years, the number of people 65 and older is estimated to grow by nearly 50 percent, which is about 4.75 million people. The fastest growing group will be those above age 85. (AgeUK.) Older people use the services provided by the NHS more often. They have more illnesses, and their health conditions are often complicated and expensive to treat.

In 2019, the largest age group in the United Kingdom was 50–54, a group that is approaching retirement age. The working population has grown more slowly, reducing the growth of tax revenue available to pay for the NHS. Demographic pressure on the NHS will likely lead to efforts to reform the system by reducing services, encouraging more competition, or increasing privatization.

The United Kingdom and the Future

The United Kingdom is likely to remain a stable liberal democracy. As a high-income country, the United Kingdom has large middle class. However, the Brexit referendum, coupled with COVID-19, will likely slow economic growth.

People in the United Kingdom enjoy extensive civil liberties and have a strong sense of political efficacy. If the government does not deliver on its promises, voters will hold it accountable through free and fair elections.

Despite being a consolidated democracy, the United Kingdom faces continued challenges. An aging population will strain the health-care system. Immigrants, nonwhites, Jews, and Muslims have been the targets of violence, hate speech, and discrimination. Nationalist movements, particularly in Scotland, will likely continue to advocate for autonomy and even independence. The government in the United Kingdom will have to find ways to ensure equal treatment for everyone and appease nationalist sentiments.

The United Kingdom left the European Union as a response to a vote by the people. Time will tell whether the citizens made a wise decision, as the United Kingdom seeks to protect its sovereignty while maintaining its place in the global economy and its connection with the rest of Europe.

Section 5.5 Review

Remember

- The government in the United Kingdom actively managed the economy and established a welfare state after World War II.
- The United Kingdom adopted neoliberal economic reforms in the late twentieth century.
- The social welfare state in the United Kingdom includes the National Health Service.
- Immigration and an aging population are sources of demographic change in the United Kingdom.

- Although it is a stable democracy, the United Kingdom will face challenges to its democratic ideals in the future.

Know

- *Regulated market economy:* an economy in which wages, prices, and production are mostly set by supply and demand, with some regulation, and mostly private control of businesses and natural resources. (p. 150)
- *National Health Service (NHS):* the government-financed and managed health-care system in the United Kingdom. (p. 150)
- *Austerity measures:* raising taxes and/or cutting spending in an effort to reduce the deficit and the national debt. (p. 152)

Think

- What are the biggest social and economic challenges the United Kingdom will face in the future?

Free-Response Question: Conceptual Analysis

Answer A, B, C, and D.

A. Define economic liberalization.

B. Describe an economic-liberalization policy in the United Kingdom.

C. Explain why the United Kingdom maintains a welfare state.

D. Explain how demographic pressures may impact the welfare state in the United Kingdom.

AP® KEY CONCEPTS

- Civil-service system (p. 129)
- Welfare state (p. 129)
- Parliamentary sovereignty (p. 129)
- Monarch (p. 132)
- House of Commons (p. 135)
- House of Lords (p. 135)
- Supreme Court (p. 136)
- First-past-the-post (FPTP) electoral system (p. 139)
- Referendum (p. 144)
- Regulated market economy (p. 150)
- National Health Service (NHS) (p. 150)
- Austerity measures (p. 152)

AP® EXAM MULTIPLE-CHOICE PRACTICE QUESTIONS

1. Which of the following is an accurate statement comparing the executive in Mexico and the United Kingdom?

    A. The head of state in Mexico is a ceremonial position, and the head of state in the United Kingdom is in charge of policymaking.

    B. The president in Mexico is a member of the legislature, and the prime minister in the United Kingdom is separate from the legislature.

    C. The term limit for the executive in Mexico is six years, and the term limit for the prime minister in the United Kingdom is five years.

    D. The prime minister in the United Kingdom is indirectly elected, and the executive in Mexico is elected directly.

2. Which of the following is an accurate statement about the legislature in the United Kingdom?

    A. Both chambers are elected directly and have significant policymaking authority.

    B. The upper house represents the elite and has more power over policymaking than the lower house.

    C. The lower house has the authority to pass legislation, and the upper house has the power to delay legislation and suggest amendments.

    D. Law Lords in the upper house serve on the Supreme Court and have the power to strike down legislation passed in the House of Commons.

Questions 3 and 4 refer to the graphic.

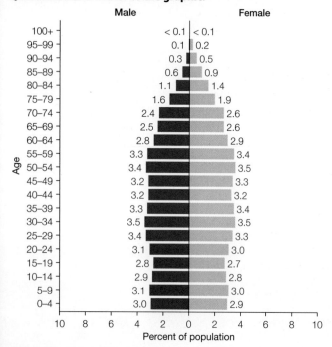

Data are 2019 figures from populationpyramid.net

3. Which of the following is an accurate statement according to the graphic?
   A. The fastest-growing age group in the United Kingdom is people from 90 to 94.
   B. There are fewer people aged 20–24 than aged 50–54.
   C. The birth rate in the United Kingdom dropped in every five-year period since 1990.
   D. In the United Kingdom, men, on average, live longer than women.

4. Which of the following is an implication of the graphic?
   A. The National Health Service will face challenges from an aging population.
   B. People under the age of 30 will have difficulty finding employment in the next two decades.
   C. The National Health Service provides better medical care to men than it does to women.
   D. Slow economic growth has resulted in a low birth rate in the United Kingdom.

5. Which of the following is the most serious threat to sovereignty in the United Kingdom?
   A. There is a strong seccessionist movement in Wales.
   B. Brexit has reduced the ability of the United Kingdom to make economic policies.
   C. Despite a failed referendum on independence, Scottish nationalism remains strong.
   D. New immigrants from Africa and the Caribbean are seeking increased autonomy.

6. Which of the following accurately describes the judiciary in the United Kingdom?
   A. The courts are based upon a code legal system, and the Supreme Court has the power to overturn acts of Parliament.
   B. Judges lack independence because they are appointed based on their political views.
   C. The United Kingdom uses a common-law system, which enhances rule by law.
   D. The Supreme Court has the authority to overturn administrative actions that violate civil liberties.

Questions 7 and 8 refer to the quote.

> For decades, British companies have struggled to respond to competition from elsewhere in the EU, with some household names disappearing. British Leyland, the once mighty car manufacturer, and ICI, the industrial conglomerate, are just two of the titans that have collapsed. But those that have survived have often emerged stronger.
>
> —Chris Giles, "What Has the EU Done for the UK?" *Financial Times*, March 31, 2017

7. Which of the following is supported by the main idea of the passage?
   A. U.K. membership in the EU harmed noncompetitive British businesses.
   B. Membership in the EU benefits large industries and harms small, local businesses.
   C. Increased competition within the EU damages the global market for manufactured goods.
   D. Voters supported Brexit because the EU reduced market competition.

8. Which of the following is an implication of the argument made in the passage?
   A. The United Kingdom should have remained in the EU, because the benefits of membership outweigh the drawbacks.
   B. Leaving the European Union will likely cause a recession in the United Kingdom.
   C. As a result of EU policies, noncompetitive businesses were weeded out, and those that remained benefited.
   D. British voters supported Brexit because they were unfamiliar with the brand names of products produced in other European countries.

9. Which of the following accurately describes the executive's ability to make policy in presidential or parliamentary systems?

   A. The executive's ability to make policy in a presidential system is limited by the cabinet.

   B. A prime minister is better able to get policies passed than a president because a prime minister is a member of the majority party or majority party coalition.

   C. Presidents have the power to propose a program to the legislature, which makes it easier for them to pass policies than prime ministers, who must rely on the cabinet to propose policy.

   D. The cabinet in a presidential system may pass legislation without the approval of Congress, but in a parliamentary system, the executive must rely on parliament to pass legislation.

10. Which of the following describes a social policy in the United Kingdom?

    A. Citizens who live below the poverty level are guaranteed a certain level of benefits for life.

    B. Health care is free only for those citizens who cannot afford it.

    C. Tuition is free for students who meet certain academic standards and pass national assessments.

    D. Medical care is state-sponsored and available to everyone at no direct cost.

AP® EXAM PRACTICE ARGUMENT ESSAY

Develop an argument as to whether unitary or federal systems result in more effective policymaking.

Use one or more of the following course concepts in your response:

- Devolution
- Authority
- Legitimacy

In your response, do the following:

- Respond to the prompt with a defensible claim or thesis that establishes a line of reasoning using one or more of the provided course concepts.
- Support your claim with at least TWO pieces of specific and relevant evidence from your study of the United Kingdom. The evidence should be relevant to one or more of the provided course concepts.
- Use reasoning to explain why your evidence supports your claim or thesis, using one or more of the provided course concepts.
- Respond to an opposing or alternate perspective, using refutation, concession, or rebuttal.

For a complete list of the sources of information cited in this chapter, turn to the Works Cited appendix.

① Mexico

② United Kingdom

○ Russia

○ Nigeria

○ China

○ Iran

NOTE TO STUDENTS:

Unit 2 Review covers what you learned in Chapters 1 through 5. As you continue on in the book, unit reviews become more cumulative. For example, the Unit 2 Review focuses mostly on what you learned in Chapters 4 and 5, but it will also test your knowledge from Unit 1.

As you complete each unit, you will have more knowledge and be able to make more connections between concepts and countries. As your knowledge and skills build over time, the unit reviews become more complex, and the questions cover more of the content you will encounter on the AP® Exam.

AP® EXAM PRACTICE QUESTIONS

Section 1: Multiple Choice

Some of these review questions refer to the six countries studied in AP® Comparative Government and Politics. You have studied only Mexico and the United Kingdom. Because some of the questions in this unit review are conceptual, knowledge about the other countries is not necessary to answer the questions.

1. Which of the following statements is a correlation?
   A. A single-member district system results in the creation of two dominant political parties.
   B. The Gini coefficient measures the level of income inequality in a country.
   C. Newly created democracies should adopt parliamentary systems of government because these systems rarely encounter gridlock in policymaking.
   D. A coup occurs when a high-ranking military official takes over government, replacing the current leader.

Questions 2 and 3 refer to the passage.

> The government did not restrict or disrupt access to the internet or censor online content, and there were no credible reports that the government monitored private online communications without appropriate legal authority. The [United Kingdom] has no blanket laws covering internet blocking, but the courts have issued blocking injunctions against various categories of content such as depictions of child sexual abuse, promotion of extremism and terrorism, and materials infringing on copyrights.
>
> By law the electronic surveillance powers of the country's intelligence community and police allow them, among other things, to check internet communications records as part of an investigation without a warrant.
>
> —U.S. Department of State, *2019 Country Reports on Human Rights Practices: United Kingdom*

2. Which of the following is supported by the main idea of the passage?
   A. The government of the United Kingdom does not censor the internet, and there are no restrictions on electronic content.
   B. Although the United Kingdom provides for freedom of expression, government authorities actively monitor citizens' use of the internet.
   C. Certain types of harmful content are not protected by free-speech laws in the United Kingdom.
   D. The Supreme Court in the United Kingdom has the power to overturn administrative actions that violate citizens' rights to freedom of expression in the internet.

3. Which of the following statements is an implication of the passage?
   A. The United Kingdom is not a liberal democracy, because it restricts certain types of expression.
   B. Laws in the United Kingdom try to balance civil liberties with the need for order and safety.
   C. Citizens who believe their reputation has been damaged by online content have the right to bring a lawsuit in civil court.
   D. The judiciary in the United Kingdom is subservient to Parliament, which has the power to pass legislation limiting the authority of the courts over the internet.

4. Which of the following is the most accurate measure of transparency and accountability in government?
   A. GDP per capita, because it serves as a rough measure of average income, allowing citizens to see how well they are doing financially compared to others.
   B. The Corruption Perceptions Index, because it measures citizens' beliefs about whether government officials are abusing their power.
   C. The Human Development Index, because it is an aggregate measure that takes several factors into account.
   D. The Gini coefficient, because it measures income inequality, which enables citizens to see the economic impact of government policies.

5. Which of the following is an accurate statement about an executive in a country studied in AP® Comparative Government and Politics?
   A. The legislature is separate from the executive in Mexico, while there is a fusion of executive and legislative power in the United Kingdom.
   B. The prime minister in the United Kingdom is more powerful than the president in Mexico, because the prime minister has the power to rule by decree.
   C. Mexico's president has the power to deploy troops, but the prime minister in the United Kingdom must rely on the minister of defense to deploy troops.
   D. Mexico's president is the head of government, and the prime minister in the United Kingdom is the head of state.

Questions 6 and 7 refer to the table.

Countries Ranked by Gross Domestic Product

Country	2020 GDP (in millions/USD)	Rank (out of 195)
China	14,860,775	2
United Kingdom	2,638,296	5
Russia	1,464,078	11
Mexico	1,040,372	16
Iran	610,662	22
Nigeria	442,976	27

Data from International Monetary Fund, 2020 estimates.

6. Which of the following is accurate according to the table?
   A. China has the highest-ranked GDP of the countries shown.
   B. Iran and Nigeria are both middle-income countries.
   C. The United Kingdom no longer has one of the top-ten world economies.
   D. Democratic states have lower GDPs than authoritarian states.

7. Which of the following is a limitation of the data shown in the table?
   A. The table is biased toward countries that adopt economic-liberalization policies.
   B. The data do not provide information about economic growth rates, which makes it difficult to measure the economic trajectory of each country.
   C. GDP per capita is a vague measure, because each country uses a different formula to calculate GDP per capita.
   D. The table does not provide an explanation of how country rankings were determined.

8. Which of the following is an accurate statement about an economic concept studied in AP® Comparative Government and Politics?
   A. Import substitution industrialization policies encourage foreign direct investment.
   B. Austerity measures improve the lives of citizens by lowering taxes and increasing social spending.
   C. Economic-liberalization policies reduce government regulations on businesses and encourage free trade.
   D. Democratic governments do not nationalize health care, because nationalized health care is a socialist policy.

9. Which of the following is an accurate statement about a concept studied in AP® Comparative Government and Politics?
   A. Charismatic leadership is the main source of legitimacy in the United Kingdom.
   B. Scotland is a state, because the Scottish people share a strong sense of history, culture, and identity.
   C. President López Obrador's election in 2018 represents regime change in Mexico, because a new political party gained control of the government.
   D. A change in government occurred when the Conservative Party in the United Kingdom replaced Prime Minister Theresa May with Boris Johnson.

10. Which of the following best explains why the United Kingdom is considered to be a liberal democracy?
    A. The United Kingdom is classified as a very stable state, and it is free from serious internal divisions.
    B. It has a high level of human development, with a large middle class.
    C. The executive in charge of policymaking is directly elected by the people.
    D. Free and fair elections are held for the House of Commons, and civil rights and liberties are protected by the government.

Questions 11 and 12 refer to the passage.

> It's just not codified. It's not drawn together in any single form. But like any other nation, we have a lot of statutes; that is, acts of Parliament that bind. And we go along with quite a number of conventions as well that constrain, that people comply with. They have no legal force, but they are complied with because they're morally correct. They're necessary . . . to make the system work.
>
> —Lord Phillip Norton, National Public Radio, September 5, 2019

11. Which of the following is supported by the main idea of the passage?
    A. The United Kingdom has an unwritten constitution, which provides a framework for the political system.
    B. Acts of Parliament are binding laws that are not part of the constitution in the United Kingdom.
    C. A convention must be held to amend the British constitution.
    D. People in the United Kingdom comply with the law, even though their civil rights and liberties are not formally protected.

12. Which of the following is an implication of the passage?

  A. An unwritten constitution makes it difficult for citizens to determine which rights and liberties are protected, leading to uncertainty in the judicial system.

  B. The political system in the United Kingdom works effectively, in the absence of a single constitutional document.

  C. Although the British people are accustomed to having an unwritten constitution, they would prefer a single written document.

  D. An unwritten constitution works well in the United Kingdom, but other democracies could not function without a single written constitution.

13. Which of the following is an accurate statement regarding a concept studied in AP® Comparative Government and Politics?

  A. A nation is a set of institutions with control over territory.

  B. A civil-service system enhances democracy, because it provides a way for citizens to participate in politics.

  C. Without the power of judicial review, courts cannot act independently.

  D. Power is the ability of a government to make citizens do something they might not otherwise do.

14. Which of the following is an accurate statement about sovereignty?

  A. States voluntarily give up some sovereignty when they join supranational organizations.

  B. The free press in Mexico challenges the sovereignty of the government by criticizing the actions of government officials.

  C. The United Kingdom lost some sovereignty over trade policies by leaving the European Union.

  D. The Scottish independence movement is not a threat to sovereignty in the United Kingdom, because the government might voluntarily allow Scotland to leave the United Kingdom.

15. Which of the following best describes the relationship between the national government and regions in course countries studied in AP® Comparative Government and Politics?

  A. Mexico and the United Kingdom are unitary governments, with significant devolution of power to regional and state assemblies.

  B. Mexico has always been a federal system, and the United Kingdom became a federal system when it devolved power to regional assemblies in Northern Ireland, Scotland, and Wales.

  C. State power is constitutionally protected in Mexico, but in the United Kingdom, Parliament may take back powers devolved to regions.

  D. In both Mexico and the United Kingdom, power is becoming more centralized in the national government.

16. Which of the following best describes the system for electing the House of Commons?

  A. MPs are elected through a plurality, single-member district system.

  B. MPs are appointed by the monarch, based on a recommendation of the prime minister and an independent commission.

  C. The House of Commons uses a mixed electoral system, in which individual candidates run for office in single-member districts and some seats are awarded through proportional representation.

  D. To win a seat in the House of Commons, a candidate must earn more than 50 percent of the vote.

Questions 17 and 18 refer to the graph.

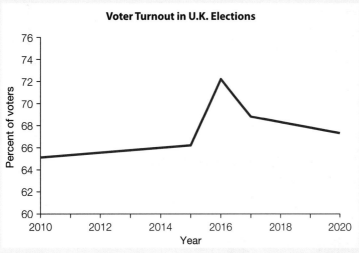

Voter Turnout in U.K. Elections

Data from Statista.
Note: Parliamentary elections took place in 2010, 2015, 2017, and 2019, and the Brexit referendum was held in 2016.

17. Which of the following is an accurate statement according to the graph?

   A. Voter turnout in the United Kingdom is lower than turnout in most liberal democracies.

   B. Voter turnout in parliamentary elections has varied significantly from election to election.

   C. The lowest level of voter turnout occurred in 2015.

   D. The highest level of voter turnout occurred in 2016.

18. Which of the following is an implication of the graph?

   A. Referendums are not an effective method of increasing political efficacy.

   B. Voters were more engaged in the Brexit referendum than they have been during elections for Parliament.

   C. Turnout is lower in elections when the party in power is likely to win.

   D. Voter turnout would likely increase if British citizens could directly elect the prime minister.

19. Which of the following describes a significant demographic change in a course country studied in AP° Comparative Government and Politics?

   A. Following the Brexit referendum, the government in the United Kingdom voted to stop new immigration from countries with predominantly Muslim populations.

   B. The aging population in the United Kingdom increases the unemployment rate, because older workers are retiring at high rates.

   C. People in Mexico are migrating from the south to the north, and from rural areas to urban areas.

   D. In both Mexico and the United Kingdom, emigration rates exceed immigration rates, because people are seeking better economic opportunities in neighboring countries.

20. Which of the following statements regarding term limits is true?

   A. There are no term limits for the head of government in either Mexico or the United Kingdom.

   B. In the United Kingdom, there is a term limit for the head of government, but the head of state serves for life.

   C. In Mexico, the president is limited to a single term, while in the United Kingdom, the head of government can serve multiple terms.

   D. In both Mexico and the United Kingdom, the lower house has the power to pass legislation extending executive term limits.

Section 2: Free Response

Conceptual Analysis

Answer A, B, C, and D.

A. Define legitimacy.

B. Describe a source of legitimacy.

C. Describe a measure a state could take to strengthen legitimacy.

D. Explain how separatist movements impact legitimacy.

Quantitative Analysis

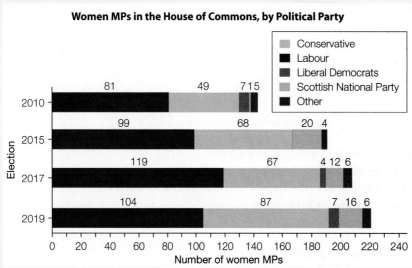

Women MPs in the House of Commons, by Political Party

Data from House of Commons Library.

Answer A, B, C, D, and E.

A. Using the data in the bar chart, identify the year with the highest number of women from the Labour Party in the House of Commons.

B. Using the data in the bar chart, describe a trend in the number of women serving in the House of Commons.

C. Describe the electoral system for the House of Commons.

D. Using your knowledge of the electoral system and the data in the bar chart, draw a conclusion about why most of the women in the House of Commons are from the Labour and Conservative parties.

E. Explain how the government in the United Kingdom could increase the number of women serving in Parliament.

Comparative Analysis

The protection of civil rights and liberties varies depending on regime type.

A. Define civil liberties.

B. Explain how the governments in two of the course countries studied in AP® Comparative Government and Politics protect civil liberties.

C. Explain why each of the two AP® Comparative Government and Politics course countries described in (B) would choose to constrain civil liberties.

Argument Essay

Develop an argument as to whether referendums increase or decrease the strength of the state.

Use one or more of the following course concepts in your response:

- Sovereignty
- Legitimacy
- Nationalism

In your response, do the following:

- Respond to the prompt with a defensible claim or thesis that establishes a line of reasoning using one or more of the provided course concepts.
- Support your claim with at least TWO pieces of specific and relevant evidence from one or more course countries. The evidence should be relevant to one or more of the provided course concepts.
- Use reasoning to explain why your evidence supports your claim or thesis, using one or more of the provided course concepts.
- Respond to an opposing or alternate perspective, using refutation, concession, or rebuttal

For a complete list of the sources of information cited, turn to the Works Cited appendix.

UNIT 3

Political Culture and Participation

In this unit, you will learn about the influence of citizens and their associations on governments. In studying Russia, you should consider the country's long history of religious, ethnic, and linguistic diversity, which sometimes has turned into political cleavages. The city of Kazan is a center of Islam and Orthodox Christianity. Note the minarets in the foreground and the church steeples in the background. About half of the local population speaks Russian and half Tatar.

Extreme-Photographer/iStock/Getty Images

Chapter 6
Political Culture
and Participation

Chapter 7
Case Study:
Russia

Participation

In Unit 3, you will learn how the state and society interact and how this interaction impacts government. Citizens participate in politics both individually and in groups. You will also study how cleavages within the population, such as ethnicity, religion, or class, become political. Unit 3 also examines civil society, which consists of voluntary associations separate from the state. You will learn about participation in both authoritarian and democratic regimes and how regime type affects the methods of participation. This unit explains how and why these processes, systems, associations, and demographics relate to one another. Using these concepts, you will continue to refine the skills necessary for success on the AP® Exam.

After completing Unit 3, you will be able to:

- Describe how civil society interacts with government
- Define political culture
- Explain the difference between political ideology, culture, and beliefs
- Describe formal and informal political participation
- Define civil rights and describe their status in different regimes
- Define civil liberties and describe their status in different regimes
- Describe a political cleavage
- Explain how social cleavages such as ethnicity, religion, and class impact government and politics
- Explain how political and social cleavages impact citizen participation
- Examine government and politics in Russia

Book fairs are a place to hear stories. The Tehran International Book Fair began in 1988 and has been held yearly since (with an interruption by the COVID-19 pandemic). Book fairs are a place for people to connect informally, as members of civil society. Readers can meet authors, and publishers can interact directly with their readerships.

Armin Karami/Middle East Images/Redux

6 Political Culture and Participation

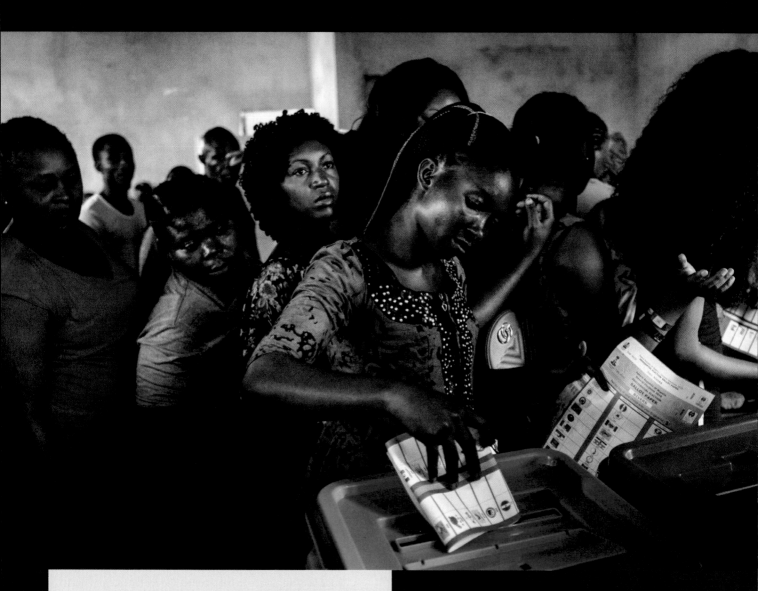

A woman in Port Harcourt, Nigeria, casts her ballot in the presidential and legislative elections on February 23, 2019. Voting is the most common form of political participation.

Yasuyoshi Chiba/AFP/Getty Images

Victory Volunteers of Russia: The Immortal Regiment

Opportunities and forms of political engagement vary by regime type. In democratic countries, participation includes voting in free and fair elections, free speech, freedom of assembly, the right to lobby, to protest, and the right to join all sorts of organizations—some of which may be politically motivated advocacy groups. However, each of these forms of participation can vary. For example, in presidential systems, citizens typically elect the executive directly, while in a parliamentary system, citizens do not directly elect the executive.

Just as there is no one way to organize a democracy, opportunities and forms of civic engagement also vary among authoritarian states. Citizens in authoritarian states often have the right to vote for national officials, although the list of candidates may be restricted. Groups that do form in authoritarian states bear an extra burden, whether they are charitable or political, because they may be suspected as threats to the regime.

Not all groups bear this burden. Some kinds of groups can be used to foster loyalty to the governing regime or to give the impression of widespread public support. By celebrating symbols of nationhood, patriotism can become an effective political tool to build support for political leaders. Even in democratic nations, political leaders ritualistically evoke the symbols of patriotism and nationhood on national holidays.

Leaders in authoritarian regimes often fear that independent groups can develop into influential political challengers. Fear of opposition groups within the nation or from political strife observed in other countries is always present. Russia is an example of an authoritarian state that restricts some forms of citizen participation, to control opposition to the regime. One important example is a 2006 law that lets state authorities deny official registration to any organization that may "create a threat to the sovereignty, political independence, territorial integrity, national unity, unique character, cultural heritage, and national interests of the Russian Federation." (Carnegie.)

Further crackdowns on civil society increased after opposition protests in 2011 that followed contested parliamentary elections. Those groups receiving foreign funding must register as "foreign agents," follow restrictive administrative requirements, and identify themselves in all communication as foreign agents. (Carnegie.)

Yet some groups within Russia have received government support. One example of a spontaneous, citizen-led demonstration that has gained such support is the May 9 observance called the Immortal Regiment that emerged to honor those who fought and died in World War II, known in Russia as the Great Patriotic War. The Immortal Regiment commemorates Russian sacrifices during its war against Nazi aggression from Germany and its allies. This patriotic effort is enthusiastically supported by state officials.

During the Great Patriotic War, 7 million Russian soldiers and civilians died in repulsing the German invasion. Victory Day celebrations were regularly held during the Soviet

A disabled veteran who fought in World War II participates in the Victory Day holiday. Volunteers often present veterans with flowers. In Russia, World War II is known as the Great Patriotic War.

Elena Peremet/Alamy

era, but by the early 1990s, large demonstrations were becoming a thing of the past, and as time went on, fewer and fewer veterans were alive and able to participate.

The Victory Volunteers saw the May 9 Victory Day parades as empty rituals that had more in common with carnivals and flash mobs than a celebration of those who had sacrificed for their country. (Kurilla.) In 2012, they developed an alternative known as the Immortal Regiment to highlight those who fought in the war. To accomplish this, participants were asked to march with photos of their family members, parents, and grandparents, who had fought in the war. Photos of veterans were enlarged, laminated, and attached to poles carried by family members. Although marching with photos of the dead was not completely new, this time, they were immortalized under the banner of the Immortal Regiment.

The 2012 march was televised across the nation, and by 2014, almost a half a million participated. Soon thereafter, Russian authorities took what had been a spontaneous volunteer effort and made it a state-sponsored event. The movement has grown across Russia, the former republics of the Soviet Union, and around the world.

In 2015, on the seventieth anniversary of the end of the war, the Immortal Regiment was granted permission to march across Red Square, the symbolic heart of the country, and Russian President Vladimir Putin joined the march carrying a photo of his father. Putin framed the march as a democratization of Victory Day, which had been previously centered on the Russian military. The Immortal Regiment had become an expression of Russian national unity, and Putin's participation represented his role of head of the Russian family. "I think that my father, just like millions and millions of simple soldiers, he was a simple soldier, had the right to march across this square . . . And hundreds of others, and thousands of other simple people, simple soldiers, laborers [on the homefront], can now take their place on Red Square . . . they've earned this." (Fedor.) By 2019, more than 12 million people, in eighty countries, participated in celebrations honoring Victory Day.

Interpretations vary as to the meaning of the Immortal Regiment and how it has been used by Russian authorities. For some, it is a healthy sign of grassroots participation and family memory. For others, it was a quasi-death cult celebrating war. Still others have noted that Putin's interest came soon after the 2014 Russian annexation of Crimea.

Crimea is a peninsula with an important port that juts into the Black Sea and provides access to the Mediterranean. The Crimean region has had a complicated history of shifting political control. Conquered by the Russians in the late 1700s, it was part of the Russian Republic of the Soviet Union. In the 1950s it became part of the Ukrainian Republic of the Soviet Union, and the majority of its residents are ethnic Russians. With the collapse of the Soviet Union, it had been recognized as part of Ukraine. Russia's annexation of Crimea was condemned as a violation of international law by nations around the world, but within Russia, it became a way to shore up patriotic support for the regime. (Kurilla.)

Mass demonstrations that are independent of state authorities have not been part of Russian politics since the 1917 Revolution. Official state support transformed the Immortal Regiment into a tame form of civic participation. Local officials competed to have the largest marches and handed out photos to be carried by those who do not have relatives to commemorate.

The size of these marches dwarfed periodic anti-government protests. In fact, they represent the largest processions in Russian history, and they have been used by state officials as a sign of political support. Putin's appearance at Victory Day celebrations and references to his father's military service may be a tactic to bolster his legitimacy.

For some, the Immortal Regiment has become a symbol of public unity, but for others, it is seen as a symbol of Russian nationalism in light of the international backlash against the annexation of Crimea. One Russian journalist commented that "[Victory Day] always had a lot of official pomposity, but we were always able to separate our personal feelings from that pomposity. . . . Now it has become harder to do that because the holiday has become suffused with something else. It was always a holiday of memory, of mourning. A holiday full of pain, a holiday with tears in our eyes, as the poet said so well. But now it is full of aggression." (Prokopyeva.)

More generally, the Immortal Regiment has become for some a celebration of a new form of Russian nationalism, as the grassroots movement was co-opted—which means it was taken over by the government to serve the government's purposes. In 2017, one former member of the parliament noted: "The Immortal Regiment was doomed from the moment of its birth. The likelihood that the authorities would tolerate an independent grassroots movement that was becoming national and even international was precisely zero. The transformation of a grassroots initiative into a state ritual and part of the quasi-religious cult of 'victory' began already in 2014. . . . That was the end of the human story of the Immortal Regiment and the beginning of the story of a state ritualistic cult." (Prokopyeva.)

Nevertheless, for many Russians, the Immortal Regiment remains a potent symbol of history, memory, and family, which are important aspects of political culture. The Immortal Regiment and Victory Day marches are also examples of widespread citizen participation that can take place, even in authoritarian regimes.

6.1 Organizations, Culture, and Beliefs

Learning Targets

After reading this section, you should be able to do the following:

1. Explain how civil society contributes to democratic government.

2. Explain how political culture impacts government and politics.

3. Explain how the political ideologies of individualism, neoliberalism, communism, socialism, fascism, and populism differ.

Several factors outside the structure of government can have an impact on the state. These include civil society organizations, which seek to influence government policy. States are also influenced by individual beliefs and a shared political culture.

Civil Society

One of the hallmarks of democratic government is a lively **civil society**—the ability of citizens to form groups outside the government's control. One example of civil-society organizations in democratic governments is interest groups. Similar to political parties, interest groups bring together like-minded individuals to achieve a goal, but interest groups do not run candidates for office. Rather, these associations of individuals or businesses attempt to influence government, and most claim to represent clearly defined interests that their members share, such as protecting the environment, advancing civil rights, or representing various industries. Citizens join interest groups to amplify their voices beyond what a single individual can accomplish in the political process. Such associations also are

Civil society
Groups that form outside the government's control.

often regulated by the government and have to follow certain rules and procedures, such as laws that require the disclosure of campaign contributions. In a pluralist system, interest groups are visible, have relatively large and active memberships, and have a significant voice on the issues in which they are interested.

Competition among interest groups may require policy makers to compromise, which limits the power of government. In theory, if interest groups are effective in carrying out their functions, the political system becomes more responsive and inclusive.

Modern interest groups emerged in the nineteenth century. Labor, business, and agriculture became key interest groups, because they represented the three key sectors of the economy. As more citizens became involved in the political process, other interest groups emerged. Civil-rights interest groups focus on issues important to women, racial, ethnic, and religious minorities, the disabled, older people, and LGBTQ citizens. Other interest groups focus on broad issues, such as animal rights, immigration reform, and protecting the environment.

As more countries become democratic, varied types of civil-society organizations arise. Some civil-society groups have political goals, while others, like a soccer team, are focused on getting people together to share a common, nonpolitical interest. The types and strength of different kinds of groups in civil society have important effects on the health of a democracy.

Analysts have grown increasingly concerned about the strength of civil society, even in well-established democracies. Robert Putnam (2000) expressed concern about a decline in social capital—that is, the social networks and the norms of reciprocity that are crucial to democratic participation. Even apparently nonpolitical organizations (such as the local Little League or parent-teacher organizations) in civil society, he argued, create social networks and mutual trust among members. But face-to-face organizations seem to be declining, weakening one of the bonds of democratic government.

Critics of Putnam argue that new forms of activity have arisen to replace those that have declined. Much of this activity takes place online and involves the use of social media to raise public awareness of issues and to advocate for change.

Civil society in democratic regimes takes place in the public sphere, in which open debate is possible. There are few governmental constraints on either the groups that form or their activities, as long as they engage in nonviolent actions.

Although authoritarian regimes allow civil society to exist, it is limited and repressed. Civil society in authoritarian states is tightly controlled and monitored by the government. Authoritarian states encourage groups that benefit the regime and limit or ban groups critical of the regime. Authoritarian states may require NGOs to register with the government and closely monitor their behavior.

Nevertheless, civil-society groups in authoritarian states may attempt to challenge the government through protests (when possible), and through the internet and social media. These efforts may be effective in calling the government's

Members of the Nigerian women's soccer team celebrate. The Super Falcons won the 2018 Women's Africa Cup of Nations tournament, their ninth time in twenty years. Sports teams are an example of civil-society organizations, which are groups that operate outside government control. Civil-society organizations contribute to democratic government, even when they are not political, because they bond citizens together based on common interests.

AP Images/Alade Omowunmi

attention to local problems, especially on issues in which the government has expressed an interest, such as pollution and corruption.

Authoritarian states may pass vague laws that allow the state to target groups critical of the government. Groups that go too far in criticizing the government may be disbanded, and their leaders may face prosecution. By reducing or eliminating negative information about the government, authoritarian regimes seek to maintain their legitimacy and power.

Political Culture, Ideology, and Beliefs

A **political culture** is a set of widely held attitudes, values, and beliefs about government and politics. It provides people with ways to understand government and politics. Political culture develops throughout the history of the state. It can change over time, although it usually changes slowly because it is often deeply embedded in a society through cultural or religious traditions. Political culture can also be influenced by geography, including the kinds of regimes in neighboring states.

The way states interact with citizens has an impact on political culture. In authoritarian regimes, the government uses rule by law to reinforce its power and authority. Citizens may come to expect and accept a certain level of corruption within the state. In democratic states, with accountability and transparency, citizens expect rule of law, where the law is applied fairly and no one is above the law.

Political culture is partly a result of **political socialization**, the process through which an individual learns about politics and is taught about society's common political values and beliefs. Political socialization is a lifelong process. An agent of socialization is a person or group that transmits political values. Agents of socialization include families, schools, peers, religion, the government, and the media. In authoritarian regimes, there is more pressure to conform to a specific set of beliefs than there is in democratic regimes.

Some political scientists believe that clear attitudes, values, and beliefs can be identified within any particular political culture. The best-known example of this is Gabriel Almond and Sidney Verba's 1963 book *The Civic Culture*. They argued that more stable and democratic countries, such as the United Kingdom, have a democratic civic culture. This means that their citizens hold the democratic values and beliefs that supported their democracies. These attitudes lead citizens to participate actively in politics, but also to defer enough to the leadership to let it govern effectively. In contrast, the authors described twentieth-century Mexico as an authoritarian culture in which citizens viewed themselves as subjects with few rights to control their government, suggesting that these attitudes helped to produce the electoral authoritarian regime under the PRI that ruled the country until 2000.

Other political scientists question the idea of a universal, slowly changing political culture within states. They note that subcultures—distinct political cultures of particular groups—exist in all societies. Racial or religious minorities, for instance, may not fully share the political attitudes and values of the majority. The assumption that we can identify a single, unified political culture that is key to understanding a particular country can mask some of the most important political conflicts within the country. Furthermore, political attitudes themselves may be symptoms rather than causes of political activity or a governmental system. For example, Mexican citizens in the 1960s may not have viewed themselves as active participants in government for a reason they arrived at rationally: They had lived for forty years under one party that had effectively suppressed all meaningful opposition and participation.

Political culture
A set of collectively held attitudes, values, and beliefs about government and politics.

Political socialization
The process through which an individual learns about politics and is taught about society's common political values and beliefs.

AP® TIP

Students often confuse political culture, political socialization, and political ideology on the AP® Exam. Make sure you are able to define and differentiate among these concepts.

Postmaterialism
A set of values in a society in which most citizens are economically secure enough to move beyond immediate economic (materialist) concerns to "quality of life" issues like human rights, civil rights, women's rights, environmentalism, and moral values.

Individualism
The belief that people should be free to make their own decisions and that the government should not unnecessarily regulate individual behavior or restrict civil liberties.

Political ideology
An individual's set of beliefs and values about government, politics, and policy.

Neoliberalism
A philosophy favoring economic policies that support the free market and reduce trade barriers.

Political cultures change over time. Ronald Inglehart (1971) coined the term **postmaterialism** in the 1970s to describe what he saw as a new predominant element in political culture in advanced industrial democracies. He argued that as a result of the post–World War II economic expansion, by the 1960s and 1970s, most citizens in wealthy societies were less concerned about economic (materialist) issues and more concerned about "quality of life" issues.

They had become "postmaterialist." Economic growth had allowed most citizens to attain a level of material comfort that led to a change in attitudes and values. Individuals had become more concerned with ideas like human rights, civil rights, women's rights, environmentalism, and moral values.

Individualism is the belief that people should be free to make their own decisions and that the government should not regulate individual behavior or restrict civil liberties unnecessarily. If you took AP® U.S. Government and Politics, you may have studied individualism as one of the core American political values. Leaders of major businesses are often depicted as "self-made" individuals whom many citizens admire.

Democratic states, such as the United Kingdom, are more likely to have individualistic belief systems than authoritarian states, where there is usually more pressure to adhere to communal values. Individualism can impact a wide range of political beliefs, including support for lower tax rates and fewer government regulations, as well as less support for a welfare state. Even in democratic states, there is a debate about how to balance the protection of individualism with doing what is best for the community.

Understanding a state's political culture helps explain behavior at the broadest level, but individual beliefs and behaviors also impact government and politics. **Political ideology** is an individual's set of beliefs and values about government, politics, and policies. Political ideologies typically are deeply held, because they include a person's worldview and ideas about the role of government. Some prominent political ideologies are individualism, neoliberalism, communism, socialism, fascism, and populism. Some of these ideologies are mostly political, others are mostly economic, and some are both.

Economic Ideologies

Neoliberalism is similar to individualism, because both beliefs emphasize freedom. While individualism focuses on individuals, neoliberalism is a broader belief in limiting government intervention in the economy. Neoliberalism focuses on free trade, deregulation, eliminating state subsidies, and privatizing businesses. Neoliberals believe that government intervention to steer the economy is ineffective and often harmful. Instead, neoliberal economists argue that government should minimize intervention in the free market so that the market can allocate resources as efficiently as possible to maximize the generation of wealth.

Neoliberal theorists also favor cutting back most government regulations. They oppose government efforts to reduce pollution, protect the safety of consumers and workers, and regulate business activities, such as banking. Neoliberal economists believe that the free market is more effective in addressing these issues than the government is. Neoliberal economists believe government regulations constrain business investment and waste precious resources. Neoliberals want to reduce regulations and the overall size of government and balance government budgets by eliminating deficit spending. Neoliberalism is opposed to statism, which is government control of economic and social policies. Neoliberalism is a term used to describe an economic philosophy. Economic liberalization refers to policies put in place that are consistent with neoliberal philosophy, such as reducing economic regulations on businesses and encouraging free trade.

You have already encountered examples of economic-liberalization policies, including Mexico's transition away from import-substitution industrialization policies in favor of the free market. NAFTA and the USMCA are also examples of neoliberal economic reform that reduced trade barriers among the United States, Mexico, and Canada. Another example of economic liberalization occurred in the United Kingdom under Prime Minister Thatcher, when many major industries were privatized.

Compared to individualism and neoliberalism, **communism** is a political ideology that advocates state ownership of all property, with the government exercising complete control over the economy. Communism is both an economic and political philosophy. Karl Marx, the originator of communism, grounded his philosophy in the belief that economic forces are the prime movers of history and politics. Feudalism produced all-powerful lords and monarchs, who kept the peasants in their place. Industrialization led to the rise of the bourgeoisie, the owners of capital, who gained political power. Many peasants were forced off their land to work for a daily wage in cities.

Marx saw the transition from feudalism to capitalism as part of a process of social revolution. Because of what he viewed as the exploitative nature of capitalism, he believed capitalist economies would expand the division between the bourgeoisie and the workers, which he called the proletariat. This class division would create an economic crisis that would usher in a new era of social revolution.

Marx believed that a revolution led by the proletariat would generate a communist society that would abolish class distinctions, with collective ownership of the means of production. Marx believed that the government would eventually be abolished. (Marx and Engels.)

In states that adopted communism, the opposite occurred. In communist states, authoritarian governments restricted individual rights and liberties, abolished private property, and took total control of the economy, setting standards for wages, prices, and production. Although China was a communist system under Mao, it is now an authoritarian state that has transitioned to what the government calls a "market socialist" economy.

Socialism is a political ideology between neoliberalism and communism. Economic equality is a core value of socialism, along with the belief that government ownership of the major means of production is a way to reduce income inequality within the state. In a socialist state, private individuals own property and most businesses, but key industries, such as steel, coal, energy, and telecommunications, may be nationalized. A socialist economic philosophy is based on the belief that government ownership of the major means of production is a way of reducing income inequality within the state. Socialist countries often have extensive welfare states where the government provides medical care, childcare, unemployment benefits, and pensions.

Keep in mind that socialism is an economic term. A state can be classified as a liberal democracy, with free and fair elections and the protection of civil rights and liberties, and still have a socialist economy. This is called democratic socialism.

Political Ideologies

While socialism is an economic belief system, **fascism** is a political ideology. Fascism relies on a strong sense of nationalism to support authoritarian rule. The rights of the ethnic and political majorities are favored, and ethnic and political minorities are oppressed. The result is strong authoritarian rule, with severe restrictions on civil rights and liberties, including civil society. The state is central to and dominant within society.

Communism
An ideology that advocates state ownership of all property, with the government exercising complete control over the economy.

Socialism
A political ideology in which economic equality is a core value, with the belief that government ownership of the major means of production is a way to reduce income inequality within the state.

Fascism
A nationalist political ideology in which nationalism and the primacy of the state are the core beliefs. It emphasizes the rights of the majority, oppresses the minority, and supports strong authoritarian rule.

AP® POLITICAL SCIENCE PRACTICES

Analyzing Limitations of Data: Question Wording and Its Effects

Questioning Capitalism
Percent of respondents agreeing with statement, "Capitalism as it exists today does more harm than good in the world."

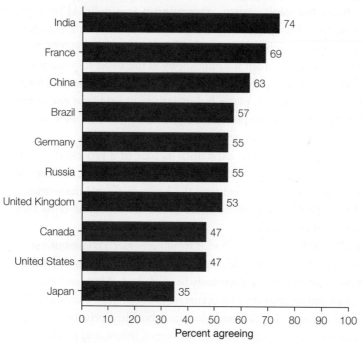

Data from Edelman Data & Intelligence, from a survey of 34,000 respondents in 28 countries taken October 19–November 18, 2019.

Reliable polling information requires that respondents be asked a non-leading question that does not encourage a particular response. An example of a non-leading question is, "Do you agree or disagree with the way Vladimir Putin is doing his job as president?"

Read carefully through the information on the bar chart and answer the following questions.

1. Identify wording that might impact the results of the survey.

2. Explain how the wording you identified in part 1 may affect the survey results.

3. Describe one factor, other than wording, that may impact the validity of a public opinion poll.

Totalitarianism
A political ideology that emphasizes domination of the state over citizens. In totalitarian systems, the government has complete control over citizens' lives.

Italian fascist leader Benito Mussolini, in *Fascism: Doctrine and Institutions*, argued that "the State is all-embracing; outside of it no human or spiritual values can exist." (Mussolini.) Fascists are intensely nationalistic, and they believe that the individual is subservient to the state. The interests of the state are dominant over both individual citizens and civil society. This state is led by one man who becomes a powerful leader and embodies the spirit of the nation. He rules on behalf of the society so that it can function properly.

Germany under Adolf Hitler and Italy under Benito Mussolini are examples of fascist states. Fascists, like communists, justify the elimination of civil society, but in contrast to communists, Mussolini openly admitted that the fascist state should be **totalitarian**, with the government having complete control over people's lives.

In contrast to communism and fascism, which place the will of the elite over the interests of citizens, **populism** is the ideology that the government should put the rights and interests of the common people above the elites. Populism is often based on the beliefs that traditional political elites are unpatriotic and corrupt, that the country faces a crisis, that the media and experts cannot be trusted, and that only a strong leader can save the country. (Frantz, 2018, 99–101.)

Populist movements often arise when people develop grievances against their government. Members of populist groups may believe that they are not getting what they deserve compared to what others have. Race, ethnicity, gender, and class can be powerful sources of populism. As you saw in your study of Mexico, President López Obrador ran a populist campaign by claiming to represent the interests of the common people against a corrupt elite.

People's political ideologies are powerful factors that influence the selection of leaders and the policy decisions of government. These belief systems can bolster the rights of citizens and democratic government, or they can be used to justify discrimination and authoritarianism.

Populism
A political ideology based on the idea that the government should put the rights and interests of the common people above the elites.

Section 6.1 Review

Each section's main ideas are reflected in the Learning Targets. By reviewing after each section, you should be able to

Remember the key points,

Know terms that are central to the topic, and

Think critically about what you have learned.

Remember

- Civil society contributes to democratic government by allowing groups outside of the government's control to advocate for policies.

- Political culture consists of citizens' shared beliefs and values, and it impacts a citizen's interactions with government and politics.

- The political ideologies of individualism, neoliberalism, communism, socialism, fascism, and populism are different philosophies about how the government and economy should operate.

Know

- *Civil society:* groups that form outside the government's control. (p. 173)

- *Political culture:* a set of widely held attitudes, values, and beliefs about government and politics. (p. 175)

- *Political socialization:* the process through which an individual learns about politics and is taught about society's common political values and beliefs. (p. 175)

- *Postmaterialism:* a set of values in a society in which most citizens are economically secure enough to move beyond immediate economic (materialist) concerns to "quality of life" issues like human rights, civil rights, women's rights, environmentalism, and moral values. (p. 176)

- *Individualism:* the belief that people should be free to make their own decisions and that the government should not unnecessarily regulate individual behavior or restrict civil liberties. (p. 176)

- *Political ideology:* an individual's set of beliefs and values about government, politics, and policy. (p. 176)

- *Neoliberalism:* a philosophy favoring economic policies that support the free market and reduce trade barriers. (p. 176)
- *Communism:* an ideology that advocates state ownership of all property, with the government exercising complete control over the economy. (p. 177)
- *Socialism:* a political ideology in which economic equality is a core value, with the belief that government ownership of the major means of production is a way to reduce income inequality within the state. (p. 177)
- *Fascism:* a nationalist political ideology in which nationalism and the primacy of the state are the core beliefs. It emphasizes the rights of the majority, oppresses the minority, and supports strong authoritarian rule. (p. 177)
- *Totalitarianism:* a political ideology that emphasizes domination of the state over citizens. In totalitarian systems, the government has complete control over citizens' lives. (p. 178)
- *Populism:* a political ideology based on the idea that the government should put the rights and interests of the common people above the elites. (p. 179)

Think

- Is civil society declining in democratic states or are new forms of civil society emerging?
- Why are certain ideologies more likely to arise in democratic or authoritarian states?

Free-Response Question: Quantitative Analysis

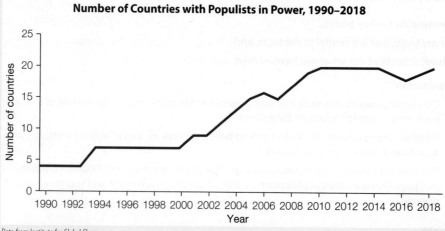

Number of Countries with Populists in Power, 1990–2018

Data from Institute for Global Change.

Answer A, B, C, D, and E.

A. Using the data in the graph, identify the time period with the lowest number of countries led by populists.

B. Using the data in the graph, identify a trend in the number of populists in power from 2000 to 2015.

C. Define populism.

D. Using your knowledge of populism and the data in the graph, draw a conclusion about the reasons for the trend you described in part B.

E. Explain why some critics of populism argue that it may lead to authoritarianism.

6.2 Participation

Learning Targets

After reading this section, you should be able to do the following:

1. Explain how formal participation impacts government and politics.

2. Explain how informal political participation impacts government and politics.

3. Explain how political participation differs in democratic and authoritarian states.

People participate politically as individuals and by joining groups, such as interest groups and political parties. In democratic states, political participation is voluntary. Authoritarian states may use **coercion**, which is when a government uses force or threats to pressure people into engaging in political activities that support the regime.

Coercion
A government's use of force or threats to pressure individual behavior.

Formal Political Participation

There are two main categories of political participation—formal and informal. **Formal political participation** includes activities such as voting in elections or on referendums, and contacting government officials with proposals, complaints, or concerns. Other methods of formal participation include joining an interest group or political party, working on a campaign, and donating money to support a candidate or cause.

Formal political participation
Voting in elections and on referendums, contacting government officials, joining political groups, working on a campaign, and donating money to a cause or candidate.

Voting is the most common form of participation. In democratic states, voters choose leaders through free and fair elections and, as a consequence, have an impact on policy-making. In democratic states, voters can remove office holders at the end of their terms and replace them with candidates whose policies they favor. People are free to join interest groups, petition their governments for a change in policies, contribute to political campaigns, run for office, and criticize the government without fear of retribution. Elected officials in democratic governments know that they must respond to citizens' concerns, or they risk losing the next election.

In authoritarian states, competition is limited, and candidates who oppose the regime may not be allowed to run for office. When opposition candidates are allowed to run, authoritarian governments may intervene to make sure the candidates favored by the regime win the election. Both democratic and authoritarian states hold elections to give citizens a sense of political efficacy and to increase the regime's legitimacy. By winning elections, even when they are rigged, leaders in authoritarian states can claim widespread popular support.

Both types of regimes restrict access to voting, although there are more restrictions in authoritarian regimes. Most states have universal suffrage, allowing citizens to vote in national elections, once they have reached the minimum voting age. Democratic states often require voter identification to prevent fraud at the polls. Authoritarian regimes may further restrict access to voting by making it more difficult for members of minority groups to run for office or vote in elections.

Referendums in both democratic and authoritarian states are another way citizens participate in politics. Referendums are policy issues sent by the government to the voters.

They allow citizens a way to participate directly in policymaking. In some states, they are a way for an executive to circumvent the legislature by taking an issue directly to the voters. Citizens can make decisions that are difficult or unpopular with government officials.

As you saw in Chapter 5, voters in the United Kingdom have been able to participate in policymaking through referendums on the devolution of power, alternative voting, and Brexit. Voters in Scotland rejected a referendum on independence. The Russian constitution was approved by voters in a referendum in 1993, and in 2020, new constitutional amendments were approved. Amendments to the Iranian constitution were approved by voters in 1989. Sending these referendums to voters increased the legitimacy of both democratic and authoritarian regimes.

In addition to voting in elections and on referendums, formal participation includes contacting government officials. In both democratic and authoritarian systems, people can write to, call, and email government officials as well as contact them through social media. In authoritarian states, government officials want to learn about problems and corruption, especially at the local level, so that they can address the issue and maintain legitimacy. In both kinds of regimes, the government provides an outlet for citizens to air their grievances as a way to reduce unrest and discontent. However, authoritarian states, such as Iran, China, and Russia, are much less tolerant of criticism against high-level officials.

The rise of new communications technology, especially social media, provides new ways for citizens to participate in politics. Social media allow activists to disseminate ideas to other like-minded individuals. Social media lower the costs of creating and organizing movements. Cellular phones led to the rise of citizen journalists who can record events and share them online. Social media also allow people to organize without requiring the participants to be in the same place at the same time. Seeing posts from people with similar grievances and knowing that others plan to show up to protest may help people overcome their fears of participating. (Earl and Kimport, 2011.)

The internet and social media can also have negative consequences. Authoritarian governments, most notably China, have increasingly made use of new technology to more effectively gather intelligence about citizens.

Informal Political Participation

Informal political participation
Protest, civil disobedience, and political violence, including terrorism.

Protest
A public demonstration against a policy or in response to an event, often targeting the government.

Informal political participation includes protest, civil disobedience, and political violence, including terrorism. Civil disobedience is intentionally breaking the law to call attention to government policies, and it occurs in both democratic and authoritarian states, although the penalties for civil disobedience are often harsher in authoritarian states.

Protests occur in both democratic and authoritarian states. Protests are public demonstrations against a policy or in response to an event. Protests often voice objections to government actions. In democratic states, the constitution protects civil liberties, including freedom of speech and assembly. As long as protests comply with reasonable restrictions, such as obtaining a permit, they are constitutionally protected activities, so long as they do not become violent.

Authoritarian states are more likely to restrict protests. They may allow small protests to provide a "safety valve" for people who are unhappy, as long as the protests do not become too large or threaten stability. Authoritarian states may encourage or coerce people to rally in favor of the regime or to intimidate the opposition. For example, in China under Mao's rule, people were forced to participate in pro-regime rallies, and encouraged to turn in their neighbors for perceived anti-government sentiments and to participate in mass campaigns to eradicate opponents of the regime. Authoritarian states may organize protests against ethnic and religious minorities and in favor of government policies that discriminate against these groups.

Many people have sympathy for social movements that engage in peaceful protest, but they have different feelings toward groups that engage in violence. This is especially true in liberal democracies, where peaceful protest is a well-established action within the bounds of civil society, but violence is seen as illegitimate. Violence takes many forms, from small-scale protests using physical force to terrorism.

Political violence is the use of physical force by non-state actors for political ends. Social movements are likely to be more peaceful in democracies, where they have greater opportunity to achieve their goals. Repression can produce violent responses. As you studied in Chapter 3, the Zapatista movement in Mexico was a response to the perception that the central government's development policies failed to address poverty in the state of Chiapas. If police escalate their response to peaceful protest, and especially if protesters see that response as brutal, a violent response is more likely. Riots typically occur when grievances among a particular group have been growing, and a "spark," almost always involving repressive actions by the police or the military, is met with violence by a group of protesters. (Waddington 2017.)

Terrorism is political violence or the threat of violence that deliberately targets civilians to influence the behavior and actions of the government. (Nacos, 2012, 32.) The key distinction between terrorism and other forms of political violence is who is targeted. Groups that become violent in opposition to a particular government typically target that government directly by destroying government buildings and assassinating officials. Terrorists, on the other hand, target civilians who are not directly responsible for the targeted state's policies. They try to sow fear in a general population through seemingly random acts of violence to influence a particular government or population. Terrorist groups are almost always clandestine, while other groups engaging in political violence are usually more public.

Many types of groups have used terrorism. As you learned in Chapter 5, one of the longest-standing terrorist groups, which no longer uses violence, was the Irish Republican Army (IRA), which fought a campaign to free Northern Ireland from British rule. Today,

Political violence
The use of physical force by non-state actors for political ends.

Terrorism
Political violence or the threat of violence that deliberately targets civilians to influence the behavior and actions of the government.

The aftermath of an April 2014 terrorist attack on the Nyanya bus station on the outskirts of Abuja, the national capital of Nigeria. Boko Haram was suspected of carrying out the attack, which killed more than seventy persons. Boko Haram is a separatist Islamic terror group. Terrorism is a form of political violence designed to target citizens and generate fear.

STR/AFP/Getty Images

much attention is focused on militant groups, such as Chechen terror groups in Russia, which you will study in Chapter 7, and Boko Haram in northern Nigeria, which you will study in Chapter 9.

Political participation in democracies influences who governs, the political agenda, and how government policies impact people's lives. In both democratic and authoritarian states, political participation, even if it is not effective at changing policy, may give people a greater sense of political efficacy and a set of political skills they can use in the future. Authoritarian governments allow less political participation, and it is unlikely to significantly impact the regime or its policies. Nevertheless, as you will learn later in studying the Iranian revolution of 1979, if enough people become dissatisfied with any government, political participation may lead to regime change, even in an authoritarian state.

Section 6.2 Review

Remember

- Formal participation in democratic states impacts who is elected and the policies enacted by government.
- Formal participation in authoritarian states is restricted, but some participation by citizens is allowed in an effort to increase legitimacy.
- Informal participation includes protest, civil disobedience, and violence, including terrorism.

Know

- *Coercion:* a government's use of force or threats to pressure individual behavior. (p. 181)
- *Formal political participation:* voting in elections and on referendums, contacting government officials, joining political groups, working on a campaign, and donating money to a cause or candidate. (p. 181)
- *Informal political participation:* protest, civil disobedience, and political violence, including terrorism. (p. 182)
- *Protest:* a public demonstration against a policy or in response to an event, often targeting the government. (p. 182)
- *Political violence:* the use of physical force by non-state actors for political ends. (p. 183)
- *Terrorism:* political violence or the threat of violence that deliberately targets civilians to influence the behavior and actions of the government. (p. 183)

Think

- What are the advantages and disadvantages of using informal political participation as a way of influencing government and politics?
- Is political violence ever an effective method of achieving political change?

....

Free-Response Question: Conceptual Analysis

Answer A, B, C, and D.

A. Define political participation.

B. Explain how formal political participation differs from informal political participation.

C. Explain why an authoritarian state would allow some forms of political participation.

D. Explain why a democratic state would restrict some forms of political participation.

6.3 Civil Rights and Civil Liberties

Learning Targets

After reading this section, you should be able to do the following:

1. Compare civil rights and civil liberties in democratic and authoritarian states.

2. Explain how civil liberties provide accountability and transparency in democratic states.

3. Describe policies that guarantee and expand civil rights.

Civil liberties are fundamental rights and freedoms protected from infringement by the government, including freedom of expression, freedom of the press, and the right to peaceably assemble. Civil liberties also include due process of law, which guarantees protections in the legal system, specifically the fair application of the law and restrictions against arbitrary government actions. Due process protections include the right of criminal defendants to be informed of the charges against them, the right to an attorney, access to a trial by jury, a public and speedy trial, the right to confront witnesses, and protections against double jeopardy. Authoritarian states, which operate under rule *by* law rather than rule *of* law, often deny due process protections to defendants, preferring secret legal proceedings.

Civil rights are positive actions taken by the government to prevent people from being discriminated against when engaging in fundamental political actions, such as voting. Civil rights protect individuals against discrimination based on their membership in a particular group, such as ethnic and religious minorities. In protecting civil rights, the government steps in to protect members of groups that face discrimination.

One of the key differences between democratic and authoritarian states is the ability to exercise civil rights and civil liberties. Civil liberties have strong protections in liberal democracies and are highly restricted in authoritarian states. Illiberal or flawed democracies, which are sometimes called competitive authoritarian regimes, are hybrid regimes—combining elements of democratic and authoritarian states. Elections in illiberal democracies have limited competitiveness, and civil liberties are restricted but not eliminated. Some political scientists classify Russia as an illiberal, hybrid regime, while others believe that the Russian state has restricted civil liberties so much that it should be classified as a competitive authoritarian state.

Civil liberties
Fundamental rights and freedoms protected from infringement by the government.

Civil rights
Positive actions taken by the government to prevent people from being discriminated against when engaged in fundamental political actions, such as voting.

Civil Liberties

In this chapter, we focus on those civil liberties that involve the right to participate in the political process. Civil liberties include certain political rights, such as the right to form political parties and interest groups, run for office, and make contributions of time or money to political campaigns.

Freedom of the press is one of the most important civil liberties, because it encourages political discussion and debate and is a way of holding the government accountable. Democratic regimes have greater transparency than authoritarian regimes, because people and the media have the right to access information about the activities of government, including

AP® POLITICAL SCIENCE PRACTICES

Interpreting Maps

People Power under Attack

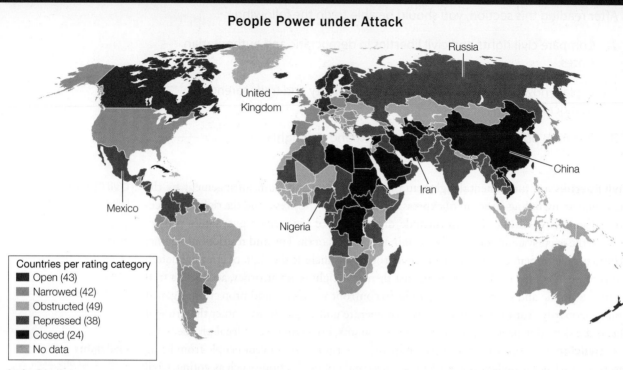

Countries per rating category
- ■ Open (43)
- ■ Narrowed (42)
- ■ Obstructed (49)
- ■ Repressed (38)
- ■ Closed (24)
- ■ No data

Data from Civicus Monitor.

Geographical representations of data can be useful tools in exploring important topics in political science. The first thing to look at in analyzing a map is the title. In this case, the title is "People Power under Attack." This map shows the parts of the world where civil society is repressed, but you cannot tell what the map measures from the title. The color-coded key shows how each country is rated. Maps like this one may not provide detailed information about the data within each country, but they are a good way of visualizing broader characteristics or trends.

Use the map and your knowledge of comparative government and politics to answer the questions.

1. Which regions are most restrictive of civil society?

2. What information is missing from the key?

3. What are the benefits and drawbacks of this map in conveying information about restrictions on civil society?

AP® TIP

Students often confuse civil rights and civil liberties. Civil rights are *positive actions taken by the government* to protect citizens from discrimination, while civil liberties are fundamental freedoms *protected from government action*. Make sure you are able to define and differentiate these concepts on the AP® Exam.

information about how the public's money is being spent. Policymaking in authoritarian states is less transparent, often taking place in secret. A free press is an important check on corruption, because it is more difficult for officials to hide their activities

According to a report issued by Freedom House in 2019, media freedom is declining, even in democratic countries. Unlike authoritarian regimes, democratic states do not throw journalists in jail for their reporting the news. Freedom of the media is threatened in democratic regimes because people are receiving biased news and misinformation or even disinformation.

As is true in some authoritarian regimes, some democratically elected leaders portray critical media as dishonest, with the goal of furthering trust in the leader and distrust in a free and independent media. Leaders in some democratic countries tell their supporters to follow some media outlets, and they criticize others, denouncing journalists who report negative information about the government.

Populist leaders, such as President López Obrador in Mexico, portray themselves as victims of liberal elites, whom they often associate with the mainstream media. These leaders believe that their interests are more important than the freedom of the press and transparency. (Repucci.)

Authoritarian states place more direct restrictions on media freedom, and the state sponsors newspapers and TV stations. The Chinese government has created a digital firewall that blocks information that might damage the regime, including information about national leaders. It has also created state-controlled social-media platforms where citizens interact under the watchful eye of government officials. Authoritarian regimes may suspend media licenses or nationalize the media in an effort to control the public's access to information. All of these tactics limit transparency, making it difficult for citizens and journalists in authoritarian states to find and share information that will hold governments accountable for policies. Figure 6.1 shows the level of internet freedom as of 2019.

This political cartoon illustrates China's monitoring of the internet. Hundreds of censors monitor activity that might pose a challenge to the state, such as searches including the terms *human rights* and *democracy*. An internet filter, known as the Great Firewall, blocks searches for items that authorities deem threats to the state.

Civil Rights

Civil rights are positive actions taken by the government to prevent people from being discriminated against when engaged in fundamental political actions such as voting. Ensuring access to the ballot by prohibiting discrimination based on characteristics such as race,

FIGURE 6.1

Internet Freedom Worldwide, 2019

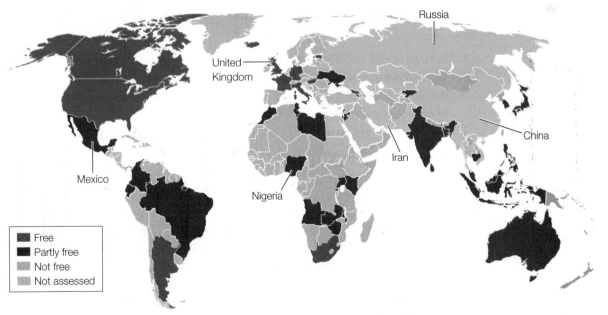

Legend:
- Free
- Partly free
- Not free
- Not assessed

Data from Freedom House, from a study of developments from June 2018 to May 2019 in the 65 countries that account for 87 percent of users of the internet.

religion, gender, age, disability, and sexual identity is an example of a positive action government takes to guarantee voting rights. Many scholars argue that truly equal citizenship requires that citizens treat each other as equals, giving each other full respect as members of the community.

Social movement
A large group organized to advocate for political change.

Social movements are large, often loosely organized, groups organized to advocate for political change. Social movements focusing on civil rights advocate for legal rights at least equal to those of other citizens. Despite the existence of national and international movements advocating for equality, discrimination still exists. For example, legal discrimination against women, especially in areas of property ownership and family law, remains fairly common. Discrimination against the LGBTQ community remains the norm in most of the world.

Disadvantaged groups often seek representation and full participation in the political process. As long as they accept the basic integrity of the state and view themselves as part of the political community, they will advocate for representation and participation. This may appear to be a simple legal matter of ensuring basic political rights, but it often becomes more complicated and controversial as groups question whether they are truly allowed to participate on an equal footing with other citizens.

Sometimes, institutional changes are necessary for disadvantaged groups to achieve equality. The Mexican law that requires political parties to run at least 50 percent female candidates is an example of a state response to demands for equality. Laws providing equal protection for women were not enough to break barriers to running for office, so a law was enacted to achieve greater representation by women.

Virtually all disadvantaged groups that mobilize to demand changes begin in a socially marginalized position. They are typically poorer and less educated than the average citizen and may be socially segregated as well. They argue that they need better education and economic positions as well as greater respect from and acceptance in society as a whole. The protection of civil rights goes beyond laws guaranteeing equality, requiring policies that support the social structures that make equality a reality, rather than just a goal.

Some people argue in favor of policies that target the distinct needs and weak social positions of particular groups. To fully protect civil rights, they argue that policies should:

1. Recognize and actively support the preservation of distinct cultures;
2. Grant some degree of governing autonomy to particular groups;
3. Reform representative institutions, such as electoral systems and political parties, to enhance or guarantee participation and representation; and
4. Actively intervene to improve the socioeconomic status of distinct groups.

Political theorist Will Kymlicka contended that without recognition and protection of their distinct cultures, disadvantaged groups will not be able to participate completely in the larger society and make the choices on which democratic citizenship depends. (Kymlicka.) Critics argue that respecting cultural differences might undermine individual rights, especially freedom of expression and gender equality. Questions about how to best protect civil rights are more common in democratic systems than in authoritarian ones, where states often actively discriminate against women and minority groups.

Section 6.3 Review

Remember

- Civil rights and liberties are constitutionally protected in democratic states, while authoritarian and illiberal or hybrid states restrict rights and liberties.
- Media freedom protects democratic government by increasing transparency and accountability.
- While authoritarian states restrict civil rights, some democratic states go beyond legal protections against discrimination and enact policies to actively promote equality.

Know

- *Civil liberties:* fundamental rights and freedoms protected from infringement by the government. (p. 185)
- *Civil rights:* positive actions taken by the government to prevent people from being discriminated against when engaged in fundamental political actions, such as voting. (p. 185)
- *Social movement:* a large group organized to advocate for political change. (p. 188)

Think

- Why are civil liberties crucial to the protection of democratic government?
- Why do most authoritarian states provide their citizens with some civil rights and liberties?

....

Free-Response Question: Quantitative Analysis

Measuring the Importance of Media Freedom

Percent who say that it is very important that media can report news in their country without government censorship

Data from Pew Research Center, 2019 Global Attitudes Survey.

Answer A, B, C, D, and E.

A. Using the data shown on the map, identify the country studied in AP® Comparative Government and Politics with the highest percentage of respondents who think that an independent press is important.

B. Using the data shown on the map, identify the country studied in AP® Comparative Government and Politics with the lowest percentage of respondents who think that an independent press is important.

C. Define an independent press.

D. Using the data on the map, draw a conclusion about why the countries you identified in parts A and B have different results in the polling data.

E. Explain why civil liberties, other than an independent press, are important in democratic states.

6.4 Cleavages

Learning Targets

After reading this section, you should be able to do the following:

1. Explain the similarities between social and political cleavages.

2. Explain how the state's response to cleavages impacts legitimacy.

3. Explain how ethnic, racial, and social class cleavages impact government and politics.

Social and Political Cleavages

Social cleavage
Division based on ethnicity, race, religion, class, or territory.

Political cleavage
Division based on different ideas about the role of government and policymaking goals.

Cleavages are divisions within a society. **Social cleavages** are divisions based on ethnicity, race, religion, class, or territory. **Political cleavages** are divisions based on different ideas about the role of government and goals in policymaking. Social and political cleavages can overlap. For example, a region such as Scotland has cultural and territorial differences with the rest of the United Kingdom, representing a social cleavage. The desire for an independent Scotland is a political cleavage.

Cleavages may weaken society by emphasizing disagreements and discrepancies between groups. State stability may be challenged by groups that pressure the regime for autonomy or that want to secede to form their own state. Groups that believe the state will not meet at least some of their demands may engage in violence, terrorism, or civil war. Cleavages can weaken state sovereignty to the point where neighboring states encroach on territory, either to expand the neighboring state's territory or for defensive purposes.

It may seem counterintuitive, but some cleavages can strengthen the state. For example, parties represent a political cleavage. When different groups compete in the political process, opportunities arise to share viewpoints and new ideas. In democratic states, groups may have to compromise, which may result in policy that is more deliberate and effective. Competition among political cleavages slows down the policymaking process, making it more deliberative. If you took AP® U.S. Government and Politics, you may remember James Madison's argument in *Federalist* No. 10 that the best way to manage the inevitable factions that arise in a democracy is to create a pluralist system in which different groups compete in the policymaking process.

Governments can respond to cleavages in several ways. Democratic governments ensure civil rights and liberties that enable groups to compete in the political process. Federal systems allow regions where an ethnic or religious group predominates to make local policies. In many federal systems, the upper house of the legislature represents regions, which means that regional interests have almost guaranteed representation in the national legislature. As you saw in the study of the United Kingdom in Chapter 5, referendums can also provide regions with autonomy or independence.

Ethnic or religious diversity may incentivize political leaders to broaden their appeal beyond their particular group. Electoral systems can encourage this by requiring winning candidates to gain votes over a broad geographic area containing multiple religious or ethnic groups. For example, in Nigeria, presidential candidates must win 25 percent of the votes in two-thirds of the states to win the election.

Some states respond to cleavages by guaranteeing representation for ethnic and religious groups in the legislature or bureaucracy. In Iran, for example, five of the 290 seats are set aside in the legislature for specified non-Muslim minorities. Also, rules for recognition of parties can require them to have representation and leadership across ethnic or other identity lines. Creating ethnically or religiously mixed states or provinces in a federal system can also encourage compromise within each state, moderating tensions. As you will see in Chapter 9, Nigeria is a classic example of this approach.

Authoritarian states are more likely to repress ethnic or religious minorities. Members of these groups may not be allowed to vote or run for office. Authoritarian states may brutally repress groups that are seen as a threat to the political or cultural stability of the state. As you will learn in Chapter 11, China's repression of Tibetans, and its creation of reeducation camps for Uyghurs, are striking examples of an authoritarian state repressing cleavages.

Governments must consider several factors in responding to cleavages, because the state's response may impact its legitimacy. Democratic governments that successfully incorporate different groups in the policymaking process may be seen as more legitimate, but some groups may hold values that go against a country's democratic ideals. For example, democratic states may be hesitant to welcome groups that oppose equal rights or advocate authoritarianism. At the same time, governments may face a backlash from the majority if they give in to the demands of unpopular minority groups, even when those groups advocate democratic values. In both democratic and authoritarian states, the threat of violence and terrorism from long-standing cleavages also threatens the stability and legitimacy of the state.

To better understand the impact of cleavages, we will examine three major sources of division—ethnicity, race, and social class.

This is a traditional Uyghur dance performance in the Xinjiang Uygur Autonomous Region of China. The Uyghurs are a minority ethnic group, who are also largely Muslim. The Chinese government faces criticism in the international community for putting Uyghurs in reeducation camps.

Guang Niu/Getty Images News/Getty Images

Ethnic Cleavages

Ethnic groups are united by one or more cultural attributes or a sense of common history. Ethnicity is a fluid concept and is based mostly on perception. Ethnic groups may be based on shared attributes, such as a common language, but even these are subject to perception and change. For example, different ethnic groups may share a common language but use a different dialect.

Ethnic group
A group of people who see themselves as united by one or more cultural attributes or a common history.

For ethnic groups, recognition may take the form of official state support of cultural events, school instruction in their language, official recognition of their language as one of the national languages, or inclusion of the ethnic group's history in the history curriculum. (Kymlicka and Norman.) If an ethnic group resides mainly in one area, it also may demand some type of regional autonomy, such as a federal system of government in which its leaders can control their own state or province. Even when an ethnic group is not regionally concentrated, it will typically demand greater representation and participation in government, perhaps through a political party that represents its interests.

Ethnicity is not always political. Irish Americans, for example, may be proud of their heritage and identify culturally with Ireland, but few feel any common political interests based on that identification. An ethnic cleavage can become a political cleavage if a strong leader emerges. A leader who can tie ethnic identity to political demands may gain tremendous support.

If a group believes that those in power have discriminated against it economically, socially, or politically, members may see their political interests and ethnic identity as one and the same. Their history, which they may pass from parent to child, is one of discrimination at the hands of the powerful "other." If an ethnic group is based in a particular region that has a valuable resource such as petroleum, group members may feel that they should receive more benefits from what they see as "their" resource.

Fear is also a common source of ethnic mobilization. With the fall of communism in eastern Europe and the former Soviet Union, many people felt great fear about the future. The old institutions had collapsed, and the new ones were untested. In this situation, it is relatively easy for a political leader to mobilize support with an ethnic or nationalist appeal by suggesting that other groups will take advantage of the uncertain situation and try to dominate. Our case study of Nigeria in Chapter 9 will illustrate many of these elements of ethnic politics.

Racial Cleavages

Race
A group of people socially defined mainly on the basis of one or more perceived common physical characteristics.

A **race** is group of people socially defined on the basis of perceived common physical characteristics. (Cornell and Hartman.) In 2011, the Human Genome Project demonstrated that all humans share 99.9 percent of the same genetic material. Race is based on perception rather than scientific differences.

Most ethnic groups represent people who claim a common identity. Race, in contrast, originates in the imposition of a classification by others. Race in its modern sense began with Europeans' expansion around the globe in the late 1400s and their encounters with different peoples. Mainly to justify European domination and the enslavement of others, European explorers and colonists classified the native populations of the lands they conquered as distinct races. Racial classifications represented differences in the power structure. Like race, ethnicity may also represent differences in a power structure, as you will see in Chapter 9 in studying Nigeria.

Ethnicity and race, then, usually differ in how they are determined (culture versus physical characteristics) and their origins (self-identification versus external imposition). Races are constructed by focusing on particular differences, such as skin color, and ignoring the many similarities among groups of people.

Given its inherent power dynamic, racial classification is always political and not scientifically based. Groups in a minority or subordinate position are more likely to view their political interests as tied to their racial identity, in part because they face discrimination on that basis. Racial classifications give certain groups more power than others. Like ethnicity, political mobilization on the basis of race depends on the ability of leaders to articulate a common agenda by using the symbols of racial identity or discrimination in a compelling way.

Politicized racial groups usually desire recognition, representation, and improved social status. Autonomy is a less common goal because racial groups often do not share a defined geographical home. Recognition usually means official governmental acknowledgment of the race as a socially important group through such means as inclusion on a census form, the teaching of the group's historical role in the larger national history, and the celebration of its leaders and contribution to the nation's culture. In addition, racial groups desire representation and full participation in their government and society, including improved social status. The demands of racial groups typically focus on inclusion in public and private employment, political offices, and the educational system.

Groups may argue that past discrimination justifies some type of targeted system to achieve representation equal to their share of the population and greater socioeconomic equality. This might include numerical targets or goals for hiring, increased funding for training and education, or adjustments to the electoral system that make the election of minorities more likely or guaranteed.

Social-Class Cleavages

Social class may be defined by measurable criteria, such as wealth, or by applying social norms. One way to distinguish between social classes is to draw lines between different classes at different income levels. But social class is more complicated than that. A **social class** is a group of people who perceive themselves as sharing a social status based on a common level of wealth, income, type of work, or education. Clearly delineating between social classes is tricky.

Income is the most straightforward way to differentiate social classes because groups can be divided into categories, such as the top, upper middle, lower middle, and bottom fourth of the population (quartiles). Similarly, educational attainment can be categorized, such as less than high school, high-school graduate, and college graduate. Type of employment is more complicated, but typical divisions refer to (1) salaried employees who do not work for an hourly wage, tend to be more educated, and have some control over their working hours; (2) employees who get paid hourly and have less education and control over their work; (3) farmers; (4) small-business owners who work for themselves; and (5) large-scale business executives who own or control big corporations.

Income level and type of employment result in different conceptions of social class. A skilled tradesperson might consider themself to be a member of the working class, even though their yearly income is twice that of a person who works in an office and defines themself as a member of the professional class.

Like ethnicity, social class is often politically important, but it is not always evident. Upper classes typically do not assert their political interests by referring to themselves as members of the upper class, especially in democracies in which equal citizenship is a goal of the political system. Nevertheless, wealthy individuals, groups, and major businesses are active everywhere in trying to influence governments.

Conscious working-class political action has usually taken place through labor unions and allied political parties, such as the Labour Party in the United Kingdom. The percentage of the population who are union members, however, has declined precipitously for decades: According to the OECD (Organisation for Economic Co-operation and

Social class
A group of people who perceive themselves as sharing a social status based on a common level of wealth, income, type of work, or education.

Development, a group that includes almost all wealthy democracies, including the United Kingdom), the average percentage of the population who are union members declined from about 35 percent in 1985 to about 17 percent in the early 2020s.

With unions declining, many working-class voters have turned to nationalism and right-wing parties, believing that their problems are caused by immigrants and globalization. In effect, these voters have shifted their political activity from a class-based focus to other types of identity policies, such as race and ethnicity.

States face challenges from divisions within society, because social and political cleavages can weaken the state by creating an "us versus them" mentality. Cleavages can also provide an opportunity to listen and incorporate diverse voices into the policymaking process. Governments must carefully consider how to respond to cleavages, because the failure to successfully address them can weaken the state and impair its legitimacy.

Section 6.4 Review

Remember

- Social and political cleavages may weaken the state through demands for autonomy or independence, but they may strengthen the state by representing competing interests in the policymaking process.
- Democratic governments protect civil rights and ensure civil liberties, which allow groups to advocate for their rights, while authoritarian states are more likely to repress ethnic or minority groups.
- Ethnic, racial, and social class cleavages impact government and politics, and a state's response to these divisions may impact its legitimacy.

Know

- *Social cleavage:* division based on ethnicity, race, religion, class, or territory. (p. 190)
- *Political cleavage:* division based on different ideas about the role of government and policy-making goals. (p. 190)
- *Ethnic group:* a group of people who see themselves as united by one or more cultural attributes or a common history. (p. 191)
- *Race:* a group of people socially defined mainly on the basis of one or more perceived common physical characteristics. (p. 192)
- *Social class:* a group of people who perceive themselves as sharing a social status based on a common level of wealth, income, type of work, or education. (p. 193)

Think

- What challenges do governments face in responding to political or social cleavages?
- Are political cleavages or social cleavages more likely to weaken state legitimacy?

Free-Response Question: Conceptual Analysis

Answer A, B, C, and D.

A. Define political cleavage.

B. Explain how an authoritarian state might respond to a political cleavage.

C. Explain how a democratic state could respond to a political cleavage.

D. Explain how political cleavages impact legitimacy.

AP® KEY CONCEPTS

- Civil society (p. 173)
- Political culture (p. 175)
- Political socialization (p. 175)
- Postmaterialism (p. 176)
- Individualism (p. 176)
- Political ideology (p. 176)
- Neoliberalism (p. 176)
- Communism (p. 177)
- Socialism (p. 177)

- Fascism (p. 177)
- Totalitarianism (p. 178)
- Populism (p. 179)
- Coercion (p. 181)
- Formal political participation (p. 181)
- Informal political participation (p. 182)
- Protest (p. 182)
- Political violence (p. 183)
- Terrorism (p. 183)

- Civil liberties (p. 185)
- Civil rights (p. 185)
- Social movement (p. 188)
- Social cleavage (p. 190)
- Political cleavage (p. 190)
- Ethnic group (p. 191)
- Race (p. 192)
- Social class (p. 193)

AP® EXAM MULTIPLE-CHOICE PRACTICE QUESTIONS

1. Which of the following is an example of a civil-society organization?

    A. A state-sponsored farmers' group in China

    B. MORENA in Mexico

    C. An environmental group in Nigeria

    D. The United Russia Party

Questions 2 and 3 refer to the passage.

> Political leaders are also using the pandemic as a pretext to censor unfavorable news, arrest critics, and scapegoat ethnic and religious groups. In at least 45 countries, activists, journalists, and other members of the public were arrested or charged with criminal offenses for online speech related to the pandemic. Governments in at least 28 countries censored websites and social media posts to suppress unfavorable health statistics, corruption allegations, and other COVID-19-related content.
>
> No government has taken a more aggressive approach to the public health crisis than China's, which was found to be the world's worst abuser of internet freedom for a sixth consecutive year. Chinese authorities combined low- and high-tech tools not only to manage the outbreak of the coronavirus, but also to deter internet users from sharing information from independent sources and challenging the official narrative. The pandemic is normalizing the sort of digital authoritarianism that the Chinese Communist Party has long sought to mainstream.
>
> —*Report: Global Internet Freedom Declines in Shadow of Pandemic*, Freedom House, October 14, 2020

2. Which of the following is supported by the main idea of the passage?

    A. The pandemic has led to the spread of misinformation, and governments censor inaccurate information in an effort to protect public health.

    B. Authoritarian governments have used the pandemic as an excuse to violate civil liberties.

    C. Democratic governments do not censor information about public health, even when the information is critical of the government.

    D. Once the pandemic abates, governments are likely to allow greater access to public health information.

3. Which of the following is an implication of the passage?

    A. The Chinese government is unlikely to reduce government censorship once the pandemic abates.

    B. Authoritarian governments will follow China's lead in censoring public health information on the internet.

    C. In the future, both democratic and authoritarian governments will use the high- and low-tech tools developed by China to censor the media.

    D. China is the leader in developing sophisticated information technology.

4. Which of the following best describes a response of democratic and authoritarian states to social and political cleavages?

   A. Both types of regime censor the expression of cleavages that challenge the government's right to rule.

   B. Democratic and authoritarian regimes are more likely to suppress ethnic cleavages than racial cleavages.

   C. Authoritarian regimes are more likely to use class cleavages to unite the nation than democratic regimes.

   D. Both types of regime limit the rights of groups when they pose a threat to public safety.

Questions 5 and 6 refer to the map.

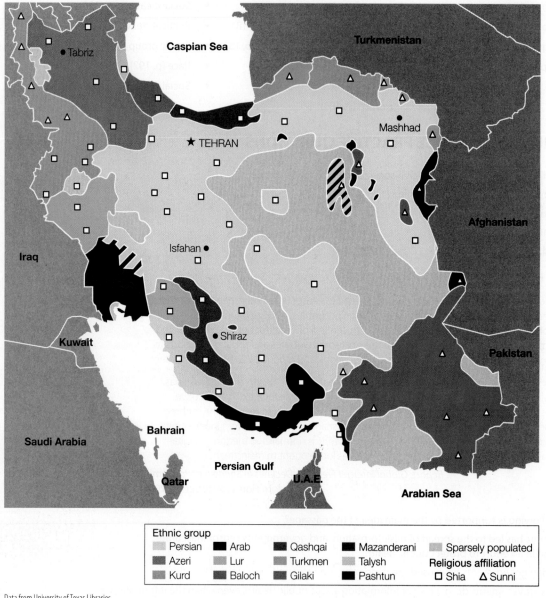

Iran's Ethnic and Religious Groups

Ethnic group
- Persian
- Azeri
- Kurd
- Arab
- Lur
- Baloch
- Qashqai
- Turkmen
- Gilaki
- Mazanderani
- Talysh
- Pashtun
- Sparsely populated

Religious affiliation
- □ Shia
- △ Sunni

Data from University of Texas Libraries.

5. Which of the following is supported by the map?

   A. Iran has many ethnic groups and a predominantly Shia population.

   B. Most Iranians are Arab and Muslim.

   C. Iran's ethnic diversity is a source of conflict within government.

   D. The central and eastern portions of Iran are very diverse, and no single ethnic group predominates.

6. Which of the following is an implication of the map?
   A. Secessionist movements are a threat to the government's sovereignty.
   B. Iran has a federal system of government, so that ethnic regions will be represented in the legislature.
   C. The religious values of the state are consistent with the religious beliefs of most of the population.
   D. Ethnic minorities in Iran face a significant level of discrimination.

7. Which of the following is typical of elections in a hybrid regime?
   A. An independent election commission oversees voting.
   B. Elections are held, but competition is limited.
   C. The regime decides who can run for office.
   D. Multiple parties and candidates compete and have the opportunity to win.

8. Which of the following is predominantly a political cleavage?
   A. The division between Sunni and Shia Muslims in Iran
   B. A rivalry between soccer teams representing different countries
   C. Policy differences between the PAN and PRI in Mexico
   D. Economic disparities between the upper class and the upper-middle class in the United Kingdom

9. Which of the following statements accurately describes restrictions on the media in democratic countries?
   A. Democratic states do not restrict media content.
   B. Social media is heavily regulated in democratic states, because it is owned by private businesses.
   C. Some democratic states do not protect media content that constitutes hate speech.
   D. Democratic states require that political parties have equal access to the media to protect electoral competition.

10. Which of the following is an example of a common form of formal political participation in both authoritarian and democratic states?
   A. Contacting a representative to express dissatisfaction with a local policy
   B. Protesting against national leaders
   C. Intentionally breaking a law to call attention to injustice
   D. Voting in a competitive and fair national election

AP® EXAM PRACTICE ARGUMENT ESSAY

Develop an argument about whether government responses to informal participation in authoritarian regimes increase or decrease state legitimacy.

Use one or more of the following course concepts in your response:

- Sovereignty
- Power
- Civil liberties

In your response, do the following:

- Respond to the prompt with a defensible claim or thesis that establishes a line of reasoning using one or more of the provided course concepts.
- Support your claim with at least *TWO* pieces of specific and relevant evidence from your study of one or more course countries. The evidence should be relevant to one or more of the provided course concepts.
- Use reasoning to explain why your evidence supports your claim or thesis, using one or more of the provided course concepts.
- Respond to an opposing or alternate perspective, using refutation, concession, or rebuttal.

For a complete list of the sources of information cited in this chapter, turn to the Works Cited appendix.

7 Case Study: Russia

Participation

May 1 is a holiday in Russia in honor of spring and of labor. This gathering takes place in Red Square in the Moscow Kremlin, a citadel that is also the seat of the Russian government. Saint Basil's Cathedral, built in the mid-1500s, is in the background, illustrating the close connection between the government and the Russian Orthodox Church.

Vladimir Putin: A Long Career

Vladimir Vladimirovich Putin is already the second longest serving leader of the Russian Federation, or its predecessor state the Soviet Union, surpassed only by Joseph Stalin who ruled from 1927 until his death in 1953. Putin became acting president in 1999 after the resignation of Boris Yeltsin, and in 2000, he was elected to his first four-year term as president. He was reelected in 2004, but term limits barred him from running in 2008. He then moved into the position of prime minister where he exercised essentially the same powers as president. While Putin was prime minister, the presidential term of office was extended to six years. Putin was elected to a third term as president in 2012 and a fourth term in 2018. In 2020, constitutional amendments reset term limits so that Putin can run again in 2024, and again in 2030, at which time he will be 83 years old and will have been in power for thirty-six years, a decade longer than Stalin.

Putin was born in 1952, seven years after the end of World War II (in Russia, called the Great Patriotic War) in what was then Leningrad (now called Saint Petersburg). Putin came from a poor family, but one that had connections with the Soviet Union's top leaders. Putin's grandfather was a cook for both Lenin and Stalin.

Leningrad is the site of one of the most brutal battles of World War II. The Siege of Leningrad lasted for 872 days and was one of the bloodiest episodes of the war. Some historians have labeled it genocide because of the Nazis' intentional targeting of civilians. More than a million people died.

Putin's father, a soldier, was wounded and severely disabled for the rest of his life. His mother barely survived and a young son, born before Putin, died. Putin's early years were spent in an apartment that did not have its own kitchen. A communal kitchen was shared among three families, as was a toilet that was built into part of the stairwell. The Putin family's apartment was a room twelve by fifteen feet, which was considered large by Soviet standards of the time.

The building had a courtyard where he spent much of his youth. A long-time friend described what it was like in the courtyard. "Thugs all. Unwashed, unshaven guys with cigarettes and bottles of cheap wine. Constant drinking, cursing, fistfights. And there was Putin in the middle of all this." Putin, never large for his age, was quick to defend himself. "If anyone ever insulted him in any way, [Putin] would immediately jump on the guy, scratch him, bite him, rip his hair out by the clump—do anything at all never to allow anyone to humiliate him in any way." (Gessen.) Even in grade school he was prone to fighting, and as punishment, the school initially prevented him from joining the Young Pioneers, officially known as the Vladimir Lenin All-Union Pioneer Organization.

Putin has never been shy about discussing his turbulent youth. In 2000, when asked why he had not been allowed in the Young Pioneers, he responded: "Of course. I was no Pioneer. I was a hooligan . . . I was a real thug." (Gessen.) For three years, he was the only child in the school prevented from joining. When he was finally allowed to join the Young Pioneers, he was elected class chairman.

Part of his transformation from hooligan to leader was his embrace of martial arts. At age eleven he started practicing Sambo, a Russian combination of judo, karate, and wrestling. By his early twenties, he had become Leningrad's judo champion.

As a teenager, Putin unsuccessfully tried to join the KGB, the Soviet security service that functioned as an intelligence agency that sought out foreign spies and repressed domestic dissent. He was subsequently recruited upon graduation from Leningrad State University (now Saint Petersburg State University) with a degree in international law.

Putin rose to the rank of lieutenant colonel during his sixteen years as an officer in the KGB. He resigned after the 1991 attempted military coup against Mikhail Gorbachev and returned to Leningrad, where he began his political career.

In 1996, Putin moved to Moscow after the mayor he worked for lost reelection. His rise to national power was rapid. He was appointed to an administrative position that was responsible for transferring assets owned by the Soviet Union to the newly independent Russia. Within a year, he was appointed to President Boris Yeltsin's staff. By 1999, he was the acting and then the appointed prime minister. At the end of the year, he became acting president after Yeltsin resigned, and in early 2000, he was elected to his first term as president.

Over his two decades in office, Putin has remained remarkably popular, although in recent years his popularity has not remained at its previous high levels. There are at least five elements to his continuing ability to rule: (1) management of the economy; (2) assertive foreign policy; (3) embrace of Russian nationalism and religion; (4) a vigorous strongman image; and (5) repression of dissent.

Putin stepped into office as president with the economy in freefall. The transition to a market economy disrupted Russian life. Economic output declined by almost half in the 1990s, life expectancy declined, alcoholism soared, and poverty was widespread.

Putin had the good fortune to take charge just as world energy prices shot up. He also ushered in some key economic reforms drafted by the Yeltsin administration that contributed to the state's ability to collect revenues, such as a 13 percent flat tax.

Russia is one of the largest energy producers in the world (oil, natural gas, coal). Oil prices surged from a low of $10 a barrel to almost $150 a barrel during his first ten years in office. Putin was able to use export revenue to improve and modernize the economy. During his first decade in office, Russia had extraordinary economic growth. In the ten years from 1999 to 2008, the Russian GDP almost doubled. Putin's popularity soared.

Putin's popularity before 2011–12 was due to elections and the appearance of party competition, which led most Russians to think that their system was democratic. That façade was called into question with protests against elections in 2011 and 2012, and the regime began to pivot toward nationalism and conservative traditionalism.

The upheaval in Ukraine in 2013–14 provided an unexpected opening for the Putin administration to increase its popularity. The collapse of the Soviet Union reduced Russia's global influence. Putin has been aggressive in asserting Russia's interests and role in the world.

Crimea, a part of the Russian Empire since the eighteenth century, became part of the Ukrainian Republic of the Soviet Union in the 1950s. With the dissolution of the Soviet Union, Crimea remained part of the now-independent nation of Ukraine. Putin saw Crimea as part of Russia's national identity and key to its interests. It contains a strategic port on the Black Sea, and the majority of the population is ethnic Russian.

In the early 2000s, Ukraine's government sought closer ties to the European Union. Russian leadership eventually came to see Ukraine's Western orientation as a threat, particularly after a pro-Western candidate claimed election fraud in the 2004 election, resulting in a protest movement called the Orange Revolution. The Russian government became even more concerned after NATO offered Membership Action Plans to Ukraine and Georgia in 2008. In 2014, protests ousted the Ukrainian president who had rejected closer relations with the EU in favor of closer relations with Russia. The Russian military, which had tens of thousands of troops stationed in Crimea as part of an agreement with Ukraine, launched a covert operation.

Crimea was subsequently annexed to Russia. In February 2020, Russia invaded Ukraine, launching a brutal assault, which resulted in international condemnation and a refugee crisis as hundreds of thousands fled Ukraine. The capture of Crimea and the subsequent war in Ukraine were justified by the state media and celebrated by the regime as an expression of Russian nationalism. Russia has been accused of crimes against humanity for targeting and killing civilians. As of the time of this writing, the war in Ukraine continues, several cities have been destroyed, and thousands of people have died.

Putin has also positioned himself as not only the defender of Russian nationalism, but also of the Russian Orthodox Church. During the Soviet era, the Church did not have a prominent public role. Official state policy was atheism. Putin has appeared at church celebrations and directed funds to rebuild churches. Putin has been critical of Western multiculturalism, endorsed traditional family values, and put into effect an anti-gay propaganda law that bans the "promotion of nontraditional sexual relations to minors" and covers the press, television, radio, and the internet. One feature of the 2020 constitutional amendments bans same-sex marriage.

Throughout his political career, Putin has sought to maintain a public image of masculine virility. He regularly appears for photographs hunting, fishing, diving, racing cars, and playing hockey and judo. In 2016, he authored a book on judo that was distributed to 7 million school children in the first through fourth grades.

Putin also hosts an annual call-in show, where average Russians can talk to the president directly. Reports of how these events are managed and how calls are pre-screened have raised questions that they are staged. Regardless, Putin's image as a strong, effective leader stands in stark contrast to Boris Yeltsin who was viewed as a weak leader and heavy drinker by the end of his time in office.

In recent years, repression of the opposition has also been common. Dissidents have been jailed and independent journalists harassed. Prominent opponents have died under mysterious circumstances, some poisoned, some shot, others due to unexplained causes. Putin's government has control of each of the national television networks. Not content to

Russian President Vladimir Putin addresses journalists in a video press conference on December 17, 2020. The size of the image illustrates Putin's power and influence over the Russian state and its citizens.

control the news of the day, Putin tightened his grip on history with a feature of the 2020 constitutional amendments that prohibits questioning of the official history of World War II.

Putin looms so large over Russia, having ruled for two-thirds of its time as an independent nation, that Vyacheslav Volodin, the Kremlin's deputy chief of staff, stated: "There is no Russia today if there is no Putin."

Russia (formally named the Russian Federation) has a long history of authoritarian rule. Freedom House classifies the state as "not free," and the political system has been described as authoritarian, competitive authoritarian, a hybrid regime, and an illiberal democracy. Although it holds elections, competition is limited, and one party, United Russia, won a majority of legislative seats from 2003 to 2021. Under President Vladimir Putin, power has become more centralized in both the national government and in the executive. In recent years, citizens' civil rights and liberties have come under attack, and the state has weak rule of law along with high levels of corruption.

BY THE NUMBERS	RUSSIA
Land area	17,098,242 sq. km
Population	142,320,790 (July 2021 est.)
Urban population	74.8% (2020)
Life expectancy	Male 66.6 Female 78 (2021 est.)
Literacy rate	Male 99.7% Female 99.7% (2018)
HDI	0.824 (2020)
HDI ranking	52/189 (2020)
GDP	$1,464,078,000,000 (2020)
GDP ranking	11/195 (2020)
GDP per capita	$10,127 (2020)
Internet users	80.86% (2018)
Internet users ranking	5/229 (2018)
Gini index (coefficient)	37.5 (2019)
Freedom House rating	Not Free (2020)
Corruption Perceptions ranking	136/180 (2021)
Fragile States Index classification	Elevated Warning (2020)

Data from *CIA World Factbook*, World Bank, Freedom House, Transparency International, Fragile States Index.

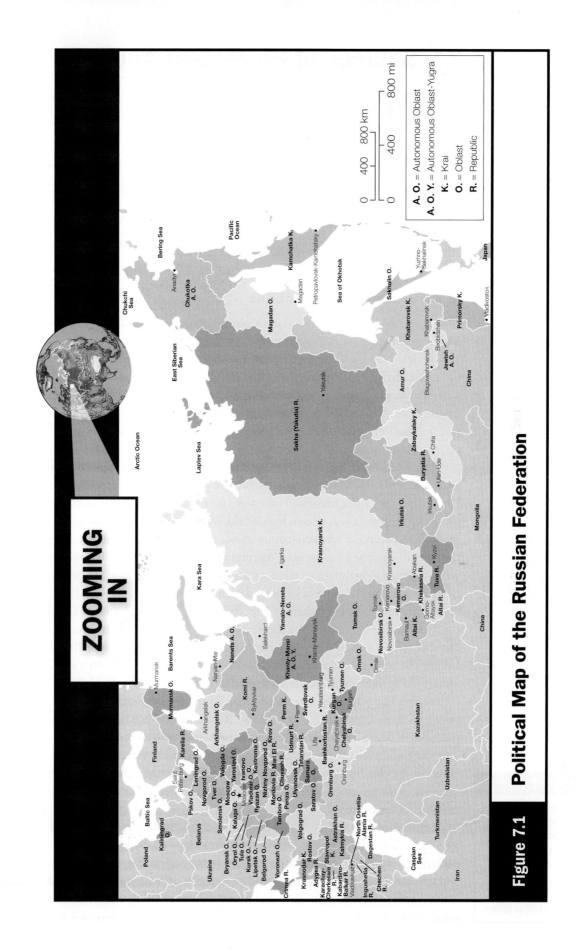

ZOOMING
IN

Figure 7.1 **Political Map of the Russian Federation**

A. O. = Autonomous Oblast
A. O. Y. = Autonomous Oblast-Yugra
K. = Krai
O. = Oblast
R. = Republic

0   400   800 km
0   400   800 mi

7.1 Sources of Power and Authority

Learning Targets

After reading this section, you should be able to do the following:

1. Explain why Russia failed to democratize.

2. Describe federalism in Russia.

3. Describe challenges facing the Russian state.

A Brief History of Russia

The story of Vladimir Putin's rise to power is consistent with Russia's long history of authoritarian rule, which was broken by brief attempts at democratization. Ivan IV Vasilyevich (Ivan the Terrible) took the Russian title "tsar" (emperor) in 1547 and greatly increased the monarch's power and the state's territory. By 1660, Russia was geographically the largest country in the world. The country became a vast, multinational state where more than one hundred languages were spoken, governed by a monarchy. The tsar was an absolutist ruler with even greater power than most monarchs in Europe. Russia began to industrialize, and cities grew.

Tsar Nicholas II was forced to agree to the creation of an elected legislature, the State Duma, in 1905. However, the tsar could rule by emergency decree, and he dissolved the Duma after only three months. There were four Dumas from 1906 until 1917.

In 1914, Russia was drawn into World War I, which was economically disastrous for the empire. Because it was still mainly a poor and agricultural society, soldiers were sent to the front ill equipped and hungry. As conditions worsened, mass desertions occurred. The state struggled to maintain its territory and military, undermining legitimacy. The makings of another electoral democracy emerged with a revolution in February 1917, when the tsar abdicated, only to be overtaken by a second, communist revolution in October.

Vladimir Lenin, inspired by the writings of Karl Marx, led his forces to victory in the October Revolution of 1917 and created the world's first communist regime, the Soviet Union. The communists assassinated the tsar and his family, and many non-Russian provinces of the former empire declared their independence. By the end of the civil war in 1921, the communists had re-incorporated much of the territory of the former empire. A new state called the Union of Soviet Socialist Republics (U.S.S.R.), or the Soviet Union, was established, which became a brutal but nonetheless modern state.

The Communist Party created a single-party dictatorship. Lenin claimed that a small group of the elite had legitimacy because it understood Marxism and could represent the interests of the majority. The Communist Party claimed it was justified in ruthlessly suppressing all opposition.

Lenin died in January 1924, and after a succession struggle, Joseph Stalin came to power. Stalin launched a plan to institute state control of the economy and take ownership of virtually all land. He rapidly industrialized the country, moving resources and laborers from the countryside and completely controlling all economic activity. The result was rapid industrialization that transformed the Soviet Union from an underdeveloped agrarian economy into an industrial powerhouse and superpower by World War II.

Under Stalin, the secret police dealt harshly with anyone who opposed the government's methods, creating an oppressive and ruthless police state that controlled an extensive network of prison camps (known as the *gulags*). Estimates of deaths range from 2 million to 20 million. Stalin created a totalitarian state that eliminated independent civil society and crushed dissent. However, the totalitarian state was difficult to maintain because it was costly for the state to police citizens constantly.

After Stalin's death in 1953, another succession struggle ensued, with Nikita Khrushchev taking the reins of leadership in 1956. Under Khrushchev, the Communist Party reasserted its control over the state, reduced the power of the secret police, and instituted de-Stalinization reforms that reduced state terror and repression.

Although the Party maintained centralized control over the economy, there was greater emphasis on producing consumer goods that would improve Soviet citizens' lives. By the mid-to-late 1970s, the inefficiencies of central planning and state economic control contributed to economic stagnation and an overall decline in the wealth and productivity of the Soviet Union compared to Western countries.

By the mid-1980s, a new generation of leaders led by General Secretary of the Communist Party Mikhail Gorbachev realized the Soviet Union had to increase economic productivity and allow some open political debate to survive. Gorbachev launched political and economic reforms, including glasnost, which allowed more citizen criticism of the state, and perestroika, a restructuring of the U.S.S.R.'s political and economic systems.

Instead of strengthening the economy and political system, Gorbachev's reforms contributed to an economic and political crisis of monumental proportions. Economic production stalled, inflation skyrocketed, and several non-Russian regions clamored for independence. As a result, Gorbachev and his policies became very unpopular among many Soviet citizens as well as Communist Party elites.

In August 1991, Soviet military and secret-police leaders attempted a coup d'état meant to restore some of the old order. Boris Yeltsin, the leader of the Russian Republic within the Soviet Union, stood up to the tanks and denounced the coup plotters. The military, faced with mass demonstrations in the streets, and under the watchful eye of the international press, backed down.

The Scarlet Sails festival in June celebrates the end of the school year. The city of St. Petersburg was founded in 1703 by Tsar Peter the Great, who made the city the capital of the Russian Empire. The city is a cultural gem, and its museums contain some of the finest art collections in the world. It is the second largest in population of Russia's cities and the place where President Putin was born.

Anton Vaganov/Alamy

The coup had failed, as had political and economic reforms intended to resuscitate the U.S.S.R. under Communist Party leadership. In December 1991, leaders of Russia, Ukraine, and Belarus signed an agreement dissolving the Soviet Union, and fifteen separate states, including the Russian Federation, emerged from the remnants. On December 25, 1991, the red Soviet flag was lowered over the Moscow Kremlin for the last time.

Failed Democratization

Following the dissolution of the Soviet Union, Russia appeared to be transitioning from communism to democracy and capitalism. Yeltsin had been elected as the first president of the Russian Republic in 1990. However, the 1990s in Russia were chaotic, both politically and economically. Yeltsin presided over a rapid but painful transition to a market economy that harmed his popular support.

On the advice of Western economists, Russia rapidly switched from a command economy to more of a free-market economy by adopting a policy known as shock therapy. Shock therapy is the immediate removal of all state intervention from an economy. Examples of such interventions include price supports, subsidies, trade tariffs, and currency controls. Shock therapy also called for severe cuts to the government's budget and envisioned the swift privatization of state-owned industries.

Russia's economy was in crisis, and a rapid transformation into a free-market system was seen as the way to stop the free-fall and to get Western financial assistance and political support. Instead, shock-therapy policies contributed to a steep fall in production, soaring prices, and a rapid rise in unemployment. Most citizens saw the value of their savings decline as they had to pay more for goods and services due to inflation. Furthermore, many experienced job loss or salary cuts.

As part of the shift away from a command economy, the Yeltsin government developed a plan for privatizing industries that it hoped would lessen the impact of shock therapy. People were given vouchers to buy shares in formerly state-owned enterprises (SOEs). In theory, newly privatized businesses would be owned by many shareholders. However, ordinary citizens often did not understand the purpose of the vouchers, and most did not have the financial reserves necessary to allow them to hold these shares until the economy stabilized. Many sold their vouchers, often to former enterprise managers who had enough money to take advantage of the plan and become major shareholders of key businesses. This created a small number of very powerful businessmen, known as oligarchs.

Oligarchs are people whose ownership of large businesses translates into a significant amount of control over a country's economy. Because the central government was desperate for cash, these powerful men were able to buy up companies in key economic sectors, such as oil and minerals, for a fraction of what they were worth. As a result, they were accused of amassing wealth and rising to power through corruption, particularly because they were also closely associated with the Yeltsin government.

The result of shock therapy in Russia was disastrous. Inflation skyrocketed, and the value of the ruble plummeted. The economic recession that followed destabilized the Yeltsin government.

By the late 1990s, Yeltsin had very little support. He resigned on December 31, 1999, a few weeks after the Duma election and six months before the June presidential election. His prime minister at the time, Vladimir Putin, became acting president and ran the state as the incumbent president. The presidential election was moved up three months, to March 2000, which hampered the opposition's ability to launch an effective campaign.

Putin, whose popularity as prime minister had soared as he decisively directed Russia's second military offensive in the breakaway region of Chechnya, promised to strengthen the state and create order. He won the presidential election handily in March 2000. Putin strengthened the state by increasing power in the executive, strengthening the central government's power over regional governments, reducing crime, and restoring order. In the process, however, he effectively eliminated the electoral democracy that had been forged during the Yeltsin era.

Putin rapidly created an electoral authoritarian regime, though he referred to it as "managed democracy," saying he supported democracy but only if it did not produce disorder and weakness. In the 2000s, this regime was characterized by somewhat competitive elections and an electoral system that favored the pro-Putin party, United Russia.

Bolstered by an economic upswing and soaring oil prices, Putin's government also promoted members of the intelligence services to important state positions, stripped opponents of their assets, and centralized the Russian state. In the 2010s, after successfully riding out the mass protests organized in response to fraudulent legislative elections in 2011, Putin's regime began to rely more on nationalism and traditional values to appeal to citizens.

Putin had worked in the KGB, the main security agency of the Soviet Union from 1975 to 1991, and became the director of the Federal Security Service (FSB, the successor to the KGB) in 1998. As president, he placed several former FSB agents in key ministries and agencies throughout the executive branch, appointed them as governors of regions, and gave them control of many important companies. (Hesli, 2007.) They were his closest, most reliable allies. As they gained power and positions, their loyalty was also cemented through opportunities for corruption, with many becoming very wealthy.

Putin's most powerful potential enemies were the oligarchs—the wealthiest and most influential of whom were in the energy and media sectors. Most famous was Mikhail Khodorkovsky, head of the giant Yukos oil firm. By 2003, he was becoming increasingly open about his plans to enter politics against Putin. Putin used selective enforcement of anticorruption laws and the tax code to eliminate Khodorkovsky, who was charged with corruption and ultimately jailed by a compliant judiciary whose judges Putin mostly appointed. The government took control of Yukos, placing it firmly in the hands of the state oil company, led by loyal Putin supporters.

More recently, Putin has increasingly championed nationalism as a basis for legitimacy, most famously in Russia's successful annexation in 2014 of the Crimean Peninsula, a mainly Russian-speaking region of Ukraine. Putin successfully strengthened Russia's external sovereignty, but he has undermined the rule of law and weakened the state in other ways. Russia scores very poorly on the Fragile States Index on "group grievances," "human rights," and the quality of the "security apparatus." In addition, Freedom House rates Russia as "not free."

Federalism

Russia is a multiethnic state, with a federal system of government that gives some power, at least in theory, to the various regions, about one-quarter of which are defined loosely along ethnic lines. The Russian constitution of 1993 created a federal system with eighty-nine (later consolidated to eighty-five) subnational units. It gave the greatest powers, however, to the central government, reserving only a handful of powers for joint national-local control, such as social and educational services. The central government also has most of the taxation power, leaving regions with little ability to raise their own revenue.

The status of *republic* is given to regions deemed ethnically non-Russian. On paper, republics used to have more power than other federal units, including more power over state property and trade. This produced what is called **asymmetrical federalism**, because some regions had more formal power than others. Asymmetrical federalism in the 1990s gave way to centralizing reforms in the 2000s that established greater institutional and legal uniformity across the regions. (Sakwa, 2021.)

Asymmetrical federalism
A system in which some regions have more formal power and autonomy than others.

In the 1990s, ethnic nationalism was a severe challenge for the Russian state, as different regions demanded varying degrees of autonomy. The most serious was Chechnya's demand for independence, which resulted in two wars between Russia's military and Chechen rebels in the 1990s and 2000s.

Today, the predominantly Muslim region of Chechnya remains under Russian rule through the control of a local government that has the backing of the federal government to ruthlessly suppress rebel opposition. While the wars in Chechnya were the only conflicts to produce widespread violence, similar tensions across the country resulted in repeated efforts to recognize ethnically defined governments while preserving the Russian Federation as a whole.

Vladimir Putin came to power with a goal of centralizing power. Seven federal districts were created in 2000, each run by an appointee of the president. An eighth district, North Caucasus, was created in 2010, following the Second Chechen War. These districts are not mentioned in the constitution, and they were created so that the federal government could more effectively oversee Russia's vast territory. Putin appoints presidential representatives, known as super-governors, who oversee the eight districts. As the economy boomed in the early 2000s, revenue poured into the central state's treasury, which Putin distributed to regions based on their political loyalty.

In 2000, Putin's government launched reforms to tame the powerful regional governors by supporting legislation to reform the upper house of parliament. Governors were no longer automatically members of the Federation Council, and instead those positions were appointed by governors and heads of regional legislatures.

In 2004, Putin moved to gut regional autonomy nearly completely by introducing reforms that allowed him to cancel gubernatorial elections in favor of presidential appointment, further centralizing power. President Dmitry Medvedev restored elections for governors in early 2012. However, the Putin administration has the authority to dismiss regional governors who have little public support and replace them with people who are more likely to win the next election. (Zubarevich, 2017.)

Putin succeeded in transforming Russia from a weak democracy to an electoral authoritarian regime. Nevertheless, federalism places some limits on central authority. With formal institutions so weak, powerful leaders have arisen in the least democratic regions. These leaders don't face much opposition, and they have the support of local elites. They bargain with central government authorities for greater autonomy and resources. (Obydenkova and Swenden.) Putin formed a State Council, which is made up of the leaders of regional governments, to utilize their power and to advise the president on important national issues. Weaker local leaders such as mayors of cities outside Moscow and St. Petersburg, though, have little autonomy.

Legitimacy and Challenges to the State

With his allies in control of key state agencies, the oligarchs tamed, and the ruling party established, Putin eliminated almost all traces of real democracy. In addition to increasing the powers of the presidency over the regions, his government harassed and closed down many independent media outlets and gradually undermined the independence of civil-society groups. He has remained in power since 1999, and amendments to the constitution approved by voters in 2020 will allow him to rule until at least 2036.

President Putin won his fourth presidential election in March 2018. Here, he is taking the oath of office in the inauguration ceremony at the Grand Kremlin Palace.

Kremlin Pool/Planetpix/Alamy

Centralizing so much power in one person means that finding a successor will pose a challenge. Russia may face a power vacuum when Putin leaves office and members of the elite vie for control. In the meantime, Russia faces other problems.

In 2014, during the crisis in Ukraine, the United States, other countries, and the European Union imposed financial sanctions against Russian officials, citizens, and businesses, such as financial institutions. The sanctions damaged the Russian economy and weakened the ruble. In 2017, the United States imposed additional sanctions against Russia for interfering in the 2016 presidential election and to punish Russia for its actions in Syria and Ukraine. Additional sanctions were imposed in 2018, and the United States, Western countries, and NATO expelled Russian diplomats after a Russian who was working for the British intelligence service was poisoned. In response to the 2022 invasion of Ukraine, the European Union, United States, and other countries issued broad economic sanctions against Russia. Foreign assets owned by Putin and other members of the elite were frozen. These actions were an attempt to damage the Russian economy and pressure the government to end the war. In addition, Western powers sent military aid, including weapons, to Ukraine.

Russia also faces pressure from NGOs to improve its record on human rights. The recent crackdown began in 2012, grew worse in 2014, and has intensified since 2017. Human Rights Watch reported that, in 2019, the Russian government responded to civic activism with violence, detentions, and prosecutions that lacked due process of law. For example, Alexei Navalny has been a vocal critic since about 2010 and has pursued various anti-government and anticorruption campaigns for at least a decade. Navalny was poisoned in 2020 and sent to prison in 2021 based on a 2014 conviction of fraud. International human-rights organizations widely publicize Russia's abuses of civil liberties and have led worldwide campaigns to pressure Russia to release political prisoners from jail. (Human Rights Watch, 2018.)

The Russian state consolidated power in both the executive and in the central government. Nevertheless, it will likely continue to face both internal and external challenges to its sovereignty and legitimacy.

Section 7.1 Review

Each section's main ideas are reflected in the Learning Targets. By reviewing after each section, you should be able to

Remember the key points,

Know terms that are central to the topic, and

Think critically about what you have learned.

Remember

- Russia has a long history of authoritarian rule, and brief attempts at democratization have been unsuccessful.
- Putin strengthened the state by increasing power in the executive, strengthening the central government's power over regional governments, reducing crime, and appealing to nationalism.
- Although Russia has a federal system, some regions used to have greater autonomy than others, and the national government has centralized power.
- Russia faces challenges, including a potential leadership vacuum when Putin leaves office and international pressure to end human-rights abuses.

Know

- *Asymmetrical federalism:* a system in which some regions have more formal power and autonomy than others. (p. 207)

Think

- Why was the Putin administration able to centralize power in a strong executive?
- Why is federalism weak in Russia?

7.2 Institutions of Government

Learning Targets

After reading this section, you should be able to do the following:

1. Describe a semi-presidential system of government.

2. Explain why the Russian president has strong powers.

3. Describe the powers of the Duma and Federation Council.

4. Explain why the judiciary is ineffective in checking executive power.

The Russian constitution adopted in 1993 created a semi-presidential system with an exceptionally strong presidency. The legislature and judicial institutions are relatively weak, and they do not serve as an effective check on executive power.

The Executive

Russia's semi-presidential system has a dual executive, with both a president and a prime minister. The president is the head of state, and the prime minister is the head of government. The constitution stipulates that the president is directly elected by citizens and may serve for two consecutive six-year terms. With the 2020 constitutional reforms, President Putin is eligible to run for two more consecutive six-year terms after his current term ends in 2024.

Russia's semi-presidential system differs from most semi-presidential systems. First, the prime minister is appointed by the president and can be easily removed by the president, making the prime minister more accountable to the president than the legislature, which is not the case in most semi-presidential systems that require a legislative majority to support the prime minister's removal. Second, the prime minister is not a member of the legislature in Russia, which also runs contrary to many semi-presidential systems.

The president appoints the prime minister with the approval of the Duma (the lower house of parliament), but if the Duma votes against the president's candidate for prime minister three times, the Duma is automatically dissolved, and new elections are called. This means that unless the president's opponents in the Duma think they will gain a significant number of seats in the election, they will hesitate before opposing his nominee. The president also appoints all cabinet members, without the approval of the Duma. Neither the prime minister nor the rest of the cabinet has to be members of the Duma, and the vast majority has not been. This structure frees the president to appoint anyone he pleases to the cabinet, regardless of which party controls parliament. Although the president has the power to oversee cabinet meetings, he usually delegates this task to the prime minister.

The president is the commander-in-chief, and he conducts foreign policy. He has direct control over several key ministries (foreign affairs, defense, and interior) and the Federal Security Service. In these areas, his authority bypasses the prime minister and the cabinet altogether. Perhaps most important, the president can issue decrees that have the force of law and cannot be vetoed by the Duma or challenged in court, which gives him the power to bypass the legislature in making policy.

Legislation adopted in 2000 gave the president the power to dismiss all governors of Russia's eighty-five regions. The governors appoint half of the members of the Federation Council, the upper house of parliament. Gubernatorial elections were canceled in 2004 and then restored in 2012. The law was amended in 2013 to allow the president to present a list of gubernatorial candidates to regional authorities, returning significant power to the president.

The Duma can initiate a vote of no confidence in the prime minister but must do so twice to remove him from office. The Duma and the Federation Council can also impeach the president by a two-thirds vote in each chamber, but this has been attempted only once, in 1999, and failed.

Upon assuming office in 2000, Putin announced goals of establishing order, increasing the strength of the state, and furthering market-oriented economic reforms. After a decade of chaos and weakness, the public was ready for order and strength, and Putin won the 2000 election with 53 percent of the vote in the first round. Putin successfully undermined the power of the parliament by encouraging voters to support the United Russia party and gained complete control of the Federation Council, which became a rubber stamp for his proposals.

As the head of government, the prime minister oversees the cabinet for the president and is in charge of policy implementation, including domestic and foreign policies, presidential decrees, and international agreements. (Reuters.) Russia's prime minister is more of a manager than a politician, and he does not have an independent power base. If the president becomes incapacitated or resigns, as Yeltsin did in late 1999, the prime minister becomes the acting president, and a presidential election is held within three months. Given the extensive nature of presidential power in Russia's unique semi-presidential system, the prime minister is subservient to the president.

The Legislature

Russia's bicameral parliament consists of the Duma and the Federation Council. The **Duma** is the directly elected lower house, and it represents the people. It has the power to debate and pass laws. It also has the power to confirm or reject the president's nominee for prime minister, although as mentioned earlier, if the Duma rejects the president's nominee for prime minister three times, the Duma is dissolved, and new elections are called.

The Duma has the power to appoint and dismiss heads of the Central Bank and of the Commission on Human Rights. (State Duma Web site.) Although the Duma has the power to investigate actions by the executive branch and impeach the president, it is unlikely to do so, because United Russia, Putin's political party, has been the majority party in the Duma since 2003.

The **Federation Council** is the appointed upper house. As is typical in federal systems with bicameral legislatures, Russia's upper house represents regions. Each of Russia's

Duma
The directly elected lower house of the Russian parliament that represents the people and has the power to pass laws, confirm the prime minister, and begin impeachment proceeding against the president.

Federation Council
The appointed upper house of the Russian parliament that represents the regions and has the power to initiate, review, and amend legislation, approve troop deployments, and remove the president.

Russians Assess Putin and Their Country's Direction

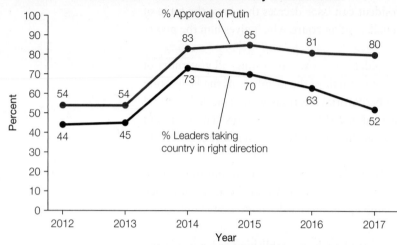

Data from Gallup World Poll.

The quantitative free-response question will provide you with a table, chart, graph, map, or other visual representation of data. Answering the quantitative FRQ requires you to demonstrate an understanding of the data and then apply your understanding to concepts you have learned in the course.

Some parts of the question will include the phrase, "using the data in the . . ." Whenever you see this language on the AP® Exam, you should pull numbers directly from the map, graph, chart, or table and use them in your response. Here is a sample part A:

"Using the data in the graph, identify the year with the highest percentage of support for Putin's leadership."

A strong response would state, "Putin had the most support in 2015, with an 85 percent approval rating."

This is a good response, because it identifies both the year with the highest rating and the percentage of support for Putin.

Here is a sample part B:

"Using the data in the graph, describe a trend in the approval ratings of President Putin."

A weak response would state, "President Putin's approval rating went down."

This is a weak response because it doesn't address the time period of the decline, and it doesn't use the data from the graph as supporting evidence.

A strong response would state, "President Putin's approval ratings remained relatively steady from 2014 to 2017, with ratings of 83 percent in 2014, 85 percent in 2015, 81 percent in 2016, and 80 percent in 2017."

An alternative strong response would state, "President Putin's approval rating declined slightly from 85 percent in 2015 to 80 percent in 2017.

Both of these are good responses, because they use both the years and the percentages in the answer.

Answer the following questions.

1. Using the data from the graph, draw a conclusion about the level of public approval for the Russian president.

2. Using the data from the graph, draw a conclusion about the stability of the Russian regime.

3. Explain why it is important to use specific data points in answering the quantitative free-response question on the AP® Comparative Government and Politics exam.

eighty-five administrative units has two senators in the Federation Council. Since 2000, one senator is selected by the regional governor (who since 2004 is usually appointed by the president) and confirmed by the regional legislature. The other senator is selected by the regional legislature.

The Federation Council has the power to draft laws and initiate legislation. It reviews laws passed by the Duma that involve the federal budget and monetary policy. The Federation Council has the power to reject laws passed by the Duma, but a law that has been rejected by the Federation Council can still be passed by the Duma with a two-thirds vote. It also has the exclusive power to approve troop deployments abroad, ratify treaties, and modify regional boundaries. The Federation Council approves the

FIGURE 7.2

The Structure of the Government of Russia

Power in a System with Asymmetric Federalism

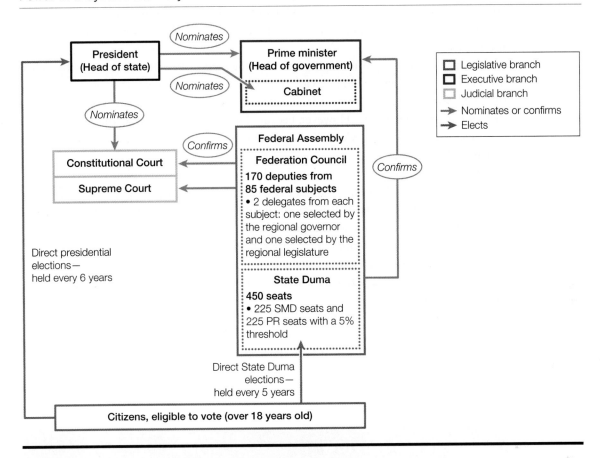

president's nomination of judges to Russia's Constitutional and Supreme Courts. Under constitutional amendments approved by voters in 2020, the Federation Council has the power to remove federal judges on recommendation of the president. (Federation Council Web site.)

The Federation Council has the power to remove the president from office, following impeachment proceedings in the Duma. In 1999, communists in the Duma attempted to impeach Boris Yeltsin on a number of charges of "high crimes," including waging war against the breakaway region of Chechnya. The impeachment was unsuccessful because all charges fell short of the two-thirds vote required in the Duma. Given the close connections between members of both legislative chambers and the Putin administration, impeachment is extremely unlikely in today's Russia.

Figure 7.2 shows the structure of the bicameral legislature of Russia. It also shows the relation between the executive and the judiciary, as well as who has the power of appointment and confirmation.

The Judiciary

Federal court justices in Russia are appointed for life. Russia has a system of trial courts, appeals courts, and two high courts. The Supreme Court serves as a final court of appeals for cases that have worked their way through the legal system. It is a court of concrete review, which means that it rules in specific cases that have been brought before it. The Constitutional Court has the power of concrete review and of abstract review, which means it may rule on an issue without having a case before it. A 2020 constitutional amendment limits the Constitutional Court's power of abstract review to those cases where the president requests the Court to review a bill before he signs it into law.

On paper, the Constitutional Court has the power to overrule actions by other branches of government, including violations of civil rights and civil liberties. The Constitutional Court also has the power of judicial review to overturn laws and executive actions that violate the constitution. However, because judges are appointed by the president and confirmed by a Federation Council that is strongly influenced by the president, judicial review is not exercised.

As the case of Mikhail Khodorkovsky illustrates, the Russian regime is characterized by rule by law, and the judicial system is used to target and prosecute political opponents. For example, in 2012, Russian authorities arrested and detained five members of a female punk rock band on charges of hooliganism after the band performed songs at a cathedral near the Kremlin criticizing the connection between the Russian Orthodox Church and the Putin government. Two members of the band were sentenced to two years in prison. In 2021, after a series of arrests, members of the band fled Russia. (Kishkovsky, 2021.)

Rampant corruption, including bribery, undue influence from politicians, and the fabrication of evidence in criminal cases undermines the rule of law. (Risk and Compliance Portal.) In Russia, independence of both the legislative and judicial branches is weak, and neither serves as an effective check on executive power.

Section 7.2 Review

Remember

- In Russia's semi-presidential system, the president is directly elected, and the prime minister is appointed by the president and confirmed by the Duma.
- The Russian president has strong powers, including the power to rule by decree.
- The Russian parliament is bicameral, with an elected Duma representing the people and an appointed Federation Council representing the regions.
- Russia has very weak rule of law and lacks judicial independence.

Know

- *Duma:* the directly elected lower house of the Russian parliament that represents the people and has the power to pass laws, confirm the prime minister, and begin impeachment proceeding against the president. (p. 211)
- *Federation Council:* the appointed upper house of the Russian parliament that represents the regions and has the power to initiate, review, and amend legislation, approve troop deployments, and remove the president. (p. 211)

Think

- Under what circumstances could Russia's legislative and judicial branches gain greater autonomy and independence from the executive?

7.3 Electoral System, Political Parties, and Civil Society

Learning Targets

After reading this section, you should be able to do the following:

1. Describe the system for electing the Russian president.

2. Describe the system for electing the Duma.

3. Explain why Russia became a single-party dominant system.

4. Explain how social movements in Russia advocate for change, despite restrictions on civil society.

Although elections are not free and fair, Russians directly elect the president and the lower house of the legislature. Over time, Russia's party system has changed from a multiparty system to a system dominated by the United Russia party. Despite limitations on civil-society groups, social movements have formed and protested against the regime.

Preparing to vote in the March 2018 presidential election, a woman with a dog reads her ballot at a polling station in Moscow.

Alexander Nemenov/AFP/Getty Images

Elections

Russia holds national elections for the president and members of the Duma. The president is directly elected to a six-year term. The term under the Russian constitution was four years, but in 2008, it was increased to six years, effective in 2012. There was a maximum of two consecutive terms until 2020, when voters approved constitutional amendments resetting presidential terms, allowing Vladimir Putin to run for two more terms.

If no presidential candidate wins a majority in the first round of the election, a second round is held between the top two candidates. As you saw in studying Mexico, executives who are elected with less than a majority of the votes may lack a mandate to carry out their policies. By making sure that the Russian president is elected by a majority of the voters, the Russian president may have a mandate to get his programs enacted.

Since Putin has been president, he has won every election with a majority of the votes, so there has been no need for a second round of elections. Putin won 53 percent of the vote in the first-round election in 2000 and 71 percent of the vote in 2004. (Russia Votes.) Putin faced a constitutional limit of two consecutive terms as president, and he left the office of the presidency in 2008.

Dmitry Medvedev, the prime minister in the Putin administration, was elected president in May 2008, with 71 percent of the vote. Medvedev named Putin as prime minister and head of the United Russia party. Putin retained power informally, even though he was not the president.

After one term, Putin and Medvedev switched roles again, with Putin running for and winning the presidency in 2012 and Medvedev returning to the prime minister position. In 2008, during the Medvedev presidency, a successful constitutional amendment had lengthened the presidential term to two six-year terms (effective as of 2012), allowing him to remain president until 2024.

In the December 2011 legislative election, United Russia's majority of votes cast for seats in the Duma was reduced from 70 to 53 percent. The March 2012 presidential election took place during large-scale opposition demonstrations over alleged electoral fraud and opposition to Putin returning to the presidency. Putin's share of the vote declined slightly to 65 percent. Once Putin had secured his re-election, the Duma passed laws greatly increasing the penalties for unauthorized gatherings, intensifying regulations on and reporting requirements for civil-society organizations, and restricting internet content.

Putin handily won reelection in 2018, with 77 percent of the vote. His most serious rival, Alexei Navalny, known for organizing nationwide anticorruption campaigns, was barred from running. Interestingly, Putin also distanced himself from United Russia, running as an independent in hopes this would increase his margin of victory in a noncompetitive race. The government also engaged in a massive get-out-the-vote campaign and scheduled the election for the anniversary of the annexation of the Crimea to appeal to voters who like Putin's "tough guy" foreign policy. The opposition once again alleged and documented fraud, but Putin's dominance seemed secure, ensuring that his presidency would continue until his term ends in 2024. Under constitutional amendments approved in 2020, Putin may run for office again in 2024.

The Duma is also directly elected, and the chamber has 450 seats. Members of the Duma serve five-year terms, and there is no term limit. The electoral system for the Duma has been changed twice, each time with the goal of increasing the ability of United Russia to win seats. Under the most recent change, enacted in 2013, the Duma uses a mixed electoral system, with 225 seats elected through SMD and 225 seats chosen through PR. This is similar to the mixed electoral system used in Mexico. While this system would seem to provide opportunities for multiple parties to run candidates and win seats in legislative elections, elections in single-member districts and registration rules for parties heavily favor United Russia. The threshold to receive PR seats in the Duma is 5 percent, which shuts out smaller parties.

Furthermore, candidates from United Russia have an advantage in name recognition and resources in their districts, and United Russia offers incentives for independent candidates to join the majority party in the Duma. (Herszenhorn.) Because United Russia was the only party capable of running candidates in all SMD constituencies in the 2021 Duma election, the electoral system led it to win 324 of 450 seats, even though it won slightly under 50 percent of the popular vote.

While citizens in Russia elect both the president and the Duma, the rules for elections have enabled Putin and the United Russia party to strengthen their hold on the political system.

Political Parties

After the formation of the Russian Federation, the first election for seats in the Duma was held in 1993. Twelve political parties won more than one seat in the Duma. Since the beginning of the Putin administration in 1999, the number of political parties has dropped. In the 2021 election, only five parties won more than one seat in the Duma.

There are several reasons why the number of political parties in Russia has dwindled. It is difficult for small parties to meet the 5 percent threshold needed to win PR seats in the legislature. It is also difficult for parties to register with the Central Election Commission, which has the power to reject candidates. Parties already serving in the Duma have the right to nominate a list of candidates. Other parties must obtain 200,000 signatures, and no more than 7,000 signatures can come from one region. (Federal Law on Elections of Deputies to the State Duma of the Federal Assembly of the Russian Federation, 2014.) Although candidates who are rejected by the Central Election Commission may appeal to the Supreme Court, the court is controlled by allies of United Russia, and judicial decisions selectively disqualify opposing candidates. As a result of these tactics, Russia has become a single-party dominant system. This is similar to the single-party dominant system that existed under PRI control in Mexico before 2000.

The Formation of United Russia

Shortly after becoming acting president in 1999, Putin encouraged a couple of smaller parties in the Duma to merge to create United Russia. United Russia (formerly called Unity) was founded in 2001, and it is a conservative and nationalist party that supports Putin. At its peak in 2013, it had more than 2 million members, although that number stalled and has likely fallen since. (Sakwa, 2021). Putin built the party, and its main goal is supporting the regime. (Oversloot and Verheul, 2006.)

The key task in creating a single dominant party was overcoming the independent strength of regional elites. Putin offered regional elites incentives to join United Russia, promising them access to the state resources, which they could use to build loyalty through a patronage system. Those with the fewest local resources and weakest networks joined first, and eventually, most regional leaders joined United Russia. United Russia nearly won a majority of seats in the Duma in 2003, with 223 seats, and the party has won the majority of seats in the Duma since 2007.

Like Mexico under PRI rule until 2000, Russia allows other parties to run candidates and win some legislative seats, but the system is structured so that one party dominates the legislature. By the late 2000s, the party controlled most seats not only in the Duma but in legislatures in virtually all eighty-five regional governments, as well as almost all governorships. The Putin administration rewards loyal supporters and punishes those who are disloyal or ineffective. Putin built United Russia by constructing an electoral and legal framework that gives United Russia an advantage and makes it difficult for other parties to register for elections. Legislation also prohibits regional parties.

Putin also manipulated the electoral system. Under the mixed electoral system he inherited, his most significant opposition came from independent MPs elected in the single-member districts. In 2003, the electoral system was changed to a purely PR system, with a 7 percent threshold, to eliminate independent candidates. This significantly reduced the number of political parties in the Duma from 12 in 2003 to four in 2011. (Central Election Commission.)

As mentioned above, in 2013, the electoral system was changed to a mixed system with a 5 percent threshold for PR seats. United Russia dominated the SMD portion of seats in the legislature and maintained a significant majority in the Duma. The reduction in the number of parties was part of a broader process of weakening the legislature's potential for opposing the executive.

Despite United Russia's dominance, four other political parties won seats in the 2021 Duma elections. The Communist Party of the Russian Federation (CPRF), the successor party to the Communist Party of the Soviet Union (CPSU), formed by politicians from the former Soviet Union, is the second largest party in Russia, with more than 160,000 members. The party's ideology is a mix of nationalistic, imperialistic, and communist tendencies. The CPRF accepts the free market, although it wants to the government to constrain some of the negative effects of a free-market economy. (Sakwa, 2021.) The Communist Party won 57 seats, nearly 19 percent, in the Duma in the 2021 election. (Central Election Commission.)

The Liberal Democratic Party of Russia is a nationalist party that is neither liberal nor democratic. The Liberal Democrats are led by Vladimir Zhirinovsky, who has called for Russia to take Alaska back from the United States. He has also encouraged the United States to take steps to preserve the white race. The Liberal Democratic Party of Russia supports state regulation of a mixed economy and a foreign policy of expansionism. (Johnson.) It won 21 seats in the 2021 election. (Central Election Commission.)

A Just Russia is a pro-welfare socialist party created to lure voters away from the CPRF. Several center-left parties merged to form A Just Russia, which claims to represent the interest of the Russian people instead of the elite in power. Yet at the same time, the party has also declared its support for Putin. (Sakwa, 2021.) The party advocates a welfare state, with an economic system that fosters equality and fairness. (Johnson.) A Just Russia won 27 of the seats in the Duma in the 2021 election, about 6 percent. (Central Election Commission.)

A fourth party, New People, made its debut, winning 13 seats in the 2021 election. Although other parties continue to compete in elections and win some seats in the Duma, increased regulations make it more difficult for parties to get candidates on the ballot, and the emergence of United Russia as a dominant party is consistent with democratic backsliding and consolidation of the authoritarian regime.

Interest Groups and Social Movements

Interest groups in Russia are relatively weak. Groups that criticize the government are portrayed as disloyal. A law passed in 2012 requires groups that participate in political activity and receive any foreign assistance to register as "foreign agents." (Human Rights Watch, 2018.) Nonpolitical groups have greater leeway to form, especially those that support the regime or are viewed by the state as consistent with Russian cultural values. (Carnegie.) Despite restrictions on civil society, social movements focused on voting rights and LGBTQ issues have formed in Russia.

The parliamentary elections in December 2011 were marred by widespread fraud, some of it captured on video and posted on the internet. Although there were protests in the mid-2000s, Russian civil society became more active in criticizing the government. Protests of tens of thousands of people demanding fairer elections took place repeatedly from December 2011 to March 2012. The regime successfully resisted most of the protesters' demands, although some concessions were made such as electoral reforms and promises to return to gubernatorial election. Nevertheless, Putin was elected president in March 2012, having legally eliminated most serious opponents.

Fearing fraudulent parliamentary elections in 2015, Navalny's Smart Vote Campaign used social media to encourage supporters to vote for any party but United Russia, and United Russia's control was reduced from 70 to 53 percent of the seats in the Duma, despite widespread fraud. (Gel'man, 2015, 117.)

As the government made it more difficult for political parties opposed to United Russia to place candidates on the ballot, it also instituted new laws that dramatically increased the fines for unauthorized demonstrations and placed greater legal restrictions on NGOs. Nevertheless, protests in 2011 and 2012 against election fraud and street protests in 2017 and 2018 against corruption demonstrate that Russian civil society lies beneath the surface of government restrictions. Protesters garnered worldwide attention, highlighting irregularities in Russia's elections.

The social movement for LGBTQ rights in Russia is another example of citizens organizing to defend their rights and oppose state policies. Putin has closely aligned himself with the Russian Orthodox Church and has used the church's emphasis on traditional values to enact anti-LGBTQ laws. An "anti-gay propaganda" law, passed in 2013, prohibits information that the state believes promotes homosexuality to minors, including counseling services for young people who identify as LGBTQ.

On July 1, 2020, voters approved a constitutional amendment stipulating that marriage is between one man and one woman, banning same-sex marriage. (Lovetsky.) That same year, the Duma considered a law that would ban transgender people from changing the sex on their birth certificates, negatively impacting their legal ability to marry and raise children. (Human Rights Watch, 2020.)

Russian LGBTQ activists used social media to galvanize support and protest the proposed changes. Medical professionals who specialize in gender transitions also publicly opposed the law. High-profile figures, including popular actors and playwrights, criticized the law, giving interviews on Russia's remaining independent media outlets. Parliament scrapped the law in November 2020. (Roache.) Parliament's rejection of the law eliminating legal recognition for transgender people does not reduce the level of discrimination against LGBTQ people in Russia, but it may demonstrate the power of civil-society activism, even in authoritarian states.

Section 7.3 Review

Remember

- The Russian president is elected in a two-round system, for a six-year term, with a limit of two consecutive terms.
- The Duma is directly elected through a mixed system, with a 5 percent threshold for PR seats.
- Russia has a single-party dominant system.
- Although civil society is restricted in Russia, social movements have protested against election fraud and in favor of LGBTQ rights.

Think

- What caused Russia's transition from a multiparty system to a dominant party system?
- Why does civil society in Russia persist despite significant government restrictions?

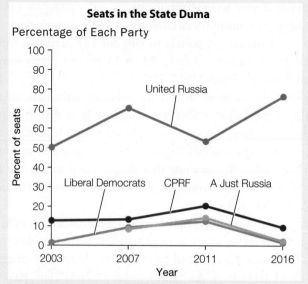

Seats in the State Duma

Percentage of Each Party

Note: Fractions are rounded up to the nearest percentage.
Data from Central Election Commission, Russia.

Answer A, B, C, D, and E.

A. Using the data in the graph, identify the political party with the largest number of seats in the Duma in 2016.

B. Using the data in the graph, describe a trend in the number of seats held by a political party in the Duma from 2003 to 2016.

C. Define single-party dominant system.

D. Using your knowledge of a single-party dominant system and the data in the graph, draw a conclusion about the level of political competition in Russia.

E. Explain how a single-party dominant system impacts democratization.

7.4 Political Culture and Participation

Learning Targets

After reading this section, you should be able to do the following:

1. Explain how Russian political authorities have used referendums to demonstrate public support for the regime and increase legitimacy.

2. Explain how Russian political authorities have created government-sponsored organizations to encourage support for the regime.

3. Describe Russia's restrictions on civil rights and liberties.

4. Explain how the conflict in Chechnya has impacted the Russian state.

Russia's long history of authoritarian rule is reflected in its political culture. Civil society in Russia is relatively weak, and the government places significant restrictions on civil rights and liberties. The government provides citizens with opportunities to participate in the political system as a way of strengthening the regime.

Referendums

Nondemocratic regimes use referendums to provide citizens with an opportunity to show their support for the regime. In April 1993, Boris Yeltsin sent a four-part referendum to voters in which they were asked (1) whether or not they had confidence in the president, (2) whether or not they supported the country's social and economic policies, (3) whether or not an early election should be held for president, and (4) whether or not an early election should be held for parliament. The first, second, and fourth questions were approved, but the outcome for the third was not binding because voter turnout was under 50 percent of all registered voters (Sakwa, 2021.) Voters rejected the proposal to move up the presidential election.

In December of the same year, the new constitution of the Russian Federation, which created a strong executive, was sent by President Yeltsin to voters, who approved the document with a vote of 58 percent. The referendum allowed Yeltsin to bypass the legislature, which opposed strengthening the executive. Despite questions about the turnout figures and results due to the immediate destruction of paper ballots, the referendum on the constitution gave the regime, and the president in particular, legitimacy in setting up the new semi-presidential system.

The Putin administration has also used a referendum to underscore public support for its policies. In summer 2020, voters approved a package of constitutional amendments that reset presidential terms from the date of the amendment. This means that the earlier terms in office of Putin and Medvedev do not count as terms subject to limits, and they can both run again for two six-year terms. The reforms also confirmed a guaranteed minimum pension, defined marriage as being between one man and one woman, included "belief in God" as a core value, and stated that Russian law supersedes international law. The government offered citizens prizes for voting, including entry into a raffle for gift certificates for cars and apartments. The amendments were approved by 78 percent of the voters. Putin critic Alexei Navalny and other opponents of the amendments claimed the referendum results were inflated and the result of an unfair process where the media favored the administration and opposition voices were silenced. (Deutsche Welle.)

Russia's referendums demonstrate how nondemocratic regimes can use referendums to rally public support to strengthen the regime. One of the crucial differences between democratic and authoritarian regimes is that in democratic systems, the rights of unpopular and minority groups are protected from the will of the majority. In authoritarian regimes, the government may use the principle of "majority rule" to restrict civil rights and liberties and consolidate power. Referendums are a good way to do this.

Civil Rights and Civil Liberties

Under Putin, the government has tried to limit the formation of civil-society groups by forming government-sanctioned associations. Oligarchs and other businesses received favorable treatment if they joined particular, regime-approved business associations, so most did. One of the best-known government-sponsored groups was a Putin-supporting youth group called *Nashi* (Ours) that staged mass rallies in support of the president, complete with its own pamphlets, other propaganda, and uniforms. The Victory Volunteers,

> ### AP® TIP
>
> People participate politically in both democratic and authoritarian states. Make sure you are able to describe the similarities and differences in participation in different kinds of regimes on the AP® Exam.

who are featured in the story that begins Chapter 6, is another example of a government-sponsored youth group that encourages young people's allegiance to the regime.

Massive protests broke out in December 2011 in the wake of the evident fraud in the Duma election and fraud in previous presidential elections. Given the restrictions on civil society, the protests took everyone, including the regime, by surprise. Middle-class citizens were awakened by economic decline and the realization that Putin was likely to win a third term as president in an election marred by fraud. Citizens took to the internet for information, then to the streets. The regime did not respond mainly with force. Instead, it made limited concessions and promised cleaner elections in the future. It also restricted NGO activity, reducing potential sources of conflict in the future.

In recent years, civil rights and liberties have been attacked with greater intensity. The regime has forced out most independent media outlets to eliminate widespread criticism, and journalists who have opposed the regime have been prosecuted on charges related to treason. In 2020, Svetlana Prokopyeva was assessed a large fine for arguing in a radio broadcast that Russia's limitations on free speech were causing young people to radicalize. She was not allowed to leave the country, and her assets have been frozen. (Committee to Protect Journalists.) Several dozen journalists have been detained during peaceful protests in Moscow and other places, even though they were clearly identified as members of the press. (Human Rights Watch, Events 2019, 2020.)

The regime has also targeted artists under a 2020 law banning disrespect to authorities. Most of the charges involved people who expressed negative opinions or made unflattering images of Putin. In August 2020, artist Alexander Shabarchin was sentenced to two years in prison on charges of hooliganism for placing a life-sized doll with Putin's face in a public square with signs reading "War Criminal" and "Liar." His sentence was later suspended by the court. Theater director Kirill Serebrennikov, whose work has been critical of the regime, was convicted on charges of embezzlement. (Human Rights Watch, 2020.) In early 2020, the state opened up an investigation against Alexander Dolgopolov, a stand-up comedian, for offending religion. He fled the country. (Zlobina.)

The treatment of Alexei Navalny, an outspoken critic of the Putin administration, further illustrates the perils of speaking out. Navalny made his name by using online platforms including a blog, YouTube, and Twitter to publish evidence of corruption among government officials and to organize political protests. He was permitted to run in Moscow's 2013 mayoral election but was banned from running in the 2016 presidential election. In 2020, Navalny was poisoned, allegedly by FSB agents. (UN News.) In February 2021, Navalny was sentenced to prison for violating the terms of a 2014 fraud conviction by not checking in with authorities while in Germany for treatment for symptoms of the poisoning. Following the sentencing, protests broke out in more than 90 cities, and more than 5,600 people were detained. (Kim, 2021.)

In recent years, the government has stepped up its efforts to control the internet to preempt criticism and limit the ability of people to organize. In 2018, Freedom House ranked Russia as "Not Free" on internet freedom. "Internet freedom declined for the sixth year in a row," the organization reported, noting the many new pieces of legislation introduced in the lead-up to the 2018 presidential election aimed at restricting anonymity and increasing censorship online. In 2018, the government blocked the popular platform Telegram, although the block was lifted by 2020. Laws that went into effect in July 2018 require internet companies to store users' communications for six months and provide the Federal Security Service with access to the files. (Freedom House, 2018.)

In 2019, proposals to restrict speech on the internet passed the lower house of the Federal Assembly with Putin's support. These would introduce jail sentences for insulting the government or spreading "fake news" online. (Nechepurenko, 2019.) Most of these measures have sparked demonstrations, but as yet no formal organization has emerged to consolidate the opposition.

Divisions in Russia

Social cleavages in Russia have emerged along the lines of ethnicity and religion. There are more than 180 ethnic groups or nationalities in the Russian Federation. More than 100 different languages are spoken across the country. Ethnic Russians make up 81 percent of the population. Other large ethnic groups include Tatar (3.9 percent), Ukrainian (1.4 percent), Bashkir (1.2 percent), Chuvash (1.1 percent), Chechen (1 percent), and Armenian (0.9 percent). (Minority Rights Group International.)

The two wars in Chechnya demonstrate the major ethnic and religious divisions within Russia. Chechens make up about 1 percent of Russia's population—about 1.5 million people—and most are Muslim. When the Soviet Union collapsed in 1991, Chechnya, one of the republics within the Russian Federation, declared its independence. President Yeltsin worried that allowing Chechnya to secede would inspire additional independence movements within the Russian Federation.

In the First Chechen War, the Russian army invaded Chechnya in December 1994. After some initial gains, Russian troops were met with heavy resistance. Thousands of Russian troops were killed, and even more Chechen civilians died. (BBC, Chechnya.) A peace agreement was signed that kept Chechnya as part of the Russian state but gave the region significant autonomy.

The agreement lasted until 1999, after Chechen separatists were suspected of carrying out bombings in Moscow and other cities. Putin, who became prime minister in 1999, launched a new military operation that marked the onset of the Second Chechen War. The Second Chechen War lasted from 1999 to 2009. Russian troops were accused of committing atrocities, including killing, looting, arson, and rape, against Chechen civilians. The Russian military prevailed in Chechnya, and Putin's approval ratings increased dramatically.

In 2002, Chechen terrorists stormed the Moscow Opera House, taking more than 800 people hostage. After four days, Russian special forces stormed the theater, firing their weapons and releasing chemicals into the air. All of the hostage takers were killed, along with at least 130 hostages, although some estimates are higher. In 2004, Chechen terrorists held more than a thousand hostages at a school in Beslan in the neighboring republic of North Ossetia-Alania. Nearly 330 people, including 186 children, were killed when Russian troops stormed the building. Following unflattering coverage of the attack, the Russian government took over most major media outlets, curtailed civil liberties, and strengthened the national government's power over regions. (Mirovalev.)

Two women check their smartphones near a fountain in rebuilt Grozny, the capital and main city of Chechnya.

After the Second Chechen War, the separatists were driven underground. In 2010, terror attacks occurred when bombs exploded in Moscow and other cities, targeting public buildings and transportation.

The Russian government has rebuilt Grozny, the Chechen capital. It is now home to steel-and-glass skyscrapers and a modern infrastructure. Eighty percent of Chechnya's revenue comes from the national government. The head of the Chechen region, Ramzan Kadyrov, fought alongside Chechen rebels against the Russian army during the first war. At the beginning of the second war, he was co-opted by the government and is now an ally of the Putin regime. Political opponents and gay rights activists have accused his administration of human rights violations, including torture. (Human Rights Watch, 2019.)

The Chechen conflict demonstrates the difficulty in making policies to address ethnic and religious divisions, especially when they lead to violence. Although the Russian state used massive military force to put down the conflict, it also invested in infrastructure and in improving the economy of the region, resulting in more stability.

Section 7.4 Review

Remember

- The Russian state has used referendums to demonstrate public support for the regime, in an effort to increase legitimacy.
- The Russian state has developed government-sponsored organizations to encourage support for the regime.
- Russia places significant restrictions on civil rights and liberties.
- The conflict in Chechnya is an example of an ethnic-religious division.

Think

- To what extent do state-sponsored associations provide citizens with meaningful political participation?
- Does responding to independence movements with violence increase or decrease state stability?

Free-Response Question: Conceptual Analysis

Answer A, B, C, and D.

A. Define civil society.

B. Explain how an authoritarian state could limit civil society.

C. Explain why an authoritarian state might take the measure described in part B.

D. Other than joining organizations, explain how citizens participate in government in authoritarian regimes.

7.5 Economic and Social Change and Development

Learning Targets

After reading this section, you should be able to do the following:

1. Explain how the Putin administration has responded to globalization.

2. Explain how being a rentier state impacts Russia's government and economy.

3. Describe social policies in Russia.

4. Describe the demographic pressures facing Russia.

5. Describe the challenges facing Russia in the future.

Russia faces challenges arising from globalization and its status as a rentier state. These challenges affect the state's capacity to provide social welfare benefits to citizens. The welfare system is also being strained by a declining and aging population.

Globalization

When Putin came to power, the government faced severe economic problems. President Putin has blamed the U.S. government along with the governments in Western Europe for failing to partner with Russia following the Cold War and for trying to take advantage of Russia when it was economically weakened. In his view, the West created a political and economic structure that benefits unelected bureaucrats in the European Union and the elite. Putin points to slowing income growth, less poverty reduction, and rising income inequality to support his contention that globalization has failed. In 2021, a group of Russian experts called globalization "destructive economically, culturally, and politically and responsible for sparking a worldwide revolt." (Yale Global, Weitz.)

In response to a belief that Western governments have used globalization to manipulate the rules in their favor, Russia is charting its own path. Russia wants to strengthen the United Nations, and in particular the Security Council. Russia is one of the five permanent members of the U.N. Security Council, each of which has the power to unilaterally veto proposed actions.

Russia is not an isolationist country. Rather, Russia seeks to reform what it sees as defects in the Western version of globalization, with an emphasis on national sovereignty. (Glaser.) The constitutional amendments approved in 2020 provide that Russia's constitution supersedes international laws. By creating its own version of how globalization should operate, Russia seeks to maintain its status as a powerful player on the world stage. (Yale Global, Weitz.)

The Recent Russian Economy

In his first two terms as president, Putin took steps to stimulate economic growth. As mentioned earlier, the administration charged several key oligarchs with corruption. Those who were convicted had their media and energy-sector assets confiscated by the state, which took control over the media and much of the state's oil and natural gas production.

The process of re-nationalizing Russia's vast oil reserves has provided an important source of revenue for the government. Russia is a **rentier state**, which relies on the revenues from export of oil (or from the leasing of land to foreign entities to extract resources) as a significant source of government revenue. Access to oil revenue increases opportunities for patronage and corruption and decreases government transparency.

Ironically, the abundance of a valuable national resource, such as oil, is known as the **resource curse**. In countries where oil is abundant, governments are tempted toward over-reliance on natural resources for government revenue, failing to diversify their economies. Oil and gas prices rise and fall at the mercy of the world market, making national budgets

Rentier state
A state that relies on the export of oil or from the leasing of resources to foreign entities as a significant source of government revenue.

Resource curse
A problem faced by countries that have a valuable and abundant natural resource, which limits diversification of the economy, makes government revenue dependent on the world market, increases opportunities for corruption, and lessens the government's responsiveness to citizens.

unpredictable and unstable. States that rely on a natural resource as a major source of revenue are less reliant on tax dollars. Consequently, they are less responsive to the demands of citizens, potentially making them less democratic.

During periods when oil prices are high, the Russian government has used the proceeds from nationalized oil and gas to fund programs to raise the standard of living. By the end of Putin's first two terms in 2008, Russia's GDP growth rate was 6.9 percent per year, average real wages had increased by 10.5 percent, and disposable income had grown by 7.9 percent. This period of prosperity was stimulated by high prices for oil. (Johnston.)

A global recession in 2008 proved that Russia is not immune from the global economy. As energy prices declined and global investment in Russia slowed, the Russian stock market plummeted. Industrial production slowed, and unemployment increased. International investors started pulling money out of Russia. The government passed a $200 billion stimulus package. By spring 2009, oil prices were climbing, and the economy slowly began to improve. (Center for Strategic and International Studies.)

During his second two terms in office, the Putin administration continued to consolidate the government's control over the oil industry. (Frum.) Nationalization of the oil and gas industry increased the power of the national government and decreased the influence of foreign governments and multinational corporations. During Putin's second terms, GDP growth was relatively slow, with a high of 4.5 percent in 2010 and a low of 1.3 percent in 2019, before the COVID-19 pandemic. Russia's social policies, such as universal health care, pension benefits, and unemployment income, provide some relief during economic downturns. (World Bank Report.) Nevertheless, the economic crisis of 2008, coupled with sanctions by the United States, EU, and other countries, damaged the Russian economy and highlighted internal problems, including overreliance on oil as a source of government revenue.

Social Policies

Russia has a welfare state that provides benefits to improve the lives of citizens. The two largest social programs are pensions for retirees and universal health care.

The Russian constitution guarantees citizens the right to health care provided by the government. People also have an opportunity to purchase additional insurance on the private market, and many of the elite use this option. The national health-care system is funded through payroll taxes and contributions from regional and local governments.

During the 1990s, health-care spending declined due to economic instability. In 2006, the government created the National Priority Project–Health to improve funding for medical equipment in hospitals and clinics. New medical clinics were built, and vaccination programs that had been scrapped during the economic downturn were relaunched. (PMLive, Overview.)

Despite efforts to improve the health-care system, access to high-quality health care is dependent on socioeconomic status and location, and those in rural areas often lack access to high-quality care. A 2020 report found that a third of the medical facilities in Russia lack running water, 52 percent lack hot water, and 40 percent do not have central heat. (Cordell and Gershkovich.) In 2016, Bloomberg ranked Russia's health-care system last out of 55 developed countries.

Another key part of Russia's social welfare program is the pension system, which provides monthly payments after retirement. In 2004 and 2005, pensioners protested a new law that took away the benefit of free travel on public transportation. The government reinstated the benefit and doubled an increase in pension payments. (Bigg, 2005).

These two elderly Russian women in St. Petersburg have newspapers and seem to be talking about current events. Russia's aging population is predicted to strain the health-care and pension systems.

Peter Titmuss/Alamy

The original retirement age was relatively low—55 for women and 60 for men. The system is becoming unsustainable because of an aging population and a shrinking number of people of working age. In 2018, right before Russia held the World Cup soccer matches (which garnered the public's attention), the government announced it was raising the retirement age to 65 years for men and 60 years for women. (Bauer.) Despite a public backlash, economists and policy analysts believed raising the retirement age was necessary to reduce the financial strain on the pension system. (Sokhey.)

The constitutional amendments approved by voters in 2020 confirmed Russia's commitment to social insurance, including support for the health-care and pension systems. These amendments may raise expectations that quality of life will improve. If the state meets these expectations, it may remain stable and increase legitimacy.

Shifting Demographics

Russia's population is aging and shrinking. Many industrialized nations are facing similar pressures, but Russia's demographic shifts are often described as a crisis. In the early 1990s, Russia's population peaked at about 148 million. By 2050, demographers predict that Russia's population will decline to 136 million. Two main factors have led to this population challenge—declining fertility rates and a high mortality rate.

Russia's population is aging. In the ten years from 2010 to 2020, life expectancy increased from 67.9 to 72.9 years, although it is below the OECD average of 80.6 years. (Seligmann.) About 15 percent of Russia's population is over the age of 65, and that percentage is expected to increase in the next forty years. Russia's working-age population is decreasing, from 61 percent of the population in 2020 to a projected 55 percent by 2050. (Seligmann.) This means fewer people will be working to support retirees drawing pensions.

One of the reasons for this trend is the decline in fertility rates. By 2018, the fertility rate had fallen to 1.57. (World Bank Report.) Falling fertility rates are common in industrialized countries as more women join the workforce, but the situation is exacerbated in Russia. It is difficult for many women to obtain contraceptives, and until recently, abortion was the main method of birth control. The procedure was often performed in unsafe medical clinics and sometimes left women sterile. In recent years, birth control has become more widely available, and abortion rates have declined. (DaVanzo and Grammich.)

As part of a program to increase birth rates, the Putin administration provides cash incentives for couples who have more than one child. Furthermore, in 2006, the governor of the Ulyanovsk region created the National Day of Conception, which takes place yearly on September 12. Couples are given the day off work. Those who have a child on June 12 (nine months later) are registered for prizes, including SUVs, video cameras, refrigerators, washing machines, and TVs. (Weaver.) Although the birth rate increased slightly following these programs, it declined again in 2017. In 2020, Putin announced a new program to give families tax breaks amounting to about $7,600 a year and other benefits, such as free school lunches for low-income children. (BBC, Birth Rate.)

AP® POLITICAL SCIENCE PRACTICES

Analyzing Population Pyramids

A population pyramid is a way of showing how much of a country's population is made up of certain age groups. Population pyramids also show the similarities or differences between the number of men and women in each age group. The term "pyramid" is misleading, because it implies that most of the population will be concentrated in younger age categories, with fewer old people at the top of the pyramid. These representations will look different for countries with a smaller number of young people and relatively more middle and older people, which results in a shape that looks more like a population coffin.

To interpret a population pyramid, it's important to look at several factors. Take a look at the year in which the representation was created. An outdated pyramid may not reflect current demographic trends within a country. Consider how age groups are distributed. In this pyramid, age groups are broken into five-year increments. Compare the number of men and women in each age group. This population pyramid indicates that after age 55, there are more women than men in each age group.

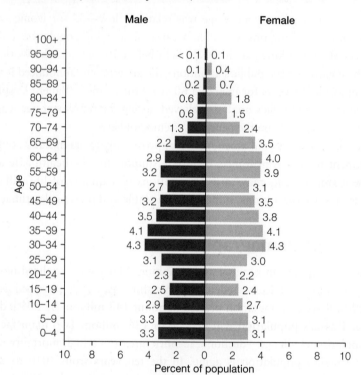

Russia, Population Pyramid, 2020

Data from U.N. Department of Economic and Social Affairs, Population Division.

Keep in mind that population pyramids are useful in representing demographic patterns, but they do not explain why those patterns occur. To figure out the reason for a trend, use math to determine today's age of the people who lived through a particular event. It is also important to understanding how historical events are likely to impact demographics. For example, wars kill more men than women. Fewer children are born during difficult economic times. Smaller demographic groups lead to smaller "echo" groups later.

Understanding these factors will help you put population pyramids in context.

Answer the following questions.

1. Describe a pattern in the population pyramid.

2. Draw a conclusion about the impact of Russia's age distribution on its pension program.

3. Explain how the Russian government could use demographic information to create public policy.

Besides low fertility rates, the decline in Russia's population is caused by a high mortality rate. Compared to the rest of the world, Russians have a high rate of death by non-natural causes, such as homicide and suicide. High rates of alcoholism and smoking are contributing factors. Increasing incidence of cancer, respiratory illness, and heart disease strain the health-care system. (Adamson and DeVanzo.)

There are several steps Russia might take to reverse these demographic trends. Russia is actively encouraging families to have more children. It could invest more in education and preventive health to encourage citizens to eat healthy food and exercise. Modernizing and improving Russia's health-care system would also help the state meet these demographic challenges. (Adamson and DeVanzo.)

Russia and the Future

Along with the rest of the world, the Russian state faced unprecedented challenges as a result of the COVID-19 pandemic. Russia closed schools and universities in cities in March 2020 and transitioned to online learning. The city of Moscow was placed on lockdown. Putin projected a positive image, claiming that the government was well prepared for the pandemic, but limited testing took place, and reported numbers of infections were likely underestimated. (Adamson and DeVanzo.) A poll conducted in March 2020 indicated that 48 percent of Russians did not believe the health-care system was prepared for a pandemic. (Levada.)

The global recession caused by the COVID-19 pandemic hit Russia's economy hard. It was projected that 2020 GDP would contract by 6 percent and hit its lowest point in eleven years. (World Bank, Economy.) In 2020, the manufacturing, mining, and transportation sectors all experienced negative growth. Plummeting crude oil prices made the problem even worse, because, as a rentier state, Russia relies on its nationalized oil industry for a significant portion of government revenue. (World Bank, Economy.) There was some positive news in August 2020, however, when Russia announced the approval of Sputnik V, the world's first official vaccine against COVID-19.

Russia's economy may improve when the pandemic ends, but the state's reliance on oil as a source of revenue may limit the government's ability to manage the budget. In addition, Russia will continue to face challenges as a result of its aging population and a slow or negative population growth rate.

In the near future, Russia is likely to remain an authoritarian state with power centralized in the executive and the national government. Russians have a strong sense of national pride in their culture and heritage, and support for the regime may continue. However, the war in Ukraine, human rights abuses, and corruption may cause future protests and unrest. Given the personalized nature of the Putin regime, the long-term stability of the political system remains uncertain.

Section 7.5 Review

Remember

- The Putin administration has criticized Western-style globalization and emphasized the importance of national sovereignty.
- Russia is a rentier state that derives government revenue from the renationalized oil and gas industry.
- Russia's social-welfare system provides pensions and health care, although access to high-quality medical care depends on socioeconomic status and location.

- Russia is facing demographic pressure due to low fertility rates, high mortality rates, and an aging population.
- Russia's authoritarian state may face challenges in the future related to its economy, human rights abuses, and corruption.

Know

- *Rentier state:* a state that relies on the export of oil or from the leasing of resources to foreign entities as a significant source of government revenue. (p. 225)
- *Resource curse:* a problem faced by countries that have a valuable and abundant natural resource, which limits diversification of the economy, makes government revenue dependent on the world market, increases opportunities for corruption, and lessens the government's responsiveness to citizens. (p. 225)

Think

- What are the advantages and disadvantages for states that have abundant natural resources?
- What strategies could the Russian government use to address its demographic challenges?

....

Free-Response Question: Quantitative Analysis

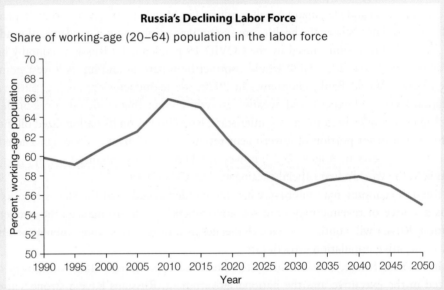

Russia's Declining Labor Force

Share of working-age (20–64) population in the labor force

Data from U.N. Department of Economic and Social Affairs, Population Division. 2019, middle scenario.

Answer A, B, C, D, and E.

A. Using the data in the graph, identify the year in which Russia had the highest percentage of people in the working-age population.

B. Using the data in the graph, describe a trend in the percentage of people in the working population from 2009 to 2050 (projected).

C. Describe social-welfare policy.

D. Using the data in the graph, draw a conclusion about the impact of demographic trends on social welfare policy in Russia.

E. Explain how the Russian government could address the impact on social welfare policy discussed in part D.

Participation

AP® KEY CONCEPTS

- Asymmetrical federalism (p. 207)
- Duma (p. 211)
- Federation Council (p. 211)
- Rentier state (p. 225)
- Resource curse (p. 225)

AP® EXAM MULTIPLE-CHOICE PRACTICE QUESTIONS

1. Which of the following accurately describes the executive in two AP® Comparative Government and Politics course countries?
   A. In both Russia and Mexico, the president is head of government, and the prime minister is the head of state.
   B. Both the United Kingdom and Russia have an elected head of government and an unelected head of state.
   C. In both the United Kingdom and Russia, the head of state is more powerful than the head of government.
   D. In both Russia and the United Kingdom, the prime minister is the head of government.

Questions 2 and 3 refer to the passage.

> In other words, millions of people even in wealthy countries have stopped hoping for an increase of their incomes. In the meantime, they are faced with the problem of how to keep themselves and their parents healthy and how to provide their children with a decent education . . .
>
> [In] 2019, 21 percent or 267 million young people in the world did not study or work anywhere. Even among those who had jobs . . . 30 percent had an income below $3.20 per day in terms of purchasing power parity. . . .
>
> These imbalances in global socioeconomic development are a direct result of the policy pursued in the 1980s, which was often vulgar or dogmatic. This policy rested on the so-called Washington Consensus with its unwritten rules, when the priority was given to the economic growth based on private debt in conditions of deregulation and low taxes on the wealthy and the corporations.
>
> —Russian President Vladimir Putin's Speech at the World Economic Forum, January 2021

2. Which of the following is supported by the main idea of the passage?
   A. Economic-liberalization policies were successful in lifting millions out of poverty.
   B. Western-style economic reforms benefit the wealthy and do not provide economic opportunity for the poor and middle class.
   C. Communism is preferable to capitalism as an economic system.
   D. The rules of neoliberal economic reform are unwritten, and policies change over time.

3. Which of the following is an implication of the argument presented in the passage?
   A. States should focus on citizens' social welfare in adopting economic policies.
   B. Widening income gaps in developed countries are likely to result in social unrest.
   C. Most of the world's young people lack access to adequate education and job opportunities.
   D. International organizations should prioritize development aid over military security.

4. Which of the following best describes the judicial system in Russia?
   A. The Constitutional Court exercises significant power, because it can overturn unconstitutional actions by the executive and legislature.
   B. The Supreme Court has more power than the Constitutional Court, because it is a final court of appeal.
   C. Although the Constitutional Court has the formal power of judicial review, the judiciary lacks autonomy.
   D. Rule by law enhances judicial independence.

5. Which of the following accurately describes a social cleavage in two AP® Comparative Government and Politics course countries?
   A. Regional cleavages based on nationalism exist in both the United Kingdom and Russia.
   B. In both Mexico and Russia, religion is an important source of political cleavages.
   C. In the United Kingdom and Russia, Muslim regions seek greater autonomy and independence.
   D. Both Mexico and the United Kingdom have devolved power to regions in an effort to lessen tensions caused by religious cleavages.

6. Which of the following accurately describes the electoral system in two AP® Comparative Government and Politics course countries?
   A. Both the United Kingdom and Russia use proportional representation to fill some seats in the national legislature.
   B. In both Russia and Mexico, the upper house of the legislature is selected through a single-member district system.
   C. Both Russia and Mexico use mixed systems to elect members of the lower house of the legislature.
   D. In both the United Kingdom and Russia, the upper house of the legislature is selected by the head of government.

Questions 7 and 8 refer to the line graph.

Attitudes toward Putin as President

Would you like to see Vladimir Putin as president of Russia after his current term expires in 2024?

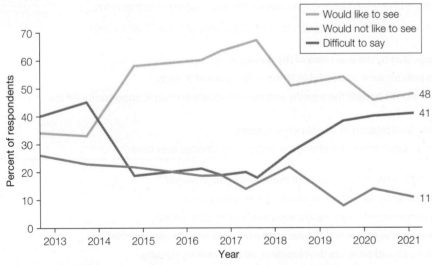

Data from the Levada Analytical Center.

7. Which of the following is accurate according to the line graph?

    A. In January 2021, the majority of Russian citizens polled supported extending the number of terms Putin can serve as president.

    B. The percentage of people who did not support allowing Putin to serve as president after 2024 rose from 2017 to 2021.

    C. In January 2021, 11 percent of Russians did not follow news stories about government and politics.

    D. The majority of Russian citizens opposes extending Putin's term beyond 2024.

8. Which of the following is an implication of the line graph?

    A. An economic recession, caused by a drop in oil prices, decreased popular support for the regime.

    B. The Russian regime lacks legitimacy, because its leader does not have widespread popular support.

    C. Although many Russians supported extending executive term limits, a majority opposed or was uncertain about extending term limits.

    D. Public opinion polling in Russia is untrustworthy, because it is conducted by government officials.

9. Russia's party system is most like which of the following?

    A. The dominant two-party system in the United Kingdom, with small regional parties winning some seats in the legislature

    B. China's one-party system for filling seats in the National People's Congress

    C. The Communist Party system in the Soviet Union before 1991

    D. The single-party dominant system in Mexico before 2000

10. Which of the following accurately describes the result of the system for selecting the executive in a course country studied in AP® Comparative Government and Politics?

    A. The Russian president usually faces a run-off election, which reduces the number of candidates to the two most popular.

    B. The prime minister in the United Kingdom often faces divided government, because they are chosen from a party coalition.

    C. The Russian constitution requires that the prime minister be from the majority party in parliament, which eliminates the possibility of divided government.

    D. The president in Mexico is elected by a plurality, which means they may not have a mandate to carry out proposed policies.

AP® EXAM PRACTICE ARGUMENT ESSAY

Develop an argument as to whether restrictions on civil liberties strengthen or weaken stability in authoritarian states.

Use one for more of the following course concepts in your response:

- Legitimacy
- Sovereignty
- Civil society

In your response, do the following:

- Respond to the prompt with a defensible claim or thesis that establishes a line of reasoning using one or more of the provided course concepts.
- Support your claim with at least *TWO* pieces of specific and relevant evidence from your study of the one or more course countries. The evidence should be relevant to one or more of the provided course concepts.
- Use reasoning to explain why your evidence supports your claim or thesis, using one or more of the provided course concepts.
- Respond to an opposing or alternate perspective, using refutation, concession, or rebuttal.

For a complete list of the sources of information cited in this chapter, turn to the Works Cited appendix.

UNIT ③ REVIEW

① **Mexico**

② **United Kingdom**

③ **Russia**

④ Nigeria

⑤ China

⑥ Iran

NOTE TO STUDENTS:

As you complete each unit, you will have more knowledge and be able to make more connections among concepts and cases. As your knowledge and skills build over time, the unit reviews become more complex, and the questions cover more of the content you will encounter on the AP® Exam.

AP® EXAM PRACTICE QUESTIONS

Section 1: Multiple Choice

Some of these review questions refer to the six countries studied in AP® Comparative Government and Politics. You have only studied Mexico, the United Kingdom, and Russia. Because the questions in this unit review are conceptual, knowledge about the other countries is not necessary to answer the questions.

1. Which of the following best describes a civil-society group?
   A. A government-sponsored youth organization in Russia
   B. The Labour Party in the United Kingdom
   C. An organized group of citizens protesting against corruption in Russia
   D. The National Health Service in the United Kingdom

Questions 2 and 3 refer to the passage.

> *New Eastern Outlook* is a pseudo-academic publication of the Russian Academy of Science's Institute of Oriental Studies that promotes disinformation and propaganda focused primarily on the Middle East, Asia, and Africa. It combines pro-Kremlin views of Russian academics with anti-U.S. views of Western fringe voices and conspiracy theorists. *New Eastern Outlook* appears to want to benefit from the veneer of respectability offered by the Russian academics it features, while also obscuring its links to state-funded institutions.
>
> —Global Engagement Center, Special Report. U.S. Department of State. August 2020

2. Which of the following is supported by the main idea of the passage?
   A. *New Eastern Outlook* is a publication favorable to the Putin regime.
   B. Most respected academics in Russia support the Putin regime.
   C. The Russian government uses control of the broadcast media to support the goals of the regime.
   D. Russians are interested in world affairs, particularly in the Middle East, Asia, and Africa.

3. Which of the following statements is an implication of the passage?
   A. The Russian Academy of Science is not a well-respected academic institution.
   B. The state's relationship with *New Eastern Outlook* is not transparent to the public.
   C. Anti-Western views in the Russian media are a response to the European Union's criticism of the Putin regime.
   D. Dissenting voices are censored by the Russian state, and critics of the regime are denied positions at prestigious universities.

4. Which of the following best describes political culture?

    A. Political culture is a product of a country's economic system, and it reflects individual beliefs about the government's role in the economy.

    B. Peers are the main source of transmitting political culture to young people.

    C. It describes an individual's set of beliefs and behaviors about the role of government.

    D. Political culture consists of the beliefs, attitudes, and values of citizens as a whole.

5. Which of the following is an accurate statement about an ideology studied in AP® Comparative Government and Politics?

    A. Populism is the belief that elected officials should represent the majority, while protecting the rights of the minority.

    B. Neoliberalism is the economic belief that governments should enact tariffs to protect domestic manufacturing.

    C. Socialism is the economic belief that the government should own the major means of production to provide for the welfare of citizens.

    D. Communism is the belief that capitalism should never have developed, because it leads to authoritarian rule.

Questions 6 and 7 refer to the graph.

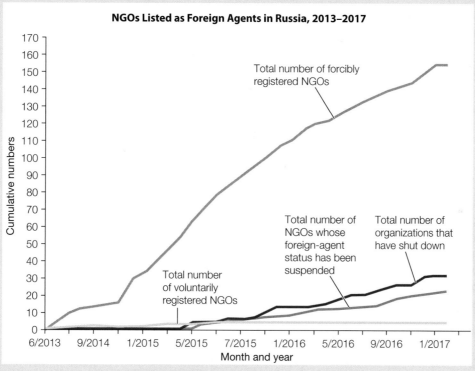

Data from Human Rights Watch, "Russia: Government vs. Civil Society: The Battle Chronicle," 2017.

6. Which of the following is accurate according to the line graph?

    A. From 2013 to 2017, the number of NGOs forcibly registered with the Russian government climbed from zero to more than 150.

    B. From 2013 to 2017, the number of NGOs working in Russia increased from zero to more than 150.

    C. Before July 2013, there were no NGOs working in Russia.

    D. Beginning in 2013, NGOs have been permitted to operate in Russia, as long as they do not criticize the state.

7. Which of the following is an implication of the data shown on the line graph?

    A. From 2013 to 2017, Russia has been more welcoming to NGOs than it was before 2013.

    B. The Russian government suspends NGOs when it suspects them of spying on behalf of foreign entities.

    C. The Russian government requires NGOs to register with the government in an effort to monitor their activities.

    D. Most of the NGOs registered in Russia are sponsored by the government, and funding for them has increased since 2013.

8. Which of the following is an accurate statement about political participation in different regime types?

    A. Authoritarian states encourage formal participation and prohibit informal participation.

    B. Democratic states encourage citizens to vote in elections, and authoritarian states discourage voting.

    C. Democratic states do not impose restrictions on political participation.

    D. Citizens in both democratic and authoritarian states engage in formal and informal participation.

9. Which of the following is an accurate statement about cleavages in course countries studied in AP® Comparative Government and Politics?

    A. In both Mexico and Russia, political parties have formed on the basis of social class.

    B. Regional movements by religious minorities seeking autonomy have occurred in both the United Kingdom and Russia.

    C. Cleavages between Christian-dominated and Muslim-dominated areas have arisen in the United Kingdom and Mexico.

    D. Cleavages between rural and urban areas in the United Kingdom and Russia have resulted in the devolution of power to regional governments.

10. Which of the following best describes the party system in Russia?

    A. It has a two-party system.

    B. Russia is a one-party state.

    C. There is a single dominant party, with a few smaller parties.

    D. Russia has a multiparty system.

Questions 11 and 12 refer to the passage.

> [Support for the Russian government] is falling short in an environment shaped by economic stagnation. . . . While the July 2020 vote showed strong support for the amendments to the constitution . . . Just one month prior to the vote, polls demonstrated that public opinion was split: only 44 percent of those polled backed the amendments versus 32 percent who opposed them. However, among those who intended to vote, supporters of the amendments outnumbered those who opposed them by a margin of 55 to 25 percent.
>
> —Andrei Kolesnikov and Denis Volkov, Carnegie Moscow Center, September 12, 2020

11. Which of the following is supported by the main idea of the passage?

    A. Voter turnout was greater among those who supported the 2020 amendments than among those who opposed them.

    B. The majority of Russian citizens favored extending President Putin's term limits.

    C. Russians have a high level of political efficacy.

    D. Russians have a strong sense of nationalism and a distrust of the West.

12. Which of the following is an implication of the argument presented in the passage?

    A. Citizens are unaware of corruption among the elites, because the Russian government is not transparent.

    B. The majority of citizens blames Russia's economic problems on the West.

    C. Most Russians will continue to support the regime as long as Putin is president.

    D. The Putin government is likely to lose legitimacy if the Russian economy does not improve.

13. Which of the following is an accurate statement regarding concepts studied in AP® Comparative Government and Politics?

    A. Legitimacy is the state's ability to control territory free of internal or external influence.

    B. In a rule-of-law system, citizens are treated equally by the courts, and in a rule-by-law system, the government uses the judiciary to target political opponents.

    C. Civil society consists of groups that treat one another fairly, without violence or discrimination.

    D. A corporatist system is one in which businesses pick the leader of the government and control the economy.

14. Which of the following is an accurate statement about legitimacy?

    A. The United Kingdom lacks rational legal legitimacy, because it does not have a written constitution.

    B. Mexico's legitimacy is based on the rule of law.

    C. Legitimacy in Russia is based partly on charismatic leadership.

    D. Legitimacy in both Russia and the United Kingdom is based on free and fair elections.

15. Which of the following best describes the relationship between the national government and regions in course countries studied in AP° Comparative Government and Politics?

    A. Russia and the United Kingdom are unitary systems.

    B. Mexico and the United Kingdom are unitary systems.

    C. Russia and Mexico are federal systems.

    D. Russia and the United Kingdom are federal systems, with devolution of power to regional assemblies.

16. Which of the following best describes the system for electing the Duma?

    A. Members are elected through a plurality, single-member district system.

    B. Members are appointed by the president, based on a recommendation of the prime minister and the United Russia party.

    C. The Duma uses a mixed electoral system, in which individual candidates run for single-member district seats and half of the seats are awarded through proportional representation, with a threshold that must be met for a party to win seats.

    D. To win a seat in the Duma, a candidate must earn more than 50 percent of the vote, which requires runoff elections in some districts.

Questions 17 and 18 refer to the bar chart.

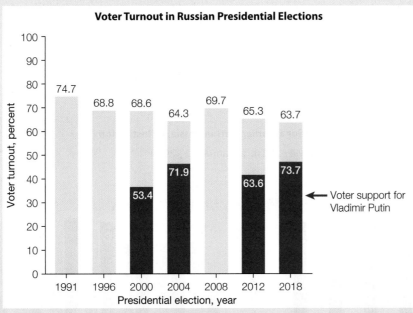

Note: Parliamentary elections took place in 2010, 2015, 2017, and 2019.
Data from Russian Central Election Commission and Radio Free Europe/Radio Liberty.

17. Which of the following is true according to the bar chart?

    A. Voter turnout in Russia was lower in 2018 than in any year since the formation of the Russian Federation in 1999.

    B. Voter turnout in Russia declined every year from 1991 to 2018.

    C. The percentage of votes earned by President Putin is consistently higher than 70 percent.

    D. Fraud was prevalent in the 2008 presidential election in Russia.

18. Which of the following is an implication of the bar chart?
    A. Rates of formal political participation in Russia are relatively low.
    B. Russians vote out of a strong sense of nationalism.
    C. Since 2012, the Putin government has gradually lost legitimacy.
    D. Political efficacy has declined in Russia since 2008.

19. Which of the following describes a significant demographic change in a course country studied in AP® Comparative Government and Politics?
    A. Contraception is not readily available in Mexico and Russia, resulting in high birth rates.
    B. The aging populations in Russia and the United Kingdom will challenge the states' health-care systems.
    C. People in Mexico and Russia are migrating from urban areas to rural areas in an effort to avoid environmental pollution.
    D. Both Russia and the United Kingdom have high mortality rates, due to the prevalence of alcoholism.

20. Which of the following statements regarding term limits is true?
    A. There are no term limits for the head of state in Mexico and the United Kingdom.
    B. In both Mexico and Russia, executives are limited to one term.
    C. Term limits have been constitutionally extended in Russia, and in the United Kingdom, there is no term limit.
    D. The heads of government in Russia and in the United Kingdom are appointed by the head of state and serve for life.

Section 2: Free Response

Conceptual Analysis

Answer A, B, C, and D.
A. Define informal political participation.
B. Describe a method of informal participation.
C. Explain why a state would limit informal participation.
D. Explain how limiting informal participation impacts state legitimacy.

Quantitative Analysis

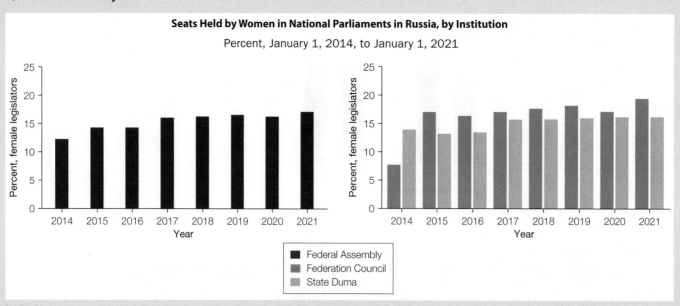

Data from Statista.

Answer A, B, C, D, and E.

A. Using the data in the bar chart, identify the year with the highest number of women in both the Duma and the Federation Council.

B. Using the data in the bar chart, describe a trend in the number of women serving in the Duma.

C. Describe the electoral system for the Duma.

D. Using your knowledge of the electoral system and the data in the bar chart, draw a conclusion about the reason for the trend you identified in part B.

E. Explain why an authoritarian state might want to increase the number of women serving in the legislature.

Comparative Analysis

Systems for electing the legislature vary and are impacted by regime type.

A. Describe the difference between a single-member district system and a proportional representation system.

B. Describe the system for electing the legislature in two of the course countries studied in AP® Comparative Government and Politics.

C. Explain how regime type impacts the system for electing the legislature in the two AP® Comparative Government and Politics course countries described in part B.

Argument Essay

Develop an argument as to whether democratic or authoritarian states are more effective in responding to political cleavages.

Use one or more of the following course concepts in your response:

- Power
- Legitimacy
- Nationalism

In your response, do the following:

- Respond to the prompt with a defensible claim or thesis that establishes a line of reasoning using one or more of the provided course concepts.
- Support your claim with at least *TWO* pieces of specific and relevant evidence from one or more course countries. The evidence should be relevant to one or more of the provided course concepts.
- Use reasoning to explain why your evidence supports your claim or thesis, using one or more of the provided course concepts.
- Respond to an opposing or alternate perspective, using refutation, concession, or rebuttal.

For a complete list of the sources of information cited, turn to the Works Cited appendix.

UNIT 4

Party and Electoral Systems and Citizen Organizations

The Wall of Kindness seems to have started in the city of Mashhad, in northeastern Iran. Someone (the inventor has remained anonymous) installed a few hooks and hangers on a wall, adding the words: "If you don't need it, leave it. If you need it, take it." Donations of coats, scarves, and other warm clothing started to appear. The idea quickly spread to other cities, fueled by the thousands of Iranians on social media. Social media have had a profound effect on how citizens organize, particularly in states that try to limit civil liberties.

Isabelle Eshraghi/Agence VU/Redux

Chapter 8
Party and Electoral Systems
and Citizen Organizations

Chapter 9
Case Study:
Nigeria

Elections

T o gain influence and power in government, individuals and groups use many tactics. Unit 4 highlights organizations such as political parties, social movements, and interest groups. There are various ways of exercising political power in the six course countries, and you will compare countries with both similar and different avenues for citizen participation. This unit breaks down the larger concepts about political institutions studied in Unit 2 and examines how individuals, parties, and citizen organizations influence policymaking. Using the concepts examined in this unit, you will continue to refine the skills necessary for success on the AP® Exam.

After completing Unit 4, you will be able to:

- Compare two or more course countries based on their political systems, policies, and institutions
- Explain how electoral systems differ among the course countries
- Define a party system
- Explain how to find a pattern or trend in a display of data
- Describe similarities and differences in citizen participation among the course countries
- Define a social movement and explain how social movements impact policymaking
- Define an interest group and explain how interest groups gain influence in the policymaking process
- Compare pluralist and corporatist interest-group systems
- Examine government and politics in Nigeria

Homero Gómez González was known as the defender of monarch butterflies. Formerly a logger, he managed the El Rosario reserve in Michoacán and advocated conservation rather than exploitation of the forests. In January 2020, he was kidnapped and murdered. His death shows what can happen to civil-society activists when major economic interests are at stake.

Elections

Nigeria has a long-standing tradition of citizen organizations, many of which contested military rule in the 1990s. Here, members of the Nigeria Labour Congress, the nation's umbrella group for labor unions, protest in favor of a better minimum-wage law. As the chapter's story illustrates, citizen organizations have also played a role in Mexican politics—most recently in the election of Andrés Manuel López Obrador as president.

Emmanuel Osodi/Majority World CIC/Alamy

AMLO: A Peculiar Savior

Andrés Manuel López Obrador (AMLO) was elected president of Mexico in 2018 on his third try, having failed in 2006 and 2012. During his long political career, he has been a member, and at times a key figure, in three of Mexico's prominent political parties.

In the 1970s AMLO was a member of the PRI, Mexico's ruling party from 1929 until 2000. He left the PRI unhappy with its role in rigging the 1988 election. He then joined the PRD, a left-of-center social-democratic party, and in 1994 he was its candidate for governor of Tabasco, his home state, but lost. He headed the party from 1996 to 1999. In 2000, as its candidate, he was elected mayor of Mexico City. He was its candidate for president in 2006 and lost. He then left the PRD and in 2014, he founded MORENA. López Obrador was elected as the MORENA candidate for the presidency in 2018. The only major party that he has not been a member of is PAN, Mexico's conservative political party.

Before 2000, the Mexican government was controlled by the PRI, although other parties existed. The PRI had dominated Mexico through a combination of shifting ideology, adaptation to changing circumstances, electoral fraud, and, sometimes, violent repression. Corruption was systemic. During the 1980s and 1990s, pressure from citizens for electoral reforms and subsequent changes set up the conditions for other parties to be able to challenge the PRI's electoral dominance, which the PAN did successfully in the 2000 presidential election. The 2000 election toppled the PRI's hold on power. Since that time, Mexico has developed more democratic political arrangements, with competitive political parties vying for and alternating in power. Corruption is still widespread.

Political parties and democracy intertwine. In fact, leading scholars of political parties have long argued that political parties created democracy and that democracy is unthinkable without parties. In modern democracies, competition between parties provides voters with the ability to choose among the alternatives of public policy. In this way, political parties make mass democracy possible.

Political parties serve four broad functions, each of which is essential for a healthy democratic political system: (1) nation-building by organizing conflicting groups; (2) filling offices through elite recruitment for public positions; (3) political socialization and education of the electorate; and (4) policymaking through coordination of government officials with shared goals.

López Obrador was born in 1953 into modest circumstances. His parents owned and operated a small store where he worked. His maternal grandparents emigrated from northern Spain, while his paternal grandparents had indigenous and African roots. Throughout his career, AMLO has presented himself as a defender of the common folk. In an address to thousands upon taking the presidential oath of office, he repeated this commitment: "We are going to govern for everyone, but we are going to give preference to the most impoverished and vulnerable. For the good of all, the poor come first." ("AMLO Promises.")

In a nod to his indigenous political base, the day that he was inaugurated as president, one journalist reported that "he received a spiritual cleansing by indigenous leaders as part of the festivities, in which traditional healers brushed him with bunches of herbs and blew incense smoke over him. They invoked the spirits of their ancestors and the land to liberate him from any bad influences." ("AMLO Promises.")

López Obrador's 2018 victory was an extraordinary turn in Mexico's political party dynamics. AMLO's MORENA party received over 53 percent of the vote, while an alliance between the PAN and PRD accounted for 22 percent and the PRI candidate 16 percent, with minor party support accounting for the rest. While MORENA is made up of elements of Mexico's left, it also includes conservative religious groups and has increasingly close

Candidate Andrés Manuel López Obrador talks to supporters at Jardín Guerrero in Querétaro, Mexico, during the closing days of his 2018 electoral campaign. AMLO campaigned using populist appeals.

Carlos Tischler/Getty Images News/Getty Images

ties to the military. In his campaign, López Obrador emphasized rooting out corruption and the rejection of the neoliberal economic reforms of his predecessors. The most notable of the reforms was the 2014 partial privatization of much of Mexico's energy sector, including the state-owned oil company Pemex.

AMLO's victory was also a personal triumph stemming from discontent with three key factors: (1) glaring inequality and widespread poverty; (2) escalating crime; and (3) rampant corruption. (Greene and Sanchez-Talanquer.) His election was a vote for change.

As his history of moving from one party to the next indicates, AMLO is not a typical politician. He relishes contact with crowds. He regularly wades into large groups with little, if any, security. He flies coach, dresses humbly, often speaks in unpretentious, vernacular Spanish, and he took a pay cut upon becoming president. He has sold off bulletproof and luxury vehicles of past presidents. He even tried to sell off the presidential jet plane but has not been able to find a buyer. "Money has never interested me," he said. "I fight for ideals, for principles."

Obrador's policies as president included raising the minimum wage three times and making direct cash payments to 23 million low-income individuals. For some, he has become the Great Benefactor. (Dresser.) To meet the challenges of Mexico's uneven development, with more than 40 percent of the population (about 50 million people) living in poverty, he has increasingly centralized power in the office of the presidency.

Meanwhile, he believes criticism of his government is a challenge to the righteousness of his cause. He has criticized women protesting femicide (the intentional murder of women) as simply tools of his conservative opponents. He also dismissed environmentalists' concerns about his cuts to renewable-energy programs. "There's a lot of deception. I would tell you that they have grabbed the flag of clean energy in the same way they grab the flag of feminism or human rights. Since when are conservatives concerned about the environment?" (Stillman and De Halvedang.)

AMLO's response to COVID-19 frustrated public-health officials. He refused to wear a mask and continued to hold rallies. He suggested carrying amulets and images of saints, and he even claimed that refraining from lying, stealing, or cheating would help prevent infection. In January 2021, he contracted the virus with mild symptoms.

AMLO is a charismatic nationalist leader who has instilled a kind of loyalty that is rare for a politician. This fervor was captured in a statement by a supporter who said: "Here Andrés Manuel is like a belief. We ask for things from him when we are in church." A sign greeting his arrival at a local community echoed this feeling. "Mexico Needs a Messiah and López Obrador Has Arrived." (Krauze, "Tropical Messiah.")

One American biographer summed up AMLO as a secular messiah, characterized by the factors that explain the rise of such leaders:

1. Weak, unrepresentative political institutions;
2. A lack of confidence in traditional politicians;
3. The yearning for a message of hope;
4. An individual who offers himself as a leader of the masses unrestrained by institutional arrangements;
5. Adeptness at capturing media attention; and
6. Vague proposals complemented by symbolic acts that respond to the needs of the masses. (Grayson, 9–10.)

López Obrador's victory disrupted Mexico's party system. With widespread voter discontent, Mexico, like other nations, could see voters "turn to personalistic outsiders, engage in serial protest voting against incumbents, or turn away from electoral politics to voice their discontent outside current institutions." (Greene and Sanchez-Talanquer.) It is also possible that a recomposition of the major parties is underway, with MORENA replacing the PRD as the party of the left, PAN as the party of the right, and with uncertainty about where the PRI fits ideologically. The Mexican party system has experienced a major disruption.

For now, MORENA is held together by the force of López Obrador's leadership and charisma. In 2019, he pledged not to seek a change to Mexico's term limit that prohibits a president from running for reelection, stating, "I think that six years are enough to uproot corruption and impunity. And to transform Mexico into a prosperous, democratic, and fraternal republic."

Virtually all regimes allow some participation and representation. Democratic regimes all claim to value and promote widespread participation and representation, and they differ in how they promote involvement and represent citizens' interests. Authoritarian regimes also allow some forms of political participation, often in an effort to maintain legitimacy.

This chapter will examine the three key aspects of representation and participation—electoral systems, parties and party systems, and civil society. Different electoral systems affect the strength and number of political parties, and they have an impact on citizen participation. An understanding of electoral systems and their impact is one of the most important concepts in AP® Comparative Government and Politics.

8.1 Elections

Learning Targets

After reading this section, you should be able to do the following:

1. Define electoral system.

2. Describe the difference between plurality and two-round systems for electing the executive.

3. Describe single-member district (SMD), proportional representation (PR), and mixed systems for electing the legislature.

4. Describe the benefits and drawbacks of different kinds of electoral systems.

Electoral system
The formal rules and procedures for selecting the executive or members of the legislature.

You learned about different election systems in studying Mexico, the United Kingdom, and Russia. In this section, you will review some of what you have already learned about how elections work, revisit vocabulary, and explore electoral systems in more depth. **Electoral systems** are the formal rules and procedures for selecting the executive or members of the legislature.

In almost all elections, citizens vote for people who will represent them rather than voting directly on policy. As you learned in studying the United Kingdom and Russia, sometimes citizens vote on referendums, but referendums are rare compared to elections for the legislature and executive.

There are two main systems for the direct election of the executive. In a plurality system, the candidate who wins the most votes in a single election becomes president. As you learned earlier, the Mexican president is elected through this kind of system. This means the Mexican president may enter office without having won a majority of the vote. This may make it difficult for the winner to claim a **mandate**—the broad support of the people to carry out proposed policies.

Mandate
The broad support of the people to carry out proposed policies.

Runoff election
A second and final election held between the top two vote-getters when no candidate wins a majority of the votes in the first round of voting.

In a two-round system for electing an executive, if no candidate earns a majority of the vote in the first round, a second election, called a **runoff election**, is held between the top two vote-getters. After the second round of voting, the candidate with the majority of the votes wins the election, making it easier for him or her to claim a mandate. Russia has a two-round system for electing the president, although Putin has always won more than a majority of the votes in the first round. Nigeria and Iran also have two-round systems for electing the executive.

Electoral systems also create a process for translating citizens' votes into seats in the legislature. One common choice is to divide territory into geographic units, with each unit electing one or more representatives. In single-member district (SMD) systems, one representative is elected per district. In **multimember district (MMD) systems**, two or more representatives are elected in each geographical area. SMD and MMD systems rest on the assumption that citizens can best be represented through their membership in geographically defined communities.

Multimember district (MMD) system
A method for electing members of a legislature in which two or more representatives are elected from a district.

In contrast, some countries elect their legislatures nationally by having citizens vote for a political party. This system assumes that citizens best express their beliefs through political parties, rather than geographic areas. Some countries choose to represent specific groups within society. After an ethnic conflict, for instance, a country may decide to provide special representation for ethnic minorities. Some countries have also legally reserved seats in parliament specifically for women to ensure that they are represented.

Electoral systems have important effects on government because they affect which parties serve in the legislature and the executive branch. Proportional representation systems that encourage many parties in the legislature provide representation of diverse views, but they may make effective government difficult due to the instability of coalition governments in parliamentary systems or gridlock in presidential systems. They also require regular negotiation, which may serve to moderate policy. Without such negotiation, policymaking may be impeded or the governing coalition might fail, which is not in the interest of coalition members. Gridlock in Mexican politics is one example, because the legislature and executive institutions are often controlled by different political parties. Systems that encourage fewer parties tend to have the opposite effect—policymaking may be more efficient, but fewer viewpoints are represented.

Single-Member Districts

As you learned in Chapter 5, the United Kingdom uses a **single-member district (SMD) system** to select MPs in the House of Commons. The country is divided into geographical districts, with roughly equal populations, and each district elects a single representative. The United Kingdom uses a **plurality** system. The candidate with the most votes wins the election, even if he or she doesn't earn at least 50 percent of the votes. In a race with more than two contestants, the winner can be elected with a relatively low percentage of the vote total. This system is often called **"first-past-the-post" (FPTP)** because, as in a horse race, the winner merely needs to edge out the next closest competitor to win a seat in the legislature.

Advocates of SMD systems argue they give constituents a strong sense of connection with their representative. Each voter has a specific representative from his or her district to hold accountable for government actions. Even if you didn't vote for your representative and you disagree with her, she is still expected to work for you. Representatives in SMD systems have staff in their districts to help constituents with problems and listen to their concerns.

Critics of the SMD system make two main arguments against it. First, because most single-member district candidates are selecting using the plurality or first-past-the-post rule, many votes are "wasted," in the sense that the winning candidate does not represent the views of the voters who did not vote for him. This is especially true in systems with more than two major parties. If only 30 or 35 percent of voters favored the winner, the votes of the majority did not have an impact on the result. This may be one reason why voter participation tends to be lower in countries with SMD systems than in countries with other systems. Minority voices are less likely to be heard. Voters—especially those who prefer minor parties—may believe voting is a waste of time.

A second criticism of SMD systems is that they overrepresent major parties. Consider a case in which a third party wins a significant share of the votes in many districts but a plurality in only one. The party would win a lot of votes but get only one seat in the legislature. Conversely, if a large number of candidates from a particular party win by a very small plurality in their districts, that party's vote in the legislature will be inflated. The number of its representatives will suggest an overwhelming national consensus, when in fact the party may not even have won a majority of the vote nationwide.

Table 8.1 on page 248 gives an example from the United Kingdom's 2019 election, in which the Conservative Party won 43.6 percent of the votes—less than a majority—but was awarded 56 percent of the seats in the House of Commons.

Apsana Begum, a member of the Labour Party in the House of Commons, launches her 2019 campaign to represent the district of Poplar and Limehouse in East London. The MPs in the House of Commons are elected through an SMD system. In addition to making laws that apply nationwide, MPs represent the constituents within their own districts.

Jess Hurd/Report Digital-Rea/Redux

Single-member district (SMD) system
A system for electing members of the legislature in which the candidate who earns the most votes in a district wins a seat in the legislature.

Plurality
The most votes, but not necessarily a majority.

"First-past-the-post" (FPTP)
An election rule in an SMD system in which the candidate with a plurality of votes wins a seat in the legislature.

AP® TIP

Single-member district (SMD), proportional representation (PR), and mixed system *always* refer to the election of representatives in the legislature. Do not confuse these terms with methods for selecting the executive.

TABLE 8.1 Results of the 2019 United Kingdom Parliamentary Election

Party	Percent of vote	Party	Percent of seats
Conservative	43.6	Conservative	56
Labour	32.2	Labour	31
Liberal Democrat	11.5	Liberal Democrat	1.6
Other parties	12.7	Other parties	12.4

In parliamentary governments, SMD systems may promote efficient, stable policy-making by allowing decisive legislative action—but this advantage in policymaking may come at the cost of accurate representation of the citizens' preferences.

Proportional Representation

Proportional representation (PR) system
A system for electing members of the legislature in which seats are awarded according to the percentage of votes a party receives.

In a **proportional representation (PR) system**, representatives are chosen nationally and seats in the legislature are allocated proportionally according to the percentage of vote for each party. Most PR systems include a minimal electoral threshold—for example, 3 or 5 percent of the vote—to gain representation in parliament. As you learned in your study of Russia, the 5 percent threshold makes it difficult for small parties to win seats in the Duma.

A PR system translates each party's share of the votes into a similar share of legislative seats. Multiple parties are likely to be represented in the legislature, and in parliamentary systems, coalition government is common.

PR systems vary. In one common form of PR system, each party presents a ranked list of candidates for all the seats in the legislature. Voters can see the list and know who the top candidates are, but they vote for the party. If party X gets ten seats in the legislature, then the top ten candidates on the party list occupy those seats. PR assumes that voters mainly want their ideas and values represented. Voters are represented by the party they support in the legislature, regardless of where each member of the legislature lives.

PR systems have some advantages over SMD systems. First, very few votes are wasted because even small parties can usually gain some seats, depending on the threshold. Voters know that at least some members of their party are representing their interests in the legislature. However, smaller parties can usually have some impact on policy only by forming coalitions with larger parties. Because fewer votes are wasted, participation rates in countries with PR systems are higher, as Figure 8.1 shows.

Proponents of PR systems argue that it is more democratic, because larger percentages of voters participate and most have their views represented by their preferred party in the legislature. PR systems also tend to result in the election of more women and members of ethnic or racial minorities than SMD systems. Party leaders often feel compelled (and, in some countries like Mexico, are required by law) to include women or minority candidates on their party lists; see Table 8.2. Finally, PR systems may provide a greater range of party positions and information for voters. (Orellana, 2014.)

Critics of PR systems point to the indirect nature of PR elections—voters don't choose individual representatives. Party officials decide a candidate's fate because they assign the ranking on the party list. As a result, legislators are less likely to open local offices or focus on local issues. (Shugart, 2005.) Critics also question whether PR systems really result in voters expressing their beliefs more clearly. In PR systems with multiple parties, policy is based on negotiated compromises after the election. Voters may compensate for this by

FIGURE 8.1

Voter Turnout by Electoral System

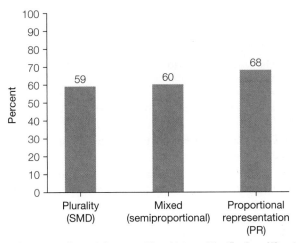

Data from International Institute for Democracy and Electoral Assistance, "What Affects Turnout?," Figure 25.

voting for parties more ideologically extreme than their own positions, assuming negotiations will result in more moderate policy.

In addition, critics of PR systems argue that having a broad range of parties in a legislature often has negative effects. Small parties, as noted above, often have little voice unless they join coalitions, but small extremist parties may gain inordinate power if they are able to negotiate key roles in ruling coalitions. Coalitions can be hard to form in such a fragmented environment, and where they do form, they may be unstable.

TABLE 8.2 Women in World Legislatures, 2018

Country	Percent, women in lower house	Type of electoral system
Iran	5.9	SMD/MMD
Mexico	48.2	Mixed
Russia	15.8	Mixed
Nigeria	5.6	SMD
United Kingdom	32	SMD

Data from Inter-Parliamentary Union, "Women in National Parliaments," World Classification Table (www.ipu .org/wmn-e/classif.htm). Based on figures for lower or single house.

Mixed Systems

Some countries, like Mexico and Russia, combine elements of SMD and PR into their electoral systems. The resulting hybrid is called a **mixed system**. Voters cast two ballots—one for a representative from their district, with the winner being the individual who gains a plurality, and a second for a party list.

Mixed systems share some of the advantages of SMD and PR systems. Because they waste fewer votes, participation rates tend to be slightly higher, as in PR systems. Citizens are also guaranteed a personal representative who can perform constituent services within their district. The SMD component in mixed systems tends to reinforce the dominance of a couple of large parties that find it easier to win a significant number of individual seats. This is the case in Russia, where the United Russia party dominates the SMD portion of seats in the Duma. In addition, the threshold in the PR portion of Russia's electoral system shuts out small parties and encourages the development of a dominant party.

Electoral systems influence the type and extent of representation citizens have, and all systems involve trade-offs. Electoral systems also have an important impact on political parties and party systems.

Mixed electoral system
A system for electing members of the legislature that includes both single-member districts and seats awarded through proportional representation.

Each section's main ideas are reflected in the Learning Targets. By reviewing after each section, you should be able to

Remember the key points,

Know terms that are central to the topic, and

Think critically about what you have learned.

Remember

- An electoral system is the process voters use to select the executive or members of the legislature.
- Presidents elected with a majority of the vote tend to have stronger mandates to govern than those elected through plurality systems.
- In a single-member district (SMD) plurality system, voters choose one representative, by plurality vote, where the winner of the most votes wins the seats, to represent citizens living in a geographical area known as a district.
- In a proportional representation (PR) system, parties receive a percentage of seats in the legislature according to the percentage of votes received in a national election.
- In parliamentary governments, SMD systems may result in fewer parties and less gridlock, but fewer interests are represented.
- A mixed system for electing the legislature includes both SMD and PR seats.

Know

- *Electoral system:* the formal rules and procedures for selecting the executive or members of the legislature. (p. 246)
- *Mandate:* the broad support of the people to carry out proposed policies. (p. 246)
- *Runoff election:* a second and final election held between the top two vote-getters when no candidate wins a majority of the votes in the first round of voting. (p. 246)
- *Multimember district (MMD) system:* a method for electing members of a legislature in which two or more representatives are elected from a district. (p. 246)
- *Single-member district (SMD) system:* a system for electing members of the legislature in which the candidate who earns the most votes in a district wins a seat in the legislature. (p. 247)
- *Plurality:* the most votes, but not necessarily a majority. (p. 247)
- *"First-past-the-post" (FPTP):* an election rule in an SMD system in which the candidate with a plurality of votes wins a seat in the legislature. (p. 247)
- *Proportional representation (PR) system:* a system for electing members of the legislature in which seats are awarded according to the percentage of votes a party receives. (p. 248)
- *Mixed electoral system:* a system for electing members of the legislature that includes both single-member districts and seats awarded through proportional representation. (p. 249)

Think

- Which type of electoral system is most effective in representing citizens' interests?

··

Free-Response Question: Conceptual Analysis

Answer A, B, C, and D.

A. Define electoral system.

B. Describe the difference between two types of systems for selecting the executive.

C. Describe the difference between the three types of systems for electing the legislatures.

D. Explain why a government would adopt one of the electoral systems described in part C.

8.2 Political Parties

Learning Targets

After reading this section, you should be able to do the following:

1. Explain why the number of and strength of political parties vary among countries.

2. Explain why democratic countries have two or more political parties.

3. Explain why SMD systems tend to result in the creation of two major parties.

4. Describe the different types of party systems.

5. Explain why political parties are weakening in wealthy democracies.

Political parties in both democratic and authoritarian states link citizens with government. Several factors impact the strength and competitiveness of political parties.

Types of Party Systems

The term **party system** refers to the number and strength of political parties within a country. By definition, democratic regimes have at least two parties, and most democratic systems have more than two parties. This is because democratic states have free and fair elections, which require competition between political parties. At the other extreme, some authoritarian states—like China—allow only one party to control government. These are called **one-party states**. In some countries, multiple parties exist,

Party system
The number of and strength of political parties within a country.

One-party state
A country where only one party is allowed to control the government.

A rally in Ciudad Juarez, Mexico, before López Obrador's victory in 2018. MORENA is one of three major parties in Mexico's multiparty system.

Jose Luis Gonzalez/Alamy

Dominant party system
A party system in which multiple parties exist, but one party dominates the executive branch and wins most of the seats in the legislature.

Two-party system
A party system in which only two parties are able to garner enough votes to win an election, although more may compete.

Multiparty system
A party system in which more than two parties can win a national election and control the government.

but one party dominates the executive branch and wins the most seats in the legislature, although other parties have some representation. These are called **dominant party systems**. Mexico under PRI rule before 2000 and modern-day Russia are two examples. In dominant party systems, the ruling party maintains power not only through its popularity but also by manipulating the electoral system, controlling government resources, and intimidating other parties.

In a **two-party system**, only two parties are able to garner enough votes to win an election and control the government, although more may compete. The United Kingdom is the classic case of a two-party system. Broad-based third parties, such as the Liberal Democrats, compete in elections, but they never win enough seats to control the legislature. The same is true of regional parties, such as the Scottish National Party, which have regional, but not national, appeal.

Finally, **multiparty systems** are those in which more than two parties can win a national election and control the government. Mexico is an example. It has three major parties and a few smaller parties, which sometimes form coalitions in the legislature.

Impact of Electoral System on the Number of Parties

A country's electoral system shapes both the number and strength of parties. French political scientist Maurice Duverger concluded that the logic of competition in SMD electoral systems results in the long-term survival of only two parties. (Duverger, 1969.) Multiple parties are unlikely to survive because all political parties must gain a plurality in a particular district to win that district's legislative seat. Successful parties will be those with broad enough appeal to gain the most support in a district. These two major parties are called **catch-all parties** because they take ideologically diverse, usually middle-of-the road, positions to capture as many voters as possible. Relying on a small, ideologically committed core group will yield no legislative seats. Voters don't want to "waste" their votes on parties that can't win seats. Over time, ambitious politicians gravitate toward established major parties to win elections rather than join small parties or create new ones. The concept that SMD systems lead to two major catch-all parties is known as Duverger's Law.

Party systems have important implications for the stability of governments. An SMD/plurality system with two catch-all parties may make governing easier and policy more coherent, because there are only two competing ideologies to consider in policymaking. In contrast, PR systems tend to create more parties and parties that are more ideologically distinct than SMD/plurality systems. Multiparty systems give more voice to diverse opinions in the legislature but can produce coalition governments, which sometimes become unstable.

Sometimes, politicians in SMD systems have to cater to a small group of supporters, because they cannot risk losing even a few voters. (Moosbrugger, 2012.) In multiparty PR systems, on the other hand, politicians are less threatened by the loss of a particular, small group upset over one issue. Farmers, for example, were able to prevent widely supported environment policies more effectively in SMD than in PR systems.

Declining Citizen Support for Political Parties

Although political parties in democracies still have faithful members and continue to control elections, they face growing skepticism. A survey of citizens in twenty-one countries found that while 80 percent supported democracy, only about 20 percent had confidence

AP® TIP

You don't have to remember the name of Duverger's Law to do well on the AP® Exam, but it's important to understand the principle that SMD plurality electoral systems tend to result in the creation of two major parties.

The third free-response question on the AP® Exam is a comparative-analysis question which, as the name implies, requires you to compare countries. The comparative-analysis question will begin with a short introduction, such as "Compare judicial independence in two different AP® Comparative Government and Politics course countries." The purpose of the introduction is to focus your attention on the subject of the question. Make sure you read it carefully.

The question is divided into three parts, and part A of the question usually requires a definition or description. For example, "Describe judicial independence." This part of the question focuses on a broad concept. You do not have to include country-specific information in part A.

Parts B and C require you to compare two countries. For example, part B might ask, "Explain how judicial independence impacts policymaking in two different AP® Comparative Government and Politics course countries." Part C might ask something like, "Explain why each of the two AP® Comparative Government and Politics course countries

described in (B) would choose to encourage or constrain judicial independence."

Think carefully about the countries you will chose in answering parts B and C. The best strategy may be to compare countries that are dissimilar, because they provide a better contrast between government systems. Don't just pick the first two countries that come to mind. Instead, provide examples that will prove to the reader that you understand the concept and are able to explain how it applies in different countries.

Use the sample question discussed in the paragraphs above to answer the questions:

1. Describe judicial independence.

2. Pick two countries to discuss in parts B and C, and explain why you chose those two countries.

3. Answer parts B and C of the question.

4. How did your strategy in picking two countries help you to fully answer the free-response question?

---

in political parties. Parties are central to democracy, but support for traditional major parties has declined in the past two decades, and their weakening raises great concern. (Scarrow and Webb, 2017, 2.)

At least since the 1980s, the ideological difference between traditional European parties on the left and right has been shrinking. (Maravall, 2016, 52.) While they remain distinct, they do not offer voters the stark choice they did a half century ago. In the mid-twentieth century, major parties appealed to voters not by their ideological distinctions but by offering them more government aid and services, especially in Europe's more developed welfare states.

Political scientists Richard S. Katz and Peter Mair argued that by the late twentieth century, this strategy was meeting budget constraints. (Katz and Mair, 2017.) Governments were no longer able to expand social programs, so parties could no longer offer benefits to attract voters. Major parties used the media and money from the government to maintain their power and the status quo. This hurt citizens' sense of political efficacy, the feeling that their participation can have a political impact. (Pardos-Prado and Riera, 2016.) This gave populist parties an opportunity to mobilize voters against the elite, whom they accused of using established political parties to take advantage of ordinary citizens.

As the traditional parties have declined, new parties have arisen. On the left, green parties focused on the environment now exist across Europe, especially in countries with PR electoral systems. Parties that question the benefits of EU membership have also arisen.

A more powerful trend has been the rise of far-right parties, many of which focus on a charismatic leader. Far-right parties generally focus on economic decline and oppose immigration, often blaming the EU and globalization for both. The United Kingdom Independence Party (UKIP) is one example. In the mid-2010s, UKIP, led by Nigel Farage, focused on a nationalist agenda, favoring the United Kingdom's withdrawal from the EU, opposing immigration, and supporting a return to traditional British culture. The party declined after the Brexit referendum in 2016, partly as a result of turmoil within its leadership.

The development of parties on the far left and far right raises questions about whether they can serve the traditional functions of parties in Western democracies—giving voters clear ideological choices, providing citizens with a way to participate in politics, and creating stable coalitions of interests that can govern effectively.

A common explanation for the decline of traditional political parties has focused on economic changes. The decline of manufacturing in wealthy democracies that accompanied globalization reduced job opportunities and incomes for less-educated workers. The European migrant crisis of 2015–2016 saw a million Middle Eastern refugees arrive in Europe in a matter of months, significantly strengthening far-right parties. Workers in manufacturing plants felt abandoned by the economic policies supported by major parties, and these workers supported the new, far-right parties who tied their grievances to support for reduced trade, a reduced role for the EU, and reduced immigration. (Rucht, 2018.)

Technology may also contribute to the decline of political parties. Major parties used to serve two key functions: educating voters about political issues, and simplifying voters' choices. As media outlets (including social media) have multiplied, voters no longer need parties to educate them. Parties now run campaigns through national and social media rather than by grassroots efforts to mobilize voters. (Dalton and Wattenberg, 2000.) Furthermore, as voters' preferences changed, the traditional parties didn't keep up.

The decline of traditional political parties raises concerns for the future of democratic systems. However, it also presents opportunities. As established parties evolve and new ones emerge, political parties have an opportunity to appeal to voters on both the left and right on important issues like the environment, race relations, and gender roles. (Dalton, 2017.)

Section 8.2 Review

Remember

- The number of and strength of political parties vary among countries
- Democratic countries have two or more political parties.
- SMD systems tend to result in the creation of two major parties.
- Party systems include one-party, dominant party, two-party, and multiparty systems.
- Political parties are weakening in wealthy democracies.

Know

- *Party system:* the number of and strength of political parties within a country. (p. 251)
- *One-party state:* a country where only one party is allowed to control the government. (p. 251)
- *Dominant party system:* a party system in which multiple parties exist, but one party dominates the executive branch and wins most of the seats in the legislature. (p. 252)
- *Two-party system:* a party system in which only two parties are able to garner enough votes to win an election, although more may compete. (p. 252)

- *Multiparty system:* a party system in which more than two parties can win a national election and control the government. (p. 252)
- *Catch-all party:* a party that takes ideologically diverse, usually middle-of-the-road, positions to capture as many voters as possible. (p. 252)

Think

- What are the advantages and disadvantages for democratic government in having a multi-party state?

....

Free-Response Question: Quantitative Analysis

Political Parties in the Lower House of the Legislature, as of March 2021

Chamber	Number of Parties	Number of Major Parties
Mexico Chamber of Deputies	9	3
Nigeria House of Representatives	10	2
Russia Duma	6	1
United Kingdom House of Commons	12	2

Note: This table does not include information about the number of seats held by independents.
Sources: Central Election Commission of Russia, U.K. Parliament, Independent Nigerian Electoral Commission, National Election Institute of Mexico.

Answer A, B, C, D, and E.

A. Using the data in the table, identify the country with the largest number of major political parties.

B. Using the data in the table, describe one difference in the party system in the country identified in part A and the party system in another country shown on the table.

C. Describe party system.

D. Using your knowledge of party systems and the data in the table, draw a conclusion about the relationship between the type of electoral system and the number of parties in the legislature.

E. Explain how the number of political parties impacts regime type.

8.3 Interest Groups and Social Movements

Learning Targets

After reading the section, you should be able to do the following:

1. Explain how interest groups attempt to influence government policy.

2. Compare pluralist and corporatist interest-group systems.

3. Explain how social movements seek to promote socioeconomic and cultural change.

Citizens participate in the political process by joining interest groups and social movements in an effort to influence government and politics. These groups differ in their tactics and in their ability to accomplish their goals. Civil society in democratic states is stronger than it is in authoritarian states. However, in both types of regimes, citizens join groups and use collective action in an effort to influence policy.

Interest Groups

Interest group
An association of individuals or businesses that attempts to influence government.

Our definition of civil society includes all groups not controlled by the government, including interest groups. **Interest groups** are associations of individuals or businesses that attempt to influence government. Most claim to represent clearly defined interests that their members share, such as protecting the environment, advancing civil rights, or representing a profession or industry. Interest groups are formal organizations, and they are often regulated by the government. Well-established interest groups are visible, have relatively big and active memberships, and have a significant voice on the issues in which they are interested.

Interest groups bring together like-minded individuals to achieve a goal, but interest groups do not run candidates for office, which is one of the ways they are different from political parties. In theory, if they are effective in carrying out their functions, the political system becomes more responsive and inclusive.

Modern interest groups emerged in the nineteenth century. Labor, business, and agriculture represented the three key sectors of the economy. For example, the Nigerian Labour Congress, whose members are pictured at the beginning of this chapter, is an umbrella organization that advocates for legislation benefiting workers, such as an increase in the minimum wage.

As more citizens became more involved in the political process, other interest groups emerged, including groups focused on expanding rights for women and racial minorities. In ethnically and religiously divided societies, ethnic or religious organizations are often more politically important than unions or other economic groups. As countries become more democratic, more and varied types of civil society organizations arise, making the study of their impact on democracy increasingly important and interesting. The types and strength of different kinds of groups in civil society have important effects on the strength of a democracy.

As is true for political parties, there is also growing concern about weakening of civil society, even in well-established democracies. Civil society consists of groups outside of the government's control, such as groups formed by people who share a common interest. Robert Putnam lamented a decline in social capital—the networks and norms of trust that are crucial to democratic participation. (Putnam, 2000.) Even apparently "nonpolitical" organizations (such as the local Little League or parent-teacher organizations), he argued, create social networks and mutual trust among members, which can be used for political action. However, face-to-face organizations seem to be declining. Theda Skocpol argued that groups that rely on members for financial support and for occasional phone calls, emails, or presence at rallies, have replaced active local branches that regularly bring members together. (Skocpol, 2003.)

Critics of Putnam and Skocpol argue that while levels of trust and membership in formal organizations have declined, involvement in political activities has not. (Dalton, 2017.) New forms of activity have arisen to replace some of those that have declined. (Lemann, 1996.) Much of this activity takes place through social movements and involves the use of social media. However, people move relatively quickly among different issues and movements and may not develop the strong ties with a group that they would have developed in a more traditional group setting.

AP® TIP

There is a difference between interest groups and civil society. Civil society consists of citizen organizations outside of the government's control. Civil society groups may or may not have a political focus. Interest groups participate in the political process in an effort to get the policies they favor enacted into law. While interest groups are one form of a civil society organization, civil society is much broader in scope. A soccer club, for example, is part of civil society, but it is not an interest group.

Pluralism and Corporatism

The formal and informal relationships that interest groups have with government are crucial to how they operate and their effectiveness. As you learned in your study of Mexico, the two major models of government–interest group interaction are corporatism and pluralism.

Interest-Group Pluralism

Pluralism means a system in which groups are allowed to form and advocate for their interests outside government control. Under a pluralist system, many groups may exist to represent the same broad interest, and all groups can compete to gain influence. The government, at least in theory, is neutral and does not give preferential access and power to any one group or allow it to be the official representative of a particular interest. Alternative groups have the right to organize and advocate for the policy positions they favor. In a pluralist system, multiple groups interact with the government, even on a single issue.

Pluralism
A system in which groups are allowed to form and advocate for their interests outside government control.

Corporatism

The major alternative to pluralism is corporatism. In general, corporatism is less democratic than pluralism. As you learned in studying Mexico under the single-party dominance of PRI, in a **corporatist** system, the state controls interest groups and chooses the ones it wishes to recognize.

In corporatist systems, **single-peak associations** represent the major interests in society by bringing together numerous local groups, and government works closely with fewer, larger, and more highly organized peak associations than under pluralism. Peak associations maintain their unity and institutional strength through internal rules that ensure local organizations will abide by the decisions of the national body. By negotiating binding agreements with them, the state recognizes the peak associations as the official representatives of their sectors. Dissatisfied members may try to change the association's policies or create alternative organizations, but these tactics are often unsuccessful because membership in the peak association provides direct access to government.

Corporatism
A system in which the state controls interest groups and chooses the ones it wishes to recognize.

Single-peak association
An organization that brings together all interest groups in a particular sector to influence and negotiate agreements with the government.

Corporatist systems can create efficiency in policymaking, because they limit the flow of information to decision makers, who do not become overwhelmed with input from multiple perspectives. In comparison, in pluralist systems, all groups compete, and information flows are unconstrained. In the corporatist approach, some important information may not make it to government, just as in a pluralist system, important information may be lost in the background noise made by many groups competing for access.

If a peak association has strong mechanisms of internal democracy, such as open elections for leadership positions and member participation in setting organizational policies, its leaders can legitimately claim to represent members' views. If the association does not, it may have significant access to government and influence, but it may not really represent its members' views.

The ability of interest groups to influence policymaking depends on their resources. Well-established interest groups may have more members and more money to influence the government. These factors increase their potential clout. No government treats each kind of group equally. In market systems, business interests are crucial for the well-being of the economy. The government in a market economy will pay more attention to business interests than to others, no matter how effectively others organize. (Lindblom, 1977.) Nevertheless, governments in democratic systems have incentives to respond to

Education for all Nigerians (EAN) is an interest group that advocates for more funding for schools. Its mission includes increasing the infrastructure for education and decreasing corruption, which diverts money from the educational system.

the demands of interest groups in order to benefit from their expertise and financial and electoral support.

Social Movements

Social movement
A group that has a loosely defined organizational structure and seeks major socioeconomic or political change through collective action.

Grassroots movement
Citizens at the local level banding together to advocate for a cause.

Social movements are groups that have a loosely defined organizational structure and seek major socioeconomic or political changes through collective action. A **grassroots movement** is created when citizens at the local level band together to advocate for a cause.

Social movements arose at least a century ago, but they became much more common during and after the 1960s. In that decade in much of the Western world, growing numbers of citizens, particularly young "baby boomers," came to feel that their governments, political parties, and interest groups were not providing adequate forms of participation and representation. They believed that political institutions were led by the elite. In response, social movements led by racial minorities, women, antiwar activists, and environmentalists arose, challenging the status quo. These groups have since been joined by many others, such as the anti-globalization movement and the Black Lives Matter movement in response to police violence against people of color.

While they exist throughout the world, social movements are most common and have arguably had the greatest impact in liberal democracies. Social movements increased the political participation and representation of women. Racial minorities united to challenge discriminatory policies. Gay-rights activists have succeeded in getting a number of Western governments to redefine marriage and international organizations to think of LGBT rights as part of universal human rights. And in the age of global climate change, environmentalists have put their concerns on the agenda of national and international institutions.

Social movements are often seen as pursuing progressive social change favored by the left, but conservative social movements also exist. The Brexit movement in the United Kingdom that resulted in separation from the European Union is similar to other conservative movements in Europe that emphasize nationalism. Similar movements have arisen in response to increased immigration from Muslim countries and support far-right populist parties.

The fourth free-response question on the AP® Exam is the argument essay. You will respond to the other three free-response questions using a short-answer format, but the argument question requires a traditional essay, with a thesis and supporting paragraphs as evidence.

The argument essay follows a standard format. First, the question asks you to develop an argument about a topic, such as, "Develop an argument as to whether interest groups or social movements are more effective in changing government policy."

The next part of the prompt is a list of concepts, and you must use one or more of them in your response. Here is an example:

Use one or more of the following course concepts in your response:

- Civil society
- Civil liberties
- Political efficacy

Write a very short introduction and define the concept in the prompt as well as the concept or concepts from the list that you will discuss in the essay. This helps the exam reader know that you understand the meaning of the concepts that you will discuss later. Your thesis statement will be the last sentence in this short introductory paragraph.

The rest of the prompt explains how to organize your essay. It begins with, "Respond to the prompt with a defensible claim or thesis that establishes a line of reasoning using one or more of the provided course concepts." Your thesis statement should include at least one of the listed course concepts and include a *because* statement that sets forth your reasoning. Your thesis may look something like this:

Thesis: Interest groups are more effective than social movements in changing government policy *because* [link to evidence and refer to one or more concepts].

The thesis statement will be the last sentence of your short introductory paragraph.

Next, the prompt instructs you to support your claim with at least two pieces of evidence from one or more course

countries. You must relate the evidence to one or more of the listed concepts. Pick countries strategically. For example, in an essay about social movements, you might pick democratic countries over authoritarian ones, because social movements are likely to have a greater impact in democratic regimes.

Next, the prompt instructs you to use reasoning to explain why the evidence you presented supports your thesis, referring to the course concept. The easiest way to do this is to write two separate evidence paragraphs that look this this:

Evidence One	**Evidence Two**
Specific and relevant	Specific and relevant
Links to concept	Links to concept
Connects to thesis	Connects to thesis

The last part of the essay is a response to an opposing or alternate perspective using refutation, concession, or rebuttal. This requires you to do two things: (1) state another perspective, and (2) respond to that perspective. It is usually easiest to use refutation or rebuttal, because it can be hard to respond after you have conceded an argument. Your rebuttal will be the last paragraph of your essay, and it might be structured like this:

Rebuttal: Opponents of my thesis would argue that . . . because . . . (Don't just state the opposing viewpoint—explain how an opponent would support that viewpoint.) However, this is incorrect because . . .

Practice using the same structure for every argument essay you write while taking this course. By the time you take the AP® Exam, you will be able to focus on providing strong content in your essay, because you will have the structure memorized.

1. Write a generic outline for the argument-essay prompt.

2. Fill in the outline with information specific to the essay prompt above.

3. Explain how to choose the appropriate countries to use as evidence.

Most social movements focus on changing government policy, and sometimes they fail. A social movement may lack an identifiable leader, and without strong organization, it may fall apart because of internal divisions. Nevertheless, social movements can create access to the political system and impact the political agenda as well as how existing policy is funded and implemented. (Giugni, 2004, 7.) Social movements can change cultural attitudes and opinions or the practices of institutions outside government, such as large corporations. Participation in social movements, even when it is not effective at changing policy, often affects those involved, giving them a greater sense of political efficacy and providing them with political skills they can use in the future.

8.3 Section Review

Remember

- Interest groups attempt to influence government policy.
- In a pluralist system, many groups complete in the policymaking process.
- In a corporatist system, the state sponsors interest groups and chooses certain groups to include in the policymaking process.
- Social movements are groups of loosely organized people who seek major changes to the political or economic system.

Know

- *Interest group:* an association of individuals or businesses that attempts to influence government. (p. 256)
- *Pluralism:* a system in which groups are allowed to form and advocate for their interests outside government control. (p. 257)
- *Corporatism:* a system in which the state controls interest groups and chooses the ones it wishes to recognize. (p. 257)
- *Single-peak association:* an organization that brings together all interest groups in a particular sector to influence and negotiate agreements with the government. (p. 257)
- *Social movement:* a group that has a loosely defined organizational structure and seeks major socioeconomic or political change through collective action. (p. 258)
- *Grassroots movement:* citizens at the local level banding together to advocate for a cause. (p. 258)

Think

- Why are some interest groups more successful than others in getting their preferred policies enacted by the government?
- What are the benefits and drawbacks of social movements in comparison to interest groups in advocating for change?

Free-Response Question: Conceptual Analysis

Interest groups and social movements seek to influence policymaking.

A. Define a pluralist interest-group system.

B. Describe the relationship between interest groups and the government in a corporatist interest-group system.

C. Explain why democratic regimes are likely to have pluralist interest-group systems.

D. Explain how social movements seek to influence policymaking

Chapter 8 Review

Elections

AP® KEY CONCEPTS

- Electoral system (p. 246)
- Mandate (p. 246)
- Runoff election (p. 246)
- Multimember district (MMD) system (p. 246)
- Single-member district (SMD) system (p. 247)
- Plurality (p. 247)

- "First-past-the-post" (FPTP) (p. 247)
- Proportional representation (PR) system (p. 248)
- Mixed electoral system (p. 249)
- Party system (p. 251)
- One-party state (p. 251)
- Dominant party system (p. 252)
- Two-party system (p. 252)

- Multiparty system (p. 252)
- Catch-all party (p. 252)
- Interest group (p. 256)
- Pluralism (p. 257)
- Corporatism (p. 257)
- Single-peak association (p. 257)
- Social movement (p. 258)
- Grassroots movement (p. 258)

AP® EXAM MULTIPLE-CHOICE PRACTICE QUESTIONS

1. Which of the following describes a result of a two-round system for electing the executive?

   A. The president may be elected by less than a majority of the voters.

   B. Voter efficacy is lower, because citizens often do not support the top two vote-getters.

   C. The president is elected by a majority, increasing the likelihood he or she will have a mandate to carry out proposed policies.

   D. Election fraud is more likely, because there are more opportunities for ballot stuffing.

Questions 2 and 3 refer to the passage.

> [Civil society organizations (CSOs)] have also proven very useful partners to accountability institutions (such as anticorruption agencies and supreme audit institutions), which often operate with limited funding and can benefit from approaches that maximise their outreach and impact. In that regard, CSOs with specific anti-corruption expertise, community-based networks and the media have all been important partners to such institutions. The diversity within civil society groups has also been a key element of its usefulness in the fight against corruption. Corruption is often most harmful to those who are most vulnerable within society, for example, indigenous groups, women, low income workers, and the rural poor. The capacity of civil society groups to build trust within such communities and champion their issues has given voice and power to such groups to ensure that corruption around issues such as land rights, resource extraction, public service access, and labour entitlements has been exposed and addressed.
>
> —"Civil Society Participation, Public Accountability, and the UN Convention Against Corruption," Transparency International, December 2015

2. Which of the following is supported by the main idea of the passage?

   A. Interest groups can bring people together in an effort to fight government corruption.

   B. Labor unions are a large source of corruption, even though they are a part of civil society.

   C. Authoritarian governments prevent civil society groups from forming in an effort to prevent the disclosure of official corruption.

   D. Large-scale anti-corruption groups, such as Transparency International, are more effective in battling corruption than smaller local groups.

Chapter 8 • Review   **261**

3. Which of the following is an implication of the argument presented in the passage?

   A. Corruption will continue unless international organizations pressure states for more transparency.

   B. Grassroots movements are effective in calling attention to corruption.

   C. Interest groups are more effective in fighting corruption than social movements, because interest groups are more focused on a common goal.

   D. Authoritarian regimes establish state-sanctioned groups and reward them with benefits in an effort to prevent transparency.

4. Which of the following is a disadvantage of a proportional representation (PR) system in representing the interests of citizens?

   A. PR systems result in fewer political parties, which means citizens must choose between middle-of-the-road ideologies.

   B. In PR systems, citizens do not have a representative in their district who can provide them with constituent service.

   C. In PR systems, voters do not know which candidates are on the list the party will use to fill seats in the legislature.

   D. PR systems take power away from the party elite, because candidates cannot run independent campaigns.

5. Which of the following best describes the impact of the electoral system on the party system in a country studied in AP® Comparative Government and Politics?

   A. Russia's mixed electoral system results in multiple, competitive parties in the Duma.

   B. Mexico's mixed electoral system results in two-party control of the Chamber of Deputies, with representation of small regional parties.

   C. The United Kingdom's single-member district system results in the Labour and Conservative parties being awarded a disproportionate share of seats in the House of Commons.

   D. The high threshold for being awarded seats in Russia's Duma results in a one-party state.

6. Which of the following is a catch-all party?

   A. United Russia

   B. The Scottish National Party

   C. The Liberal Democrats in Russia

   D. The Conservative Party in the United Kingdom

Questions 7 and 8 refer to the line graph.

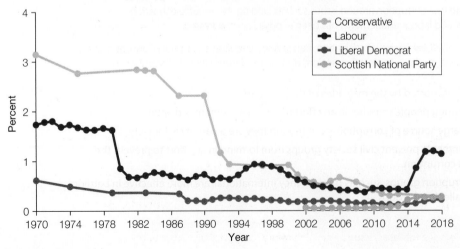

Party Membership as a Proportion of the U.K. Electorate, 1970–2018

Data from House of Commons Library.

7. Which of the following describes a trend in the graph?

    A. Membership as a percentage of the electorate in the two major parties in the United Kingdom declined significantly from 2000 to 2014.

    B. People who left the Labour and Conservative parties from 1970 to 2018 joined the Liberal Democrats.

    C. From 2014 to 2018, the Scottish National Party saw the largest increase in membership as a percentage of the electorate of all of the parties shown on the graph.

    D. Of the two major parties in the United Kingdom, the Conservative Party saw the biggest decrease in membership as a percentage of the electorate from 1970 to 2018.

8. Which of the following describes a limitation of the data shown on the graph?

    A. The graph does not account for the rise of new political parties, such as the United Kingdom Independence Party (UKIP).

    B. The vertical axis is drawn in increments that overestimate trends shown in the graph.

    C. The horizontal axis is drawn using increments of one year, and it does not focus on years when elections took place.

    D. The graph is based on the self-reporting of citizens regarding party membership, and it may not reflect the actual membership of the party.

9. Which of the following describes a difference between an interest group and a social movement?

    A. Interest groups run candidates for office, and social movements do not run candidates for office.

    B. Social movements focus on narrow issues, such as the environment, and interest groups focus on broad issues, such as worker pay.

    C. Social movements are more effective in getting their proposed policies enacted, because they have more members than interest groups do.

    D. Interest groups are more organized and have an identifiable leadership structure in comparison to social movements.

10. Which of the following is an example of interest-group corporatism in a country studied in AP® Comparative Government and Politics?

    A. In Mexico under PRI rule, the state recognized and negotiated with specific large groups representing business and labor.

    B. In the United Kingdom, the National Health Service is supported by the government, and it represents the interests of medical professionals in the policymaking process.

    C. The United Russia party claims to represent the interest of all Russian citizens, including interest groups.

    D. Interest groups in Russia are required to register with the government, which has the power to disband groups for extremism.

AP® EXAM PRACTICE ARGUMENT ESSAY

Develop an argument about whether single-member district, or mixed electoral systems are more effective in representing citizens' interests in the legislature.

Use one or more of the following course concepts in your response:

    • Party system   • Accountability   • Legitimacy

In your response, do the following:

    • Respond to the prompt with a defensible claim or thesis that establishes a line of reasoning using one or more of the provided course concepts.

    • Support your claim with at least TWO pieces of specific and relevant evidence from your study of one or more course countries. The evidence should be relevant to one or more of the provided course concepts.

    • Use reasoning to explain why your evidence supports your claim or thesis, using one or more of the provided course concepts.

    • Respond to an opposing or alternate perspective, using refutation, concession, or rebuttal.

For a complete list of the sources of information cited in this chapter, turn to the Works Cited appendix.

9 Case Study: Nigeria

Elections

The large population of Nigeria has led to the growth of mass media since independence. The Nigerian film industry is now an economic force and increasingly influential worldwide. Vendors at Alaba International Market in the city of Ojo in Lagos State are a major source of films. Although piracy of films is an issue, the size of the market shows the appetite for film among Nigerians.

Andrew Esiebo

Nollywood, Mo Abudu, and Nigeria's Vibrant Media Industry

Since their development in the late nineteenth century, motion pictures have captivated audiences with images of life, fantasy, and wonder. In 2019, before the COVID-19 pandemic, more than 5 billion tickets were sold to movies worldwide. In Africa, the Nigerian film industry, nicknamed Nollywood, has become one of the largest film producers in the world.

The rise of Nollywood is attributed to several factors. Among them is the development of the VCR, which allowed low-cost production and duplication. People could watch movies at home, which was less expensive than going to a theater. Economic problems in the 1980s led to a rise in crime that made attendance at movie theaters dangerous. Problems with reliable electricity made things even more difficult. (Witt.) Even as recently as 2004 there were no movie houses in Lagos, which, at 8.5 million people, is the largest city in Africa's most populous country. The accessibility and affordability of VCR tapes, coupled with the perils and hassles of going to a theater, propelled Nollywood's popularity.

While there were popular Nigerian films before 1992, *Living in Bondage* is often seen as Nollywood's first big hit. It was an Igbo-language film with English subtitles. Hundreds of thousands of copies were sold, mostly on videocassette. The story revolves around a main character who sacrifices his wife to a satanic cult in exchange for wealth, something each of his more successful friends had already done. Made on a shoestring budget with poor production values, it spoke to the postcolonial experience of many Nigerians. Today, Nollywood has developed into a popular economic powerhouse, producing more than 2,500 movies in 2020. (Statista.)

Nollywood's films have contributed to a sense of African identity. According to one commentator, "Nollywood deserves credit for its roles as a chronicler of social history, as an organ of cultural and moral response to the extreme provocations and dislocations of contemporary Nigeria, and, as a bearer of a true nationalism." (Hayes, xxvii.) In an interview, Femi Odugbemi, a noted Nigerian documentary film maker, summarized the contribution of Nollywood films:

> [They] recognized our existence as a distinct culture, as a distinct civilization, a distinct aspiration. We were just defined in one single [image] . . . The little boy starving with big inflated stomach defined our narrative. Well guess what? It was from Nollywood that people first realized that we built houses with huge big columns and we could afford it. It was from Nollywood that we first realized that we had people that bought seven, eight cars, and they only had one wife. . . . Nollywood . . . became our voice, our documentary. We did not need you to create a space for us. (Witt, 17–18.)

Exemplifying the global reach of Nigeria's media industry is Mosunmola Abudu, who goes by the name Mo Abudu. Born in 1964 in the United Kingdom to Nigerian parents, she has created an international media empire.

At age seven, Abudu and her family moved back to Nigeria to her grandparents' cacao farm. At age twelve, after the death of her father, she returned to the United Kingdom for school. After completing college, she earned a master's degree in human resources from the University of Westminster in London, and in her late twenties, she returned to Nigeria. At age nineteen, she was also a brand ambassador for Avon cosmetics for Africa. Her HR

Mo Abudu is a multimedia "mogul." She is active in television, film, and education. As of 2021, her film company had produced four of the ten Nigerian movies that have made the most money. She chaired the forty-seventh International Emmy Awards gala and was the first African to do so.

Angela Weiss/AFP/Getty Images

This poster advertises the movie, *Loud*, a high-school musical. The film—reputedly the first high-school musical made in Nigeria—was directed by Umanu Elijah and released in 2020.

career included time as head of human resources and administration for the oil giant Esso Exploration and Production Nigeria Limited (ExxonMobil). She left Exxon in 2000 to open her own HR consulting company.

In her forties, Abudu decided to make a career change. By 2008, without any TV experience, she developed, produced, and hosted a talk show, the first syndicated daily talk show on African regional television to present Africa's stories.

From her talk show, which she turned over to another host in 2013, she has expanded her media empire. Her company, EbonyLife Media, includes EbonyLife TV, Africa's first global Black entertainment and lifestyle network that aims to narrate African stories on global platforms. Her company now includes other divisions: EbonyLife Films, EbonyLife ON, EbonyLife Studios, and EbonyLife Productions Limited (U.K.).

In 2015, EbonyLife TV's first feature film, *Fifty*, about four women friends in Lagos, was released worldwide. In 2020, she signed a multi-film deal with Netflix, becoming the first African production company to partner with Netflix. She also signed a deal with the American entertainment company AMC to develop a science-fiction show, and she has signed a two-series, one-movie agreement with Will Smith and Jada Pinkett Smith's Westbrook Studios.

In 2013, the *Hollywood Reporter* included Abudu on the list of the 25 Most Powerful Women in Global Television. In 2015, *Forbes* magazine described her as "Africa's Most Successful Woman," and CNN described her as "Africa's Queen of Media who conquered the continent." She was on The Powerlist, a U.K. list of the 100 most influential people of African and Caribbean heritage, in 2018. She was selected in 2021 to join the producer category of the Academy of Motion Picture Arts and Sciences (Oscars). She is the only African in that category.

While some people have labeled her "The African Oprah," Abudu is firm about establishing her own identity. In 2019, she was the first African to receive the *médaille d'honneur* from the trade group MIPTV, at a ceremony in Cannes, France. It is given to senior executives for their impact on the global television industry. Upon receiving the award, she said: "My big dream was and still is, to change the narrative about my continent. As a continent, Africa has remained creatively silent for centuries, our stories seldom told outside of our families and villages and often from the perspective of 'someone' looking in." (The Guardian, 2019.)

The success of Nollywood and the story of Mo Abudu demonstrate that Nigeria is a vibrant and complex country. Nollywood has the potential to bring people together through shared experiences and strengthen national pride. Furthermore, the expansion of the media in Nigeria has the potential to further democratization by allowing Nigerians to share their voices and impact the direction of the country.

Freedom House categorizes Nigeria as partially free. It holds lively elections with competitive political parties, and power has been transferred peacefully between political parties. However, election fraud, corruption, and human-rights abuses prevent Nigeria from being a liberal democracy. Like many countries, Nigeria has economic inequality, with some people living very well and many others living in poverty. Nigeria has a growing middle class, but 40 percent of Nigerians live below the poverty line. (World Bank, 2019.) Over 40 percent of all income goes to the top 10 percent of income earners. (World Inequality Database.)

Despite the country's problems, Nigerians have reasons to be optimistic about the future of their oil-rich country. Nevertheless, the state faces significant obstacles that have prevented Nigeria from fully realizing its democratic potential.

BY THE NUMBERS	NIGERIA
Land area	910,768 sq. km
Population	219,463,862 (July 2021 est.)
Urban population	52% (2020)
Life expectancy	Male 59.07 Female 62.78 (2021 est.)
Literacy rate	Male 71.3% Female 52.7% (2018)
HDI	0.539 (2020)
HDI ranking	74/189 (2020)
GDP	$448,120,000,000 (2020)
GDP ranking	26/190 (2020)
GDP per capita	$2,097 (2019)
Internet users	42% (2018)
Internet users ranking	8/229 (2018)
Gini index (coefficient)	35.1 (2019)
Freedom House rating	Partially free (2020)
Corruption Perceptions ranking	154/180 (2021)
Fragile States Index classification	Alert (2020)

Data from *CIA World Factbook*, World Bank, Freedom House, Transparency International, Fragile States Index.

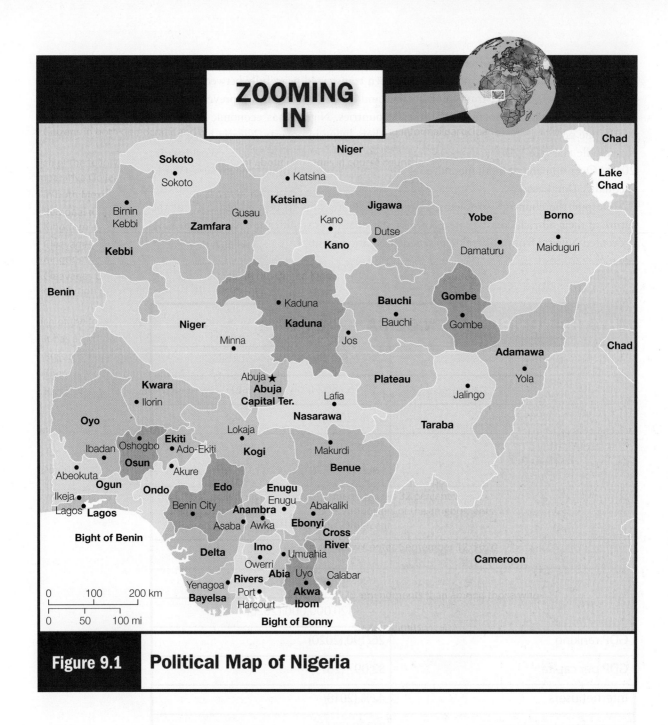

Figure 9.1 | **Political Map of Nigeria**

9.1 Sources of Power and Authority

Learning Targets

After reading this section, you should be able to do the following:

1. Explain how the British colonized Nigeria.

2. Explain why, during the postcolonial period, Nigeria alternated between military rule and democratic government.

3. Explain how Nigeria's democracy has survived and grown since 1999.

4. Describe Nigeria's federal system of government.

5. Describe the challenges facing the Nigerian state.

A Brief History of Nigeria

Before it became a British colony, the territory that is now Nigeria was home to numerous and varied societies. The northern half was mainly Muslim and had been ruled by Islamic emirs (religious rulers) based in twelve separate city-states since the 1300s. The southern half consisted of many societies, the two biggest of which were the Yoruba and Igbo. The Yoruba lived in the southwest in groups of small kingdoms, and they shared a common language and religion. The Igbo in the southeast also shared a common language and culture and were governed at the local level by councils of respected community members.

Slavery existed in precolonial Nigeria. Before the arrival of the British, enslaved persons usually worked closely with those who had enslaved them, commonly living in the same household. The transatlantic slave trade transformed the practice of slavery in the region that became Nigeria and had a major impact on the country's social structure, government, and economy. Enslaved people were forced onto crowded, unsanitary ships, and they faced disease and violence from their captors.

According to the Watson Institute for Internal and Public Affairs at Brown University, more than 2 million Africans died in the passage across the Atlantic. Nigerian ports played an important role in the trade of people who had been enslaved. Although Britain abolished the slave trade in 1807, it continued until 1834, with dire consequences for Nigerian societies. The Nigerian economy relied on slavery, but only a small group benefited, increasing the income gap. Slavery increased violence among groups, ripped families apart, and resulted in a major loss of population. (Choices Program.)

The British colonization of Nigeria began in the middle of the nineteenth century, as part of what came to be known as the Scramble for Africa. The boundaries of Nigeria were created by the British, without regard to religion or ethnic identity, pulling together groups that may have had little in common with one another.

The British eventually established indirect rule, under which colonial authorities, in theory, left precolonial kingdoms to be ruled by local leaders. In northern Nigeria, this meant ruling through the emirs, who in general accepted British oversight as long as they were left to run their internal affairs mostly as they pleased. In the south, the British used established leaders to carry out their policies, but where there were no formal leaders, the British appointed someone to lead. British colonialism gave local rulers more power than they had before, in exchange for their implementation of unpopular policies, such as forced labor and tax collection. Colonialism undermined the legitimacy of those who had been precolonial rulers and prevented newly appointed leaders from gaining legitimacy.

The colonial state required people with formal education to staff its bureaucracy. In the south, Christianity and Western education expanded rapidly, and southerners filled most of the positions in the colonial state. The northern emirs, on the other hand, convinced colonial authorities to keep out Christian education to preserve Islam, the basis of their legitimacy.

The educated elite became the leadership of the nationalist movement after World War II. Given the history of divisions in the country, it is no surprise that the nationalist movement was split along ethnic and religious lines, and groups were brought together by feelings of anticolonialism rather than genuine belonging.

The British ultimately negotiated a new government for an independent country. The new Nigerian state would be federal, with three regions corresponding to the three major ethnic groups—the Hausa-Fulani, Yoruba, and Igbo—and political parties formed mainly along regional and ethnic lines. Nigeria was a state, but many questioned whether Nigerians had the bonds to call themselves a nation.

The new government was fragile. The British began introducing the institutions of British-style democracy just a few years before full independence on October 1, 1960. Nigeria's First Republic had very weak institutions and grew increasingly chaotic. The population was larger in the north than it was in the south, which gave the northern region control of the government at independence. After government officials manipulated two elections, citizens in the western region, who thought the northern-dominated government had stolen control of the country, turned violent. By late 1965, the national government had lost effective control of the western region, and general lawlessness was spreading throughout the country.

In response to fraudulent elections and anti-Igbo violence, the army overthrew the elected government in January 1966 in the first of six military coups. Most of the leaders of the coup were ethnic Igbo from the eastern region, including General Johnson T. U. Aguiyi-Ironsi, who became Nigeria's military ruler. The leaders of the coup killed several important northern and western political and military figures but no eastern ones. Aguiyi-Ironsi abolished all parties and ethnic associations. He ended Nigeria's fractured federalism, creating a unitary state. Northerners saw the coup and Ironsi's elimination of federalism as an attempt by the eastern, Igbo military elite to centralize power.

Nigerians celebrate independence from the British and the swearing in of Sir Abubakar Tafawa Balewa, who became the prime minister of Nigeria's First Republic.

Express Newspapers/Archive Photos/Getty Images

Six months later, in July 1966, the northerners responded with a countercoup that brought army chief of staff Yakubu Gowon to power. Gowon was backed by northern top military leaders. Gowon immediately re-created a federal system, with twelve states replacing the former three regions. Eastern military leaders rebelled, proclaiming themselves the leaders of the independent Republic of Biafra in May 1967. Large-scale oil production had just begun, and the oil wells were in the area claimed as Biafra. A three-year civil war ensued that cost the lives of a million people. Gowon received much credit for winning the war and helping reconcile the nation afterward.

Like all of Nigeria's military leaders, Gowon promised a return to democracy. By the mid-1970s, however, he and the military governors of the states were seen as increasingly corrupt, stealing from Nigeria's rapidly growing oil revenues and delaying the promised return to democracy. Other northern military leaders overthrew him in 1975 and returned the country to democracy in 1979.

That democracy would last until 1983. The Second Republic government that was elected in 1979 and reelected in 1983 was again dominated by the northern region. By 1983, it was both corrupt and ineffective. Nigeria's economy was declining as the level of corruption seemed to be skyrocketing and world oil prices were plummeting. The 1983 election in which incumbent president Shehu Shagari was reelected was widely viewed as fraudulent, resulting in another military coup.

The military ruled Nigeria continuously from 1983 to 1999 (except for the four-month interim government in 1993) under three different leaders. Each one ruled through repression and used Nigeria's vast oil wealth to buy the support of other military leaders and many prominent civilians. Throughout this era, the institutions of government declined as corruption rose, but they never collapsed. Some freedom of political expression was tolerated.

The last of Nigeria's six military coups took place in November 1993. The country had been in turmoil since June, when its military leader annulled the results of what most observers saw as a free and fair election. Northerners had led almost all of Nigeria's regimes, both civilian and military. A westerner had won the election. The incumbent military leader refused to accept the results. He appointed a handpicked interim government headed by a civilian but with one of the top military leaders, General Sani Abacha, in the position of secretary of defense. Large protests involving millions of Nigerians took place over the next months, as the country demanded that the fairest elections in its history be respected. By November, Abacha overthrew the interim government in a bloodless coup, promising to restore democracy.

Abacha quickly proved himself much more ruthless than earlier leaders. During his first two years in office, he eliminated much of the judiciary's autonomy, assassinated or imprisoned many political opponents (including the winner of the 1993 election), and banned many civil-society organizations. These abuses of civil liberties culminated in the conviction by military tribunal and hanging of the famed poet and leader of the Ogoni ethnic and environmental movement, Ken Saro-Wiwa. Saro-Wiwa's death led to nearly universal international condemnation of the regime.

Corruption was the other hallmark of Abacha's personalist regime. He and his closest associates looted the Nigerian treasury of an estimated $3 billion during his six years in power, some of which the subsequent democratic government was able to recover from British and Swiss banks. As repression increased, both civilian and military political leaders faced the choice of working with the government and becoming wealthy, fleeing the country (which thousands did), or becoming victims of the repression.

> **AP® TIP**
>
> You do not have to memorize the names of the people who have led Nigeria or know the details about each transition of power. The important point is that beginning in the postcolonial era in the 1960s until 1999, Nigeria had a series of military coups that alternated with democratic governments.

Abacha's rule was the final and most extreme stage of this long saga of alternation in government between democracy and military dictatorship. By the time of his sudden death in 1998, many military leaders were glad to see the end of the regime. The military leadership that took power immediately promised and carried out democratic elections, ushering in the Fourth Republic—the democratic regime still in power today.

Democratization

Nigeria's transition toward democracy demonstrates that democratization is a process that evolves over time, and it often takes decades for a state to consolidate as a liberal democracy. In 1999, Nigeria held its first free and fair election in twenty years, electing Olusegun Obasanjo, a former general, as president.

Nigeria has held five elections since, and in 2015, executive power was transferred peacefully between political parties. This means that the Nigerian presidency has been controlled by more than one political party.

Elections are overseen by the Independent National Electoral Commission (INEC). The INEC supervises elections through independent observers, registers and monitors political parties and candidates, and audits campaign finances. While many observers have questioned the integrity of some of the elections, Nigeria's democracy has survived, and there is little threat of further military intervention. Democracy has become the basis of the government's legitimacy. Election fraud still occurs (although it has lessened), and some civil rights and liberties are restricted, making Nigeria an illiberal democracy.

Along with the electoral commission, civilian control of the military has strengthened democracy. Military leaders backed Obasanjo for president in 1999 because they assumed they could control him after he took office. After becoming president, however, he quickly removed the most politically active generals and replaced them with less politically active officers.

Several years later, when president Umaru Yar'Adua's prolonged illness left him incapacitated, there were rumors that the military would take over the government, but the armed forces remained in their barracks. When the National Assembly determined that Yar'Adua was incapacitated, his vice president, Goodluck Jonathan, assumed office, and democratic government continued. President Muhammadu Buhari, who was the military head of state from 1983 to 1985, defeated Jonathan in the 2015 presidential race, where power transferred peacefully between political parties. Buhari was reelected in 2019.

The Nigerian government has faced growing religious tension in the northern states, many of which have adopted **sharia law**—a legal system based on principles derived from Islam. A violent Islamist group, Boko Haram, initiated an armed insurgency that has killed thousands, mostly in the northwestern part of the country, since 2010. Buhari's government began a military campaign that severely weakened the group, but it continues to conduct terror attacks and mass kidnappings targeting women and girls. Furthermore, in the oil-rich areas of the former Biafra, ethnic militias have demanded greater economic and social benefits for the region.

Nigeria continues to face challenges, but the Fourth Republic has existed since 1999, giving the country the time and experience to deepen the roots of democracy.

Federalism

Today, Nigeria has a federal system of government that divides political authority between the central government and the states. Nigeria has thirty-six states, and a separate federal territory for the capital of Abuja, that have the constitutional power to make local laws.

Sharia law
A legal system based on principles derived from Islam.

Unlike many federal systems, such as the United States, Nigeria's states are drawn roughly along ethnic lines. The goal of this system is to reduce conflict by allowing ethnic and religious groups some measure of autonomy over issues such as social and educational services. However, as Nigeria's postcolonial politics has shown, ethnically based federalism can also lead to disunity and conflicting laws.

Nigeria is a rentier state, which makes it difficult to predict state revenue. States rely on the national government for funding, and they have few resources to carry out policies independently. The national government controls the electrical grid. This means that local governments have little control over crucial infrastructure. (Campbell.) States compete against each other for access to resources, and this can intensify ethnic and religious conflicts.

Federalism in Nigeria is reflected in its system for staffing government jobs. Under the Federal Character Principle, high-level government jobs and the national bureaucracy must be filled with people who reflect the geographic, linguistic, ethnic, and religious diversity of the country. The purpose of the Federal Character Principle is to prevent a few major ethnic groups from gaining control of the national government and to make sure that every state has a fair share of power in the national government. (Babalola.)

As a result of Nigeria's federal system, states can create their own legal systems. The 1999 constitution allows states to set their own legal codes within national law, and Nigeria has long allowed dual civil-law codes based on religion. Immediately after the transition to democracy, twelve northern states adopted sharia law for both civil and criminal law. The establishment of sharia law in the north led to confrontations with Christian minorities in several of these states and opposition from the south in general. Long-standing northern and Muslim control of national politics has left southerners and Christians fearful of Islamic movements.

Because of federalism, each state's version of sharia is slightly different. Some states apply some Muslim laws to non-Muslims, and other states do not, while some include the harshest penalties, such as stoning, and others do not. So far, national courts have not revoked states' rights to implement sharia law, and there is no uniform legal code that state courts must follow.

Legitimacy and Challenges to the State

Although democracy in Nigeria is a basis for legitimacy, rampant corruption undermines the people's trust in government and poses a significant challenge to the state. Transparency International's 1999 Corruption Perception Index ranked Nigeria as the second most corrupt country in the world (after Cameroon). In 2020, in a ranking from least to most corrupt, Nigeria was 149th of 168 countries studied, showing modest but noticeable improvement since 1999. This is due in part to an anticorruption drive Obasanjo launched that received great praise in the early years of the Fourth Republic.

In 2003, the government created the Economic and Financial Crimes Commission (EFCC) to investigate financial crimes, prosecute those accused of wrongdoing, and recover government funds diverted for personal benefit. Government reports found that approximately $1.5 billion of oil revenue failed to reach the treasury in 2012–2013, and as much as $16 billion has been missing since. According to an article in *The Guardian*, in the first ten months of 2020, the EFCC secured 646 convictions and recovered nearly $29 million in monetary assets. (The Guardian, 2020.)

President Buhari has made some strides in prosecuting corruption. Critics contend that he is only targeting opponents. However, Buhari does not seem to be amassing personal wealth. (Mbaku, 2019.) As part of Buhari's anticorruption efforts, Ibrahim Magu, chairman of the EFCC, was removed from office in 2020 following an investigation into corruption, including the diversion of government funds. (Adeshoken.)

Continued corruption has weakened state institutions, harmed the ability of the INEC to conduct proper elections, and prevented people in the oil-producing states from benefiting from the resources located in their regions. The future of Nigeria's democracy may rest on its ability to tackle the pervasive issue of corruption, and the government is taking strides to reduce the problem in an effort to increase citizens' trust and confidence.

Section 9.1 Review

Each section's main ideas are reflected in the Learning Targets. By reviewing after each section, you should be able to

Remember the key points,

Know terms that are central to the topic, and

Think critically about what you have learned.

Remember

- Nigeria's contemporary borders were created by the British as part of the "Scramble for Africa," and until 1960, Nigeria was a British colony.
- From 1965 until 1999, Nigeria alternated between military rule, which weakened government institutions, and democratic government.
- Nigeria's democracy has survived and grown since the Fourth Republic was established in 1999, partly due to the INEC and EFCC.
- Nigeria has a federal system of government, and several northern states have adopted sharia law.
- Democracy is a basis for Nigeria's legitimacy, but state legitimacy is undermined by rampant corruption.

Know

- *Sharia law:* a legal system based on principles derived from Islam. (p. 272)

Think

- How does the legacy of colonialism contribute to corruption in Nigeria?
- What steps could Nigeria take to become a consolidated, liberal democracy?

....

Free-Response Question: Quantitative Analysis

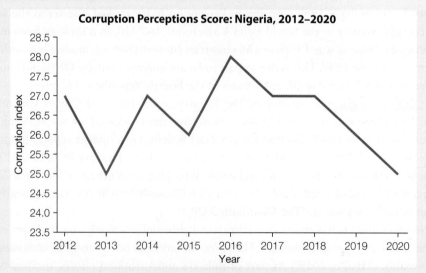

Corruption Perceptions Score: Nigeria, 2012–2020

Note: A score of 100 indicates the absence of corruption, and a score of 0 indicates a high level of corruption.
Data from Transparency International

Answer A, B, C, D, and E.

A. Using the data in the graph, identify the year in which Nigeria has the lowest level of perceived corruption.

B. Using the data in the graph, describe a trend in the level of perceived corruption in Nigeria from 2012 to 2020.

C. Define corruption.

D. Draw a conclusion about an action taken by the Nigerian government to limit corruption.

E. Explain a limitation of the graph in measuring the level of corruption in Nigeria.

9.2 Institutions of Government

Learning Targets

After reading this section, you should be able to do the following:

1. Describe the formal powers of the Nigerian president.

2. Describe the formal powers of both houses of the Nigerian National Assembly.

3. Describe the powers of the Supreme Court in Nigeria and explain why the judiciary lacks some autonomy and independence.

Nigeria has a presidential system of government, with a single chief executive, a bicameral legislature, and a separate judicial branch.

The Executive

Nigeria's president is directly elected and serves as both head of government and head of state. The president runs the executive branch and also symbolizes the nation. The president serves for a four-year term, with a limit of two terms. The president has executive powers typical of a presidential system, including the power to submit a budget, propose a program of legislation, and sign bills into law. He appoints cabinet heads, with Senate approval, and oversees the federal bureaucracy. He serves as commander-in-chief of the military. In addition, he is the chief diplomat and has the power to negotiate treaties, subject to approval by the National Assembly. Based on the recommendation of a special judicial council, the president appoints justices to the Supreme Court, subject to confirmation in the Senate. (Library of Congress.)

Nigeria has a patronage-based system with oil revenue available to reward supporters, so the presidency is very powerful and has the potential to be lucrative. Nevertheless, the two-term limit serves as a check on executive power.

The limits of presidential power have been tested in Nigeria. The first test came when President Obasanjo launched a campaign to revoke the two-term limit for the presidency. Amending the constitution to allow Obasanjo a third term required Senate approval. Reportedly, he and his supporters tried to bribe senators, with inducements totaling more than $500 million, to vote in favor of the amendment. (Campbell, 2018.) The population

As leader of Africa's most populous nation, President Muhammadu Buhari is also influential on the world stage. Here, President Buhari attends the third day of the twenty-sixth U.N. Climate Change Conference held in November 2021, in Glasgow, Scotland.

Adrian Dennis/ Pool/Getty Images

overwhelmingly opposed the move, and in May 2006, the Senate voted down the extension of term limits, despite the pressure and bribes. Obasanjo agreed to accept the result of the vote in the Senate. Democratization is furthered when key players accept the outcome of the political process.

The second major institutional challenge began in 2009, when President Yar'Adua became gravely ill and left the country for treatment in Saudi Arabia. An incapacitated president is supposed to turn over his powers to his vice president, but Yar'Adua refused. His wife and closest aides did not let any Nigerians see him and released no information about his health. For two months, the country was without an acting president.

Amid growing domestic and international pressure to clarify the situation, Yar'Adua gave a radio interview in which he said in a weak voice that he hoped to return to work soon. The National Assembly took that as a public statement that he was incapacitated and appointed Vice President Goodluck Jonathan as acting president. Once again, the sitting president and his closest aides were rebuffed in an attempt to retain power, because the legislature served to check presidential power.

The Legislature

National Assembly
Nigeria's bicameral legislature.

House of Representatives
The lower house of the National Assembly, which represents the people.

Senate
The upper house of the National Assembly, which represents the states.

As is typical in federal systems, Nigeria's legislature—the **National Assembly**—is bicameral. The **House of Representatives** is the lower house, and it represents the people. The **Senate** is the upper house, and it represents the states.

The House of Representatives consists of 360 members, and it is led by a Speaker of the House. The Senate has 109 members, three from each state, and one from the Federal Capital Territory. Both chambers have the power to debate and pass national legislation, and bills must pass in both chambers to be sent to the president's desk for signature. A committee system, similar to the one you studied if you took AP® U.S. Government and Politics, refines legislation before it is sent to the full chamber. The National Assembly also has the power to approve the federal budget.

Both chambers have the authority to conduct oversight hearings into the actions of other officials, including government agencies and private businesses. The Senate has additional powers, including the authority to confirm appointments to the cabinet and justices of Nigeria's Supreme Court.

The National Assembly has the authority to check executive power. It has the power to override a presidential veto with a two-thirds vote of both houses. The National Assembly has the power to conduct investigations and oversight hearings into the bureaucracy and to impeach and remove cabinet members and the president for gross misconduct by a two-thirds vote of both houses. ("How to Impeach.")

On paper, the National Assembly is a powerful policymaking body with the power to check other institutions of government. However, the National Assembly in Nigeria is fragmented, and some people believe it is the weakest link in Nigeria's democratic system. It has been criticized for not doing enough to improve citizens' lives and for exercising insufficient oversight into the bureaucracy to ensure that the bureaucracy is implementing legislation once it has been enacted.

Relations between the executive and legislature are poor, making it difficult to coordinate policy. Furthermore, relations between individual members of the legislature are frequently contentious, making it difficult to get laws passed. High-profile cases involving corruption among legislators have damaged the body's public image. In addition, some members of the legislature have flaunted a wealthy lifestyle, angering their constituents.

In general, legislators have been accused of failing to read the public mood and ignoring the demands of the people they serve. (Saliu and Bakare, 2020.) The National Assembly's full democratic potential has yet to be realized. Figure 9.2 on page 278 shows the structure of the federal government of Nigeria.

The Judiciary

Because Nigeria has a federal system, there are separate court systems at the state and national levels. The federal judiciary includes trial courts, appeals courts, and the Supreme Court, which serves as the final court of appeal. Judges are required to have formal legal training and to have been in the profession for at least ten years.

The Supreme Court in Nigeria is made up of the chief justice and a group of associate justices, with the total number not exceeding twenty-one. As of March 2021, eighteen justices sat on the Nigerian Supreme Court. Similar to the Supreme Court in the United States, it has original jurisdiction in cases between states. On paper, the Supreme Court has the power of judicial review. (Supreme Court of Nigeria Web site.)

When Nigeria was under military rule, the judiciary deferred to the executive. The constitution for the Fourth Republic created a National Judicial Council that has helped insulate the judiciary from pressures from elected officials. The president nominates justices based on the recommendation of the council, and the Senate confirms the nominees.

The Supreme Court has made several important rulings that demonstrated its autonomy. In disputes between the national and state governments about control over oil revenues, the court ruled in some key cases in favor of the oil-producing states and in others in favor of the federal government, indicating a certain degree of autonomy from political pressure from either side. After the faulty 2007 election, the courts ruled several gubernatorial victories invalid and required new elections. In 2017, the judiciary set up a series of special courts designed to hear complaints of corruption within its own ranks, one of the greatest impediments to its independence and legitimacy.

FIGURE 9.2

The Structure of the Federal Government of Nigeria
Division of Power and Responsibilities

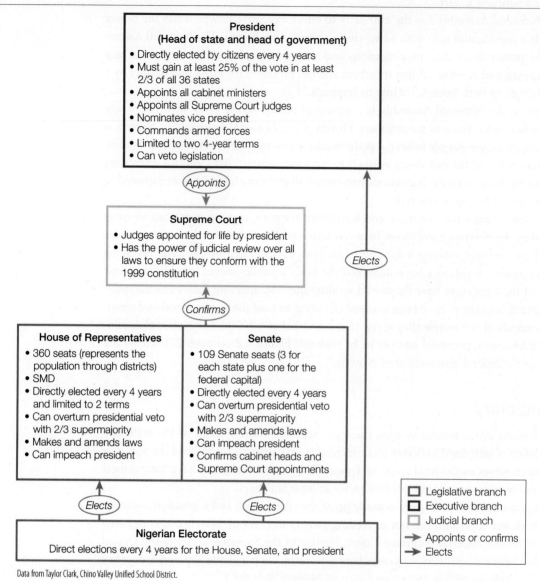

President
(Head of state and head of government)
- Directly elected by citizens every 4 years
- Must gain at least 25% of the vote in at least 2/3 of all 36 states
- Appoints all cabinet ministers
- Appoints all Supreme Court judges
- Nominates vice president
- Commands armed forces
- Limited to two 4-year terms
- Can veto legislation

Appoints

Supreme Court
- Judges appointed for life by president
- Has the power of judicial review over all laws to ensure they conform with the 1999 constitution

Elects

Confirms

House of Representatives
- 360 seats (represents the population through districts)
- SMD
- Directly elected every 4 years and limited to 2 terms
- Can overturn presidential veto with 2/3 supermajority
- Makes and amends laws
- Can impeach president

Senate
- 109 Senate seats (3 for each state plus one for the federal capital)
- Directly elected every 4 years
- Can overturn presidential veto with 2/3 supermajority
- Makes and amends laws
- Can impeach president
- Confirms cabinet heads and Supreme Court appointments

Elects   *Elects*

Nigerian Electorate
Direct elections every 4 years for the House, Senate, and president

☐ Legislative branch
☐ Executive branch
☐ Judicial branch
→ Appoints or confirms
→ Elects

Data from Taylor Clark, Chino Valley Unified School District.

Three weeks before the 2019 presidential election, however, Buhari suspended Chief Justice Walter Onnoghen, a key player in electoral appeals and disputes. This raised international concern over the fairness of the election and about the executive's respect for the independence of the judiciary. (BBC.) In April 2019, Onnoghen was convicted of failing to disclose cash in foreign bank accounts and banned from holding public office for ten years, raising questions about whether he was selected for prosecution based on political motivations. (Al Jazeera.)

Like the legislature, the Nigerian judiciary has the potential to further democratization. It remains to be seen whether efforts to professionalize the judiciary, such as the Judicial Council, will be effective in insulating it from executive influence.

Remember

- The Nigerian president is directly elected and has the power to submit a budget, propose a program of legislation, act as chief diplomat, and serve as commander-in-chief of the military.
- The National Assembly is bicameral and consists of a House of Representatives and a Senate.
- The National Assembly has the power to debate and pass laws, approve the budget, pass treaties into law, hold oversight hearings, and impeach and remove the president.
- The Senate has the power to confirm cabinet heads and Supreme Court nominees.
- Members of the Supreme Court are appointed by the president, based on the recommendation of a Judicial Council and confirmed by the Senate.
- The Nigerian Supreme Court has the power of judicial review, but it lacks full autonomy and independence.

Know

- *National Assembly:* Nigeria's bicameral legislature. (p. 276)
- *House of Representatives:* the lower house of the National Assembly, which represents the people. (p. 276)
- *Senate:* the upper house of the National Assembly, which represents the states. (p. 276)

Think

- What steps could Nigeria take to strengthen the power of the legislature and judiciary relative to the executive?

....

Free-Response Question: Comparative Analysis

Compare legislative constraints on executive power in two different AP® Comparative Government and Politics course countries.

A. Describe legislative constraints on executive power.

B. Explain how legislative constraints on executive power differ in two different AP® Comparative Government and Politics course countries.

C. Explain why each of the two AP® Comparative Government and Politics course countries described in part B would allow or prevent the legislature from constraining executive power.

9.3 Electoral System, Political Parties, and Civil Society

Learning Targets

After reading this section, you should be able to do the following:

1. Describe the system for electing the president in Nigeria.

2. Describe the system for electing the Nigerian House of Representatives and Senate.

3. Explain why Nigeria has developed a two-party system.

4. Explain why civil society in Nigeria is growing but still faces obstacles.

AP® TIP

Country-specific rules—like Nigeria's requirement that the president earn at least 25 percent of the vote in two-thirds of the states and Mexico's requirement that women make up 50 percent of candidates run by parties for single-member district seats and on party lists for proportional representation—are likely to appear on the AP® Exam.

As of the 2019 election, Nigeria has held six presidential elections since the Fourth Republic was founded in 1999. Competitive political parties have emerged, and civil society is growing.

Elections

Nigerians directly elect the president and both houses of the National Assembly. Presidential elections are held every four years, and executives are limited to two terms in office.

Nigeria follows a unique rule in selecting the president. The winning candidate must obtain a plurality of the votes and at least 25 percent of the vote in two-thirds of the states to assume the presidency. The purpose of this rule is to ensure that a candidate who appeals to only one region cannot win office. The rule encourages candidates to campaign throughout the country to generate support from diverse groups of voters. If no candidate wins in the first round with at least 25 percent of the votes in two-thirds of the states, then a second-round runoff election is held between the top two vote-getters.

Elections for the House of Representatives are held every four years. The House consists of 360 representatives from electoral districts that are roughly equal in population. An SMD system is used to fill seats in the House. Members of the Senate also serve four-year terms. Each state is divided into three districts, and one senator is elected from each district, for a total of three senators per state. One senator is elected from the Federal Capital Territory of Abuja. (Library of Congress.)

Election fraud has been a problem since the founding of Nigeria's Fourth Republic, but the situation may be improving. In the earlier years of the Fourth Republic, elections were deemed free and fair in only about one-third of Nigeria's states. (Kew, 2004.) In many others, "the elections were marred by extraordinary displays of rigging and the intimidation of voters." (Rawlence and Albin-Lackey, 2007, 497.) In quite a few states, no elections took place at all: Officials simply fabricated results in favor of the ruling party, and observers saw officials openly stuffing ballot boxes in a number of cases.

AP® TIP

Both Mexico and Nigeria have created independent electoral commissions in an effort to reduce fraud at the polls and further democratization. Both countries have developed processes to make it more difficult to engage in voter fraud. Mexico requires identification to vote, and Nigeria authenticates voters' identities through fingerprints. Efforts by Mexico and Nigeria to make voting fairer would make a good comparison on the AP® Exam.

The INEC has become more effective in overseeing elections. President Jonathan appointed a well-known democracy advocate and scholar to head the electoral commission, substantially improving the credibility of the 2011 and 2015 elections. In 2015, fraud still occurred but was reduced enough to allow an opposition party to win the presidency for the first time. (Lewis and Kew, 2015.)

In 2019, the sixth election since the democratic transition, was plagued with problems. These problems included Buhari's delay and eventual veto of legislation to improve electoral transparency, his suspension of the chief justice weeks before the election, threats from a Boko Haram offshoot in the north, droughts elsewhere, and a weeklong delay in voting.

Election observers concluded, however, that these irregularities were not significant enough to undermine the vote. The INEC declared Buhari the winner with 56 percent of the vote compared to the 41 percent of the vote earned by Atiku Abubakar, his opponent. The delay and suspension of the chief justice created suspicions of unfairness. Abubakar called the election a sham, but there was no popular outcry. (Mbaku, 2019.) Voters were

authenticated through fingerprinting at the polls, reducing the opportunity to engage in election fraud.

Political Parties

On April 1, 2015, Nigeria's incumbent president, Goodluck Jonathan of the long-ruling People's Democratic Party (PDP), did something no Nigerian president had ever done before: He publicly congratulated his opponent, Muhammadu Buhari of the All Progressives Congress (APC) for winning the election and conceded defeat. This occurrence, a regular event in well-established democracies, was a milestone for Nigeria, because it represented the first peaceful transfer of power in the executive from one political party to another.

Given Nigeria's diversity, it is not surprising that there were more than ninety parties registered with the INEC in the 2019 election. (Freedom House.) However, as you learned in Chapter 8, SMD systems for electing the legislature tend to result in two catch-all parties, and that is what happened in Nigeria. Beginning with the Fourth Republic's first election in 1999, the PDP dominated the executive branch. In regionally, ethnically, and religiously divided Nigeria, the PDP became dominant partly by agreeing that political offices would alternate among regions. There was a tradition (but not a requirement) that major political parties nominate someone from the north to run in a presidential election, and then in the next election (if they are not running an incumbent) parties nominate a candidate from the south.

President Obasanjo, who won the elections in 1999 and 2003, is from the south. President Yar'Adua, who was elected in 2003 and 2007, was from the north. Yar'Adua became gravely ill and died in March 2010. He was succeeded by his vice president, Goodluck Jonathan, who was from the southeast. This violated the informal principle of north–south alternation. For Jonathan's critics, Nigeria prematurely alternated to a southern president.

The argument question on the AP® Exam requires you to build an analytical thesis. Simply restating the question or taking a position is not enough to earn the thesis point on the AP® Exam. Your thesis must also establish a line of reasoning and refer to at least one of the concepts listed in the question. It is very important to practice this skill, because if you do not earn the thesis point, your essay cannot earn more than two points (out of five) on this portion of the exam. Without a thesis, you can at most earn two points for evidence, but nothing else.

Here is a sample prompt:

Develop an argument as to whether democratic or authoritarian governments are better at maintaining stability in a country.

Use one or more of the following course concepts in your response:

- Legitimacy
- Power
- Authority

To earn the thesis point, you must do three things: (1) take a position, (2) use the course concept, and (3) establish a line of reasoning.

Here is an example of what **not** to do:

"Both democratic and authoritarian states maintain stability within a country."

The prompt requires you to pick a type of system and explain why it is better at maintaining stability. This thesis statement does not take a position.

Take a look at this thesis statement:

"Authoritarian governments are better at maintaining stability in a country."

This thesis statement would not earn a point, because it is not analytical. The statement takes a position, but it is not supported with a line of reasoning, and it does not refer to a course concept.

Here is another thesis statement.

"Democratic regimes are better at maintaining stability and legitimacy."

Again, this thesis statement would not earn a point. Although it refers to the course concept of legitimacy, it does not establish a line of reasoning.

Here is a much better thesis statement:

"Authoritarian regimes are better than democratic governments at maintaining stability because they have more power to use force against citizen unrest, which prevents uprisings."

This thesis uses the concept of power in context and supports the thesis with the line of reasoning that authoritarian states can prevent uprisings because they can use force against citizens.

Here is another sample prompt:

Develop an argument as to whether single-member district or mixed systems provide citizens with more effective representation in the legislature.

1. Write a factual thesis that responds to the prompt, without taking a position or establishing a line of reasoning.
2. Write a thesis that responds to the prompt and takes a position, without a line of reasoning.
3. Write an analytical thesis that responds to the prompt and includes a line of reasoning and includes the concept of political efficacy.

Many in the north believed that Yar'Adua should have been succeeded by another president from the north and given the chance to complete two terms in office.

Initially, northern party leaders resisted Jonathan's desire to run for a full presidential term in 2011. After extensive behind-the-scenes campaigning, which allegedly included funneling oil money to key governors to gain their support, the ruling party allowed Jonathan to stand for office, effectively ending the policy of alternating the presidency between north and south. Muhammadu Buhari, the major opposition candidate and a northerner, gained support because of this, but the PDP held together and won the 2011 election, with a reduced majority in the legislature.

In 2013, however, the PDP split when a former vice president and seven state governors stormed out of the party convention because their candidates were not given key party positions. Most who left were from the north and opposed President Jonathan's planned reelection bid in 2015. They believed he was moving to gain greater control of the party to ensure another term as president. Ultimately, the PDP defectors built an opposition coalition with several smaller parties that nominated Buhari as its presidential candidate, setting up the 2015 election as the most competitive in the country's history.

The newly united opposition party, the All Progressives Congress (APC), took advantage of President Jonathan's increasing unpopularity, largely a result of his inability or unwillingness (as some northerners alleged) to defeat Boko Haram in the north. They also opposed the government's continuing massive corruption and the declining economy suffering from the dramatic drop in world oil prices. The APC campaigned on security, improving the economy, reducing corruption, and improving the quality of elections. Buhari, a former military general, won 54 percent of the popular vote nationwide, sweeping all northern and most southwestern states, leaving Jonathan with only his native southeast and a few other states.

The APC also won majorities in both houses of the National Assembly. International and domestic observers deemed the election credible. While some PDP leaders wanted to resist handing over power, international governments and civil society demanded the results be respected, and Jonathan made his historic concession. (Lewis and Kew, 2015.)

In 2019, Buhari won the presidency again with 55.6 percent of the vote. In the House of Representatives, the APC won 212 seats (59 percent), the PDP won 127 seats (35 percent), and eight smaller parties won 21 seats (6 percent). In the Senate, the APC won 64 seats (48 percent), and the PDP won 44 seats (42 percent). (INEC.)

A two-party system has established itself in Nigeria, and this may bode well for democracy. Both parties must consider the interests of diverse groups of voters and appeal to people in both the north and the south. As a result, political parties have the potential to serve as a unifying factor in the Nigerian political system.

Interest Groups and Social Movements

Civil society existed in Nigeria since before independence. However, decades of military rule delayed the development of Nigerian civil society. Civil-rights violations against critics of the government prevented groups from advocating for change. Because government institutions were weak and did not respond to citizens' demands, it was difficult for interest groups and social movements to impact government policy. As Nigeria has democratized, civil society has broadened and become more robust. (Freedom House.)

There are five broad categories of interest groups operating in Nigeria: (1) regional, ethnic, and religious; (2) professional and labor groups; (3) grassroots organizations; (4) issue-based groups; and (5) NGOs. (Ikelegbe, 2013.)

One example of a regional interest group is the Arewa Consultative Forum, a powerful political group that advocates for the interests of northern Nigeria. Professional and labor groups include the Nigerian Medical Association, the Nigerian Bar Association, the Nigeria Labour Congress, and the Nigeria Union of Journalists. Grassroots organizations, such as the Grassroots Health Organization of Nigeria, focus on issues affecting their communities, such as lack of basic health care and alleviating poverty. Issue-based organizations include groups advocating for students, the environment, and human rights. There are more than 30,000 NGOs in Nigeria, many of which focus on providing social and welfare services to Nigeria's poorest citizens. (Abah and Tanko.)

Despite the number of interest groups in Nigeria, there are obstacles to strengthening civil society. Weak government institutions make it difficult for interest groups to advocate for policies and get them enacted. In addition, distrust between groups weakens social

Members of the Facebook group Female IN (or FIN), which comes from the group's earliest name, Female in Nigeria, meet up in person. The group provides an online forum for women and girls in Nigeria to discuss issues and to provide support. Started in 2015, by 2021 Female IN had more than 1.7 million members.

Courtesy Lola Omolola

capital. Because the government relies on oil as a source of revenue, some officials have little incentive to work with civil-society groups for the betterment of society. (Songonuga.) As a result of these factors, civil society in Nigeria has not reached its full potential in creating a pluralistic and democratic system.

In addition to organized interest groups, social movements in Nigeria seek to influence government policies. Two of the most recognized are the Movement for the Survival of the Ogoni People (MOSOP) and the Movement for the Emancipation of the Niger Delta (MEND). The Niger Delta is an oil-rich region in southeast Nigeria where international oil companies have enormous facilities that drill for oil and pipelines that transport oil to tankers.

MOSOP is an ethnic organization based in the Niger River Delta that is made up of several member groups and represents the Ogoni people in advocating for improved social, economic, and environmental conditions. It is a cultural and political organization that seeks self-determination and protection for traditional practices of the Ogoni people. MOSOP promotes nonviolence and supports democratic government.

The Ogoni, the Ijaw, and other ethnic groups living in the region complained that Shell, Mobil (which is now known as ExxonMobil), Chevron, and other foreign oil companies were using their political influence with the national government to profit at the expense of local communities, destroying the environment. Amnesty International describes the Niger River Delta region as one of the most polluted places on Earth.

In the 1990s, people living in the Niger Delta region began protesting and engaging in minor sabotage. Following the hanging of MOSOP founder and environmental activist Ken Saro-Wiwa by the Nigerian government in 1995, groups in the Niger River Delta became more radical, kidnapping oil workers and holding them for ransom. Militant groups also engaged in "bunkering," which is illegally tapping into pipelines and selling oil locally or to tankers offshore.

In 2006, MEND emerged under the leadership of Henry Okah, who was arrested a year later for buying illegal weapons in Angola. MEND is mainly a regional (rather than ethnic) movement, and it consists of several loosely coordinated groups, without a clear leader. MEND's tactics are lucrative, and it has attracted wealthy financial backers. MEND is equipped with speedboats, body armor, assault rifles, machine guns, and rocket-propelled grenade launchers. (Hallmark.) The group consists mostly of young Ijaw men, and some of its leaders have college educations. The organizational structure is fluid, and the movement works in secrecy, with the help of sympathetic local communities. (Hanson.)

MEND's goal is to make it impossible for the government to produce and export oil by threatening international companies, and their workers, operating in the Niger River Delta. One of its major tactics is taking oil workers hostage and releasing them unharmed once ransom is paid. Kidnappings have the added benefit of generating publicity. In addition, the International Crisis Group reports that oil companies pay militants money in exchange for security. (Hanson.) Some estimates place the costs of MEND's attacks at billions of dollars in lost oil income.

The Nigerian military has attempted to capture the rebels, but the terrain is difficult to navigate. In 2009, the government announced an amnesty program, paid militants millions of dollars, and released Okah from jail. Okah was tried for terrorism in South Africa and found guilty in 2013.

In February 2016, a new group, the Niger Delta Avengers (NDA), was formed. Its targets have included a pipeline owned by Shell Oil, a platform owned by Chevron, and ExxonMobil's terminal, the largest terminal for oil in Nigeria. The attacks had an immense effect on Nigeria's oil production, which dropped from 2.2 million barrels per day to 1.4 million in 2016, its lowest level in twenty years. (Hallmark.)

The standoff between international oil companies, the Nigerian government, and militant groups in the Niger River Delta continues. Oil companies are not going to leave Nigeria's lucrative market. The military cannot protect workers and the assets owned by foreign companies. It is unlikely that a settlement will be reached between militants and the government without a commitment to clean up the environment and provide compensation for local communities impacted by the oil industry. (Hallmark.) The conflict over the Niger River Delta demonstrates both the success of this social movement in calling attention to an issue and the failure to reach a long-term solution to the conflict.

Section 9.3 Review

Remember

- The president in Nigeria is directly elected through a plurality of the vote and must receive 25 percent of the votes in two-thirds of the states, and if no candidate meets this requirement, then a second-round election is held between the top two vote-getters.

- The House of Representatives is elected using an SMD system, and three senators are elected from each state, with one senator representing the Federal Capital Territory.

- Although many parties are registered with the INEC, Nigeria has two major parties—the People's Democratic Party (PDP) and the All Progressives Congress (APC).

- Civil society is growing in Nigeria, but it is hindered by a lack of trust and confidence in government and among citizens.

Think

- What steps could the Nigerian government take to strengthen civil society?

Free-Response Question: Quantitative Analysis

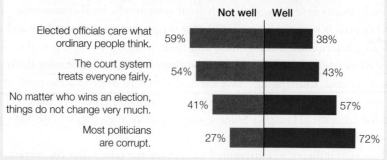

Nigerians Assess Their Political System, 2018
How well does this statement describe Nigeria?

	Not well	Well
Elected officials care what ordinary people think.	59%	38%
The court system treats everyone fairly.	54%	43%
No matter who wins an election, things do not change very much.	41%	57%
Most politicians are corrupt.	27%	72%

Data from Pew Research Center based on a survey of Nigerian adults conducted June 25–July 30, 2018.

Answer A, B, C, D, and E.

A. Using the data in the bar chart, identify the statement with the highest percentage of respondents who believed it described Nigeria well.

B. Using the data in the bar chart, describe the level of trust Nigerian citizens have in government.

C. Define political efficacy.

D. Using your knowledge of political efficacy and the data in the bar chart, draw a conclusion about the strength of civil society in Nigeria.

E. Explain what the data illustrate about the citizens' level of trust and confidence in government in illiberal democracies.

9.4 Political Culture and Participation

Learning Targets

After reading this section, you should be able to do the following:

1. Describe Nigeria's constitutional protections of civil rights and liberties.

2. Explain why women are underrepresented in the Nigerian government.

3. Describe human-rights violations in Nigeria.

4. Explain why Boko Haram arose in northern Nigeria and describe the government's response to Boko Haram.

Nigerians have the right to vote and otherwise participate in the political process. However, women are underrepresented in government positions. In addition, government officials have engaged in serious human-rights violations. Divisions within society have also hindered democratization in Nigeria.

Civil Rights and Civil Liberties

The Nigerian Constitution provides extensive protections for civil liberties, including due process rights for those accused of crimes, freedom of expression, assembly, and the press, the right to practice religion, and the right to privacy. The constitution also protects civil rights, including freedom from discrimination based on a "particular community, ethnic group, place of origin, sex, religion, or public opinion." (Constitution of the Federal Republic of Nigeria, article 42.)

Although Nigeria's constitution provides for equal rights for women, few women are represented in government. Nigerian women have the right to vote and run for office, but as Figure 9.3 demonstrates, women are underrepresented in the government. Although women make up 47 percent of registered voters in Nigeria, no woman has ever served as president or as the governor of a state. Six women ran for the presidency (out of seventy-three candidates) in 2019, and all of them dropped out before the election was held. (Akwagyiram and Carsten, 2019.)

According to a 2015 report written by Oloyede Oluyemi of the Nigerian National Bureau of Statistics, several factors account for the small number of women serving in elected positions. Nigeria has a history of being a patriarchal society, where women were expected to take care of the household and not become involved in political matters. Women may not want to participate in politics because of the stigma that politicians are untrustworthy. Female literacy rates (52.7 percent) are below those of men (71.3 percent), making it more difficult for women to participate in politics. Women who live in poverty have difficulty finding the time to engage in political activities along with taking care of

FIGURE 9.3

Makeup of the Nigerian House of Representatives

Gender, 1999–2019

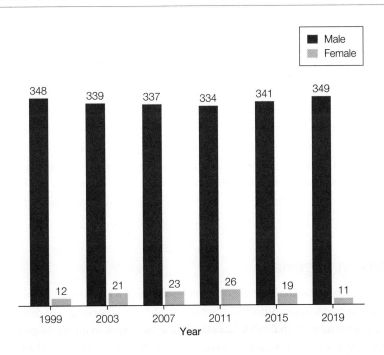

the home and earning a living. Furthermore, women have more difficulty raising money for political campaigns, and they may face hate speech and political violence during political events because of their gender.

Although civil liberties are protected on paper, they are not protected in practice. For example, while Nigerians are free to engage in lively discussions of political issues, they have less freedom to criticize leaders and the military, or to address sensitive topics such as religion and ethnicity. In 2017, Maurice Fangnon, a human-rights activist, was detained by the national intelligence and investigations agency after reporting that members of the Otodo-Gbame waterfront community in Lagos State were being forcibly evicted from their homes. In February 2019, Maryam Awaisu, from the #ArewaMeToo movement, was arrested by the national government's Special Anti-Robbery Squad after seeking justice for sexual-assault victims. Human-rights activists claim that both arrests were an attempt by the government to silence its critics. (Human Rights Watch.)

Reporters Without Borders deems Nigeria to be a dangerous place for journalists. According to a report by Amnesty International, journalists, bloggers, and human-rights activists who criticize the government or report about human-rights abuses have been threatened, detained, and arrested by police and national security forces.

In January 2019, the offices of the *Daily Trust*, a newspaper in the capital city of Abuja and the northeastern city of Maiduguri, were raided by the military. The newspaper's bureau chief, Uthman Abubakar and a reporter, Ibrahim Sawab, were detained. Both were held for two days without charges and then released. In November, during a protest against security officials in front of the headquarters for the Department of State Security (DSS), security forces shot at journalists who were covering the event. (Amnesty International.) In August 2019, Omoyele Sowore, who organized a #RevolutionNow protest over election fraud, was arrested by security forces. He was released, but in January 2021, Sowore was beaten at another protest and arrested again. (MSN.)

Amnesty International reports that, besides targeting journalists and human-rights activists, the Nigerian government has engaged in serious due process violations of those accused of crimes, including arbitrary arrest and detention, torture, and executions. For example, Sambo Dasuki, a former national security advisor, was arrested on charges of corruption in 2015. Four different court rulings ordered his release, but he was held until December 2019. Human Rights Watch also reports that thousands of children, who were suspected of supporting non-state armed groups (such as Boko Haram) have been held in detention facilities, without access to education, and subject to abuse by soldiers.

Despite formal protections for civil rights and liberties, Freedom House classifies Nigeria as partially free, with scores of 21/40 for political rights and 24/60 for civil liberties. (Higher scores indicate freer societies.) LBGTQ Nigerians face significant restrictions on their civil liberties, including a ban on same-sex marriage and laws penalizing sexual relations between members of the same gender, with violations resulting in prison sentences. Human-rights abuses by the Nigerian government have hindered the country's democratization.

Divisions in Nigeria

In Section 9.3, you learned about two groups in the Niger Delta—the Ogoni and Ijaw—who are advocating for more autonomy in the region. The experiences of these two groups represent a microcosm of the more than 250 ethnic groups living in Nigeria. The three largest ethnic groups in Nigeria are the Hausa-Fulani, Yoruba, and Igbo. The Hausa-Fulani live in the north and are mainly Muslim. The Yoruba live in the southwest and the Igbo

You may worry that you don't have time to carefully read passages on the multiple-choice portion on the AP® Exam. However, your score may suffer if you don't slow down and focus on what you are reading. This is especially true for the source-analysis portion of the exam, where you are expected to be able to understand an author's point of view.

Here is a passage from an article about Nigeria:

In a July decision, the African Union unanimously endorsed the appointment of President Buhari as its anti-corruption champion. The Nigerian president, who has introduced a zero tolerance policy on corruption in his own administration, is expected to lead an African Union summit on anti-corruption next year.

This appointment is a welcome recognition of President Buhari's own efforts against corruption in Nigeria, and a sign of Africa's determination to rid itself of a crime that blights development and progress.

—Statement by Spokesman for the United Nations Office of Drugs and Crime, "UNODC Congratulates Nigerian President Muhammadu Buhari on His Anti-Corruption Efforts"

Here is a sample multiple-choice question based on the passage:

Which of the following is the main idea of the passage?

A. Nigeria has a high level of corruption, which blights development and progress.
B. In the year after the passage was written, Nigeria was expected to be a leader in Africa in battling corruption.
C. Nigeria's status as a rentier state makes it difficult for the country to battle corruption.
D. The African Union commended Buhari based on his strong stance against corruption.

You may be tempted to choose option A, because the passage refers to corruption as a crime that "blights corruption and progress," and this language is used in the prompt. However, option A is not the correct answer to this question, because, if you read the passage carefully, you will know that most of the passage is about the African Union's

decision to endorse Buhari as its anti-corruption champion. Option A does not convey the main idea of the passage.

Option B may look tempting, because based on the passage, president Buhari was expected to lead a summit on corruption sponsored by the African Union. However, an executive leading a conference is not the same as a country being a leader in the region. Unless you carefully read the passage, you might have missed the reference to the summit.

You may be tempted to choose option C, because based on your study of Nigeria and of comparative government and politics, you know that rentier states tend to have high levels of corruption. However, option C is not the correct answer to this question, because it does not convey the main idea of the passage. Be wary of true information that is not the focus of the passage.

Option D is the correct response, because the passage focuses on the African Union's support for Buhari based on his pledge to tackle corruption.

Here is another passage about Nigeria:

In 2011, Nigerians participated in what were arguably the most credible and transparent elections since the country's independence. USAID capitalized on this positive momentum to improve elections by supporting the organizational development of political parties and the independence of the electoral commission, and by increasing civil society input into electoral and constitutional reform dialogue. In 2015, the Independent National Electoral Commission working with civil society organizations—which ran parallel vote tabulations—Nigeria helped usher in the first peaceful, democratic transition of power between two parties.

—"Democracy, Human Rights, and Governance," USAID

1. What is the main idea of the passage?
2. What evidence is used to support the main idea of the passage?
3. What is an implication of the passage about the future of democratization in Nigeria?

in the southeast. Both groups are mainly Christian and animist, although there is a sizable minority of Yoruba who are Muslims. More than 500 languages are spoken in Nigeria, with English being the official language. (Translators Without Borders.)

Colonization in Nigeria created great ethnic strife. The British created a country where none existed previously. The British drew Nigeria's boundaries without consideration of the diverse ethnic, linguistic, and religious groups living there, many of which had little in common. Furthermore, the British in Nigeria offered advantages to local rulers who carried out unpopular policies that benefited the colonizers and pitted ethnic groups against each other by rewarding some groups at the expense of others. This set the stage for personalized rule and ethnic, religious, and regional conflict. As a result of its diversity and history, Nigeria has many social and political cleavages.

The most extreme example of religious conflict in present-day Nigeria is Boko Haram, an Islamic separatist movement in the northern region. Most westerners first heard of Boko Haram in April 2014, when members kidnapped 276 secondary-school girls from the town of Chibok. An international Twitter campaign ensued, demanding the girls' return to their families, and Western governments vowed to do all they could to secure their release. The Nigerian military launched a mission to search for the girls, along with local volunteer groups. Five years later, over a hundred were still missing.

The kidnapping happened in the fifth year of the group's violent struggle with the Nigerian government and neighboring states, at the height of the group's greatest military strength. Lying behind the insurgency is a long history of poverty and political marginalization.

Boko Haram was founded by Mohammed Yusuf in 2002. The name Boko Haram, which means "Western education is sinful," is a pejorative term that local detractors used to describe the group. Boko Haram, though, has become the common name by which it is known around the world. It began in Borno—the most northeastern state of Nigeria—and mainly operates there and in two neighboring states, plus the neighboring countries of Niger, Chad, and Cameroon. The northeastern states where Boko Haram arose remain among the poorest and most economically unequal in the country. Although the Nigerian government developed programs to reduce youth unemployment, they were poorly implemented, creating resentment among poor, young men in the region.

Although Borno and other northern states had already adopted sharia as their source of civil law under Nigeria's democracy, Yusuf thought that they had not implemented it in a pure enough form. He eventually argued that true believers should not work with the secular state in any way. From 2001 to 2009, Yusuf and Boko Haram operated openly in the Borno area. Yusuf became a well-known preacher in Maiduguri and formed an alliance with the state governor until a disagreement in 2007. After that, Yusuf was arrested more than once and Boko Haram continued to radicalize, training its members militarily. In 2009, it attempted to lead an uprising in the city that failed. Yusuf was captured and executed by the military. (Thurston, 2018.)

Remnants of the group quickly re-formed under the leadership of one of Yusuf's assistants, Abubakar Shekau, moved to rural areas, and began a much broader campaign of violence, targeting Christian churches, schools, and state institutions such as police stations and prisons. The group became a terrorist organization, targeting innocent civilians. Boko Haram has killed several thousand people. The fighting has displaced several million, though the Nigerian military's counterattacks have killed and displaced many people as well.

The government declared states of emergency in 2011 and 2013, eliminating civil rights in the key northeastern states. In 2013, the military was widely reported to have gone on a rampage, indiscriminately killing hundreds of civilians in one village, in response to a Boko Haram attack that killed soldiers. In 2014–2015, Boko Haram controlled territory the size of Maryland in the northeastern corner of Nigeria. In 2015, it was declared the most violent terrorist group in the world. (Searcey and Santora.) A spiral of vengeful attacks began between the group and the Nigerian military.

The election in 2015 of Buhari, a northern Muslim and former military dictator, helped turn the tide of the battle. He reorganized the military and cracked down on corruption.

The neighboring countries of Chad and Cameroon, where Boko Haram also operated, were allowed to join the battle in Nigeria. Local citizens' militias also formed and were instrumental in weakening the group. Chad's military, which had fought its way into power in earlier years, was particularly effective. In 2018 and 2019, the military sometimes emptied entire villages of their populations to ensure there were no Boko Haram members among them. By 2019, the Nigerian military, with the help of neighboring countries, had eliminated Boko Haram's control of territory, but it continued to operate as a mobile terrorist organization throughout the region.

Despite Nigerian president Buhari's repeated claims of victory, Boko Haram has continued attacks, including kidnapping more than one hundred schoolgirls in February 2018 (and releasing almost all of them a few days later). Boko Haram has made the region insecure.

The group, which had broken into factions, attacked military garrisons in the region for supplies. It engages in kidnapping for ransom and bank robberies to raise funds. Several reports said that most recent recruits were victims of kidnapping rather than people who joined voluntarily. Some members of Boko Haram may not believe in or understand the organization's theology. Often, lack of alternative opportunities, desire for revenge in local political battles, or just a sense of belonging to something larger than themselves motivate young men to join and remain in such groups.

By 2019, a fragmented Boko Haram had lost control of most of its territory, but instability in the region continues. In February 2021, 279 schoolgirls were kidnapped by bandits in the northwestern state of Zamfara. They were released following negotiations between the government and the kidnappers. (Akinwotu, 2021.) As of 2021, Boko Haram had been weakened, but it continues its operations in the northern region, which remains dangerous and unstable.

Section 9.4 Review

Remember

- Although the Nigerian Constitution protects civil rights and civil liberties, women are underrepresented in government, and the Nigerian government has engaged in serious human-rights abuses.
- Nigeria is a diverse society, including the Hausa-Fulani, Yoruba, and Igbo, along with 250 smaller ethnic groups.
- Boko Haram is an Islamic terrorist and separatist group operating in northern Nigeria and surrounding countries.

Think

- What steps could the Nigerian government take to increase female representation in government?

Free-Response Question: Comparative Analysis

Compare the government's response to social cleavages in two different AP® Comparative Government and Politics course countries. In your response, you should do the following:

A. Define social cleavage.

B. Describe a social cleavage in two different AP® Comparative Government and Politics course countries.

C. Explain how the government in two different AP® Comparative Government and Politics course countries responded to the cleavages described in part B.

9.5 Economic and Social Change and Development

Learning Targets

After reading this section, you should be able to do the following:

1. Describe the impact of British colonization on Nigeria's economic development.

2. Explain how Nigeria's status as a rentier state impacts economic growth.

3. Explain how Boko Haram has destabilized northeastern Nigeria.

4. Describe social welfare programs in Nigeria and explain why few citizens benefit from them.

5. Explain how Nigeria's large population of young people will impact the government's ability to provide economic opportunities.

Globalization

Globalization impacted the Nigerian region long before colonization, but British colonial rule had an outsized impact on the Nigerian society and economy. As was true throughout sub-Saharan Africa, colonial rulers in Nigeria used the region to benefit themselves. Under British rule, Nigerians' economic opportunities were limited. Peasant farmers were encouraged to produce food and export crops, but Nigerians were not allowed significant opportunity in industry. Foreign businesses controlled what little industry there was.

Nigerians' best route to economic advancement was education and employment in the colonial government. At independence, the educated elite were mainly employed in government and had virtually no involvement or expertise in private industry. They believed the expansion of the government's role in the economy would improve development in Nigeria and further their own interests.

During colonial rule, the government had a monopoly over marketing of key export crops, which it bought from farmers at low prices and then sold internationally at much higher prices. Most of the revenue went to the regional governments, which used the money to build infrastructure and encourage industrialization, causing wasteful duplication between regions. Export crop revenues also became an early source of corruption, further undermining development.

Nigeria was a poor, agricultural country with little industry when it gained independence in 1960. As much as 98 percent of the population worked in agriculture, producing 65 percent of the country's GDP and 70 percent of its exports. Since then, the Nigerian government has invested almost nothing in agriculture, which has declined from being the most important sector of the economy to one that continues to employ many people but produces very little.

Like Mexico, the Nigerian government initially attempted to industrialize by adopting import substitution industrialization (ISI) policies. By the 1970s, the government had rapidly expanded its investment in large-scale industry. Most of the private Nigerian investors were government officials or political leaders, so participation in the government and politics remained the key means of acquiring wealth.

In 1961, money from oil exports constituted less than 8 percent of government revenue. By 1974, it was 80 percent, following the quadrupling of world oil prices. The state-owned Nigerian National Petroleum Corporation (NNPC) formed joint investments with foreign companies to extract and produce oil.

By the mid-1970s, Nigeria had become a rentier state. Oil production and revenue had overwhelmed all other aspects of the economy and made the government dangerously dependent on the global oil market for political and economic survival. The government stopped investing in other sectors of the economy.

Jobs in the petroleum sector drew away labor from other sectors, making it difficult for other sections of the economy to survive and preventing new sectors from emerging. As other sectors of the economy collapse, or never emerge in the first place, petroleum becomes a larger and larger part of the economy until eventually the economy is dependent on petroleum. The huge influx of oil revenue and the active involvement of the government in the economy helped make Nigeria one of the most corrupt societies in the world, as it struggled to deal with the resource curse.

The governments of the 1970s used oil wealth to invest in large-scale infrastructure projects, borrowing money against future oil revenues to do so. When the oil market collapsed in the mid-1980s, the government was unable to pay back its loans and faced bankruptcy. In the mid-1980s Nigeria negotiated a loan from the International Monetary Fund. To receive the money, the Nigerian state was required to adopt economic-liberalization policies, including restructuring the national budget to raise taxes and reduce expenditures, privatizing state-owned companies, reducing tariffs, and reducing subsidies for domestic industries. This is known as a **structural adjustment program**. Reducing the government's size was politically and socially painful, because structural adjustment policies tend to negatively affect the poorest and most vulnerable citizens, such as children and the elderly.

Structural adjustment program
Requirements for receiving assistance from international lenders (such as the IMF), including the privatization of state-owned companies, reducing tariffs, and reducing subsidies for domestic industries.

The Recent Nigerian Economy

The democratic government's economic policies have oscillated between reforms aimed at reducing corruption and improving economic performance, and policies that allow political leaders to use oil and other revenues as patronage for electoral purposes. (Lewis, 2018.) The government of the Fourth Republic used its international support to gain financial aid and debt relief from Western donors but in turn was required to make substantial progress in adopting economic-liberalization policies.

By 2006, the country's overall debt had dropped to less than one-tenth of what it had been two years earlier. (Gillies, 2007, 575.) The government used monetary policy to control inflation, stabilized government spending and the country's currency, and reduced various tariff barriers. It created a sovereign wealth fund, which is meant to act as a "rainy day" fund that sets aside oil revenues above a certain level so that they can be spent when oil prices fall, helping to stabilize the government budget. Donors responded not only with debt relief but also with a major increase in aid, from less than $200 million in 2000 to more than $6 billion in 2005. Debt relief and aid, combined with rapidly increasing world oil prices, substantially improved economic growth, which averaged around 5 percent in the decade after 2000, with non-oil-sector growth at an impressive 9 percent from 2003 to 2009. (Ajakaiye, Collier, and Ekpo, 2011.)

Nigeria's oil wealth allowed it to weather the immediate effects of the 2007 recession without an economic downturn. High oil prices kept its growth rate at a robust 7 percent in 2009 before falling to 6.7 percent in 2011—still a high growth rate by global standards.

Oil dependence continues to cause problems, however. The economy was devastated by the drop in oil prices that began in 2014. With global oil prices falling by 50 percent, Nigeria entered a recession in 2016 for the first time in more than twenty years. The economy contracted by 1.5 percent, and the government, facing a revenue crisis, considered selling off some of its ownership of the oil sector. The government failed to follow through on its promise to set aside money in the sovereign wealth fund in 2012 when oil prices were high, and it spent the revenue instead. When prices collapsed after 2014, the budget deficit and international debt increased. The IMF ranked the Nigerian sovereign wealth fund as the second-worst managed in the world in 2019.

The collapse of oil revenue may have finally provided some incentive for the government to reduce corruption in the oil sector. In 2012, President Goodluck Jonathan commissioned a study of the oil sector that found a combination of domestic and foreign malfeasance had cost the government more than $100 billion in the previous decade, a figure that shocked the nation. In 2018, the National Assembly passed a reform bill to provide more transparency and accountability in the oil sector, but President Buhari refused to sign it into law, arguing the bill did not go far enough in preventing corruption.

As of 2021, the NNPC produced 1.6 million barrels of crude oil a day, but the Nigerian government imports almost all of the state's petroleum from other countries, because of the country's limited capacity to refine oil. Refined petroleum purchased abroad is then sold within Nigeria at a subsidized price. These subsidies cost nearly $300 million a month. Eliminating these expensive subsidies would be difficult politically because they keep gas prices low, have widespread popular support, and prevent protest and unrest. (Olurounbi and Clowes, 2021.)

Buhari proposed an Economic Recovery and Growth Plan (ERGP) to "give firms a competitive edge through access to raw materials, skilled labor, technology, and materials." (African Development Bank Group, 2019.) In 2017, a portion of the ERGP, the Power Sector Recovery Plan, was passed by the legislature with the goal of attracting investment and expanding the country's power infrastructure. Legislation to make financial systems, personnel, and payroll processes more transparent was also passed.

Real GDP growth rebounded slightly in 2017 but remained under 1 percent. In 2018, it reached nearly 2 percent and was driven by non-oil sectors, especially services, mining, and some manufacturing. Agriculture remained stagnant, in part due to the herder–farmer conflicts in the Middle Belt states and the Boko Haram insurgency in the northeast.

Many Nigerians have responded to the economic challenges facing the economy by going into business for themselves. According to a report by Global Entrepreneurship Monitoring, Nigeria leads the world in entrepreneurship. (Copeland.) This is particularly true among Nigeria's young people, many of whom view Nigeria as ripe for starting businesses. On one list of the top ten African startups to watch, half of the companies have offices in Nigeria. (Mitchell.) Nigerian entrepreneurs have created businesses in diverse fields such as advertising, business strategies, magazine publishing, fashion, computer repair, smartphones, and furniture. (Adejo.)

Despite the ongoing economic challenges facing the country, many Nigerians remain optimistic about the future. In 2017, a Pew Research Survey indicated that 72 percent of Nigerians believed that their children would be better off than their parents. Buhari's decisive reelection in 2019 raised some hopes that implementation of the ERGP, particularly aspects that would improve the investment environment and adjust trade policies, would

Bilikiss Adebiyi is the founder or Wecyclers, a company based in Lagos that gives low-income communities the opportunity to clean up their neighborhoods and earn income from recycling. Adebiyi has an M.B.A. from MIT and a master's degree from Vanderbilt University.

increase growth. (World Bank, 2019.) However, falling oil prices and the 2020 COVID-19 pandemic have threatened Nigeria's economic growth.

Social Policies

The Nigerian Constitution guarantees social policies that enhance citizens' quality of life. (Constitution of the Federal Republic of Nigeria, Chapter 2, Sections 16 and 17.) Under the constitution, the government pledges to provide citizens with suitable shelter, adequate food, a reasonable minimum wage, and benefits for the elderly, unemployed, and disabled. The constitution also guarantees the right to earn a livelihood, including access to jobs. Despite these provisions, the welfare system in Nigeria is underdeveloped, and few Nigerians benefit from social programs. (World Bank, 2019.)

In 2005, the National Health Insurance Scheme (NHIS) was implemented. Unlike the NHS in the United Kingdom, which is state-run, the NHIS sets up a system where people pre-pay a fixed amount, which goes into a health maintenance organization (HMO). Those needing medical attention can access services through the HMO. According to a 2018 report by the World Bank, only 16 percent of Nigerians use the NHIS system, and health-care coverage in rural areas is only 11 percent. Most workers in the informal sector, such as street vendors, do not have health insurance. Most people pay for health care out of their own pockets, making up more than 70 percent of national health-care expenses. About 60 percent of people in Nigeria are not enrolled in pension plans. (World Bank, 2019.)

In 2015, the Nigerian government created the National Social Investment Programmes (NSIP). NSIP created a framework for delivering welfare services in education, health, housing, employment, social insurance, and family and community support. Under the programs, the government pledged to provide free meals to students in elementary schools and to provide cash transfer payments to support children with disabilities or living in poverty. In addition, the government would provide more access to the NHIS as well as free health-care services for pregnant women, children under five, the elderly, and the disabled. (Friedrich Ebert Stiftung.)

The NSIP includes a number of programs to improve the economy. One program provides farmers and small businesses with access to financial services. Another program provides childcare for kids under five, giving their parents more opportunities to earn a living. The Youth Employment and Social Support Operations develops job-training programs for young people and helps them find employment. The National Cash Transfer Programme provides for cash transfer payments to families facing emergencies. The Community and Social Development Project was created to help local communities devise development strategies. (Friedrich Ebert Stiftung.) Most of these programs involve NGOs as stakeholders and sources of funding. (World Bank, 2020.)

Enactment of the NSIP was an important step in furthering an agenda to help the poor, but it did little to improve social welfare services in Nigeria. Implementation of the NSIP has been fragmented, and there is a lack of coordination among the national and state governments, NGOs, and local communities. More importantly, Nigeria spends only 2.6 percent of its GDP on social programs and only 0.3 percent on social-safety nets, partly because fuel subsidies drain the budget of money that could be made available for social welfare programs. (World Bank, 2019.)

Only a small percentage of Nigerians are covered by social-protection programs. For example, in 2016, only 2.1 percent of households received benefits from safety-net programs. (World Bank, 2020.) The government has had difficulty identifying and targeting individuals and families who qualify. Different agencies produce different reports, and limited data are available. The last demographic survey took place in 2006, making it hard to estimate the size and distribution of the population. (World Bank, 2020.)

Furthermore, job-training programs and employment opportunities are particularly scarce for women, northerners, and those lacking a primary education. People engaged in subsistence agriculture lack access to both public and private safety nets.

Shifting Demographics

Nigeria's population growth rate will further strain the country's limited social welfare system. Nigeria's population is projected to grow from about 219 million in 2021 to 392 million in 2050, which would make it the most populous country in Africa and the fourth most populous country in the world. (*CIA World Factbook*, 2021.)

Nigeria has a high fertility rate, a slightly declining mortality rate, and a large population of young people. In 2017, the total fertility rate was 5.8 percent, with rates over 6 percent in the north. Although the rate has come down in recent years, it still means that the average woman bears five children. Women living in cities or who have more education have fewer children. As of 2017, fewer than 11 percent of married women used a modern method of contraception.

Studies show that educating girls lowers fertility rates and increases economic productivity. Yet in Nigeria, girls have less access to secondary education. Twenty-eight percent of girls aged 15–18 are already married, and 23 percent are already mothers. Education and job creation for females are top priorities in lowering the fertility rate.

Several factors prevent children in Nigeria from living comfortably and from having an economically productive future. Children in Nigeria have high rates of malnutrition, and 37 percent of children under five have slow growth rates. Lack of health coverage puts children at risk for infectious diseases, and only a third of mothers reports seeking health care for children sick with respiratory viruses or diarrhea. (Population Reference Bureau.)

As a result of these demographic factors, 23 percent of Nigerians are under the age of 18, and the total number of adolescents is expected to more than double to 84 million in 2050. (Population Reference Bureau.) Nigeria's young population poses challenges for the state in providing education, health care, and job training. Unless the fertility rate is lowered, Nigeria's youth will not be prepared for a comfortable and economically productive future, and high youth unemployment rates have the potential to destabilize the political system.

Nigeria and the Future

Thirty years into its democratic transition, Nigeria's democracy faces several enduring problems, including poverty, corruption at the local and national levels, environmental damage, and internal divisions.

The country remains deeply divided along regional, ethnic, and religious lines. In the northeast, Boko Haram continues to wreak havoc, though President Buhari reorganized the military and, working with neighboring countries, greatly reduced Boko Haram's territory. In the southeast, the battle over control of oil revenues has been both violent and tied to ethnic demands. Addressing the security issues arising from these conflicts will be crucial to Nigeria's democratization. (Mbaku, 2019.)

Despite challenges, Nigeria has held six democratic elections since 1999 and created an independent election commission. Power in the executive has peacefully changed hands between political parties. Although the economy remains dependent on oil, Nigerians are known for their entrepreneurial spirit, and new independent ventures are creating jobs. Despite continuing and serious problems, there is reason to be hopeful about the future of Nigeria.

Section 9.5 Review

Remember

1. British colonization had a significant impact on Nigeria's economic development.

2. Nigeria is a rentier state, and a major source of government revenue comes from the rent generated by leasing land for the extraction of oil.

3. Boko Haram is an Islamic terrorist organization that has destabilized northeastern Nigeria.

4. Although Nigeria has adopted programs to provide social welfare, few citizens benefit from them.

5. Nigerians are known for their entrepreneurial spirit.

6. Nigeria has a large population of young people, which will make it difficult for the country to provide economic opportunities for this demographic group.

Know

- *Structural adjustment program:* requirements for receiving assistance from international lenders (such as the IMF), including the privatization of state-owned companies, reducing tariffs, and reducing subsidies for domestic industries. (p. 293)

Think

- What steps could the Nigerian government take to make its social welfare programs more effective in providing aid to the poor and disadvantaged?

- What steps could the Nigerian government adopt to lower the fertility rate?

Free-Response Question: Quantitative Analysis

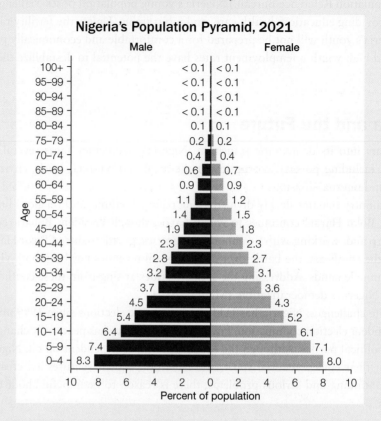

Nigeria's Population Pyramid, 2021

Answer A, B, C, D, and E

A. Using the data in the population pyramid, identify the demographic group that makes up the largest percentage of Nigeria's population in 2021.

B. Using the data in the population pyramid, identify a trend in the age structure in Nigeria in 2021.

C. Describe social welfare policies.

D. Draw a conclusion about how the age structure of Nigeria's population will impact social programs.

E. Explain how the Nigerian government could address the age structure in Nigeria.

AP® KEY CONCEPTS

- Sharia law (p. 272)
- National Assembly (p. 276)
- House of Representatives (p. 276)
- Senate (p. 276)
- Structural adjustment program (p. 293)

AP® EXAM MULTIPLE-CHOICE PRACTICE QUESTIONS

1. Which of the following best describes the impact of oil reserves on the Nigerian economy?

   A. Oil is difficult to access in Nigeria because oil reserves are located in territory controlled by Boko Haram.

   B. Insurgents in the Niger Delta region divert oil from pipelines, making oil production unprofitable.

   C. The Nigerian economy is diversified, and the proceeds from oil production do not make up a significant percentage of government revenue.

   D. Nigeria is a rentier state, and government revenues are subject to fluctuations in the world market for oil.

Questions 2 and 3 refer to the infographic.

Nigerian General Elections, 2019
Women as Candidates, by the Numbers

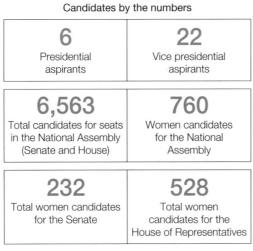

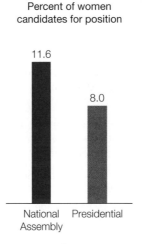

Note: Numbers refer to the number of candidates running for office.
Data from Premium Times (www.premiumtimesng.com)

2. Which of the following is supported by the infographic?

   A. Women are not allowed to run for office in Nigeria.

   B. Nigerian women are more likely to win seats in the Senate than in the House of Representatives.

   C. Women are more likely to run for vice president rather than president.

   D. The percentage of female presidential candidates was higher than the percentage of female candidates for the National Assembly.

3. Which of the following is an implication of the data?
   A. Women are underrepresented in elected government offices in Nigeria.
   B. Female participation in government in Nigeria is likely to increase over the next two decades.
   C. Nigeria uses a federal character principle, which requires political parties to place a quota of women on the ballot.
   D. Voter turnout among women in Nigeria is low compared to voter turnout among women in Mexico.

4. Rentier states face which of the following problems?
   A. Lack of valuable natural resources, which is known as the "resource curse"
   B. Difficulty in predicting future government revenues
   C. A low level of home ownership because most people lease apartments
   D. Overdiversification of the economy, making it difficult to focus on one economic sector

5. Which of the following describes a similarity in electing the executive in two course countries studies in AP® Comparative Government and Politics?
   A. A second round of elections is possible in Nigeria and Russia.
   B. The prime minister is elected directly in Russia and the United Kingdom.
   C. The presidents in Mexico and Nigeria must win by a majority of the votes.
   D. Because of the federal systems in Russia and Nigeria, the winning candidate must receive a majority of the votes in two-thirds of the states.

Questions 6 and 7 refer to the passage.

(1) The sharia Court of Appeal of a State shall, in addition to such other jurisdiction as may be conferred upon it by the law of the State, exercise such appellate and supervisory jurisdiction in civil proceedings involving questions of Islamic personal Law which the court is competent to decide in accordance with the provisions of subsection (2) of this section.

(2) For the purposes of subsection (1) of this section, the sharia Court of Appeal shall be competent to decide—

(a) any question of Islamic personal Law regarding a marriage concluded in accordance with that Law, including a question relating to the validity or dissolution of such a marriage or a question that depends on such a marriage and relating to family relationship or the guardianship of an infant;

(b) where all the parties to the proceedings are Muslims, any question of Islamic personal Law regarding a marriage, including the validity or dissolution of that marriage, or regarding family relationship, a founding or the guarding of an infant . . .

—Constitution of the Federal Republic of Nigeria, Section 277

6. Which of the following is supported by the passage?
   A. The Nigerian Constitution established sharia law as the national legal system.
   B. Some northern states in Nigeria have implemented sharia law, while southern states use a common-law system.
   C. In states that have adopted sharia law, courts of appeal have jurisdiction over divorce and child custody matters.
   D. Decisions issued by state sharia courts have precedence over decisions issued by the Nigerian Supreme Court.

7. Which of the following is an implication of the passage?
   A. Sharia law is applied consistently in northern states.
   B. Non-Muslims living in northern Nigeria face discrimination in the legal system.
   C. Members of the sharia Court of Appeal must be well-versed in Islamic law.
   D. Nigeria follows rule of law because it has a standard legal code.

8. Which of the following describes the legislature in two course countries studied in AP® Comparative Government and Politics?

    A. In the United Kingdom and Nigeria, the lower house represents population districts, and the upper house represents the elite.

    B. In Mexico and Russia, the lower house is directly elected, and the upper house is appointed by state legislatures.

    C. In Mexico and Nigeria, a quota system requires parties to run female candidates for office.

    D. In Mexico and Russia, the lower house represents the population, and the upper house represents the states.

9. Which of the following describes the impact of electoral systems on party systems in the legislature in two countries studied in AP® Comparative Government and Politics?

    A. In Mexico and Russia, proportional representation has led to a multiparty system.

    B. In Nigeria and the United Kingdom, a single-member district system has led to more than two parties winning seats in the legislature.

    C. In Russia and the United Kingdom, a threshold for gaining proportional representation seats has led to a single-party dominant system.

    D. In Russia and Nigeria, a mixed electoral system resulted in a multiparty system in the legislature.

10. Which of the following describes separatist movements in two course countries studied in AP® Comparative Government and Politics?

    A. Separatist movements in Russia and Nigeria are based on ethnicity and religion.

    B. In the United Kingdom and Mexico, separatist movements are based on religion.

    C. In Mexico and Nigeria, regional separatist movements are based in oil-rich regions.

    D. In the United Kingdom and Russia, Muslims have led regional independence movements.

AP® EXAM PRACTICE ARGUMENT ESSAY

Develop an argument as to whether a state's response to perceived threats with violence increases or decreases legitimacy.

Use one or more of the following course concepts in your response:

- Civil liberties
- Social divisions
- Sovereignty

In your response, do the following:

- Respond to the prompt with a defensible claim or thesis that establishes a line of reasoning using one or more of the provided course concepts.
- Support your claim with at least TWO pieces of specific and relevant evidence from your study of one or more course countries. The evidence should be relevant to one or more of the provided course concepts.
- Use reasoning to explain why your evidence supports your claim or thesis, using one or more of the provided course concepts.
- Respond to an opposing or alternate perspective, using refutation, concession, or rebuttal.

For a complete list of the sources of information cited in this chapter, turn to the Works Cited appendix.

① Mexico

② United Kingdom

③ Russia

④ Nigeria

⑤ China

⑥ Iran

NOTE TO STUDENTS:

As you complete each unit, you will have more knowledge and be able to make more connections between concepts and countries. As your knowledge and skills build over time, the unit reviews become more complex, and the questions cover more of the content you will encounter on the AP® Exam.

AP® EXAM PRACTICE QUESTIONS

Section 1: Multiple Choice

1. Which of the following accurately describes the electoral system for the lower house of the legislature in two course countries studied in AP® Comparative Government and Politics?
   A. The United Kingdom and Russia use proportional representation systems.
   B. Russia and Mexico have mixed electoral systems.
   C. Thresholds are used for filling proportional representation seats in Nigeria and Russia.
   D. Mexico and Nigeria use quota systems to ensure adequate female representation.

Questions 2 and 3 refer to the bar chart.

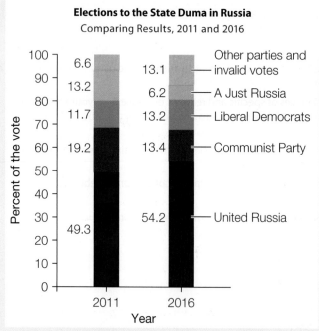

Elections to the State Duma in Russia
Comparing Results, 2011 and 2016

Data from the Central Election Commission, Russian Federation, with 99.4 percent of votes counted.

2. Which of the following statements is supported by the bar chart?
   A. United Russia held a majority of seats in the Duma following the 2011 and 2016 elections.
   B. The Liberal Democrats are the second most popular party in Russia.
   C. United Russia received a larger percentage of the votes in the 2016 election than it did in the 2011 election.
   D. In the 2016 election, more than 13 percent of the votes were invalidated.

3. Which of the following is an implication of the bar chart?
   A. Coalition government occurs frequently in the Duma.
   B. Russia is likely to become a one-party state in the next decade.
   C. United Russia controls policymaking in the Duma.
   D. The Communist Party works closely with United Russia in the policymaking process.

4. Which of the following accurately describes the system for electing the executive in a course country studied in AP® Comparative Government and Politics?
   A. The Nigerian president must earn a plurality of the votes and at least 25 percent of the votes in two-thirds of the states, or a runoff election is held.
   B. The president in Russia is selected in a single-round election, by a plurality of the votes.
   C. The prime minister in the United Kingdom is selected by the majority party in the House of Commons, with confirmation by the House of Lords.
   D. The president in Mexico must win with a majority of the votes to avoid a runoff election.

5. Which of the following accurately describes a policy enacted to make elections more free and fair?
   A. The House of Lords in the United Kingdom certifies election results.
   B. The Federation Council in Russia approves candidates for office, in an effort to prevent extremism.
   C. The Guardian Council in Iran may remove candidates for office who do not comply with Islamic principles.
   D. Electoral commissions have been established in Mexico and Nigeria to oversee voting.

Questions 6 and 7 refer to the passage.

> In the case of the newly democratised countries at the end of the twentieth century, unfortunately few introduced mechanisms aimed at preventing corruption after they transitioned from autocracies. In these newly democratised countries, however, intense partisan competition often leads to higher rates of corruption as new political parties promise state jobs, contracts and other resources to their potential supporters . . . This may have contributed to how little progress has been made in these countries to improve the quality of their democracies.
>
> —Pring and Vrushi. "Tackling the Crisis of Democracy, Promoting Rule of Law and Fighting Corruption." Transparency International. January 19, 2019. (Licensed under CC-BY-ND 4.0.)

6. Which of the following is supported by the main idea of the passage?
   A. The consolidation of parties improves political competition, fostering democratization.
   B. Competition between political parties does not necessarily lead to democratization and increases opportunities for corruption.
   C. Countries with well-established political parties have more corruption than one-party states.
   D. Political parties hinder democratization and should be abolished in favor of candidates running independently.

7. Which of the following is a criticism of the argument presented in the passage?
   A. Although parties can lead to corruption, competitive elections between political parties are crucial in democratic states.
   B. The passage implies that authoritarian states are more effective in limiting corruption than democratic states, which is inaccurate.
   C. It is difficult for political parties to engage in corruption in democratic states, because democratic states provide transparency in government.
   D. States that engage in patron-clientelism democratize as quickly as states that use a merit-based system for awarding government jobs and contracts.

8. Which of the following accurately describes the system for filling seats in the upper house of the legislature in a course country studied in AP® Comparative Government and Politics?
   A. All members of the House of Lords in the United Kingdom are selected through heredity.
   B. Senators in Nigeria are selected by state legislatures.
   C. Senators in Mexico are appointed by the president and confirmed by state governors.
   D. Members of the Federation Council in Russia are appointed by regional governors and approved by regional legislatures.

9. Which of the following describes the party system in a course country studied in AP® Comparative Government and Politics?
   A. The United Kingdom has a multiparty system, and the House of Commons is typically controlled by a coalition government.
   B. Mexico has a two-party system, with the PRI and MORENA alternating control of the legislature.
   C. Nigeria has a two-party system, with small regional parties earning some seats in the legislature.
   D. Russia is a one-party state.

10. Which of the following political parties is most disadvantaged by the electoral system in a course country studied in AP® Comparative Government and Politics?
   A. The Liberal Democrats in the United Kingdom
   B. United Russia
   C. The PAN party in Mexico
   D. The People's Democratic Party in Nigeria

Questions 11 and 12 refer to the graph.

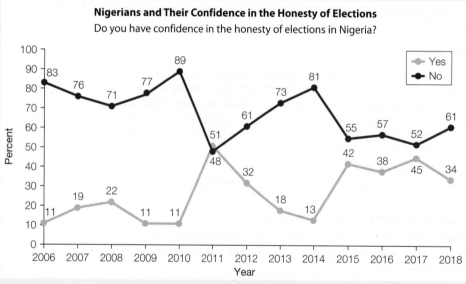

Data from Gallup World Poll, January 2019.

11. Which of the following statements is supported by the graph?
   A. From 2006 to 2018, trust and confidence in Nigerian elections have never been above 50 percent.
   B. Nigerians' trust and confidence in elections decreased between 2017 and 2018.
   C. Trust and confidence in elections are lower in Nigeria than in most illiberal democracies.
   D. From 2006 to 2018, there was a steady rise in trust and confidence in Nigerian elections.

12. Which of the following is an implication of the data presented in the graph?
    A. Elections in Nigeria are often accompanied by allegations of fraud.
    B. The Independent National Election Commission has been very effective in preventing fraud in Nigeria's elections.
    C. Because of high rates of fraud at the polls, a majority of Nigerians does not vote in national elections.
    D. Nigerian democracy has weakened significantly since 2011.

13. Which of the following is an example of a religious separatist movement in a course country studied in AP® Comparative Government and Politics?
    A. The Movement for the Survival of the Ogoni People (MOSOP) in Nigeria
    B. The Zapatistas in Mexico
    C. The Scottish independence movement in the United Kingdom
    D. Boko Haram in Nigeria

14. Which of the following best describes petroleum policy in course countries studied in AP® Comparative Government and Politics?
    A. Oil and gas production is nationalized in the United Kingdom and Mexico.
    B. Mexico and Russia are in the process of privatizing the petroleum industry.
    C. Russia and Nigeria have state-owned petroleum organizations.
    D. Mexico and Russia put quotas on the amount of petroleum they sell on the world market, in an effort to control state revenue.

15. Which of the following is a consequence of Nigeria's status as a rentier state?
    A. Multinational petroleum corporations influence Nigeria's lax environmental policies.
    B. Nigeria has a large source of predictable government revenue to support social programs.
    C. Nigeria has developed a diverse economy, including a thriving service industry.
    D. Oil revenue has been used to improve infrastructure in rural areas, decreasing the income gap.

16. Which of the following accurately describes the judicial system in Nigeria?
    A. Sharia law in the north is not subject to decisions of the Supreme Court, because religious law supersedes secular law.
    B. The judiciary is being professionalized, and the Supreme Court has the formal power of judicial review.
    C. Bribery and corruption are common and are the most prevalent at the highest levels of the court system.
    D. The president appoints Supreme Court justices and may remove them at will, giving the executive strong power over the court system.

Questions 17 and 18 refer to the passage.

> The Nigerian government promotes entrepreneurship because it is a bedrock of economic growth, but it also needs to provide an enabling environment for founders and their innovations to scale because the entrepreneurial success of any nation depends on the policies of the government. Policies that address infrastructural, financial, and fiscal challenges must have mechanisms in place for effective implementation.
>
> —"Trends in National Entrepreneurship Policies." Endeavor Nigeria. June 26, 2020

17. Which of the following is supported by the main idea of the passage?
    A. The Nigerian government's reliance on oil as a source of income hinders economic diversification.
    B. The government in Nigeria does not support the growth and development of independent businesses.
    C. Underdeveloped infrastructure and banking systems hinder business development in Nigeria.
    D. Although the Nigerian government supports independent businesses, corruption in government hinders economic growth.

18. Which of the following is an implication of the passage?

    A. Government policies are important in impacting economic growth and diversification.

    B. Entrepreneurs should rely on their own creativity and talent in building their businesses, because they cannot rely on government support.

    C. Although the entrepreneurial spirit is strong in Nigeria, most small businesses fail due to lack of trust and confidence in the economy.

    D. Nigeria's status as a rentier state makes it difficult for small businesses to obtain loans.

19. Which of the following best describes the relationship between the electoral system and the party system in Nigeria?

    A. The proportional representation system has led to multiple parties controlling both houses of the legislature.

    B. A mixed electoral system has led to coalition government in the legislature.

    C. A single-member district system resulted in the formation of two major catch-all parties.

    D. Nigeria's one-party state is a result of the electoral system established during military rule.

20. Which of the following best describes colonization in a course country studied in AP® Comparative Government and Politics?

    A. Nigeria's current parliamentary system is a legacy of British colonization.

    B. Ethnicity played a bigger role in the colonization of Nigeria than it did in the colonization of Mexico.

    C. Russia's colonization of Chechnya resulted in ethnic and religious conflict.

    D. Nigeria's unitary system was established by the British before independence.

Section 2: Free Response

Conceptual Analysis

Answer A, B, C, and D.

A. Define party system.

B. Explain how party systems differ in democratic and authoritarian regimes.

C. Explain how electoral systems impact the number of political parties that gain seats in the legislature.

D. Explain how the type of party system impacts policymaking in the legislature.

Quantitative Analysis

Distribution of Wealth in Nigeria
GDP by State

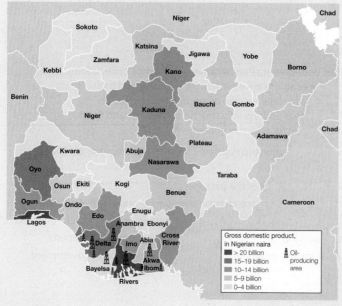

Data from BBC News and Congressional Research Service.

Answer A, B, C, D, and E.

A. Using the data in the map, identify the two wealthiest regions in Nigeria.

B. Using the data in the map, describe a pattern of wealth distribution in Nigeria.

C. Define rentier state.

D. Draw a conclusion about the relationship between Nigeria's status as a rentier state and wealth distribution.

E. Explain what the data illustrate about federalism in Nigeria.

Comparative Analysis

A. Define social movement.

B. Describe a social movement in two different AP® Comparative Government and Politics course countries.

C. Explain how the government in each of the two AP® Comparative Government and Politics course countries responded to the social movements described in part B.

Argument Essay

Develop an argument about whether corporatist or pluralist systems result in more effective policymaking.

Use one or more of the following course concepts in your response:

- Legitimacy
- Civil society
- Representation

In your response, do the following:

- Respond to the prompt with a defensible claim or thesis that establishes a line of reasoning using one or more of the provided course concepts.
- Support your claim with at least TWO pieces of specific and relevant evidence from your study of one or more course countries. The evidence should be relevant to one or more of the provided course concepts.
- Use reasoning to explain why your evidence supports your claim or thesis, using one or more of the provided course concepts.
- Respond to an opposing or alternate perspective, using refutation, concession, or rebuttal.

For a complete list of the sources of information cited in this review, turn to the Works Cited appendix.

UNIT 5

Political and Economic Changes and Development

Petroleum may come to mind right away when thinking of Iran. Yet its economy also relies on agriculture, even though only about 15 percent of the mountainous country is suitable for growing crops. Thinking about natural resources means thinking about quality of soil, availability of freshwater, and precipitation. Here, young Iranian farmers in the northeast harvest crocus flowers to gather their stigmas to make saffron.

Economics

This unit is a culmination that introduces some new concepts and brings together many of the concepts you have studied. Its theme is the interaction of political and economic changes within and across the course countries and how these changes affect political policies and behaviors. Every country studied in this course has experienced profound economic and political change over the past thirty years. You will examine the economic impact of globalization on citizens and on relationships between countries, as well as how countries have responded to changing economic circumstances. In short, you will apply what you have learned about government and politics in course countries to understand how they have adapted in a globally interconnected world. Relying on concepts in this unit, you will continue to refine skills necessary for success on the AP® Exam.

After completing Unit 5, you will be able to:

- Explain how countries have responded politically and economically to globalization
- Describe the role of international and supranational organizations
- Explain how countries have adapted social policies to deal with impacts of globalization
- Describe the effects of social policies on legitimacy and stability
- Describe different approaches to economic development and industrialization
- Describe causes and effects of demographic changes
- Explain how the abundance or lack of natural resources affects policymaking
- Examine government and politics in China and Iran

One of the newest phenomena in globalization and social media is the influencer. This category did not exist in the West—or in China—until recently. Papi Jiang has been called "No. 1 Internet Celebrity" in China. She started as a vlogger posting sharp, satiric videos. She is now a fashion influencer, too. In 2018, *Vogue* magazine estimated her followers on the platform Weibo at 28 million and on TikTok at 24 million.

10 Globalization

Economics

Shanghai is an economic and cultural powerhouse. It is the most populous city in China and one of the wealthiest. Although more than a thousand years old, the city began a growth spurt in the early 1800s, rising in prominence. Shanghai is a gateway city—from China to the outside world, as well as a place for outside influences to enter China.

Yuen Man Cheung/Alamy

The Ups and Downs of Jack Ma

China's economic growth over the past forty years has, for many, made it synonymous with globalization. It is the world's leading exporter, accounting for almost 15 percent of exports worldwide. In some industries, its share of exports is double that number.

China, officially known as the People's Republic of China, is a one-party state led by its communist party. China's embrace of markets and private property—in other words, capitalism—seems at odds with its official communist doctrine. Yet its government has officially called its public-private arrangement as "socialism with Chinese characteristics." Thirty years ago, the Chinese introduced the term "market socialism," to describe the mix of public and private enterprise within its economy. China is best described as a unique system "balancing the imperatives of globalizing capitalism and the demands of explosive, market-led growth with the maintenance of virtually total political control . . ." (Peck and Zhang, 374.)

China's mix of public and private ownership, with a vibrant private sector, is responsible for its unparalleled economic growth over the past forty years. Since 2010, it has become the world's second-largest economy, and its gross domestic product is on pace to surpass the GDP of the United States within the next ten years. According to the World Economic Forum, China's private sector contributes 60 percent of China's GDP, 70 percent of its innovation, 80 percent of its urban employment, 90 percent of new jobs and exports, and, overall, 70 percent of investment. China accounts for almost 30 percent of global manufacturing.

China's unparalleled economic growth has lifted an estimated 800 million people out of poverty, produced a middle class of roughly 400 million, and created hundreds of billionaires, second only to the United States. By way of comparison, there were no billionaires in China in 1999.

China's most visible billionaire is Jack Ma, whose Chinese name is Ma Yun (in Chinese practice, the family name goes before one's given name). Born in 1964, in 2020 he was the richest man in China. At one point, he had an estimated net worth of just under $60 billion.

Ma was raised in an ordinary family. At an early age, he sought to learn English. Beginning at age twelve, Ma rode his bicycle 40 minutes to an international tourist hotel and offered to give free tours to practice English. He chose the name Jack as his "American" first name.

He did not attend one of China's prestigious universities. Instead, it took him three tries to pass the university entrance exam because he failed the math portion twice. Once accepted, he studied English at the Hangzhou Teacher's Institute. After he graduated, he applied for thirty different jobs and was rejected by all. One of those jobs was at KFC. Of the twenty-four applicants, he was the only one not hired.

Although his teaching career lasted only a few years, he put his English skills to work by establishing a translation business that eventually led him to come to the United States. In 1995, while visiting a friend in Seattle, he saw his first personal computer and discovered the internet. Without any technical training, he returned to China and established one of China's first internet businesses, China Yellow Pages, a short-lived effort focused on building Web sites.

In 1999, with the help of Wall Street investors, he launched Alibaba, which has grown into an internet giant. Alibaba is a Chinese technology company that is often compared to Amazon but with a far greater reach. It is China's largest technology company, and its online marketplace is estimated to offer almost a billion products.

China's Jack Ma, looking like a rock star at a celebration of the twentieth anniversary of Alibaba, the e-commerce company he founded. In early 2021, though, his company was hit with a record-breaking fine by China's antitrust regulatory agency.

STR/AFP/Getty Images

Ma also created the world's largest fintech (financial technology) company. Hundreds of millions of Chinese use his companies daily. Users can make direct payments in stores for both small and large purchases. This feature, known as Alipay, is used by more than 700 million people every month. It also functions like a credit card and has become China's largest consumer-credit lender, in 2020 making about 10 percent of all consumer loans. Another feature allows users to put savings into investments, which has become one of the world's largest money-market funds. All of this is outside of the formal banking sector.

The media in China labeled the growing tech sector "The era of Ma Yun." In 2019, Ma stepped down as chairman of the board of Alibaba. In 2020, Ma was set to sell stock to the public of his fintech company Ant Group (the owner of Alipay). It was slated to be the largest IPO (initial public offering of stocks) ever, valued at $37 billion. Two days before the scheduled sale, in a stunning turn of events, the Chinese government canceled the sale.

Months before, in a very public forum, Ma had criticized China's regulators for stifling innovation. Ma had grown so famous that polls showed him more recognizable outside of China than Xi Jinping, China's president. At the same time, many in the banking sector argued that he was a threat to their business.

As a result of the canceled IPO, Ant's value plummeted. To further reduce Ma's influence and power, the company was reorganized, and Ant's ownership stake was reduced, with half of the company's ownership handed out to new partners selected by the government. Shortly after the canceled IPO, the official *People's Daily* Web site posted an article with the title, "There Is No So-Called Era of Ma Yun. Ma Yun Is Only Part of the Era."

To further punish Ma, and reduce his influence, he was removed in 2021 as president of Hupan University, an elite private business school that he had founded and endowed. The school was then reorganized without Ma.

Regulators also fined Alibaba $2.8 billion for monopolistic practices. After the canceled IPO, Ma retreated from public view. Normally, a flamboyant showman who loved the spotlight, by the summer of 2021, he was seldom seen. When he was, it was by means of low-key, scripted comments.

The Chinese government's treatment of Ma sent a clear signal to the nation's private sector that, despite its growing prominence, it was still under government control.

"The greatest lesson for the legions of Chinese entrepreneurs he's inspired may be reminding them that the Communist Party reigns supreme and that any private business, no matter how strategically important to the country's future, will be brought to heel if it is perceived to jeopardize the party." (McMorrow and Yu.)

The lesson from Ma's treatment is that despite a flourishing private sector, the Chinese Communist Party is firmly in control of the country's authoritarian state.

10.1 Impact of Global and Technological Forces

Learning Targets

After reading this section, you should be able to do the following:

1. Define globalization and explain how technology has increased the pace of globalization.

2. Explain how multinational corporations impact government policies and the lives of citizens.

3. Describe the benefits and drawbacks of state membership in international and supranational organizations.

4. Explain how individuals and civil-society groups, including NGOs, have responded to globalization and economic-liberalization policies.

In this chapter, you will learn more about globalization, which has been taking place for centuries but has been accelerated by the pace of rapid technological change. You learned about the impact of globalization in studying Mexico, the United Kingdom, Russia, and Nigeria. In this chapter, you will review some of what you have already learned, revisit vocabulary, and explore the impact of globalization in more depth.

Economic Globalization

Globalization is the increased interconnectedness of people, states, and economies. Globalization includes the flow of economic activity, technology, and communications around the world. It results in the increased sharing of cultural symbols, political ideas, and social movements across countries. Economic activity across borders has increased over the last generation: Between 1980 and 2010, trade as a share of global GDP increased from 30 percent to 56 percent, foreign direct investment more than quadrupled, and annual minutes of international phone calls from the United States went from 2 billion to 75 billion. (Dadush and Dervis, 2013.)

Technology is one of the driving forces of globalization. The costs of communication and transportation have dropped dramatically over the past two decades. Air travel, once a luxury enjoyed mostly by the elite, is now common for citizens of wealthy countries. Advances in containerization and just-in-time manufacturing have allowed more rapid and efficient shipment of goods. Personal computers, cell phones, and the internet have created instantaneous global communications capabilities while reducing costs. All of

Globalization
The increased interconnectedness of people, states, and economies.

this has allowed businesses to expand across national borders at unprecedented rates and created a new set of highly skilled, knowledge-based workers.

This communications and transportation revolution allows multinational corporations to coordinate complex production processes for both goods and services across multiple countries in new ways. Shoes may be designed in Portland, Oregon, and produced in Malaysia, using Bangladeshi labor and material inputs from Vietnam and China, all coordinated by "just-in-time" manufacturing to deliver the number of shoes that are likely to sell in your local shopping mall this month.

Globalization has produced dramatically different levels of economic development around the world. There are three key features of economic globalization: **Foreign direct investment (FDI)** is investment from abroad in economic activity in another country, such as building a factory. **Trade** is the import and export of goods and services, and **international capital flow** is the movement of money across national borders.

Multinational Corporations

Multinational corporations (MNCs) are companies that have facilities or assets in more than one country. Companies may be headquartered in one country but operate production facilities in another country, due to lower labor costs. Figure 10.1 is a map showing the number of MNCs in the world in 2018.

Foreign direct investment (FDI)
Investment from abroad in economic activity in another country.

Trade
The flow of goods and services across national borders.

International capital flow
Movement of money across international borders.

Multinational corporation (MNC)
A company with facilities or assets in more than one country.

FIGURE 10.1

The 2,000 Largest Multinational Corporations, 2017
By Country, Market Capitalization, and Change in Market Capitalization

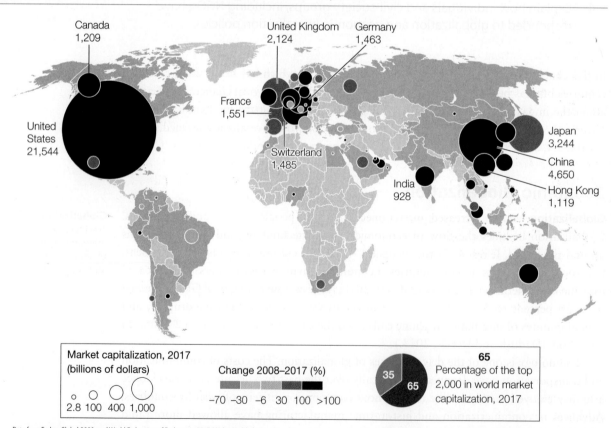

Canada 1,209
United Kingdom 2,124
Germany 1,463
France 1,551
Switzerland 1,485
United States 21,544
India 928
Japan 3,244
China 4,650
Hong Kong 1,119

Market capitalization, 2017 (billions of dollars)
2.8 100 400 1,000

Change 2008–2017 (%)
−70 −30 −6 30 100 >100

35 65
65 Percentage of the top 2,000 in world market capitalization, 2017

Data from Forbes Global 2000; and World Federation of Exchanges, 2017 Market Highlights.

MNCs often have multiple offices throughout the world to take advantage of a large pool of talented people with specialized knowledge. MNCs locate their distribution facilities to make the supply chain more efficient, by bringing goods and services closer to their targeted customers. You are probably familiar with many multinational brands, such as McDonalds, Starbucks, and Nike. MNCs change their offerings to fit local tastes. One particularly strange example is McDonald's German sausage double beef burger, which is available in China.

There are economic benefits for developing countries that attract MNCs. MNCs increase capital growth and provide jobs. Although wages are lower in developing countries than they are in developed countries, people in developing countries may prefer working for an MNC to the available alternatives in the local economy. Workers may develop new skills. MNCs may spend money on infrastructure, such as roads, which benefits local communities. In addition, developing countries that attract MNCs may be able to diversify their economies. This is particularly true in **rentier states** that rely on the export of oil or from the leasing of resources to foreign entities as a significant source of government revenue.

There are also drawbacks for developing countries that attract MNCs. Most of the profit made by MNCs in developing countries goes abroad. Furthermore, MNCs may rely on skilled labor from developed countries, instead of improving the skills of local people working in their facilities.

Working conditions in factories are often very difficult, and some people argue that employees working in sweatshops should be paid more for their labor, even when local wage rates are low. Critics of MNCs argue that host countries have little incentive to pass laws raising the minimum wage or regulating working conditions for fear that foreign companies will leave.

In addition, developing countries may offer tax incentives to foreign businesses, decreasing the potential revenue available to the government. Some states may even take land from citizens without fair compensation so that foreign companies can build facilities. Manufactured goods compete with locally made products, which are usually more expensive, running small companies out of business.

MNCs often damage the environment. MNCs often close manufacturing facilities in developed countries with strict environment standards and move them to other counties. Developing countries compete to attract MNCs by reducing or eliminating their own environmental standards, in a process called the "race to the bottom." As you learned in your study of Nigeria in Chapter 9, the extraction of raw materials by foreign companies can cause significant environmental damage.

A Kentucky Fried Chicken restaurant in China features the image of Colonel Sanders, a character now familiar to people worldwide.

Megapress/Alamy

Rentier state
A state that relies on the export of oil or from the leasing of resources to foreign entities as a significant source of government revenue.

International and Supranational Organizations

Like MNCs, international and supranational organizations have played a key role in globalization. An **international organization**, such as the International Monetary Fund (IMF) or World Bank, is a body established by a treaty or other agreement among countries. Countries that join international organizations voluntarily give up some sovereignty

International organization
A body established by a treaty or other agreement among countries.

in exchange for the benefits of membership. The creation of the World Trade Organization (WTO) in 1995 accelerated a process, started after World War II, of lowering tariffs on imports and exports and liberalizing the global economy. Both the World Bank and the International Monetary Fund support economic-liberalization policies.

Before adopting economic-liberalization policies, many developing countries, such as Mexico, utilized **import substitution industrialization (ISI)** policies. As you learned in your study of Mexico (Section 3.6), ISI policies were adopted to reduce a country's dependency on other countries by raising tariffs and providing incentives to encourage domestic manufacturing. Countries using ISI strategies often nationalized key industries. The shift to **economic-liberalization policies** significantly reduced the role of most governments in regulating economic transactions, especially across their borders.

The World Bank and IMF lend money to member states in an effort to reduce debt and improve economic circumstances in developing and underdeveloped countries, with the long-range goal of reducing poverty and improving citizens' well-being. As you learned in your study of Nigeria (Section 9.5), in exchange for the funds, the borrower country is required to meet certain conditions, such as liberalizing its economy and adopting **structural adjustment programs** to reduce tariffs and subsidies and privatize nationally owned industries.

Critics of economic-liberalization policies, and of structural adjustment programs in particular, argue that the elimination of subsidies and cuts to social programs have a disproportionate and negative impact on the most vulnerable citizens, including children and the elderly. Advocates of these programs argue that reducing state debt improves economic conditions in the long term.

Supranational organizations have even more policymaking authority than international organizations. In **supranational organizations**, representatives of member countries have some say in governing the institution and give up sovereignty over issues that affect the organization as a whole. In joining supranational organizations, member countries agree to abide by the rules of the organization, even when doing so means changing internal policies. Supranational organizations raise fundamental questions about globalization and state sovereignty over economic policy. (Iversen and Soskice, 2019.) Some examples include the Economic Community of West African States, a free-trade organization with fifteen member states, including Nigeria, and the World Trade Organization, which negotiates trade agreements and settles disputes among its more than 160 members, representing 98 percent of world trade.

As you learned in your study of political systems in Chapter 2 and the United Kingdom in Chapter 5, the European Union is another example of a supranational organization. Initially, EU member states did not yield substantial sovereignty because each state retained an effective veto over Europe-wide policies. That changed with the Single European Act of 1987, which limited a single state's veto power. Instead, several states must vote together to block a decision, which means that individual states have given up their sovereignty over key economic decisions.

The next and biggest step was the Maastricht Treaty of 1992, which created the euro, controlled by a new European Central Bank (ECB). The nineteen states that have so far agreed to adopt the euro voluntarily gave up their ability to control their own monetary policy and agreed to limits on their fiscal policies, reducing their ability to set their own economic policies. The United Kingdom never adopted the euro for fear of losing control over its currency. On the other hand, countries that adopted the euro believed that joining the eurozone would improve their economies because of the strength of the euro as a currency. The ECB controls the money supply and, therefore, monetary policy for these states.

Import substitution industrialization (ISI)
Enacting high tariffs and providing incentives to encourage the growth of domestic manufacturing.

Economic-liberalization policy
Policy that reduces the role of government in the economy, supports the free market, and reduces trade barriers.

Structural adjustment program
Requirements for receiving assistance from international lenders (such as the IMF), including the privatization of state-owned companies, reducing tariffs, and reducing subsidies for domestic industries.

Supranational organization
A body in which member countries have some say in governing and give up some sovereignty over issues affecting the organization as a whole.

Nigerians protest against the government's removal of a fuel subsidy, which raised gas prices. This protest in May 2016 demonstrates how citizens may respond when governments enact economic-liberalization policies.

Pius Utomi Ekpei/AFP/Getty Images

In addition to monetary policy, the EU sets policies regarding product standards and the environment. The 1985 Schengen Agreement provides that EU citizens can freely travel between member countries. As you learned in your study of the United Kingdom in Chapter 5, dissatisfaction with the EU's immigration and border security policies was a driving force behind the Brexit referendum.

Citizen Response to Globalization and Economic-Liberalization Policies

Citizens have responded to globalization by forming civil-society organizations. Some of these groups are regional, such as the Movement for the Survival of the Ogoni People in Nigeria, which arose in response to the presence of foreign oil companies in the Niger Delta and the environmental damage caused by drilling for oil. The Zapatista movement in Mexico, which arose in response to NAFTA, is another example of a regional civil-society organization that drew the world's attention to the plight of disenfranchised citizens who perceived themselves as left behind in the wake of economic liberalization.

The rise of new communications technology and especially social media has provided new ways of organizing civil-society groups to challenge state policies. However, some observers fear online communications erode social capital—the social networks and the norms of reciprocity that are crucial to democratic participation—by isolating individuals, limiting their likely participation in face-to-face social movements and threatening the continued existence of the movements themselves. Other skeptics see online activity as "slacktivism"—low-cost, low-commitment activism that has little impact. At the other extreme, some scholars argue that "the networked social movements of the digital age represent a new species of social movement." (Castells, 2012, 15.)

Social media, in particular, allow activists to bypass their traditional reliance on "mainstream media" to disseminate their ideas. Social media also allow all individuals, regardless of past involvement or leadership, to express their grievances to larger audiences and to find and form networks with like-minded people. Social media create a more public space in which social movements can form and act.

The internet has two elements that can cause transformation. First, the internet lowers the costs of creating and organizing movements. Second, it provides a way for people to act collectively without requiring the participants to be in the same time and place. Seeing posts from people with similar grievances and knowing that others plan to show up to protest may help people overcome fears and join a movement. Meeting virtually instead of in person can cut resource costs dramatically, reducing the need for expensive infrastructure such as offices and paid staff. (Earl and Kimport, 2011.) When movements are able to harness these benefits, they create new and powerful models than can challenge the state.

The new technologies can also have negative consequences. Authoritarian governments, such as China, have increasingly made use of new technology to surveil their

AP® POLITICAL SCIENCE PRACTICES

Defining Concepts in Free-Response Questions

The four types of free-response questions use terms specific to political science as part of the prompt. You have already studied many specific political science terms, which appear in this book in bold in the running text and in boxes in the page margins.

Sometimes, a question may ask you to define a specific term. For example, a conceptual-analysis question might be built around the concept of sovereignty, and part A may ask you to define the term. It is important that you clearly and precisely define terms to receive credit for your response. Here is an example of a sample response that needs improvement:

"Sovereignty means a country can do whatever it wants."

This response indicates an understanding of the term, but it overstates the concept and is not specific enough. Even the governments of countries with a high degree of sovereignty cannot do whatever they want at any time, especially if the countries are members of international organizations. Furthermore, the sample response does not indicate that challenges to sovereignty can come from inside or outside of a country. Here is another response:

"Sovereignty is a state's ability to act without internal or external interference."

This is a better definition, because it explains several things: (1) *states* are the actors related to sovereignty, (2) sovereignty impacts state *actions*, (3) both *internal and external actors* can influence the degree of sovereignty, and (4) sovereignty exists when there is little *interference*.

It is much more important to understand and be able to apply political science concepts than it is to memorize

definitions word for word. It's also crucial to know all of the parts of the concept so that you can express it clearly. Here is another response:

"Sovereignty means states can carry out policies without infringement by people or groups inside or outside the country."

Although this definition does not use the same words as the more formal definition, it still covers all aspects of sovereignty and shows clear understanding of the concept.

Sometimes, a free-response question may use a political science term without asking you to define it. Make it a personal practice to define key political science terms, even when the prompt does not specifically ask for a definition. For example, the argument question asks you to "Use one or more of the following course concepts in your response." After you choose the course concept or concepts you are going to use in your response, make sure to define each one. This will prove to the AP® Exam Reader that you know what you are writing about and make it easier for the Reader to award points for your response.

Answer the following questions about how to incorporate key concepts on the AP® Exam:

1. Describe the strategy you will use to remember and articulate your understanding of key concepts.

2. Explain why it is more important to understand the key concepts and be able to apply them to various scenarios than it is to memorize exact definitions.

3. Explain why you should define key terms, even when the prompt does not specifically ask you to do so.

population more effectively. Facial-recognition software enables governments to identify protesters. Authoritarian governments monitor social-media posts by critics and use the information to arrest, detain, and prosecute dissidents.

Transnational Activism

Global communication has become easier through the internet. Further, a growing number of issues, such as trade, human rights, and environmental protection, seems to require global action. These two factors have led to the rise of transnational social movements.

Transnational activism provides new opportunities for advocacy. It enables groups to target international organizations instead of, or in addition to, national governments. Wealthy and more experienced groups can share their knowledge and resources with newer and weaker groups in other countries. Groups can also share their strategies across borders much more easily, as global norms around issues such as human rights create a sense of collective purpose. These changes have been particularly important for groups in poorer countries and under authoritarian regimes. Their ability to appeal to and borrow tactics and resources from groups in wealthier countries can help them survive. Entire networks of like-minded organizations have formed to engage in parallel actions around the world.

Some groups, such as the global justice movement (GJM), target international organizations, while others use global resources to fight domestic battles. The GJM is a well-known example of new "transnational advocacy networks" of activists working together to use global resources to force policy change. (Keck and Sikkink, 1998.)

Protests against economic-liberalization policies have garnered worldwide attention. One of the most famous examples occurred during a WTO Ministerial Conference in Seattle, Washington, in January 1999. Protesters opposed the WTO's policies on workers' rights, the environment, and social issues. On the first morning of the conference, thousands of protesters blocked streets and intersections. They were met by tear gas and rubber bullets fired by overwhelmed police, who arrested more than fifteen people. Downtown businesses were vandalized. The conference was temporarily postponed. The city was criticized for its lack of preparedness and for mishandling the protests. (Seattle.gov.)

The protests in Seattle increased awareness of the backlash against globalization. Global protests against globalization and economic-liberalization policies have been joined by very diverse groups, including nationalists, people opposed to immigration, labor unions, artists, feminists, environmentalists, students, civil and human-rights groups, socialists, and anarchists. (Warner, 2005.)

Globalization has made it easier for international civil-society organizations to form. **Nongovernmental organizations (NGOs)** are not-for-profit organizations outside of government that usually focus on social or political issues. One example is Friends of the Earth, which has about 5,000 local groups and more than 2 million activists globally. It challenges corporate policies that damage the environment and encourages companies to engage in practices to protect the earth. Technology, especially social media, has provided these organizations with the unprecedented ability to increase public awareness, organize supporters, and raise funds. The increased ability of citizens to connect with one another over political and social issues poses challenges to the state, especially in authoritarian regimes.

As you will learn in your study of China in the next chapter, authoritarian states restrict social media in an effort to prevent domestic and international civil-society groups from organizing and sharing ideas critical of the state. One example is Amnesty International, an NGO that publicizes violations of civil rights and civil liberties and encourages its grassroots members worldwide to pressure governments to respect human rights. Amnesty

Nongovernmental organization (NGO)
A nonprofit group outside government control that usually focuses on social or political issues.

Analyzing a Table with Data

Tables can provide many data in a single format, and they may appear in the multiple-choice and quantitative free-response portions of the AP® Exam. Unfortunately, tables can provide so many data that they might seem overwhelming. Here is an example of a table that includes many numerical data:

TABLE 10.1 Profile of Eleven of the Largest NGOs

In alphabetical order

Organization	Income 2011 (in U.S. dollars)	Staff numbers	Geographic reach
ActionAid Johannesburg, South Africa	$314 million	2,328	45 countries 25 million people
Aga Khan Development Network Geneva, Switzerland	Development activities budget $450 million (2008)	60,000	25 countries
CARE International Geneva, Switzerland	$780 million	12,000	87 countries 60 million people 12 national members
Catholic Relief Services (CRS) Baltimore, Maryland, U.S.A.	$823 million	5,211	100 countries 130 million people
Christian Aid London, U.K.	$148 million	758	45 countries
Médecins Sans Frontières Geneva, Switzerland	$1.24 billion	22,000	60 countries
Mercy Corps Portland, Oregon, U.S.A.	$301 million	3,700	40 countries
Oxfam International Oxford, U.K.	$1.25 billion	6,000	98 countries 14 member organizations
Plan International Woking, U.K.	$827 million	8,131	48 countries
Save the Children London, U.K.	$1.4 billion	14,000	120 countries 29 national organizations 80 million children
World Vision International Monrovia, California, U.S.A.	$2.79 billion	40,000	120 countries 100 million people

Data from U.N. Development Programme and the NGO annual reports and Web sites, as of 2011. Data about staffing and geographic reach are from 2008.

There are three initial steps in analyzing a table.

1. The first step in analyzing a table is to look at the title. The title of this table indicates that the data are from some top NGOs. Because the title uses the word "eleven," you can infer that not all of the wealthiest NGOs are included in the table. The title also tells you that the table is organized alphabetically, which means it is not organized by income (given in U.S. dollars), the number

of people on staff, or how many countries or people each NGO serves.

2. The second step is to look at the source of the table. In this case, the source is the U.N. Development Programme.

3. The third initial step is to look at any notes under the table. In this case, the data in the table come from annual reports and Web sites. The data about income are from 2011, but

data about staffing and geography are from 2008. The use of data from two different years does not mean that the table is not useful, but it is something to keep in mind.

After reviewing preliminary information, it is time to dig into the table. Look at the column headings to get a sense of the kinds of information conveyed. In this case, the columns include the names of NGOs (and where they are headquartered), income in 2011, staffing numbers, and geographic reach.

You should read tables both horizontally and vertically. By reading the table horizontally, for example, you will learn that Save the Children is based in London, had $1.4 billion in income in 2011, had a staff of 14,000 people in 2008, and works in 120 countries, with 29 national organizations, and serves 80 million children. By reading vertically, you can identify patterns in the data. For example, by looking at staffing data, you can determine that of the top NGOs listed in the table, only three had more than 20,000 staff members in 2008.

In analyzing tables on the AP® Exam, it's important not to let yourself be overwhelmed by the amount of data conveyed. By looking at the title, notes, rows, and columns before you begin to answer the questions, you will be well prepared to find the appropriate data and answer the question.

Answer the following questions about how to analyze data in a table.

1. What are some advantages of using a table, instead of a graph, in conveying data?

2. What are some disadvantages of using a table to convey data?

3. What are some strategies you can use in finding patterns in data that are represented in a table?

International claims that in 2020 alone, it helped free more than 150 people wrongfully detained by their governments. The organization seeks to change laws regarding refugees, LGBTQ equality, freedom of expression, capital punishment, and due process rights. In January 2009, China blocked Amnesty International's Web site. (Amnesty International.)

As the world becomes more connected, citizens, civil-society organizations, and governments have responded in an effort to protect their interests in an increasingly globalized world.

Section 10.1 Review

Each section's main ideas are reflected in the Learning Targets. By reviewing after each section, you should be able to

Remember the key points,

Know terms that are central to the topic, and

Think critically about what you have learned.

Remember

- Globalization is the increased interconnectedness of people, states, and economies, and technology has increased the pace of globalization.
- Multinational corporations do business in more than one country and impact government policies and the lives of citizens.
- States join international and supranational organizations, giving up some sovereignty in exchange for the benefits of membership.
- Individuals and civil-society groups, including NGOs, have been formed in response to globalization and economic liberalization.

Know

- *Globalization:* the increased interconnectedness of people, states, and economies. (p. 313)
- *Foreign direct investment (FDI):* investment from abroad in economic activity in another country. (p. 314)

- *Trade:* the flow of goods and services across national borders. (p. 314)

- *International capital flow:* movement of money across international borders. (p. 314)

- *Multinational corporation:* a company with facilities or assets in more than one country. (p. 314)

- *Rentier state:* a state that relies on the export of oil or from the leasing of resources to foreign entities as a significant source of government revenue. (p. 315)

- *International organization:* a body established by a treaty or other agreement among countries. (p. 315)

- *Import substitution industrialization (ISI):* enacting high tariffs and providing incentives to encourage the growth of domestic manufacturing. (p. 316)

- *Economic-liberalization policy:* policy that reduces the role of government in the economy, supports the free market, and reduces trade barriers. (p. 316)

- *Structural adjustment program:* requirements for receiving assistance from international lenders (such as the IMF), including the privatization of state-owned companies, reducing tariffs, and reducing subsidies for domestic industries. (p. 316)

- *Supranational organization:* a body in which member countries have some say in governing and give up some sovereignty over issues affecting the organization as a whole. (p. 316)

- *Nongovernmental organization (NGO):* a nonprofit group outside government control that usually focuses on social or political issues. (p. 319)

Think

1. What types of policies can governments in developing countries pass to benefit economically from globalization while minimizing its negative impact on the unique culture and history of their citizens?

Free-Response Question: Comparative Analysis

Compare how globalization has impacted the formation of civil-society groups in two different AP® Comparative Government and Politics course countries. In your response, do the following:

A. Define globalization.

B. Explain how civil-society groups in two different AP® Comparative Government and Politics course countries have responded to globalization.

C. Explain how the governments in two different AP® Comparative Government and Politics course countries responded to the civil-society movements explained in part B.

10.2 Political Responses to Globalization

Learning Targets

After reading this section, you should be able to do the following:

1. Explain why some countries have responded to globalization by adopting policies favoring economic liberalization, while other countries have been hesitant to fully liberalize their economics.

2. Explain how states develop economic policies in response to pressure from citizens.

3. Describe the varying degrees of privatization of natural resources in the six course countries.

International and supranational organizations, multinational corporations, and nongovernmental organizations increasingly impact the global economy. Nevertheless, states are still very important economic actors, and they have developed varied responses to globalization and economic liberalization. States respond to global economic forces in an effort to maintain or increase their power domestically and internationally.

Globalization and Politics

States develop economic policies in an effort to navigate global markets. Although some problems, such as a worldwide recession, may require global solutions, countries must adopt policies to address issues that directly affect the state, such as inflation, GDP growth, and unemployment. Countries can choose to address these issues through state control of the economy or by adopting policies that reduce the role of the state and support economic liberalization.

Countries that adopt economic-liberalization policies try to keep inflation low so that prices are stable. Countries embracing economic liberalization keep corporate taxes low to attract direct foreign investment. However, if taxes are too low, the government may receive less revenue. When that happens, then government spending must be reduced, and social welfare programs also have to be cut. Economic liberalization requires a flexible labor force, which means countries must do what they can to keep labor unions from making too many demands. Rigid contracts with labor unions and rules that guarantee jobs or benefits for long periods discourage investment. And, of course, countries that adopt economic-liberalization policies must keep tariffs and other barriers to the entry and exit of goods, capital, and people at a minimum.

Many countries have not fully adopted economic-liberalization policies. Long-established political and economic institutions heavily influence how each country can and will respond to globalization. As you learned in your study of shock therapy in Russia, it is difficult for countries to quickly and dramatically change their economic systems. Countries like China, which moved more slowly in adopting market reforms, have had more time to develop the institutions and mechanisms to facilitate economic change. As you will learn in Chapter 11, one of China's first market initiatives was the creation of special economic zones to encourage foreign investment. Special economic zones provided investors with necessary infrastructure, an abundant labor force, and the promise of reduced bureaucracy and red tape.

Failure to meet citizens' economic demands for food, housing, and jobs decreases state legitimacy and increases the likelihood of unrest. In October 2020, for example, protests erupted throughout Nigeria after the government raised the price of fuel and electricity. (Anadolu Agency.) As shown in Figure 10.2 on page 324, fuel subsidies cost the Nigerian government 1.19 trillion naira (about $260 million) in 2018. Despite the negative impact of fuel subsidies on the federal budget, reducing subsidies and raising fuel prices risk further unrest. Similar protests over fuel prices occurred in Iran in November 2019. (BBC.) Despite global pressures to adopt free-market policies, states must respond to counter-pressures from their own citizens.

Privatization

Privatization is a key aspect of economic liberalization. Among the six countries studied in AP® Comparative Government and Politics, there are varying degrees of private ownership of property and capital. Under the leadership of Prime Minister Margaret Thatcher, the United Kingdom privatized key industries, such as steel and coal. However, although

FIGURE 10.2

Nigeria's Expenditures on Subsidies for Imported Gasoline
Years 2006 through 2018, in Nigerian Naira

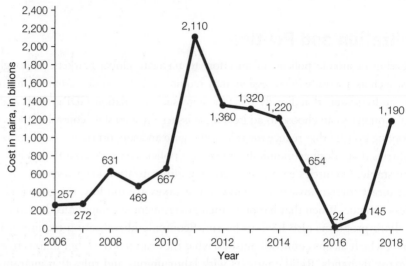

Data from *Daily Trust* newspaper and Nigeria National Petroleum Corporation monthly reports.

the natural-resources industry is privatized in the United Kingdom, the British government retains ownership of the NHS, including medical clinics and hospitals.

Like the United Kingdom, Mexico has privatized key industries over the past four decades. However, the Mexican government retains the largest share of ownership in Pemex, the national oil company, which was opened up to some private investment in 2014. President Obrador proposed strengthening Pemex by building a new oil refinery. In Nigeria, the National Petroleum Company has set up joint ventures with foreign companies to collaborate in oil extraction and production.

Government control over natural resources varies among the six course countries studied in AP® Comparative Government. The United Kingdom has the least government control over the natural resources within its borders. The governments of China and Iran maintain government control of natural resources. Russia re-nationalized the oil and natural gas industries and imposes restrictions on foreign oil and gas companies in an effort to increase government revenue and control over oil production. China, Iran, and Russia have maintained nationalized natural resources in an effort to extend their regional and international influence.

Section 10.2 Review

Remember

- Some countries have responded to globalization by adopting economic-liberalization policies, but other countries have been hesitant to fully liberalize their economics.
- States develop economic policies in response to pressure from citizens, in an effort to maintain legitimacy and prevent unrest.
- The six core countries have allowed varying degrees of privatization of natural resources.

10.3 Challenges from Globalization

Learning Targets

After reading this section, you should be able to do the following:

1. Explain how the actions of multinational corporations can threaten state sovereignty.

2. Explain how globalization weakens state sovereignty over monetary policy.

3. Explain how globalization can weaken traditional cultural values and practices.

4. Explain how technology can provide a way for communities to preserve their heritage.

Globalization poses challenges for states in maintaining their economic and political sovereignty. In addition, globalization has the potential to weaken traditional cultural values and practices.

Globalization and Sovereignty

Globalization's earliest supporters saw it as the beginning of a fundamental change in how the world would operate. Japanese scholar Kenichi Ohmae argued that globalization would result in the "end of the nation-state," claiming that the rapid flow of money, goods, and services around the world will eventually make the nation-state irrelevant. (Ohmae, 1995.) According to Ohmae, regional and international actors would eventually take over roles currently played by the state. The flow of ideas and culture would severely weaken national identity, as the internet in particular would allow people to form identities not linked to territories and their immediate local communities. All of these changes ultimately would require political responses in the form of strengthened international organizations for global governance and a new global civil society to respond to global problems with global solutions.

Ohmae argued that globalization significantly increased capital mobility so that businesses can credibly threaten to leave a country much more easily now than they could in the 1970s and 1980s. Capital's greatest weapon has been its mobility. Businesses can often threaten to move if they do not obtain the benefits they want from a state.

These textile workers are at a Chinese-owned factory in the Hawassa Industrial Park in the city of Hawassa, Ethiopia. China, once a source of labor in manufacturing, is outsourcing jobs to Africa, where labor is less expensive.

Joerg Boethling/Alamy

The state, in sharp contrast, is tied to a territory. The mobility of capital increased the power of businesses in relation to states. In trying to manage their economies, policymakers have to worry about preserving the investments they have and attracting new ones. Businesses can move relatively easily, and states compete with one another to attract new investments.

States, especially those that are small and poor, must base monetary and fiscal policy not only on domestic concerns but also on how global markets might react. States that borrow money from the International Monetary Fund must also agree to structural adjustment policies that often require them to develop budgets that raise revenues and cut expenditures. This decreases their sovereignty over economic decision making within the state.

Some political scientists question whether globalization has weakened the power of the state. Torben Iversen and David Soskice argued that the new, knowledge-based economy that arose with the communication and technology revolutions is based on particular kinds of skilled labor. (Iversen and Soskice, 2019.) This specialized skilled labor is concentrated in certain places (such as Silicon Valley) and is not very mobile. Iversen and Soskice argued that states remain powerful in establishing the policies that enhance their position in new markets, supported by educated citizens from their own countries who benefit the most from globalization.

Deindustrialization in developed countries occurred as trade policies allowed older industries to take advantage of lower production costs in developing countries and move manufacturing plants out of wealthy countries. Hundreds of thousands of workers in advanced economies, long reliant on relatively well-paying and secure jobs in such industries as automobile manufacturing and steel, faced unemployment and bleak prospects as their jobs were outsourced to countries with lower labor costs. At the same time, the tech industry boomed, creating a thriving job market for workers with strong skills in technology. Some argue that although the global economy has resulted in winners and losers within countries, states remain the driving force in the world.

In the new millennium, the scholarly consensus has moved away from Ohmae's view of globalization toward a more modest assessment of its effects on state sovereignty. Many agree that globalization has weakened the nation-state, but few believe that globalization will destroy it. Any state interested in the economic well-being of its populace must negotiate the rapidly expanding global markets and bargain with international actors to increase economic growth while protecting state sovereignty and maintaining legitimacy.

The state's bargaining power depends on its resources. Developing countries struggle to achieve economic development that can continue over the long term. If nonrenewable resources are being used quickly, development may not be sustainable. As demand for food and land increases, for instance, farmers and ranchers clear forested areas. This gives them nutrient-rich soil on which to grow crops and graze cattle, as well as valuable wood to sell on the global market. After a few years, new land must be cleared because the old land is exhausted.

The result is rapidly disappearing forests and development that is unsustainable in the long run. Deforestation also increases climate change because trees absorb and retain carbon. Farmers' and ranchers' rational response to growing global demand for agricultural products has created unsustainable development. Globalization-induced pollution of air and water and rapid use of nonrenewable resources make the goal of sustainable development challenging for many poor countries.

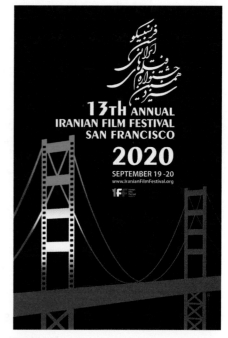

WE'RE GOING TO HAVE TO LET YOU GO...WE'VE FOUND SOMEONE IN CHINA WHO IS 45% BETTER AT BEING YOU FOR 24% LESS

This cartoon demonstrates the impact of outsourcing, when companies move jobs out of advanced economies in an effort to find replacement labor at lower costs.

Fran/Cartoonstock

Globalization and Culture

Globalization has both positive and negative cultural consequences. International marketing campaigns have created a global consumer culture. Many people have unprecedented access to new foods, goods, and services. However, mass-produced items may displace local restaurants, traditional clothing, and unique handmade items. On the other hand, artisans from throughout the world can use the internet to reach new customers. (UNESCO.) Globalization also creates new markets for movies and other forms of entertainment. For example, international film festivals, such as the Iranian Film Festival, which is held in San Francisco each year, expose moviegoers to new cultures and provide a way to share stories and cultural traditions with a broad audience.

Globalization can also impact societal norms and values. Technology offers communities a way to preserve their heritage and culture through Web sites, blogs, and podcasts. The Zapatistas in Mexico, for example, have their own radio station, and past broadcasts on a variety of topics are available on the station's Web site. However, technology spreads Western values, including individualism and an emphasis on "modernization," that may come into conflict with traditional conservative viewpoints and communal norms. Technology has the power to open educational opportunities in remote and underserved areas, but as you saw in your study of Boko Haram in Nigeria (Chapter 9), access to education may produce a backlash. The impact of globalization is complex, and it has the potential to simultaneously challenge and reinforce cultural norms and values.

Iranian Film Festival–San Francisco holds a contest each year for its poster to introduce to the U.S. public some of the best graphic artists from Iran. The winner in 2020 was Omid Khazra Jafari, who created a design based on the famous Golden Gate Bridge in San Francisco, using the colors of the Iranian flag.

Courtesy of Iranian Film Festival–San Francisco, design by Omid Khazra Jafari

Remember

- Globalization challenges state sovereignty, because businesses can threaten to move if the state does not meet their demands.
- The global market for currency weakens state sovereignty over monetary policy.
- Globalization can weaken traditional cultural values and practices, but technology can provide a way for communities to preserve their heritage.

Think

- Why are states still important international actors, despite pressures from globalization?

....

Free-Response Question: Quantitative Analysis

Five Eras of Globalization

As Measured by the Trade Openness Index, 1870–2017

Note: The Trade Openness Index measures the ratio of world exports to world GDP.

Data from Peterson Institute for International Economics and Our World in Data.

Answer A, B, C, D, and E.

A. Using the data in the graphic, identify the year with the highest level on the Trade Openness Index.

B. Using the data in the graphic, describe a pattern in the data.

C. Define globalization.

D. Using the data in the graphic and your knowledge of globalization, draw a conclusion about how the trend you described in part B impacts globalization.

E. Describe a factor, other than exports and trade, that impacts globalization.

Chapter 10 Review

Economics

AP® KEY CONCEPTS

- Globalization (p. 313)
- Foreign direct investment (FDI) (p. 314)
- Trade (p. 314)
- International capital flow (p. 314)
- Multinational corporation (p. 314)
- Rentier state (p. 315)
- International organization (p. 315)
- Import substitution industrialization (ISI) (p. 316)
- Economic-liberalization policy (p. 316)
- Structural adjustment program (p. 316)
- Supranational organization (p. 316)
- Nongovernmental organization (NGO) (p. 319)

AP® EXAM MULTIPLE-CHOICE PRACTICE QUESTIONS

1. Which of the following is a policy promoted by the World Bank and International Monetary Fund?
   A. Fuel subsidies to keep domestic prices low
   B. Reduction of tariffs and other trade barriers
   C. Import substitution industrialization policies to protect domestic manufacturing
   D. Renationalization of oil and gas to protect sources of government revenue

Questions 2 and 3 refer to the passage.

> [W]e need to do more to make the case for globalization and interconnectedness, and convey to our citizens the opportunities of collaboration and integration. Too many people in the developed world see only a loss of jobs to lower wage destinations. Too many people fear that immigration is compromising their economic well-being.
>
> Too few see clearly the pay-offs—poverty reduction, the innovation that comes from shared ideas, higher living standards from greater access to trade, and higher returns to the wealthy world from investment partnerships with developing countries.
>
> —David Lipton, "Can Globalization Still Deliver?," Speech, Stavros Niarchos Foundation Lecture, May 24, 2016. Reproduced with permission of the International Monetary Fund.

2. Which of the following is supported by the main idea of the passage?
   A. International organizations have not done enough to reduce poverty.
   B. Globalization has led to the outsourcing of jobs to lower-cost locations.
   C. There should be more education about the benefits of globalization.
   D. People in the developed world have been more negatively impacted by globalization than people in developing countries.

3. Which of the following is an implication of the argument made in the passage?
   A. Economic-liberalization policies raise living standards.
   B. Wealthy countries benefit more from free trade than poor countries.
   C. Globalization improves economic conditions, at the expense of state sovereignty.
   D. Outsourcing provides new opportunities for workers to find employment in other countries.

4. Which of the following is a supranational organization?
   A. The European Union
   B. Doctors Without Borders
   C. The Nike Corporation
   D. The North American Free Trade Agreement

5. Which of the following describes the impact of joining an international organization on state sovereignty?

 A. State sovereignty increases by joining international organizations, because states are not required to follow directives issued by international organizations.

 B. International organizations do not impact sovereignty, because states join them voluntarily.

 C. States lose political sovereignty by joining international organizations, but states retain sovereignty over economic policies.

 D. States give up some sovereignty by joining international organizations, in exchange for the benefits of membership.

6. Which of the following is an example of the influence of a supranational organization?

 A. Countries that have adopted the euro have given up the authority to make monetary policy.

 B. Boko Haram influenced authorities in northern Nigeria to adopt sharia law.

 C. Amnesty International pressures countries to end human-rights abuses and release political prisoners.

 D. Mass-produced goods have created a consumer culture and reduced demand for goods produced by local artisans.

Questions 7 and 8 refer to the graphic.

What Is Globalization?

Focus Groups Describe Relationships among Concepts and Characteristics

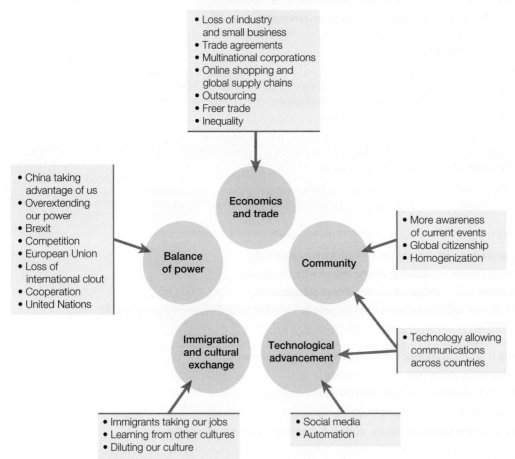

Data from Pew Research Center from focus groups conducted August 19–November 20, 2019.

7. The graphic supports which of the following statements?
   A. Globalization weakens people's sense of community.
   B. Globalization involves both cooperation and competition.
   C. New media sources spread disinformation, making people less informed.
   D. Technology allows small businesses to compete with big corporations by selling their products online.

8. Which of the following is an implication of the graphic?
   A. Most respondents have little understanding of the term *globalization*.
   B. Focus-group participants have more knowledge about globalization than people chosen at random.
   C. The people surveyed identified both positive and negative attributes of globalization.
   D. People in developed countries are more likely to have a negative view of globalization than people in developing countries.

9. Which of the following is an accurate example of a response by civil society to economic-liberalization policies?
   A. Protests against the removal of fuel subsidies in Nigeria
   B. The movement for Scottish independence
   C. The secessionist movement in Chechnya
   D. Advocacy by peasant groups in Mexico in favor of the United States–Mexico–Canada agreement

10. Which of the following accurately describes a state response to globalization?
    A. Mexico's privatization of the oil industry, after failed joint ventures with foreign companies
    B. Russia's recent decision to privatize the oil industry, in an effort to attract foreign direct investment
    C. China's censorship of the internet, in an effort to monitor and prevent criticism of the government
    D. Privatization of the National Health Service in the United Kingdom

AP® EXAM PRACTICE ARGUMENT ESSAY

Develop an argument about whether globalization has significantly reduced state sovereignty.

Use one or more of the following course concepts in your response:

- Supranational organizations
- Multinational corporations
- Nongovernmental organizations

In your response, do the following:

- Respond to the prompt with a defensible claim or thesis that establishes a line of reasoning using one or more of the provided course concepts.
- Support your claim with at least TWO pieces of specific and relevant evidence from your study of one or more course countries. The evidence should be relevant to one or more of the provided course concepts.
- Use reasoning to explain why your evidence supports your claim or thesis, using one or more of the provided course concepts.
- Respond to an opposing or alternate perspective, using refutation, concession, or rebuttal.

For a complete list of the sources of information cited in this chapter, turn to the Works Cited appendix.

11 Case Study: China

Economics

Although China's long history includes periods of disorder, the country has benefited from a strong central government and a talented bureaucracy to administer the state. The Grand Canal is an example of longstanding attention to infrastructure. Work began around 486 BCE, with major improvements and many extensions since. The Grand Canal extends 1,100 miles—the longest canal in the world—and connects Hangzhou in the east to Beijing in the north.

Keren Su/China Span/Alamy

Rebiya Kadeer: Calling Attention to the Plight of the Uyghurs

In the past ten years, China has been accused of cultural genocide of its Uyghur minority. By some accounts, 1 million, or about 10 percent of Uyghurs living in the Xinjiang region, are interned in "reeducation camps" subject to forced labor, torture, constant surveillance, and efforts to strip them of their cultural identity, in the largest mass incarceration of a minority group in the world today. In 2021, Chinese authorities called this claim the "biggest lie of the century."

The Chinese state officially recognizes fifty-five minority ethnic groups along with its Han majority, who make up 91.5 percent of the population. One of the largest minority groups is the Uyghurs, who live mainly in the northwest region known as Xinjiang, officially, the Xinjiang Uygur Autonomous Region. The Uyghurs are a Turkic ethnic group whose main language is part of the Turkic family of languages and is written using modern Arabic script. Largely Muslim, the Uyghurs embraced Islam in the tenth century and trace their history in the region back thousands of years.

Conflicts between the Chinese state and the Uyghurs have a long history. China first invaded Xinjiang two thousand years ago, but it was not until the mid-eighteenth century that the region was brought under Chinese rule. In the early and mid-twentieth century, the region had two short periods of secession and independence and has continued to wage on-again, off-again struggles over autonomy and identity. The Uyghurs do not consider themselves Chinese and even reject the name Xinjiang for their region. Instead, they refer to the region as East Turkestan. (Dillon.)

Chinese authorities have viewed Uyghur demands for autonomy as a threat to the nation's sovereignty. The Chinese blame the conflict on "three evils": separatism, religious extremism, and terrorism. If left unchecked, Chinese authorities believe, China could follow the path of the former Soviet Union where non-Russian republics achieved independence.

China also has strategic interests in Xinjiang. Several key elements of the Belt and Road Initiative, a major global infrastructure development strategy undertaken by the Chinese government, run through the region. In addition, Xinjiang is rich in natural resources. It contains China's largest reserves of coal and natural gas. It also produces more than 45 percent of the world's supply of polysilicon, a key refined material that makes up 95 percent of solar panels. Chinese companies account for about 80 percent of worldwide production of solar panels.

Chinese authorities have refused international requests to allow outside observers to visit Xinjiang. Reports of the harsh treatment of the Uyghurs have included the destruction of mosques and cemeteries, bans on religious practices, forced labor, placing officials to live in the homes of Uyghur families, forced marriages of Uyghur women to Han Chinese men, forced sterilization, and torture. (Khatchadourian.) The expansion of so-called reeducation camps has been justified as necessary to teach Mandarin, Chinese laws and customs, and vocational skills. Another stated goal of the Chinese government in running the reeducation camps is to prevent the spread of extremist ideas that contribute to terrorism. Human-rights organizations have countered that the only "crime" Uyghurs have committed is being Muslim. (Human Rights Watch.)

China's treatment of the Uyghurs has been called genocide. International law defines genocide as acts "committed with intent to destroy, in whole or in part, a national, ethnical, racial or religious group, as such." China's actions, while clearly a violation of human rights, may not qualify as genocide because the government's intent is unclear. Is it to turn

Rebiya Kadeer, a Uyghur activist, and the Dalai Lama, an exiled Tibetan monk and spiritual leader. Both of them seek independence for their regions and publicize China's human-rights abuses against some ethnic minorities.

Michal Cizek/AFP/Getty Images

the Uyghurs into patriotic Chinese citizens who conform to the official atheist doctrine, society, and customs of the Han Chinese majority, or is it to destroy them as an ethnic and religious group? (Flaherty.)

Rebiya Kadeer is the former president of the World Uyghur Congress, an exile group that seeks to represent the Uyghurs. She was once the richest woman, and among the ten richest people, in China. Born in 1946, Kadeer comes from a long line of those who fought to free themselves from foreign domination, including her grandfather and father.

Seeking a way out of desperate poverty, she married at fifteen to a man of twenty-seven but refused to wear his wedding ring. At age thirty-one, after giving birth to six children, she divorced him. She showed her entrepreneurial skill while married to her first husband when she sewed clothes that were sold on the black market. Once divorced, she sought ways to support herself and her children by at first washing clothes and then by trading goods such as lamb hides, timber, and fabric from one location to another.

She then built a bazaar for others to sell their wares, and eventually, she built a seven-story department store that became a regional commercial hub. It was the beginning of her focus on real estate. With each step, she sought to empower the lives of Uyghur women through her business dealings and extensive philanthropy.

During the 1990s, Kadeer continued to travel and gain prominence in Xinjiang and in greater China. She was seen by Chinese authorities as a model of Uyghur success and given prominent positions to highlight how women and minorities were treated. In 1992, she was elected to the National People's Congress, officially China's chief legislative body. In 1995, she was one of China's delegates to the U.N. World Conference on Women held in Beijing. As she gained more prominence, she tried to bring attention to the poverty and harassment facing the Uyghurs.

In 1996, as Chinese authorities were arresting scholars of Uyghur history, Kadeer worried that her husband, a university professor who had already spent time in jail, was in jeopardy. Under the pretense of going on a vacation, they flew to the United States. Upon their arrival, she told him that for his safety, he could not return to China with her. He subsequently found employment with the U.S.-based Radio Free Asia and Voice of America as a pro-independence broadcaster.

Kadeer continued to speak out about the treatment of the Uyghurs even in speeches before the National People's Congress with China's president present. In 1997, her passport was revoked, and she was stripped of her position in the National People's Congress. In 1999, when she was to meet with researchers from the U.S. Congressional Research Service to complain about political prisoners in Xinjiang, she was arrested for endangering state security by passing state secrets to foreigners. All she had with her were newspaper clippings. In early 2000, after a fifteen-minute trial, she was sentenced to eight years in jail.

Bowing to international diplomatic pressure, in 2005, with eighteen months left on her sentence, China released her into the custody of the U.S. Department of State. Once in the United States, Kadeer continued to advocate Uyghur independence, and from 2006 to 2017, she was the president of the World Uyghur Congress. During that time, she testified

BY THE NUMBERS	CHINA
Land area	9,326,410 sq. km
Population	1,397,897,720 (July 2021 est.)
Urban population	61.4% (2020)
Life expectancy	Male 74.23 Female 78.62 (2021 est.)
Literacy rate	Male 98.5% Female 95.2% (2018)
HDI	0.761 (2020)
HDI ranking	85/189 (2020)
GDP	$14,860,775,000,000 (2020)
GDP ranking	2/195 (2020)
GDP per capita	$10,500 (2020)
Internet users	54.3% (2018)
Internet users ranking	1/229 (2018)
Gini index (coefficient)	38.2 (2019)
Freedom House rating	Not free (2020)
Corruption Perceptions ranking	66/180 (2021)
Fragile States Index classification	Warning (2020)

Data from *CIA World Factbook*, World Bank, Freedom House, Transparency International, Fragile States Index.

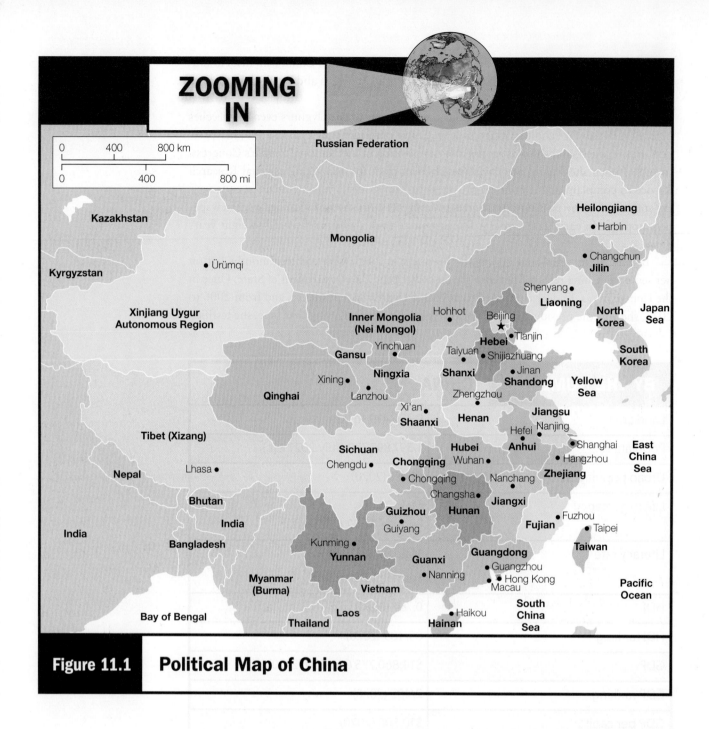

ZOOMING IN

Russian Federation

Kazakhstan

Kyrgyzstan

Mongolia

Ürümqi

Xinjiang Uygur
Autonomous Region

Inner Mongolia
(Nei Mongol)

Hohhot

Heilongjiang

• Harbin

• Changchun
Jilin

Shenyang •

Liaoning

Beijing ★
• Tianjin

North
Korea

Japan
Sea

South
Korea

Yinchuan

Gansu

Hebei

Ningxia

Taiyuan

• Shijiazhuang

Xining •

Qinghai

Lanzhou •

Xi'an •

Shaanxi

Zhengzhou •

Henan

Jinan •

Shandong

Yellow
Sea

Jiangsu

Hefei • Nanjing

Shanghai

East
China
Sea

Tibet (Xizang)

Nepal

Lhasa •

Bhutan

India

Bangladesh

Sichuan

Chengdu •

Chongqing

• Chongqing

Hubei

Wuhan •

Anhui

Hangzhou

Zhejiang

Changsha •

Jiangxi

Nanchang •

Hunan

Guizhou

Guiyang •

Kunming •

Yunnan

Myanmar
(Burma)

India

Vietnam

Bay of Bengal

Thailand

Laos

Guanxi

• Nanning

Fujian

Fuzhou

• Taipei

Taiwan

Guangdong

• Guangzhou

Hong Kong
Macau

Pacific
Ocean

• Haikou

Hainan

South
China
Sea

0   400   800 km
0   400   800 mi

Figure 11.1 | **Political Map of China**

before a U.S. congressional committee and met with President George W. Bush to highlight the longstanding effort by the Chinese to harass, torture, and dilute the cultural identity of the Uyghur people. In her 2009 autobiography, she wrote:

> For as long as I can remember, Uyghur people have been tortured and subjugated by foreign powers. We have always been menaced by persecution and murder. Truly, I come from a land that has been fighting for its independence and freedom for a long time—today more than ever before. Until now, however, the world has little known about the Uyghur nation. I speak and fight for the approximately twenty million Uyghurs worldwide, from whom almost all forms of cultural, economic, and religious autonomy have been stripped away. I want to be the mother of all Uyghurs, the medicine for their ills, the cloth with which they dry their tears, and the cloak to protect them from the rain. My name is Rebiya Kadeer. (Kadeer, 4.)

CHAPTER 11 • Case Study: China

Rebiya Kadeer's story, and the treatment of the Uyghurs, illustrate the power of China's authoritarian state in suppressing dissent to maintain the power of the Han majority and prevent perceived threats to state sovereignty.

The last two countries you will study are China and Iran. Both are authoritarian and unitary states. Both countries have **dual rule**, which means that the state is run by two different authorities—in China's case, both the government and the Chinese Communist Party administer the state. China is an interesting case study, because it is an economic powerhouse that liberalized its economy without democratizing its political system.

Dual rule
A system in which two different groups with authority run a state.

11.1 Sources of Power and Authority

Learning Targets

After reading this section, you should be able to do the following:

1. Describe the events that led to Mao Zedong's leadership of China and describe the government's policies during the Mao era.

2. Describe China's gradual shift away from a command economy and its adoption of market reforms.

3. Explain how the Chinese regime has resisted democratization.

4. Describe China's unitary state.

5. Describe the basis for the legitimacy of China's regime and describe challenges to legitimacy.

China has a long history of authoritarian government. The regime's legitimacy is based on tradition, longstanding rule by the Chinese Communist Party, and economic growth that has lifted millions of Chinese citizens out of poverty.

A Brief History of China

China is one of the oldest countries in the world, with a history that spans five thousand years. The Chinese empire was united in 221 BCE and "built a centralized, merit-based bureaucracy that was able to register its population, levy uniform taxes, control the military, and regulate society some eighteen hundred years before a similar state was to emerge in Europe." (Fukuyama, 2014, 354.) While it was not a fully modern state, China developed some elements of a modern state very early.

The empire's demise began in the mid-nineteenth century. While trade with the outside world had existed for a long time, the United States and European powers demanded greater access to Chinese markets, leading to the Opium Wars from 1839 to 1860 that gave Western powers sovereignty over key areas of the country.

China, which had been one of the strongest states in the world, was dramatically weakened. Foreign domination and economic stagnation produced growing discontent. The peasantry, which constituted the great majority of the population, had longstanding grievances and a tradition of revolting against local landlords who became too repressive. During the late nineteenth and early twentieth centuries, the peasantry faced greater impoverishment as the empire declined and lost control of much of its territory to Japanese and Western interests. A younger generation of intellectuals increasingly questioned the legitimacy of the empire. And the ruling dynasty failed to deliver on its promises to the people.

Sun Yat-sen, a physician who had received some of his schooling in Hawaii, started a nationalist movement that opposed the imperial Chinese regime. Young military leaders in the provinces shared these sentiments and led the 1911 rebellion that eventually created Sun Yat-sen's nationalist-led Republic of China. By 1911, military uprisings signaled the empire's imminent collapse, and on January 1, 1912, the last emperor abdicated. The Republic of China was established.

The new nationalist government quickly became a dictatorship after Sun Yat-sen's resignation from the presidency, ushering in more than a decade of chaos and war. Warlords gained control of various parts of the country as the Chinese state's sovereignty and territorial control crumbled.

In the 1920s, the nationalists slowly regained control with the help of an alliance with a new political force, the **Chinese Communist Party (CCP)**. Once fully back in power, the nationalists turned against the Communists. The state's sovereignty, however, was seriously compromised by warlords, by continuous threats of civil war with the CCP, and by Japanese invasion in 1937. The nationalists ruled a very weak state.

Inspired by *The Communist Manifesto*, written by Karl Marx and Friedrich Engels, Mao Zedong created a new version of communist philosophy by arguing that a revolution could be led by peasants, instead of industrial workers, as Marx had envisioned. **Communism** is an ideology that advocates state ownership of all property, with the government exercising complete control over the economy.

Starting in 1927, the nationalists broke the alliance with the communists and turned against them. Nationalist troops launched military campaigns against the communists, and the communists suffered heavy losses. Mao fought back and led an uprising in China's southeast provinces of Hunan and Jiangxi, which was put down by the government. Following this initial defeat, Mao began assembling a "Red Army" of Chinese workers and peasants who began an intermittent civil war with the government.

In 1934–1935, Mao led the famous Long March, a six-thousand-mile trek by the Red Army. The CCP took control over a section of Shaanxi Province in the northwest and began creating a model of its future communist regime. For the first time in a century, peasants saw their situation in life at least stabilize, if not improve. They became the backbone of support for the Communist Party. Mao also built up the party, welcoming intellectuals, elites, and peasants. An estimated 85,000 troops began the march, and about 8,000 remained at the end of the journey. (History Channel.)

Japan invaded China in 1937, dividing the country's territory and sovereignty between the CCP, the nationalist government, and Japan. The communists' guerrilla tactics proved effective against the Japanese occupiers during World War II as well as popular with the Chinese public. The communists gained a reputation as defenders of the beleaguered nation. After the Japanese withdrawal at the end of World War II, a communist revolution led by Mao triumphed in 1949, despite U.S. military support for the nationalists, who fled to the island of Taiwan and formed a government there.

The communist revolution in China in 1949 resulted from discontent among the peasants, the creation of the Communist Party that could mobilize popular discontent,

---

Chinese Communist Party (CCP)
The political party that has ruled China from 1949 to the present.

Communism
An ideology that advocates state ownership of all property, with the government exercising complete control over the economy.

and an extremely weak state. Communist victory ushered in a new state that completely changed Chinese society—a full revolution had occurred at the grassroots level. It resulted in an authoritarian state. Mao's government quickly eliminated people who had supported the revolution but were not communists, along with people who were communists but opposed Mao's policies. The People's Republic of China became a dictatorship.

Communist rule created the first modern Chinese state, but at a big cost to citizens. The new government instituted large-scale campaigns against corruption, opium use, and other socially harmful practices, but at the cost of human rights. It also took control of the economy. The state seized land in rural areas and created collective farms. China created a Soviet-style command economy with a massive bureaucracy, which attempted to industrialize the world's largest agrarian society through a program called the Great Leap Forward. The result was a famine, which killed at least 20 million people, and political purges that sent many others to "re-education camps," prison, or execution.

During the Cultural Revolution from 1966 to 1976, Mao mobilized his followers against what he saw as entrenched bureaucrats in his own party and state, causing widespread political uncertainty, violence, repression, and destruction of property (including priceless historical artifacts) as well as economic and social dislocation.

The Cultural Revolution ended with Mao's death in 1976. Deng Xiaoping, one of Mao's earliest comrades, who had been removed from power during the Cultural Revolution, established his supremacy over the party and state in 1979. Deng initiated a series of slow but ultimately sweeping reforms that reduced the state's direct control of the economy. He also began to reestablish organized control by the party over the state and enact more uniform laws to govern the country.

This propaganda poster is entitled Long Live the Red Sun of the World's People, Chairman Mao, written in Chinese and Mongol characters. The poster portrays Mao's extraordinary influence over China's government, economy, and culture. The Little Red Book of Mao's sayings was required reading in schools.

David Pollack/Corbis Historical/Getty Images

These reforms continue today, a four-decade process of introducing a market economy and stronger state institutions that is still not complete. The result has been the fastest economic growth in the world that has moved millions of Chinese out of poverty, spurred a huge exodus from rural areas to cities, and widened the income gap.

Resistance to Democratization

While rebuilding a modern bureaucracy, Deng and his successors have resisted efforts to make China freer and more democratic. The Chinese state still claims to be communist, and some of its legitimacy rests on the long history of rule by the CCP. However, China has pursued "market socialism," which means economic-liberalization policies that are at odds with traditional communist theory.

A key to the state's legitimacy is its ability to modernize the economy and provide wealth. Thus, China is a modernizing authoritarian regime. Many observers see a fundamental contradiction between allowing economic freedoms and denying political ones. They argue that the CCP will eventually have to allow much greater political freedom. Others argue that economic reform does not necessarily lead to political reform and that the move to the market strengthened China's authoritarian state. In addition, the Chinese state has used military force against its citizens to maintain the regime.

The most famous case is the Tiananmen Square protest in 1989. The protest was a gathering to memorialize the death of Hu Yaobang, a reform-oriented elite. Over the course of a week, small student demonstrations grew into daily protests by upward of 200,000 students demanding government accountability, release of jailed dissidents, and freedom of the press. Although the protesters' goals evolved over time, it is an overstatement to characterize the Tiananmen Square protests as "pro-democracy." Protesters did not demand fully competitive electoral democracy.

After making some minor concessions, the government declared martial law in the city and called in the army. At least a million citizens poured into the streets to try to prevent the army from entering the square, without success. In the middle of the night, the army opened fire on the remaining dissidents, killing between 1,000 and 3,000 students and civilians. Worldwide condemnation followed, but the regime survived.

Another large-scale protest against the regime occurred in 2019, when opposition to a controversial extradition law led to months of mobilization and demonstrations in Hong Kong, including a forced shutdown of the airport for two days. Hong Kong retained its own political and legal systems, including the right to protest and freedom of the press and speech, when the British returned it to China's jurisdiction in 1997. Those rights were supposed to be guaranteed for fifty years after the transfer, under a principle commonly known as "one country, two systems."

Many Hong Kong residents believe the government in Beijing is increasingly encroaching on those civil liberties. As protests continued and escalated throughout the summer of 2019, Beijing faced a grave dilemma over how much it should tolerate them and whether to use force as it had in Tiananmen Square to quell them. The government increasingly denounced the protesters as foreign-backed terrorists and criminals and asserted in August 2019 that it would declare a state of emergency if unrest continued, but it did not take such drastic action.

Under the latest general secretary of the CCP and president of the republic, Xi Jinping, the regime has restricted freedoms further and intervened in the economy more in response to declining growth. This, along with the social and environmental effects of extremely rapid economic growth, widespread corruption, and growing inequality, are major weaknesses facing China's authoritarian state today.

The Unitary State

Like the United Kingdom and Iran, China is a unitary state, with power concentrated at the national level. Unitary states often result in more uniform policies throughout the country and a more efficient policymaking process than federal systems. China is divided into subgovernments, including autonomous regions, prefectures, prefecture-level cities, counties, and administrative divisions called banners. Most of China's major ethnic minorities are geographically concentrated in the five autonomous regions.

People's congresses within each subgovernment are granted some authority over laws and policies affecting local communities. Regional governments can ask for permission to tailor national policies to meet local needs, under the guidance of the national government. Local government can administer programs related to education, culture, and public health and request technical assistance from the state.

Direct, competitive elections are held to select the leaders of townships and villages. More than one candidate may be allowed to run for office, and candidates may have different policy platforms, but they may not challenge CCP rule in China's one-party state. Local authorities have some limited policymaking ability, yet in contrast to a federal system, their powers are not guaranteed. The Chinese state is more centralized that the other countries you have studied so far.

Legitimacy and Challenges to the State

Much of China's legitimacy rests on the country's economic growth. China's transition to a market economy created much greater inequality than in the past, and the income gap between urban areas and poor rural areas has widened. Nevertheless, China's economic reforms benefited many segments of society. The regime has earned the support of entrepreneurs and professionals, many of whom have gained great wealth under market reforms. In addition, workers in the private sector and even workers in the declining state-owned sector, who still have some social welfare protections from the state, fear that they would be worse off if the ruling party were no longer in power.

In 2016, overall satisfaction with the central government was high, with 95 percent of those surveyed reporting that they were "highly satisfied" or "somewhat satisfied" with the national government. At the same time, satisfaction with local governments was much lower, with slightly over 11 percent being "highly satisfied." (Saich, 2016.)

The Chinese government is wary of influences that might undermine its legitimacy. In 2013, Xi Jinping started a campaign within the party to warn members about key ideas that would undermine the party's grip on power. At the top of the list were "constitutional democracy" and "universal human rights." The current leadership has no intention of yielding to demands for democracy anytime soon, and outside Hong Kong, there seems to be little demand from Chinese citizens for democratic reforms.

One of the biggest threats to the CCP is corruption. The government's legitimacy is now heavily based on its economic performance, which corruption directly damages. Dickson conducted an extensive public opinion survey that found that rising personal incomes increased the regime's popular support, while personal experiences with corruption lowered it. (Dickson, 2016.)

The party leadership demands that local officials achieve economic growth while maintaining social stability. In the world's most populated country, however, much authority is left in the hands of local party leaders. As long as they deliver on the key items of growth and stability, they are likely to retain their positions. They are also free to pursue their own interests. This has produced corruption and the personalization of power in the hands of local leaders.

The party's Central Commission for Discipline Inspection is charged with ferreting out corruption within the party, and the Chinese leadership is emphasizing eradication of corruption more strongly than in the past. President Xi launched a massive anticorruption crusade in 2013, which reached high into the ruling elite and helped him purge potential opponents. By 2016, an estimated 300,000 people had faced corruption charges, including close to 150 high-level office holders.

The very top leadership itself had avoided accountability until the case of Bo Xilai, a provincial party secretary and a rising star in the party. In 2012, one of Bo's top aides made accusations of major corruption, and Bo's wife was implicated in a murder that Bo may have been trying to cover up. His very public removal from office exposed high-level intrigue and corruption in the party unlike anything the country had ever witnessed.

The anticorruption drive has made Xi very popular with average citizens. The anticorruption efforts seem to be having some effect, too. In 1995, Transparency International ranked China as the fourth most corrupt country in the world, but by 2020, it was ranked eightieth, in the middle of the global spectrum. Despite the country's progress, corruption, especially at the local level, reduces citizens' trust in government and poses a challenge to state legitimacy.

Section 11.1 Review

Each section's main ideas are reflected in the Learning Targets. By reviewing after each section, you should be able to

Remember the key points,

Know terms that are central to the topic, and

Think critically about what you have learned.

Remember

- Since Mao Zedong became the leader of China in 1949, the state has been run by the Chinese Communist Party.
- After Mao's death, China gradually shifted away from a command economy and adopted market reforms.
- Although China has liberalized its economy, it has not democratized its political system.
- China is a unitary state, although regional governments are given some limited autonomy.
- Most of China's ethnic minorities are concentrated in five autonomous regions.
- Much of China's legitimacy is based on economic performance, although corruption undermines state legitimacy.

Know

- *Dual rule:* a system in which two different groups with authority run a state. (p. 337)
- *Chinese Communist Party (CCP):* the political party that has ruled China from 1949 to the present. (p. 338)

- *Communism:* an ideology that advocates state ownership of all property, with the government exercising complete control over the economy. (p. 338)

Think

- Will market reforms in China eventually lead to democratization? Why or why not?
- Is corruption at the local level or at the national level more damaging to the legitimacy of the state?

Free-Response Question: Quantitative Analysis

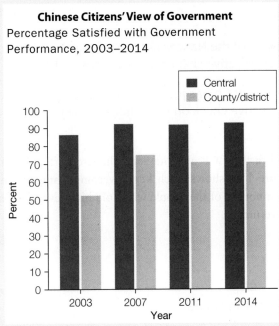

Chinese Citizens' View of Government
Percentage Satisfied with Government
Performance, 2003–2014

Data from surveys by Anthony Saich, Harvard Kennedy School.

Answer A, B, C, D, and E.

A. Using the data in the bar chart, identify the year in which Chinese citizens had the lowest level of satisfaction with county/district government.

B. Using the data in the bar chart, compare the levels of satisfaction among Chinese citizens with the central government and county/district governments.

C. Define corruption.

D. Using the data in the bar chart and your knowledge of AP® Comparative Government and Politics, draw a conclusion about how corruption impacts citizen satisfaction with government.

E. Explain how a factor, other than corruption, impacts citizen satisfaction with government.

11.2 Institutions of Government

Learning Targets

After reading this section, you should be able to do the following:

1. Explain how China is ruled by both the CCP and the formal institutions of government.

2. Describe the structure of the CCP.

3. Describe the structure of the government.

4. Describe the role of the National People's Congress and explain why it does not serve as an effective check on the actions of the CCP.

5. Describe the role of China's judiciary and explain why the judiciary does not serve as an effective check on the actions of the CCP.

China is ruled by both the CCP and officials who are part of the formal structure of government. As Figure 11.2 shows, each key governing institution has a parallel party institution. Many, but not all, of the people who hold high-level positions in the CCP also hold positions in government.

FIGURE 11.2

Parallel Institutions of Party and Government in China

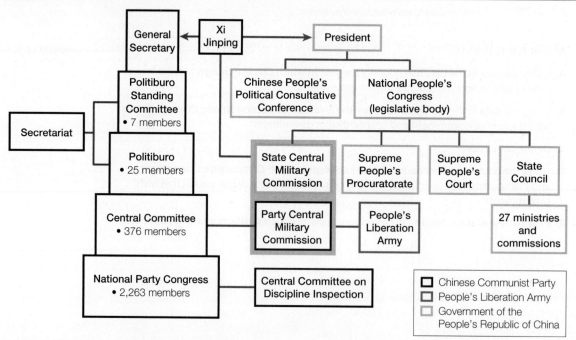

Note: Party structures are depicted as a pyramid. The structure of government is shown as a flow chart.

Organization of the Chinese Communist Party

The CCP is the most important authority in China. Constitutionally, the National Party Congress is the official decision-making body of the party. The **National Party Congress** is elected by provincial and local party congresses, which are elected by citizens who are members of the CCP.

Candidates for the National Party Congress are selected by high-level officials within the CCP, ensuring that they will pass the policies put forth by the elite within the party. The Central Committee elected at each Party Congress routinely includes about 60 percent new members, with each Party Congress seeing a significant shift toward younger and more highly educated members. (Shambaugh, 2008, 153.)

The Party Congress, on its surface, works uniformly, with nearly unanimous votes on every issue and leader. But behind the scenes, key leaders jockey to get their people into top positions. Xi Jinping's rise to power was a carefully orchestrated compromise between the two previous leaders and their followers. Xi's vice president is from an opposing faction. Political elites engage in bargaining and compromise to maintain party unity.

Party congresses happen once every five years. In November 2012, the Party Congress selected Xi Jinping as the general secretary of the party and head of the party military commission. He was appointed president of the country a few months later. Xi's rise to the top was not a surprise. The 2007 Party Congress had clearly signaled Xi's position as the next leader by appointing him vice president.

The internal process for selecting China's leader is not transparent, but it has been fairly predictable since the 1990s. Presidents Jiang Zemin and Hu Jintao were chosen by Deng. Xi broke with past precedent by not revealing his successor at the 2017 Party Congress, which also amended the constitution to remove presidential term limits, fueling speculation that Xi might try to hold power longer than the two terms that have become the norm.

Real power lies in the party's **Politburo** and even more so in a smaller subgroup—the **Politburo Standing Committee (PSC)**. (Refer to Figure 11.2 and its parallel structures.) The PSC sets the legislative agenda and develops a program of legislation when the legislature is not in session, and it supervises elections for the legislature. Although it is not part of the judiciary, the PSC has the authority to interpret laws and the constitution. While the workings of the Politburo and the PSC are secret, reports suggest that a great deal of open discussion occurs within these highest levels of power, and their members represent all of the important factions among the top elite. Factions within the elite limit one another's power as the top leaders in the country.

At the top of the party is the **general secretary**, Xi Jinping, who is also China's president. The general secretary is the head of China's Central Military Commission, making him the most powerful person in China. The military has long been a crucial factor in Chinese politics but also has been subordinate to the civilian leadership of the party. The vast majority of the army—and certainly all of its top leaders—are ruling party members, trained to support the party and its ideals.

No military leaders have been in the top organs of the country's leadership since the 1990s. While the military has channels to let its voice be heard, it does so mainly in areas of direct relevance to it such as defense and foreign policy. The People's Liberation Army (PLA) remains an important faction behind the scenes, and its purpose is to protect the CCP. The top leadership controls the PLA, eliminating a potential threat to the survival of the CCP and the state that is common in authoritarian regimes.

As mentioned earlier, both the party and the government rule China. In 2020, CCP membership stood at about 92 million, which is about 6.5 percent of China's population.

National Party Congress
A body within the CCP that acts as a legislature, passing policies put forth by the party elite.

Politburo
A powerful body of elite policymakers within the CCP.

Politburo Standing Committee
A subgroup of the Politburo, consisting of the most powerful people in the CCP.

General secretary
The head of the CCP and the most powerful individual in China.

State Council
The cabinet that leads the formal bureaucracy in China.

National People's Congress
China's unicameral legislature.

We now turn our attention away from the structure of the CCP to discuss the structure of government, which is shown on the right side of Figure 11.2 on page 344.

The Executive

Under the formal structure of government, the executive consists of a president and a premier. The premier is the head of government and has the power to oversee the actions of the **State Council**, which is the cabinet that leads the formal bureaucracy.

Xi Jinping, the general secretary of the CCP, also serves as president. Although the general secretary of the CCP and the president of the country are two different positions, both have been filled by a single individual since 1993, which consolidates executive power. As president, Xi is the head of state and has the power to appoint and dismiss the premier of the legislature. The president also has the power to propose a program of legislation, dismiss ministers of the State Council, grant pardons, and declare a state of emergency. The president is the chief diplomat, and he has the power to sign treaties.

The Legislature

The **National People's Congress (NPC)** is China's unicameral legislature. Similar to the National Party Congress, members of the legislature are not directly elected. They are chosen from municipal, regional, and provincial people's congresses. The National People's Congress meets once a year for about two weeks. In 2018, 2,980 deputies were elected to sit in the National People's Congress.

Under the constitution, the National People's Congress is the most powerful government body in China. However, in reality, the NPC is a "rubber stamp" body that confirms office holders and approves legislation drafted by the Standing Committee.

On rare occasions, the NPC has exercised some independence and delayed legislation. This occurred in 1999, when the legislature was presented with an unpopular fuel tax. (BBC, 2012.) Sometimes, the NPC pushes for substantial changes in bills before voting on them. This occurred in 2016, when the NPC was presented with a law regulating NGOs. A significantly revised law was passed after some behind-the-scenes wrangling. (NPC Observer.) Nevertheless, because the CCP controls candidates for delegate positions in the NPC, the legislature does not serve as an effective check on the actions of the executive and the party.

The Judiciary

The judiciary in China, and especially the civil system, has become institutionalized—which means it has established a uniform set of rules by which it operates. However, the Chinese legal system does not protect basic human rights, and rule of law is weak. The Supreme People's Court, the country's highest court, has the right to interpret the law and the constitution but not to overturn decisions of the National People's Congress.

In China's criminal system, defendants lack many due process rights. People convicted of crimes face harsh punishments, including forced labor and the imposition of the death penalty for a wide variety of offenses, ranging from murder and treason to robbery and bribery. (China Justice Observer.) Amnesty International ranks China as the world's leader in executions, and 2016 estimates put China's executions at more than 1,000 a year. (Amnesty International.) China's most common methods of execution are firing squads and lethal injections, which are administered by mobile death vans. (Micklethwaite.)

A woman on a bicycle rides near a police van, passing a billboard that advocates China's rule by law.

AP Images/Andy Wong

There have been some limited reforms to China's criminal justice system. A 1996 law provides criminal defendants with some due process rights, including the right to an attorney during investigations and trials, except in cases involving "state secrets." Trials are now supposed to be open to the public, and most are, but the government still prevents the public from attending high-profile political cases. The trial of the popular regional leader Bo Xilai on corruption charges in 2013 was not open to the public but included the release of edited transcripts. Police are not required to read suspects their rights, and there is no rule prohibiting admission of evidence obtained through police misconduct. (Chu, 2000.) Overall, defendants lack significant due process protections, and the Chinese criminal system lacks rule of law.

China's civil court system was modernized in the late 1980s, partly due to market reforms. A 1989 reform of administrative law increased citizens' ability to take local government agencies to court for not doing their jobs properly. A broad survey found rapidly growing use of and trust in courts among Chinese citizens in the new millennium, especially for handling civil disputes. (Landry, 2008.)

By the early 2000s, the courts became overwhelmed, and the central government issued an order to reduce the number of cases accepted. Therefore, Chinese citizens with complaints against local government took petitions directly to authorities rather than trying to sue. In response, the Supreme Court announced a five-year plan in 2014 to improve court efficiency. The number of court cases since has increased.

One reason for reform of China's civil courts is the desire to attract foreign investors. A study of the civil-court system argued that stronger courts and rule of law exist mainly so that civil and economic law can meet the demands of businesses and attract foreign investors. (Wong, 2013.) In 2017, reforms were enacted to increase the independence of trial judges, who no longer have to submit their decisions to their superiors before rendering a judgment. (Wang, 2020.)

Despite some reforms in both the criminal and civil court systems, China's judiciary is not independent. In 2017, Chief Justice Zhou Qiang told a gathering of high-ranking court officials, "Bare your swords towards false western ideals like judicial independence," warning against democratization and checks and balances. (Reuters, 2017.) He reminded judges that reforms were meant to rein in local officials and strengthen the rule of the CCP. (Reuters, 2017.) China's courts have held secret trials of human-rights activists, including prominent lawyer Wang Quanzhang. (Lum, 2019.) Lack of transparency in government is one of the reasons China is classified as an authoritarian state.

Section 11.2 Review

Remember

- China is ruled by both the Chinese Communist Party and the formal institutions of government.
- The Politburo Standing Committee of the CCP is made up of the most powerful individuals in China.
- The general secretary is the leader of the CCP and the most powerful individual in China.
- The executive in China consists of a president, who serves as head of state, and a premier, who serves as head of government.
- The National People's Congress is formally the most powerful governing body in China, but it is a rubber-stamp institution that approves policies presented to it by the CCP.
- The criminal justice system in China lacks rule of law, but the civil court system has been institutionalized.
- China's judiciary is not independent and does not serve as an effective check on the actions of the CCP.

Know

- *National Party Congress:* a body within the CCP that acts as a legislature, passing policies put forth by the party elite. (p. 345)
- *Politburo:* a powerful body of elite policymakers within the CCP. (p. 345)
- *Politburo Standing Committee:* a subgroup of the Politburo, consisting of the most powerful people in the CCP. (p. 345)
- *General secretary:* the head of the CCP and the most powerful individual in China. (p. 345)
- *State Council:* the cabinet that leads the formal bureaucracy in China. (p. 346)
- *National People's Congress:* China's unicameral legislature. (p. 346)

Think

- What are the advantages and disadvantages of a dual rule system in the policymaking process?

Free-Response Question: Comparative Analysis

Compare the level of judicial independence in two different AP® Comparative Government and Politics course countries. In your response, you should do the following:

A. Define judicial independence.

B. Describe the level of judicial independence in two different AP® Comparative Government and Politics course countries.

C. Explain why each of the two AP® Comparative Government and Politics course countries described in part B protects or restricts judicial independence.

11.3 Electoral System, Political Parties, and Civil Society

Learning Targets

After reading this section, you should be able to do the following:

1. Describe one-party rule by the CCP in China.

2. Describe the process for selecting high-ranking officials in the government and the CCP.

3. Explain how the Chinese government limits civil society.

China is a **one-party state**, ruled by the CCP, which is the only political party allowed to control the government. Officials at the national level are selected indirectly by local and regional congresses. Civil society is closely monitored by the state.

One-party state
A country where only one party is allowed to control the government.

Elections

Elections for national leaders of both the party and the government are indirect, and the CCP is the only party allowed to control government. The general secretary of the CCP is chosen by the National Party Congress, based on a recommendation of the Standing Committee. Members of the National Party Congress are selected by party members at local and regional congresses. The president is chosen by the National People's Congress in a similar process. The National People's Congress approves of the presidential candidate selected by the party elite. Members of the National People's Congress are chosen by local and regional government bodies.

Changes to the electoral system for local-level congresses have provided opportunities for voter participation and representation within the strict confines of the ruling party. China holds direct elections for the most local level of government—village committees. Candidates can be nominated by the party, other local organizations, or any group of ten citizens. Sometimes, local officials severely limit the level of competition.

Estimates are that the elections are fairly competitive in about half of the country. Hundreds of thousands of candidates have run in village elections since 1999, and 48 percent of elected village officials are not CCP members. (Landry, Davis, and Wang, 2010, 766.) One survey in the late 1990s found that more than half of voters had attended a campaign event, and nearly 20 percent had participated in nominating a candidate. (Shi, 2006, 365.)

Melanie Manion (2015) surveyed members of local congresses and voters and concluded that while local congresses remain firmly under the control of the CCP, local representatives are able to provide the party with knowledge of local concerns. (Manion, 2015.) Local party leaders are responsive to the concerns of their constituents because their career advancement requires maintaining social stability. Voters attempt to choose candidates they think will honestly represent local interests and help bring government investment to the area. The CCP uses local elections to provide it with information about local concerns, address those concerns, and maintain legitimacy.

> **AP® TIP**
>
> It's important to know the difference between a one-party state and a single-party dominant state. In a one-party state, like China, only one party is allowed to control the government, although smaller, state-sponsored parties are allowed to exist. In a single-party dominant state, like Russia, multiple parties exist, but the same party dominates the executive branch and wins most of the seats in the legislature.

Citizens in China elect local officials. This election is for delegates to a local people's congress. People do not have the ability to directly elect high-ranking government officials, who are selected from among the elite within the CCP.

Chen Fuping/VCG/Getty Images

Political Parties

The CCP has been in power since 1949. The government has sanctioned eight other political parties, such as the Chinese Peasants' and Workers' Democratic Party. However, these parties are not allowed to run candidates for national office or to control the government. In practice, China's state-endorsed parties act as interest groups representing specific interests and consulting with the government. Despite the formal existence of other parties, China is classified as a one-party state, because the CCP has complete control over the state.

The CCP has changed profoundly since Mao's death in 1976. Although communist in name, China has become a modernizing authoritarian regime by successfully encouraging state-led, capitalist development while maintaining a firm one-party hold on political power.

This is a far cry from the early days of the regime. Communist rule under Mao developed into a full-blown personality cult. CCP membership was also the sole road ambitious citizens could travel to political, social, or economic success. Yet fewer than 10 percent of citizens were party members. With the complete ban on any independent organizations, citizens had little ability to demand changes in government policy or to petition the government about issues of concern.

China has not permitted an open opposition party, but it has expanded participation within the ruling party. Membership in the CCP has changed, as the growing market economy has produced new elites. After the country's opening to the world market, farmers' and workers' share of party membership dropped from 63 percent in 1994 to 44 percent in 2003. Large numbers of scientists, engineers, and other intellectuals joined the party. By 1997, technocrats made up about three-quarters of top Chinese leaders, a share that has since shrunk as they have been replaced by lawyers and entrepreneurs.

In 2001, the party leadership decided to allow private entrepreneurs, including successful capitalists, into the Communist Party, the ultimate irony in a system that still describes itself as communist. (Dickson, 2003.) By 2011, an estimated 40 percent of

Chinese entrepreneurs were party members. With the booming economy, party membership is a key means of patronage, and "90 percent of China's millionaires are the children of high-ranking officials." (Saich, 2013, 110.)

The political implications of these changes to the CCP's membership are not clear. Dickson surveyed China's new entrepreneurs and found that their political attitudes do not suggest they will help expand democracy. (Dickson, 2003.) Entrepreneurs agree with party officials that political participation should be limited to the elite to maintain stability. Chen and Lu surveyed middle-class citizens and found similar results. (Chen and Lu, 2011.) They did not have a particularly strong preference for democracy, and the more economically dependent they were on the state, the less support they showed for democracy.

The World Values Survey, on the other hand, found that 71 percent of Chinese thought democracy was "very good" or "fairly good," and those with university educations, who would likely be middle class, supported it even more strongly, at least in principle. (McAllister and White, 2018.)

Under Xi, the CCP has returned to actively propagating an official ideology. Xi began making major ideological pronouncements shortly after gaining power. He has tried to rehabilitate Mao's image by saying that both Mao's and Deng's eras were equally important in understanding China today. Xi has also expanded the role of nationalism and Confucianism as ideological supports for the regime. In 2017, the Party Congress enshrined *Xi Jinping Thought on Socialism with Chinese Characteristics for a New Era* (known simply as *Xi Jinping Thought*), in the constitution, as *Mao Zedong Thought* and *Deng Xiaoping Thought* were earlier. In 2019, the regime created a smartphone "app" of *Xi Jinping Thought* that is interactive. Under Xi, the CCP has emphasized both economic growth and ideology in maintaining its hold on power.

Interest Groups and Social Movements

Under Mao's rule, the CCP completely controlled society. At the height of the Mao era, the state controlled the entire economy, including the allocation of jobs, houses, and other services. Appearing loyal to the regime was crucial to one's success in the system. Networks of supporters, including family and other social connections, known as *guanxi*, connected citizens with government officials. Relatives and friends in the system could get you a better job or apartment or keep you out of trouble with local authorities. People within the CCP used *guanxi* to advance their careers. While the reforms since 1980 have profoundly changed the system, *guanxi* have not disappeared. Even with the recent expansion of civil society, clientelism remains important.

China's modernizing authoritarian regime places significant limits on the ability of groups to form outside the government's control, but the CCP no longer has complete control over the formation and activities of groups. Labor unions are one example of how civil society has changed since Mao's rule. The All-China Federation of Trade Unions (ACFTU) was the sole legal union during Mao's rule, with mandatory branches in any enterprise with more than one hundred employees. The rapid expansion of private companies has made it difficult for the party to maintain its monopoly on labor organizations, but the ACFTU remains tightly controlled by and supportive of the government. A revised labor law enacted in 2008 made arbitration and court cases by workers easier. The number of such cases more than doubled, and in the most industrialized regions, the system is overwhelmed with cases.

Lee and Friedman argued that the global economy reduces workers' ability to secure rights. (Lee and Friedman, 2009.) Forty percent of urban workers were part-time, casual, or temporary employees who have great difficulty demanding better treatment. Nearly half of them reported not receiving wages on time.

Like labor unions, NGOs are closely monitored by the government. The number of officially registered NGOs in China more than tripled between 2000 and 2012, to about half a million. (Dickson, 2016, 125.) To control these organizations, the government created a registration system for NGOs and approved only one organization of each type in each administrative region. As the government became more comfortable with its ability to control NGOs, it allowed more groups to register and eliminated a requirement that each NGO have a government agency as a sponsor.

Lu Yiyi studied urban NGOs providing social services and found that even though NGOs depend on the state for financing and information, they can achieve a degree of autonomy. (Lu, 2009.) NGOs can develop personal relationships with local bureaucrats who can protect them from the more burdensome demands of the state. Hildebrandt argued that NGO leaders limit their own demands to what will be politically acceptable in a particular community. (Hildebrandt, 2013.)

Bruce Dickson and others divide Chinese civil society into two categories. (Dickson, 2016.) The first category includes the NGOs focused on economic, cultural, sports, and charitable work. The second category consists of groups that seek political changes, which the regime sees as threatening. Nonpolitical civil-society groups are often welcomed by local government and can influence the direction of government policy, though mostly at the local level. Local branches of the ACFTU have successfully supported workers' strikes on a number of occasions, and the national organization helped to get a five-day workweek approved.

President Xi has cracked down on NGOs that might threaten the regime. A new law in 2016 required the 7,000 foreign NGOs operating in China to register with the government and reveal their funding sources, giving the government the potential to deny legal status to those it believed might threaten regime stability. It also restricted contact between foreign and Chinese NGOs and made it nearly impossible for Chinese NGOs to get international funding. A similar law regulating religious organizations was passed in late 2016, limiting their contact with like-minded foreign groups and requiring them to register with the state. Xi has restricted civil society further by requiring that all NGOs allow members of the CCP to observe their operations, acting as watchdogs for the regime.

Section 11.3 Review

Remember

- Although China has eight state-sanctioned parties other than the CCP, China is a one-party state that has been ruled by the CCP since 1949.
- Elections for high-ranking party and government officials are indirect through the National Party Congress and National People's Congress, whose members are chosen by party members and citizens through local congresses.
- Civil society is limited in China because it is difficult to create and register NGOs, and their continued operation is restricted by government monitoring.

Know

- *One-party state:* a country where only one party is allowed to control the government. (p. 349)

Free-Response Question: Comparative Analysis

Compare the party systems in two different AP® Comparative Government and Politics course countries. In your response, you should do the following:

A. Define party system.

B. Describe party systems differ in two different AP® Comparative Government and Politics course countries that have authoritarian regimes.

C. Explain why the authoritarian regimes described in part B have different types of party systems.

11.4 Political Culture and Participation

Learning Targets

After reading this section, you should be able to do the following:

1. Explain why China, as an authoritarian state that restricts civil liberties, allows some civil liberties at the local level.

2. Explain how the Great Firewall of China is a system to allow government officials to monitor people's online presence and censor content critical of the regime.

3. Describe the continuing conflict over China's sovereignty in Tibet.

4. Explain how China has restricted the civil liberties of the Uyghurs living in the Xinjiang Autonomous Region.

Civil Rights and Civil Liberties

China is an authoritarian regime. As the massacre at Tiananmen Square showed, the government is willing to use repression and force against citizens when it perceives a threat to the regime. Civil liberties are restricted in China, but citizens have some avenues for expressing their viewpoints.

Although the Chinese government restricts the right to protest, some kinds of protest are allowed. The regime has successfully eliminated most large-scale protests on the Chinese mainland. (As discussed earlier, large-scale protests have happened in Hong Kong.)

Many local protests, which the Ministry of Public Security (MPS) calls "mass incidents," continue. Most protests do not criticize the national government but target corruption and inefficiency by local officials. In the past, the MPS reported data about the number of annual protests in China. In 2006, the MPS reported 87,000 mass incidents, which was almost twice the number reported in 2003. The government has not reported the number of protests since 2006, but it appears that a significant number of protests take place in China each year. (The Economist, 2018.)

A key organizational tool for protesters and petitioners is to use the media or dramatic protests to get the attention of the central government, a tactic often referred to as "troublemaking." The central government may make concessions to those who protest against local government officials. Locally focused protests—like local elections, courts, and the media—can provide the regime information to help root out corruption at the local level and maintain legitimacy. (Chen, 2012.)

Bruce Dickson argued that China has a long history of easing and tightening repression as needed to control problems at minimal cost. (Dickson, 2016.) The latest tightening began in the lead-up to the 2008 Olympics and accelerated once Xi became president. Crackdowns against human-rights activists and others increased significantly as the Olympics approached. The government also increased restrictions in Tibet, a region whose populace desires greater autonomy or independence. You will learn more about Tibet later in this section.

China uses surveillance to track people. China now has an estimated 200 million cameras around the country to watch the population—one camera for every seven people. (Economy, 2019.)

China initiated a "social credit" system in 2014 that was supposed to include every citizen by 2020, although its implementation was delayed by COVID-19. (Donnelly, 2021.) This system is a vast network of data collection that gives citizens "social credit" for positive behavior, such as making supportive statements about the regime online, and demerits for poor behavior, such as failing to repay loans. Along with a growing collection of citizens' DNA and facial recognition technology, the system raises the possibility of using artificial intelligence to gather, retain, and use information on each citizen to ensure that his or her behavior is consistent with the expectations of the regime. This data-collection effort allows the government to monitor people to a degree never before possible in human history. (Qiang, 2019.)

This political cartoon comments on how the Great Firewall in China is used by authorities to monitor citizens' online activity.

Chinese media expanded dramatically in the past generation. Professional journalists generate online news critical of the regime, but they must be careful to stay within certain boundaries. The regime generally tolerates criticisms of local officials' malfeasance in mainstream media because the media's criticism of local government helps the regime gain information about what is happening "on the ground." (Stockman, 2012.)

Yet political criticism of the top leadership can result in harsh consequences. Xi has mandated ideological training for journalists. The government has arrested many professionals who dared to criticize the regime, including university faculty, lawyers, and editors. (Zhao, 2016.) In 2018, the international NGO, Reporters Without Borders, ranked China the fourth-worst country in the world on press freedom.

The biggest venue for criticism of the regime has been the internet, and the government has created the Great Firewall of China to prevent internet users from accessing information on sensitive topics. Since a major speech by Xi in 2013, the regime has actively centralized and expanded its efforts to monitor and limit the internet, calling cybersecurity a key element of national security. A 2016 cybersecurity law required internet service providers to provide data to the government upon request and internet users to register all accounts with their real names to root out anonymous criticism of the regime.

A new profession of "public opinion analysts" has arisen, hired by the government to monitor citizens' online activity. The regime employs tens of thousands of cyber-police and sophisticated security programs to constantly monitor internet use and has eliminated virtually all of the major global internet providers, such as Google, Facebook, and YouTube, replacing them with more easily controlled Chinese alternatives.

Nonetheless, Chinese "netizens," initially led by professional journalists, created active online communities and techniques to evade censorship. Some of the tactics to avoid censorship include new Chinese-language characters that can bypass filtering systems, Web sites based on foreign servers, and meetings held in secret chat rooms. Lei Ya-Wen concluded that the government's steps to control the media and internet are only partially successful but curtail the most contentious political speech. (Lei, 2018.)

Divisions in China

A large majority of China's population—more than 90 percent—is Han Chinese, an East Asian ethnic group that originated along the Yellow River, which is the largest ethnic group in the world. China is also home to more than fifty-five other ethnic groups. Some ethnic minority groups, particularly in the Tibet and Xinjiang autonomous regions, are repressed by the Chinese government. At the same time, dissidents from ethnic minority groups, such as Rebiya Kadeer, who is featured at the beginning of this chapter, are becoming more visible.

The conflict in Tibet stems from differing claims over sovereignty. China claims sovereignty over the Tibet Autonomous Region, but the Dalai Lama, an exiled Tibetan spiritual leader, claims that Tibet is an independent state. Those opposed to Chinese rule claim that the government has violated the rights of Tibetans and engaged in a campaign of ethnic and religious repression, with the goal of weakening traditional Tibetan culture, because thousands of ethnic Chinese have migrated to the Tibetan region.

The Chinese government argues that conditions in Tibet have improved due to the government policies that have resulted in significant economic development in the region, including a new railroad linking Lhasa, the capital of the Tibetan region, with Qinghai, a neighboring Chinese province. (BBC, 2019.)

China has also been accused of serious and sustained human-rights violations against the Muslim, Turkic-speaking Uyghur minority in the Xinjiang Uygur Autonomous Region in northwestern China. Xinjiang is the only region in China in which the majority is Muslim, and the Chinese government has historically maintained strict control over the region. Xinjiang's population includes members of the Uyghur, Kazakh, and Kyrgyz ethnic groups. (Human Rights Watch.) Xinjiang is rich in minerals and on the strategically and economically important route to Central Asia, and many view the Chinese state's repression of the Uyghurs as an effort to secure central control over the area for economic reasons. In 2016, the Chinese government announced an investment of $17 billion in more than 100 projects in Xinjiang. (Reuters, 2016.)

In May 2014, a car-bomb attack at an outdoor market in Urumqi, the capital of the region, killed thirty-one people and injured more than ninety. The Chinese government concluded that the terrorist attack was carried out by the East Turkestan Islamic Movement (now known as the Turkistan Islamic Movement), an extremist Uyghur group.

Writing Evidence Paragraphs in the Argument Essay

In Chapter 8, you learned about how to structure your argument essay. In this practice, we will go into more depth about how to write evidence paragraphs.

There are two parts of the prompt that refer to the evidence paragraphs. The first part states:

Support your claim with at least TWO pieces of specific and relevant evidence from one or more course countries. The evidence should be relevant to one or more of the provided course concepts.

The second part of the prompt that refers to the evidence paragraphs states:

Use reasoning to explain why your evidence supports your claim or thesis, using one or more of the provided course concepts.

Taken together, these instructions tell you how to construct an evidence paragraph. Here is the formula:

1. Describe specific and relevant evidence from a course country,

2. Explain how the evidence relates to one of the listed course concepts, and

3. Explain why the evidence supports your thesis, using the course concept.

You will follow the same formula in your second evidence paragraph, using different evidence from the same course country or evidence from a different course country. You can use the same concept that you discussed in the first evidence paragraph, or you can use a different course concept from the list.

Suppose the essay asks you to take a position about whether democratic or authoritarian regimes are better at maintaining legitimacy, and the listed course concepts are power, representation, and civil liberties. In this example, suppose you have written an analytical thesis that states, "Authoritarian states are better than democratic states at maintaining legitimacy, because they do not protect civil liberties and can censor information that might undermine the regime, which helps them maintain legitimacy."

Here is an example of an evidence paragraph that meets the requirements of the prompt, with explanations between

brackets of how sentences succeed in responding to the prompt:

"China is an example of an authoritarian state that maintains legitimacy by restricting civil liberties. In China, the internet is censored through the Great Firewall, and information critical of the government is prevented from reaching public view. [*This sentence provides specific and relevant information about the Great Firewall.*] This is a restriction of civil liberties, which are protections individuals have from government interference, such as protections of freedom of expression and the press. By restricting civil liberties through the Great Firewall, the Chinese government prevents negative information about the regime and promotes positive information. [*These sentences provide information about the course concept of civil liberties.*] The Great Firewall enhances legitimacy, because citizens only see a favorable view of the government, enhancing their belief that the government has the right to rule. [*This sentence uses reasoning to support the thesis.*]"

An easy way to make sure you have included reasoning in your evidence paragraph is to make sure you have a *because* statement linking your evidence to your thesis.

Practice writing the second evidence paragraph of this argument essay by doing the following:

1. Write a sentence or two using a different piece of specific and relevant evidence about China or another course country.

2. Write a sentence or two explaining how your evidence relates to civil liberties or to one of the other course concepts provided in the prompt (power and representation).

3. Write a sentence or two, including a *because* statement, explaining why the evidence supports your thesis and relates to the course concept.

Note: This is a practice exercise, but on the AP® Exam, you might need to revise the thesis stated above, depending on the evidence and concept used in the second evidence paragraph.

President Xi vowed to punish the terrorists and to take action to stabilize the region. (Panda, 2014.)

China detained an estimated 800,000 to 2 million Uyghurs in "reeducation centers" in 2018, according to the U.S. State Department. China claims the camps are "vocational training centers" and are a "necessary counterterror measure." (Hollingsworth, 2019.) According to a report issued by Human Rights Watch, the Chinese government has engaged in crimes against humanity against the Uyghurs, including disappearances, murder, torture, forced labor, and sexual violence. (Human Rights Watch.) The Chinese government is also reportedly using advanced facial recognition technology through a growing network of surveillance cameras to track Uyghurs, not only in Xinjiang, but also in a number of large cities outside the region. (Mozur, 2019.)

The U.N. Human Rights Council has condemned the Chinese government's policy in the Xinjiang region. The United States, United Kingdom, and European Union have imposed economic and travel sanctions against high-ranking Chinese government officials, including the director of the Xinjiang Public Security Bureau. (Muhammad.)

China has invested billions of dollars in regions populated predominantly by ethnic minorities. Nevertheless, China's treatment of ethnic minorities, particularly in Tibet and Xinjiang, demonstrates that the state is willing to use repression against perceived threats to the stability of the regime. Freedom House ranks China as "not free," and despite international sanctions, it is unlikely that China will significantly improve its human-rights record in the foreseeable future.

Section 11.4 Review

Remember

- Although China is an authoritarian state that restricts civil liberties, some protests are allowed, especially to point out corruption and inefficiency at the local level.
- The Great Firewall of China is a system that allows government officials to monitor people's online presence and censors content critical of the regime.
- China claims the Tibet Autonomous Region under its sovereignty, and some Tibetans, including the Dalai Lama, advocate Tibetan autonomy and independence.
- China has restricted the civil liberties of the Uyghurs living in the Xinjiang Uygur Autonomous Region, and the government has been accused of human-rights violations for placing Uyghurs in "reeducation" camps.

Think

- To what extent has the repression of civil rights in China decreased the legitimacy of the state?
- Why haven't international sanctions against China been effective in encouraging the government to change its policies in Xinjiang autonomous region?

Free-Response Question: Conceptual Analysis

Answer A, B, C, and D.

A. Define sovereignty.

B. Describe a measure that an authoritarian government could use to protect state sovereignty.

C. Explain how the measures used by authoritarian governments to protect state sovereignty differ from the measures used by democratic governments to protect state sovereignty.

D. Explain how a measure adopted by an authoritarian state to protect state sovereignty might impact the state's legitimacy.

11.5 Economic and Social Change and Development

Learning Targets

After reading this section, you should be able to do the following:

1. Describe China's shift to a market socialist economic policy.

2. Explain how China's economic growth has affected the standard of living of citizens.

3. Describe the benefits and limitations of China's social policies.

4. Describe the impact of the one-child policy, and explain why the Chinese government now allows families to have three children.

5. Explain why environmental degradation is a serious problem in China.

In the late 1970s, China shifted its economic policy away from the command economy that existed under Mao's communism to market socialism. China's dramatic economic growth over the past forty years lifted millions out of poverty. Nevertheless, China faces challenges, including a widening income gap and environmental degradation.

Globalization

When Mao Zedong died in 1976, China was one of the poorest and most chaotic societies in the world. A three-year power struggle ensued upon his death, pitting those who wished to continue his legacy against those who saw the need to change direction, especially in economic policy.

In 1979, Deng Xiaoping set out to move the country away from Mao's ideology of a communist command economy to a more pragmatic economic system, called "market socialism." As Deng famously said, "It doesn't matter whether the cat is black or white, so long as it catches mice." What he meant was that it does not matter how a country describes its economic system, as long as the system raises citizens' standard of living.

China's reforms under Deng began gradually and remain incomplete nearly five decades later. While China has changed its economic system to compete in the global market, it has not completely adopted a market economy, and the state still plays a key role in the economy.

Household responsibility system
An agricultural reform that allowed farmers more control over their own production.

The first economic policy changes focused on agriculture. The **household responsibility system** converted the management of many of China's collective farms into arrangements allowing families to lease and cultivate farmland. Families offer their surplus crops on the open market, giving them a financial incentive to be more productive. Between 1978 and 1984, nearly all farming households converted to this system. Agricultural production grew at an unprecedented rate of 7 percent per year, and per-capita rural incomes increased by more than 50 percent. In rural areas, **township and village enterprises (TVEs)**, factories and other businesses mostly owned by local governments, were given greater freedom to produce what they could for a profit. Their production rose fivefold between 1983 and 1988. (Qian, 2006, 235–237.)

Township and village enterprise (TVE)
Factories and other businesses mostly owned by local governments.

At the same time, the government gradually began to open to the market, domestically and internationally. **State-owned enterprises (SOEs)** sold their products at set prices until they met the official production quota, but they were free to sell their surplus at whatever market price they could get. In 1995, the government announced the start of privatization, selling off the vast majority of SOEs to private investors. The process resulted in the layoffs of at least 20 million workers from 1995 to 1997, but the growing economy was able to employ many of them, and the government created a pension system for the unemployed, so layoffs did not cause widespread unrest. (Frazier, 2010; Qian, 2006, 243.) A decade later, the private sector constituted 70 percent of the economy.

Throughout the 1990s, the government gradually but systematically lowered tariffs on imports and loosened restrictions on companies' rights to import and export. China joined the World Trade Organization (WTO) in 2001, furthering its commitment to free trade. The result has been an explosion of international trade for the country. Chinese exports and imports increased nearly tenfold between 2000 and 2014.

As part of its transition toward a market economy, China encouraged **foreign direct investment** by people and businesses outside of China. The government began large-scale spending on infrastructure expansion and improvements, showing its financial commitment to both domestic and foreign private investment.

As part of its effort to attract foreign investors, the Chinese government in 1979 created **special economic zones (SEZs)**, strategically located areas with large labor pools, well-developed infrastructure, and tax incentives, such as exemptions from paying income tax and customs duties. Initially, SEZs were located in coastal cities, but the economic model has been so successful in attracting foreign capital that China has expanded the program throughout the country.

China has started to focus more on expanding SEZs westward. In 2014, the government began building railroads, roads, and pipelines to connect the east and west. In 2017, the project was named the Belt and Road Initiative, and ambitious plans were announced to build infrastructure connecting China with countries in Central Asia, Europe, the Middle East, and east Africa. The Belt and Road Initiative is an attempt by China to integrate its presence into Central Asia and assert influence internationally. (Chatzky and McBride, 2020.) China's investment in the Belt and Road Initiative may be mainly an effort to strengthen legitimacy by accessing resources that will contribute to economic growth, or the initiative may be part of a greater plan to extend China's political and economic influence in Central Asia.

China has become a key player in the global economy, but the state retains control of a significant amount of economic activity. A 2019 estimate places the contribution of SOEs to China's GDP at about 23 percent. (Zhang, 2019.) SOEs still control entire sectors that are considered strategic, such as energy and military industry. Some SOEs compete with private firms in sectors such as pharmaceuticals and chemicals. (Pearson, 2015.) After the 2007 recession, SOEs' share of the economy increased slightly because the government channeled most of its large stimulus package into infrastructure built mainly by SOEs. China's state sector remains the largest in the world and is a crucial element in the state's effort to guide investment into certain areas.

The government also controls much of the banking system, although it faces competition from private financing and international banks. When China began the shift toward a market economy, the government created a central bank. Four other government-owned banks are used to direct large-scale investment in key areas such as energy, steel, and natural resources. The growing private sector finances most of its investment with its own profits, and the number of international banks in China is growing. (Knight and Ding, 2013.)

State-owned enterprise (SOE)
A factory or other business owned by the government.

Foreign direct investment
The creation of or investment in a business in one country by an entity from another country.

Special economic zone (SEZ)
A strategically located area in China with a large labor pool, well-developed infrastructure, and tax incentives to attract foreign companies.

The Recent Chinese Economy

China's economic success since 1979, measured in terms of economic growth, per-capita income, and poverty reduction, is spectacular. The GDP per capita in China rose from $195 in 1980 to $10,839 in 2020. (World Bank.) The World Bank estimates that 850 million people have been lifted out of extreme poverty in China since 1981. According to a survey conducted by Ipsos in 2018, 84 percent of adults and 92 percent of young people believe their generation is better off than their parents. (Zhou, 2018.) Rising incomes provide members of China's middle and upper-middle classes with opportunities to travel internationally for work and education.

While China's economic policies have improved most citizens' standards of living, they have widened the income gap. China's overall inequality as measured by the Gini index was 0.465 in 2019, near that of the United States (which was 0.48)—a sharp increase from the communist era. According to the Pew Research Center poll shown in Figure 11.3, 48 percent of respondents said that the rising income gap in China is a very big problem.

Since the early 1990s, the urban-rural gap has grown considerably, as foreign investment and manufacturing in coastal cities have exploded. Even though most households have gained from the expanding economy, the wealthiest 20 percent gained far more than their poorer neighbors until about 2010. Since then, the pattern began to reverse, and per-capita income of the bottom 40 percent began to grow more quickly than that of the top 20 percent. (Kroeber, 2016, 202.)

The booming coastal regions also have become much wealthier than the distant interior provinces, which remain largely rural and poor. One result has been the massive migration to the coastal cities of workers in search of jobs. Although the state has long tried to regulate this movement, it has been only partially successful. Privatization and migration from the countryside have produced considerable urban unemployment in recent years.

FIGURE 11.3

Chinese Citizens' Concerns about Corruption, Inequality, and Food Safety
Percent Responding That the Issue Is a "Very Big Problem"

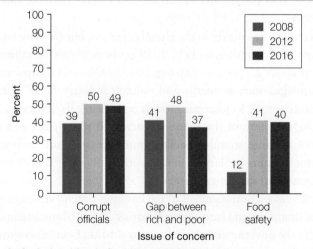

Data from Pew Research Center, based on the 2012 and 2018 Pew Global Attitudes survey.

China recovered from the great recession of 2008–2009 much more quickly than the United States and Europe. China surpassed Japan in 2010 to become the second-largest economy in the world. Part of this success is credited to the government's very large stimulus program in 2009, which invested heavily in infrastructure, including renewable energy and improved road and rail networks. It also used credit from key government-aligned banks to stimulate growth in selected high-technology sectors. (Naughton, 2015, 124.)

After 2012, growth dropped below 8 percent. By 2015, economic analysts became increasingly concerned about whether China could maintain its exceptional economic growth. The global slowdown in the demand for goods hurt its exports, the heart of its growth model. In 2018 growth dipped to 6.6 percent, still high by world standards but the lowest in China since 1990. Manufacturing and exports, the heart of the economy, seemed to be slowing particularly quickly. Rising wages in the manufacturing sector threaten China's status as the world's main producer of goods, as manufacturing plants seek less expensive labor elsewhere.

In early 2019, the United States imposed tariffs on imports from China. China placed retaliatory tariffs on U.S. goods. In 2020, the United States prohibited eleven Chinese companies from purchasing American products and technology without a special license on grounds that the companies were complicit in human-rights violations against the Uyghurs. (Swanson, 2020.)

Despite its remarkable economic success over the past four decades, it is not clear whether China can continue its impressive economic growth in the face of increasing global competition and international sanctions.

Social Policies

China's social welfare program includes medical insurance and some protections for workers. However, it is difficult for some citizens, particularly migrants and people living in rural areas, to access benefits.

A key problem in providing social services is the *hukou* system, which requires every citizen to carry identification stating where they are legally allowed to live, which is part of the state's effort to control population movements. The *hukou* system is the key to receiving benefits for Chinese citizens who are legally registered in the city where they work. A 2014 survey found that more than 80 percent of legal residents in cities had medical insurance, as opposed to as few as 20 percent of residents without documentation, and urban residents generally have far better insurance than rural residents. (Dickson, 2016, 195.)

Changing one's *hukou* is difficult, so many migrant workers do not legally reside in the cities where they work. In 2020, the Chinese government relaxed residency restrictions to encourage migration to most cities in Guangdong Province, except for Shenzhen and Guangzhou. (Reuters, 2020.)

As you learned earlier in this chapter, protests have been increasing in China for years, including among workers. In 2008, the government revised the national labor law to respond to growing worker unrest. The 2008 law gave full-time workers rights to longer and more secure contracts and streamlined the arbitration process through which workers could demand better wages and working conditions. However, Chinese law still does not allow workers to form their own unions, preserving the monopoly of the official state-sanctioned union.

A woman rides her scooter with two children in Henan Province. China's controversial one-child policy has been replaced with a policy allowing most families to have three children.

STR/AFP/Getty Images

Migrant workers not recognized as legal in the *hukou* system are particularly subject to low wages and poor working conditions, and they are not able to avail themselves of the limited worker protections Chinese law allows.

In the early twenty-first century, the Chinese government began providing greater social services for workers, including payments for unemployed people and pensions for retired workers. These covered nearly half the workforce by 2005. In 2010, the government passed a comprehensive Social Insurance Law that is designed to guarantee all citizens a right to a pension, medical insurance, employment injury insurance, unemployment insurance, and maternity insurance—a policy that will take years to implement fully.

The largest antipoverty program, known as *dibao*, provides a "bare-bones" level of assistance for those without other means of support, including families, which are still expected to support impoverished relatives. While it has reduced the depth of poverty, it is too limited to raise many people out of poverty. (Gao, 2017.)

Social welfare programs are a way for the government to reduce poverty and to keep social and political peace by providing income to those not benefiting from China's dramatic economic transformation.

Shifting Demographics

China's demographics have shifted significantly in the past four decades. The move toward the market economy generated a migration from rural areas to cities and from the west to the coastal cities in the east. To expand urbanization but ensure the government still maintains control, the government announced a plan in 2013 to move 250 million people from rural areas to newly built cities by 2025. (Weller, 2015.) If achieved, the ambitious effort would be by far the biggest planned urbanization in human history.

The most dramatic shift in China's demographics has occurred in its population growth rates. In the late 1970s, China's population was rapidly approaching 1 billion, at a rate that would outpace its economic growth. In 1979, Deng Xiaoping introduced a family-planning policy, known as the one-child policy, to reverse the trend and decrease the population growth rate. The policy applied to most of China's population, except for people living in ethnic autonomous regions.

Under the policy, families who limited themselves to one child were provided with financial and employment benefits. Contraceptives and education about birth control were made widely available. Couples who had more than one child were penalized with fines. The policy was also enforced using coercion, including mass sterilizations, and forced abortions, which generated condemnation from human-rights advocates. The policy disproportionately impacted the poor and middle class. Wealthy families could simply pay the fines and have more than one child.

The one-child policy skewed the ratio of men to women in China. In many areas, male children were preferred. Because families were limited to one child, they wanted a boy, which led to sex-selective abortions following an ultrasound. Large numbers of girls were abandoned, placed in orphanages, and, in some cases, killed at birth. (BBC, 2015.)

According to National Census Data released in 2021, the sex ratio in China was 111 boys to 100 girls. (Xinhua, 2021.) As of 2021, China had a surplus of about 30 million men. (Chen, 2021.) This uneven sex ratio means that many men have difficulty finding female partners, a situation that increased sex trafficking. (Fetterly, 2014.)

The Chinese government relaxed the one-child policy in 2016, allowing couples to have two children. Despite the new policy, China's birth rate continued to decline. (BBC, 2019.) In 2021, China revised the policy to allow couples to have three children. Couples are no longer required to get the government's approval to have a child, and the government is becoming less involved in reproductive decisions. (BBC, Child Policy, 2021.)

Changes to China's population policy were made because China is facing pressures from an aging population and a decline in the working-age population. The one-child policy was in effect for thirty-five years, and it has had a lasting effect on China's social fabric. It is unclear whether a generation of only children will be interested in having more than one child and raising China's population growth rate.

China and the Future

China has made great strides in lifting millions of out of poverty, and its authoritarian state remains strong. Nevertheless, China faces significant challenges.

Environmental Degradation

As the 2008 Summer Olympics approached, commentators around the world began to question whether Beijing was an appropriate host, not because of a lack of infrastructure or resources, but because of the quality of the air the athletes would be breathing. The government enacted several policies to reduce air pollution, including (1) removing half of Beijing's 3.3 million vehicles from its highways, (2) banning 300,000 aging vehicles found to be especially heavy polluters, (3) encouraging commuters to bike to work, (4) opening three new subway lines, and (5) setting up many new bus lines. Nevertheless, some athletes still bowed out of the competition.

China's environmental degradation and problems are staggering. By 2018, 15.5 percent of the nation's water was unfit for human or agricultural use. Beijing's peak daily air-quality index in 2020 was 262, a level rated as seriously unhealthy by the U.S. Environmental

An infographic is a collection of images to visualize a topic. Infographics can convey much information in an eye-catching format, and they can be fun to look at. Take a look at the example at right.

There are several steps in interpreting an infographic. This infographic does not have a title, so you will have to look at the different parts of the infographic to determine its topic. In the upper left corner, there is some background on China's one-child policy, which means the infographic is most likely about China's population policies. In the upper right corner, there is a projection of how large China's population would have been if the one-child policy had not been enacted.

As you look at each part of the infographic, look for any important information that is missing. For example, the projection in the upper right corner is missing a year, so we do not know when China's population was projected to reach 1.7 billion without the one-child policy.

Remember that while infographics may look pretty, like other visual representations of data, they can be biased or inaccurate. Carefully analyze the bottom half of the infographic and answer the following questions.

1. When is China's population expected to reach 1.6 billion?

2. Why is it difficult to determine whether the one-child policy was effective in reducing China's population growth rate based on the information in the infographic?

China's **one-child** policy was **introduced** in
1979
although it was **preceded** by other similar **policies** to keep the **population** down from **1971** onwards.

China's population is

1.3 billion

Those who back the **one-child policy claim** it would now be **1.7 billion** had it not been in place.

1.7 billion

An **estimated**
336 million
abortions and
222 million
sterilizations have taken place in China since **1971.**

China's **population** is expected to reach
1.6 billion
by **2030.**

56% of **Chinese parents** said they wanted a **second** child in a recent **poll.**

Lifting the **one-child ban** could result in an additional
9.5 million
births every year.

Birth rates in China dropped from

4.77 children per woman in the early **1970s** to

1.64 children per woman in **2011.**

China's **workforce** shrank by
3 million
last year (2012).

There will be an **estimated labor shortage** of almost
140 million
workers by the early **2030s** in **China.**

Data from International Monetary Fund, Southern Metropolis Daily, Chinese Health Ministry, Bureau of Statistics of China, United Nations.

3. What is the point of view about the one-child policy conveyed in the infographic? Explain how you reached your conclusion.

Protection Agency. (Center for Strategic and International Studies, 2020.) Pilots flying into Beijing Capital International Airport typically rely on their navigation systems to make landings because they cannot see the runways because of smog. (Reuters, 2013.)

The result is skyrocketing health problems. Air pollution in China is estimated to have caused 1.4 million premature deaths in 2019. (Center for Strategic and International

Studies, 2020.) In Beijing, where the most polluted days reach forty times the internationally recommended maximum level of air particulates, residents regularly wear facemasks to protect themselves from air pollution. Those who can afford to do so will choose apartments and schools based partly on the quality of the air filtration system they use.

Facing mounting public pressure, the government announced a major new initiative in September 2013 that set upper limits on air particulate levels in major cities, banned the most heavily polluting vehicles, and slightly reduced the nation's dependence on coal. By 2015, the average Chinese citizen's exposure to harmful particles in the air had dropped 47 percent from a decade earlier, although most of the decrease was due to households switching fuel sources (away from coal) rather than restrictions on industry. (Yu, 2018.) Because of an economic resurgence in major cities, pollution levels increased in 2017 and 2018.

Since 2002, the Chinese leadership has made a significant commitment to environmental protection. In 2008, the Ministry of Environmental Protection (MEP) was elevated to a full cabinet ministry and its funding doubled. In 2015, with greater central government concern about pollution, the MEP set up a new monitoring unit that publicly disciplined over one thousand local officials for violation of environmental regulations.

A further reorganization in 2018 created the Ministry of Ecology and Environment, subsuming the work of MEP and several other agencies under one umbrella that the government said would be far more powerful at reducing pollution than MEP had been. While it has had energetic leaders and has been a bureaucratic advocate for the environment, it had limited ability to enforce China's environmental laws because it was dependent on local governments for most of its funding and staff. Local government leaders are rewarded in China's system mainly for their ability to further rapid economic growth, so they have little incentive to slow growth in favor of protecting the environment.

Concern about the environment among Chinese citizens has grown over the years, with three-quarters saying air and water pollution and climate change were "very big" or "moderately big" problems in 2015. (Gao, 2017.) In March 2015, a video called "Under the Dome: Investigating China's Smog" went viral on the internet, attracting 150 million viewers before the government shut it down.

The COVID-19 Pandemic

COVID-19 was the second pandemic to begin in China in the twenty-first century. From 2002 to 2003, an outbreak of Severe Acute Respiratory Disease (SARS) began in China, and it took several months to warn the public of the outbreak, prompting criticism that the government responded too slowly to the crisis. (Stanway, 2020.)

The first cases of COVID-19 were reported in late December 2019. Chinese authorities detected the virus in Wuhan, Hubei Province, in central China. Most of the infected people were connected to Huanan Seafood Market. In early January 2020, Chinese authorities notified the World Health Organization about the virus. On January 23, 2020, just before the Lunar New Year, the government announced a lockdown in the region. The government reported more than 80,000 infections by the end of February. (Thomala, 2021.) By April 2020, more than 100 countries reported cases of COVID-19, and the world was in the grip of a pandemic. (LaFee, 2021.)

The Chinese government responded to outbreaks in major cities, such as Beijing and Shanghai, with lockdowns and widespread testing. Those who tested positive were required to quarantine, and travel was prohibited. As of January 2021, China reported about 100,000 infections and 4,500 deaths. (BBC, Wuhan, 2021.)

China has been criticized for a lack of transparency in reporting about COVID-19. Authorities appear to have been slow in responding to the new virus when it first appeared in Wuhan. Doctors who shared information about the virus faced recriminations from the government. Dr. Li Wenliang, who warned the world about COVID-19 on social media, died from the virus. (BBC, Wuhan, 2021.)

China's handling of SARS and COVID-19 demonstrates the power of an authoritarian state to control citizens' behavior in an effort to reduce disease transmission. At the same time, it demonstrates how authoritarian states seek to limit the spread of potentially damaging information.

China will continue to face challenges, including those related to economic growth, human rights, and the environment. Nevertheless, China is one of the most powerful countries in the world, and its authoritarian regime remains stable.

Section 11.5 Review

Remember

- Beginning in 1979, China started to move its economy toward market socialism, an economy with elements of a market economy but with significant state ownership of industries and natural resources.
- China's remarkable economic growth has lifted millions of people out of poverty, but the income gap has widened.
- China provides its citizens with social programs, including medical care, unemployment payments, and pensions, but migrants and people living in rural areas have less access to these programs.
- China allows families to have three children, but because of the previous one-child policy, the gender ratio is skewed toward men.
- Environmental degradation is a serious problem in China.

Know

- *Household responsibility system:* an agricultural reform that allowed farmers more control over their own production. (p. 358)
- *Township and village enterprise (TVE):* factories and other businesses mostly owned by local governments. (p. 358)
- *State-owned enterprise (SOE):* a factory or other business owned by the government. (p. 359)
- *Foreign direct investment:* the creation of or investment in a business in one country by an entity from another country. (p. 359)
- *Special economic zone (SEZ):* a strategically located area in China with a large labor pool, well-developed infrastructure, and tax incentives to attract foreign companies. (p. 359)

Think

- Why was China's shift to more of a market-based economy more successful than shock therapy in Russia?
- What is the most significant challenge facing the Chinese government in the future?

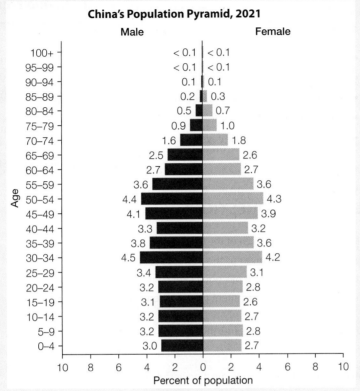

China's Population Pyramid, 2021

Data from PopulationPyramid.net.

Answer A, B, C, D, and E.

A. Using the data in the population pyramid, identify the largest age group in China in 2021.

B. Using the data in the population pyramid, describe a pattern in the age distribution in China.

C. Describe China's current population policy.

D. Using your knowledge of China's current population policy and the data in the population pyramid, draw a conclusion about how China's age distribution is likely to change in the future.

E. Explain how China's population policies over the past 40 years have impacted the ratio of men to women.

AP® KEY CONCEPTS

- Dual rule (p. 337)
- Chinese Communist Party (CCP) (p. 338)
- Communism (p. 338)
- National Party Congress (p. 345)
- Politburo (p. 345)
- Politburo Standing Committee (p. 345)

- General secretary (p. 345)
- State Council (p. 346)
- National People's Congress (p. 346)
- One-party state (p. 349)
- Household responsibility system (p. 358)

- Township and village enterprise (TVE) (p. 358)
- State-owned enterprise (SOE) (p. 359)
- Foreign direct investment (p. 359)
- Special economic zone (SEZ) (p. 359)

AP® EXAM MULTIPLE-CHOICE PRACTICE QUESTIONS

1. The structure of the government in China is most similar to which of the following?

   A. The presidential system in Mexico, where a single executive has the power to propose legislation.

   B. The federal system in Russia, where the central government has significant control over regions.

   C. The unitary system in the United Kingdom, where subgovernment power is determined by the central government.

   D. The dual executive in Nigeria, where the head of state represents the country, and the head of government proposes policy.

2. According to the Chinese constitution, which of the following is the most powerful institution?

   A. The general secretary of the CCP

   B. The National People's Congress

   C. The National Party Congress

   D. The president

Questions 3 and 4 refer to the quote.

> Freedom and order must be upheld side by side in both cyberspace and the physical world. Freedom is the purpose of order, and order the guarantee of freedom . . . We need to fully respect netizens' rights to express themselves, while at the same time, ensure a sound cyberspace order to better protect the lawful rights and interests of all netizens . . .
>
> —Interview with Chinese President Xi Jinping, *The Wall Street Journal*, September 22, 2015

3. Which of the following is supported by the main idea of the passage?

   A. China balances order and freedom in monitoring the internet.

   B. The Chinese government supports internet freedom.

   C. China monitors the internet to prevent cyberattacks by foreign entities.

   D. The Great Firewall is a method for restricting liberties in China.

4. Which of the following is an implication of the passage?

   A. The Chinese government is repressive, and citizens who use the internet to criticize the regime face criminal charges.

   B. The Great Firewall monitors citizens' use of the internet, and some criticism of local government is allowed.

   C. Although China censors the internet, the government is not completely effective in blocking critical Web sites.

   D. The Chinese government believes that individual freedom has the potential to threaten community stability.

5. Which of the following best describes a party system in a country studied in AP® Comparative Government and Politics?

   A. The United Kingdom has a two-party system.

   B. Russia is a one-party state.

   C. China is a single-party dominant state, with eight authorized minor parties.

   D. Mexico has a two-party system.

6. Which of the following best describes the judiciary in China?

   A. The civil court system is characterized by rule of law, and the criminal system is characterized by rule by law.

   B. The Supreme Court is the highest court of appeal and has the power of judicial review.

   C. Neither the civil nor the criminal system is well-developed, and both systems lack rule of law.

   D. The government exerts more control over the judicial system than the CCP does.

Questions 7 and 8 refer to the table.

Chinese Students' Opinions on Democracy

	Strongly disagree	Disagree	Neutral	Agree	Strongly agree
Democracy is indecisive and has too much quibbling.	18.9%	26.5%	36.7%	12.6%	5.3%
Democracy is not good at maintaining order.	35.6%	31.6%	23.5%	6.0%	3.3%
Democracy may have problems, but it's better than any other form of government.	10.5%	17.6%	35.2%	23.5%	13.2%
Social order is more important than individual freedom.	10.1%	20.2%	32.8%	22.3%	14.6%

Data from Purdue University survey of Chinese students, 2016.

7. Which of the following statements is accurate according to the table?

   A. A majority of Chinese students believe that democracy is not good at maintaining order.

   B. More than half of Chinese students believe democracy is the best form of government.

   C. More than a third of Chinese students believe that social order is more important than individual freedom.

   D. The majority of Chinese students is neutral about which form of government they prefer.

8. Which of the following is an implication of the table?

   A. Young people in China are more likely to support democratization than older adults.

   B. Most young people in China are not likely to advocate that the country become more democratic in the future.

   C. People in China are afraid to criticize the government, and the poll results are most likely inaccurate.

   D. Chinese people enjoy living in an authoritarian state, because the regime provides order and stability.

9. Which of the following best describes China's economic policy?

   A. China is renationalizing industries in an effort to maintain the central government's control over the economy.

   B. The state limits foreign direct investment to prevent outside influences from weakening the government's control over the economy.

   C. China has fully embraced market reforms and is in the process of privatizing all state-owned industries.

   D. China's economic policy combines free market principles with nationalized industries.

10. Which of the following best describes population policies in two AP® Comparative Government and Politics course countries?

    A. Mexico and Russia limit access to birth control in an effort to increase population growth rates.

    B. The United Kingdom and Nigeria encourage large families to provide support for aging populations.

    C. In the past decade, Russia and China have enacted programs to increase the birth rate.

    D. Mexico and Nigeria restrict access to birth control, which is a result of citizens' religious beliefs.

AP® EXAM PRACTICE ARGUMENT ESSAY

Develop an argument about whether authoritarian states that adopt market economic policies are likely to democratize.

Use one or more of the following course concepts in your response:

- Legitimacy
- Civil Liberties
- Sovereignty

In your response, do the following:

- Respond to the prompt with a defensible claim or thesis that establishes a line of reasoning using one or more of the provided course concepts.
- Support your claim with at least TWO pieces of specific and relevant evidence from your study of one or more course countries. The evidence should be relevant to one or more of the provided course concepts.
- Use reasoning to explain why your evidence supports your claim or thesis, using one or more of the provided course concepts.
- Respond to an opposing or alternate perspective, using refutation, concession, or rebuttal.

For a complete list of the sources of information cited in this chapter, turn to the Works Cited appendix.

12 Political and Economic Change and Development

Economics

People interact with an owl and its handler at a celebration of Bird Day in Moscow. The holiday is observed on April 1 in Russia. The purpose of the holiday is to raise awareness of conserving species of birds. In a rentier state like Russia, though, the revenues from extractive industries mean that natural resources like birds and their habitats are in constant competition with economic forces. The trade-off between protecting the environment and encouraging economic development is discussed in Section 12.3.

Mladen Antonov/AFP/Getty Images

The NHS and Universal Health Care

A major aspect of all advanced democracies is the modern welfare state, which includes retirement security, unemployment insurance, aid to the poor and disabled, and health care, among other programs. Worldwide, the overwhelming majority of nations offers universal health care to their citizens. All wealthy democracies do so, except for the United States.

The United Kingdom's system of universal health care was the result of planning for the future of the country that happened as World War II was ending. During the war, British labor unions pushed for a comprehensive system of health care, and in 1941, the Parliament established a commission to examine the future of social-insurance policy, including health care. A year later, the Beveridge Report, named after its author, William Beveridge, was issued. It became the cornerstone of the postwar welfare state in the United Kingdom.

More than 500,000 copies of the 300-page report were printed—the largest number of any U.K. government report in the twentieth century—and copies were even distributed to British armed forces to build morale. Beveridge sought a fundamental, comprehensive reorganization of welfare-state programs. Social progress, he argued, required that five issues be addressed: "Want, Disease, Ignorance, Squalor, and Idleness." (Beveridge Report.)

The report was greeted with widespread public support. Conservative Party leader and Prime Minister Winston Churchill objected to committing funds to such an ambitious project. His stance contributed to his defeat in the 1945 election. Once the Labour Party was in power, Parliament in 1946 acted to create the National Health Service (NHS).

The NHS was established to provide health care for all as a right regardless of employment status or income. Comprehensive care is free to the user. There are no bills, co-payments, or deductibles.

Government revenue funds almost all of the NHS budget. Although private health insurance in the United Kingdom does exist, only about 10 percent of the public carry private insurance. Overall, health-care expenditures are approximately 9.6 percent of GDP,

Health-care workers outside the Royal Victoria Infirmary in Newcastle, England, celebrate the seventy-second anniversary of the foundation of the National Health Service in the United Kingdom.

AP Images/Owen Humphreys

about the average for OECD nations. The United States, by contrast, spends 17.1 percent of GDP on health care, more than any other nation, yet the outcomes in health care for the two countries are almost the same.

A 2021 independent evaluation of eleven high-income nations rated the U.K. health-care system as the best. The evaluation measured five factors: access to health care, care process, administrative efficiency, equity, and health-care outcomes. (Commonwealth Fund.)

Of course, no health-care system is without flaws. Complaints are regularly heard of NHS underfunding and of long waits for patients to gain access to certain procedures. However, its key feature is that care is based on clinical need. Care is not rationed by ability to pay, nor does it leave those who are sick with the burden of navigating the complexity of insurance coverage or paying bills.

Hospitals are publicly owned, and health-care providers are paid from NHS funds. Some physicians are self-employed private contractors, while others are salaried employees of hospitals. Patients choose their doctor and their hospital for care.

Wildly popular, the National Health Service is a point of national pride. When the 2012 Olympics were held in London, the opening ceremony included a celebration of the NHS featuring dancing and roller-skating nurses.

The experience of identical twin sisters, one living in London and the other living in Washington, D.C., each diagnosed and treated for breast cancer, highlights the differences between the health-care systems in the United Kingdom and the United States. Nora Ellen Groce is a medical anthropologist and a professor in the Department of Epidemiology and Health Care at University College London. Nancy Groce is a folklore specialist for the Library of Congress in Washington, D.C.

In 2008 at age 55, Nora moved to the United Kingdom and enrolled in the NHS. Given her family history of breast cancer, her regular doctor referred her for genetic counseling, which included yearly mammograms. In 2012, tests confirmed that she had breast cancer. Given the complexity of her case, Nora elected to have a double mastectomy that involved a six-day stay in the hospital and six weeks off from work. Her salary was fully covered by her employer. She could have taken off more time if she had chosen to do so.

Most importantly, she never received a bill for her care. The only paperwork she filled out was a form to grant permission to operate. The social welfare system in the United Kingdom even paid for the taxi ride home from the hospital. (Groce, Twin Study.)

Nancy's experience with breast cancer was quite different, but not because her medical case was more complicated. First, an earlier bout with cancer in 1994 meant that she had a "previously existing condition." At that time, only certain states required insurance companies to cover such conditions. The result was that Nancy had to keep her legal residence in the state of New York even though she had moved to Washington, D.C., in 2007 to work for the federal government. When she moved, she was given a choice of health insurance plans and chose one with a high deductible because it offered fuller coverage in cases like hers. She paid 40 percent of the total yearly premiums or $3,500. (Groce, Twin Study.)

In 2017, she was diagnosed with cancer and underwent treatment that included several MRIs, two biopsies, an outpatient lumpectomy, and a month-long course of radiation. She also had to deal with a flurry of bills and insurance-company decisions.

> Insurance inexplicably covered some things, denied others, and required complex paperwork for it all. What the insurance company would or wouldn't cover was unclear. Nancy was regularly forced to negotiate directly with hospital labs and doctors' offices to sort out bills.
>
> And there were dozens of bills. Nancy needed a spreadsheet to keep track of them. Every bill had to be reviewed, often negotiated, and frequently paid immediately. (Groce, Bills.)

Sometimes, Nancy received bills by mistake. She received one for $40,000 from the hospital where she received her radiation treatment. They had erred in submitting her insurance information, and she was deemed to be without insurance. It took weeks to clear up. Her out-of-pocket expenses, the amount her insurance did not cover, came to $14,000. Six months after her surgery, she was still receiving bills.

Nancy and Nora both agreed that in the end they each received good medical care, but Nora never had any paperwork to deal with and could concentrate on her illness and recovery. Nancy was fortunate that she could negotiate bills with her providers and also could afford the bills for which she was responsible. When they wrote about their experiences in 2020, each was cancer free.

The NHS is one example of a social welfare policy. Social welfare policies, which are addressed in Section 12.2 of this chapter, are designed to reduce poverty and improve citizens' health. Before we study social welfare policies, however, we turn our attention to economic policies.

12.1 Economic Policies

Learning Targets

After reading this section, you should be able to do the following:

1. Explain how countries use import substitution industrialization policies to encourage domestic manufacturing.

2. Describe economic-liberalization policies.

3. Describe structural adjustment programs and austerity measures, and explain how they impact state budgets, citizens, and economic growth.

In this chapter, you will revisit many of the economic concepts you studied throughout this book, learning about several key ones in greater depth. This section focuses on economic-liberalization policies, such as reducing tariffs and subsidies, privatizing state-owned industries, and encouraging foreign investment. Before adopting policies favored by **neoliberal** economists, some states used import substitution industrialization strategies.

Neoliberalism
An economic ideology favoring policies that support the free market and reduce trade barriers.

Import Substitution Industrialization

Many developing countries did not adopt economic-liberalization policies until the late twentieth century, preferring **protectionist economic policies** instead. As you learned in Chapter 3, in the 1980s, Mexico pursued import substitution industrialization (ISI) policies to stimulate rapid industrialization and growth. Mexico adopted protectionist policies to protect businesses in the domestic economy from more competitive international businesses.

Protectionist economic policy
A policy designed to shelter domestic industry from competition and reduce foreign influence on sectors of the economy.

Agriculture is a good example. Farmers in Mexico in the 1970s were not mechanized at a comparable level to U.S. farmers (or other advanced industrial agricultural producers). Opening up Mexico's economy to international competition would have caused Mexican producers to go out of business, potentially making Mexico dependent on external food production. These factors caused the Mexican government to adopt protectionist ISI policies. Iran, which we will study in the next chapter, also adopted ISI during the 1960s and 1970s.

The economic philosophy behind **import substitution industrialization (ISI)** is that a developing country should protect its new industries by placing restrictions on international trade. This allows new domestic industries to grow until they are strong enough to compete on the international market. By limiting the number of imported manufactured products or placing tariffs on them, governments could encourage domestic and international investment in new industries in their countries. Many developing countries pursued these policies, with the support of Western governments and the World Bank, from the 1950s to the 1970s. Some governments created state-owned industries that supplied the domestic market with key goods, such as fuel and electricity.

At first, ISI was relatively successful in creating new industries. Countries such as Mexico saw rapid economic growth throughout the 1950s and 1960s. By the 1970s, economic growth slowed. Protecting industries from competition helped them get started, but in the long run, protection resulted in inefficient industries that could not compete in the international market. These industries and their employees put political pressure on governments to preserve the protections they enjoyed.

When oil prices quadrupled in 1973, countries that were not oil producers had to pay much more for oil and other key imports, but because their industries could not compete globally, they could not export enough goods to pay for the imports. They were forced to take out international loans to cover the trade imbalance. When oil prices increased again in 1979, governments had to borrow even more money from international lenders. Some reached the brink of bankruptcy, and Mexico's declaration in 1982 that it was unable to meet its international debt obligations began a global "debt crisis," which ushered in a new era in development policy.

> **Import substitution industrialization (ISI)**
> Enacting high tariffs and providing incentives to encourage the growth of domestic manufacturing.

> **AP® TIP**
> Make sure you understand the differences between ISI and neoliberal economic policies. Both terms are likely to appear on the exam.

Neoliberal Policies

Neoliberal economic policies support the free market and reduce trade barriers. Countries adopt economic-liberalization policies to reduce unemployment, increase productivity, and lower trade deficits. Rentier states, like Nigeria, enact economic-liberalization policies to diversify their economies and reduce the state's dependence on finite natural resources, such as gold and silver, natural gas, and petroleum, as a source of government revenue.

Supporters of neoliberalism argue that government intervention to steer the economy is at best ineffective and often harmful. Instead, neoliberal economists such as Milton Friedman and Friedrich Hayek argued that governments should minimize intervention in the free market so that the market can allocate resources as efficiently as possible to maximize wealth generation. Friedman argued that government borrowing and deficit spending simply "crowd out" private-sector borrowing, impeding the ability of businesses to invest and reducing long-term growth.

Neoliberal theorists also favor cutting back most government regulations. Government efforts to reduce pollution, protect consumers' and workers' safety, and regulate business activities, such as banking, put constraints on businesses' ability to invest wisely and waste precious resources. Neoliberal economists call for a reduction in regulations and the overall size of government, in addition to balancing government budgets by eliminating deficit spending.

As you learned in your study of the United Kingdom, neoliberalism was the basis for the economic policies of Prime Minister Margaret Thatcher. In the early 1980s, the Thatcher government radically reduced the size and scope of the British government's intervention in the economy (Section 5.5). The government closed or privatized many previously nationalized industries and passed laws weakening the power of labor unions.

Following Thatcher's policies, the economy grew, until the recession of 2008–2009. Even when the Labour Party came to power in the 1990s, it continued mostly to pursue economic-liberalization policies. Neoliberal ideas and policies spread to many other countries. They became particularly powerful in poorer countries.

Neoliberal economists argued that developing countries were no different from wealthy ones and should follow the same basic policies. These economists compiled a package of policies that came to be known as **structural adjustment programs (SAPs)**.

Structural adjustment program (SAP)
Requirements for receiving assistance from international lenders (such as the IMF), including the privatization of state-owned companies, reducing tariffs, and reducing subsidies for domestic industries.

The debt crisis that began in 1982 caused many governments, such as Mexico, to ask the IMF for emergency financial assistance. Working together, the IMF and World Bank demanded that the governments receiving assistance in the 1980s and 1990s implement SAPs. As you learned in your study of Nigeria (Section 9.5), SAPs required countries borrowing from international lenders to end government protection of domestic industries and other restrictions on free trade, reduce subsidies, privatize government-owned industries, and reduce budget deficits.

SAPs required budget cuts and far less government intervention in the economy. The idea was that if a country could endure short-term economic pain, the new policies would maximize efficiency and encourage new investment, producing economic growth in the long term. This was a slow process in many countries. SAP policies were politically unpopular because they initially resulted in high inflation, increased unemployment, and drastic cuts in government services, including education, health care, and programs to alleviate poverty. Cuts in social programs have the potential to lead to widespread unrest, which undermines the stability of the regime.

Austerity measures
Cuts to social services, which might include programs to help women, children, the poor, and the elderly, in an effort to reduce government debt.

To secure necessary debt relief, poor countries had to accept **austerity measures** that the IMF and World Bank imposed, including cuts to social services, such as programs designed to help women, children, the poor, and the elderly. Austerity measures often result in cuts to programs aimed at leveling the economic playing field for disadvantaged citizens and tend to negatively and disproportionally impact the poor. States agreed to make certain policy changes over a period of about three years, and the IMF/World Bank subsequently monitored how the countries followed through on their promises. Often, political leaders only partially fulfilled their obligations, so everything went back to the drawing board. This resulted in very slow and partial implementation of neoliberal policies as countries went through several rounds of negotiation and implementation with the IMF/World Bank.

Wealthy countries, such as the United Kingdom, also have adopted austerity measures. Unlike countries that adopt austerity measures as a condition of borrowing money from the IMF and World Bank, wealthy countries voluntarily pass austerity measures. For example, following the 2007–2008 recession, the Conservative government in the United Kingdom cut public spending and passed several tax increases in an effort to reduce government deficits.

Overall, the effects of SAPs were mixed. On one of the most common measures of development, gross domestic product per capita, developing countries grew more quickly than wealthy countries from 1965 to 1980, indicating that development policies before the implementation of SAPs had been helping to accelerate development. In the 1980s and 1990s, however, developing countries grew more slowly than wealthy countries, suggesting SAPs might have made things worse or at least did not help them overcome other factors slowing their growth. (Ocampo and Vos, 2008, 10.)

The growth of GDP per capita varied by region. East Asia grew much faster than the world average. However, Africa suffered economic contraction through most of the

A bustling street in Shenzhen, China. Shenzhen was one of China's first special economic zones, created to attract investors as part of the country's move toward a more liberal economic system.

Tuul and Bruno Morandi/Alamy

period, and Latin America contracted in the 1980s and saw very low growth of only 1.3 percent per year during the 1990s.

Changes in poverty mirrored the changes in growth. The percentage of the world's population living in extreme poverty (earning less than a dollar per day) was cut nearly in half over the two decades, from just over 40 percent to about 22 percent. Almost all of that decline, however, took place in East and South Asia. Given population growth, the total number of people living in extreme poverty increased in Africa and Latin America and very slightly declined in South Asia. Yet the numbers were cut by nearly three-quarters in East Asia, which includes rapidly growing China. As you saw in your study of China, the country's extraordinary economic growth since partially adopting economic-liberalization policies lifted millions out of poverty and is a source of legitimacy for the CCP and the regime (Sections 11.1 and 11.5).

Drawbacks of Neoliberalism

Some critics argue that neoliberalism undermines the fundamentals of long-term development in infrastructure and **human capital**, the education, skills, training, and other positive attributes that people bring to the economy. Critics contend that states can best develop their economies by providing government funds for infrastructure—especially efficient transportation and communications systems—and for human capital, an educated and healthy workforce.

SAPs demand fiscal austerity, typically by cutting government spending. For countries with weak infrastructure, education, and health care, austerity measures are counterproductive. Critics also point out that neoliberal economic reforms have not reduced the persistent corruption that exists in many developing countries.

Although economic liberalization policies can stimulate economic growth, they also result in urban sprawl and environmental pollution, uneven economic development, and a widening income gap. Urban sprawl increases fuel consumption, depletes fossil fuels, and

Human capital
The education, skills, training, and other positive attributes that people bring to the economy.

Writing a Response to an Opposing or Alternate Perspective Using Refutation, Concession, or Rebuttal

The final part of the argument essay requires you to describe an opposing perspective and respond to it using refutation, concession, or rebuttal (RCR). As you learned in the AP® Political Science Practices feature in Section 2.5, refutation is using evidence to prove that an opponent's contention is false, rebuttal means discrediting an argument by offering a different point of view, and concession means acknowledging a point and demonstrating an understanding of a differing viewpoint.

The last part of the prompt in the argument essay asks you to do the following:

Respond to an opposing or alternate perspective, using refutation, concession, or rebuttal.

Note that the prompt requires you to do TWO things: (1) describe an opposing or alternate perspective to your thesis, and (2) respond to the perspective you described. In other words, you have to give an argument that would be made by someone who disagrees with your thesis, and then you have to explain why your argument is better (or why the other perspective is wrong).

Suppose the argument essay prompt asks you to take a position on whether economic-liberalization policies will lead to democratization in authoritarian states. To start, you write your thesis as,

Economic-liberalization policies are not likely to lead to democratization in authoritarian states, because these policies improve economic performance and citizens' standards of living and increase the legitimacy of the state.

First, make a clear transition to your RCR paragraph, and then describe an opposing argument. Here is an example:

An opponent of my argument might claim that economic-liberalization policies open countries to free trade and the exchange of ideas, including ideas about democracy. Because economic-liberalization policies allow exposure to democratic ideals, citizens in authoritarian states will advocate for more freedom and democratic government.

It is important that you clearly indicate that this is the beginning of your RCR discussion. In this case, the paragraph begins with, "An opponent of my argument might claim . . ."

After the discussion of the opposing or alternative perspective, make a clear transition to your response, and provide a specific response. Here is an example:

This opposing argument is not accurate, because although economic-liberalization policies may allow exposure to democratic systems, people in authoritarian states will also learn about the drawbacks of democracy, such as the protection of hate speech. Therefore, economic-liberalization policies are not likely to lead authoritarian states to democratize, because after their citizens learn about some of the negative aspects of democracy, they may prefer the security and order provided in an authoritarian state.

This is an example of a concession argument because it agrees with the notion that economic-liberalization policies result in exposure to new ideas, but it provides a different perspective from the opposing argument about how citizens might react to learning more about democracy.

The sample response is specific. Do not state only that your opponent is wrong, and do not simply restate your thesis. For example, a response that stated, "The opposing argument is inaccurate because economic-liberalization policies lead to more democracy," simply restates the thesis. It does not provide evidence refuting the opposing argument.

Answer the following questions based on an essay prompt that asks you to develop an argument about whether structural adjustment policies increase or decrease state sovereignty in the long run.

1. Write an analytical thesis.
2. Describe an opposing or alternate perspective.
3. Respond to the opposing or alternate perspective using refutation, concession, or rebuttal.

contributes to air pollution. As you saw in your study of Nigeria, lack of environmental regulation led to devastating pollution in the Niger Delta (Section 9.3). Neoliberal policies encourage states to engage in a "race to the bottom" by reducing regulations on labor conditions and the environment.

Economic-liberalization policies also impact migration patterns. Countries with urban industrial centers, such as China and Mexico, have seen increased migration from rural to urban areas, as well as a migration from the south to the north in Mexico and from the west to the east in China. Internal migration strains housing and social services. Furthermore, rural areas may be omitted from development plans and continue to struggle with lack of infrastructure and access to social services.

A broader review of the effect of economic-liberalization policies concluded that "liberalizing countries see significant poverty reduction if and when they have beneficial initial conditions, such as good geography, large endowments of low-skilled labor (rather than unskilled labor), and strong institutions," such as the protection of property rights and the rule of law. (Rudra and Tobin, 2017, 302.) The World Bank set forth an agenda of "good governance," arguing that states need to take an active role in providing security, property rights, contract enforcement, and infrastructure. They also must enhance human capital and development potential by providing essential health and education services to the poor. Many now believe that some state intervention in the economy is appropriate, especially to alleviate poverty.

Section 12.1 Review

Each section's main ideas are reflected in the Learning Targets. By reviewing after each section, you should be able to

Remember the key points,

Know terms that are central to the topic, and

Think critically about what you have learned.

Remember

- Countries use import-substitution industrialization policies to encourage domestic manufacturing.
- Economic-liberalization policies encourage the reduction of tariffs, free trade, privatization of industry, and a reduction of regulations on businesses.
- Structural-adjustment programs and austerity measures are designed to improve the budgets of countries by increasing state revenue and decreasing expenses.

Know

- *Neoliberalism:* an economic ideology favoring policies that support the free market and reduce trade barriers. (p. 374)
- *Protectionist economic policy:* a policy designed to shelter domestic industry from competition and reduce foreign influence on sectors of the economy. (p. 374)
- *Import substitution industrialization (ISI):* enacting high tariffs and providing incentives to encourage the growth of domestic manufacturing. (p. 375)
- *Structural adjustment program (SAP):* requirements for receiving assistance from international lenders (such as the IMF), including the privatization of state-owned companies, reducing tariffs, and reducing subsidies for domestic industries. (p. 376)
- *Austerity measures:* cuts to social services, which might include programs to help women, children, the poor, and the elderly, in an effort to reduce government debt. (p. 376)
- *Human capital:* the education, skills, training, and other positive attributes that people bring to the economy. (p. 377)

Think

- What are the advantages and drawbacks of economic-liberalization policies?
- Why might different economic policies be appropriate for states, depending on their level of development?

12.2 Social Policies

Learning Targets

After reading this section, you should be able to do the following:

1. Explain how the women's movement has impacted gender equity.

2. Describe the types of social welfare programs.

3. Describe the types of health-care programs.

Social policies include programs to promote gender equity and provide access to education and health care. Governments enact social welfare programs to alleviate poverty and make people healthier. By providing these programs, states decrease the likelihood of unrest and instability and increase their legitimacy.

Gender Equity

Changes in women's political and social status in the last generation have been dramatic, especially in liberal democracies. Women can vote and run for office in all six countries studied in AP® Comparative Government and Politics. In liberal democracies, the number of women in the workforce, in professional positions, and in higher education has skyrocketed since the 1960s. (Kirkpatrick, 1974.)

While still underrepresented in the executive, legislative, and executive institutions, the number of women holding high office is growing in democracies. For example, as you learned in Section 3.3, Mexico requires parties to run 50 percent female candidates. In illiberal democracies, such as Nigeria, and in authoritarian states, such as Russia, China, and Iran, women are underrepresented at the highest levels of government.

While women have made many gains, their social and legal status is still not uniformly equal to men's. Women's groups worldwide have sought greater access to education and participation in the labor force. The gender gap in educational access and attainment has narrowed substantially in most Latin American and African countries and in some Asian ones as well. However, rates of female participation in the paid workforce are still lower than the employment rates for men. Overall, democracies provide more equality for women, including countries that have recently undergone democratic transitions. (Tripp, 2013.) Figure 12.1 is a world map of gender inequality rankings.

FIGURE 12.1

Gender Inequality

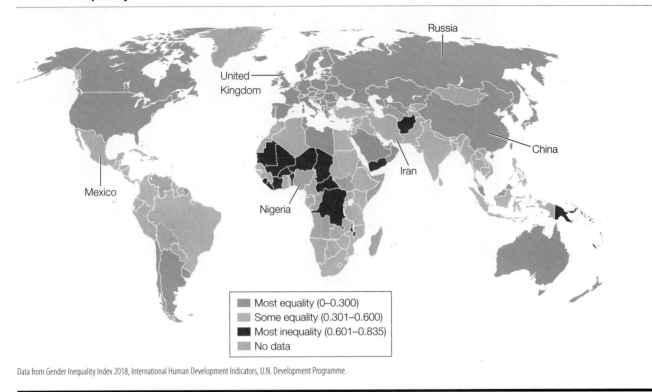

Most equality (0–0.300)
Some equality (0.301–0.600)
Most inequality (0.601–0.835)
No data

Data from Gender Inequality Index 2018, International Human Development Indicators, U.N. Development Programme.

Concerns about achieving greater social and economic status have led women to demand access to contraception and state support for childbearing and child rearing. Women's movements have successfully fought for access to contraception in much of the world, and birth rates have fallen significantly in most countries over the last generation.

Abortion remains a controversial subject, with women leading successful efforts to legalize it. For example, even though Mexico is a predominantly Catholic country, abortion is legal in some states. In 2021, Mexico's Supreme Court ruled that laws criminalizing abortion are unconstitutional. However, abortion is illegal in many countries due to moral and religious objections.

Women, especially in wealthier countries, have also demanded greater state support for childbearing and childrearing. Social welfare programs to benefit parents include paid and unpaid maternity leave, paid and unpaid paternity leave (for fathers to help with child rearing), and access to affordable and high-quality childcare.

Women's groups worldwide advocate equal status in family law (including child custody), land ownership, and inheritance of family property. This goal has been achieved in almost all liberal democracies. However, in many illiberal or hybrid regimes and authoritarian states, women still face legal inequalities that prevent them from independently owning land or inheriting property. In some cases, women are even restricted from having independent access to banking and travel. While virtually all countries have active women's movements working toward these goals, women in most developing countries remain poorer and less educated, on average, than in developed countries.

A meeting of mostly female activists in Iran, planning a protest against the 2015 arrest of Narges Mohammadi, a human-rights activist. The women's movement in Iran seeks to improve their legal status.

After a long struggle, women have gained recognition as a group with legitimate concerns and basic political rights in some countries. Yet in many countries, the law does not grant women equal status with men.

Social Welfare

The main goals of social welfare policies are to reduce poverty and income inequality and to stabilize individual or family income. Governments may want to alleviate poverty on purely humanitarian grounds. States might also be concerned about social and political stability. High poverty rates and economic instability can threaten a state's legitimacy, and poverty is associated with higher levels of crime.

Of the different types of social welfare policies, some programs provided by the government are available to all citizens equally, usually funded by taxes. A free public education is one example. Another kind of social welfare is a social-insurance program. Social insurance provides benefits to people who have contributed to a public fund. In most cases, both workers and their employers must contribute to the funds, which pay for disability benefits, pensions, and unemployment insurance. Workers can then benefit from the fund when they need it—after retirement, when temporarily unemployed, or if they become disabled.

Means-tested social assistance programs are available only to individuals who fall below a specific income level. These programs can include monthly cash payments and food and housing assistance. Some countries, like the United Kingdom, impose requirements for receiving public assistance, such as work requirements or time limits. While means-tested assistance is an effective way to reduce poverty, it can be expensive for governments to administer means-tested programs.

Conditional cash transfer (CCT) programs are innovative forms of social welfare designed to improve health and education. These programs, such as the Prospera program in Mexico, provide cash grants to the poor in exchange for recipients sending their children to school and to health clinics. These programs are means-tested and target the poorest households to gain the maximum impact. CCT programs in Latin America reduced poverty and have increased both school enrollment and use of health-care services. (Ferreira and Robalino, 2011.)

Health Care

There are three basic types of health-care systems. One common type is a national health system (NHS). NHS is a government-financed and managed system. The government creates a system into which all citizens pay. The classic example of this type of system is in the United Kingdom, which established its NHS after World War II. China, Russia, Iran, and Nigeria have adopted versions of NHS systems. In most NHS countries, most medical professionals receive their income directly from the government, which controls the cost of medical care through payments for procedures, equipment, and drugs. Private insurance is often available for people who want to supplement the medical coverage provided by the state.

Most poor countries have an NHS through which the government provides medical care through hospitals and local clinics and in which doctors are direct government employees. As you saw in your study of Nigeria, however, poor countries lack adequate clinics and doctors, and many people lack access to or must wait long periods for what is often low-quality care.

Another common health-care model is an NHI system, in which the government requires citizens to purchase health insurance. Since the government mandates the insurance, it also regulates the system, setting or limiting premiums and payments to medical providers. In many NHI systems, access to health care is not specific to an employer, so workers can keep their insurance when they switch jobs.

A market-based private-insurance system is the least common health-care system. Mexico is an example of a country that relies on private insurance for the bulk of its health care. In a market-based system, citizens gain insurance through their employment, and medical care is provided mostly by private clinics and hospitals. Government programs often exist in market-based systems to cover specific groups without private insurance, such as the poor, the unemployed, and the self-employed. Market-based systems do not guarantee access to health care to all citizens, and even in the wealthiest of these countries, a sizable minority lack insurance.

Developed countries are most concerned about cost because health-care costs are rising faster than incomes. People in developed countries demand advanced medical care, and expensive technology emerges to help provide that care. Developed countries have relatively low birth rates and high life expectancies, so the proportion of the population that is elderly increases over time, which increases the need for health care.

Access is a much greater problem than rising costs in the less developed countries, where limited resources mean smaller numbers of doctors, hospitals, and clinics per capita. Even though individuals might formally be covered by a government health plan, they cannot gain access to health care if facilities and providers are not available. As a result of limited access and costs that are too high for the poor majority, preventable and easily treatable diseases continue to shorten life spans and cause loss of income and productivity in much of the world.

Remember

- The women's movement has increased gender equity, but women still face unequal treatment in many countries.

- Social welfare programs are designed to reduce poverty and provide benefits to citizens, such as pensions and payments to the unemployed and disabled.

- Health-care systems vary among countries, and while wealthy countries worry about cost, poorer countries are concerned about access.

Think

- To what extent does state stability depend on the ability to provide citizens with social programs?

....

Free-Response Question: Quantitative Analysis

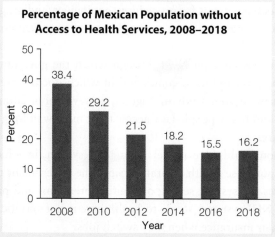

Percentage of Mexican Population without Access to Health Services, 2008–2018

Data from Statista and Ana María Ríos, August 26, 2020.

Answer A, B, C, D, and E.

A. Using the data in the bar chart, identify the year in which the largest percentage of the Mexican population lacked access to health care.

B. Using the data in the bar chart, describe a trend in the percentage of the Mexican population considered vulnerable due to lack of access to health care between 2008 and 2018.

C. Describe a social welfare program in Mexico.

D. Draw a conclusion about how social welfare programs impact poverty rates.

E. Describe a factor, other than social welfare programs, that impacts poverty rates.

12.3 Causes and Effects of Economic Policies

Learning Targets

After reading this section, you should be able to do the following:

1. Explain how globalization and industrialization impact the environment.

2. Explain why countries nationalize resources.

3. Explain why countries with an abundant natural resource often face negative economic and political consequences, a situation known as the resource curse.

Industrialization has both benefits and drawbacks. It can improve economic growth and raise citizens' standard of living. It also increases the demand for fossil fuels, such as coal, oil, and natural gas. Rapid development caused by industrialization results in environmental pollution, which damages health and increases the potential for instability.

Impact of Industrialization

Globalization has produced industrialization in many developing countries, improving economic growth rates, but increasing pollution in previously agrarian societies. Some people believe global competition has produced a "race to the bottom," as countries use lax environmental rules to attract foreign capital. Those who believe there is a race to the bottom argue that rich countries are outsourcing not only factories and jobs but pollution as well. For example, the quality of the air and water around Pittsburgh has dramatically improved as the city's steel industry has declined, while China, now the world's largest steel producer, faces a major problem with pollution.

Rapidly industrializing countries face dramatically expanding environmental problems. The southeastern region of Nigeria is dotted with nearly 1,500 oil wells, which for many years provided an estimated 40 percent of U.S. oil imports. From 2008 to 2018, Nigeria had 9,343 documented oil spills, and an estimated 9 to 13 million barrels of oil have been spilled into the Niger River Delta in the past five decades. This is fifty times the amount of the *Exxon Valdez* oil spill in Alaska, which is generally considered to be one of the worst oil spills in history. (Oshienenmen, Amaratunga, and Haigh, 2018.)

Analyzing the World Values Survey, Dunlap and York found the citizens of both poor and wealthy countries express concern for the environment. (Dunlap and York, 2012.) Using a large, quantitative analysis, Gabriele Spilker found that foreign direct investment is associated with more pollution in developing countries. (Spilker, 2013.) However, governments can lessen the impact of globalization on pollution. One way to reduce the impact of globalization on pollution is by membership in key international organizations that could help the government respond to environmental problems. For example, the United Nations has adopted seventeen Sustainable Development Goals, which intertwine policies to support the economy, social well-being, and environmental protections. Another way to reduce the impact of globalization on pollution is through a well-established democracy, in which people can demand stronger policies to protect the environment.

Also tied to globalization are "third-generation" environmental problems. These problems are global and, therefore, require global responses. Air and water pollution have always crossed borders. The source of the pollution does not matter, because its effects are global. Scientists have demonstrated measurable effects of China's air pollution on the west coast of the United States. The major third-generation problem, though, is climate change, which is addressed below.

Development always involves increased use of resources, but if nonrenewable resources are being used quickly, development won't be sustainable. As demand for food and land increases, farmers and ranchers clear forested areas throughout the tropics. This gives them nutrient-rich soil on which to grow crops and graze cattle, as well as valuable wood to sell on the global market, but tropical rainforest soils are thin and are quickly depleted. After a few years, new land must be cleared as the soil is exhausted. The result is rapidly disappearing forests and development that is unsustainable in the long run. Deforestation also increases climate change because trees absorb and retain carbon.

Farmers' and ranchers' rational response to growing global demand for agricultural products has created unsustainable development and more global warming. Globalization-induced air and water pollution and rapid use of nonrenewable resources make the goal of sustainable development ever more challenging for many poor countries.

States can enact several policies to reduce the impact of globalization and industrialization on the environment. China has become a global leader in renewable energy, generating the largest share of wind and solar energy in the world. Its Thirteenth Five-Year Plan for Electricity (2016–2020) had the goal of raising the percentage of production from non-fuels, and the National Energy Administration and National Development and Reform Commission planned to spend more than $360 billion on renewable energy development by 2020. (Chiu, 2017.)

AP® POLITICAL SCIENCE PRACTICES

Interpreting a Pie Chart

A pie chart is one of the most basic methods to display data visually. The pie represents 100 percent of something, and each slice represents a fraction of the whole. Pie charts can be used to summarize large amounts of data, but if they include too many categories of information, they get crowded, and it becomes difficult to understand each "slice" of data.

Pie charts that do not include data references (numbers next to each slice) make it hard to determine the exact value of each piece of data. One of the biggest drawbacks of pie charts is that a single chart does not show change over time, and several pie charts would be required to show trends in the data.

As in most visual representations, the title of a pie chart is your starting point for analysis. Next, look at the area of the slices, especially the biggest ones. Dig deeper into the numbers by looking at any values next to the slices. Finally, consider the source of the data, which may give clues about the perspective of the person or organization that created the pie chart.

Use the pie chart to answer the following questions.

1. Describe what the pie chart measures.

2. Describe one drawback of the pie chart.

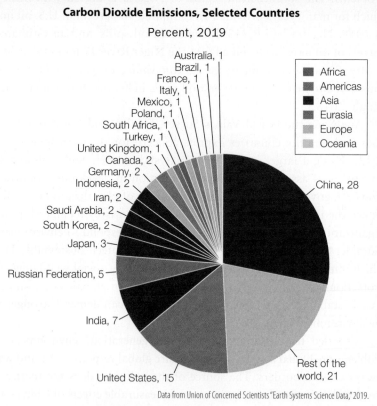

Carbon Dioxide Emissions, Selected Countries

Percent, 2019

Australia, 1
Brazil, 1
France, 1
Italy, 1
Mexico, 1
Poland, 1
South Africa, 1
Turkey, 1
United Kingdom, 1
Canada, 2
Germany, 2
Indonesia, 2
Iran, 2
Saudi Arabia, 2
South Korea, 2
Japan, 3
Russian Federation, 5
India, 7
United States, 15

China, 28
Rest of the world, 21

Legend:
- Africa
- Americas
- Asia
- Eurasia
- Europe
- Oceania

Data from Union of Concerned Scientists "Earth Systems Science Data," 2019.

3. Explain whether a pie chart is the best way to represent the data.

Mexico City's ECOBICI bike-sharing program is an easy way to get around and reduces traffic congestion and air pollution.

Paul Christian Gordon/Alamy

China is also shutting down industrial regions known for air pollution. In 2017, the Ministry of Environment inspected factories throughout the country, levied fines, and used criminal enforcement to punish the worst polluters. Entire industrial regions are being shuttered and some companies have moved their production facilities away from China.

China's emphasis on cleaning up the environment has both social and political causes. Air pollution poses harmful health risks. China has an air quality monitoring system to help citizens make decisions about outdoor activity. (Schmitz, 2017.) Furthermore, by improving air quality, the state can increase legitimacy, reduce the potential for unrest, and increase state security by relying less on other countries for energy. (Chiu, 2017.)

Many countries have passed laws to reduce air pollution caused by vehicles, such as offering financial incentives for buying battery-powered or hybrid vehicles. Mexico City was a pioneer in developing bike-share programs to reduce traffic congestion and auto emissions. ECOBICI is a program that allows people to pay for access to bikes for a few days, a week, or a year. Bike stations throughout the city allow users to take bikes and return them elsewhere for 45-minute trips. The system allows commuters to save the time they would otherwise be sitting in traffic jams, improve their health, and protect the environment.

Despite the global challenge of environmental degradation, many governments are taking steps to protect natural resources and the health of their citizens.

Nationalized Resources

Natural resources are nationalized, which means they are owned and managed by the government, in Mexico, Russia, Nigeria, China, and Iran. Controlling key sectors of the economy allows government to consolidate its power and provides a source of government revenue. States that set artificially low prices for nationalized resources provide citizens with a financial benefit and may be more likely to maintain their legitimacy. As you saw in studying Nigeria, however, fuel subsidies are a drain on the government's budget, and the threat to remove them resulted in widespread protests.

State ownership of natural resources increases sovereignty because foreign investors and MNCs have little control over the production and use of those resources. Some resources, such as coal and steel, are crucial for industrial development. Ownership of key natural resources increases the state's control over economic development. Russia, for example, renationalized its oil industry. Although Mexico allows some private investment in Pemex, the government retains a majority share of ownership.

Privatization of national resources may make production more efficient because private companies must invest in new technologies and improve infrastructure to compete on the world market. However, privatization of natural resources decreases the government's control over their extraction and production, increases the wealth gap, and may decrease state sovereignty.

The Resource Curse

Rentier state
A state that relies on the export of oil or from the leasing of resources to foreign entities as a significant source of government revenue.

Resource curse
A problem faced by countries that have a valuable and abundant natural resource that limits diversification of the economy, makes government revenue dependent on the world market, increases opportunities for corruption, and lessens the government's responsiveness to citizens.

As you learned in your study of Russia and Nigeria, states with a large amount of a valuable natural resource, such as oil, often become **rentier states**, where a significant percentage of government revenue comes from the export of oil and gas or from leasing land to foreign companies that extract the resource.

Although it may seem counterintuitive, having large quantities of a valuable natural resource does not mean a state will have positive economic and political outcomes. This is known as the **resource curse**. Countries with an abundant natural resource face negative economic and political consequences. Neither the government nor the private sector is incentivized to diversity and modernize their economies, because they already have a steady source of government revenue. However, that revenue is subject to change depending on a fluctuating world market, which makes it difficult to predict revenue and plan budgets. Spending anticipated future revenue on government projects results in budget deficits, trade imbalances, and overvalued currency when commodities prices fall. Revenue from the sale of resources tends to benefit the economic elite, widening the gap between the rich and the poor.

Rentier states present opportunities for corruption by government officials who divert the revenue from natural resources away from the treasury. This is at least in part because citizens are less invested in overseeing how a government uses funds from a commodity compared to the attention citizens give when the government is funded by tax revenues from their citizens. It is a straightforward pocketbook issue. But, as you saw in studying the Niger Delta region of Nigeria, the resource curse can also lead to conflict when the extraction of resources results in environmental damages and when people do not believe they are receiving the benefits of the resources extracted from their communities.

The resource curse affects how a country is governed. Rentier states tend not to rely on income tax as a major source of revenue. Citizens who do not pay taxes may have less sense of political efficacy. The leaders of rentier states may not be willing to cooperate with regional or international organizations in following policies that would increase transparency. In addition, authoritarian states may use the revenues from natural resources to strengthen their institutional power, making the regime more durable. (Ross, 2015.)

Economic policies, including industrialization and control over natural resources, have social and political consequences. Their impact on citizens can increase or diminish the state's ability to rule.

Section 12.3 Review

Remember

- Globalization and industrialization have resulted in environmental damage, which harms public health, increases the potential for instability, and decreases state legitimacy.
- Many countries have enacted policies to reduce pollution, including closing factories, monitoring air quality, and investing in sources of renewable energy.
- Countries nationalize industries to maintain control over key sectors of the economy.
- Countries with an abundant natural resource often face negative economic and political consequences, a situation known as the resource curse.

Know

- *Rentier state:* a state that relies on the export of oil or from the leasing of resources to foreign entities as a significant source of government revenue. (p. 388)
- *Resource curse:* a problem faced by countries that have a valuable and abundant natural resource that limits diversification of the economy, makes government revenue dependent on the world market, increases opportunities for corruption, and lessens the government's responsiveness to citizens. (p. 388)

Think

- What policies can states adopt to maintain economic growth while protecting the environment?

....

Free-Response Question: Conceptual Analysis

Answer A, B, C, and D.

A. Define rentier state.

B. Explain how a rentier state could improve economic growth.

C. Explain how a country's status as a rentier state impacts legitimacy.

D. Explain why having an abundant natural resource can negatively impact a state's economy.

AP® KEY CONCEPTS

- Neoliberalism (p. 374)
- Protectionist economic policy (p. 374)
- Import substitution industrialization (ISI) (p. 375)
- Structural adjustment program (SAP) (p. 376)
- Austerity measures (p. 376)
- Human capital (p. 377)
- Rentier state (p. 388)
- Resource curse (p. 388)

AP® EXAM MULTIPLE-CHOICE PRACTICE QUESTIONS

1. In which of the following countries does the government have the least control over natural resources?

   A. Mexico

   B. Russia

   C. Nigeria

   D. The United Kingdom

2. Which of the following is an economic-liberalization policy adopted in a course country studied in AP® Comparative Government and Politics?

   A. Russia's renationalization of the oil industry

   B. Nigeria's creation of fuel subsidies

   C. Partial privatization of Pemex in Mexico

   D. China's creation of state-owned industries

Questions 3 and 4 refer to the infographic.

China Dialogue

3. The infographic supports which of the following statements?

   A. Nearly three-fourths of Chinese consumers are willing to pay more for products that are environmentally friendly.

   B. Only 29 percent of people in China have some knowledge of the low-carbon transition.

   C. Seventy-seven percent of people living in rural areas are satisfied with the low-carbon performance of their region.

   D. More than three-fourths of the respondents believe it is mainly the responsibility of the government to address climate change.

4. Which of the following is an implication of the information presented in the infographic?

   A. People in China are more concerned about economic growth than climate change.

   B. People living in China are aware of possible solutions to address climate change.

   C. The Chinese government limits access to information about climate change.

   D. The Chinese government has developed programs to address climate change to increase its international legitimacy.

5. Which of the following is a political consequence of a country's status as a rentier state?

   A. Increased environmental degradation

   B. Lack of diversity in the economy

   C. Increased opportunities for corruption

   D. Increased transparency in accounting for oil revenue

Questions 6 and 7 refer to the passage.

> [These programs] share a common objective: to move countries away from self-directed models of national development that focus on the domestic market and toward outward-looking development . . . [t]he neoliberal philosophy of economic development revived the old precepts of economic liberalism, which hold that an unregulated free market and private sector are the engines for unrestricted growth, the benefits of which will trickle down from the owners of capital to the entire population.
>
> —Jason Oringer and Carol Welch, Institute for Policy Studies, April 1, 1998

6. Which of the following economic policies is the topic of the passage?

   A. Import-substitution industrialization

   B. Nationalization of key industries

   C. Structural-adjustment policies

   D. Tariffs to protect domestic industries

7. Which of the following is a criticism of the economic policies described in the passage?

   A. They result in cuts to social services that hurt the most vulnerable.

   B. They focus on short-term benefits instead of long-term economic goals.

   C. The policies discourage direct foreign investment.

   D. The policies narrow the income gap by taking money from the wealthy.

8. Which of the following countries is the leader in the creation of renewable energy?

   A. The United Kingdom

   B. Nigeria

   C. Mexico

   D. China

9. Which two AP® Comparative Government and Politics course countries are rentier states?

    A. The United Kingdom and Russia

    B. Mexico and Nigeria

    C. Nigeria and Russia

    D. The United Kingdom and China

10. Which of the following is a potential drawback of nationalized industries?

    A. It is difficult for the state to control production levels.

    B. Nationalized industries are often understaffed due to low wages and poor working conditions.

    C. Government-controlled industries increase unemployment rates.

    D. Nationalized industries have less incentive than privatized industries to modernize and adopt new technology.

AP® EXAM PRACTICE ARGUMENT ESSAY

Develop an argument about whether being a rentier state increases or decreases legitimacy.

Use one or more of the following course concepts in your response:

- Structural adjustment programs
- Resource curse
- Sovereignty

In your response, do the following:

- Respond to the prompt with a defensible claim or thesis that establishes a line of reasoning using one or more of the provided course concepts.
- Support your claim with at least TWO pieces of specific and relevant evidence from your study of one or more course countries. The evidence should be relevant to one or more of the provided course concepts.
- Use reasoning to explain why your evidence supports your claim or thesis, using one or more of the provided course concepts.
- Respond to an opposing or alternate perspective, using refutation, concession, or rebuttal.

For a complete list of the sources of information cited in this chapter, turn to the Works Cited appendix.

Economics

13 Case Study: Iran

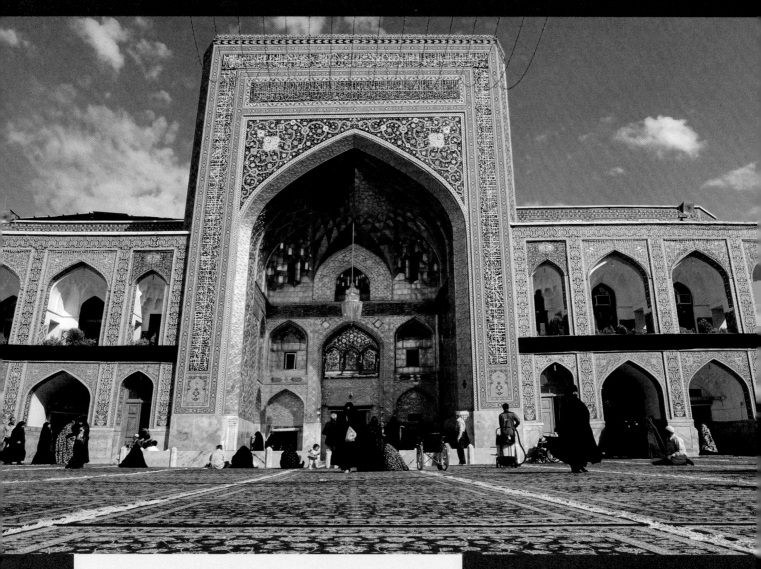

Iran has been an important crossroads for thousands of years. The Silk Road was long lived and particularly famous. One of its routes traversed northern Iran, through what are now the two largest cities, Tehran and Mashhad. The Imam Reza Shrine in Mashhad, shown here, is still a major destination of pilgrims.

Mehdi Langari/Alamy

Social Media and Music: Challenging Cultural Norms in Iran

For the leader of Iran's 1979 revolution, Ayatollah Ruhollah Khomeini (1900–1989), installing religious authority was central to his mission. "We did not make the revolution for cheap melons," he said, "We made it for Islam." (Farhi.) Khomeini targeted culture: "the road to reform in a country goes through its culture, so one has to start with cultural reform." (Rastovac.)

As you will learn in Section 13.1, there were many reasons for the revolution, and not all revolutionaries were religious fundamentalists. However, some of the revolutionaries were Islamic fundamentalists who rejected Western ideologies of secularism and individualism. When they prevailed, they put religious leaders in place and gave them extensive political power. Religious edicts, backed by state power, are one of the key attributes of post-revolutionary Iran. Restrictions on women's public appearance, and the censoring of music and dance, are two key features of Iran's moral politics.

Since the 1979 revolution, enforcement of religious commands has varied depending on the amount of political power held by those who favor reform. In recent years, moral codes have been enforced strictly, sparking street protests throughout the country, and leading to arrests and shutdowns of social media, because it has been used as a form of virtual protest. Since the constitutional system enshrines religious authority at the top of the state, challenges to this authority, including postings on social media, undercut its legitimacy. Social media posts critical of the state's regulation of moral behavior are seen as a threat to the political power of the clerical regime.

Battles over perceived immoral behavior have included the imposition of strict enforcement of public dress codes, particularly focused on women, strict separation of men from women in public, and bans on dancing and certain kinds of music. More recently, the state has banned social media platforms such as Facebook, Twitter, and YouTube, as well as many Western news sources.

Dressing modestly in public has been a requirement since the revolution. The requirement to wear the hijab, a headscarf that covers the hair of females after the age of ten, includes those who are not Muslim or Iranian. The hijab has long been a source of contention in Iran. Veiling in the form of a hijab has a long history in Iran going back more than 500 years, but in the twentieth century, the practice been subject to different mandates. (Mahmoudi.) In 1936, Iran's leader ordered women to remove their hijab in an effort to Westernize Iran, only to retreat from this position five years later in the face of protests. Between 1941 and 1979, veiling was an individual choice, but often subject to the approval of male family members.

In the 1970s, wearing a veil came to be seen as a sign of virtue and even opposition to the Shah. After the revolution, Khomeini noted that

> [T]he women who contributed to the revolution were and are women who wear modest clothes. These coquettish women, who wear makeup and put their necks, hair and bodies on display in the streets, did not fight the Shah. They have done nothing righteous. They do not know how to be useful, neither to society, nor politically or vocationally. And the reason is because they distract and anger people by exposing themselves. (Fallaci.)

Two weeks after assuming power, Khomeini mandated wearing the veil in public and in private when male nonfamily members were present. The day after the edict was announced, women protested. In Tehran, for example, more than 100,000 women took to the streets.

Despite periodic protests, wearing a veil is enforced through police checkpoints in major cities and a paramilitary force of tens of thousands. Penalties for not wearing a hijab include jail terms of ten days to two months and fines. Sometimes greater penalties have been given, including flogging.

Social media, such as Facebook and Instagram, have become a new tactic to protest against laws mandating the hijab. In 2014, Masih Alinejad, a journalist who left Iran in 2009 for London, posted a photo of herself on Facebook running down a London street with her long hair flowing in the wind. Within a month the post garnered 500,000 likes and led to a Web site, My Stealthy Freedom, where women in Iran post photos of themselves without headscarves. (Maloney and Katz.)

Protests against veiling continued, and in 2017, a new movement with the hashtag, Girls of Revolution Street, spread throughout the country. It was sparked by a thirty-one-year-old mother, Vida Movahed, who stood atop a utility box on one of Tehran's busiest streets and took off her headscarf waiving it on a stick like a flag. She was imprisoned and eventually sentenced to one year in jail but then pardoned.

The photo went viral, and others followed her example. Within months, dozens of women were arrested. Some were charged with more serious crimes than simply violating the headscarf mandate. Some were charged with "assembly and collusion to act against national security," "propaganda against the regime," as well as "encouraging and preparing the grounds for corruption and prostitution." Lengthier sentences were handed down, some as long as twenty years, although most sentences have been reduced.

A "street style" develops in most big cities, and the cities in Iran are no exception. Like others worldwide, Iranian women and men invent trends and follow fashion to express their individuality. Iranian law requires women to dress modestly and cover their hair in public.

Only France/Alamy

Iran's president at the time, Hassan Rouhani, a moderate reformer, seemed to be sympathetic to the protesters and released a survey that showed that at least half the country did not support laws that mandated wearing the hijab. Overall, in recent years, millions of Iranian women have received official warnings for not wearing the hijab properly, and in one year, 18,000 cases were prosecuted. (Maloney and Katz.)

In 2021, after the presidential election of conservative cleric Ebrahim Raisi, Iran's legislature moved to further restrict virtual protests against the state and restricted social media, including access to Instagram. Following the ban on another messaging app, Telegram, which was used by over half of the population, Instagram use spread throughout the country. Instagram is used by half of businesses and by three-quarters of Iranians, more than 60 million people.

On Instagram, women have posted pictures of themselves walking down public streets without a hijab, dressing immodestly, and wearing make-up. One seventeen-year-old said, "We dress up for Instagram. We show the best side of ourselves and our lives. But who I am on Instagram is closer to my reality than the person I am when I walk on the streets." (Nadeem.)

Iranians have found ways to circumvent restrictions on their social behavior. In the face of official efforts to prevent the use of many types of social media, many Iranians have found ways around the bans through VPNs and satellite dishes. Other types of illicit behavior, such as parties with women not wearing headscarves, loud music, and alcohol take place with a small bribe to the police.

Music is another realm of self-expression, and there are official efforts to stifle it. Although the Koran, the central scripture of Islam, does not explicitly condemn music,

Iranian authorities have often seen it as corrupting youth. According to Supreme Leader Khomeini,

> ... music is like a drug, whoever acquires the habit can no longer devote himself to important activities. It changes people to the point of yielding people to vice or to preoccupations pertaining to the world of music alone. We must eliminate music because it means betraying our country and our youth. We must completely eliminate it. (Rastovac.)

After the revolution, public concerts, solo female singing, and television broadcasts of both Western and Iranian pop music were banned. While some of these restrictions were loosened in the early 1990s, musical instruments still cannot be shown on television, and they must be blurred if a concert is broadcast. Women cannot sing solo to a mixed audience. Singing and dancing are not illegal but can be prosecuted if deemed indecent or immoral. Zumba, the fitness program set to Latin music, was banned in 2017.

Despite these restrictions, an underground music scene continues to flourish, including rap, rock, heavy metal, and other genres. Some of this music is produced in Los Angeles, California, which has the largest Iranian population outside Iran, and is the home of a

BY THE NUMBERS	IRAN
Land area	1,648,195 sq. km
Population	85,888,910 (July 2021 est.)
Urban population	76.3% (2020)
Life expectancy	Male 73.71 Female 76.48 (2021 est.)
Literacy rate	Male 90.4% Female 80.8% (2016)
HDI	0.783 (2020)
HDI ranking	70/189 (2020)
GDP	$610,662,000,000 (2020)
GDP ranking	21/195 (2020)
GDP per capita	$20,422 (2020)
Internet users	70% (2018)
Internet users ranking	14/229 (2018)
Gini index (coefficient)	40.9 (2019)
Freedom House rating	Not free (2020)
Corruption Perceptions ranking	150/180 (2021)
Fragile States Index classification	High Warning (2020)

Data from *CIA World Factbook*, World Bank, International Monetary Fund, Freedom House, Transparency International, Fragile States Index.

distinctive form of Iranian pop that is broadcast via satellite and the internet to Iran to circumvent censorship.

One of Iran's most popular underground singers, Sasan Heidari Yafteh, known as Sasy, has had continuing run-ins with Iran's censors. Born in 1988, he left Iran after being arrested for immoral dancing and now lives in Los Angeles. In 2019, he ran afoul of Iran's censors with a video that showed schoolchildren dancing. The song was played over 100 million times on the Persian-language music Web site Radio Javan.

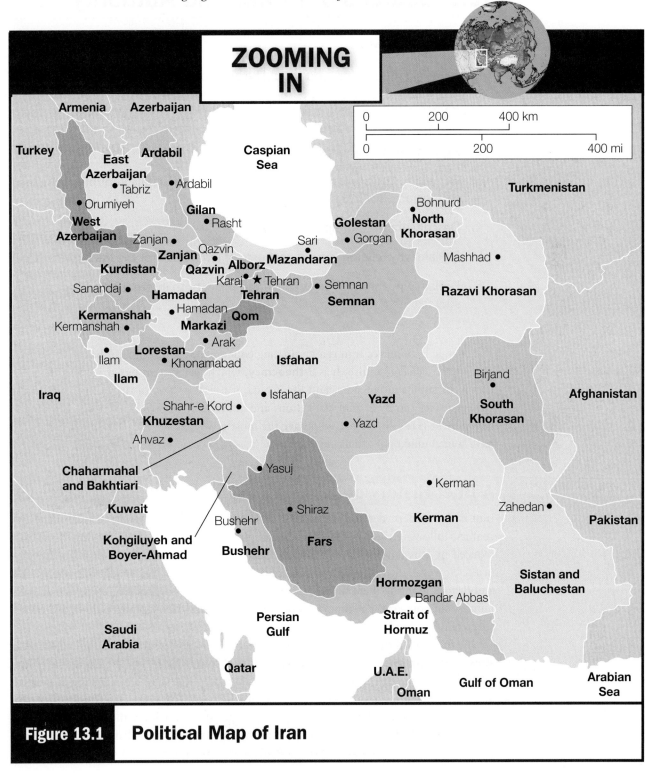

ZOOMING IN

Figure 13.1   Political Map of Iran

The continuing attempts by some Iranians to circumvent morality laws, and the government's crackdowns on illicit behavior, highlight tension within Iran's authoritarian state. The government seeks to maintain power and control over social behavior, but by doing so, it may risk losing some legitimacy among Iranians seeking self-expression.

13.1 Sources of Power and Authority

Learning Targets

After reading this section, you should be able to do the following:

1. Describe Iran's government under Shah Mohammad Reza Pahlavi, who ruled from 1953 to 1979.

2. Explain why the shah was overthrown in a revolution.

3. Explain how Ayatollah Khomeini established the Islamic Republic of Iran as a theocracy.

4. Describe Iran's centralized unitary state.

5. Explain why religion is a major source of legitimacy for the Iranian regime.

6. Explain why the state faces challenges from both internal and external sources.

Theocracy
A system based on religious rule.

The Islamic Republic of Iran is a fascinating country to study because it has a rich history and unique Persian culture. It is a **theocracy**, which is a system based on religious rule. Iran is an authoritarian state, and like China, it uses a system of dual rule in which the government is run by formal institutions and another, more powerful group. The Iranian government is run by clerics, who have the most power, along with elected officials, who have some limited policymaking authority.

A Brief History of Iran

Iran is the modern descendant of the great ancient empire of Persia. In the nineteenth century, following the discovery of oil, the power of the Persian empire was drastically reduced by Russian and British imperialism. Like China, Iran was never formally colonized. However, the Persian government became economically dependent on the Russians and British, granting them favorable terms for key resources, such as oil, in exchange for military support for the regime. European imperialism severely compromised the empire's sovereignty and reduced its territory.

By the start of the twentieth century, popular discontent with foreign influence led to street demonstrations from citizens demanding a new constitution. In 1906 the shah, a hereditary ruler, allowed the creation of a legislature, but the state remained weak, divided, and heavily influenced by Russia and the United Kingdom.

In 1921, Colonel Reza Khan led a coup d'état that overthrew the weakened empire and established what came to be known as the Pahlavi dynasty, ruled first by Reza Shah and then by his son, Mohammed Reza Pahlavi, who ruled from 1941 to 1979.

The Pahlavis created the first truly modern Persian state, renaming the country Iran in 1935. During their rule, the Pahlavis increased the size of the central army tenfold, dramatically expanded the bureaucracy, and gained full control over the provinces. The Pahlavis established an authoritarian regime, expanding both the state and the economy, increasing agricultural and industrial production, and building a significant amount of infrastructure, through state-led development. They welcomed extensive foreign investment, especially in the growing oil sector. They also centralized power in their hands. There was still an elected legislature with an elected prime minister, but its power was greatly reduced.

Following World War II, the United States built a close relationship with the Iranian government. The United States and its allies, and the Soviet Union and its allies, were trying to build good relationships with nonaligned countries during the Cold War period, and the United States also wanted access to Iran's oil reserves. In 1953, Iran's elected prime minister, Mohammed Mosaddeq, who wanted to nationalize Iran's oil industry, was ousted in a coup backed by the United States and the United Kingdom. Shah Mohammad Reza Pahlavi, who was friendly to Western powers, took power. The United States provided the Pahlavi government with economic and military aid, and Iran's military became one of the most powerful in the Middle East. (CBC, 2009.)

Social and Economic Policies under the Shah

From 1953 to 1979, the shah launched a series of social and economic reforms to modernize Iranian society, which further expanded the power of the state and its bureaucracy. The shah encouraged foreign investment, mechanization of agriculture, and access to higher education. These policies, however, did not benefit everyone. They favored larger over smaller enterprises, foreign over domestic investors, and urban over rural interests.

While economic growth and personal incomes rose noticeably on average, the poor observed the elite's conspicuous consumption, which they compared with their own very small gains. The 1973 quadrupling of world oil prices brought Iran a glut of wealth but skewed wealth distribution even further. Modernization of agriculture drove rural migrants to the cities, and there they joined the longstanding *bazaari* groups (traders in Iran's traditional bazaars). *Bazaaris* felt threatened by modernization as well, because the shah encouraged Western shops and banks to open to cater to the growing urban middle class, reducing the *bazaaris'* sales opportunities. (Clawson and Rubin, 2005.)

The shah pursued secularization, reducing the role of Islamic law in a country where the vast majority is Muslim. Domestic opposition mounted. SAVAK (the acronym in Farsi for the Organization for Intelligence and Security), a state secret police force, engaged in human-rights violations, including the torture and execution of critics of the regime, which was growing increasingly authoritarian. (Karimi and Gambrell, 2019.) SAVAK became one of the most feared and hated features of the shah's regime.

Opposition to and Overthrow of the Shah

Opposition to the shah had survived underground ever since the early 1950s but was divided along ideological lines among liberal reformers, Marxists, and religious groups. Secular intellectuals wrote anonymous letters and circulated pamphlets calling for the overthrow of the shah. The Islamic clergy opposed the shah's Westernization policies as a threat to Islam.

One of the country's major religious leaders, Ayatollah Ruhollah Khomeini, emerged as a major spokesperson and leader of this opposition. Jailed in 1963 and forced into exile in 1964 in neighboring Iraq and then France, Khomeini was the symbol and most popular leader of the opposition to the shah.

The worldwide economic downturn in the 1970s further highlighted problems in the Iranian government and economy. The public resented foreign ownership of oil production and the opportunities it presented for corruption among officials.

U.S. president Jimmy Carter, who was inaugurated in 1977, announced a new foreign policy emphasizing civil rights and liberties and criticized the shah's regime for violating human rights. The United States had strongly supported the regime for decades, so even the hint of willingness by leaders in the United States to consider regime change in Iran inspired the opposition to act. Social protests kicked into high gear after the Carter administration stopped pressing the shah for further reform.

The shah was diagnosed with cancer in 1974. In early 1978, his public appearances stopped. The shah's poor health, along with widespread public opposition to his policies, led to a perception that the shah's regime was weak, which was a crucial element in igniting the revolution. Protests spread through the streets and mosques, and local Islamic militias took over entire neighborhoods. The *bazaaris* and recent urban migrants, along with students and workers, became key supporters of revolution.

In January 1978, the government arranged for publication of a newspaper article attacking Khomeini. The following day, theology students organized a large demonstration in protest in the holy city of Qom. The shah's police responded with violence, and at least seventy people were killed. The religious opposition, joined by students and the *bazaaris*, then used the traditional mourning gatherings for those killed to organize greater demonstrations. By September, a demonstration of more than a million people took place in Tehran, and the shah once again reacted with the use of force: More than five hundred people were killed. The government declared martial law shortly afterward, shutting down universities and newspapers. This led to greater opposition as the urban working class joined the movement by organizing strikes, including in the country's crucial oil sector.

By December 1978, the shah had tried to respond to the rising revolt by replacing his prime minister, but this was not nearly enough to satisfy the growing opposition. In January 1979, the new prime minister managed to get the shah to leave office "temporarily" and began dismantling the shah's hated secret police. Facing growing opposition, the shah went into what was termed a temporary exile in January 1979 but would never return, completely eliminating any remaining legitimacy.

The opposition insisted on Khomeini's return from exile, a demand the government continued to resist. Returning to Iran on February 1, 1979, Khomeini immediately declared one of his supporters the "real prime minister," a claim the government rejected. The opposition mobilized its followers to invade prisons, police stations, and military bases on February 10 and 11 to take them over in the name of the revolution. After two bloody days in which hundreds were killed, the revolutionaries succeeded in taking power. Khomeini and other revolutionaries then established the Islamic Republic of Iran, the first theocratic government in the modern era, in April 1979.

Resistance to Democratization

The revolution of 1979 that created the Islamic Republic of Iran was a stark ideological contrast to the revolution led by the CCP in China, because the revolution in Iran was based partly on religion, which became an important source of state legitimacy. Like Mao in China, Ayatollah Khomeini was a charismatic leader who became the symbol of the revolution.

Unlike the Chinese revolution, no single political organization had control of the revolutionary movement in Iran. Khomeini was the charismatic and symbolic leader, but the revolutionary forces that came to power were ideologically diverse, including religious groups that followed Khomeini, Marxists, communists, and secular liberal nationalists who argued for democracy. Over the course of the first year following the revolution, Khomeini systematically put his supporters in charge of key institutions and called for an early referendum on the creation of an Islamic republic. The population overwhelmingly approved this move, and the new constitution was adopted in December 1979, furthering the state's legitimacy. The constitution creates a theocracy based on the principle of the jurist's guardianship (*valayat-e faqih*), where clerical rule would ensure that the government rules according to Islamic values.

Over the next few years, Khomeini and his religious supporters increasingly repressed the other factions of the revolutionary movement, jailing and executing people who were perceived as threats to the regime. Khomeini and his supporters took firm control of the government and created Iran's authoritarian Islamic theocracy.

In September 1980, Iraq, led by Saddam Hussein, and with the support of the United States, attacked Iran. The Iraqi and U.S. governments feared the revolutionary spirit in Iran would spread across the Middle East. The Iraqi government hoped to win the war quickly by capturing Iran's oil facilities, but the effort stalled. Tens of thousands were killed in a war that lasted eight years and was fought to a stalemate. The invasion spurred patriotism and nationalism, consolidating support for the ayatollah's regime. (Watson Institute for International Studies.)

The Unitary State

Iran is a unitary state, with power concentrated in the central government. As you learned throughout this textbook, policymaking in unitary states has the potential to be more uniform and efficient that it is in federal systems. Unitary systems provide authoritarian governments with significant control over the enactment and enforcement of national policies.

Iran is divided into thirty-one provinces. Although the leaders of the 1979 revolution claimed they would provide autonomy to provinces, regions have very little power. Each province has a capital, which is usually the largest city in the province. The minister of the interior appoints the governors of each province, subject to the approval of the cabinet. (Iranian Chamber Society.)

Cities and villages hold direct elections for mayors and councils. In April 2017, the Guardian Council, one of Iran's religious institutions of government, declared that non-Muslims could not run for local office in regions with Muslim majorities. (Jafari, 2017.) Despite the Guardian Council's declaration, in May 2017, Sepanta Niknam, a member of the Zoroastrian religious minority, ran as a candidate and was reelected as a municipal councilor in the city of Yazd. Later that year, Iran's parliament, the Majles, passed a law giving religious minorities the right to nominate candidates for local offices. (Iran Project, 2017.) In 2018, the Expediency Council, a powerful institution of government that moderates disputes between the Guardian Council and the Majles, backed the law allowing members of religious minorities to run for city councils, settling the issue. (Reuters, 2018.)

Legitimacy and Challenges to the State

Religion is a key source of legitimacy for the Iranian state, and it can be a powerful source in maintaining the people's belief that the government has the right to rule. Nevertheless, Iran's government faces internal and external challenges to its legitimacy. External challenges include economic sanctions imposed in response to Iran's development of a nuclear program and international condemnation of Iran's record on human rights, including discrimination against ethnic and religious minorities and women, which undermines rule of law.

Drug trafficking poses another serious external challenge to the Iranian state. Iran shares its eastern border with Afghanistan, the world's largest producer of illegal opium, making it a corridor for international trafficking in illegal drugs. The government has spent millions of dollars on border control, including the construction of expensive barriers on both the eastern and western borders. In the past three decades, more than 3,700 law enforcement personnel have been killed in narcotics operations. In addition to the opium trade, Iranian authorities have reported increased trafficking in methamphetamines since 2014. (United Nations Office of Drugs and Crime.)

Iran is not just a corridor for illegal drugs. It is a destination for them. Illicit drugs pose both an external and internal challenge to the Iranian state. Iran is usually ranked first or second (along with Afghanistan) in the number of opioid users. It is estimated that more than 10,000 people have been executed in Iran for drug offenses since the founding of the republic, and the system responds harshly to those actively involved in the drug trade. (A moratorium was placed on capital punishment for drug offenses in 2017.) Iran is also a leader in providing state-sponsored treatment for those using illegal drugs, however, including therapy and programs to provide sterile syringes. Yet corruption by officials running drug treatment facilities has undermined their effectiveness. (Global Initiative against Transnational Organized Crime, 2020.)

Poor economic performance, caused by several factors, including corruption and the impact of international economic sanctions against Iran, also poses an internal challenge to the state. As shown in Figure 13.2, in a poll taken in December 2019, 73 percent of Iranians rated the economy as bad.

Yet another challenge to the state may come from a large generation of young people who have little psychological connection to the 1979 revolution. In a population as young as that of Iran, many are not as likely to recall the revolution and see it as an important source of state legitimacy.

Another potentially serious threat to state legitimacy and stability is separatist movements and unrest in provinces that have ethnic majorities. The Baluchi minority is one

FIGURE 13.2

Iranians Assess the Economy, 2015–2019
How good or bad is our country's economic situation?

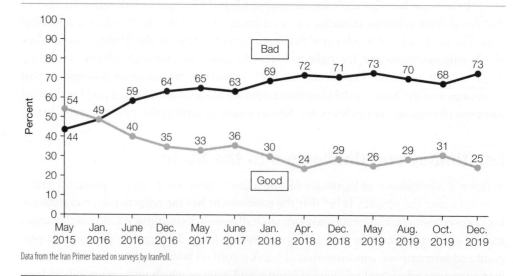

Data from the Iran Primer based on surveys by IranPoll.

example. In Sistan and Baluchestan, a province with a large Baluchi population, underdeveloped infrastructure limits access to social services, such as health care and education. The Baluchi are Sunni Muslims, and the Shiite government in Iran has implemented programs to convert the Baluchi to Shi'ism, closing and sometimes destroying Sunni mosques.

In response to the Iranian government's tactics in the province, an Islamic militant group, Jaish ul-Adl (JUA), which translates into "Army of Justice," has attacked government security forces. Its tactics include kidnappings, assassinations, car bombs, and land mines. The JUA's base of operations is in Pakistan, and the United States has listed it as a terrorist organization. In 2015, the Iranian government arrested Javid Dehghan Khald, an ethnic Baluch, and accused him of being a leader of the JUA. He was convicted of killing two members of Iran's elite military force, the Revolutionary Guard. Amnesty International claimed the government obtained Dehghan's confession through torture. Despite a request from the U.N. Human Rights Office to review the trial, Dehghan was executed on January 30, 2021. (Nada, 2021.) The potential for terrorism from separatist groups is a continuing threat to the legitimacy of the regime in Iran.

Section 13.1 Review

Each section's main ideas are reflected in the Learning Targets. By reviewing after each section, you should be able to

Remember the key points,

Know terms that are central to the topic, and

Think critically about what you have learned.

Remember

- From 1953 until 1979, Iran was governed by a shah who ruled an authoritarian state that was favorable to the West and emphasized economic modernization and secularization.
- In 1979, the shah was overthrown in a revolution, and under Ayatollah Khomeini, the Islamic Republic of Iran was established as a theocracy.
- Iran is a unitary state, and provinces have little power, although mayors and town councils are directly elected.
- Religion is a major source of legitimacy for the Iranian regime, although the state faces challenges from both internal and external sources.

Know

- *Theocracy:* a system based on religious rule. (p. 398)

Think

- What is the most serious challenge to legitimacy faced by the Iranian state?

Free-Response Question: Conceptual Analysis

Answer A, B, C, and D.

A. Define legitimacy.

B. Explain how internal legitimacy differs from external legitimacy.

C. Explain how an authoritarian state could increase internal legitimacy.

D. Explain why an authoritarian state would choose not to adopt the measure explained in part C.

13.2 Institutions of Government

Learning Targets

After reading this section, you should be able to do the following:

1. Explain how the Iranian constitution creates a system where clerics run government and share some power with elected officials.

2. Describe the powers of Iran's supreme leader.

3. Compare the unelected and elected institutions of government in Iran.

4. Describe the function and powers of the Guardian Council and Expediency Council.

5. Describe the function and powers of the president in Iran.

6. Describe the function and powers of the Majles, Iran's unicameral legislature.

7. Describe the role of the Assembly of Experts.

Supreme leader
The executive who is a cleric and the most powerful person in Iran.

The Islamic Republic of Iran created a unique set of political institutions based on theocratic principles with significant participatory elements. Under this system of dual rule, the clergy maintains central control of the regime while giving some limited authority to officials elected to represent the people. Elected officials have the power to pass and implement laws and voice some public criticism, but clerical authority is final. So, despite its distinctive institutions, the Iranian government rules like many other authoritarian regimes, limiting citizens' choice of leaders and repressing civil rights and liberties.

Iran's system of government includes a unique set of political institutions. Some of them, like the legislature, are similar to institutions you studied in other countries. Other Iranian institutions do not fit neatly into the three branches of government you are used to studying. Figure 13.3 provides an overview of these institutions. First, we will focus on the institutions of government that are not directly elected and have the most power in Iran. Then, we will turn our attention to the directly elected institutions of government.

The Supreme Leader

The new constitution of December 1979 established Iran as an Islamic republic that specifically followed the Shiite denomination of Islam and declared Allah (God) as sovereign. One of Khomeini's most important contributions to Iran's theocracy was the concept of the **supreme leader**. He argued that one leader with enough religious authority and popular support should be the topmost guide of the Islamic state, with the power to veto any law. The supreme leader is both the legal and spiritual guide of the country.

First occupied by Khomeini himself and since Khomeini's death in 1989 by Ayatollah Ali Khamenei, the office has the power to appoint the heads of the armed forces, the head of the judiciary, directors of television and radio, the head of the National Security

FIGURE 13.3

Elected and Unelected Institutions in Iran

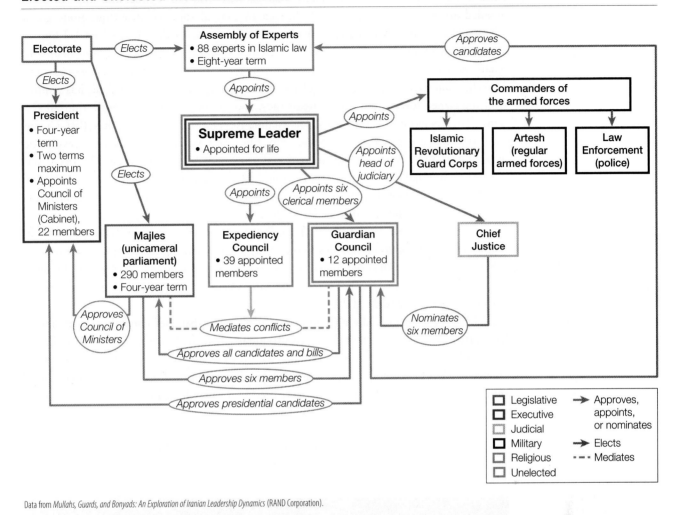

Data from *Mullahs, Guards, and Bonyads: An Exploration of Iranian Leadership Dynamics* (RAND Corporation).

Council, six of the twelve members of the Guardian Council, all of the members of the Expediency Council, and the leaders of Friday prayers at mosques (refer to Figure 13.3). These powers mean that the supreme leader sets the political agenda, making him the most powerful figure in the country. The supreme leader serves for life unless he is deemed to be incapacitated by the Assembly of Experts.

Khomeini's popularity and power were based not only on the traditional legitimacy he enjoyed as a grand ayatollah, one of a handful of the highest religious authorities in Shiite Islam, but they also flowed from his charismatic legitimacy as the leader of the revolution. Khomeini and other leaders did not believe that any of the other grand ayatollahs could fully replace him as the supreme leader. To avert a potential crisis, a constitutional amendment eliminated the requirement that the supreme leader come from only among the most high-ranking clergy. This allowed the regime to select then-president Ali Khamenei to become the new supreme leader upon Khomeini's death. He was only a mid-level cleric and was raised overnight to the rank of ayatollah (still below grand ayatollah), an attempt to give him greater religious authority.

Khomeini and his advisers chose someone who understood politics rather than a leading religious authority. The other grand ayatollahs did not fight Khamenei's rise to power because they had become increasingly disillusioned with the regime, and most of them avoided an active role in politics. Still, lack of clerical support raised questions about Khamanei's legitimacy as supreme leader, which was one of the factors that led him to strengthen the power of the Revolutionary Guard, a military force loyal to him personally. Khamanei's position as the supreme leader—the most powerful person in Iran—is secure.

The dual executive, consisting of the supreme leader and the president, has control over the armed forces, judiciary, bureaucracy, and military. Like many authoritarian systems, Iran has more than one army. The Islamic Revolutionary Guard Corps (IRGC) was formed as the armed wing of the revolution. Khomeini maintained it after the revolution as a military unit separate from the national army, which he didn't trust. The IRGC has become an internal security force that maintains the power of the regime.

By 2010, the IRGC had become one of the wealthiest organizations in Iran, controlling between one-third and two-thirds of the official economy and the black market. Ali Ansari, an expert on Iran, called the IRCC "a business conglomerate with guns." (Borger and Tait, 2010.) The IRGC owns companies in oil and gas, construction, telecommunications, and other key industries. The government takes good care of the large and ideologically loyal Guard as well—the 2021–2022 budget allocates one-fifth of total public expenditures to the IRGC. (Khodabandeh, 2020.)

The Iranian regime, like all authoritarian regimes, also uses clientelism to maintain its control. Quasi-governmental religious foundations (called *bonyads*) have become key avenues for sharing the nation's oil wealth with regime supporters. The foundations were created as charities to help the poor and marginalized, and they often receive government funding. Bonyads are not required to make their budgets public, and many are tax exempt. Some engage in commercial activities. One example is Bonyad Mostazafan, which has more than 150 holdings in key economic sectors, including banking, oil and gas, mining, and construction. Although some bonyads engage in meaningful work to improve the lives

The Vakil Mosque in Shiraz. Iran's Shia theocracy influences government and society. Like the intricate design of the mosque, Iran's history and culture are complex.

Hermes Images/AGF/Getty Images

of Iranian citizens, others are used by the elite to reward supporters, enrich themselves, and target political enemies. (United States Department of the Treasury, 2020.)

The Guardian Council

A **Guardian Council** of twelve clergy is a watchdog over elected officials in government. The council must approve or reject every law the parliament passes, as well as approve all candidates for office. The Guardian Council has the power to review and eliminate any candidate for president, the Majles, local government councils, and the Assembly of Experts. The Guardian Council has a great deal of power in deciding who can run for office, and it can remove candidates on the basis that they are not adequately committed to the goals of the Islamic revolution. Because candidates can be eliminated from competing, and there is a lack of transparency in the vetting process, elections are not free and fair.

Six of the members of the Guardian Council are appointed directly by the supreme leader and six are nominated by the judiciary appointed by the supreme leader, making the body a pillar of clerical authority that preserves the will of the supreme leader.

Guardian Council
A twelve-member body in Iran that has the power to reject or approve legislation and reviews candidates for the presidency, parliament, local councils, and the Assembly of Experts.

The Expediency Council

In 1989, following Ayatollah Khomeini's death, the Iranian constitution was amended, and a new government body—the **Expediency Council**—was created. The Expediency Council is an advisory body to the supreme leader. It has the power to resolve disputes between parliament and the Guardian Council, and its rulings are final. It also has the authority to rewrite legislation and enact new policies into law without the consent of the parliament or president. The supreme leader appoints all of its members, so it is an additional way for him to control elected officials.

Expediency Council
A body appointed by the supreme leader to act as an advisory council that has the power to reject and rewrite proposed legislation and create new laws without parliamentary approval.

The Judiciary

The constitution establishes *sharia* as the predominant source of law, and clergy head all major courts. The supreme leader appoints the head of the judiciary, who in turn appoints all of the judges under him. Other than nominating half of the Guardian Council, the judiciary has no formal political role. The Supreme Court does not have the traditional power of judicial review, but it does have the power of religious review, based on the Koran. Because the courts are religious bodies, judges are trained in sharia law. They interpret and enforce the Islamic legal code in criminal and civil cases.

The supreme leader has used the judiciary repeatedly to repress political opponents. Many political activists, journalists, and students were prosecuted on charges such as treason after large demonstrations following a presidential election in 2009. In recent years, hundreds of human-rights activists and protesters have been detained and arrested, and many have been sentenced to long prison terms. (Human Rights Watch.)

AP® TIP

Most systems with a dual executive have a clear delineation between the head of state and the head of government. In Iran, the president is the head of government, and the traditional powers of the head of state are divided between the president and supreme leader. If you are asked about the difference between the head of state and the head of government, don't pick Iran to use as an example. Pick the United Kingdom, Russia, or China instead.

The President

Although clerics have strong control over Iran's government, some policymaking authority is shared with elected officials. The supreme leader shares formal executive power with a directly elected president, who serves as head of government. The president appoints a cabinet, which the parliament must approve and can remove, and administers the daily affairs of government. The president is the chief diplomat and has the power to sign treaties. The president is selected in a direct election and can serve two four-year terms, which the last four presidents have done.

The dual executive creates the possibility of tension between the president and the supreme leader. For example, when President Mohammad Khatami, who favored reform, served from 1997 to 2005, he clashed regularly with the supreme leader and the institutions like the Guardian Council that limit the president's power.

The next president, Mahmoud Ahmadinejad (2005–2013), increasingly used secular nationalist rhetoric that threatened to go against the Islamist basis for the regime's legitimacy. He built up an independent base of support by appointing supporters to key government positions. Ultimately, the supreme leader opposed him, and his supporters lost the next parliamentary and presidential elections. The Guardian Council barred Ahmadinejad from running for a third, nonconsecutive term in 2017.

Rouhani, who was elected in 2013 and reelected in 2017, represented a change for Iran. He was more moderate than Ahmadinejad and ran as a reformist candidate. Given that the supreme leader has great influence over who can run for president, the election of Rouhani indicates that the supreme leader was willing to allow a more moderate president. The 2021 election of Ebrahim Raisi shifted the presidency back to a conservative hardliner.

Although Iran's president has the power to propose a program of domestic policy and conduct foreign policy, his power is checked, and his actions can be overridden, by the supreme leader.

The Majles

Majles
Iran's unicameral legislature.

In creating the Islamic republic, Ayatollah Khomeini allowed an elected unicameral parliament, the **Majles**. The Majles (a Persian and Arabic term meaning assembly or council) has the power to pass laws, subject to the approval of the supreme leader and other clerical institutions. Despite the limits on its powers, debate in the Majles can become lively and heated. In addition to passing legislation, the Majles has the power to approve cabinet nominees and confirm half of nominees (appointed by the chief justice) to the Guardian Council, and it can investigate the executive's implementation of the law. It has used its oversight powers to expose corruption in the bureaucracy.

The autonomy and strength of the Majles are severely limited, even though its formal powers look significant. The power of the appointed clerics always lurks behind the actions of the Majles. The Guardian Council disqualified thousands of mostly moderate and reformist candidates for the 2020 parliamentary election. (Karimi, 2020.) Furthermore, when the clerics disapprove of significant legislation, they reject it in the Guardian Council and rewrite it in the Expediency Council.

The Assembly of Experts

Assembly of Experts
An elected body that has the power to select the supreme leader and remove him if he is unable to perform his duties.

An **Assembly of Experts** is composed of eighty-eight members who are masters of Islamic law. Candidates must pass written and oral exams and be approved by the Guardian Council. (Borden, Religious Experts.) The Assembly is popularly elected by citizens for an eight-year term. The Assembly of Experts does not have authority to make policy. Its only tasks are appointing the supreme leader and monitoring his performance. The Assembly of Experts does not have the power to challenge the supreme leader based on policy decisions, but on paper, it has the right to remove him if he is unable to perform his duties (becomes incapacitated). Despite its limited duties, the Assembly of Experts, as a directly elected institution of government, serves as at least a theoretical check on clerical power.

Iran is ruled by unelected theocratic bodies that share some power with elected institutions. This combination of theocratic government with quasi-democratic elements is unique in the world and makes the system both intricate and fascinating.

Section 13.2 Review

Remember

- Iran's constitution creates a system in which clerics run government and share some power with elected officials.
- The supreme leader is the most powerful person in Iran, and he sets the political agenda.
- Iran's unelected bodies include the supreme leader, the Guardian Council, the Expediency Council, and the judiciary.
- The Guardian Council has the power to approve and reject legislation and to vet candidates for office.
- The Expediency Council has the power to reject or rewrite legislation and to create new legislation without approval of the legislature.
- The Iranian president is directly elected and has the power to administer the government and conduct foreign policy.
- The Majles is a directly elected unicameral legislature with the power to pass laws, approve the budget, and conduct oversight hearings into the actions of the bureaucracy.
- The Assembly of Experts consists of directly elected members who appoint, monitor, and have the power to remove the supreme leader.

Know

- *Supreme leader:* the executive who is a cleric and the most powerful person in Iran. (p. 404)
- *Guardian Council:* a twelve-member body in Iran that has the power to reject or approve legislation and reviews candidates for the presidency, parliament, local councils, and the Assembly of Experts. (p. 407)
- *Expediency Council:* a body appointed by the supreme leader to act as an advisory council that has the power to reject and rewrite proposed legislation and create new laws without parliamentary approval. (p. 407)
- *Majles:* Iran's unicameral legislature. (p. 408)
- *Assembly of Experts:* an elected body that has the power to select the supreme leader and remove him if he is unable to perform his duties. (p. 408)

Think

- How does having a system of both clerical rule and elected representatives impact the legitimacy of the Iranian regime?

Free-Response Question: Comparative Analysis

Compare how the structure of the executive institution impacts policymaking in two different AP® Comparative Government and Politics course countries. In your response, you should do the following:

A. Describe the function of the executive institution.

B. Describe the structure of the executive institution in two different AP® Comparative Government and Politics course countries.

C. Explain how the structure of the executive institution in each of the AP® Comparative Government and Politics course countries described in part B impacts policymaking.

13.3 Electoral System, Political Parties, and Civil Society

Learning Targets

After reading this section, you should be able to do the following:

1. Describe the process for electing the president, Majles, and Assembly of Experts.

2. Explain why Iranian elections are not considered to be free and fair.

3. Explain why Iran's political party system is weak.

4. Describe the economic and political factions in Iran.

5. Describe the Green Movement protests that arose as a result of claims of fraud in the 2009 presidential election and explain how the government responded.

Regular elections for president and parliament have been held on schedule since the regime was founded. However, the Guardian Council excludes candidates favoring reform. This reduces electoral competition and representation. Iranian political parties are weak, and they are loosely formed alliances, divided into economic and political factions. Although Iran's elections are not free and fair, multiple candidates compete for office, and elections are sometimes lively.

Elections

Iran's regime has allowed limited but competitive elections since it began, though the degree of competition has varied. The 290-member Majles is elected using a mixed single-member district and **multimember district (MMD) system**. In MMDs, there is more than one representative elected in a district. Citizens in MMDs can vote for the same number of candidates as the number of seats available in the district. In an MMD system, several separate elections are held at the same time. If a district has thirty seats, citizens have thirty votes to cast. Candidates who earn 25 percent of the vote are awarded a seat. If seats are left over, a runoff election is held within the MMD. (O'Neil, Fields, and Share.)

Multimember district (MMD) system
A system in which two or more representatives are elected from a district.

Religious minorities are guaranteed a small amount of representation in the Majles—two seats for Armenian Christians, one seat to Assyrian and Chaldean Christians, one seat for Jews, and one seat for Zoroastrians. (Borden, Demystifying.)

Elections for the Majles are held every four years, and while none has been truly free and fair because the Guardian Council uses its authority to prevent candidates from running for office, the Guardian Council at times has allowed significant competition. A similar mixed SMD/MMD system is used to elect the Assembly of Experts, which serves for an eight-year term.

A two-round system is used for Iran's presidential elections. Like presidential elections in Russia, a candidate is declared the winner in Iran if he wins a majority of the vote in the first round. If no candidate earns more than 50 percent of the vote in the first round,

Supporters of incumbent President Rouhani at a campaign rally in Tehran in May 2017 when he was running for his second term in office.

AP Images/Ebrahim Noroozi

a second round of elections is held between the top two vote-getters. Countries use a two-round election system to give the winner a mandate to pursue his policy proposals, because more than half of the voters showed support for the candidate, at least in the second round.

Although Iran's elections are often competitive (at least among the candidates who are allowed to run for office by the Guardian Council), elected officials have limited ability to make policy. In the 1997 presidential election, Mohammad Khatami, a reformist cleric, won a sweeping victory that many observers saw as the start of a major liberalization of the political system. Until 2000, however, conservatives in parliament were numerous enough to block major reforms.

In the 2000 Majles election, the Guardian Council did not prevent reformist candidates from running because of Khatami's popularity, and reformists won 80 percent of the vote. The new parliament passed reforms involving greater freedoms of expression, women's rights, human rights in general, and market-oriented economic policies. The Guardian Council, however, vetoed many of these, arguing that they violated sharia law.

The Guardian Council later also blocked some of Ahmadinejad's policy proposals after they were passed by the Majles. Through its power to veto laws passed by the Majles, the Guardian Council serves as a clerical check on the actions of the elected officials.

The Guardian Council banned thousands of candidates in the 2004 and 2008 elections. On June 12, 2009, Iran's president Mahmoud Ahmadinejad faced reelection. Early on, he was predicted to win easily, but he fared poorly in a televised debate, and suddenly, his opponents and their supporters believed he was vulnerable. Interest in the election skyrocketed, and predictions shifted to a possible opposition victory. The morning after the election, the government announced the results with only two-thirds of the votes counted, claiming the president had won 62 percent of the vote, clearly a fraudulent outcome. The number-two candidate, reformist Mir-Hossein Mousavi, called on his supporters to protest, and within a day more than 1 million people marched through the streets of Tehran in the largest demonstration since the 1979 revolution.

After weeks of demonstrations, the government finally and effectively cracked down, arresting as many as five thousand protesters, putting more than one hundred of them on televised trials on fabricated charges, and allegedly torturing and raping some in prison. The dramatic events of 2009 were a powerful moment in the long battle between conservative supporters of Iran's theocratic regime, who want power kept in clerical hands, and reformist elements, who want to strengthen the regime's quasi-democratic institutions.

The Guardian Council has repeatedly banned reformist candidates, leading the major reformist party to boycott the 2012 Majles election. The 2013 presidential election once again showed the power of the Guardian Council to enforce the interests of the supreme leader. Forty candidates put their names forward, but the council approved only eight, six of whom were conservative supporters of the clerical leadership. Both the preferred candidate of term-limited President Ahmadinejad and the leading reformist candidate, former president Hashemi Rafsanjani, were banned. As the campaign developed, Rafsanjani endorsed Hassan Rouhani as closest to being a true reformist candidate, and he won with just over 50 percent of the vote. The election showed both the continuing popular demand for change and the clerical leadership's ability to limit reformers' efforts.

Once in office, President Rouhani had limited success, especially on domestic policy. He supported the nuclear accord with the United States that many hardliners opposed, which resulted in a partial lifting of economic sanctions. The accord was subsequently reversed by the United States under President Donald Trump. Rouhani's initial efforts at opening the economy were resisted by opponents in parliament and the Revolutionary Guard, whose economic influence remains large. Rouhani's moderate reformist coalition won majority control of the Majles in 2016, although the Guardian Council prevented hundreds of more radical reformist candidates from running for office.

After a grueling campaign in which conservatives fought hard against him, including alleging that he and members of his government engaged in corruption, Rouhani won reelection in 2017 with 57 percent of the vote, with more than 70 percent of Iran's voters participating. In 2020, the Guardian Council's mass disqualification of reform candidates, along with concerns about the spread of COVID-19, likely contributed to a low voter turnout of 42.57 percent in the Majles elections. (Azizi, 2020.)

In the 2021 election, 592 candidates submitted their names to run for the presidency. The Guardian Council approved seven mostly hardline candidates. Ebrahim Raisi was the frontrunner. Several well-known Iranian politicians, including the serving vice president and a former head of Iran's parliament, were barred from running. By blocking moderate candidates, the Guardian Council ensured a victory for hardline conservatives. (BBC, 2021.)

Raisi won the election with 72 percent of the vote. The Iranian government reported that voter turnout was 48 percent. The 2021 election demonstrates the power of the clerical officials in government to influence the outcome of elections and their ability to restrict moderate voices within the regime.

Political Parties

Iranian political parties are weak. The authoritarian regime of the shah seldom allowed significant political participation, so the country has no continuing history of political parties. This serves as a stark contrast with Mexico, which had stable political parties during authoritarianism.

Despite the Islamic constitution's guarantee of a right to form parties, Khomeini banned them in 1987, claiming they produced unnecessary divisions. Reformist president Khatami successfully legalized parties again in 1998. The government banned the two leading reformist parties after the 2009 election. Parties continue to exist but as loose coalitions around individual leaders, not as enduring organizations with which citizens identify. The Guardian Council's power to vet candidates for office also undermines the strength of political parties by blocking their preferred candidates.

In the absence of strong parties, ideological factions are central to understanding Iranian political shifts over time. Iranian political scientist Payam Mohseni described two main ideological factions in Iran—one economic and one political. (Mohseni, 2016.) The economic division is the familiar division that arises in many countries between those who favor economic policies emphasizing greater market forces and those who favor a greater role for the state, such as using oil revenue to fund programs for the poor.

The political division is unique to Iran—it distinguishes those who believe in the nearly absolute power of the supreme leader, with legitimacy coming solely from religion, and those who believe legitimacy should also stem from citizens' preferences expressed in elections. Mohseni argues that the 2017 election shows conservative clerics' determination to resist the formation of a consensus among moderate, reformist, and conservative elites who embrace a less stringent Islamist ideology and want to integrate Iran into the global system. He foresees a polarization of Iranian politics as conservative hardliners prevent reformers from running for office, block moderate reforms, and work to energize their base of voters. (Mohseni, 2017.)

In the 2020 Majles election, conservatives swept the election, winning 230 seats. The election has been deemed the least competitive in years. In addition to the impact of COVID-19, the wholesale exclusion of moderate candidates resulted in an official voter turnout rate of 42.57 percent—the lowest in the history of the regime. (Azizi, 2020.) The exclusion of moderate candidates decreased political efficacy among their supporters, lowering voter turnout.

Interest Groups and Social Movements

Despite some periods of greater openness, the Iranian government places significant limits on citizens' ability to voice opinions and engage in political activity. Nonetheless, the country has seen growing pressure for change. Iran has a more active civil society than is present in many Middle Eastern countries.

Yet like political parties, civil society is not particularly strong in Iran. The Islamic theocratic regime requires citizen organizations to function within limits imposed by its version of Islam. In the 1990s, a reformist movement arose that did not reject the clerics' right to rule but argued for a more open and tolerant interpretation of Islam, one that would allow wider discussion and action.

The 1997 election of reformist president Khatami inspired hope that Iran would become a more open society. However, in 2005, Iranians elected President Ahmadinejad, a hardline conservative. Nevertheless, the reformist movement survived and became the catalyst for the Green Movement protests of 2009.

The Green Movement emerged in response to allegations of fraud in the 2009 election and showed both the strength and weakness of Iran's civil society. As mentioned in the story that begins this chapter, Iranians use social media as a way of connecting with one another around various interests. A decentralized organizing system using Twitter and Facebook became the main means of communicating about the 2009 election, aided by

The two Political Science Practice features in this chapter are longer and differ from the others you have encountered in this book. Instead of asking you to complete tasks that build political science skills, these boxes summarize what you have already learned about taking the AP® Exam and provide test-taking tips for both portions of the exam.

The multiple-choice portion of the AP® Comparative Government and Politics exam consists of fifty-five questions. You will have sixty minutes to complete the multiple-choice portion of the AP® Exam, and multiple-choice questions are worth 50 percent of your AP® Exam score. There is no penalty for guessing on the AP® Exam, so answer every question.

There are five basic types of multiple-choice questions on this exam: conceptual, country-specific, country comparison, data analysis, and text-based analysis.

Conceptual Question

Here is an example of a conceptual question:

Which of the following is most likely to cause a change in government in a democratic regime?

A. A revolution

B. A military coup

C. An election

D. Rule by decree

Test-Taking Tips

Conceptual questions require understanding key terms (which have appeared in bold throughout this textbook) and being able to apply them. In this sample question, the key concepts are "change in government" and "democratic regime." Concepts can be phrased in different ways, so it's important not to just memorize definitions. In this case, you know that a change in government is a change in leaders without a fundamental change in the system. You also know that democratic regimes hold free and fair elections. Putting these two concepts together, the correct answer is C.

Country-Specific Question

A country-specific question focuses on one country. Here is a sample question:

Which of the following best describes how Iran's president is chosen?

A. He is selected by the majority party or majority party coalition in the Majles.

B. The president is directly elected by citizens through a plurality vote.

C. He is selected by the supreme leader and confirmed by the Guardian Council.

D. The president is directly elected, and a second-round election is held if no candidate receives a majority of votes in the first round.

Test-Taking Tips

It's important to remember specific facts about each country studied in the course. The Countries at a Glance tables at the end of this book will help you recall some of these details.

Don't pick the first answer that appeals to you. Choice B might distract you because you know that the Iranian president is directly elected. However, when you finish reading the answers, you will realize that answer D is correct because it refers to Iran's two-round election system.

Country-Comparison Question

Country-comparison questions ask you about similarities or differences between two countries. Here is a sample question:

Which of the following accurately describes legislative powers in two different AP® Comparative Government and Politics course countries?

A. The House of Commons in the United Kingdom and the Chamber of Deputies in Mexico have the power to debate laws.

B. The Duma in Russia and the House of Commons in the United Kingdom have the power to select the prime minister.

C. The Senate in Mexico and the Federation Council in Russia have the power to select regional governors.

D. The Majles in Iran and the House of Representatives in Nigeria have the power to confirm cabinet members.

Test-Taking Tips

Like country-specific questions, country-comparison questions require you to remember details. The correct answer must be true for both countries. For example, in choice B, the House of Commons in the United Kingdom has the power to select the prime minister, but in Russia, the prime minister is selected by the president and confirmed by the Duma. Even though part of choice B is accurate, it is the wrong answer. Both statements in choice C are incorrect. In choice D, although the Majles in Iran confirms cabinet members (making the first half of the statement correct), in Nigeria, the Senate, not the House of Representatives, confirms members of the cabinet (making the second half of the statement incorrect). The correct answer is A, because the House of

Commons in the United Kingdom and the Chamber of Deputies in Mexico both have the power to debate laws.

Data-Analysis Question

Data-analysis questions include graphs, tables, maps, and infographics. The multiple-choice portion of the AP® Exam will contain three sets of data-analysis questions, with two or three questions per set. You encountered data-analysis questions throughout this textbook. AP® Political Science Practice features in Chapters 3, 5, 6, 7, 10, 11, and 12 helped prepare you for this type of question. Here is an example of a data-analysis question, taken from the Chapter 6 Review:

Iran's Ethnic and Religious Groups

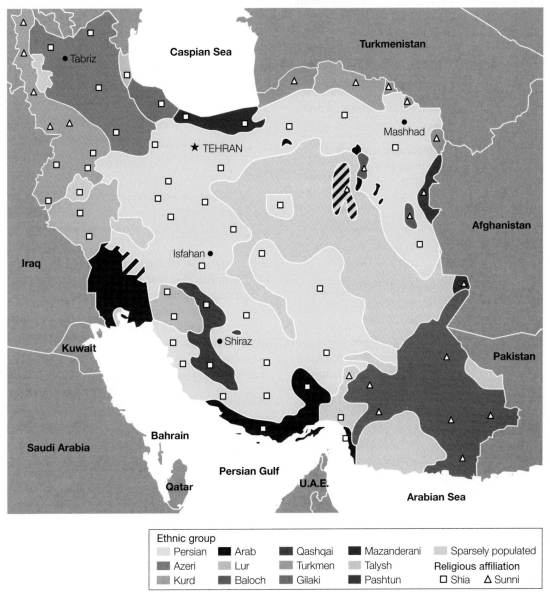

Ethnic group

Persian	Arab	Qashqai	Mazanderani	Sparsely populated
Azeri	Lur	Turkmen	Talysh	**Religious affiliation**
Kurd	Baloch	Gilaki	Pashtun	□ Shia △ Sunni

Data from University of Texas Libraries.

1. Which of the following is supported by the map?

   A. Iran has many ethnic groups and a predominantly Shia population.

   B. Most Iranians are Arab and Muslim.

   C. Iran's ethnic diversity is a source of conflict within government.

   D. The central and eastern portions of Iran are very diverse, and no single ethnic group predominates.

2. Which of the following is an implication of the map?

   A. Secessionist movements are a threat to the government's sovereignty.

   B. Iran has a federal system of government, so that ethnic regions will be represented in the legislature.

   C. The religious values of the state are consistent with the religious beliefs of most of the population.

   D. Ethnic minorities in Iran face a significant level of discrimination.

Test-Taking Tips

The first question following the data can usually be answered directly from the chart, graph, table, map, or infographic. In this case, the map shows that there are many ethnic groups in Iran, and the open squares show that most Iranians are Shia, so the answer is A. You may be able to easily rule out answers that are not likely to be shown on a map, such as choice C, which is about conflict within government and not the distribution of the population.

After the first question, subsequent questions are usually a bit harder and require you to draw inferences from what you have studied. For example, you know from your study of Iran that it is a theocracy run by Shia clerics, so the correct answer is C. None of the other answer choices can be determined from looking at the map.

Don't get bogged down in complicated graphics. If you are having a hard time picking through a graph, table, map, or infographic, look through the answer choices and find the answer you think is best. Check your first-choice answer against the graphic before you check the other answers.

Text-Based Analysis Question

Text-based analysis questions require you to analyze a passage. The multiple-choice portion of the AP® Exam will contain two sets of text-based analysis questions, with two or three questions per set. You encountered text-based analysis questions throughout this textbook. AP® Political Science Practice features in Chapters 1, 3, 4, and 9 helped prepare you for this type of question. Here is an example, taken from the Chapter 9 Review:

> (1) The sharia Court of Appeal of a State shall, in addition to such other jurisdiction as may be conferred upon it by the law of the State, exercise such appellate and supervisory jurisdiction in civil proceedings involving questions of Islamic personal Law which the court is competent to decide in accordance with the provisions of subsection (2) of this section.
>
> (2) For the purposes of subsection (1) of this section, the sharia Court of Appeal shall be competent to decide—
>
> (a) any question of Islamic personal Law regarding a marriage concluded in accordance with that Law, including a question relating to the validity or dissolution of such a marriage or a question that depends on such a marriage and relating to family relationship or the guardianship of an infant;

> (b) where all the parties to the proceedings are Muslims, any question of Islamic personal Law regarding a marriage, including the validity or dissolution of that marriage, or regarding family relationship, a founding or the guarding of an infant . . .
>
> —Constitution of the Federal Republic of Nigeria, Section 277

1. Which of the following is supported by the passage?

    A. The Nigerian constitution established sharia law as the national legal system.

    B. Some northern states in Nigeria have implemented sharia law, while southern states use a common-law system.

    C. In states that have adopted sharia law, courts of appeal have jurisdiction over divorce and child custody matters.

    D. Decisions issued by state sharia courts have precedence over decisions issued by the Nigerian Supreme Court.

2. Which of the following is an implication of the passage?

    A. Sharia law is applied consistently in northern states.

    B. Non-Muslims living in northern Nigeria face discrimination in the legal system.

    C. Members of Nigeria's Court of Appeals must be well-versed in Islamic law.

    D. Nigeria follows rule of law because it has a standard legal code.

The first question following a passage is usually a comprehension question, so read carefully. Highlight key phrases. This passage from the Nigerian constitution indicates that states may adopt sharia law (Section 1) and that Courts of Appeal have jurisdiction over matters of family law (Section 2.a). After carefully reading the passage, the correct answer to question 1 is C. Note that the passage does not directly address the issues raised in choices A, B, and D.

As with data-analysis questions, after the first questions, subsequent source-analysis questions are usually a bit harder and require you to draw inferences from what you have studied. For example, you know from your study of Nigeria that judges in northern states that adopted sharia law apply Islamic law, so the correct answer is C. Choice A is incorrect because the passage does not imply that the law is applied in the same manner in all northern states. The passage does not directly address the statements made in choices B and D.

Don't get bogged down in long, complicated passages. If you are having a hard time understanding a passage, look through the answer choices and find the answer you think is best. Consider your first-choice answer in the context of the passage before you check the other answers.

public statements and occasional public appearances by reformist leaders. At least a million people marched in the streets of Tehran, but the demonstrations did not have much effect in the countryside. The movement had no clear formal organization. Protests continued for weeks, giving youthful participants hope that change was possible, but the government successfully repressed protesters despite widespread international condemnation.

Mousavi, the leading reformer, called for demonstrations again in February 2011 in support of the Arab Spring movements protesting dictatorships in Egypt and Tunisia. Tens of thousands of Iranians turned out, but the government responded with force, disbanding the demonstrations, and arresting their leaders. As of February 2021, Mousavi and his wife, Zahra Rahnavard, had been under house arrest for ten years. (Iran International, 2021.)

Even after these huge demonstrations, and despite reformers' partial victory in the 2013 presidential election and 2016 parliamentary election, the reform movement is severely limited. Reformers supported the more moderate forces around President Rouhani, but those demanding more fundamental changes in the regime have been silenced.

Despite restrictions on civil society, activists continue to challenge the regime. In March 2020, the Iranian judiciary ordered Mohammad Rasoulof, a filmmaker, to serve a year in prison based on charges of "propaganda against the system" because of the content of his movies, including a film titled *There Is No Evil*, about the death penalty in Iran. Rasoulof was banned from traveling to the Berlin Film Festival and was ordered not to produce any movies for two years. (Freemuse, 2020.)

Without the ability to openly engage with the regime, civil society organizations and activists have moved underground and online. (Milani, 2015.) Many underground media and internet sites exist. Millions of people have Facebook and Instagram accounts, even though both are banned.

Section 13.3 Review

Remember

- Iran holds direct elections for the president, Majles, and Assembly of Experts.
- Iranian elections are not free and fair, because the Guardian Council vets candidates for office, preventing many reformists and moderates from running.
- The Majles is elected through a mixed SMD/MMD system.
- Iran's president is elected in a two-round system, in an effort to provide the winner with a mandate.
- Iranian political parties are weak, and factions are divided about the government's role in managing the economy and sources of the regime's political legitimacy.
- The Green Movement protests arose because of claims of fraud in the 2009 presidential election, and the government responded by repressing protests and arresting demonstrators.

Know

- *Multimember district (MMD) system:* a system in which two or more representatives are elected from a district. (p. 410)

Think

- Why does the Guardian Council allow multiple candidates to run for the presidency?

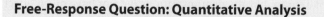

Free-Response Question: Quantitative Analysis

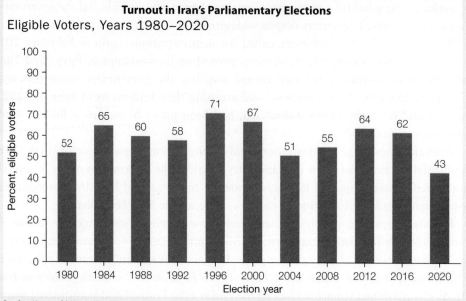

Turnout in Iran's Parliamentary Elections

Eligible Voters, Years 1980–2020

Data from Ministry of the Interior, Iran.

Answer A, B, C, D, and E.

A. Using the data in the bar chart, identify the year with the lowest voter turnout in Majles elections.

B. Using the data in the bar chart, describe a trend in voter turnout in Majles elections.

C. Define political efficacy.

D. Using your knowledge of political efficacy and the data in the bar chart, draw a conclusion about why the trend you identified in part B occurred.

E. Describe a factor, other than political efficacy, that impacts voter turnout.

13.4 Political Culture and Participation

Learning Targets

After reading this section, you should be able to do the following:

1. Explain how the Iranian government represses speech critical of the regime.

2. Explain how women's political, educational, economic, and social rights in Iran have varied over time.

3. Describe Iran's treatment of dissidents.

4. Describe the legal protections in Iran for Jews, Chaldean and Assyrian Christians, Zoroastrians, and Sunni Muslims.

5. Describe the repression of the Bahá'í religious group by the Iranian government.

Civil Rights and Civil Liberties

Iran is an authoritarian state with significant restrictions on civil rights and liberties. The state restricts the media as well as the rights of women and religious minorities.

Restrictions on the Press

The Iranian government's treatment of the press has varied over time. Whenever the government has allowed it, a very active press has emerged, but whenever this press begins to question the goals of the regime beyond certain limits, religious authorities close it down and begin a period of repression. Leading up to the 2000 Majles election, many newspapers emerged, and an exceptionally open political debate occurred. Since that time, religious authorities have repressed newspapers, closing them down for criticizing the government too harshly and drastically reducing public debate.

Since 2009, many political activists and journalists have been arrested and jailed, and key journalistic and legal associations were banned. The government created a new "cyberpolice force" to monitor the internet and disrupt bloggers and social media sites critical of the regime. It also restricted Facebook and Instagram.

These restrictions, however, have not kept Iranians off social media. Forty-five million Iranians have Facebook accounts, including Supreme Leader Khamenei. (Milani, 2015, 58.) Anti-government protests in January 2018 led authorities to slow down internet connections, block servers outside Iran, and block Instagram and Telegram, an instant-messaging app. Telegram was declared a security threat and was permanently blocked in April 2018. The Iranian state does not appear to have the ability to restrict the internet as effectively as the Chinese state, but it continues to exert control and block access, leading Freedom House to classify it as not free with a score only slightly better than China's. (Freedom House, 2020.)

Human-Rights Abuses

The Iranian state represses citizens and organizations that are deemed a threat to the regime, often labeling critics as terrorists. Iranian authorities are willing to use violence to target dissidents living within the country and abroad. The government's tactics include unlawful detentions, online intimidation, spyware, and assassinations. The Iranian government has used these tools against citizens living in other countries in the Middle East, the United States, and Europe. (Freedom House.)

The government has shut businesses and frozen assets of journalists who work in independent media outlets in other countries. The family members of dissidents, including children and elderly parents, have been intimidated, interrogated, arrested, and detained. (Amnesty International.)

Within the country, hundreds of journalists, dissidents, writers, and human-rights activists have been arbitrarily detained. Those accused of security-related crimes have been denied access to an attorney, and their trials have been held in secret. Prisoners face torture, such as flogging, and other human-rights abuses, such as the denial of medical treatment. Iran has the second-highest number of executions in the world (behind China), executing nearly 300 people in 2019. (Death Penalty Information Center.)

Women's Status

The status of women in Iran has evolved since the revolution, altering their political, educational, economic, and social rights. One of the first acts of the Ayatollah Khomeini and Islamist clerics who consolidated their power in 1979–1980 was to reverse the shah's Family Protection Law, which had Westernized much of the country's family law and improved the status of women. The theocratic regime eliminated women's right to divorce while giving men nearly an unlimited right to leave their wives, required women to wear the hijab (the Islamic headscarf) in public, forced women out of the legal profession, restricted them from several other professions, banned contraception, and segregated the education system. Many women who had been active in the revolution felt betrayed and protested these changes, including hundreds of thousands who took to the streets in March 1979.

At the same time, the newly adopted Islamic constitution gave women full rights to participate in politics, including voting and running for office, except for holding the office of the president. Under the reformist government in the 1990s, more women entered parliament, but when the Guardian Council undermined the reformists in 2000, their numbers dropped, recovering only in 2016, when more women were allowed to run for office and a record seventeen women were elected. Seventeen women were also elected to serve in the Majles in 2020.

From the start of the Islamic Republic, most of the small number of women in the Majles worked actively to achieve greater equality for women. In the area of family law, women were granted more rights to divorce and greater rights over guardianship of children, which came with child allowances from the government. Such legal victories, though, have remained relatively rare and minor.

Women's educational opportunities have improved since the founding of the regime. The absence of men during the Iran–Iraq War (1980–1988) gave women an opportunity to enter school at all levels to an unprecedented degree, which the government encouraged as part of a literacy campaign. The regime's gender segregation of schools increased girls' enrollment, as conservative parents were more willing to send their daughters to all-female schools. Political activity critical of the government was still severely repressed, but women found new paths to enter the public arena through the education system.

Spurred by a renewed women's movement and economic necessity, the government partially and gradually reversed most restrictions on what women could study. Universities had appeal to young women in part because they were places where they could get away from restrictions imposed on them at home and in the larger society. The rapid educational gains by women led to a conservative backlash that put quotas on the number of women allowed in certain fields of study and at universities away from their homes. (Aryan.) In 2012, the government banned women from seventy-seven college majors, including biology and engineering. Nevertheless, as of 2016, women made up about half of college students in Iran. (Kishi, 2016.)

Economic opportunities have improved somewhat for women since the regime began. In the early 1990s, the government's economic liberalization program, which is discussed in the next section, was hindered by restrictions on women's employment. The government pursued policies to open more employment opportunities, directly and indirectly, for women. For example, women were allowed to reenter the legal profession in any position except that of judge. The state actively supported access to contraception and mandated maternity leave. Fertility rates dropped, female literacy increased dramatically, women achieved higher educational levels, more women chose not to marry, and the age of first marriage increased. (Bahramitash and Kazemipour, 2006.)

Women's improved status, however, did not translate into large gains in employment. Women continue to be employed at much lower rates than men and tend to work in lower-paid sectors, especially the government and universities. As of 2020, women made up 19 percent of Iran's workforce. (Nada, 2020.) Many Iranians argue that women pursue education in such high numbers in part because few economic alternatives are open to them. (Rezai-Rashti and Moghadam, 2011.)

The social status of women has varied depending on the presidential administration, even under the same supreme leader. The Ahmadinejad government elected in 2005 restricted women's appearance in public, banned numerous women's (and dissident) publications and Web sites, and expanded gender segregation of public amenities. This crackdown, however, did not eliminate the women's movement. A women's coalition formed during the 2009 campaign, and women were active participants in the large protests that followed the elections.

Running for president in 2013, Hassan Rouhani said that he believed men and women should be treated equally. By 2019, he had appointed four women as vice presidents of government-affairs organizations and three as governors. In the same year, the government reversed a rule that women could not attend soccer matches. About 4,000 tickets to a World Cup soccer match between Cambodia and Iran were set aside for women, who were required to sit in a separate section of Azadi Stadium in Tehran. (Wamsley, 2019.)

Iranian women can participate in many sports, such as rowing, running, archery, and soccer, although female teams have difficulty in obtaining financing. The regime bans women's participation in certain athletic activities, such as cycling.

Rouhani also promised to reduce the enforcement of punishments for not complying with hijab requirements. As the story that opens this chapter shows, Rouhani's promise was put to the test in December 2017, when Vida Movahed was arrested for appearing in public without her head covering. After the images spread through social media, thirty women engaged in similar protests were arrested, and three were sentenced to prison. The authorities responded to the protests with repression. Young women took to social media to call for freedom of dress, and women parliamentarians also began to challenge gender discrimination and call for equal access to education and jobs. The women protesting on

Women attend a 2019 World Cup qualification match between Iran and Cambodia. Iran's government lifted a ban on women attending soccer matches and allowed 4,000 women to attend, although in a segregated section of the arena.

Atta Kenare/AFP/Getty Images

Basij
A voluntary paramilitary force that serves as the morality police in Iran.

Revolution Street in 2017–2018 learned, however, that the president had little control over the situation.

The **Basij**, a voluntary paramilitary force under the authority of the Revolutionary Guard, with organizations in nearly every city and town, serves as the morality police. (Alfoneh, 2010.) The Basij actively enforces the hijab requirement, so little changed for the women protesting against it. Nonetheless, the engagement of millennials on social media and the involvement of women parliamentarians may indicate that the women's movement is gaining momentum.

Protests over wearing the hijab are just the latest in the long series of conflicts over women's rights and roles in Iran. The women's movement in Iran represents a different type of feminism than that found in Western countries. Iranian feminists reject what they view as Western society's sexual objectification of women. Instead, they argue for a place of equality within Iran's traditional Islamic society.

Conservative clergy have resisted changes to laws regarding divorce, clothing, and other issues associated with religious observance, but they have allowed significant socio-economic changes in women's lives. These changes have fostered the growth of women's organizations calling for even further change.

Divisions in Iran

Iran is unusual in the Middle East because the majority of the country's population is Persian, not Arab, and major religious authorities are Shiites, not Sunnis. The Iranian constitution requires the president to be a Shiite Muslim.

Iran's minority ethnic groups include Arabs, Azeris, Kurds, and Baluchis. Iran also has several non-Shiite Muslim and non-Muslim religious groups.

In the seventh century, Islam split over who would succeed the Prophet Mohammed. Shiite Muslims believe the Prophet's son-in-law, Imam Ali, was the rightful heir to the leadership and that descendants of Imam Ali remain the only rightful religious authorities. Major Shiite religious authorities are chosen from among those who can claim to be his heirs. Sunnis, who constitute approximately 85 percent of the world's Muslims, believe that any religiously educated person with appropriate training can become an important leader in Islam, and they reject the claim that a particular bloodline should rule. Iran and Iraq are two of only four Muslim countries with Shiite majorities, and Iran is about 90 percent Shia. (Pew Research.)

Religious minorities in Iran include Sunni Muslims, Christians, Jews, Zoroastrians, and Bahá'í. Article 12 of the Iranian constitution protects the rights of Sunni Muslims to practice their religious beliefs, stating, "Other Islamic schools, including the Hanafi, Shafi'i, Maliki, Hanbali, and Zaydi are to be accorded full respect, and their followers are free to act in accordance with their own jurisprudence in performing their religious rites. These schools enjoy official status in matters pertaining to religious education, affairs of personal status (marriage, divorce, inheritance, and wills) and related litigation in courts of law."

Despite these legal protections, Sunni Muslims face discrimination in society and by the state. Molavi Abdolhamid Ismaeelzahi, Iran's highest-ranking Sunni cleric, reports that he has been harassed, intimidated, and prevented from traveling. (Rafizadeh, 2018.) The Ministry of Intelligence and local militias are used to monitor and control the country's Sunni population. (Rafizadeh, 2018.)

Some minority groups, such as Assyrian and Chaldean Christians, Jews, and Zoro-astrians (the oldest monotheistic religion in the world), are officially recognized by the

The second part of the AP® Comparative Government and Politics exam consists of four different written free-response questions. You will have ninety minutes to complete this section. You have practiced all four types of questions throughout this textbook. Here are some reminders.

Conceptual Analysis

The first free-response question is the conceptual-analysis question. It is worth 11 percent of the exam score, and the recommended writing time for this question is ten minutes. This question requires you to define or describe a concept and explain how the concept affects government and politics. AP® Political Science Practice features in Chapters 2 and 10 helped prepare you for these questions. The conceptual-analysis question has four parts, and each part is worth one point.

Here is an example from Chapter 2, Section 1:

Answer A, B, C, and D.

A. Define regime change.

B. Explain how a regime change differs from a change in government.

C. Explain why changes in government are more common than changes in regime.

D. Describe a policy a government might enact in an effort to strengthen the state.

Some Reminders

Part A usually requires you to define a key term. While you don't have to memorize definitions word for word, remember to be specific. In part A, your response should indicate that a regime change is a change in the fundamental system of government. The rest of the question will ask you to describe or explain how the key concept differs from other concepts or how the concept applies to government and politics. Use the language from the prompt in your response. Remember to use the word *because* in response to questions that use *explain* as a task verb. For example, in part B, a good response would state, "A change in regime is different from a change in government *because* a regime change is a change in the whole system of government, while a change in government is just a change in leaders, while the basic system stays the same."

In part C, a good response would state, "Changes in government are more common than changes in regime *because* it is easier to change leaders through votes of no confidence or elections than it is to change the entire system of government, which often occurs through a revolution or coup." Descriptions should be specific.

In part D, a good response would state, "A country might try to strengthen the state by expanding the civil liberties of ethnic groups so that these groups feel less disadvantaged and are less likely to rebel."

Quantitative Analysis

The second free-response question is the quantitative-analysis question. This question is worth 12.5 percent of the exam score, and the recommended writing time is twenty minutes. This type of question requires you to

1. Describe data from a graph, map, table, or infographic,

2. Describe patterns and trends and similarities and differences,

3. Define or describe course concepts,

4. Draw conclusions based on data, and

5. Explain how the data relate to government and politics.

You have encountered quantitative-analysis questions throughout the book, and AP® Political Science Practices features in Chapters 3, 5, 6, 7, 10, 11, and 12 prepare you for these questions. The quantitative-analysis free-response question has five parts, and each part is worth one point.

Measuring the Importance of Media Freedom

Percent who say that it is very important that media can report news in their country without government censorship

Data from Pew Research Center, 2019 Global Attitudes Survey.

Here is an example of a quantitative-analysis question from the Section 3 review in Chapter 6:

Answer A, B, C, D, and E.

A. Using the data shown on the map, identify the country studied in AP® Comparative Government and Politics with the highest percentage of respondents who think that an independent press is important.

B. Using the data shown on the map, describe a pattern among countries studied in AP® Comparative Government and Politics with a low percentage of respondents who think that an independent press is important and countries studied in AP® Comparative Government and Politics with a high percentage of respondents who think that an independent press is important.

C. Define an independent press.

D. Draw a conclusion about why the country you identified in part A has a higher level of agreement that an independent press is important than a country you identified in part B.

E. Explain why civil liberties, other than a free press, are important in democratic states.

Some Reminders

Parts A and B of the quantitative-analysis question require you to incorporate data from the graphic into your response. In this question, part A asks you to identify the country with the highest percentage of respondents who believe an independent press is important. In part B, a pattern is that in the United Kingdom, which is a liberal democracy, a high percentage of respondents believes an independent press is important, while in Russia, which is an authoritarian state, a lower percentage of respondents believes an independent press is important. This information comes directly from the map.

In part C, you may be asked about a key concept from the course, in this case, an independent press, which is when newspapers, TV, and other media are not restricted by the government in what they report.

Part D requires you to apply a key concept to the data in the graphic. Remember to use the language from the prompt in your answer. A good response to part D would state:

More people in the United Kingdom than in Russia believe an independent press is important, because the United Kingdom is a democratic state, and people are used to being able to get their news from a variety of sources, while in Russia, fewer people see an independent press an important because they are used to getting their news from sources sanctioned by the authoritarian state.

Part E may ask you to apply other concepts learned in the course. A good response to part E would state:

Civil liberties, other than a free press, are important in democratic states because they provide citizens with equal treatment under the law. Due-process rights, for example, protect those accused of crimes and ensure the rule of law that characterizes a democratic state.

Comparative Analysis

The third free-response question on the AP® Exam is the comparative-analysis question. It is worth 12.5 percent of the exam score, and the recommended writing time for this question is twenty minutes. The comparative-analysis question requires you to

1. Define or describe a course concept, institution, or policy,

2. Describe or explain examples of a course concept, institution, or policy in two course countries, and

3. Compare or explain two different course countries with regard to the concept, institution, or policy.

The AP® Political Science Practices feature in Chapter 8 prepared you for comparative-analysis questions. This question has three parts and is worth five points.

Here is an example of a comparative-analysis question:

Compare how the legislature and judiciary can constrain executive power in two course countries studied in AP® Comparative Government and Politics. In your response, you should do the following:

A. Define institutional independence.

B. Explain how the legislature can constrain executive power in two of the course countries studied in AP® Comparative Government and Politics.

C. Explain how the judiciary can constrain executive power in two of the course countries studied in AP® Comparative Government and Politics.

Some Reminders

Part A of the question requires you to define or describe a course concept, in this case institutional independence, which is the ability of one branch of government to operate without interference from other branches of government.

Part B requires you to compare two countries. Part B is worth two points—one for an accurate and relevant statement about each country. For example, a response would earn one point for stating, "The legislature in the United Kingdom can constrain executive power through a vote of no confidence" and a second point for stating, "The legislature in Nigeria can constrain executive power through impeachment."

Part C is also worth two points—one for an accurate and relevant statement about each country. For example, a response would earn one point for stating, "The Supreme Court in the United Kingdom can overturn actions by executive agencies that violate citizens' civil rights," and a second point for stating, "The judiciary in Nigeria has the power of judicial review to overturn executive actions that violate the Constitution." Remember to choose countries that can be easily compared using the key concept in the question.

Argument Essay

The final portion of the AP® Exam is the argument essay. It is worth 14 percent of the exam score, and the recommended writing time is forty minutes. AP® Political Science Practices

features in Chapters 2, 8, 11, and 12 prepared you for this question. Each chapter, chapter review, and unit review includes an argument essay. We will not rewrite an entire argument question here. Instead, we will offer some reminders:

Reminders and Tips for the Argument Essay

The argument question follows a standard format, which you can see in this question from the Chapter 8 Review:

Develop an argument about whether single-member district, or mixed electoral systems are more effective in representing citizens' interests in the legislature.

Use one or more of the following course concepts in your response:

- Party system
- Accountability
- Legitimacy

In your response, do the following:

- *Respond to the prompt with a defensible claim or thesis that establishes a line of reasoning using one or more of the provided course concepts.*
- *Support your claim with at least TWO pieces of specific and relevant evidence from your study of one or more course countries. The evidence should be relevant to one or more of the provided course concepts.*
- *Use reasoning to explain why your evidence supports your claim or thesis, using one or more of the provided course concepts.*
- *Respond to an opposing or alternate perspective, using refutation, concession, or rebuttal.*

The italicized language is standard and will be used in every argument question. Only the prompt and the bulleted list of concepts will change.

The argument essay is worth five points, allocated as follows:

One point for a thesis that establishes a line of reasoning and incorporates one or more course concepts from the list.

One point for each of two pieces of specific and relevant evidence.

One point for reasoning that explains how the evidence relates to a listed concept and supports the thesis.

One point for responding to an opposing argument with refutation, concession, or rebuttal.

A Few Final Reminders

Choose a thesis that is easy to support with evidence, whether or not you agree with it. Make sure your thesis refers to a listed concept and uses a *because* statement to establish a line of reasoning. Pick your country or countries carefully to use as evidence. It is often easiest to use evidence from countries that differ, but the most important consideration is your specific knowledge of the countries. Make a clear transition to your RCR paragraph, and after stating your opponent's argument, write a response explaining why your argument is better.

government. These groups are allowed to practice their faith, with some restrictions. Members of officially recognized minority religions who work in government or serve in the army are allowed to take leave to celebrate religious holidays. They can run their own schools, but the Ministry of Education approves textbooks and curriculum. However, proselytizing or attempting to convert Shiite Muslims to a different religion is a criminal offense. In July 2017, the judiciary sentenced four people to ten-year prison sentences for holding illegal gatherings to promote Christianity. (Ceasefire Centre for Civilian Rights, 2018.)

Iran has pursued a systematic program of persecution against the Bahá'í, a non-Muslim religion which emerged in the 1800s. The Iranian government views Bahá'í beliefs as heresy and fundamentally detrimental to the teachings of Islam. Members of the Bahá'í religion report that they have been forced out of their homes and that local authorities have vandalized property, confiscated land, and bulldozed the graves of their ancestors. (Deutsche Welle.) According to the representative offices of the Bahá'í International Community, more than two hundred Bahá'ís have been executed since the mid-1980s. Thousands have been interrogated, detained, and arrested. Jobs, pensions, and opportunities for education have been denied to tens of thousands of Bahá'í. (Bahá'í International Community.)

The Iranian regime lacks rule of law and engages in significant human-rights abuses. Despite international condemnation of these practices, the government uses force, including the threat of violence, as a means of maintaining its power.

Section 13.4 Review

Remember

- The Iranian government represses speech critical of the regime by harassing, arresting, and jailing journalists and shutting down newspapers and Web sites critical of the regime.
- Women's rights in Iran have varied over time, and although they make up half of all college students, women in Iran lack political, economic, and social equality.
- Iran lacks due process and rule of law, and critics of the regime face arbitrary detention, torture, and execution.
- Jews, Chaldean and Assyrian Christians, Zoroastrians, and Sunni Muslims received some legal protections under Iran's constitution, but these groups face discrimination.
- The Bahá'í religious group is repressed by the Iranian government.

Know

- *Basij:* a voluntary paramilitary force that serves as the morality police in Iran. (p. 422)

Think

- How has Iranian women's political, educational, economic, and social status changed since the revolution?

Free-Response Question: Comparative Analysis

Compare the government's response to social cleavages in two different AP® Comparative Government and Politics course countries. In your response, you should do the following:

A. Define social cleavage.

B. Describe social cleavages in two different AP® Comparative Government and Politics course countries.

C. Explain how the governments in each of the two AP® Comparative Government and Politics course countries responded to the social cleavages described in part B.

13.5 Economic and Social Change and Development

Learning Targets

After reading this section, you should be able to do the following:

1. Explain how Iran's status as a rentier state impacts its economy.

2. Describe economic liberalization in Iran.

3. Explain how sanctions imposed by Western countries impact Iran's economy.

4. Describe the social welfare state in Iran.

5. Describe the demographic changes occurring in Iran and explain how they might alter the social welfare system.

Iran is a rentier state that derives a significant amount of government revenue from rent paid by foreign concerns for access to natural resources, particularly oil. Its economy has partially transitioned away from state-led development toward a free market. However, Iran's economy has been negatively impacted by sanctions imposed by Western nations and by falling oil prices. These economic woes may make it difficult for the state to fund Iran's fairly extensive social programs, especially as birth rates continue to fall and many productive Iranians leave the country.

Globalization

Iran's theocratic regime has not shielded the country from the impact of globalization. Iran's economy has been influenced by the goals of the revolution and its status as an oil-rich rentier state. The revolutionary government nationalized many economic assets in 1980, including large private companies and banks, which became state-owned enterprises (SOEs). Property confiscated from the shah's family and close associates funded the new Islamic foundations (*bonyads*), which became a key part of revolutionary rule. The eight-year Iran–Iraq War in the 1980s pummeled the economy, with estimated losses exceeding $500 billion. (MSN Encarta.)

The 1990s saw some improvement, but this was accompanied by annual inflation of more than 20 percent and growing unemployment, which reached 16 percent by 2000. Throughout both the 1980s and 1990s, the country remained critically dependent on oil, which accounted for more than 80 percent of exports and anywhere from one-third to two-thirds of government revenue, depending on world oil prices.

The Iranian government intervened extensively in the economy, partly to decrease the influence of other countries and foreign companies and investors. Government-controlled banks set interest rates, and trade barriers were high. The government budget provided large subsidies to the *bonyads* and to the SOEs. Because they were getting so much money from the government, SOEs had little incentive to modernize or operate efficiently. Their losses from 1994 to 1999 equaled nearly 3 percent of the country's GDP. (Alizadeh, 2003, 273.)

In 1995, President Bill Clinton announced sanctions against Iran that prohibited companies based in the United States from investing in or trading with Iran. The sanctions announced by President Clinton were meant to punish Iran for its support of what the United States deemed as terrorist organizations within the region. The sanctions were also aimed at forcing Iran to change its behavior.

Facing growing economic problems, the government under President Mohammad Khatami attempted the first significant liberalization of the economy in the late 1990s. Economic liberalization was a response to pressures at home and from abroad. Iran's theocratic government took advice from the IMF in setting new policies. The most dramatic reforms included the sale of some government-controlled banks to the private sector, reduction of import and export barriers, and the privatization of some SOEs.

Elites within the regime were divided over privatization, and the supreme leader ultimately ensured that much of the equity in and control of the former SOEs ended up in the hands of the *bonyads* and similar groups with close ties to the regime. (Mohseni, 2016.) Overall, the reforms increased GDP growth in the first decade of the twenty-first century to an average of 4.5 percent per year and reduced inflation to less than 15 percent (World Bank, 2020; Statista), but unemployment and poverty levels remained largely unchanged.

In 2006, the Bush administration issued additional sanctions targeting Iran's banking industry and the United Nations adopted the first in a series of sanctions against Iran in the continuing effort to encourage Iran to stop enriching uranium. (U.N. Security Council Resolution 1727.) The Iranian government claims its uranium enrichment program is for the peaceful purpose of domestic energy production through nuclear power. Officials in the United States, the EU, and the United Nations are concerned that Iran intends to use its uranium-enrichment program to build nuclear weapons.

The EU complied with the U.N. sanctions against Iran and adopted additional restrictions on trade and banking. Because of falling oil prices during the 2008 Great Recession, Iran's oil revenue declined. Revenue from Iranian oil exports fell 24 percent in 2009, and the GDP growth rate dropped to 1 percent.

President Ahmadinejad cut subsidies to control the rapidly growing budget deficit. Past efforts to reduce subsidies had led to widespread protests and reversals of the cuts, but in late 2010, the government allowed gasoline prices to quadruple. This move was met with little protest, perhaps because of the severe crackdown on protests after the 2009 election. Ahmadinejad actively encouraged imports from countries such as India, Pakistan, and China that did not follow Western sanctions, greatly expanding consumer imports. Increased international sanctions starting in 2011 and stagnant oil prices affected the economy heavily. Growth dropped to zero by 2012, and as President Ahmadinejad handed power over to newly elected president Hassan Rouhani, inflation was estimated at over 40 percent and unemployment at around 25 percent.

The Recent Iranian Economy

Rouhani's biggest economic success was the completion of the nuclear deal with the United States, the five permanent member countries of the U.N. Security Council, and Germany that resulted in the removal of some sanctions. Within a year of the accord, Iran's oil exports doubled, and the country struck many deals with European businesses for investment. Annual growth shot up to more than 12 percent in 2016 before dropping to slightly over 3 percent in 2017—a fall that led to the massive demonstrations in December of that year. In 2018, however, the United States repudiated the nuclear accord and reimposed sanctions.

Iran was defiant and claimed it could maintain a "resistance economy." However, its vulnerable economy was hit hard with a big drop in oil production. In 2020, its GDP shrank by 6.8 percent. (World Bank, 2020.) Inflation reached 36.5 percent in 2020 (Statista), with prices of housing, many staple foods, and medical care soaring. The poorest were hit the hardest by rising prices.

China and India, two of Iran's largest oil purchasers, declared their intention to keep buying Iranian oil despite the threat of U.S. sanctions against them. But with growing budget deficits, and falling oil prices and revenues, it was unclear how long popular support for the regime's resistance economic policy could persist. (BBC News, 2019; K. Johnson, 2019.)

In another reversal, in 2021 President Biden signaled a desire to recommit to the Iran nuclear deal. Although officials in the United States, European Union, and Iran have indicated their support for the deal, as of this writing, the United States has not rejoined.

Social Policies

Iran has had a social welfare system since the 1920s. Under the government of the shah, social-insurance programs were expanded to people working for the government, in industry, and in petroleum production.

The Islamic regime created an expanded and more inclusive welfare system than the country had previously seen. Article 29 of the Iranian constitution provides that it is a universal right "to benefit from social security with respect to retirement, unemployment, old age, disability, absence of a guardian, and benefits related to being stranded, accidents, health services, and medical care and treatment."

Health care in Iran is provided by the government, the private sector, and through NGOs and charities. The health-care system in Iran is made up of a system of local clinics in villages and cities, called health houses. These clinics provide basic medical services, including treatment, health education, preventive care, and contraception. In 2014, the Ministry of Health and Medical Education launched the Health Transformation Plan (HTP), which is also called Rouhanicare. The HTP provides nearly universal health care for Iranians, and it includes a prescription drug benefit. The HTP increased the percentage of people with health insurance coverage and reduced the amount of money people had to pay for medical treatment and prescription drugs. In addition, like people living in the United Kingdom, Iranians may purchase supplemental insurance on the private market. (Landinfo, 2020.)

Iran provides other social welfare benefits to its citizens. Unemployment benefits are available to people who lose their jobs. The amount received depends on several factors, including whether the person is married and the number of dependents. Benefits are available for people who are disabled. Civil servants are guaranteed sick leave up to one full year. Maternity leave can be taken three months before birth and lasts for a total of six months.

About 75 percent of Iranian workers have a retirement pension, which is paid for by contributions from the worker, the employer, and the government. However, about a quarter of workers, mostly in the informal sector, do not have pensions. (Landinfo, 2020.)

Iran's most vulnerable citizens are served by a dual system of aid from the government and private charity. The *bonyads* served as parallel providers of social support to the poor. The Imam Khomeini Relief Foundation is a charity organization funded by donations, and it provides social services for Iran's poorest and most vulnerable citizens. The State Welfare Organization (SWO) provides targeted assistance to these groups, including women, children, and the mentally and physically disabled. The SWO provides financial and job assistance to female breadwinners. The organization also works to prevent domestic and child abuse by providing hotlines for reporting abuse and safehouses for victims. SWO skills and jobs training programs are available for people with physical or mental disabilities. (Landinfo, 2020.)

As you will learn below, Iran was hit hard by the COVID-19 pandemic, increasing its health-care costs. Coupled with the impact of economic sanctions, and lower oil prices, government revenues for 2020–2021 were 55 percent of what had been predicted in the budget. (World Bank, 2021.) As a result, the future of Iran's social welfare programs is uncertain.

Shifting Demographics

Iran is facing two key demographic changes. Its population is aging, and well-educated, highly skilled young people are emigrating to other countries—a phenomena known as brain drain.

Iran's population policies have changed over time. In 1966, the government under the shah established Iran's first family-planning program, which provided access to modern forms of contraception. The program was not effective in lowering birth rates, and by the time of the revolution in 1979, the fertility rate was above 6.0 children per woman. During the Iran–Iraq War (1980–1988), the supreme leader called upon Iranians to have big families to supply the army with future troops, and the fertility rate rose to 6.5 children in the middle of the conflict. (Cincotta and Sudjadpour, 2017.)

Once the war ended, the government reversed strategy. The oil industry and infrastructure were damaged and had to be rebuilt. Social welfare programs were a burden on the state, and economic growth was not sufficient to keep up with a rapidly growing younger population. The government announced a family-planning program to provide health education and contraception through local health clinics, staffed with female volunteers who followed up with the families they served. The state provided contraception and vasectomies free of charge, and Iran built the only state-sponsored condom factory in the Middle East. (BBC.) By 2005, the fertility rate was just above 2.0 children per woman.

Iran's population policy reversed course again with the election of President Ahmadinejad in 2005, who argued that family planning was a conspiracy by Western powers to weaken Iran. In 2010, the government began giving financial incentives for people to expand their families. By 2014, legislation was passed to eliminate free contraception and vasectomies provided by the state. (Cincotta and Sadjadpour.) However, despite efforts by the government to raise the fertility rate, by 2020, it had dropped to 1.7. (The Guardian.) The drop in the fertility rate means that fewer young people will be available to fund social programs for Iran's aging population.

A family of four travels by motorbike in Isfahan, Iran. Fertility rates have dropped in Iran since the revolution, and on average, women now have two children.

Reza Estakhrian/The Image Bank Unreleased/ Getty Images

Along with a drop in fertility rates, Iran's productive workforce is being impacted by the brain drain, the emigration of well-educated and highly skilled Iranians to other countries. Between 1979 and 2019, a staggering 3.1 million people emigrated from Iran, many of them graduate students. Hardworking and talented Iranians are admitted to universities throughout the world, and there is a perception that attending graduate school abroad provides a higher-quality education than staying in Iran. Furthermore, the job market in Iran does not offer much opportunity or hope for those earning advanced degrees. Iranian students abroad may be able to get scholarships that are not available within the country. Furthermore, getting a degree from a foreign university may provide a legal path to citizenship elsewhere. (Azadi, Mirramezani, and Mesgaran, 2020.)

There are a number of political reasons why well-educated young people leave Iran, as one student studying for his doctorate at Harvard put it: "The government is corrupt, and promotion is not merit-based. You must pretend you are more religious than you really are. If you are a woman, the scarf is mandatory in public spaces. The moral police are a pain . . . be it because you are out with your boyfriend or you are not covered up as they deem appropriate. There is a constant threat . . . of war. Serious threat. Not very pleasant or easy to live in. Finally, politics are unstable. You often hear the conspiracy theorists in the public buses saying that the current government is 'gone by next year.' This doesn't really happen. But the government fears it somewhat, and they rule with an iron fist." (Sinai, 2014.)

The brain drain puts the Iranian regime in a difficult situation. The government is willing to allow dissidents to leave the country, reducing internal threats. However, the regime does not want to fully acknowledge the extent of the problem, because the brain drain sheds light on dissatisfaction and hopelessness among Iran's well-educated young people. The exodus of this group means that Iran is losing some of its most talented and productive citizens. (Azadi, Mirramezani, and Mesgaran, 2020.)

Iran and the Future

In 2020, Iran reported a high of 25,000 COVID-19 cases per day. As of March 2021, Iran reported more than 1.7 million cases of the virus and 61,000 deaths—making it the most heavily impacted country in the Middle East and North Africa. (World Bank, 2021.) In April 2021, while vaccines were becoming more available in many countries, and especially in the West, Iran reported a surge in COVID cases, with a projected 60,000 hospitalizations.

Many Iranians gave up on social distancing to keep their jobs. Subways and buses were packed with people who could not afford to miss work. There was widespread uncertainty about vaccine availability after the supreme leader prohibited import of vaccines from the United States and United Kingdom. COVID-19, coupled with economic sanctions, has the potential to severely strain the health-care system and wreak havoc on the Iranian economy. (Al Jazeera, 2021.)

The Islamic republic has endured and remains regionally powerful. While basing its claim to legitimacy firmly in theocracy, it includes limited elements of democratic rule. However, patronage from oil revenue and corruption may be more important than elections in maintaining the government's authority.

Questions remain, however, about its legitimacy, as seen in the large street protests against the presidential election outcome in 2009. There have been many incidents of civil unrest in the past decade, including strikes and large-scale protests, such as a massive demonstration against high fuel prices in 2019. Many talented young Iranians are leaving the country in search of more personal freedom and economic opportunity.

Iran's attempt to acquire much greater nuclear capabilities has recently made the country a center of global debate. While it is an important regional player and focus of global attention, the Fragile States Index gives Iran a "high warning" designation, and the Islamic republic has become potentially less stable.

Section 13.5 Review

Remember

- Iran is a rentier state that relies on oil revenue as a significant source of government funds.
- Sanctions imposed by Western countries and declining oil prices have hindered the country's economic growth.
- Iran is a social welfare state that provides health care, unemployment benefits, pensions, and other programs to assist the disadvantaged.
- Iran's working-age population will decrease due to declining birth rates and highly skilled young people leaving the country.

Think

- What is the biggest challenge the Iranian regime will face in the future?

Free-Response Question: Quantitative Analysis

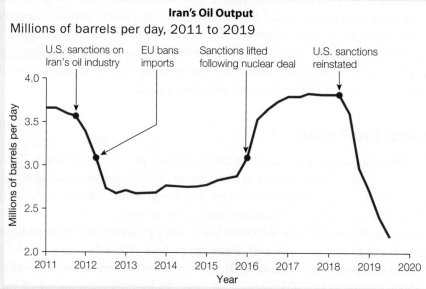

Iran's Oil Output
Millions of barrels per day, 2011 to 2019

Data from OPEC and the BBC. Data for 2019 through September.

Answer A, B, C, D, and E.

A. Using the data in the graph, identify the year in which Iran had the second highest level of oil production from 2011 to 2019.

B. Using the data in the graph, describe a trend in oil production that occurred after the period you identified in part A.

C. Define rentier state.

D. Using your knowledge of rentier states and the data in the graph, draw a conclusion about how economic sanctions could impact social programs in Iran.

E. Describe a factor, other than the factors discussed in part D, that could impact social programs in Iran.

Chapter 13 Review

AP® KEY CONCEPTS

- Theocracy (p. 398)
- Supreme leader (p. 404)
- Guardian Council (p. 407)
- Expediency Council (p. 407)
- Majles (p. 408)
- Assembly of Experts (p. 408)
- Multimember district (MMD) system (p. 410)
- Basij (p. 422)

AP® EXAM MULTIPLE-CHOICE PRACTICE QUESTIONS

1. Iran, with its system of dual rule by theocratic and elected officials, is most similar to
   A. The United Kingdom, which is ruled by a monarch and elected government.
   B. Russia, with rule by an elected president and appointed prime minister.
   C. China, which is ruled by the CCP and the government.
   D. Nigeria, which has sharia law in the north but not in the south.

Questions 2 and 3 refer to the passage.

> What we saw in the United States yesterday evening and today shows above all how fragile and vulnerable Western democracy is . . . We saw that unfortunately the ground is fertile for populism, despite the advances in science and industry . . . I hope the whole world and the next occupants of the White House will learn from it . . . to make up [for the past] and restore the country to a position worthy of the American nation, because the American nation is a great nation . . . May they return to reason, legality and their obligations. It's for their own benefit and the good of the world.
>
> —President Hassan Rouhani, speech broadcast on Iranian state television, January 7, 2021

2. Which of the following is supported by the passage?
   A. Iran's theocratic government provides more rule of law than democracy in the United States.
   B. Democracy in the United States is unstable.
   C. Sanctions imposed on Iran are illegal and were imposed to benefit Western nations.
   D. Iran's government should serve as a model for the West.

3. Which of the following arguments would be made by a critic of the point of view conveyed in the passage?
   A. Violent protests occurred in Iran following the 2009 presidential election.
   B. Western protesters who engage in violence are exercising civil liberties that are restricted in Iran, where citizens are not allowed to protest.
   C. Protesters in the United States support democracy, while protesters in Iran oppose democracy.
   D. President Rouhani should not criticize populism, because populism is the basis of the Iranian state's legitimacy.

4. Which of the following institutions in Iran is directly elected?
   A. The Guardian Council
   B. The Expediency Council
   C. The cabinet
   D. The Assembly of Experts

5. Which of the following is a similarity between Iran and Nigeria?

   A. Both have unicameral legislatures.

   B. They both set aside seats for religious minorities in the legislature.

   C. Women are not allowed to vote in certain states or provinces in both countries.

   D. Both have directly elected presidents.

6. Which of the following best describes the executive branch in two course countries studied in AP® Comparative Government and Politics?

   A. The president in Mexico and the prime minister in the United Kingdom serve as the head of state.

   B. Mexico and Nigeria have a single executive.

   C. Russia and Iran have a dual executive consisting of a president and a prime minister.

   D. In Iran, the supreme leader acts as the head of government, and in China, the head of government is the president.

Questions 7 and 8 refer to the population pyramid.

Iran's Population Pyramid, 2020

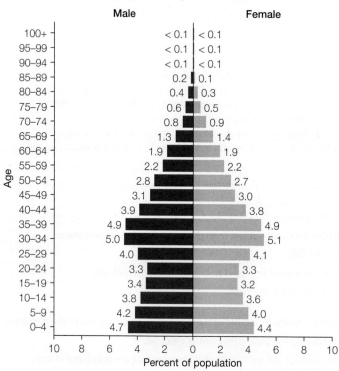

Data from PopulationPyramid.net.

7. According to the bar chart, which age group makes up the largest percentage of Iran's population in 2020?

   A. 30–34

   B. 0–4

   C. 35–39

   D. 65 and above

8. Which of the following is an implication of the data in the chart?

   A. Birth rates have remained the same in Iran in the past twenty years.

   B. The percentage of Iranians over the age of sixty-five will decline in the next twenty years.

   C. Iran's pension program will face funding challenges in the next thirty years.

   D. Life expectancy in Iran dropped due to the COVID-19 pandemic.

9. Which of the following best describes the regime type in Iran?

   A. It is a democracy because members of the executive and legislative branches are directly elected.

   B. It is a hybrid regime because the president and supreme leader share power.

   C. It is an illiberal or hybrid regime, because it holds elections, but the government restricts human rights.

   D. It is an authoritarian regime, because elections are not free and fair and civil rights and liberties are restricted.

10. Which of the following accurately describes a formal power of an institution in Iran?

    A. The president serves as commander-in-chief.

    B. The Guardian Council approves or rejects candidates who want to run for office.

    C. The Assembly of Experts reviews laws passed by the parliament to ensure they conform to sharia law.

    D. The Expediency Council serves as a cabinet and oversees each ministry.

AP® EXAM PRACTICE ARGUMENT ESSAY

Develop an argument as to whether having a single executive or a dual executive provides for the most effective policymaking within a state.

Use one or more of the following course concepts in your response:

- Legitimacy
- Authority
- Stability

In your response, do the following:

- Respond to the prompt with a defensible claim or thesis that establishes a line of reasoning using one or more of the provided course concepts.
- Support your claim with at least TWO pieces of specific and relevant evidence from your study of one or more course countries. The evidence should be relevant to one or more of the provided course concepts.
- Use reasoning to explain why your evidence supports your claim or thesis, using one or more of the provided course concepts.
- Respond to an opposing or alternate perspective, using refutation, concession, or rebuttal.

For a complete list of the sources of information cited in this chapter, turn to the Works Cited appendix.

UNIT ⑤ REVIEW

Economics

① Mexico

② United Kingdom

③ Russia

④ Nigeria

⑤ China

⑥ Iran

AP® EXAM PRACTICE QUESTIONS

Section 1: Multiple Choice

1. Which of the following conflicts was a response to neoliberal economic policies?
   A. Sanctions imposed on Iran by the United States and other Western powers
   B. The Zapatista movement in Mexico
   C. The Chinese state's internment of Uyghurs in reeducation camps
   D. Russia's conflict within the Chechen region

Questions 2 and 3 refer to the bar chart.

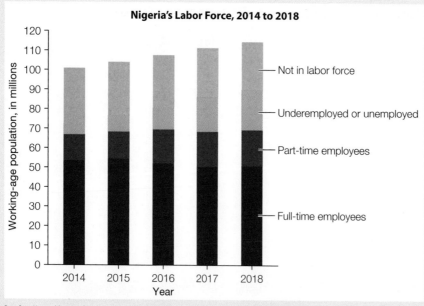

Data from National Bureau of Statistics (Nigeria), Labour Force Survey. Data are from the final quarter of 2014, 2015, 2016, and 2017, Q3 of 2018.

2. Which of the following is accurate according to the bar chart?
   A. The number of people not in the labor force in Nigeria rose between 2014 and 2018.
   B. The number of part-time employees fell between 2014 and 2018.
   C. Nigeria's total labor force remained stable between 2014 and 2018.
   D. The number of people underemployed and unemployed increased between 2014 and 2018.

3. Which of the following is an implication of the data in the bar chart?
   A. In the future, Nigeria will not have enough people employed full time to support its economy.
   B. The Nigerian economy is likely to grow at a steady pace.
   C. Most Nigerians prefer to work part time or to stay home to care for their families.
   D. The Nigerian economy is based mostly on unskilled labor.

4. Which of the following represents a departure from neoliberal economic reform?
   A. China's establishment of special economic zones
   B. The United States–Mexico–Canada trade agreement
   C. Russia's renationalization of the oil industry
   D. Nigeria's policies to encourage direct foreign investment

5. Which of the following countries has the highest degree of state control over natural resources?
   A. China
   B. Mexico
   C. Nigeria
   D. The United Kingdom

Questions 6 and 7 refer to the passage.

> Economic and environmental performance must go hand in hand. The natural environment is central to economic activity and growth, providing the resources we need to produce goods and services, and absorbing and processing unwanted by-products in the form of pollution and waste.
>
> This underpins economic activity and wellbeing, and so maintaining the condition of natural assets is a key factor in sustaining growth for the longer term. Correspondingly, economic growth contributes to the investment and dynamism needed to develop and deploy new technology, which is fundamental to both productivity growth and managing environmental assets.
>
> —Tim Everett, Mallika Ishwaran, Gian Paolo Ansaloni, and Alex Rubin,
> "Economic Growth and the Environment"

6. Which of the following is supported by the passage?
   A. There is a trade-off between economic growth and environmental damage.
   B. There is a reciprocal relationship between a healthy environment and a healthy economy.
   C. Economic and social activities pose inherent risks to the environment.
   D. Economic growth should focus on services instead of making industrial goods that create byproducts that harm the environment.

7. Which of the following is an implication of the passage?
   A. Advanced democracies should provide models for the rest of the world to follow in protecting the environment.
   B. Oil production by rentier states is a major contributor to environmental degradation.
   C. Poor countries often focus on short-term economic growth, depleting valuable natural resources.
   D. Economic growth spurs the development of green technology to protect and improve the environment.

8. Which of the following describes the party systems in China and Iran?
   A. China has a stable one-party state, and Iran has unstable multiple parties.
   B. Iran and China have multiparty systems, although government authorities in both countries can prevent candidates from running for office.
   C. Both countries have longstanding communist parties that win seats in the legislature.
   D. Neither country has political parties, which are forbidden by their authoritarian regimes.

9. Which of the following accurately describe the executives in two course countries studied in AP® Comparative Government and Politics?
   A. Russia and Iran have directly elected prime ministers.
   B. Iran and China have directly elected presidents.
   C. In both China and Russia, the executive consists of a prime minister and a president.
   D. The heads of state in Iran and the United Kingdom are symbolic and have little formal power.

10. Which of the following is a goal of economic liberalization?
    A. To increase government control over the key means of production
    B. To increase productivity and encourage direct foreign investment
    C. To decrease the influence of international organizations and multinational corporations
    D. To increase wealth and income gaps

Questions 11 and 12 are based on the graph.

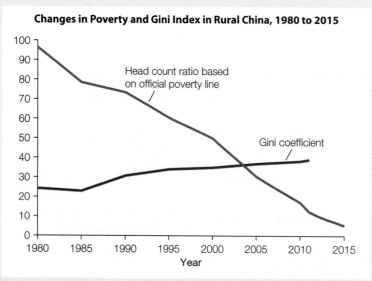

Changes in Poverty and Gini Index in Rural China, 1980 to 2015

Note: Higher Gini coefficient scores indicate greater income inequality.
Data from China National Bureau of Statistics (2015), *Poverty Monitoring Report of Rural China*, and China Statistics Press.

11. Which of the following is accurate according to the line graph?
    A. Since 1985, the number of people living in poverty in China has dropped, and income inequality increased slightly.
    B. Market reforms in China increased the number of people classified as middle class.
    C. The Gini index is not an accurate measure of economic growth within a country.
    D. Since 2005, income inequality and poverty in rural China increased.

12. Which of the following is an implication of the data in the line graph?
    A. Market reforms in China were successful in reducing the poverty level.
    B. The social welfare system in China provides a safety net for the country's poorest citizens.
    C. People living in rural areas of China are more likely to live in poverty than urban residents.
    D. Most of China's economic growth is a result of foreign direct investment.

13. Which of the following accurately describes the systems of government in China and Iran?
    A. Both are presidential and have unicameral legislatures.
    B. They both are semi-presidential and have bicameral legislatures.
    C. Both are parliamentary and federal.
    D. They both are unitary and have unicameral legislatures.

14. Which of the following is a result of the "resource curse"?
    A. A lack of foreign direct investment
    B. The ability to accurately predict government revenues
    C. Lack of economic diversification
    D. A positive trade balance, where exports exceed imports

15. Which of the following characterizes rentier states?
    A. They are among the wealthiest countries, because of the abundance of natural resources.
    B. A significant amount of government revenue is derived from natural resources.
    C. They derive revenue by leasing land to multinational corporations that manufacture consumer goods.
    D. The state owns all agricultural land, which it leases to farmers in exchange for a share of the profit from crops.

16. Which of the following accurately describes a formal power of an institution of government in Iran?
    A. The supreme leader is the chief diplomat.
    B. The Expediency Council is the upper house of the legislature.
    C. The Assembly of Experts selects the supreme leader.
    D. The Guardian Council selects the cabinet, subject to confirmation by the Majles.

Questions 17 and 18 refer to the passage.

> Iran's financial sector had already been badly mauled by existing U.S. sanctions and the flight of non-Iranian banks. The threat of being sanctioned by the United States led most reputable European and other international banks to withdraw from relationships with Iran.
>
> Some business with these banks remains legal under U.S. sanctions, but the conservative nature of many foreign banks—especially in dealing with Iran—will complicate even legitimate trade.
>
> — Richard Nephew, "The Iran Primer." U.S. Institute of Peace.
> October 11, 2020

17. Which of the following is supported by the main idea of the passage?
    A. Sanctions against Iran should be reduced or eliminated because they harm the country's most vulnerable citizens.
    B. The Iranian government has lost significant legitimacy because of sanctions imposed by Western powers.
    C. Iran's petroleum production has decreased because of sanctions, endangering the world's oil supply.
    D. Foreign banks are hesitant to do business in Iran.

18. Which of the following is an implication of the passage?

A. Sanctions imposed by the United States and other Western powers have had a significant negative effect on the Iranian economy.

B. Iranian officials can effectively circumvent sanctions by trading with non-Western powers.

C. Non-Iranian banks are leaving Iran, which provides new opportunities for banks based in Iran.

D. Sanctions block Iran from engaging in all forms of international trade.

19. Which of the following accurately describes a state response to environmental damage caused by industrialization?

A. The Iranian government prohibits journalists from reporting on environmental issues.

B. China has become the world's largest investor in green technology.

C. Nigeria has moved oil-production facilities away from the Niger Delta region.

D. Russia privatized its petroleum industry to modernize oil-production facilities and make them more environmentally friendly.

20. Which of the following is the most powerful body in their respective countries?

A. The House of Commons in the United Kingdom and the National People's Congress in China

B. The Guardian Council in Iran and the president in Mexico

C. The supreme leader in Iran and the general secretary of the CCP in China

D. The prime ministers in the United Kingdom and Russia

Section 2: Free Response

Conceptual Analysis

Answer A, B, C, and D.

A. Define social policy.

B. Describe a measure a state could take to expand social programs.

C. Explain a political reason why a government would choose to expand social programs.

D. Explain how international actors could impact a state's spending on social programs.

Quantitative Analysis

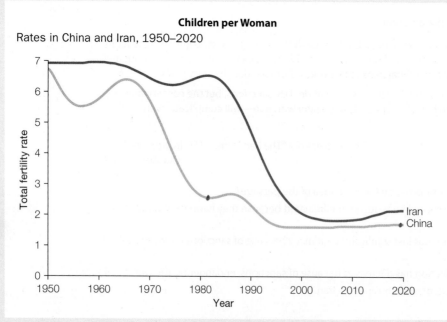

Children per Woman
Rates in China and Iran, 1950–2020

Data from U.N. Population Division.

Answer A, B, C, D, and E.

A. Using the data in the graph, identify the country with the most children per woman in 2020.

B. Using the data in the graph, identify the country that had the largest drop in its fertility rate from 1980 to 2020. ~~IRAN~~ *China*

C. Describe population policy.

D. Using your knowledge of population policy and the data in the graph, draw a conclusion about why the fertility rate dropped in the country identified in part B. *~~1 child~~ policy 1 child policy.*

E. Using your knowledge of population policy and the data in the graph, explain why fertility policies have limited effectiveness.

Comparative Analysis

Compare how the presence of an abundant natural resource impacts the state in two different AP® Comparative Government and Politics course countries. In your response, you should do the following:

A. Define rentier state.

B. Explain how being a rentier state impacts the economy in two different AP® Comparative Government and Politics course countries.

C. Explain how being a rentier state impacts legitimacy in two different AP® Comparative Government and Politics course countries.

Argument Essay

Develop an argument about whether globalization strengthens or weakens regime stability.

Use one or more of the following course concepts in your response:

- Economic liberalization
- Sovereignty
- Legitimacy

In your response, do the following:

- Respond to the prompt with a defensible claim or thesis that establishes a line of reasoning using one or more of the provided course concepts.

- Support your claim with at least TWO pieces of specific and relevant evidence from your study of one or more course countries. The evidence should be relevant to one or more of the provided course concepts.

- Use reasoning to explain why your evidence supports your claim or thesis, using one or more of the provided course concepts.

- Respond to an opposing or alternate perspective, using refutation, concession, or rebuttal.

For a complete list of the sources of information cited in this unit review, turn to the Works Cited appendix.

Section I: Multiple-Choice

Time–1 hour

55 Questions

Directions: Each of the questions or incomplete statements below is followed by four suggested answers or completions. Select the one that is best in each case and then enter the letter in the corresponding space on your answer sheet.

1. Which of the following best describes an overthrow of a regime based on widespread popular support in a course country studied in AP® Comparative Government and Politics?
   A. Coups d'état in Nigeria led by military generals
   B. The 2000 election in Mexico
   C. The Islamic Revolution in Iran
   D. Uprisings in Hong Kong to protest against China's rule

2. Which of the following describes how a legislature can act independently from other branches of government?
   A. The legislature can hold oversight hearings to investigate actions of the bureaucracy.
   B. In presidential systems, the legislature creates the budget.
   C. The legislature can overturn executive actions that violate the constitution.
   D. In a parliamentary system, the legislature has the power to impeach the prime minister.

3. Which of the following is more common in federal systems than in unitary systems?
   A. An authoritarian regime in which some provinces are created for ethnic minorities
   B. Governors and regional leaders who are appointed by the executive
   C. Referendums allowing the national government to devolve power to regional governments
   D. A legislative branch consisting of two houses

4. Which of the following referendums was passed in a course country studied in AP® Comparative Government and Politics?
   A. A measure that allows Scotland to leave the United Kingdom, with a majority vote in the Scottish National Assembly
   B. A proposal allowing President Putin in Russia to serve two additional six-year terms.
   C. A rule requiring political parties in Mexico to run women as 50 percent of candidates.
   D. The creation of the Guardian Council in Iran to reduce gridlock in policymaking in Iran.

5. Which of the following is a disadvantage of the devolution of power?
   A. The central government must treat all regions equally, even though some areas may need more support than others.
   B. Policies vary among regions, which may lead to confusion and contradictory policy approaches.
   C. Central governments are not allowed to take power back once it has been devolved to regional governments.
   D. Devolution reduces the likelihood of rebellion by placing some policymaking authority at the local level.

6. Which of the following best describes political ideology?
   A. An individual's belief about the role of government
   B. The way in which individuals acquire their beliefs about government, often from parents, the state, peers, and the media
   C. The shared values and norms of behavior within a state
   D. The people's belief that the government has the right to rule

7. Which of the following describes how the Iranian president is chosen?
   A. The president is appointed by the supreme leader and confirmed by the Majles.
   B. The president is directly elected by a plurality vote.
   C. The president is chosen by the majority party or majority-party coalition in the parliament.
   D. The president is directly elected, and if no candidate earns a majority of the votes in the first round, a second-round election is held.

8. Which of the following is a difference between democratic and authoritarian regimes?
   A. Democratic regimes hold elections for members of the legislature, and authoritarian regimes do not.
   B. Authoritarian regimes do not have market economies, and only democratic regimes adopt neoliberal economic reforms.
   C. Protests are not allowed in authoritarian regimes, and the right to protest is protected in democratic regimes.
   D. Civil society is more restricted and weaker in authoritarian regimes than it is in democratic regimes.

Questions 9–11 refer to the map.

Internet Filtering, 2020

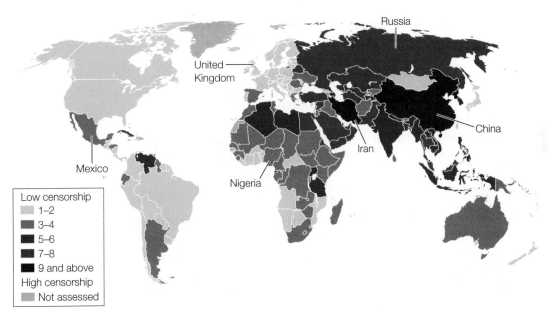

Low censorship
- 1–2
- 3–4
- 5–6
- 7–8
- 9 and above
High censorship
- Not assessed

Note: Higher scores indicate more citizenship.
Data from Comparitech.

9. According to the map, which of the following countries has the highest level of internet censorship?
   A. Mexico
   B. Russia
   C. United Kingdom
   D. China

10. Which of the following is an implication of the map regarding level of internet censorship within a country?
    A. Democratic countries do not censor information on the internet, even when the information poses a threat to national security.
    B. Authoritarian countries are more likely to monitor citizens' online behavior than democratic states.
    C. Both authoritarian and democratic states censor the internet to prevent citizens from accessing negative information about the government.
    D. Citizens in authoritarian countries do not have access to social-media platforms.

11. Which of the following is a limitation of the data in the map?
    A. There is no explanation of how censorship scores were calculated.
    B. The map does not show regional patterns in internet censorship.
    C. The map was produced in the United States and is biased against authoritarian regimes.
    D. Many countries do not report data about internet censorship, and the data are inaccurate.

12. Which of the following best describes a source of legitimacy in Mexico and Nigeria?
    A. Both countries have a long history of democratic government and rule of law.
    B. They are both rentier states, and a state's reliance on oil revenue decreases the opportunities for corruption.
    C. Commissions in both countries have been established to make elections fairer.
    D. Officials in both countries respect the due process rights of people accused of crimes.

13. Which of the following accurately describes cleavages in two AP® Comparative Government and Politics course countries?
    A. The United Kingdom and China are homogenous, and there are few ethnic divisions within either country.
    B. Mexico and Russia have significant religious cleavages, and secessionist movements have been formed based on religious identity.
    C. Heredity social class is an important cleavage in the United Kingdom and China.
    D. In Russia and Mexico, there is a significant economic cleavage between rural and urban areas.

14. Economic-liberalization policies in Mexico resulted in which of the following?
    A. The creation of farm subsidies to keep food prices low
    B. The partial privatization of Pemex, the Mexican oil company
    C. The replacement of NAFTA with the more protectionist policies of the United States–Mexico–Canada Agreement (USMCA)
    D. The imposition of tariffs to shelter domestic manufacturing from foreign competition

15. Which of the following describes a way that the prime minister in the United Kingdom may be removed?
    A. The members of the majority party in the House of Commons may vote to replace the prime minister.
    B. The prime minister may be impeached by the lower house of the legislature with a majority vote.
    C. The monarch can remove the prime minister for wrongdoing.
    D. The House of Commons can remove the prime minister through a vote of no confidence, which requires a two-thirds vote for approval.

16. Which of the following is an example of an import-substitution industrialization (ISI) economic policy?
    A. Imposing tariffs on imported goods
    B. Signing a free-trade agreement
    C. Eliminating subsidies on fuel and other necessities
    D. Privatizing state-owned industries

Gross Domestic Product per Capita in Mexico, 2009–2020

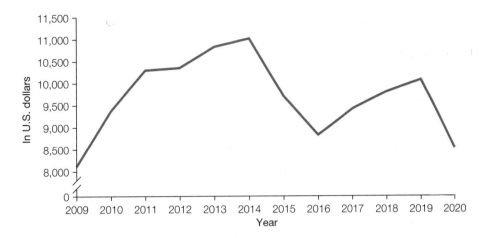

Data from CEIC Data.

17. Which of the following is supported by the data in the graph?
    A. Mexico's lowest GDP per capita occurred in 2016.
    B. Since 2016, GDP per capita in Mexico has dropped at a steady rate.
    C. GDP per capita rose in Mexico from 2009 to 2014.
    D. Most people living in Mexico are in the middle class.

18. Which of the following is an implication of the data in the graph?
    A. The adoption of neoliberal economic reforms widened the income gap in Mexico.
    B. The privatization of Pemex caused oil revenue to decrease.
    C. Mexico's economy is largely dependent on trade agreements with the United States.
    D. Mexico's economy is impacted by globalization, which causes periods of recession and recovery.

19. Which of the following would make the graph more informative?
    A. Data should be reported in Mexico pesos instead of U.S. dollars.
    B. Important economic events could be included in the graph to demonstrate causation.
    C. The graph should explain how GDP per capita was calculated.
    D. The data would be more understandable in the form of a bar chart.

20. Which of the following is an accurate description of environmental policy in a course country?
    A. Mexico has adopted policies to improve air quality.
    B. Nigeria has shifted away from petroleum production and relies significantly on green-energy technology.
    C. Voters in the United Kingdom supported Brexit because they disapproved of the EU's lax environmental policies.
    D. China has not adopted legislation protecting the environment because the government focuses on economic growth instead.

21. Which of the following best describes the judiciary in a course country studied in AP® Comparative Government and Politics?
    A. The Supreme Court in the United Kingdom has the power of judicial review, which protects the rule of law.
    B. China's judiciary has gained significant independence from the CCP.
    C. The Expediency Council in Iran has the power to overturn laws passed by the Majles that violate the Constitution.
    D. Mexico's judiciary has been professionalized to increase the rule of law.

22. Which of the following describes how members of the National People's Congress in China are selected?
    A. They are directly elected through a single-member district system.
    B. Representatives are chosen by the Politburo Standing Committee.
    C. They are indirectly elected by provincial congresses.
    D. Representatives are directly elected from a party list provided by the Committee on Elections.

23. Which of the following best explains the role of the Guardian Council in Iran?
    A. It reviews laws passed by the Majles and approves candidates for office.
    B. The Guardian Council determines whether the supreme leader is physically and mentally fit for office.
    C. It serves as an intermediary between the parliament and the Expediency Council to prevent gridlock in lawmaking.
    D. The Guardian Council has the power to impeach the president for wrongdoing.

Questions 24–26 refer to the passage.

It is very important that our young people should look to and be inspired by the achievements and victories of our outstanding ancestors and contemporaries, by their love for our Motherland, and aspiration to make a personal contribution to its development. Children should have the opportunity to explore the national history and the multinational culture, our achievements in science and technology, literature and art in advanced formats. You know, I still open certain school textbooks occasionally and am surprised at what I see there—as if what is written there has nothing to do with us at all. Who writes such textbooks? Who approves them? It is unbelievable. They mention everything, the "second front" and a lot of other facts, but not the Battle of Stalingrad—how is that possible? Amazing! I do not even want to comment.
                    —President Vladimir Putin, Address to the Federal Assembly, April 21, 2021

24. Which of the following best describes President Putin's claim in the passage?
    A. Textbooks in Russia should focus more on important military victories.
    B. The curriculum in Russian schools should encourage patriotism.
    C. Most textbooks are produced outside of Russia and have a pro-Western bias.
    D. Young Russian students are more interested in learning about science and technology than history.

25. Which of the following terms best describes the focus of the passage?
    A. Sovereignty
    B. Nationalism
    C. Political ideology
    D. Legitimacy

26. Which of the following policies would most directly address the issue mentioned in the passage?
    A. Devolving power over educational standards to regional governors
    B. Providing grant money to teachers to improve education related to science and technology
    C. Requiring multicultural education in social-science courses
    D. Adopting a national curriculum and providing resources for implementation at the local level

27. Which of the following is an accurate statement about how the legislature is chosen in two AP® Comparative Government and Politics course countries?
    A. The lower houses in the United Kingdom and Nigeria are chosen through proportional representation.
    B. Members of the unicameral legislatures in Iran and China are directly elected in single-member districts.
    C. Russia and Mexico use mixed systems to elect members of the Duma and Chamber of Deputies.
    D. Members of the upper house in Russia and the United Kingdom are appointed by the executive and confirmed by regional assemblies.

28. Which of the following describes the difference between civil rights in democratic and authoritarian regimes?
    A. In authoritarian regimes, ethnic minorities may face discrimination from the state, while democratic regimes promise equal legal treatment of ethnic minorities.
    B. Both authoritarian and democratic regimes promise equal treatment for minority groups, but only democratic regimes guarantee legislative seats for members of minority groups.
    C. Democratic regimes require a certain percentage of female members in the cabinet, while authoritarian regimes rarely include women in the cabinet.
    D. Women can vote in democratic regimes but not in authoritarian regimes.

29. Which of the following explains how the electoral system in the United Kingdom impacts political parties in the House of Commons?
    A. The single-member district system results in two major parties, along with a weaker third party and regional parties.
    B. A system of proportional representation results in numerous catch-all and regional parties serving in the legislature.
    C. A mixed system of representation results in the Labour and Conservative parties dominating Parliament, but smaller parties are still guaranteed some seats.
    D. Members of Parliament do not have to live in the district they represent, which results in single-party dominance by the Conservative Party.

30. Which of the following is a result of the system for electing the executive in Mexico?
    A. The two-round system allows voters some say in selecting the winner, even if the candidate who was their first choice is eliminated in the first round.
    B. A single-round, plurality election system may result in a winning candidate who does not have a strong popular mandate to govern.
    C. The requirement that a candidate win at least 25 percent of the vote in two-thirds of the states ensures that the winner has support from throughout the country.
    D. An electoral-college system in Mexico gives people living in small states disproportionate influence in selecting the executive.

Questions 31 and 32 refer to the passage.

If the 2015 U.K. general election had been held under a PR system, UKIP would have been the third-largest party in Parliament, with 83 seats instead of one. Good news for its supporters but worrying for those who linked the party's popularity with resurgence of xenophobia and nationalism.

Under FPTP, MPs serve the constituency they campaign in, so are more inclined to tackle important local issues. Under PR, electoral constituencies would have to be much bigger in order to have multiple seats to fill proportionately, possibly leading to local issues being overlooked.

—"Proportional Representation: The Pros and Cons." *The Week*. May 30, 2019. This article is reproduced from *The Week* and is copyright of or licensed by Future Publishing Limited, a Future plc group company, UK 2022. All rights reserved. https://www.theweek.co.uk/22271/proportional-representation-the-pros-and-cons.

31. Which of the following best describes a claim in the passage?
    A. Proportional-representation systems are more democratic than single-member district systems, because they enable small parties to earn seats in the legislature.
    B. Proportional-representation systems lead to unstable coalition governments.
    C. Legislatures selected through proportional representation are better equipped to address local issues.
    D. Proportional-representation systems result in the election of more extremist candidates.

32. Which of the following is an implication of the author's argument?
    A. Voters in the United Kingdom should have approved the referendum on alternate voting.
    B. A proportional-representation system would strengthen democracy in the United Kingdom.
    C. The United Kingdom should retain its current legislative-election system.
    D. Both legislatures and executives should be chosen through single-member district systems.

33. Which of the following describes a similarity between the role of the executive in two AP° Comparative Government and Politics course countries?
    A. The prime ministers in the United Kingdom and Russia serve as the head of government.
    B. The heads of state in Mexico and Russia are largely symbolic.
    C. Both China and Nigeria have a dual executive consisting of a president and a prime minister.
    D. The heads of state in Iran and the United Kingdom have more power over policymaking than the heads of government.

34. Which of the following is true of the bureaucracies in two AP° Comparative Government and Politics course countries?
    A. Positions in the bureaucracies in the United Kingdom and China are filled partly through a merit-based system.
    B. Nigeria and Mexico fill positions in the bureaucracy using ethnic quotas.
    C. The bureaucracies in Iran and Russia are small in comparison to bureaucracies in democratic states.
    D. The bureaucracy in the United Kingdom is subject to legislative oversight, but the legislature in Iran does not have the power to investigate the bureaucracy.

35. Which of the following describes a trend in migration in a course country studied in AP° Comparative Government and Politics?
    A. Mexican citizens are moving from urban areas to rural areas to escape drug violence.
    B. People in China are moving from rural areas to cities in search of jobs.
    C. Nigerians are moving from the south to the north in search of religious freedom.
    D. Well-educated people are moving to Iran because of increased job opportunities in business and technology.

36. Which of the following accurately describes population policies in two AP° Comparative Government and Politics course countries?
    A. Russia and the United Kingdom are encouraging people to have larger families to offset strains on the health-care system caused by an aging population.
    B. China and Nigeria substantially lowered birth rates in the past ten years by providing universal access to health care.
    C. Mexico and Iran have not adopted family-planning policies because contraception goes against the religious beliefs of the majority.
    D. China and Iran pursued family-planning policies that reduced birth rates, and both countries recently changed those policies to encourage more births.

37. Which of the following is an example of a civil-society organization?
    A. The Scottish National Party in the United Kingdom
    B. A state-sponsored women's association in Iran
    C. A group protesting the reduction of fuel subsidies in Nigeria
    D. A Chinese company doing business in Russia as a joint venture

38. Which of the following states are classified as democracies that are not consolidated?
    A. China and Iran, because both countries provide seats in the legislature for religious minorities
    B. Mexico and Nigeria, because both countries are making elections more free and fair, but they lack some civil rights and liberties
    C. Russia and China, because the constitutions in both countries create democratic structures of government
    D. The United Kingdom and Nigeria, because both countries have common-law judicial systems

Questions 39 and 40 refer to the infographic.

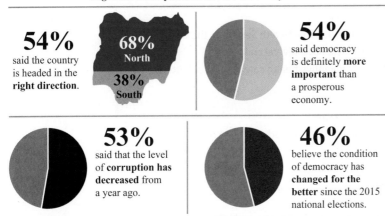

Despite Regional Divisions and Worsening Economy, Nigerians Are Optimistic about Democracy

54% said the country is headed in the **right direction**.

68% North **38%** South

54% said democracy is definitely **more important** than a prosperous economy.

53% said that the level of **corruption has decreased** from a year ago.

46% believe the condition of democracy has **changed for the better** since the 2015 national elections.

Data from NOIPolls and International Republican Institute.

39. Which of the following is accurate according to the infographic?
    A. Many Nigerians support democracy and are optimistic about the future of the country.
    B. A majority of Nigerians believes the political climate for democracy has improved since the mid-2010s.
    C. Nigerians living in the south are more likely to believe the country is headed in the right direction than those living in the north.
    D. Most Nigerians believe that corruption is the biggest factor hindering democratization.

40. Which of the following is an implication of the infographic?
    A. The presence of Boko Haram in northern Nigeria has destabilized politics within that region.
    B. Although most Nigerians support the idea of democracy, they do not believe democratic government will stabilize Nigeria.
    C. In a tradeoff between democracy and economic growth, most Nigerians choose political values.
    D. Polling in Nigeria is inaccurate, and it is difficult to determine the level of support for democratic values in Nigeria.

41. Which of the following is a consequence of a successful vote of no confidence in the House of Commons?
    A. The prime minister is replaced by a member of his or her own party.
    B. The cabinet resigns, and the shadow cabinet assumes power.
    C. Coalition government is formed.
    D. The legislature is dissolved, and new elections are called.

42. Which of the following accurately describes the party system in an AP® Comparative Government and Politics course country?
    A. Iran has a stable two-party system.
    B. Mexico has a multiparty system.
    C. Russia is a one-party state.
    D. The United Kingdom is a multiparty state.

43. Which of the following best describes a nation?
    A. It is a sense of identity based on history, language, ethnicity, religion, or other shared characteristics.
    B. A nation is a country, with defined political borders.
    C. A nation is territory governed by a recognized set of political institutions.
    D. It exists when the government has a monopoly of force over territory.

44. Which of the following is a social policy designed to reduce poverty?
    A. The introduction of market-based competition in the National Health Service in the United Kingdom
    B. Programs in Russia that offer incentives to couples who have several children
    C. Cash-transfer programs in Mexico that encourage preventive health care and school attendance
    D. The reduction of fuel subsidies in Iran

45. Which of the following best describes political parties in Iran?
    A. Iran does not have formal political parties, because they are forbidden in the Koran.
    B. Two stable, ideologically based parties have emerged.
    C. Personalistic parties tend to form around charismatic politicians.
    D. Iran is a single-party state, dominated by Islamic fundamentalists.

46. Which of the following is an advantage of the executive in a parliamentary system?
    A. Coalition government does not occur, which makes policymaking more efficient.
    B. The prime minister is elected directly by the people, which gives him or her a mandate to govern.
    C. The executive presides over a cabinet that is separate from the legislature, which enhances executive power.
    D. The prime minister does not face divided government, making it highly likely that his or her program of legislation will be enacted.

47. What is the Federal Character Principle in Nigeria?
    A. The rule that presidents must earn 25 percent of the vote in two-thirds of the states to win election
    B. An ethnic quota system for staffing the bureaucracy
    C. The practice that political parties will alternate candidates for the presidency between Muslims and Christians
    D. The principle of federalism that allowed some states in northern Nigeria to adopt sharia law

48. Which of the following is an accurate statement about the political systems in Russia and China?
    A. Both have a dual executive consisting of a president and a premier or prime minister.
    B. The countries both use dual rule by the government and by a political party.
    C. Both have bicameral legislatures, with the lower house representing the population and the upper house representing states or provinces.
    D. The countries both have unitary systems, with power concentrated in the national government.

49. Which of the following is a similarity between the legal systems of Mexico and Nigeria?
    A. In both systems, the supreme court lacks the power of judicial review.
    B. Both systems are characterized by rule of law, and bribery and corruption are rare.
    C. The countries have separate state and national judicial systems.
    D. Both countries impose the death penalty for a wide range of criminal offenses.

50. Which of the following is a normative statement?
    A. Nigeria has the lowest GDP per capita of the six countries studied in AP° Comparative Government and Politics.
    B. The Mexican government should expand social services for the poor to reduce rural poverty.
    C. Poor economic growth is likely to cause increasing instability within Iran.
    D. President Putin in Russia has consolidated power and created a dictatorship by extending term limits.

51. Which of the following describes legislative-executive relations in Nigeria and the United Kingdom?
    A. The prime minister sits in Parliament in the United Kingdom, and the prime minister in Nigeria is not a member of the National Assembly.
    B. The heads of state in the United Kingdom and Nigeria have the power to veto legislation.
    C. The president in Nigeria and the prime minister in the United Kingdom are the leaders of the majority party in the legislature.
    D. The prime minister in the United Kingdom is from the majority party in the legislature, and the president in Nigeria might not be a member of the majority party in the legislature.

52. Which of the following describes a difference between populism and communism?
    A. Populist parties are run by charismatic leaders, and the leaders of communist parties are ideological and not charismatic.
    B. Communists support a command economy, and populists support market economies.
    C. Populists favor an extreme nationalistic ideology, and communists support a unified, multiethnic state.
    D. Populism rejects rule by the elite in favor of rule by common people, and communism favors a classless society.

53. Which of the following is true of political participation in both democratic and authoritarian regimes?
    A. Both types of regime hold elections to maintain legitimacy.
    B. Both encourage strong civil society.
    C. Women and ethnic minorities are encouraged to vote and run for office in both types of systems.
    D. Both types of regimes restrict speech that is critical of the state.

54. Which of the following is a similarity between Iran and China?
    A. The countries both have bicameral legislatures.
    B. The judiciaries in both countries have the power of judicial review.
    C. Both countries have dual executives.
    D. In both countries, the legislature serves as a significant check on executive power.

55. Which of the following poses the most serious threat to sovereignty in a course country studied in AP° Comparative Government and Politics?
    A. The potential for rebellion by religious minorities in Iran
    B. The Scottish independence movement in the United Kingdom
    C. Trade agreements among Mexico, the United States, and Canada
    D. Protests in Hong Kong against the Chinese government

Section II: Free Response

Time–1 hour and 30 minutes

4 Questions

Directions: You have 1 hour and 30 minutes to answer one conceptual-analysis question, one quantitative-analysis question, one comparative-analysis question, and one argument essay. Unless the directions indicate otherwise, respond to *all* parts of *all* four questions. It is suggested that you take a few minutes to plan and outline each answer. *It is also suggested that you spend approximately 10 minutes total on question 1, 20 minutes each on questions 2 and 3, and 40 minutes total on question 4.* These suggested times do not reflect the weight of the questions as part of your AP° Exam score. In your responses, use substantive examples where appropriate.

Conceptual Analysis

Answer A, B, C, and D.

A. Define sovereignty.

B. Explain how membership in an international organization impacts state sovereignty.

C. Explain why states join international organizations.

D. Explain how state sovereignty can be impacted by a factor other than membership in an international organization.

Quantitative Analysis

Nigerian Election Figures, 1999–2019

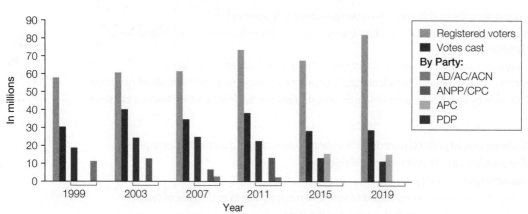

Note: The political parties that participated are abbreviated as follows.

AC, Action Congress; ACN, Action Congress of Nigeria; AD, Alliance for Democracy; ANPP, All Nigeria Peoples Party; APC, All Progressives Congress; CPC, Congress for Progressive Change; PDP, People's Democratic Party.

Data from Australian Institute of International Affairs.

Answer A, B, C, D, and E.

A. Using the data in the bar chart, describe a trend in the number of votes cast in Nigeria from 1999 to 2019.

B. Using the data in the bar chart, describe a trend in the number of registered voters in Nigeria from 1999 to 2019.

C. Define political participation.

D. Using your knowledge of political participation and the data in the bar chart, draw a conclusion about a trend you identified in part A or part B.

E. Explain how a democratic regime could increase voter turnout.

Comparative Analysis

Compare how the governments in two different AP® Comparative Government and Politics course countries have responded to social cleavages. In your response, you should do the following:

A. Define social cleavage.

B. Describe a social cleavage in two different AP® Comparative Government and Politics course countries.

C. Explain how the governments in two different AP® Comparative Government and Politics course countries have responded to the cleavages described in part B.

Argument Essay

Develop an argument about whether democratic or authoritarian regimes are more stable.

Use one or more of the following course concepts in your response:

- Legitimacy
- Power
- Civil liberties

In your response, do the following:

- Respond to the prompt with a defensible claim or thesis that establishes a line of reasoning using one or more of the provided course concepts.

- Support your claim with at least TWO pieces of specific and relevant evidence from your study of one or more course countries. The evidence should be relevant to one or more of the provided course concepts.

- Use reasoning to explain why your evidence supports your claim or thesis, using one or more of the provided course concepts.

- Respond to an opposing or alternate perspective, using refutation, concession, or rebuttal.

Course Countries at a Glance

Data and Classifications

Characteristic	China	Iran	Mexico	Nigeria	Russia	United Kingdom
Freedom House classification	Not free	Not free	Partially free	Partially free	Not free	Free
Political rights score, 2021 (out of 40)	–2	4	27	20	5	39
Civil liberties score, 2021 (out of 60)	11	10	33	23	14	54
Fragile States Index classification	Warning	High warning	Warning	Alert	Elevated warning	Very sustainable
Corruption Perceptions Index ranking, 2021 (out of 180)	66	150	124	154	136	11
Human Development Index, 2020	0.761	0.783	0.779	0.539	0.824	0.932
HDI ranking (out of 189)	85	70	74	161	52	13
Gross domestic product per capita, 2020	$10,500	$20,422	$10,919	$2,097	$10,127	$40,285
Gini index, 2019	38.2	40.9	45.4	35.1	37.5	35

Data from *CIA World Factbook,* World Bank, Freedom House, Transparency International, Fragile States Index.

Government Systems

Characteristic	China	Iran	Mexico	Nigeria	Russia	United Kingdom
Regime type	Authoritarian	Authoritarian	Democracy	Illiberal democracy	Illiberal democracy/ hybrid/ competitive authoritarian	Liberal democracy
Sources of legitimacy	Revolution, tradition, economic performance	Revolution, religion, elections, constitution	Elections, constitution	Elections, constitution	Tradition, charismatic leadership	Elections, constitution, tradition, rule of law
Unitary or federal	Unitary	Unitary	Federal	Federal	Federal	Unitary, with devolution to regional assemblies and a mayor of London
Presidential, semi-presidential, or parliamentary	Semi-presidential	Theocratic and presidential	Presidential	Presidential	Semi-presidential	Parliamentary
Single or dual executive	Dual	Dual	Single	Single	Dual	Dual
Head of state	President	Supreme leader and president/ divided powers	President	President	President	Monarch
Head of government	Premier	President	President	President	Prime minister	Prime minister
Executive election system	Indirect, by National People's Congress	Supreme leader appointed for life, selected by Assembly of Experts. President directly elected in a two-round system	Direct plurality election	Winning candidate must earn 25 percent of the vote in two-thirds of the states, two-round system	President is directly elected in a two-round system. Prime minister is appointed by president and confirmed by Duma.	Prime minister is selected from majority party or majority party coalition. Monarch is hereditary.
Executive term length and limit	Five-year terms, unlimited terms	Supreme leader serves for life. President serves a four-year term, with a limit of two consecutive terms.	One six-year term (sexenio)	Four-year term, with a two-term limit	Six-year term, with a two-term limit, extended for Putin	Elections must be called every five years, no term limits
Legislative structure	Unicameral	Unicameral	Bicameral	Bicameral	Bicameral	Bicameral
Chambers	National People's Congress	Majles	Chamber of Deputies (lower) and Senate (upper)	House of Representatives (lower) and Senate (upper)	Duma (lower) and Federation Council (upper)	House of Commons (lower) and House of Lords (upper)

Characteristic	China	Iran	Mexico	Nigeria	Russia	United Kingdom
Legislative election system	Indirect	SMD/MMD. Reserved seats for Jews, Christians, and Zoroastrians	Mixed SMD and PR, with a 2 percent threshold. Parties must run 50 percent female candidates.	SMD	Mixed SMD and PR, with a 5 percent threshold for Duma. Federation Council is appointed and indirectly elected.	SMD. House of Lords is hereditary and appointed.
Power of judicial review	No	Religious review	Yes	Yes	Yes, rarely used	Administrative review
Other bodies and rules	General secretary, Politburo Standing Committee, Central Committee	Guardian Council, Expediency Council, Assembly of Experts	National Electoral Institute	Independent National Election Commission, Federal Character Principle		
Party system	One-party	Fluid and unstable	Multiparty	Two-party	Single-party dominant	Two-party
Parties	Chinese Communist Party and eight other authorized parties		MORENA (National Regeneration Movement), PRI (Institutional Revolutionary Party), PAN (National Action Party), PRD (Party of the Democratic Revolution), small parties	APC (All Progressives Congress), PDP (People's Democratic Party), small parties.	United Russia, CPFR (Communist Party of the Russian Federation), and smaller parties	Conservative, Labour, Liberal Democrats, Scottish National Party, and other regional parties
Referenda	No	1979, Constitution ratified. 1989, Constitution amended.	No	No	1993, Constitution ratified. 2020, extended Putin's term limit.	1975, membership in European Community. 1997, devolution. 2010, alternate voting. 2014, Scottish independence. 2016, Brexit.
Major political and social cleavages	Uyghurs, Tibetans, Hong Kong, Taiwan	Sunnis, non-Persian ethnic minorities	Zapatistas	Hausa-Fulani, Yoruba, Igbo, 250 other ethnic groups	Chechens	Scottish independence

Works Cited

Chapter 1

Adichie, Chimamanda Ngozi. "The Danger of a Single Story." TED Talk, 2009, www.ted.com/talks/chimamanda_ngozi_adichie_the_danger_of_a_single_story.

Adichie, Chimamanda Ngozi. *Half of a Yellow Sun.* Alfred A. Knopf, 2006.

Adichie, Chimamanda Ngozi. "We Should All Be Feminists." TED Talk, 2012.

Adichie, Chimamanda Ngozi. Web site. Awards, www.cerep.ulg.ac.be/adichie/cnaawards.html.

Beehner, Lionel, and Joseph Young. "Is Ranking Failed or Fragile States a Futile Business?" *Washington Post*, 14 July 2014.

Chowdhury, O. H. "Human Development Index: A Critique." National Library of Medicine, 19 Sept. 1991.

Eastern Connecticut State University. "Alumna Chimamanda Ngozi Adichie to Receive Honorary Degree at Commencement." 17 Apr. 2015. www.easternct.edu/news/_stories-and-releases/2015/04-april/alumna-chimamanda-ngozi-adichie-to-receive-honorary-degree-at-commencement.html.

Investopedia. "What Are the Criticisms of the Human Development Index (HDI)?" 1 Feb. 2020.

Khamenei, Ayatollah Ali. Supreme Leader of Iran, televised speech delivered 8 Jan. 2021.

Khomeini, Ayatollah Ruhollah. Speech given on 5 Nov. 1979.

Lozovsky, Ilya. "Argument: Freedom by the Numbers." *Foreign Policy*, 29 Jan. 2016.

OECD. "Income Distribution and Poverty." *OECD. Stat*, 2020, https://stats.oecd.org/Index.aspx?DataSetCode-IDD.

The 100 Most Influential People, 2015. "Chimamanda Ngozi Adichie," by Radhika Jones. *Time*, 16 Apr. 2015, www.time.com/collection-post/3823296/chimamanda-ngozi-adichie-2015-time-100/.

Ostry, Jonathan D., Prakash Loungani, and Andrew Berg. *Confronting Inequality: How Societies Can Choose Inclusive Growth.* Columbia UP, 2019.

Risse, Thomas. "Limited Statehood: A Critical Perspective." In *Oxford Handbook of Transformations of the State,* edited by Stephan Leibfried et al., Oxford UP, 2015, pp. 152–68.

Sen, Amartya K. *Development as Freedom.* Anchor Books, 1999.

Silver, Nate. *The Signal and the Noise: Why So Many Predictions Fail, but Some Don't.* Penguin Books, 2012.

Statista. "Countries with the largest population 2021." www.statista.com/statistics/262879/countries-with-the-largest-population/.

Women's Prize for Fiction, 2021. "Announcing the Women's Prize for Fiction 'Winner of Winners,'" www.womensprizeforfiction.co.uk/features/features/news/announcing-the-womens-prize-for-fiction-winner-of-winners.

World Inequality Database. 2019. https://wid.world/data/.

Chapter 2

Bishop, Sylvia, and Anke Hoeffler. "Free and Fair Elections: A New Database." *Journal of Peace Research* (Sage Publishing), 2016.

Collier, Paul. "Culture Politics, and Economic Development," *Annual Review of Political Science*, 2017.

Collini, Stefan. "Inside the Mind of Dominic Cummings." *The Guardian*, 6 Feb. 2020.

Cummings, Dominic. "How the Brexit Referendum Was Won." *The Spectator*, 8 Jan. 2017.

Freedom House. "Freedom in the World 2021: Democracy under Siege."

Hobolt, Sara. "The Brexit Vote: A Divided Nation, a Divided Continent," *Journal of European Public Policy*, vol. 23, no. 9, (2016), pp. 1259–77.

Human Rights Watch. *Russia's War in Chechnya: Victims Speak Out.* 1995.

Huntington, Samuel. "Democracy's Third Wave." *Journal of Democracy*, vol. 2, no. 2, 1991.

Lambert, Harry. "Dominic Cummings: The Machiavel in Downing Street," *New Statesman*, 25 Sept. 2019.

Leeke, Matthew, Chris Sear, and Oonagh Gay. *An Introduction to Devolution in the UK.* Research Paper 03/84, House of Commons Library, 17 Nov. 2003.

Ottaway, Marine. *Democracy Challenged: The Rise of Electoral Authoritarianism.* Carnegie Endowment for International Peace, 2003.

Sim, Philip. "Scottish Election 2021: Results in Maps and Charts." BBC, 9 May 2021.

Smith, Noah. "Mexico Is Solidly Middle Class (No Matter What Trump Says)." *Bloomberg*, 26 Aug. 2019.

Srebrnik, Henry. "Asymmetrical Federalism in the Russian Federation." *The Guardian*, 2019.

U.S. Embassy in Nigeria, Nigeria Fact Sheet. https://ng.usembassy.gov/category/fact-sheets/.

Weber, Max. 1970. "Politics as Vocation." Translation of *Politik als Beruf* (1919) in *From Max Weber: Essays in Sociology*, edited by H. H. Gaert and C. Wright Mills. London: Routledge and Kegan Paul.

Westcott, Ben. "Tiananmen Square Massacre: How Beijing Turned on Its Own People." *CNN*, 1999.

Winke, Richard, and Shannon Schumacher. "Satisfaction with Democracy: Democratic Rights Popular Globally but Commitment to Them Not Always Strong." Pew Research Center, 2020.

World Bank. "Poverty Headcount Ratio at $1.90 a Day (2011 PPP) (% of Population) | Data."

Worldometer, Largest Countries in the World by Area.

Chapter 3

Ahmed, Azam, and Kirk Semple. "A New Revolution? Mexico Still Waiting as López-Obrador Nears Half-Year Mark." *The New York Times*, 10 May 2019.

Álvarez-Rivera, Manuel. "Election Resources on the Internet: Federal Elections in Mexico." ElectionResources.org. Accessed 2 Feb. 2021.

Amnesty International. *Mexico 2019: Annual Report.* 2019.

Camp, Roderic Ai. *Politics in Mexico: Democratic Consolidation or Decline?* 6th ed., Oxford UP, pp. 209–10.

Casar, Ma. Amparo. 2016. "Parliamentary Agenda Setting in Latin America: The Case of Mexico." In *Legislative Institutions and Lawmaking in Latin America*, edited by Eduardo Aleman and George Tsebelis, 118–174. Oxford, UK: Oxford University Press.

de Córdoba, José. "Mexico's Cartels Distribute Coronavirus Aid to Win Popular Support." *Wall Street Journal*, 14 May 2020.

Dresser, Denise. "Mexican Women Are Furious. AMLO Should Start Listening." *Foreign Affairs*, 6 Oct. 2020.

Dresser, Denise. "Mexico's New President Turns Back the Clock on Democracy." *Foreign Affairs,* May 2019.

The Economist. "A Tale of Two Mexicos North and South: Why Can't Its Stagnant Southern States Catch Up with the Rest of Mexico?" 24 Apr. 2008.

Enriquez, Diana, Sebastián Rojas Cabal, and Miguel A. Centeno. "Latin America's COVID-19 Nightmare." *Foreign Affairs*, 1 Sept. 2020.

Freedom House. *Freedom in the World: Mexico.* 2020.

Fuller, Graham, David Ronfeldt, and John Arguilla. *Zapatista Social Netwar in Mexico.* RAND Corporation, 1999.

Garcia-Navarro, LuLu. "What Happened to Mexico's Missing 43 Students in 'A Massacre in Mexico.'" *National Public Radio*, 21 Oct. 2018.

Gonzales-Barrera, Ana, and Jens Manuel Krogstad. "What We Know about Illegal Immigration from Mexico." Pew Research Center, 28 June 2019.

The Guardian. "Mexico's War on Drugs: What Has It Achieved and How Is the U.S. Involved?" 8 Dec. 2016.

Human Rights Watch. *World Report 2020: Mexico.* 2020.

Kidd, Stephen. "The Demise of Mexico's Prospera Programme: A Tragedy Foretold." *Development Pathways*, 2 June 2019.

Library of Congress. "Mexico: Constitutional Reform Regarding Crimes Committed by the President of the Republic Approved." 2020.

Magaloni, Beatriz, and Zaira Razu. "Mexico in the Grip of Violence." *Current History*, vol. 115, no. 778, 2016, pp. 57–62.

McCormick, Gladys, and Matthew Clearly. "What Ails Mexican Democracy: Too Much Hope, Too Little Change." *Foreign Affairs*, 22 Mar. 2018.

Nobel Peace Prize 2007. NobelPrize.org. Nobel Prize Outreach AB 2021. 28 June 2021. www.nobelprize.org/prizes/peace/2007/summary.

O'Neil, Shannon. "Mexico's Economic Divide." *Council on Foreign Relations*, 30 June 2015.

Piscopo, Jennifer. "Beyond Hearth and Home: Female Legislators, Feminist Policy Change, and Substantive Representation in Mexico." *Revista Uruguaya de Ciencia Política,* vol. 23, no. 2, July–Dec. 2014, pp. 87–110, www.redalyc.org/pdf/2973/297338131005.pdf.

Piscopo, Jennifer. "What Does It Take to Get Women Elected?" *Boston Review*, 3 Aug. 2020.

Pskowski, Martha. "The Long Road to Mexico City's First Elected Woman Mayor." *Bloomberg*, 6 Aug. 2018. www.bloomberg.com/news/articles /2018-08-06/claudia-sheinbaum-and-women-s-rise-in-mexican-politics.

Ramirez, Sandra. "Mexico's Female Legislators Are No Silver Bullet for Gender Inequality." *Council on Foreign Relations*, 4 Sept. 2018.

Reporters Without Borders. "Worldwide Round-Up. Journalists Killed, Detained, Held Hostage, or Missing in 2018." https://rsf.org/en/news/rsfs-2018-round -deadly-attacks-and-abuses-against-journalists-figures-all-categories.

Rodriguez, Andrés. "Ahead of Mexico's Presidential Election, Fears and Warnings over Possible Fraud." *Chicago Tribune*, 29 June 2018.

Sheridan, Mary Beth. "Mexico's Military Becomes More Powerful As the Country's Security Deteriorates." *The Washington Post*, 17 Dec. 2020.

Smith, Noah. "Mexico Is Solidly Middle Class (No Matter What Trump Says)." *Bloomberg*, 26 Aug. 2019.

Social Sciences LibreTexts. *Race Relations in Mexico—The Color Hierarchy.*

Statista. "Share of Population Living in Poverty in Mexico in 2018, by State." www.statista.com/statistics/1036147/poverty-rate-mexico-state/.

Taylor, Adam. "Leaders in Mexico and Poland Look to Curb Power of Social Media Giants after Trump Bans." *The Washington Post*, 16 Jan. 2021.

"Topline Report: 2020 Mexico National Online Survey." Latin America Public Opinion Project. Vanderbilt University.

USA Today. "Mexico's Zapatista Rebel Movement Marks 20 Years." 2 Jan. 2014.

U.S. Department of State. *Country Reports on Human Rights Practices for 2019: Mexico*. Bureau of Democracy, Human Rights, and Labor, 2019.

Versa, Maria. "Party Chaos Threatens Mexican President's Administration." AP, 13 Oct. 2020.

World Bank. "A Model from Mexico for the World." www.worldbank.org/en /news/feature/2014/11/19/un-modelo-de-mexico-para-el-mundo.

Zizumbo-Colunga, Daniel, and Ivan Flores Martinez. "Study Reveals Racial Inequality in Mexico, Disproving Its 'Race-Blind' Rhetoric." *The Conversation*, 13 Dec. 2017.

Unit 1 Review

Bermeo, Nancy. "On Democratic Backsliding." *Journal of Democracy*, vol. 27, no. 1, Jan. 2016, pp. 5–19.

Chapter 4

Amnesty International. *Blood-Soaked Secrets: Why Iran's 1988 Prison Massacres Are Ongoing Crimes against Humanity*. 2018.

Burgat, Casey. "Five Reasons to Oppose Congressional Term Limits." *Brookings*, 18 Jan. 2018.

Hafezi, Parisa. "Khomeini Protégé Wins Iran Election amid Low Voter Turnout." Reuters, 20 June 2021, https://newsinfo.inquirer.net/1448320 /khamenei-protege-wins-iran-presidential-election-amid-low-turnout.

Linz, Juan José. "The Perils of Presidentialism." *Journal of Democracy*, vol. 1, no. 1, 1990, pp. 51–69.

Lippmann, Walter. *New York Herald Tribune*, 10 Dec. 1963, p. 24.

Lumsden, Andrew. "Chief Justice Ebrahim Raisi." *American Iranian Council*, 4 Apr. 2019, http://www.us-iran.org/resources/2019/4/4/media-guide -chief-justice-ebrahim-raisi.

O'Dwyer, Conor. *Runaway State-Building: Patronage Politics and Democratic Development*. Johns Hopkins UP, 2006.

Ozkan, Gulcin, and Richard McManus. "Parliamentary Systems Do Better Economically Than Presidential Ones." *The Conversation*, 11 Feb. 2019.

Samuels, David. "Separation of Powers." In *The Oxford Handbook of Comparative Politics*, edited by Carles Boix and Susan Carol Stokes, Oxford UP, 2007, pp. 703–26.

White, Edward, and Sun Yu. "China Executes Former Asset Management Chief for Corruption." *Financial Times*, 29 Jan. 2021.

Chapter 5

AgeUK. "Briefing: Health and Care of Older People in England." 2017.

Almond, Gabriel A., and Sidney Verba. *The Civic Culture: Political Attitudes and Democracy in Five Nations*. Princeton UP, 1963.

Castle, Stephen. 2019. "Is Britain's Political System at the Breaking Point?" *New York Times,* February 20, 2019. https://www.nytimes.com/2019/02/20 /world/europe/ukconservative-party-independent-group.html.

Chartered Accountants Benevolent Association (CABA). "Understanding Benefits in the UK—the Basics Explained."

Cutts, D., M. Goodwin, and C. Milazzo. "Defeat of People's Army? The 2015 British General Election and the UK Independence Party (UKIP)." *Electoral Studies*, vol. 48, 2017, pp. 70–83.

Evans, Geoffrey, and James Tilley. *The New Politics of Class: The Political Exclusion of the British Working Class*. Oxford UP, 2017.

Faucher-King, Florence, and Patrick Le Galès. *The New Labour Experiment: Change and Reform under Blair and Brown*. Stanford UP, 2010.

Giles, Chris. "What Has the EU Done for the UK?" *Financial Times*, 31 Mar. 2017.

Ginsburg, Norman. "Globalization and the Liberal Welfare States." In *Globalization and European Welfare States: Challenges and Change,* edited by Robert Sykes, Bruno Palier, and Pauline M. Prior, with Jo Campling, Palgrave, 2001, pp. 173–92.

Ham, Chris, and Richard Murray. "Implementing the NHS Five Year Forward View: Aligning Policies with the Plan." *The King's Fund*, Feb. 2015.

Huber, Evelyne, and John D. Stephens. *Development and Crisis of the Welfare State: Parties and Policies in Global Markets*. University of Chicago Press, 2001.

Levy-Rapoport, Noga. "Teaching the Truth." *Fabian Review: The Quarterly Magazine of the Fabian Society,* summer 2019, p. 13.

Levy-Rapoport, Noga. "We Were Making History." *Book of Beasties*, 31 Mar. 2021, https://www.bookofbeasties.com/post/youth-climate-activist- noga-levy-rapoport-we-were-making-history.

McCarthy, Niall. "Poll: Majority in Northern Ireland Support Unification." Statista, 12 Sept. 2019.

McMullan, Lydia, et al. "Covid Chaos: How the UK Handled the Coronavirus Crisis." *The Guardian*, 3 Feb. 2021.

The Migration Observatory. "Migrants in the UK: An Overview." 6 Nov. 2020.

The Migration Observatory. "UK Public Opinion toward Immigration: Overall Attitudes and Level of Concern." 20 Jan. 2020.

Moosbrugger, Lorelei K. *The Vulnerability Thesis: Interest Group Influence and Institutional Design*. Yale UP, 2012.

Office for National Statistics. "Overview of the UK Population." Jan. 2021.

Piven, Frances Fox, and Richard Cloward. *Poor People's Movements: Why They Succeed, How They Fail*. Vintage Books, 1979.

Proksch, Sven-Oliver, and Jonathan B. Slapin. 2015. *The Politics of Parliamentary Debate: Parties, Rebels, and Representation*. Cambridge, UK: Cambridge UP.

Russell, M., and P. Cowley. "The Policy Power of the Westminster Parliament: The 'Parliamentary State' and the Empirical Evidence." *Governance*, vol. 29, 2016, pp. 121–37.

Savage, Michael, et al. *Social Class in the 21st Century: A Pelican Introduction*. Pelican Books, 2015.

Schleiter, Petra, and Valerie Belu. 2016. "The Decline of Majoritarianism in the UK and the Fixed-Term Parliaments Act." *Parliamentary Affairs* 69 (1): 36–52. doi:10.1093/pa/gsv002.

Statista. "United Kingdom: Real Gross Domestic Product Growth Rate from 2015 to 2025."

Tonge, J. "Supplying Confidence or Trouble? The Deal between the Democratic Unionist Party and the Conservative Party." *Political Quarterly*, vol. 88, no. 3, 2017, pp. 412–16.

U.S. Department of State. *Country Reports on Human Rights Practices for 2019: United Kingdom.* 2019.

Walker, Nigel. *Research Briefing. Brexit Timeline: Events Leading to the UK's Exit from the European Union.* House of Commons Library, 6 Jan. 2021.

Unit 2 Review

Norton, Lord Phillip. "Professor Explains Britain's Unwritten Constitution." Interview by National Public Radio, 5 Sept. 2019.

U.S. Department of State. *2019 Country Reports on Human Rights Practices: United Kingdom.* 2019.

Chapter 6

Almond, Gabriel A., and Sidney Verba. *The Civic Culture: Political Attitudes and Democracy in Five Nations.* Princeton UP, 1963.

Carnegie Endowment for International Peace. "Delegitimization and Division in Russia." 18 May 2017, https://carnegieendowment.org/2017/05/18/delegitimization-and-division-in-russia-pub-69958.

Cornell, Stephen, and Douglas Hartman. *Ethnicity and Race: Making Identities in a Changing World.* 2nd ed., Pine Forge Press, 2007.

Earl, Jennifer, and Katrina Kimport. *Digitally Enabled Social Change: Activism in the Internet Age.* MIT Press, 2011.

Fedor, Julie. "Memory, Kinship, and the Mobilization of the Dead: The Russian State and the Immortal Regiment." In *War and Memory in Russia, Ukraine, and Belarus,* edited by Fedor et al., Palgrave Macmillan, 2017.

Frantz, Erica. *Authoritarianism: What Everyone Needs to Know.* Oxford UP, 2018.

Inglehart, Ronald. "The Silent Revolution in Europe: Intergenerational Change in Post-Industrial Societies." *American Political Science Review,* vol. 65, no. 4, 1971, pp. 991–1017.

Kurilla, Ivan. "'The Immortal Regiment': A Holiday through Tears, a Parade of the Dead, or a Mass Protest," in *Russian Politics & Law,* vol. 57, nos. 5–6, 2020, pp. 150–65.

Kymlicka, Will. *Multicultural Citizenship: A Liberal Theory of Minority Rights.* Clarendon Press, 1995.

Kymlicka, Will, and Wayne Norman, editors. *Citizenship in Diverse Societies.* Oxford UP, 2000.

Marx, Karl, and Friedrich Engels. *The Marx-Engels Reader.* Edited by Robert C. Tucker. 2nd ed., Norton, 1978.

Mussolini, Benito. *Doctrine: Fascism and Institutions.* Ardita Publishers, 1935.

Nacos, Brigitte L. *Terrorism and Counterterrorism.* 4th ed., Longman, 2012.

Prokopyeva, Svetlana. "Russia's Immortal Regiment: From Grassroots to Quasi-Religious Cult." *Radio Free Europe,* 12 May 2017, https://www.rferl.org/amp/russia-immortal-regiment-grassroots-to-quasi-religious-cult/28482905.html.

Putnam, Robert D. *Bowling Alone: The Collapse and Revival of American Community.* Simon and Schuster, 2000.

Report: Global Internet Freedom Declines in Shadow of Pandemic. Freedom House, 14 Oct. 2020.

Repucci, Sarah. *Freedom and the Media, a Downward Spiral.* Freedom House, 2019.

Waddington, David. "Riots." In *The Oxford Handbook of Social Movements,* edited by Donatella della Porta and Mario Diani, Oxford UP, 2017, pp. 423–38.

Chapter 7

Adamson, David M and Julie DaVanzo. "Russia's Demographic 'Crisis': How Real Is It?" *Rand Issue Paper.* Rand Corporation.

Address by President Putin of the Russian Federation, 18 Mar. 2014.

Bauer, Elizabeth. "Putin's Russian Retirement Age Hike and U.S. Social Security." *Forbes,* 4 Oct. 2018.

BBC. "Chechnya Profile—Timeline." 17 Jan. 2018.

BBC. "Russia's Putin Seeks to Stimulate Birth Rate." 15 Jan. 2020.

Bigg, Clare. "Protests across Russia Force Putin to Double Increase in Pension Payments." *The Guardian,* 18 Jan. 2005.

Carnegie Endowment for International Peace. "Delegitimization and Division in Russia." 18 May 2017, https://carnegieendowment.org/2017/05/18/delegitimization-and-division-in-russia-pub-69958.

Center for Strategic and International Studies. "Economic Change in Russia."

Central Election Commission of the Russian Federation. http://www.cikrf.ru/eng/.

Committee to Protect Journalists. "Russian Journalist Svetlana Prokopyeva Facing Trial over Terrorism Commentary." 15 June 2020.

Cordell, Jake, and Evan Gershkovich. "We Don't Have Enough Intensive Care Beds: Coronavirus Will Test Russia's Creaking Healthcare System." *Moscow Times,* 18 Mar. 2020.

DaVanzo, Julie, and Clifford A. Grammich. "Improvements in Contraception Are Reducing Historically High Abortion Rates in Russia." *Rand Issue Paper,* Rand Corporation.

Deutsche Welle. "Russia's Putin Wins Election on Constitutional Reforms."

Federal Law on Elections of Deputies to the State Duma of the Federal Assembly of the Russian Federation, 2014.

Federation Council of the Federal Assembly of the Russian Federation: Status and Authority. http://council.gov.ru/en/structure/council/status/.

Freedom House. Freedom on the Net 2018. The Rise of Digital Authoritarianism. By Adrian Shahbaz. https://freedomhouse.org/report/freedom-net/2018/rise-digital-authoritarianism.

Frum, David. "Russia Re-Nationalizing Its Oil." *The Daily Beast,* 21 Apr. 2017.

Gel'man, Vladimir. *Authoritarian Russia: Analyzing Post-Soviet Regime Changes.* U of Pittsburgh P, 2015.

Gessen, Masha. *The Man without a Face: The Unlikely Rise of Vladimir Putin.* Riverhead Books, 2012.

Glaser, Marina. "Globalization: A Russian Perspective." *Global-e,* 31 Oct. 2019.

Herszenhorn, David M. "Putin Orders Changes in Election Rules." *The New York Times,* 2 Jan. 2013.

Hesli, Vicki L. *Government and Politics in Russia and the Post-Soviet Region.* Houghton Mifflin, 2007.

Human Rights Watch. "Russia: Government vs. Group Rights." 18 June 2018.

Human Rights Watch. "Russia: New Anti-Gay Crackdown in Chechnya: Police Detain, Torture Men in Grozny." 8 May 2019.

Human Rights Watch. "Russia: Reject Anti-LGBT 'Traditional Values' Bill." 6 Aug. 2020.

Human Rights Watch. "World Report 2020: Russia, Events of 2019."

Human Rights Watch. "World Report 2021: Russia, Events of 2020."

Johnson, Bridget. "Political Parties in Russia." ThoughtCo, 4 Nov. 2019.

Johnston, Matthew. "The Post-Soviet Union Russian Economy. Investopedia, 25 June 2019.

Kim, Lucian. "Kremlin Critic Navalny Sent to Prison on Old Conviction." National Public Radio, 2 Feb. 2021.

Kishkovsky, Sophia. "Pussy Riot Members Leave Russia after Facing Multiple Arrests amid Crackdown." *The Art Newspaper,* 4 Aug. 2021.

Levada Analytical Center. "The Coronavirus Situation in Russia," 13 Apr. 2020.

Lovetsky, Dmitri, "Russian Constitution Change Ends Hopes for Gay Marriage." *NBC News,* 13 July 2020.

Minority Rights Group International. World Directory of Minorities and Indigenous People. Russian Federation. https://minorityrights.org/country/russian-federation/.

Mirovalev, Mansur. "Chechnya, Russia, and 20 Years of Conflict: How the Tiny Region Shaped Post-Soviet Russia on the 20th Anniversary of the Start of First Chechnya War." Al Jazeera, 11 Dec. 2014.

Nechepurenko, Ivan. "Insult the Government? Russians Could Go to Jail under Proposed Law." *New York Times.* 7 Mar. 2019.

Obydenkova, Anastassia, and Wilfried Swenden. "Autocracy-Sustaining Versus Democratic Federalism: Explaining the Divergent Trajectories of Territorial Politics in Russia and Western Europe." *Territory, Politics, Governance,* vol. 1, no. 1, 2013, pp. 86–122.

Oversloot, Hans, and Ruben Verheul. "Managing Democracy: Political Parties and the State in Russia." *Journal of Communist Studies and Transition Politics,* vol. 22, no. 3, 2006, 383–405.

PMLive. "Overview of Healthcare in Russia: The Russian Healthcare System."

Reuters. "FACTBOX: Russian President and Prime Minister: Who Does What?" 7 May 2008.

Risk and Compliance Portal. *Country Risk Reports: Russia: Judicial System.* https://www.ganintegrity.com/portal/country-profiles/russia/.

Roache, Madeline. "Russian Activists Just Won an Important Battle over LGBTQ Rights. But the War Is Far from Over." *Time,* 2 Dec. 2020.

Russian President's Speech at the World Economic Forum: Complete English Translation. *Russia Briefing.* Dezan Shira & Associates, 28 Jan. 2021.

Russia Votes. "Results of Presidential Elections 1996-2004." Centre for the Study of Public Policy. University of Strathclyde, Scotland.

Sakwa, Richard. *Russian Politics and Society.* 5th ed., Routledge, 2021.

Seligmann, Renaud. "Demographic Transition—What Russia Can Learn from Other Countries." World Bank, 13 Feb. 2020.

Sokhey, Sarah Wilson. "What Does Putin Promise Russians? Russia's Authoritarian Social Policy." National Center for Biotechnology Information, 25 May 2020.

State Duma website. "Status and Powers, Composition and Regulations of the State Duma." http://duma.gov.ru/en/duma/about/.

UN News. "Russia Responsible for Navalny Poisoning, Rights Experts Say." 1 Mar. 2021.

Weaver, Matthew. "Russians Given Day Off Work to Make Babies." *The Guardian.* 12 Sept. 2007.

World Bank. "Russia Economic Report." 16 Dec. 2020.

World Bank. "Russian Economy Faces Deep Recession amid Global Pandemic and Oil Crisis, Says New World Bank Report." 6 July 2020.

Yale Global. "Russia Wants to Remake Globalization in Its Own Image." Richard Weitz. November 24, 2016. https://www.hudson.org/research/13192 -russia-wants-to-remake-globalization-in-its-own-image.

Zlobina, Anastasiia. "Jokes in Russia Are No Laughing Matter." Human Rights Watch, 24 Jan. 2020, https://www.hrw.org/news/2020/01/24/jokes-russia -are-no-laughing-matter.

Zubarevich, Natalya. "The Fall of Russia's Regional Governors." Carnegie Moscow Center, 10 Dec. 2017.

Unit 3 Review

Global Engagement Center Special Report. "Pillars of Russia's Disinformation and Propaganda Ecosystem." U.S. Department of State, Aug. 2020.

Kolesnikov, Andrei, and Denis Volkov. "Putin, Unlimited? Challenges to Russia's Regime After the Reset of Presidential Terms." Carnegie Moscow Center, 12 Sept. 2020.

Chapter 8

"AMLO Promises to 'Purify Public Life' as He Assumes Mexican Presidency." *The Guardian,* 2 Dec. 2018. https://www.theguardian.com/world/2018/dec/02 /amlo-promises-to-purify-public-life-as-he-assumes-mexican-presidency.

Dalton, Russell J. *The Participation Gap: Social Status and Political Inequality.* Oxford UP, 2017.

Dalton, Russell J., and Martin P. Wattenberg. *Parties without Partisans: Political Change in Advanced Industrial Democracies.* Oxford UP, 2000.

Dresser, Denise. "Mexico: López Obrador's 'Fourth Transformation'." *Berkeley Review of Latin American Studies,* fall 2019.

Duverger, Maurice. *Political Parties, Their Organization and Activity in the Modern State.* Methuen, 1969.

Giugni, Marco. 2004. *Social Protest and Policy Change: Ecology, Antinuclear, and Peace Movements in Comparative Perspective.* New York: Rowman and Littlefield.

Grayson, George. *Mexican Messiah.* Penn State UP, 2007.

Greene, Kenneth, and Mariano Sanchez-Talanquer. "Latin America's Shifting Politics: Mexico's Party System under Stress." *Journal of Democracy,* vol. 29, no. 4, Oct. 2018, pp. 31–42.

Katz, Richard S., and Peter Mair. 2017. *Democracy and the Cartelization of Political Parties.* Oxford UP, 2017.

Krauze, Enrique. "Tropical Messiah," *Letras Libres,* 30 June 2006, https://www .letraslibres.com/mexico/politica/tropical-messiah.

Lemann, Nicholas. "Kicking in Groups." *The Atlantic,* 1996.

Lindblom, Charles E. 1977. *Politics and Markets: The World's Political Economic Systems.* New York: Basic Books.

Maravall, Jose Maria. *Demands on Democracy.* Oxford UP, 2016.

Moosbrugger, Lorelei K. *The Vulnerability Thesis: Interest Group Influence and Institutional Design.* Yale UP, 2012.

Orellana, Salomon. *Electoral Systems and Governance: How Diversity Can Improve Policy-Making.* Routledge, 2014.

Pardos-Prado, Sergi, and Pedro Riera. "The Attitudinal Implications of the Cartel Party Thesis: Ideological Convergence and Political Efficacy in Contemporary Democracies." In *Party Politics and Democracy in Europe: Essays in Honour of Peter Mair,* edited by Ferdinand Muller-Rommel and Fernando Casal, Routledge, 2016, pp. 83–100.

Putnam, Robert. *Bowling Alone: The Collapse and Revival of American Community.* Simon and Schuster, 2000.

Rucht, Dieter. "Right-Wing Populism in Context: A Historical and Systematic Perspective." In *Populism and the Crisis of Democracy: Volume 2: Politics,*
Social Movements, and Extremism,* edited by Gregor Fitzi et al., Routledge, 2018, pp. 67–84.

Scarrow, Susan E., and Paul D. Webb. "Investigating Party Organization: Structures, Resources, and Representative Strategies." In *Organizing Political Parties: Representation, Participation, and Power,* edited by Susan E. Scarrow et al., Oxford UP, 2017, pp. 1–30.

Shugart, Matthew Soberg. 2005. "Comparative Electoral Systems Research: The Maturation of a Field and New Challenges Ahead." In *The Politics of Electoral Systems,* edited by Michael Gallagher and Paul Mitchell, 22–55. Oxford, UK: Oxford UP.

Skocpol, Theda. *Diminished Democracy: From Membership to Management in American Civic Life.* U of Oklahoma P, 2003.

Stillman, Amy, and Max De Halvedang. "Mexico Pouring Money into Pemex, at the Environment's Expense. *World Oil,* https://www.worldoil.com/news /2021/1/8/mexico-pouring-money-into-pemex-at-the-environment -s-expense.

Chapter 9

Abah, Danladi, and Adihikon Tanko. "Civil Society and Democratic Governance in Nigeria's Fourth Republic: A Historical Reflection." Benue State University, Makurdi, Nigeria, and Federal University, Wukari, Nigeria.

Adejo, Mary. "Success Stories of Entrepreneurs in Nigeria." *LegitNG,* 2019.

Adeshoken, Oluwatosin. "Nigeria's EFCC Boss Suspended from Office Following Secret Tribunal." *The Africa Report,* 17 July 2020.

African Development Bank Group, 2019.

Ajakaiye, Olu, Paul Collier, and Akpan H. Ekpo. "Management of Resource Revenue: Nigeria." In *Plundered Nations? Successes and Failures in Natural Resource Extraction,* edited by Paul Collier and Anthony J. Venables, Palgrave Macmillan, 2011, pp. 231–61.

Akinwotu, Emmanuel. "Almost 300 Schoolgirls Kidnapped in Nigeria Are Free, Says State Governor." *The Guardian,* 2 Mar. 2021.

Akwagyiram, Alexis, and Paul Carsten. "Factbox: Nigeria's 2019 Presidential Election." Reuters, 13 Feb. 2019.

Al Jazeera. "Nigeria's Chief Justice Banned from Holding Public Office." 18 Apr. 2019.

Amnesty International. "Human Rights Agenda for Nigeria." 31 May 2019.

Amnesty International. "The Niger Delta Is One of the Most Polluted Places on Earth."

Babalola, Dele. "Nigeria: Federalism Works." IPI Global Observatory, 25 Aug. 2014.

BBC. "Nigerian Chief Justice's Suspension Raises International Concerns." 26 Jan. 2019.

Campbell, John. "Nigeria's Unitary Federalism." Council on Foreign Relations, 16 Dec. 2020.

Campbell, John. "Obasanjo's Costly Failed Third-Term Bid." Council on Foreign Relations, 27 Sept. 2018.

The Choices Program. "Nigeria: History, Identity and Change." Watson Institute for International and Public Affairs, Brown University. June 2017.

CIA World Factbook. "Nigeria: Age Structure." 2021.

Constitution of the Federal Republic of Nigeria, https://www.constituteproject .org/constitution/Nigeria_2011.pdf?lang=en.

Copeland, Malu. "We've Got Entrepreneurial Spirit, Yes We Do." *Forbes,* 7 Aug. 2015.

Freedom House. "Nigeria: Country Profile." 2021.

Friedrich Ebert Stiftung. "Social Protection in Nigeria." *Frankage,* 2018.

Gillies, Alexandra. "Obasanjo, the Donor Community and Reform Implementation in Nigeria." *The Round Table,* vol. 96, no. 392, 2007, pp. 569–86.

The Guardian. "ERCC Records 646 Convictions, Recovers More Than N11 Billion in 10 Months." 7 Oct. 2020.

The Guardian. "Nigerian Media Mogul, Mo Abudu, Receives 2019 Médailles d'Honneur at Cannes." 13 Apr. 2019.

Hallmark, Terry. "Oil and Violence in the Niger Delta Isn't Talked about Much, But It Has a Global Impact." University of Houston Energy Fellows, 13 Feb. 2017.

Hanson, Stephanie. "MEND: The Niger Delta's Umbrella Militant Group." Council on Foreign Relations, 22 Mar. 2007.

Hayes, Jonathan. *Nollywood: The Creation of Nigerian Film Genres.* U of Chicago P, 2016.

"How to Impeach the President of the Federal Republic of Nigeria." Enough Is Enough: Nigeria. Nov. 2016.

Human Rights Watch. "World Report 2021: Nigeria."

Ikelegbe, A. O. *State, Civil Society, and Sustainable Development in Nigeria.* CEPED Monograph Series, No. 7, 2013.

Kew, Darren. "The 2003 Elections: Hardly Credible, but Acceptable." In *Crafting the New Nigeria,* edited by Robert I. Rotberg, pp. 139–173. Boulder, CO: Lynne Rienner, 2004.

Lewis, Peter M. "Nigeria's Petroleum Booms: A Changing Political Economy." In *The Oxford Handbook of Nigerian Politics*, edited by A. Carl LeVan and Patrick Ikata, Oxford UP, 2018, pp. 502–19.

Lewis, Peter, and Darren Kew. "Nigeria's Hopeful Election." *Journal of Democracy* 26 (3):94–109, 2015.

Library of Congress. "National Parliaments: Nigeria."

Mbaku, John Mukum. "The 2019 Nigerian Elections and Buhari's Second Chance to Provide Peace, Prosperity, and Security." *Africa in Focus*, Brookings Institution, 1 Mar. 2019.

Mitchell, Alex. "Top 10 African Startups to Watch in 2020." Medium.com, 14 Nov. 2020, https://amitch5903.medium.com/top-10-african-startups -to-watch-in-2021-e2a42d9b5d3c.

MSN. "Nigeria Arrests Journalist and Opposition Leader Sowore." MSN.com, AFP, 3 Jan. 2021.

Olurounbi, Ruth, and William Clowes. "Nigeria Fuel Subsidies Near $300 Million a Month, NNPC Says." *Bloomberg*, 25 Mar. 2021.

Oluyemi, Oloyede. "Monitoring Participation of Women in Politics in Nigeria." National Bureau of Statistics. Abuja, Nigeria, 2015.

Population Research Bureau. International Data. Nigeria. https://www.prb.org /international/geography/nigeria/.

Rawlence, Ben, and Chris Albin-Lackey. 2007. "Briefing: Nigeria's 2007 General Elections; Democracy in Retreat." *African Affairs* 106(424): 497–506. doi:10.1093/afraf/adm039.

Reporters Without Borders. "Nigeria." 2020.

Saliu, H. A., and A. Bakare. "An Analysis of the Role of the National Assembly in Nigeria's Fourth Republic and Its Possible Reform." *Studia Politica: Romanian Political Science Review*, vol. 20, no. 2, 2020, pp. 271–90.

Searcey, Dionne, and Marc Santora, "Boko Haram Ranked Ahead of ISIS for Deadliest Terror Group." *The New York Times*, 18 Nov. 2015.

Songonuga, Temitope O. "Civil Society in Nigeria: Reasons for Ineffectiveness." Naval Post-Graduate School, Monterey, CA, Mar. 2015.

Statement by Spokesman for the United Nations Office of Drugs and Crime, "UNODC Congratulates Nigerian President Muhammadu Buhari on His Anti-Corruption Efforts." United Nations.

Statista. "Number of Movies Produced and Censored by Nollywood from 2017 to 1st Quarter 2021."

Supreme Court of Nigeria. Jurisdiction of the Court. https://supremecourt.gov .ng/about/court-jurisdiction.

Thurston, Alexander. *Boko Haram: The History of an African Jihadist Movement.* Princeton UP, 2018.

Translators Without Borders. "Language Data for Nigeria."

USAID. "Democracy, Human Rights, and Governance." https://www.usaid.gov /nigeria/democracy-human-rights-and-governance.

Witt, Emily. *Nollywood: The Making of a Film Empire.* Columbia Global Reports, 2017.

World Bank. "Advancing Social Protection in a Dynamic Nigeria." 7 Aug. 2019.

World Bank. "Nigeria Releases New Report on Poverty and Inequality in Country." 28 May 2020.

World Inequality Database. "Income Inequality, Nigeria, 2019."

Unit 4 Review

Endeavor Nigeria. "Trends in National Entrepreneurship Policies." 26 June 2020.

Pring, Coralie, and Jon Vrushi. "Tackling the Crisis of Democracy, Promoting Rule of Law and Fighting Corruption." Transparency International, 19 Jan. 2019.

Chapter 10

Amnesty International. "China Blocks Amnesty International Website." 13 Jan. 2019.

Anadolu Agency. "Nigeria: Arrests in Protests against Fuel Price Hike." 9 Oct. 2020.

BBC. "Iran Petrol Price Hike: Protestors Warned That Security Forces May Intervene." 17 Nov. 2019.

Castells, Manuel. *Networks of Outrage and Hope: Social Movements in the Internet Age.* Cambridge, UK: Polity Press, 2012.

Dadush, Uri, and Kemal Dervis. "The Inequality Challenge." *Current History*, vol. 112, no. 750, 2013, pp. 13–19.

Earl, Jennifer, and Katrina Kimport. *Digitally Enabled Social Change: Activism in the Internet Age.* MIT Press, 2011.

Iverson, Torben, and David Soskice. *Democracy and Prosperity: Reinventing Capitalism Through a Turbulent Century.* Princeton UP, 2019.

Keck, Margaret E., and Kathryn Sikkink. *Activists beyond Borders: Advocacy Networks in International Politics.* Cornell UP, 1998.

Lipton, David. "Can Globalization Still Deliver?" Speech, Stavros Niarchos Foundation Lecture, Peterson Institute for International Economics, 24 May 2016.

McMorrow, Ryan, and Sun Yu, "The Vanishing Billionaire: How Jack Ma Fell Foul of Xi Jinping." *Financial Times*, 15 Apr. 2021, https://www.ft.com /content/1fe0559f-de6d-490e-b312-abba0181da1f.

Ohmae, Kenichi. *The End of the Nation State: The Rise of Regional Economies.* Simon and Schuster, 1995.

Peck, Jamie, and Jun Zhang, "A Variety of Capitalism . . . with Chinese Characteristics." *Journal of Economic Geography*, vol. 13, 2013, pp. 357–96.

Seattle.gov. "World Trade Organization Protests in Seattle." City of Seattle, Washington Archives.

UNESCO. "Culture for Sustainable Development."

Warner, Adam. "A Brief History of the Anti-Globalization Movement." *University of Miami International and Comparative Law Review*, vol. 1, no. 2, 2005, p. 237.

Chapter 11

Amnesty International. "Death Penalty: World's Biggest Executor China Must Come Clean about 'Grotesque' Level of Capital Punishment." 11 Apr. 2017.

BBC. "China Allows 3 Children in Major Policy Shift." 31 May 2021.

BBC. "How China Is Ruled: National People's Congress." 10 Nov. 2012.

BBC. "Tibet Profile." 26 Apr. 2019.

BBC. "What Was China's One-Child Policy?" 29 Oct. 2015.

BBC. "Wuhan Lockdown: A Year of China's Fight against the Covid Pandemic." 23 Jan. 2021.

Chatzky, Andrew, and James McBride. "China's Massive Belt and Road Initiative." Council on Foreign Relations, 28 Jan. 2020.

Chen, Frank. "China's Women Deficit Taking a Demographic Toll." *Asia Times*, 20 Apr. 2021.

Chen, Jie, and Chunlong Lu. 2011. "Democratization and the Middle Class in China: The Middle Class's Attitudes toward Democracy." *Political Research Quarterly* 64 (September): 705–719.

Chen, Xi. *Social Protest and Contentious Authoritarianism in China*. Cambridge UP, 2012.

China Justice Observer. "How Many Crimes Are Punishable by Death in China?: China Law in One Minute." 23 Nov. 2020.

Chu, Mike P. H. "Criminal Procedure Reforms in the People's Republic of China: The Dilemma of Crime Control and Regime Legitimacy." *Pacific Basin Law Journal*, vol. 18, no. 2, 2000.

Dickson, Bruce J. *The Dictator's Dilemma: The Chinese Communist Party's Strategy for Survival.* Oxford UP, 2016.

Dickson, Bruce J. *Red Capitalists in China: The Party, Private Entrepreneurs, and Prospects for Political Change.* Cambridge UP, 2003.

Dillon, Michael. *Xinjiang in the Twenty-First Century.* Routledge, 2019.

Donnelly, Drew. "An Introduction to the China Social Credit System." *New Horizons*, 2021.

The Economist. "Why Protests Are So Common in China." 4 Oct. 2018.

Economy, Elizabeth. "30 Years after Tiananmen: Dissent Is Not Dead." *Journal of Democracy*, vol. 30, no. 2, 2019, 57–63. Project MUSE, doi:10.1353 /jod.2019.0024.

Fetterly, Madeline. "Sex Trafficking and China's One Child Policy." *The Diplomat*, 6 Nov. 2014.

Flaherty, Martin. "Repression by Any Other Name: Xinjiang and the Genocide Debate." *The Diplomat*, 3 Aug. 2021, https://thediplomat.com/2021/08/ repression-by-any-other-name-xinjiang-and-the-genocide-debate/.

Frazier, Mark W. *Socialist Insecurity: Pensions and the Politics of Uneven Development in China.* Cornell UP, 2010.

Fukuyama, Francis. *Political Order and Political Decay: From the Industrial Revolution to the Globalization of Democracy.* New York: Farrar, Straus, and Giroux, 2014.

Gao, Qin. *Welfare, Work, and Poverty: Social Assistance in China.* Oxford UP, 2017.

Hildebrandt, Timothy. *Social Organizations and the Authoritarian State in China.* Cambridge, UK: Cambridge UP, 2013.

History Channel. *Long March.* 21 Aug. 2018.

Hollingsworth, Julia. "UN Boss Raises Xinjiang Uyghurs During His Trip to China." CNN, 29 Apr. 2019.

"How Does Water Security Affect China's Development?" Center for Strategic and International Studies. 2020.

Human Rights Watch. "Break Their Lineage, Break Their Roots: China's Crimes Against Humanity Target Uyghurs and Other Turkic Muslims." 19 Apr. 2021.

Interview with Chinese President Xi Jinping (full transcript). *The Wall Street Journal*, 22 Sept. 2015.

"Is Air Quality in China a Social Problem?" ChinaPower Project. Center for Strategic and International Studies. 2021.

Kadeer, Rebiya. *Dragon Fighter: One Woman's Struggle for Peace with China.* Kales Press, 2009.

Khatchadourian, Raffi. "Ghost Walls." *The New Yorker*, 12 Apr. 2021, pp. 30–51.

Knight, John, and Sai Ding. *China's Remarkable Economic Growth.* Oxford UP, 2013.

Kroeber, Arthur R. *China's Economy: What Everyone Needs to Know.* Oxford UP, 2016.

LaFee, Scott. "Novel Coronavirus Circulated Undetected Months before First COVID-19 Cases in Wuhan, China." UC San Diego Health, 18 Mar. 2021.

Landry, Pierre F. "The Institutional Diffusion of Courts in China: Evidence From Survey Data." In *Rule by Law: The Politics of Courts in Authoritarian Regimes,* edited by Tom Ginsburg and Tamir Moustafa, 207–234. Cambridge, UK: Cambridge UP, 2008.

Landry, Pierre F., Deborah Davis, and Shiru Wang. 2010. "Elections in Rural China: Competition Without Parties." *Comparative Political Studies* 43 (6): 763–790. doi:10.1177/0010414009359392.

Lee, Ching Kwan, and Eli Friedman. 2009. "The Labor Movement." *Journal of Democracy* 20 (3): 21–24.

Lei, Ya-Wen. *The Contentious Public Sphere: Law, Media, and Authoritarian Rule in China.* Princeton UP, 2018.

Lu, Yiyi. *Non-Governmental Organizations in China: The Rise of Dependent Autonomy.* New York: Routledge, 2009.

Lum, Alvin. "Confidence in China's Judicial System Damaged by Secret Trial of Human Rights Lawyer Wang Quanzhang, Says Hong Kong Bar Association." *South China Morning Post*, 19 Feb. 2019.

Manion, Melanie. *Information for Autocrats: Representation in Chinese Local Congresses.* Cambridge, UK: Cambridge UP, 2015.

Marx, Karl, and Friedrich Engels. *The Communist Manifesto.* Translated by Samuel Moore with Friedrich Engels. William Reeves Bookseller, 1888. Originally published as *Manifest der Kommunistischen Partei* in London in 1848.

McAllister, Ian, and Stephen White. "Economic Change and Public Support for Democracy in China and Russia." In *Authoritarian Powers: Russia and China Compared,* edited by Stephen White, Ian McAllister and Neil Munro, 76–91. New York: Routledge, 2018.

Micklethwaite, Jamie. "Death State: Inside China's Brutal Execution System with Mobile Injection Vans and Firing Squads Killing Most in the World." *The Sun*, 18 Feb. 2021.

Mozur, Paul. "One Month, 500,000 Face Scans: How China Is Using A.I. to Profile a Minority." *The New York Times*, 14 Apr. 2019.

Muhammad, Jeanette. "U.S. Joins EU in Sanctions Against China over Treatment of Uyghur Muslims." NPR, 22 Mar. 2021.

Naughton, Barry. "China and the Two Crises: From 1997 to 2009." In *Two Crises, Different Outcomes: East Asia and Global Finance,* edited by T. J. Pempel and Keiichi Tsunekawa, Cornell UP, 2015, pp. 110–36.

NPC Observer. *About: The NPC and the Blog.* Oct. 2017.

Panda, Ankit. "31 Dead in Urumqi Car Bomb Attack." *The Diplomat*, 22 May 2014.

Pearson, Margaret M. "State-Owned Business and Party-State Regulations in China's Modern Political Economy." In *State Capitalism, Institutional Adaptation, and the Chinese Miracle,* edited by Barry Naughton and Kellee S. Tsai, Cambridge UP, 2015, pp. 27–45.

Qian, Yingyi. "The Process of China's Market Transition, 1978–1998: The Evolutionary, Historical, and Comparative Perspectives." In *China's Deep Reform: Domestic Politics in Transition,* edited by Lowell Dittmer and Guoli Liu, Rowman and Littlefield, 2006, pp. 229–50.

Qiang, Xiao. "The Road to Digital Unfreedom: President Xi's Surveillance State." *Journal of Democracy*, vol. 30, no. 1, 2019, 53–67. Project MUSE, doi:10.1353/jod.2019.0004.

Reuters. "China's Most Populous Province to Loosen Grip on Internal Migration." 14 Jan. 2020.

Reuters. "China's Top Judge Warns Courts on Judicial Independence." 16 Jan. 2017.

Reuters. "China Tells Pilots to Improve Landing Skills to Deal with Beijing Smog." 22 Dec. 2013.

Reuters. "China to Invest $17 Billion in Xinjiang Projects: Xinhua." 5 Mar. 2016.

Saich, Anthony. "How China's Citizens View the Quality of Governance under Xi Jinping." *Journal of Chinese Governance*, vol. 1, no. 1, Mar. 2016, pp. 1–20.

Saich, Anthony. "Political Representation." In *Handbook of China's Governance and Domestic Politics,* edited by Chris Ogden, 109–119. New York: Routledge, 2013.

Shambaugh, David. *China's Communist Party: Atrophy and Adaptation.* Washington, DC: Woodrow Wilson Center Press, 2008.

Shi, Tianjian. "Village Committee Elections in China: Institutionalist Tactics for Democracy." In *China's Deep Reform: Domestic Politics in Transition,* edited by Lowell Dittmer and Guoli Liu, 353–380. Lanham, MD: Rowman and Littlefield, 2006.

Stanway, David. "The Shadow of SARS: China Learned the Hard Way How to Handle an Epidemic." Reuters, 22 Jan. 2020.

Stockman, Daniela. *Media Commercialization and Authoritarian Rule in China.* Cambridge UP, 2012.

Swanson, Ana. "U.S. Imposes Sanctions on 11 Chinese Companies over Human Rights." *The New York Times*, 20 July 2020.

Thomala, Lai Lin. "Key Figures of Coronavirus COVID-19 in Greater China 2021." Statista, 26 Apr. 2021.

Wang, Yueduan. "Overcoming Embeddedness: How China's Judicial Accountability Makes Its Judges More Autonomous." *Fordham Law*, 2020.

Weller, Chris. "Here's China's Genius Plan to Move 250 Million People from Farms to Cities." *Business Insider*, 5 Aug. 2015.

Wong, Edward. "In China, Widening Discontent Among the Communist Party Faithful." *New York Times,* January 19, 2013. http://www.nytimes.com/2013/01/20/world/asia/inchina- discontent-among-the-normally-faithful.html?emc=eta1.

World Bank. *China's Special Economic Zones.* 3 July 2019.

Xinhua. "China's Latest Census Reports More Balanced Gender Ratio." 11 May 2021.

Yu, Katrina. "The Good News (and Not So Good News) about China's Smoggy Air." NPR, 18 Dec. 2018.

Zhang, Chunlin. "How Much Do State-Owned Enterprises Contribute to China's GDP and Employment?" 15 July 2019.

Zhao, Suisheng. "Xi Jinping's Maoist Revival." *Journal of Democracy*, vol. 27, no. 3, 2016, 83–97.

Zhou, Viola. "China Is the World's Most Optimistic Country. Here's Why." *Inkstone News*, 2 Oct. 2018.

Chapter 12

Beveridge Report. "Social Insurance and Allied Services" (Command Paper 6404). https://archive.org/details/in.ernet.dli.2015.275849.

Chiu, Dominic. *The East Is Green: China's Global Leadership in Renewable Energy.* Center for Strategic and International Studies, 2 Oct. 2017.

Commonwealth Fund. *Mirror, Mirror 2021: Reflecting Poorly: Health Care in the U.S. Compared to Other High-Income Countries.* 4 Aug. 2021.

Dunlap, Riley E., and Richard York. "The Globalization of Environmental Concern." In *Comparative Environmental Politics: Theory, Practice, and Prospects,* edited by Paul F. Steinberg and Stacy D. VanDeveer, MIT Press, 2012, pp. 89–112.

Ferreira, Francisco H. G., and David A. Robalino. "Social Protection in Latin America: Achievements and Limitations." In *The Oxford Handbook of Latin*

American Economics, edited by José Antonio Ocampo and Jaime Ros, Oxford UP, 2011, pp. 836–62.

Groce, Nora Ellen. "'The Bills Were More Stressful Than the Cancer': US Versus UK Healthcare—a Personal Story." *The Conversation*, 20 Mar. 2020. https://theconversation.com/the-bills-were-more-stressful-than-the-cancer-us-versus-uk-healthcare-a-personal-story-133131.

Groce, Nora Ellen, and Nancy Groce, "Comparative Twin Study: Access to Healthcare Services in the NHS and the American Private Insurance System." *British Medical Journal (BMJ)*, 17 Feb. 2020, https://blogs.bmj.com/bmj/2020/02/17/comparative-twin-study-access-to-healthcare-services-in-the-nhs-and-the-american-private-insurance-system/.

Kirkpatrick, Jeane J. *Political Woman*. Basic Books, 1974.

Ocampo, José Antonio, and Rob Vos. *Uneven Economic Development*. Zed Books, 2008.

Oringer, Jason, and Carol Welch. *Structural Adjustment Policies*. Institute for Policy Studies, 1 Apr. 1998.

Oshienenmen, Albert N., Dilanthi Amaratunga, and Richard P. Haigh. "Evolution of the Impacts of Oil Spill Disaster on Communities and Its Influence on Restiveness in Niger Delta, Nigeria." *Science Direct*, 2018.

Ross, Michael L. "What Have We Learned about the Resource Curse?" *Annual Review of Political Science,* vol. 18, May 2015, pp. 239–59.

Rudra, Nita, and Jennifer Tobin. "When Does Globalization Help the Poor?" *Annual Review of Political Science*, vol. 20, 2017, pp. 287–307.

Schmitz, Rob. "China Shuts Down Tens of Thousands of Factories in Unprecedented Pollution Crackdown." *NPR*, 23 Oct. 2017.

Spilker, Gabriele. *Globalization, Political Institutions and the Environment in Developing Countries*. Routledge, 2013.

Tripp, Aili Mari. "Political Systems and Gender." In *The Oxford Handbook of Gender and Politics*, edited by Georgina Waylen et al., Oxford UP, 2013, pp. 514–35.

Chapter 13

Alfoneh, Ali. "The Basij Resistance Force." Iran Primer. United States Institute of Peace. 6 Oct. 2010.

Alizadeh, Parvin. "Iran's Quandary: Economic Reforms and the 'Structural Trap.'" *Brown Journal of World Affairs*, vol. 9, no. 2, 2003, 267–81.

Al Jazeera. "Sanctions-Battered Iran Faces Worst Coronavirus Wave." 25 Apr. 2021.

Amnesty International. "Iran 2020."

Aryan, Khadijeh. "The Boom in Women's Education." In *Women, Power, and Politics in 21st Century Iran*, edited by Tara Povey and Elaheh Rostami-Povey. Ashgate, 2012, pp. 25–53.

Azadi, Pooya, Matin Mirramezani, and Mohsen B. Mesgaran. "Migration and Brain Drain from Iran." *Stanford*, Apr. 2020.

Azizi, Arash. "Factbox: The Outcome of Iran's 2020 Parliamentary Election." *Atlantic Council*, 26 Feb. 2020.

Bahramitash, Roksana, and Shahla Kazemipour. "Myths and Realities of the Impact of Islam on Women: Changing Marital Status in Iran." *Critique: Critical Middle Eastern Studies*, vol. 15, no. 2, 2006, 111–28.

BBC. "Iran Presidential Election: Hardliners Dominate Approved Candidates List." 25 May 2021.

BBC News. "Six Charts That Show How Hard US Sanctions Have Hit Iran." 2 May 2019.

Borden, Emma. "Demystifying Iran's Parliamentary Election Process." *Brookings*, 9 Feb. 2016.

Borden, Emma. "Everything You Need to Know about Iran's Assembly of Religious Experts Election." *Brookings*, 9 Feb. 2016.

Borger, Julian, and Robert Tait, "The Financial Power of the Revolutionary Guards." *The Guardian*, 15 Feb. 2010.

CBC. "History of Iran: from Persia to Present." 29 June 2009.

Ceasefire Centre for Civilian Rights. "Rights Denied." Mar. 2018.

Cincotta, Richard, and Karim Sudjadpour. "Iran in Transition: The Implications of the Islamic Republic's Changing Demographics." *Carnegie Endowment for International Peace*, Dec. 2017.

Clawson, Patrick, and Michael Rubin. *Eternal Iran: Continuity and Chaos*. Palgrave Macmillan, 2005.

Death Penalty Information Center. "Executions around the World." 2019.

Deutsche Welle. "Baha'i in Iran Repressed and Persecuted by the State."

Fallaci, Oriana. "An Interview with Khomeini." *New York Times*, 7 Oct. 1979, sec. SM, p. 8.

Farhi, Farideh. "Cultural Practices in the Islamic Republic of Iran." https://www.wilsoncenter.org/sites/default/files/media/documents/event/FaridehFarhiFinal.pdf.

Freedom House. "Special Report 2021 Iran: Transnational Repression Case Study."

Freemuse. "Iran: Filmmaker Sentenced to Prison Because of 'Propaganda Against the System' Movies." 13 Mar. 2020.

Global Initiative Against Transnational Organized Crime. "Under the Shadow: Illicit Economies in Iran." Oct. 2020.

The Guardian. "Iran Ends Provision by State of Contraceptives and Vasectomies." *The Guardian*, 15 June 2020.

Human Rights Watch. *Iran: Events of 2019*.

Iran International. "Iran Green Movement Leaders Mark Ten Years under House Arrest." 15 Feb. 2021.

The Iran Project. "Iranian Parliament Debating Bill on Religious Minorities." 29 Nov. 2017.

Iranian Chamber Society. "Provinces of Iran." 3 May 2021.

Jafari, Saeid. "Zoroastrian Takes Center Stage on Iran's Political Scene." *Al-Monitor*, 2 Nov. 2017.

Johnson, Keith. "Iran's Economy Is Crumbling, but Collapse Is a Long Way Off." *Foreign Policy*, 13 Feb. 2019.

Karimi, Nasser. "Iran Disqualified Thousands from Running for Parliament." *Associated Press*, 14 Feb. 2020.

Karimi, Nasser, and Jon Gambrell. "Torture Still Scars Iranians 40 Years after Revolution." *Associated Press*, 6 Feb. 2019.

Khodabandeh, Bahram. "The Revolutionary Guards' Outsize Share of Iran's National Budget." *Iranwire*, 10 Dec. 2020.

Kishi, Katayoun. "Iran by the Numbers." Iran Primer. United States Institute of Peace, 25 May 2016.

Landinfo. "Iranian Welfare System." Country of Origin Information Centre, 2020.

Mahmoudi, Hoda. "Freedom and the Iranian Women's Movement." *Contexts*, vol. 18, no. 3, 2019, pp. 14–19, https://journals.sagepub.com/doi/pdf/10.1177/1536504219864953.

Maloney, Suzanne, and Katz, Eliora. "Iran and the Headscarf Protests." *Brookings*, 24 Jan. 2019, https://www.brookings.edu/opinions/iran-and-the-headscarf-protests/.

Milani, Abbas. "Iran's Paradoxical Regime." *Journal of Democracy*, vol. 26, no. 2, 2015, pp. 52–60.

Mohseni, Payam. "Factionalism, Privatization, and the Political Economic of Regime Transformation." In *Power and Change in Iran: Politics of Contentions and Conciliation*, edited by Daniel Brumberg and Farideh Farhi, Indiana University Press, 2016, pp. 37–69.

MSN Encarta. "Iran-Iraq War." 20 Aug. 1988.

Nada, Garrett. "Iran's Troubled Provinces: Baluchistan." *The Iran Primer*, United States Institute of Peace, 24 Feb. 2021.

Nada, Garrett. "Statistics on Women in Iran." *The Iran Primer*, United States Institute for Peace, 9 Dec. 2020.

Nadeem, Mehr. "Selfies and Sharia Police." *Rest of World*, 9 Nov. 2020, https://restofworld.org/2020/selfies-and-sharia-police/.

O'Neil, Patrick H., Karl Fields, and Don Share. *Comparative Politics*. Norton. 2015.

Pew Research. "Estimated Percentage of Shia by Country." Oct. 2009.

Rafizadeh, Majid. "Iran's Worsening Treatment of Religious Minorities." *Arab News*, 5 Feb. 2018.

Rastovac, Heather. "Contending with Censorship: The Underground Music Scene in Urban Iran." *Intersections Online*, vol. 10, no. 2, spring 2009, https://depts.washington.edu/chid/intersections_Spring_2009/Heather_Rastovac_The_Underground_Music_Scene_in_Urban_Iran.pdf.

Reuters. "Iran Lifts Ban on Non-Muslim City Council Member after Outcry." 21 July 2018.

Rezai-Rashti, Goli, and Valentine Moghadam. "Women and Higher Education in Iran: What Are the Implications for Employment and the 'Marriage Market'?" *International Review of Education*, vol. 57, no. 3–4, 2011, 419–41.

Rouhani, Hassan. Speech broadcast on Iranian state television, 7 Jan. 2021, https://www.youtube.com/watch?v=P0-akk7xYJU.

Sinai, Sam. "Why Does Iran Have Such a Brain Drain Problem?" *Quora*, 17 Dec. 2014.

"Situation of Baha'is in Iran." Bahá'í International Community. Aug. 2020.

Statista. "Iran: Inflation Rate 1984–2020."

United Nations Office on Drugs and Crime. "Drug Trafficking and Border Control Situation Analysis: Islamic Republic of Iran."

U.S. Department of the Treasury. "Treasury Targets Vast Supreme Leader Patronage Network and Iran's Minister of Intelligence." 18 Nov. 2020.

Wamsley, Laurel. "Thousands of Women Will At Last Be Allowed to Attend a Soccer Match in Iran." *NPR*, 9 Oct. 2019.

Watson Institute for International Studies. "Iran Through the Looking Glass: History, Reform, and Revolution." The Choices Program, Brown University, May 2012.

World Bank. "Iran's Economic Update." Oct. 2020.

World Bank. "Islamic Republic of Iran." 2021.

Unit 5 Review

Everett, Tim, et al. "Economic Growth and the Environment." Defra Evidence and Analysis Series, Paper 2, Mar. 2020.

Nephew, Richard. "Sanctions 4: The 'Chilling Effect' of U.S. Sanctions on Iran." *The Iran Primer*, United States Institute of Peace, 11 Oct. 2020.

Glossary/Glosario

This glossary includes all AP® key concepts defined and listed in the minor column of each chapter including the page number(s) where it appears. To help students keep track of the many terms used in political science, this glossary also includes terms used in the book as working vocabulary. These important terms from political science and related areas are not linked to a specific chapter or page.

English	Español
A	
Accountability The ability of the citizenry, directly or indirectly, to control political leaders and institutions.	**Rendición de cuentas** Proceso que da a la ciudadanía el poder de controlar, directa o indirectamente, a los líderes políticos y a las instituciones.
Assembly of Experts An elected body in Iran that has the power to select the supreme leader and remove him if he is unable to perform his duties. (p. 408)	**Asamblea de expertos** Cuerpo electo de Irán que posee la facultad de elegir al líder supremo y destituirlo si no es capaz de desempeñar sus funciones.
Asymmetrical federalism A system in which some regions have more formal power and autonomy than others. (p. 207)	**Federalismo asimétrico** Sistema en el cual algunas regiones tienen una mayor autonomía y poder formal que otras.
Austerity measures Raising taxes and/or cutting spending in an effort to reduce the deficit and the national debt. Measures may entail cuts to social services, which might include programs to help women, children, the poor, and the elderly, in an effort to reduce government debt. (pp. 152, 376)	**Medidas de austeridad** Subir los impuestos o recortar el gasto con el fin de reducir el déficit y la deuda nacional. Es posible que las medidas impliquen recortes en los servicios sociales (entre los cuales podrían verse afectados programas de ayuda a las mujeres, a los niños, a los pobres y a los ancianos) en un esfuerzo por reducir la deuda pública.
Authoritarian state A system without free and fair elections in which civil rights and liberties are restricted. (p. 33)	**Estado autoritario** Sistema sin elecciones libres y justas en el que se restringen los derechos y las libertades civiles.
Authority The legitimate power a state has over people within its territory. (p. 39)	**Autoridad** Poder legítimo que posee un estado sobre las personas que se encuentran en su territorio.
Autonomy The ability and right of a group to partially govern itself within a larger state.	**Autonomía** Capacidad y potestad de un grupo a tener parcialmente un gobierno propio dentro de un estado más amplio.
B	
Basij A voluntary paramilitary force under the authority of the Revolutionary Guard that serves as the morality police in Iran. (p. 422)	**Basich** Fuerza paramilitar voluntaria de Irán que, bajo la autoridad de la Guardia Revolucionaria, funciona como policía de la moral.
Bicameral A legislature with two chambers. (p. 64)	**Bicameral** Legislatura compuesta de dos cámaras.
Bureaucracy A set of appointed officials and government workers who carry out policies and implement laws. (pp. 30, 103)	**Burocracia** Conjunto de funcionarios designados en sus cargos y trabajadores gubernamentales que ponen en práctica las políticas y aplican las leyes.
C	
Cabinet The heads of major departments, or ministries, in the bureaucracy. (p. 110)	**Gabinete** Jefes de los principales ministerios o departamentos de la burocracia.
Cabinet head An official appointed to run a government department with a specific policy area. (p. 62)	**Jefe de gabinete** Funcionario que ha sido designado para dirigir un departamento gubernamental con un área política específica.
Capitalism The combination of a market economy with private property rights.	**Capitalismo** Combinación de una economía de mercado con derecho a la propiedad privada.
Catch-all party A party that takes ideologically diverse, usually middle-of-the-road, positions to capture as many voters as possible. (p. 252)	**Partido "atrápalotodo"** Partido que adopta posturas de diversas ideologías, normalmente de centro, para captar el mayor caudal posible de votantes.
Causation A statistical concept, when a change in one variable precipitates a change in another variable. (p. 10)	**Causalidad** Concepto estadístico, en el cual un cambio en una variable precipita un cambio en otra variable.
Chamber of Deputies The elected lower house of the Mexican Congress, which has the power to pass legislation, levy taxes, approve the budget, and certify elections. (p. 64)	**Cámara de Diputados** Cámara baja del Congreso mexicano, elegida por el voto, que tiene la facultad de aprobar leyes, crear impuestos, aprobar el presupuesto y certificar las elecciones.

Change in government A change in leaders, without fundamental changes in the system of government. (p. 30)	**Cambio de gobierno** Cambio de gobernantes, sin cambios fundamentales en el sistema de gobierno.
Charismatic legitimacy The right to rule based on personal virtue, heroism, or other extraordinary characteristics. (p. 42)	**Legitimidad carismática** Derecho a gobernar basado en una virtud personal, el heroísmo u otras características extraordinarias.
Chinese Communist Party (CCP) The political party that has ruled China from 1949 to the present. (p. 338)	**Partido Comunista Chino (PCC)** Partido político que ha gobernado China desde 1949 hasta la actualidad.
Citizen A member of a political community or state with certain rights and duties.	**Ciudadano** Miembro de una comunidad política o de un estado que posee ciertos derechos y obligaciones.
Civil liberties Fundamental rights and freedoms protected from infringement by the government. (pp. 75, 185)	**Libertades civiles** Derechos y libertades fundamentales que están protegidos de ser quebrantados por el gobierno.
Civil rights Positive actions taken by the government to prevent people from being discriminated against when engaged in fundamental political actions, such as voting. (p. 75, 185)	**Derechos civiles** Acciones positivas adoptadas por el gobierno para evitar que las personas sean discriminadas al realizar acciones políticas básicas, como votar.
Civil-service system A method of staffing the bureaucracy based on competitive testing results, education, and other qualifications, rather than patronage. (p. 129)	**Sistema de ingreso a la administración pública** Método para contratar personal para la burocracia que se basa en los resultados de las pruebas competitivas, la formación y otras calificaciones, en lugar de la influencia o el patrocinio.
Civil society Groups that form outside the government's control. Civil society includes voluntary organized groups, online activists, and social movements that exist independently of government institutions as well as independent media, unions, and other social and religious groups. (pp. 67, 173)	**Sociedad civil** Grupos que se forman fuera del control del gobierno. La sociedad civil incluye a los grupos organizados de manera voluntaria, a los activistas en línea y a los movimientos sociales que existen independientemente de las instituciones gubernamentales, como así también a los medios de comunicación independientes, a los sindicatos y a otros grupos sociales y religiosos.
Coalition government When two or more parties agree to work together to form a majority and select a prime minister. (p. 104)	**Gobierno de coalición** Cuando dos o más partidos acuerdan trabajar juntos para formar una mayoría y elegir un primer ministro.
Code law A legal system in which judges follow the law written by the legislatures, and previous court decisions do not serve as precedent. (p. 115)	**Código de leyes** Sistema legal en el que los jueces cumplen con las leyes redactadas por las legislaturas, y las decisiones judiciales anteriores no sirven como precedente.
Coercion The use of force, or the threat of force, to get someone to do something they would not otherwise do. Also, a government's use of force or threats to pressure individual behavior. (pp. 40, 181)	**Coacción** Uso de la fuerza, o la amenaza de usarla, para lograr que alguien haga algo que de otro modo no haría. También, el uso de la fuerza o la amenaza de usarla por parte del gobierno para ejercer presión sobre el comportamiento de los individuos.
Common law A legal system in which previous written opinions serve as precedent for future cases. (p. 115)	**Derecho común** Sistema jurídico en el cual las opiniones escritas previamente sirven de precedente para los casos futuros.
Communism An ideology that advocates state ownership of all property, with the government exercising complete control over the economy. (pp. 177, 338)	**Comunismo** Ideología que aboga por la propiedad estatal de la totalidad de los bienes, en el cual el gobierno ejerce un control absoluto sobre la economía.
Comparative method Examining the same phenomenon in several cases and reaching conclusions. (p. 10)	**Método comparativo** Examinar un mismo fenómeno en diversos casos y sacar conclusiones.
Comparative politics The study of similarities and differences between states, how different government systems operate, and why political changes occur. (p. 7)	**Política comparada** Estudio de las semejanzas y diferencias entre los estados, el funcionamiento de los distintos sistemas de gobierno y por qué ocurren los cambios políticos.
Conditional cash transfer Programs that provide cash grants to the poor and in exchange require particular beneficial behavior from the poor, such as children's attendance at school and visits to health clinics. (p. 382)	**Transferencia monetaria condicionada** Programas que entregan subsidios en efectivo a los pobres y, a cambio, exigen un comportamiento beneficioso en concreto por parte de ellos, como por ejemplo, la asistencia de los niños a la escuela y a los controles de salud.
Corporatism A system in which the state controls interest groups and chooses the ones it wishes to recognize. (pp. 70, 257)	**Corporativismo** Sistema en el cual el estado controla a los grupos de interés y elige a cuáles de ellos desea reconocer.
Correlation A statistical concept indicating an apparent connection between variables. (p. 10)	**Correlación** Concepto estadístico que indica una conexión aparente entre variables.
Corruption The abuse of official power for personal gain. (p. 19)	**Corrupción** Abuso de poder oficial en beneficio propio.

Corruption Perceptions Index A measure of how corrupt a system is believed to be. (p. 20)	**Índice de percepción de la corrupción** Medida de lo corrupto que se percibe que es un sistema.
Coup d'état (coup) An overthrow of government by a small number of people, often military leaders. (p. 30)	**Golpe de estado** Derrocamiento del gobierno por un número reducido de personas, a menudo líderes militares.

D

Deficit spending Government spending that is more than what is collected in revenue.	**Gasto deficitario** Gasto público que supera a lo que se recauda en ingresos.
Democratic backsliding Decline in the quality of democracy, including a decrease in citizen participation, rule of law, transparency, and accountability. (p. 37)	**Retroceso democrático** Retroceso de la calidad democrática, incluyendo una disminución de la participación ciudadana, el estado de derecho, la transparencia y la responsabilidad.
Democratic consolidation The process by which a regime has developed stable democratic institutions and significant protections of civil liberties and is unlikely to revert to authoritarianism. (pp. 19, 37)	**Consolidación democrática** Proceso por el cual un régimen ha desarrollado instituciones democráticas estables y protecciones significativas de las libertades civiles, y es poco probable que retorne al autoritarismo.
Democratization The process of transitioning from an authoritarian to a democratic regime. (p. 36)	**Democratización** Proceso de transición de un régimen autoritario a uno democrático.
Devolution Granting of powers by the central government to regional governments. (p. 46)	**Traspaso** Delegar competencias por parte del gobierno central a los gobiernos regionales.
Divided government When one or both houses of the legislature are controlled by a political party other than the party of the president. (p. 104)	**Gobierno dividido** Cuando una o ambas cámaras del congreso están controladas por un partido político que no es el partido al que pertenece el presidente.
Dominant party system A party system in which multiple parties exist, but the same party dominates the executive branch and wins most of the seats in the legislature. (p. 252)	**Sistema de partido hegemónico** Sistema partidista en el que existen muchos partidos, pero donde un mismo partido controla el poder ejecutivo y gana la mayoría de los escaños del congreso.
Dual rule A system in which two different groups with authority run a state. (p. 337)	**Doble regla** Sistema en el que dos grupos con autoridad gobiernan un estado.
Duma The directly elected lower house of the Russian parliament that represents the people and has the power to pass laws, confirm the prime minister, and begin impeachment proceedings against the president. (p. 211)	**Duma** Cámara baja del parlamento ruso, elegida por el voto directo, que representa al pueblo y tiene la potestad de aprobar leyes, confirmar al primer ministro e iniciar un proceso de destitución contra el presidente.
Duverger's Law The observation by political scientist Maurice Duverger that single-member district systems lead to two major catch-all parties, eliminating smaller parties. (p. 252)	**Ley de Duverger** Observación del politólogo Maurice Duverger que sostiene que los sistemas de distritos uninominales conducen a dos partidos principales "atrápalotodo", eliminando a los partidos más pequeños.

E

Economic liberalism Economic policies that support the free market and reduce trade barriers. (p. 80)	**Liberalismo económico** Políticas económicas que apoyan el libre mercado y reducen las barreras al comercio.
Economic-liberalization policy Policy that reduces the role of government in the economy, supports the free market, and reduces trade barriers. (p. 316)	**Política de liberalización económica** Política que reduce el papel del gobierno en la economía, apoya el libre mercado y reduce las barreras al comercio.
Electoral system The formal rules and procedures for selecting the executive or members of the legislature. (p. 246)	**Sistema electoral** Normas y procedimientos formales para elegir al poder ejecutivo o a los miembros del parlamento.
Elite theory Argument that societies are ruled by an economic, gender, racial, or other small group that has effective control over virtually all power; in contrast to pluralist theory.	**Teoría de la élite** Argumento que sostiene que las sociedades están gobernadas por un pequeño grupo, ya sea económico, de género, racial o de otro tipo, el cual ejerce el control real de prácticamente todo el poder; contrasta con la teoría pluralista.
Empirical statement An assertion of fact that can be proven. (p. 10)	**Enunciado empírico** Declaración de hecho que puede ser demostrada.
Ethnic group A group of people who see themselves as united by one or more cultural attributes or a common history. (p. 191)	**Grupo étnico** Grupo de personas que se consideran unidas por uno o varios atributos culturales o por una historia común.

Executive The chief political power in a state, usually a president or prime minister. (p. 103)	**Ejecutivo** Principal poder político de un estado, usualmente un presidente o primer ministro.
Expediency Council A body appointed by the supreme leader of Iran to act as an advisory council that has the power to reject and rewrite proposed legislation and create new laws without parliamentary approval. (p. 407)	**Consejo de Expedición** Órgano designado por el líder supremo de Irán para actuar como grupo de asesoría o de consulta y que tiene la facultad de rechazar y reescribir las leyes propuestas y crear leyes nuevas sin aprobación parlamentaria.

F

Failed state A state that has lost control over all or part of its territory. (p. 20)	**Estado fallido** Estado que ha perdido el control sobre todo su territorio o parte de él.
Fascism A nationalist political ideology in which nationalism and the primacy of the state are the core beliefs. It emphasizes the rights of the majority, oppresses the minority, and supports strong authoritarian rule. (p. 177)	**Fascismo** Ideología política nacionalista en la cual el nacionalismo y la primacía del estado son las creencias fundamentales. Hace hincapié en los derechos de la mayoría, oprime a las minorías y favorece un gobierno autoritario fuerte.
Federal system A political system in which a state's power is legally and constitutionally divided among more than one level of government. (p. 44)	**Sistema federal** Sistema político en el cual el poder de un estado se divide legal y constitucionalmente entre más de un nivel de gobierno.
Federation Council The appointed upper house of the Russian parliament that represents the regions and has the power to initiate, review, and amend legislation, approve troop deployments, and remove the president. (p. 211)	**Consejo de la Federación** Cámara alta del parlamento ruso que representa a las regiones y tiene la potestad de iniciar, revisar y enmendar las leyes, aprobar el despliegue de tropas y destituir al presidente.
"First-past-the-post" (FPTP) An election rule in an SMD system in which the candidate with a plurality of votes wins a seat in the legislature. (p. 247)	**Escrutinio mayoritario uninominal** Norma electoral de un sistema de circunscripción uninominal en la cual el candidato que saca la mayoría simple de votos obtiene un escaño en el congreso.
First-past-the-post (FPTP) electoral system Another term for an SMD plurality system, in which the candidate with the most votes wins the seat in a legislative district. This is also called a winner-take-all system. (p. 139)	**Sistema electoral de escrutinio mayoritario uninominal** Otro término para el sistema de circunscripción uninominal de mayoría simple, en el cual el candidato con más votos obtiene un escaño en un distrito legislativo. También se denomina "el ganador se lleva todo."
Fiscal policy Government budgetary policy, which includes how revenue is generated and how expenses are allocated.	**Política fiscal** Política presupuestaria de un gobierno, que incluye cómo se generan ingresos y en qué se destinan los gastos.
Foreign direct investment (FDI) Investment from abroad in economic activity in another country. (pp. 314, 359)	**Inversión extranjera directa (IED)** Inversión del extranjero en la actividad económica de otro país.
Formal political participation Voting in elections and on referendums, contacting government officials, joining political groups, working on a campaign, and donating money to a cause or candidate. (p. 181)	**Participación política formal** Votar en las elecciones y en los referendos, ponerse en contacto con funcionarios del gobierno, afiliarse a grupos políticos, trabajar en una campaña y donar dinero para una causa o un candidato.
Fragile States Index A measure of state strength, highlighting concerns about fragile and failed states. (p. 21)	**Índice de estados frágiles** Medida de la fortaleza de un estado, que hace hincapié en la preocupación por los estados frágiles y fallidos.
Freedom House A nongovernmental organization that advocates for democracy and human rights and measures freedom around the world. (p. 19)	*Freedom House* **(Casa de la Libertad)** Organización no gubernamental que aboga por la democracia y los derechos humanos y mide la libertad en todo el mundo.

G

General secretary The head of the CCP and the most powerful individual in China. (p. 345)	**Secretario general** Líder del PCCh; la persona más poderosa de China.
Gini Index (coefficient) A measure of income inequality within a country. (p. 16)	**Índice de Gini (coeficiente)** Medida de la desigualdad de ingresos de un país.
Globalization The increased interconnectedness of people, states, and economies. (pp. 80, 313)	**Globalización** Creciente interconexión de las personas, los estados y las economías.
Government Institutions and individuals, such as the executive, legislature, judiciary, and bureaucracy, that make legally binding decisions for the state and that have the lawful right to use power to enforce those decisions. (p. 30)	**Gobierno** Instituciones y personas físicas, como la burocracia y los poderes ejecutivo, legislativo y judicial, que toman decisiones legalmente vinculantes para el estado y que poseen el derecho legal de utilizar el poder para hacer cumplir dichas decisiones.

Grassroots movement Citizens at the local level banding together to advocate for a cause. (p. 258)	**Movimiento de base** Ciudadanos que, a nivel local, se unen en pos de una causa.
Gross domestic product (GDP) The total value of goods and services produced in a country in a year. (p. 14)	**Producto interno bruto (PIB)** Valor total de los bienes y servicios producidos por un país en un año.
GDP growth rate The percentage of GDP growth over a period of time. (p. 15)	**Tasa de crecimiento del PIB** Porcentaje de crecimiento del PIB durante un lapso de tiempo.
GDP per capita Gross domestic product divided by population. (p. 15)	**PIB per cápita** Producto interno bruto dividido por la población.
Guardian Council A twelve-member body in Iran that has the power to reject or approve legislation and reviews candidates for the presidency, parliament, local councils, and the Assembly of Experts. (p. 407)	**Consejo de Guardianes** Órgano de doce miembros de Irán que posee la potestad de aprobar o rechazar las leyes y evaluar a los candidatos a la presidencia, al parlamento, a los consejos locales y a la Asamblea de Expertos.

H

Head of government The key executive in the policymaking process. (p. 62)	**Jefe de Gobierno** Persona clave del ejecutivo en el proceso de creación y formulación de políticas.
Head of state The symbolic representative of a country. (p. 62)	**Jefe de Estado** Representante simbólico de un país.
Household responsibility system An agricultural reform that allowed farmers more control over their own production. (p. 358)	**Sistema de responsabilidad doméstica** Reforma agraria que otorgó a los agricultores más control sobre su propia producción.
House of Commons The directly elected lower house of Parliament in the United Kingdom, which holds most of the policymaking power. (p. 135)	**Cámara de los Comunes** Cámara baja del Parlamento del Reino Unido, elegida por el voto directo, que ostenta la mayor parte del poder en la creación y formulación de políticas.
House of Lords The unelected upper house of Parliament in the United Kingdom, which has the power to suggest amendments to bills and delay legislation. (p. 135)	**Cámara de los Lores** Cámara alta del Parlamento del Reino Unido, no elegida por el voto, que tiene el poder de sugerir enmiendas a los proyectos de ley y dilatar la aprobación de las leyes.
House of Representatives The lower house of Nigeria's National Assembly, which represents the people. (p. 276)	**Cámara de Representantes** Cámara baja de la Asamblea Nacional de Nigeria, que representa al pueblo.
Human capital The education, skills, training, and other positive attributes that people bring to the economy. (p. 377)	**Capital humano** Formación educativa, destrezas, capacitación y otros atributos positivos que las personas aportan a la economía.
Human Development Index (HDI) An aggregate measure of life expectancy, education, and per capita income. (p. 14)	**Índice de Desarrollo Humano (IDH)** Indicador compuesto por la esperanza de vida, la educación y el ingreso per cápita.
Hybrid democracy (See illiberal, flawed, or hybrid democracy, p. 33.)	**Democracia híbrida** (Ver democracia iliberal o híbrida, p. 33.)

I

Illiberal, flawed, or hybrid democracy A system in which elections may be marred by fraud and the state protects some civil rights and liberties but restricts others. (p. 33)	**Democracia iliberal o híbrida** Sistema en el cual las elecciones pueden verse empañadas por el fraude y donde el estado garantiza algunos derechos y libertades civiles, pero restringe otros.
Impeachment The process of removing a president from office before the end of his or her term. (p. 109)	**Destitución** Proceso de remoción del cargo de un presidente antes del final de su mandato.
Import substitution industrialization (ISI) Enacting high tariffs and providing incentives to encourage the growth of domestic manufacturing. (pp. 80, 316, 375)	**Industrialización por sustitución de importaciones (ISI)** Imponer aranceles altos y brindar incentivos para fomentar el crecimiento de la industria nacional.
Individualism The belief that people should be free to make their own decisions and that the government should not unnecessarily regulate individual behavior or restrict civil liberties. (p. 176)	**Individualismo** Tendencia a pensar que las personas deben ser libres para tomar sus propias decisiones y que el gobierno no debe regular innecesariamente el comportamiento individual o restringir las libertades civiles.
Informal political participation Protest, civil disobedience, and political violence, including terrorism. (p. 182)	**Participación política informal** Protesta, desobediencia civil y violencia política, incluyendo el terrorismo.
Institutions The executive and bureaucracy, the legislature, and the judiciary. (p. 103)	**Instituciones** La burocracia, el poder ejecutivo, el legislativo y el judicial.
Interest group An association of individuals or businesses that attempts to influence government. (p. 256)	**Grupo de interés** Agrupación de personas o empresas que intentan influir sobre el gobierno.

International capital flow Movement of money across international borders. (p. 314)	**Flujo internacional del capital** Movimiento de dinero a través de las fronteras internacionales.
International organization A body established by a treaty or other agreement among countries. (p. 315)	**Organización internacional** Organismo establecido mediante un tratado u otro acuerdo entre países.
International recognition A formal step taken by a state to grant official status to another state and begin treating it as a member of the global community. (p. 30)	**Reconocimiento internacional** Paso formal que da un estado para conceder estatus oficial a otro estado y para comenzar a tratarlo como miembro de la comunidad mundial.

J

Judicial independence The ability of judges to decide cases according to the law, free of interference from politically powerful officials or other institutions. (p. 115)	**Independencia judicial** Competencia de los jueces para tomar decisiones en los distintos casos de acuerdo con la ley, ajenos a toda interferencia de funcionarios políticamente poderosos u otras instituciones.
Judicial review The authority of the judiciary to decide whether a specific law contradicts a country's constitution. (p. 115)	**Revisión judicial** Autoridad del poder judicial para decidir si determinada ley contradice la constitución de un país.
Judiciary The system of courts that interprets the law and applies it to individual cases. (p. 103)	**Poder judicial** Sistema de cortes y tribunales que interpretan las leyes y las aplican a los casos individuales.

L

Legislative oversight The power of the legislature to hold cabinet officials and members of bureaucracy accountable for their actions and policies. (p. 110)	**Supervisión legislativa** Poder del parlamento para hacer que los miembros del gabinete y de la burocracia rindan cuentas de sus acciones y políticas.
Legislature A group of lawmakers that passes laws and represents citizens. (p. 103)	**Poder legislativo** Conjunto de legisladores que aprueba las leyes y representa a los ciudadanos.
Legitimacy The citizens' belief that the government has the right to rule. (p. 42)	**Legitimidad** Convicción extendida entre los ciudadanos de que el gobierno tiene derecho a gobernar.
Liberal democracy A system with free and fair elections in which a wide array of civil rights and civil liberties is protected. (p. 33)	**Democracia liberal** Sistema de gobierno con elecciones libres y justas en el cual se garantiza un amplio abanico de derechos y libertades civiles.
Lower house The legislative body in a bicameral system that typically has more members, shorter terms, and less prestige than the upper house, but it may be the more powerful body in the legislature. (p. 64)	**Cámara baja** Órgano legislativo de un sistema bicameral que suele tener más miembros, mandatos más cortos y menor prestigio que la cámara alta, pero que puede ser el órgano más poderoso del parlamento.

M

Majles Iran's unicameral legislature. (p. 408)	**Majles** Parlamento unicameral de Irán.
Mandate The broad support of the people to carry out proposed policies. (pp. 68, 246)	**Mandato** Amplio apoyo popular para llevar a cabo las políticas propuestas.
Market-based private insurance system A health-care system that relies on private insurance for the bulk of the population.	**Sistema de seguro privado basado en el mercado** Sistema de salud que depende de la cobertura de los seguros privados para la mayor parte de la población.
Market failure A phenomenon that occurs when markets fail to perform efficiently or fail to perform according to other widely held social values.	**Fracaso del mercado** Fenómeno que tiene lugar cuando los mercados no se comportan de forma eficiente o no lo hacen de acuerdo con otros valores sociales generalizados.
Marxism Political analysis that says that economic structures largely determine political behavior; the philosophical underpinning of communism.	**Marxismo** Análisis político que sostiene que las estructuras económicas determinan en gran parte el comportamiento político; el fundamento filosófico del comunismo.
Means-tested public assistance Social programs that provide benefits to individuals who fall below a specific income level.	**Asistencia pública condicionada a los recursos** Programas sociales que brindan prestaciones a las personas que se encuentran por debajo de un determinado nivel de ingresos.
Member of parliament (MP) A representative in the legislature elected by citizens. (p. 104)	**Parlamentario** Representante de la legislatura elegido por los ciudadanos.

Mixed electoral system A system for electing members of the legislature that includes both single-member districts and seats awarded through proportional representation. (pp. 68, 249)	**Sistema electoral mixto** Sistema para elegir miembros del parlamento que incluye tanto a los distritos uninominales como a los escaños adjudicados por representación proporcional.
Monarch A hereditary ruler who serves for life. (p. 132)	**Monarca** Gobernante que recibe su cargo por sucesión hereditaria y que gobierna de por vida.
Monetary policy The amount of money a government prints and puts into circulation and the basic interest rates the government sets.	**Política monetaria** Cantidad de dinero que un gobierno emite y pone en circulación y las tasas de interés básicas que el gobierno fija.
Multimember district (MMD) system A method for electing members of a legislature in which two or more representatives are elected from a district. (pp. 246, 410)	**Sistema de distritos plurinominales** Método para elegir a los miembros de una legislatura en donde dos o más representantes de un distrito resultan electos.
Multinational corporation (MNC) A company with facilities or assets in more than one country. (p. 314)	**Empresa multinacional (EMN)** Empresa con instalaciones o activos en más de un país.
Multiparty system A party system in which more than two parties can win a national election and control the government. (p. 252)	**Sistema multipartidario** Sistema de partidos políticos en el cual más de dos partidos pueden ganar las elecciones nacionales y asumir el control del gobierno.

N

Nation A group of people who share a sense of belonging and who often have a common language, culture, religion, race, ethnicity, political identity, or set of traditions or aspirations. (p. 31)	**Nación** Conjunto de personas que comparten un sentimiento de pertenencia y que suelen tener en común un idioma, una cultura, una religión, una raza, una etnia, una identidad política o un conjunto de tradiciones o aspiraciones.
National Assembly Nigeria's bicameral legislature. (p. 276)	**Asamblea Nacional** Poder legislativo bicameral de Nigeria.
National Health Service (NHS) The government-financed and managed health-care system in the United Kingdom. (p. 150)	**Servicio Nacional de Salud (NHS)** Sistema de salud del Reino Unido, que es financiado y gestionado por el gobierno.
Nationalism When a group has a strong sense of identity and believes it has its own destiny. (p. 31)	**Nacionalismo** Cuando un conjunto de personas tiene un fuerte sentido de identidad y cree ser dueño de su propio destino.
Nationalized industry A state-owned company controlled by the government. (p. 80)	**Industria nacionalizada** Empresa que es propiedad del estado y está controlada por el gobierno.
National Party Congress A body within the Chinese Communist Party that acts as a legislature, passing policies put forth by the party elite. (p. 345)	**Congreso Nacional del Partido** Órgano dentro del Partido Comunista de China que actúa como legislatura al aprobar las políticas presentadas por la élite del partido.
National People's Congress China's unicameral legislature. (p. 346)	**Congreso Nacional del Pueblo** Poder legislativo unicameral de China.
Neoliberalism An economic ideology favoring policies that support the free market and reduce trade barriers. (pp. 176, 374)	**Neoliberalismo** Ideología económica que favorece las políticas de libre mercado y las reduce barreras comerciales.
Nongovernmental organization (NGO) A nonprofit group outside the government's control. NGOs usually focus on social or political issues. (pp. 63, 319)	**Organización no gubernamental (ONG)** Asociación sin fines de lucro ajena al control del gobierno. En general, las ONG se dedican a temas políticos o sociales.
Normative statement A value judgment, usually in the form of a should or ought statement. (p. 11)	**Declaración normativa** Juicio de valor, que suele estar escrito como declaración sobre lo que debe o debería ser.

O

One-party state A country where only one party is allowed to control the government. (pp. 251, 349)	**Estado monopartidista** País en el que un único partido puede controlar el gobierno.

P

Parliamentary sovereignty The principle that parliament's power is supreme and extends over all aspects of the state. (p. 129)	**Soberanía parlamentaria** Principio por el cual el poder parlamentario es supremo y abarca todos los aspectos del estado.
Parliamentary system A system in which the executive and legislature are fused. (p. 104)	**Sistema parlamentario** Sistema en el cual los poderes ejecutivo y legislativo están fusionados.
Party system The number of and strength of political parties within a country. (p. 251)	**Sistema de partidos políticos** El número de partidos políticos y su poderío dentro de un país.

Patron-clientelism When those in power offer benefits to citizens in exchange for political support. (p. 58)	**Clientelismo patronal** Cuando quienes ostentan el poder ofrecen beneficios a los ciudadanos a cambio de apoyo político.
Peak association An organization authorized by the government to represent a group, such as labor, business, or agriculture. (p. 70)	**Asociación cumbre** Organización autorizada por el gobierno para representar, por ejemplo, a un grupo laboral, empresarial o agrícola.
Personalist regime A system of government in which a central leader comes to dominate a state, typically not only eliminating all opposition but also weakening the state's institutions to centralize power in his or her own hands. (p. 35)	**Régimen personalista** Sistema de gobierno en el cual un líder central llega a dominar un estado, no solo eliminando a toda la oposición, sino también debilitando las instituciones del estado para centralizar el poder en su persona.
Pluralism A system in which groups are allowed to form and advocate for their interests outside of government control. (pp. 71, 257)	**Pluralismo** Sistema en el cual se permite que se formen grupos que luchan por sus intereses ajenos al control del gobierno.
Pluralist theory The contention that society is divided into various political groups and that power is dispersed among these groups so that no group has complete or permanent power; in contrast to elite theory.	**Teoría pluralista** Argumentación que sostiene que la sociedad está dividida en varios grupos políticos y que el poder está repartido entre estos grupos de tal manera que ninguno de ellos ostenta el poder completo o de forma permanente; contrasta con la teoría de las élites.
Plurality The most votes, but not necessarily a majority. (p. 247)	**Pluralidad** La mayor cantidad de votos sin llegar necesariamente a ser una mayoría.
Politburo A powerful body of elite policymakers in a communist party, in particular within the Chinese Communist Party. (p. 345)	**Politburó** Poderoso conjunto de legisladores de élite pertenecientes a un partido comunista, en particular al Partido Comunista de China.
Politburo Standing Committee A subgroup of the Politburo, consisting of the most powerful people in the Chinese Communist Party, who act as a cabinet in making policy. (p. 345)	**Comité Permanente del Politburó** Subgrupo del Politburó, integrado por las personas más poderosas del Partido Comunista de China, que actúan como gabinete político en la formulación de políticas.
Political actor Any person or group engaged in political behavior.	**Actor político** Cualquier persona o grupo que participe en la política.
Political appointee An official who serves at the pleasure of the president or prime minister and is assigned the task of overseeing a segment of the bureaucracy.	**Persona designada por la política** Funcionario que sirve a las órdenes del presidente o primer ministro y a quien se le asigna la tarea de supervisar una parte de la burocracia.
Political cleavage A division among citizens according to political beliefs about the role of government and policymaking goals. (p. 77)	**Grieta política** División entre los ciudadanos de acuerdo con sus creencias políticas sobre el papel del gobierno y los objetivos de la formulación de políticas.
Political culture A set of collectively held attitudes, values, and beliefs about government and politics, and the norms of behavior in the political system. (pp. 75, 175)	**Cultura política** Conjunto de actitudes, valores y creencias colectivas sobre el gobierno y la política y las normas de comportamiento en el sistema político.
Political efficacy A citizen's belief that his or her actions can impact the government. (p. 42)	**Eficacia política** Creencia de los ciudadanos de que sus acciones impactan al gobierno.
Political ideology An individual's set of beliefs and values about government, politics, and policy. (p. 176)	**Ideología política** Conjunto de creencias y valores de un individuo respecto al gobierno, la política y las políticas.
Political science The systematic study of politics and power.	**Ciencias políticas** Estudio sistemático de la política y el poder.
Political socialization The process through which an individual learns about politics and is taught about society's common political values and beliefs. (p. 175)	**Socialización política** Proceso a través del cual un individuo aprende sobre la política y se le enseñan las creencias y valores políticos comunes de la sociedad.
Political violence The use of physical force by nonstate actors for political ends. (p. 183)	**Violencia política** Uso de fuerza física por parte de actores no estatales con fines políticos.
Politics The process by which human communities make collective decisions.	**Política** Proceso a través del cual las comunidades humanas toman decisiones colectivas.
Populism A political ideology based on the idea that the government should put the rights and interests of the common people above the elites. (p. 179)	**Populismo** Ideología política basada en el concepto de que el gobierno debe poner los derechos e intereses de las personas comunes por encima de las élites.

Postmaterialism A set of values in a society in which most citizens are economically secure enough to move beyond immediate economic (materialist) concerns to "quality of life" issues like human rights, civil rights, women's rights, environmentalism, and moral values. (p. 176)

Posmaterialismo Conjunto de valores de una sociedad en la cual los ciudadanos gozan de una seguridad económica que les permite dejar atrás las preocupaciones económicas (materiales) inmediatas y pensar en temas de "calidad de vida", tales como los derechos humanos, los derechos civiles, los derechos de las mujeres, el ambientalismo y los valores morales.

Power The ability to make someone do something they would not otherwise do. (p. 39)

Poder Capacidad de hacer que alguien haga algo que normalmente no haría.

Presidential system A system in which the executive and legislature are elected independently and have separate and independent powers. (p. 104)

Sistema presidencial Sistema en el cual los poderes ejecutivo y legislativo son elegidos de manera independiente y tienen poderes separados e independientes.

Prime minister (PM) The head of government in a parliamentary or semi-presidential system. In a parliamentary system, the PM is a member of the legislature and is selected by the majority party. (p. 104)

Primer ministro (PM) Jefe de gobierno de un sistema parlamentario o semipresidencialista. En un sistema parlamentario, el primer ministro es miembro de la legislatura y es elegido por el partido mayoritario.

Privatization When a government transfers ownership and control of a nationalized industry to the private sector. (p. 81)

Privatización Cuando un gobierno transfiere la propiedad y el control de una industria nacionalizada al sector privado.

Proportional representation (PR) system A system in which seats in the legislature are awarded according to the percentage of votes a party receives. (pp. 68, 248)

Sistema de representación proporcional (RP) Sistema en el cual los escaños de la legislatura se otorgan de acuerdo al porcentaje de votos obtenidos por el partido.

Protectionist economic policy A policy designed to protect domestic industry and reduce foreign influence on sectors of the economy. (pp. 80, 374)

Política económica proteccionista Política diseñada para proteger la industria nacional y reducir la influencia extranjera sobre los diversos sectores de la economía.

Protest A public demonstration against a policy or in response to an event, often targeting the government. (p. 182)

Protesta Manifestación pública contra una política o como respuesta a un evento, cuyo blanco suele ser el gobierno.

Q

Qualitative data Text-based descriptions, including explanations of how government and political institutions function. (p. 11)

Datos cualitativos Descripciones basadas en textos, que incluyen explicaciones de cómo funcionan el gobierno y las instituciones políticas.

Quantitative data Observations made using statistical techniques, which are often conveyed in charts, graphs, tables, and maps. (p. 11)

Datos cuantitativos Observaciones llevadas a cabo por medio de técnicas estadísticas, que se presentan mediante tablas, gráficas y mapas.

Quantitative statistical techniques Research method used for large-scale studies that reduces observations and data to sets of numbers so that statistical analysis can systematically compare a huge number of cases.

Técnicas estadísticas cuantitativas Método de investigación empleado en estudios de gran escala que reduce las observaciones y datos a conjuntos numéricos para que el análisis estadístico pueda comparar sistemáticamente una gran cantidad de casos.

R

Race A group of people socially defined mainly on the basis of one or more perceived common physical characteristics. (p. 192)

Raza Grupo de personas socialmente definidas a partir de una o más características físicas que se perciben como compartidas.

Rational-legal legitimacy The right to rule based on an accepted set of laws. (p. 43)

Legitimidad racional-legal Derecho a gobernar basado en un conjunto de leyes aceptadas.

Referendum A vote on a policy issue sent by the government to the people. (p. 144)

Referendo Votación sobre una cuestión política que el gobierno pone a consulta del pueblo.

Regime A type of government, such as liberal democracy or authoritarian. (p. 30)

Régimen Tipo de gobierno, tales como la democracia liberal o el autoritario.

Regime change A change in the fundamental rules and system of government. (p. 30)

Cambio de régimen Cambio en las reglas fundamentales y el sistema de gobierno.

Regulated market economy An economy in which wages, prices, and production are mostly set by supply and demand, with some regulation, and mostly private control of businesses and natural resources. (p. 150)

Economía regulada por el mercado Economía en la cual los salarios, los precios y la producción se establecen en mayor medida por la oferta y la demanda, aunque con cierta regulación, y el control de los negocios y los recursos naturales suele ser privado.

Rentier state A state that relies on the export of oil or from the leasing of resources to foreign entities as a significant source of government revenue. (pp. 225, 315, 388)	**Estado rentista** Estado que depende de la exportación de petróleo o del alquiler de recursos a entidades extranjeras como fuente importante de ingresos públicos.
Research methods Systematic processes used to ensure that the study of some phenomena is as objective and unbiased as possible.	**Métodos de investigación** Procesos sistemáticos que permiten garantizar que el estudio de fenómenos sea lo más objetivo e imparcial posible.
Resource curse A problem faced by countries that have a valuable and abundant natural resource, which limits diversification of the economy, makes government revenue dependent on the world market, increases opportunities for corruption, and lessens the government's responsiveness to citizens. (pp. 225, 388)	**Maldición de los recursos** Problema al que se enfrentan los países que poseen en abundancia un recurso natural valioso, lo cual limita la diversificación de la economía, genera dependencia en el mercado global de los ingresos del gobierno, aumenta las posibilidades de corrupción y disminuye la capacidad de respuesta del gobierno a los ciudadanos.
Revolution An overthrow of a regime based on widespread popular support. (p. 30)	**Revolución** Derrocamiento de un régimen basado en un apoyo popular generalizado.
Rule by law Where the law is applied arbitrarily, and government officials are not subject to the same rules and penalties as citizens. (p. 33)	**Imperio de la ley** Cuando la ley se aplica de manera arbitraria y los funcionarios no están sujetos a las mismas reglas y sanciones que los ciudadanos.
Rule of law A clear set of rules where government officials are subject to the same laws and penalties as citizens. (p. 33)	**Estado de derecho** Conjunto de leyes claras donde los funcionarios están sujetos a las mismas leyes y sanciones que los ciudadanos.
Runoff election A second and final election held between the top two vote-getters when no candidate wins a majority of the votes in the first round of voting. (p. 246)	**Elección de segunda vuelta** Segunda y última elección entre los dos candidatos más votados cuando ninguno de ellos obtiene la mayoría de los votos en la primera ronda electoral.

S

Semi-presidential system A system that divides executive power between a directly elected president and a prime minister. (p. 105)	**Sistema semipresidencial** Sistema que divide el poder ejecutivo entre un presidente elegido por el voto directo y un primer ministro.
Senate (Mexico) The elected upper house of the Mexican Congress, which has the power to confirm appointments, ratify treaties, and approve federal intervention in the states. (p. 64)	**Senado (México)** Cámara alta del Congreso mexicano, elegida por el voto directo, que posee la facultad de confirmar los nombramientos, ratificar los tratados y aprobar la intervención federal en los estados.
Senate (Nigeria) The upper house of the National Assembly, which represents the states. (p. 276)	**Senado (Nigeria)** Cámara alta de la Asamblea Nacional, que representa a los estados.
Separation of powers A division of power among the major branches of government. (p. 104)	**Separación de poderes** División del poder entre las principales ramas del gobierno.
Sexenio The single six-year term for the Mexican president. (p. 62)	**Sexenio** El mandato único de seis años del presidente mexicano.
Sharia law A legal system based on principles derived from Islam. (p. 272)	**Sharía** Sistema jurídico basado en los principios derivados del Islam.
Single-member district (SMD) system A system for electing members of the legislature in which the candidate who earns the most votes in a district wins a seat in the legislature. (p. 247)	**Sistema de distritos uninominales (SDU)** Sistema de elección de los miembros del poder legislativo en el cual el candidato que saca más votos en un distrito obtiene un escaño en la legislatura.
Single-member plurality system (SMD) A system in which the candidate who earns the most votes in a district wins a seat in the legislature. (p. 68)	**Sistema pluralista uninominal (SPU)** Sistema en el cual el candidato que saca más votos en un distrito obtiene un escaño en la legislatura.
Single-peak association An organization that brings together all interest groups in a particular sector to influence and negotiate agreements with the government. (p. 257)	**Agrupación sectorial** Organización que reúne a todos los grupos de interés de un sector específico para ejercer influencia y negociar acuerdos con el gobierno.
Social capital Social networks and norms of reciprocity that are important for a strong civil society.	**Capital social** Redes sociales y normas de reciprocidad que son importantes para una sociedad civil fuerte.
Social class A group of people who perceive themselves as sharing a social status based on a common level of wealth, income, type of work, or education. (p. 193)	**Clase social** Grupo de personas que perciben que comparten un estatus social basado en un nivel común de riquezas, ingresos, actividad laboral o educación.

Social cleavage A division in society among social factors such as ethnicity, class, religion, or language. (pp. 77, 190)	**Grieta social** División en la sociedad a raíz de factores sociales tales como la etnia, la clase, la religión o el idioma.
Socialism A political ideology in which economic equality is a core value, with the belief that government ownership of the major means of production is a way to reduce income inequality within the state. (p. 177)	**Socialismo** Ideología política en la cual la igualdad económica es un valor fundamental, y en la cual se cree que el gobierno debe ser el propietario de los principales medios de producción con el fin de reducir la desigualdad de ingresos en el país.
Social movement A large group organized to advocate for political change. (pp. 188, 258)	**Movimiento social** Grupo numeroso que se organiza para bregar por un cambio político.
Social policy Policy focused on reducing poverty and income inequality and stabilizing individual or family income.	**Política social** Política cuyo fin es disminuir la pobreza, la desigualdad de ingresos y estabilizar los ingresos individuales o familiares.
Source analysis Reading and analyzing text. (p. 12)	**Análisis de fuentes** Leer y analizar textos.
Sovereignty A state's ability to act without internal or external interference. (p. 30)	**Soberanía** Capacidad de un estado para actuar sin interferencias internas o externas.
Special economic zone (SEZ) A strategically located area in China with a large labor pool, well-developed infrastructure, and tax incentives to attract foreign companies. (p. 359)	**Zona económica especial (ZEE)** Área estratégicamente situada en China que cuenta con una gran reserva de mano de obra, infraestructura bien desarrollada e incentivos fiscales para atraer a empresas extranjeras.
State Political institutions with international recognition that govern a population in a territory. (p. 29)	**Estado** Instituciones políticas con reconocimiento internacional que gobiernan sobre una población que habita un territorio.
State Council The cabinet that leads the formal bureaucracy in China. (p. 346)	**Consejo de Estado** Gabinete que dirige la burocracia formal en China.
State-owned enterprise (SOE) A factory or other business owned by the government. (p. 359)	**Empresa estatal** Industria u otra empresa que es propiedad del gobierno.
Strong state A state that is capable of providing necessary government services to its citizens. (p. 20)	**Estado fuerte** Estado que es capaz de proporcionar los servicios gubernamentales necesarios a sus ciudadanos.
Structural adjustment program (SAP) Requirements for receiving assistance from international lenders (such as the IMF), including the privatization of state-owned companies, reducing tariffs, and reducing subsidies for domestic industries. (pp. 293, 316, 376)	**Programa de ajuste estructural** Requisitos para recibir asistencia de prestamistas internacionales (como el FMI), que incluye la privatización de empresas estatales, la reducción de los aranceles y la reducción de los subsidios a la industria nacional.
Supranational organization A body in which member countries have some say in governing and give up some sovereignty over issues affecting the organization as a whole. (p. 316)	**Organización supranacional** Organismo en el cual los países miembros tienen una participación acotada en el gobierno de dicho organismo y renuncian a una parte de su soberanía concerniente a las cuestiones que afectan a la organización en su conjunto.
Supreme Court A high court. In the United Kingdom, it cannot overturn acts of parliament but has the authority to protect civil rights and liberties and rule on cases involving devolution. (p. 136)	**Tribunal Supremo** Tribunal superior. En el Reino Unido, no puede anular leyes aprobadas por el parlamento, pero tiene autoridad para proteger los derechos y libertades civiles, y para juzgar en casos relacionados con los traspasos.
Supreme leader The executive who is a cleric and the most powerful person in Iran. (p. 404)	**Líder supremo** Clérigo que es jefe del ejecutivo de Irán, y es la persona más poderosa de ese país.

T

Term limit A restriction on the number of terms the executive may serve. (p. 108)	**Límite de mandatos** Limitación de la cantidad de mandatos que puede ejercer el titular del ejecutivo.
Term of office A specified number of years that an executive can serve. (p. 108)	**Duración del mandato** Cantidad determinada de años que puede ejercer el titular del ejecutivo.
Territory An area with clearly defined borders to which a state lays claim.	**Territorio** Área con fronteras claramente definidas que un estado reclama como propia.
Terrorism Political violence or the threat of violence that deliberately targets civilians to influence the behavior and actions of the government. (p. 183)	**Terrorismo** Violencia política o la amenaza de ejercerla deliberadamente contra la población civil para influir en el comportamiento y las acciones del gobierno.

Theocracy A system based on religious rule. (pp. 40, 398)	**Teocracia** Sistema basado en un gobierno ejercido por un poder religioso.
Totalitarianism A political ideology that emphasizes domination of the state over citizens. In totalitarian systems, the government has complete control over citizens' lives. (p. 178)	**Totalitarismo** Ideología política que hace hincapié en el dominio del estado sobre los ciudadanos. En los sistemas totalitarios, el gobierno ejerce un control total sobre la vida de los ciudadanos.
Totalitarian state A type of authoritarian government where the state controls nearly all aspects of citizens' lives. (p. 33)	**Estado totalitario** Tipo de gobierno autoritario en el cual el estado controla casi todos los aspectos de la vida de los ciudadanos.
Township and village enterprise (TVE) Factories and other businesses mostly owned by local governments. (p. 358)	**Empresa pública administrada por municipios y aldeas (TVE)** Industrias y otras empresas que suelen ser propiedad de los gobiernos locales.
Trade The flow of goods and services across national borders. (p. 314)	**Comercio** Flujo de bienes y servicios a través de las fronteras nacionales.
Traditional legitimacy The right to rule based on a society's long-standing patterns and practices. (p. 42)	**Legitimidad tradicional** Derecho a gobernar sobre la base de los patrones y costumbres de una sociedad arraigadas en el tiempo.
Transparency The ability of citizens to know what the government is doing. (p. 34)	**Transparencia** Capacidad de los ciudadanos de saber qué hace el gobierno.
Two-party system A party system in which only two parties are able to garner enough votes to win an election, although more may compete. (p. 252)	**Sistema bipartidista** Sistema de partidos políticos en el cual sólo dos de ellos son capaces de obtener votos suficientes para ganar las elecciones, aunque otros partidos también compitan en los comicios.

U

Unicameral legislature A legislature with one chamber. (p. 112)	**Legislatura unicameral** Legislatura que tiene una sola cámara.
Unitary system A political system in which the central government has sole constitutional sovereignty and power. (p. 44)	**Sistema unitario** Sistema político en el cual únicamente el gobierno central ejerce la soberanía y ostenta el poder constitucional.
Upper house The legislative body in a bicameral system that typically has fewer members and may have more prestige but less power than the lower house. (p. 64)	**Cámara alta** Órgano legislativo de un sistema bicameral que suele tener menos miembros y puede tener más prestigio, pero menos poder que la cámara baja.

V

Vote of no confidence In parliamentary systems, a vote by parliament to remove a government (the prime minister and cabinet) from power. (p. 104)	**Voto de censura** En los sistemas parlamentarios, una votación del parlamento con el objetivo de destituir al gobierno (al primer ministro y su gabinete).

W

Weak state A state that only partially provides political goods to its citizens.	**Estado débil** Estado que solo proporciona de forma parcial bienes políticos a sus ciudadanos.
Welfare state Government programs to benefit the health and well-being of citizens. (p. 129)	**Estado de bienestar** Programas gubernamentales en beneficio de la salud y el bienestar de los ciudadanos.

Index

Note: Page numbers followed by *f* indicate figures, and page numbers followed by *t* indicate tables.